THE NEUROTIC CHILD
AND ADOLESCENT

THE NEUROTIC CHILD AND ADOLESCENT

Edited by

M. Hossein Etezady, M.D.

JASON ARONSON INC.
Northvale, New Jersey
London

Copyright © 1990 by Jason Aronson Inc.

All rights reserved. Printed in the United States of America. No part of this book may be used or reproduced in any manner whatsoever without written permission from Jason Aronson Inc. except in the case of brief quotations in reviews for inclusion in a magazine, newspaper, or broadcast.

Library of Congress Cataloging-in-Publication Data

The Neurotic child and adolescent / edited by M. Hossein Etezady.
    p.   cm.
  Includes bibliographical references.
  ISBN 0-87668-808-3
  1. Neuroses in children. 2. Neuroses in adolescence.
I. Etezady, M. Hossein.
  [DNLM: 1. Neurotic Disorders—in adolescence. 2. Neurotic Disorders—in infancy & childhood. WS 350.6 N494]
RJ506.N48N48 1990
618.92'852—dc20
DNLM/DLC
for Library of Congress   89-18246
                                                                                                CIP

Manufactured in the United States of America. Jason Aronson Inc. offers books and cassettes. For information and catalog write to Jason Aronson Inc., 230 Livingston Street, Northvale, New Jersey 07647.

CONTENTS

Contributors   vii
Preface   xi

PART I. The Concept of Neurosis in Children

1. Childhood Neurosis at the End of the 20th Century   3
   E. James Anthony, M.D.
2. Symptomatic Disturbances and Clinical Manifestations of Neurosis in Children and Adolescents   25
   Helen R. Beiser, M.D.
3. Transference Neurosis in Childhood and Adolescence   41
   Henry Eisner, M.D.
4. Traumatic Neurosis in Children   59
   Jules Glenn, M.D.
5. The Infantile Neurosis and Neuroses in Childhood   75
   J. Alexis Burland, M.D.
6. Update on the Concept of the Neurotic Child   91
   Charles A. Sarnoff, M.D.
7. Neurotic Children in the Light of Research   101
   Aaron H. Esman, M.D.

PART II. Developmental and Etiological Considerations

8. Neurosogenesis   117
   Henri Parens, M.D.
9. Neurosis and Prevention   135
   Henri Parens, M.D.
10. Neurosis and Object Relations in Children and Adolescents   159
    Leroy J. Byerly, M.D.
11. Parent–Child Dimension of Development and Neurosogenesis   197
    G. Pirooz Sholevar, M.D.
12. Neurosis and Femininity   227
    Ruth S. Fischer, M.D.
13. The Neurotic Adolescent   241
    Robert C. Prall, M.D.
14. The Adulthood of the Neurotic Child— Developmental Perspectives   303
    Sol Altschul, M.S., M.D.

PART III. Therapeutic Issues
15. The Fantasy World of the Child as Revealed in Art, Play, and Dreams 319
    Jules Glenn, M.D., and *Isidor Bernstein*, M.D.
16. A Historical Perspective on the Treatment of Neurotic Children 349
    Bertram A. Ruttenberg, M.D.
17. The Neurotic Child and Response to Treatment 379
    Martin A. Silverman, M.D.
18. Current Perspectives on the Treatment of Neuroses in Children and Adolescents 403
    J. Alexis Burland, M.D.

Index 413

CONTRIBUTORS

Sol Altschul, M.D.

Associate Dean for Graduate Education, Training and Supervising Analyst, Director, Barr-Harris Center for the Study of Separation and Loss in Childhood, Institute for Psychoanalysis, Chicago; Associate Professor of Clinical Psychiatry, Northwestern University Medical School, Chicago.

E. James Anthony, M.D.

Director of Child and Adolescent Psychotherapy, Chestnut Lodge Hospital, Rockville, Maryland; Clinical Professor of Psychiatry and Behavioral Science, George Washington School of Medicine, Washington, DC; Training and Supervising Analyst, Washington Psychoanalytic Institute; Past president, Association for Child Psychoanalysis, Inc.

Helen R. Beiser, M.D.

Training and Supervising Analyst (adult and child), Institute for Psychoanalysis, Chicago. Clinical Professor of Psychiatry, Emeritus, University of Illinois College of Medicine.

Isidor Bernstein, M.D.

Training and Supervising Analyst, The New York Psychoanalytic Institute; Training and Supervising Analyst for Child and Adolescent Analysis, The New York Psychoanalytic Institute and The Psychoanalytic Institute, New York University Medical Center. Associate Clinical Professor of Psychiatry, New York University Medical Center.

J. Alexis Burland, M.D.

Training/Supervising Psychoanalyst, adult and child/adolescent curriculum, Philadelphia Psychoanalytic Institute, Philadelphia. Clinical Professor of Psychiatry and Human Behavior, Jefferson Medical College of

Thomas Jefferson University, Philadelphia. Member, board of trustees, Margaret S. Mahler Psychiatric Research Foundation.

LeRoy J. Byerly, M.D.

Training and Supervising Analyst (child and adult); chairman, Child Analysis Committee, Philadelphia Psychoanalytic Institute; visiting lecturer, College of Physicians and Surgeons, Columbia University, New York; Assistant Clinical Professor, Medical College of Pennsylvania.

Henry Eisner, M.D.

Member of faculty and supervising analyst in Child and Adolescent Division at Institute of Philadelphia Association for Psychoanalysis; also a member of Adult Division faculty. Associate Professor of Psychiatry and Pediatrics at the Hahnemann Medical College and Associate Professor of Psychiatry at University of Pennsylvania Medical School. Founded and chaired the Child and Adolescent Clinic of the Philadelphia Association for Psychoanalysis; also consultant to the Elwyn Institutes, the Philadelphia Department of Human Services, and the Maxicare Health Maintenance Organization. Full-time adult and child psychiatric and psychoanalytic practice.

Aaron H. Esman, M.D.

Attending Psychiatrist, New York Hospital. Professor of Clinical Psychiatry, Cornell University Medical College. Lecturer, New York Psychoanalytic Institute. Private practice. Fellow, American Psychiatric Association, American Academy of Child Psychiatry, American Society for Adolescent Psychiatry.

M. Hossein Etezady, M.D.

Board certified in adult and child psychiatry and trained in child and adult psychoanalysis. Active member of American Psychoanalytic Association, member of Association for Child Psychoanalysis, faculty member of Philadelphia Psychoanalytic Institute, assistant clinical professor at Medical College of Pennsylvania. In private practice, and clinical director of the psychiatric services at Paoli Memorial Hospital,

CONTRIBUTORS

Paoli, Pennsylvania. President of the Regional Council of Child and Adolescent Psychiatry (Eastern Pennsylvania and Southern New Jersey).

Ruth S. Fischer, M.D.

Training and supervising analyst of the Institute of the Philadelphia Psychoanalytic Society; senior attending psychiatrist, Institute of Pennsylvania Hospital; clinical faculty at the University of Pennsylvania School of Medicine.

Jules Glenn, M.D.

Clinical Professor of Psychiatry, New York University Medical Center. Training and Supervising Analyst, The Psychoanalytic Institute, New York University Medical Center. Editor, *Child Analysis and Therapist.* Co-editor, *Freud and his Self-Analysis* and *Freud and his Patients.*

Henri Parens, M.D.

Psychoanalytic training, adults and children, Philadelphia Psychoanalytic Institute; Psychiatrist and Psychoanalyst of adults and children; Director, The Infant Psychiatry Section, Department of Psychiatry, Medical College of Pennsylvania; Research Professor Psychiatry, The Medical College of Pennsylvania; Training and Supervising Analyst (adult and child analysis), Philadelphia Psychoanalytic Institute.

Robert C. Prall, M.D.

Life Fellow APA, AACAP, Life Member APsAnA, IPsAnA, Philadelphia PsAnSoc. Private practice of child, adolescent, and adult psychoanalysis and psychiatry in Austin, Texas. Visiting professor, Medical College of Pennsylvania, Philadelphia. Consulting child analyst, Austin State Hospital Children's and Adolescent Units and The Meridell Achievement Center.

Bertram A. Ruttenberg, M.D.

Graduate of the Institute of the Philadelphia Association for Psychoanalysis in adult and child psychoanalysis; also a trained and practicing adult, child, and infant psychiatrist (1953, 1960, 1980) and psychoanalyst (1961, 1970). Currently Professor of Psychiatry and Human Behavior, Jefferson University College of Medicine, and Medical Director of the Center for Autistic Children in Philadelphia.

Charles A. Sarnoff, M.D.

Lecturer, College of Physicians and Surgeons, Columbia University, Department of Psychiatry, Psychoanalytic Clinic for Training and Research, New York. Formerly Director of Child Psychiatry Fellowship Training; lecturer and supervisor in Child and Adolescent Psychiatry, Hillside Hospital, Glen Oaks, New York. Life Fellow, American Psychiatric Association; fellow, American Academy of Child Psychiatry.

G. Pirooz Sholevar, M.D.

Professor and Director, Division of Child, Adolescent and Family Psychiatry at Jefferson Medical College, Thomas Jefferson University, Philadelphia.

Martin A. Silverman, M.D.

Clinical Professor of Psychiatry, Training and Supervising Analyst, and Chairman of the Child and Adolescent Analysis section at The Psychoanalytic Institute, New York University Medical Center.

PREFACE

Neurotic conditions may be considered the field in which psychoanalysis and, subsequently, dynamic psychotherapy germinated. Freud first recognized the unconscious determinants of these disorders in his work with adult patients. He described unconscious conflicts resulting from sexual and aggressive impulses during early childhood. He found that such neurotic conflicts are derived from earlier conscious conflicts between the child and those who are significant to him. These can remain unresolved, yet removed from awareness through the mechanism of repression. Later in development, reactivation of these conflicts is manifested in symptom formation. He elaborated on the manner in which symptoms symbolically represent compromise formation between the unconscious repressed urges and the inhibitions that oppose them. In the light of these momentous discoveries, the psychological universe of children became accessible to exploration and understanding as well as to treatment. Psychoanalytic treatment of neurotic manifestations in children was first attempted when Freud supervised the treatment of Little Hans by the child's father. Ever since these beginnings, clinical experience with adults, as well as children, has supported the notion that neurotic disorders are ideally suited for application of psychoanalytic treatment and dynamic psychotherapy.

Over the past nine decades, our experience and clinical data have grown. Our concepts have evolved. As the scope of our therapeutic acumen and application has widened, refinements in technique have been introduced. Nevertheless, as our field of vision and domain of comprehension has expanded, our questions and areas of ambiguity have grown. Yet in the face of increasing complexity and diversity, no recent publication has addressed the subject of neurosis in children and adolescents as an exclusive focus in a comprehensive volume. For students, teachers, counselors, social workers, health-care professionals, and psychotherapists and psychoanalysts treating children and adolescents, we need a volume reflecting current views on the subject and providing an updated integration of new concepts and trends of our time.

The Neurotic Child and Adolescent strives to fill this gap in the literature regarding current views on the topic and to serve as a clinical guide to the understanding and treatment of neurosis in children and adolescents. In fulfilling this ambitious goal, two objectives were pursued. The first was to provide each contributing author with ample latitude in presentation, in form as well as content, allowing the full expression of each author's wealth of expertise and experience. This has resulted in a kaleidoscope of approaches and presentations with emphasis on originality and diversity rather than consistency or uniformity. The second was to maintain a clinical orientation through the use of clinical vignettes to provide the reader with an intimate glimpse of the interactions between the doctor and the young patients. It was hoped that the de-emphasis in structure and elaborate theoretical deliberation would be balanced by the impact of the immediate clinical narrative.

Questions regarding neurosogenesis, prevention, object relations, neurotic manifestations, transference neurosis, traumatic neurosis, neurosis in the adolescent or the female child, dreams, art and play in treatment, intergenerational considerations, and research are among many issues examined. Treatment and techniques of intervention have not been addressed fully here and should be the subject of a separate volume.

It is hoped that this book will be of sufficient appeal to the novice as well as to the seasoned clinician searching for familiar landmarks of a road much traveled. Perhaps incidentally this book will serve the purpose of defining more sharply the boundaries of application of dynamic psychotherapy and psychoanalytic treatment to the emotional disorders of childhood.

I am grateful to many people for their encouragement, guidance, and assistance in putting together this volume. Among them, Drs. Selma Kramer, E. James Anthony, Alex Burland, and Henri Parens were especially helpful and their guidance and continued interest were deeply appreciated. Finally, I would like to thank Ruth Dudt for her meticulous care and diligent secretarial work in helping me with the preparation of this volume.

M. Hossein Etezady, M.D.

PART I

THE CONCEPT OF NEUROSIS IN CHILDREN

1

Childhood Neurosis at the End of the 20th Century

E. James Anthony, M.D.

In view of the historical changes in the conceptualizations of childhood neurosis, it seems important to specify the historical moment in any reappraisal of the disorder. Metabletics, or the science of change, has indicated how sensitive nosology is to the prevailing scientific beliefs of the time and to the general cultural shifts that occur. These bring about shifts in the presentation, representation, and prevalence of any particular disorder. The dynamic approach to neurosis has less stability than the descriptive counterpart since it relies heavily on inferential and subjective elements, and also because of theoretical developments in the field.

The authors of the *DSM-III* (1982) decided to omit the class of neuroses, well aware that this was "a matter of great concern to many clinicians." They pointed out that Freud's use of the term "psychoneurosis" was based on both descriptive and etiological factors. They averred that there was "no consensus" in our field as to how to define "neurosis" (p. 9) and concluded that in order to avoid ambiguity the term neurotic disorder should be used only descriptively and the term neurotic process employed when the clinician wished to indicate etiological or dynamic elements. The term neurotic disorder encompassed a symptom or group of symptoms that is distressing to the individual; it is regarded as ego-dystonic, with reality testing and behavior within normal limits. It is not confined to transient reaction to stressors and not demonstrably related to organic factors. The concept of neurotic process, on the other hand, involves an etiological sequence of unconscious conflicts between opposing wishes or between wishes and prohibitions, causing unconscious perception of anticipated danger or dysphoria, leading to the use of defense mechanisms that result in symptomatic developments, personality disturbances, or both (p. 9). In this book, the contributors are mainly concerned with the neurotic process and the dynamic etiologies underlying it. These etiologies, however, have undergone significant changes as psychoanalysis has developed and acquired new insights into the preoedipal phase. It will be logical to begin at the time when Freud first conceived the notion of a neurosis of early childhood that antedated the later adult neurosis.

THE ORIGINAL FORMULATION OF AN INFANTILE NEUROSIS

By a stroke of genius, Freud pursued his conception of an infantile neurosis prospectively in the case of Little Hans (1909) and retrospectively and reconstructively in the case of the Wolf Man (1918), and these two provided the classical examples of the condition. In some ways, it was unfortunate that the qualifying term infantile was used, since in English, this suggested a disturbance in the first year or year-and-a-half of life, whereas the intention was to focus on a period of early childhood ranging between three and five years. This terminology complicated later discussions when preoedipal disturbances were seen as entering the total picture. A second problem lay in the confusion of the normal neurosis occurring as an inherent part of development with a clinical neurosis stemming from the same inherent elements as the normal neurosis, but aggravated by inborn or environmental factors. Thus, it would seem that some infantile neuroses can develop into clinical neuroses of childhood; many infantile neuroses are spontaneously cured by the forces conducing to latency, while a certain unknown number of developmental or clinical neuroses arising at this stage may remain subterranean until reactivated as an adult neurosis.

The developmental conflict or Oedipus complex may remain clinically silent and stage-limited unless the nuclear conflicts involved (between positive and negative oedipal attitudes, between masculine and feminine identifications, between feelings of love and hate occurring ambivalently toward the parents, between castration wishes and fears, and between the different structures within the personality) reach a certain threshold of intensity that is followed by regression, anxiety arising from regressive aims, the warding off of anxiety by means of defense, conflict solution through compromise, and finally, symptom formation.

It must be remembered that the infantile neurosis, when transformed into a clinical neurosis, represents one of many different types of psychopathology encountered during childhood. These psychopathologies may sometimes develop in parallel with the childhood neurosis, blurring the picture of the latter. This was the case with the Wolf Man, where the childhood pathology was diffuse and pervasive as compared with the more circumscribed, phase-specific disorder of Little Hans (Anthony 1975, 1986).

Freud began the analysis of the Wolf Man two years after the successful completion of the analysis with Little Hans. It was better for Freud that the "direct" view preceded the indirect and reconstructive one since it was more trustworthy, more convincing, and sprang to the eyes "with unmistakable distinctness" (Freud 1955, p. 9). The case of Hans was also far less severe and set within a relatively normal and expectable environment. If one was looking for the uncontaminated Oedipus complex, this was clearly the patient in which to find it. Having inspected it at close quarters, Freud was in a much better position to find his way through the complex entanglements that characterized the early psychopathology of the Wolf Man. In the relatively brief first inspection entailing Little Hans, Freud was not able to visualize the boy's bisexuality or the biphasic nature of his nuclear complex, but it is also possible that these two elements are far more subdued when development is almost within the normal range. If the Wolf Man had been treated as a child, the analysis would undoubtedly have taken much longer and presented itself with far less clarity.

Despite the less complex clinical picture, the representational competence of a small child robbed the account of some of its richness as well as some of its authenticity since "too many words and thoughts have to be lent to the child" (Freud 1955, p. 9). It is possible, however, that the circumscribed neurosis of childhood may have a less convoluted developmental complex than the diffuse neurosis even when both are examined directly through child analysis (Anthony 1986).

In the case of Little Hans, Freud separated the unconscious complexes and wishes and the repression from the reawakening or return of the unconscious that produced a clinical condition of phobia which was precipitated when he saw the horse fall down in the street. This event crystallized his diffuse anxiety that appeared to be floating around searching for some object on which to settle. Ordinary life, of course, provides many instances of this. The pure complex was formulated by Freud as follows: "Long before he was in the world, I had known that a Little Hans would come who would be so fond of his mother that he would be bound to feel afraid of his father because of it . . ." (Freud 1909, p. 42).

The predisposing factor that led to the transformation of the developmental complex (the infantile neurosis) into the clinical neurosis (the phobia) was the birth of his sister, which from that time on gave him no rest. It was a normal event that produced normal reactions: a temporary separation from his mother, a resulting diminution in the amount of care and attention he received from her, envy at the infantile gratifications experienced by his rival, a new sense of loneliness, exclusion from his parents' bedroom, the observation of the difference between the sexes, and the wish to have a baby as his mother had. He was also extremely curious about what his father did in bed with his mother and, since he slept with his mother in his father's absence, he wished that he could be rid of him as well as his sister. There was no traumatic factor associated with the start of the neurosis and the intensity of the response to horses depended on the symbolic significance that they had acquired. With Hans, it was a horse-complex while with the Wolf Man it was a wolf-complex, although the Wolf Man also had a fear of horses as he had a fear of many other things.

In the case of the Wolf Man, Freud did not separate the developmental complex from the actual neurosis since a good deal of disturbed experience preceded the grandfather's story of the tailor and the wolf. There was the primal scene observation at 1½; the "scene" with Grusha just before 2½; the screen memory of the parents' departure with his sister, leaving him alone with his nurse at 2½; his mother's lamentations to the doctor at 3¼ ("I can't go on living like this any more"); the seduction by his sister and the castration threat from his nurse at 3¼; and finally the arrival of the English governess at 3½, followed by a marked change in his behavior. At the same time, there was a refusal to eat anything except sweet things until he was threatened by a fear of death. Freud felt that this disturbance of appetite was "the very first of the patient's neurotic illnesses, and that, together with the wolf phobia and the obsessional piety, it constituted a 'complete series' of infantile disorders" which finally predisposed him to a neurotic breakdown in early adult life. It will be noted that here Freud is talking about a complete series of neurotic disorders. These transient disturbances are often "shouted down in the nursery" and mistaken for naughtiness. In fact, neurotic naughtiness often has the habit of suddenly turning into anxiety, as was the case with the butterfly phobia developed by the Wolf Man. Freud had an answer for those who would underplay the significance of trivial and transient reactions of little children.

It will be objected that few children escape such disorders as a temporary loss of appetite or an animal phobia. But this argument is exactly what I should wish for. I am ready to assert that every neurosis in an adult is built upon a neurosis which has occurred in his childhood, but has not invariably been severe enough to strike the eye and be recognized as such. This objection only serves to emphasize the theoretical importance of the part which infantile neuroses must play in our view of those later disorders which we treat as neuroses and endeavor to attribute entirely to the effects of adult life. If our present patient [the Wolf Man] had not suffered from obsessional piety in addition to his disturbance of appetite and his animal phobia, his story would not have been noticeably different from that of other children, and we should have been the poorer by the loss of precious material which may guard us against certain plausible errors." [Freud 1918, p. 99]

It is not easy to disentangle the kaleidoscopic events of early childhood or to see them all distinctly in any one case, whether at the time of occurrence in the analysis of the child or fifteen years later. First, there is the nuclear complex that has its own attendant anxieties that may amplify into an infantile neurosis, that is, according to Freud, "not severe enough to strike the eye and be recognized as such" (p. 99). Then there is the possibility of a complete series of infantile disorders. In the case of the Wolf Man they stretch from about age 3 to the final outbreak of the obsessional neurosis at 10. Finally, there is an adult neurosis at 17. Again in the case of the Wolf Man, this was precipitated by gonorrhea, which represents the aftermath of an obsessional neurosis, but was regarded by other clinicians as manic-depression. After four years of treatment, Freud regarded the Wolf Man as cured, although some time later he came back for a few months of work on an unresolved piece of transference.

The normal developmental conflict is at first largely external, stemming from incompatibilities between the child's needs and the external demands of the environment. Gradually, the external demand is internalized, and the developmental conflict disappears, since the balance is shifted from the need to gratify pleasurable impulses to the need to comply with the new internal representatives of the external order. With each resolution of conflict in the child, there is a further step to a formation of the normal adult personality, but when the conflict is unresolved, two forms of neurotic disturbance tend to occur. The first is circumscribed and restricted to the phase of conflict—that is, the premorbid history seems relatively peaceful, the parents are more helpful than harmful, constitutional factors are slight, and the prognosis is fairly good. The second and more common form is a diffuse neurotic disturbance that presents itself as a polymorphous mixture of two or more neuroses. The clinical picture lacks definition, and the pathological processes seem potentially capable of developing in several different directions that are difficult to predict. There is often gross familial pathology, with a plethora of constitutional dispositions. In contrast with the first form, the defense mechanisms used tend to be more various and primitive. As a result of the multiple fixation points, a sequence of different neurotic reactions appears during the course of development (Anthony 1975).

In his classical studies, Freud described four different types of childhood neurosis, three of which had later neurotic developments in adult life. This well-known series of cases is shown in tabulated form in Table 1-1, exemplifying some of Freud's important conclusions that neurotic reactions in the adult are associated frequently with neurotic reactions in childhood; that the connection is sometimes continuous but more often separated by a latent period of nonneurosis; and that infantile sexuality, both fantasied and real, occupies a memorable place in the early history of the patient.

There are certain differences worth noting in the four cases shown in the table. First, the phobic reactions tended to start at about 4 or 5 years old, the obsessional reactions between 6 and 7, and the conversion reactions at 8. The amount of background disturbance is greatest in the conversation reaction and the mixed neurosis, and it seems only slight in the phobic and obsessional reactions. The course of the phobic reaction seems little influenced by severe traumatic factors, whereas traumatic factors, such as sexual seductions, play an important role in the three other subgroups. At an earlier period, Freud elaborated his seduction hypothesis as the cause of neurosis, in terms of which the obsessive-compulsive and the hysterical reactions were alleged to originate in active and passive sexual experiences. Later, the actual seductions were relegated to the sphere of fantasy as the intrapsychic etiology of neurosis became paramount in Freud's theory.

One of the striking features of these classical cases is the place of animals in the genesis of the neurosis. Animal fears and anxiety dreams about animals are frequent between the ages of 3 and 5, and it is also true that frightening experiences with animal pets are not unusual in this same age group. Therefore, it would seem natural that in the search for an external object on which to displace internal danger, the animal is first choice. In his discussion of animism and totemism, Freud (1913) observed that a sense of kinship existed between children and animals,

TABLE 1-1. Classical Psychoneurotic Reactions of Childhood

	Conversion Reaction (Dora)	Phobic Reaction (Hans)	Obsessive-Compulsive Reaction (Rat Man)	Mixed Neurotic Reaction (Wolf Man)
Family history	Striking family history of psychiatric and physical illness.	Both parents treated for neurotic conflict but not severe.	No family history of mental illness.	Striking family history of psychiatric and physical illness.
Symptoms	Enuresis and masturbation, 6–8 yr. Onset of neurosis at 8. Migraine, nervous cough, and hoarseness at 12. Aphonia at 16. "Appendicitis" at 16. Convulsions at 16. Facial neuralgia at 19. Change of personality at 8 from "wild creature" to quiet child.	Compulsive questions at 3–3½ yr. in regard to sex difference. Jealous reaction to sibling birth at 3½. Overt castration threat. Overt masturbation at 3½. Overeating and constipation at 4–5. Phobic reaction at 4–5. Attack of flu at 5 worsens phobia. Tonsillectomy at 5 worsens phobia.	Naughty period at 3–4 yr. Marked timidity after beating by father at 4. Recognizing people by their smells as a child (*Renifleur*). Precocious ego development. Onset of obsessive ideas at 6–7.	Tractable and quiet up to 3¼ yr. "Naughty" period at 3¼–4 yr. Phobias at 4–5 with nightmares. Obsessional reaction at 6–7 (pious ceremonials). Disappearance of neuroses at 8.
Causes	Seduction by older man. Father's illness. Father's affair.	Seductive care by mother. Sibling birth at 3½.	Seduction by governess at 4. Death of sibling at 4. Beating by father at 4.	Seduction by older sister at 3¼. Mother's illness. Conflict between maid and governess.

Adapted from "Classical Neurotic Reactions of Childhood" by Anna Freud. IJPA, Vol. 47, 1966, pp. 116–122. Copyright © Institute of Psycho-Analysis.

as if they were not too far apart in their thinking and feeling, except for the fact, as noted by the child, that animals seem much freer in their sexual and aggressive behavior and much less hampered by social restrictions. Animals can therefore serve admirably for the projection of unacceptable feelings. Occasionally, the animal phobia gives place to a different type of phobia and in some cases, such as with the Wolf Man, it may be replaced by obsessive-compulsive reactions. As Freud came to scrutinize the childhood situation retrospectively and then directly, he began to recognize the disturbance categorized by caretakers as an authentic neurotic reaction which he saw later as an exaggeration of an underlying developmental conflict that was less discernible. He soon arrived at the conclusion that every adult neurosis was built on an infantile one but did not make the generalization, now widely accepted, that every child necessarily passes through a stage of neurosis that was normally resolved prior to latency. Subsequently, Klein (1958) added earlier stages to the Oedipus conflict, postulating an earlier appearance of the superego with guilt displaced back to the pregenital impulses and with anxiety caused by the beginning of the Oedipus conflict taking the form of a dread of being devoured and destroyed. In this view, the Oedipus complex began during the first year of life similarly with both the sexes in relation to the mother's breast, which is the essential factor that determines the whole emotional and sexual development. The gratification experienced at the breast then enables the baby to turn toward new objects, first the father's penis; this movement is given additional impetus by any frustration in the breast relationship. The imagos of breast and penis are then established within the ego and form the nucleus of the superego. Klein agreed with Freud that every child passed through a neurosis differing only in degree from one individual to another, but she would add that every infant experiences anxieties that are psychotic in content and that the infantile neurosis is the normal means of dealing with and modifying these anxieties. For her, the infantile depressive position occupied the central role in the child's development. The complex feelings, fantasies, and anxieties included under this term supported the view that the child, in his early development, went through a transitory manic-depressive state as well as a state of mourning that became modified by the infantile neurosis, and with the passing of this, the infantile depressive position is overcome. This means that the child's belief and trust in his capacity to love, in his reparative paths, and in the integration and security of his good inner world increases as a result of constant and manifold proofs gained by the testing of external reality, so that manic-omnipotence decreases along with the obsessional push toward reparation, all of which indicates that the infantile neurosis has passed.

The Kleinian addendum suggests an interlocking of psychotic and neurotic elements in the genesis of the infantile neurosis so that one would assume that where the developmental passage is clinically upset, the clinical neurotic picture will in time manifest manic-depressive and paranoid features, which is what was reported diagnostically in the case of the Wolf Man. It is far easier to see the likelihood of such developments in this case than in the case of Little Hans, so that the question of severity may be a crucial factor in determining the eventual clinical neurotic picture in the adult. However, it is not quite clear how the earlier psychotic developments lead to the phase-specific vulnerability for neurotic development or in what way they contribute to the phase-specific conflicts of the phallic-oedipal period.

The same question of predisposition can be raised with regard to the addenda proposed by Anna Freud (1954) and Greenacre (1954) relating to the prestructural phase of development. Anna Freud dealt with two types of mothering experience during the "darkest of all ages," namely the first year of the infant's life. The "seducing" mother, owing to her own strong libidinal bias, overstimulates the infant, generating fixations, and the "rejecting" mother fails to fulfill her role as the object of the child's libidinal desires, likewise creating fixations. These preoedipal influences during which primitive needs relating to eating, sleeping, eliminating, interacting, and bodily contact were either frustrated or overexcited, led to diffuse pathological developments and neurotic disorders not unlike those of the Wolf Man. Anna Freud believed that these physiological functions and dysfunctions are the first mental representatives of the body and provide the first content of the mind, which, as she sees it, is one of extreme simplicity as compared with complex operations envisaged by Klein. In her view, the child at this point is dominated by need and not by the relation to the parts object. Anna Freud insists that "the mother is not responsible for the child's neurosis, even if she causes 'chaotic' development in some instances. By rejecting and seducing, she can influence, distort, and determine development, but she cannot produce either neurosis or psychosis" (A. Freud 1954, p. 347). She also felt that the self-righting aspects of development could help to mitigate some of the environmental experiences.

Greenacre (1954) produced the novel concept of two pervading and contrasting rhythms: the one soothing and lulling and the other a steplike rise of mounting excitement and strain. The former categorizes the aggressive activities such as rocking, sucking, stroking, and so forth, while the latter is represented above all by phallic masturbation, which has a more progressive significance. Many of the child's activities contain elements of both in varying combinations. Sexual stimulation by a caretaker may produce either type of rhythm or both. It is not clear at present what impact such early activities have on the genesis or choice of neurosis.

Hartmann (1954, 1964) had some interesting things to say regarding the new developments relating to infantile neurosis. As he says, "It is actually not so easy to say what we call an infantile neurosis." He pointed out that whereas Freud rescued the diagnosis from the moral indictment of "naughtiness," almost fifty years later clinicians were confronted with the reverse situation, and every piece of naughtiness and "actually every behavior of the child that does not conform to the textbook model, every developmental step that is not according to plan," were considered "neurotic." What this meant to him was that the broad range of normal variations of behavior was not being recognized, and that the very specific features that analysts referred to as neurosis were lost sight of. As far as infantile neurosis was concerned, he felt that we had more questions than answers, but this was not cause for dismay as much more was now known about developmental psychology than at the turn of the century. What was needed was still more precise and thorough knowledge of normal development. However, he insisted that most of what Freud had said about infantile neurosis a long time ago remained true at the current time.

Hartmann made some succinct comments on the neurotic process in children: that it was generally limited to a single functional disturbance, that the step from conflict to symptom was shorter than in adult neurosis, that the differentiation of ego and id as a basic prerequisite for the development of neurosis still held true, and that the fixations and conflicts found in infantile neurosis were also frequently found at the basis of adult neurosis. In the Wolf Man, the sequence of early childhood neurosis, latency neurosis, and adult neurosis was clearly in evidence.

Hartmann also made three further observations that throw light on the infantile neuroses: that phase-adequate neurotic reactions in the child may be healthier than no such reaction, representing the best possible solution of a given childhood conflict; that the infantile neurosis may in certain instances mean calcification through the establishment of rigid fixations on certain drives or defenses; and that preoedipal events such as traumata, specific physiological frustrations, and the Greenacre rhythms may lead not to neurosis but to psychosomatic disorders and borderline states even though one can consider them pathogenic.

THE REENACTMENT OF THE INFANTILE NEUROSIS IN THE CHILD ANALYTIC TRANSFERENCE NEUROSIS

The notion of transference neurosis has evoked a great deal of controversy over the years and there are analysts, particularly Kleinian, who believe that it is a regular feature of analytic work with children. For instance, there are those who feel that it makes an intermittent appearance, but never as completely and intensely as in the case of adult patients; there are those who have observed its occurrence when the child under treatment is separated from his parent; and finally, there are those who think that transferences occur in the child analysis but never to the extent of the neurotic formation. Klein (1927) is of the opinion that the full transference neurosis occurs in children in a manner analogous to what arises with adults and that parents have reported to her that they have seen habits long since disappeared return again.

In 1930, Jenny Waelder Hall reported on the analysis of a 7-year-old boy, Anton, suffering from night terror that was published many years later in English (1946). Anton showed exhibitionistic and voyeuristic tendencies toward his analyst, told her that he loved her and that he wanted to marry her, but that since he had no money, she would not want to marry him. The analyst reported that

> the transference neurosis [sic] brought abundant material to the surface. Gradually, however, this changed into play acting and ceased to provide much material. Taking the interpretation of the transference neurosis as the starting point, I tried once more to find a connection with the first material of the analysis. But he flatly refused to tell me anything for the fear that then we would reach the end of the treatment too quickly, and he wanted to come and see me for a long time. [p. 209]

Sylvester (1945) analyzed a 4-year-old child with psychogenic anorexia and vomiting, and concluded that the structure of the disturbance was similar to the structure of depression in the making as postulated by Abraham (1924). This involved aggression against the mother, incorporative and cannibalistic impulses arising from fixations at the oral-sadistic level leading to introjective-projective defenses against good-bad objects. The little patient also went through phases in which she manifested intense wishes for gratification by the mother and for undivided possession of her, aggressive and destructive wishes toward her, identification with her, anger directed against the siblings and all the males in the family, and regressive play. Having worked through this varied preoedipal material, an intense oedipal phase was instituted, characterized by open masturbation during her session accompanied by sexual curiosity and activity. The anorexia and the vomiting were completely relinquished. Her neurosis showed at first with depression, but as she progressed, the neurotic aspects came to the forefront and the original autoplastic manifestations of her organ neurosis gave place to the alloplastic behavior that showed in the transference neurosis (p. 107).

Harley's (1967) report on transference developments in a 5-year-old demonstrated that the transference was not limited to current reactions toward the original love object but included earlier libidinal and aggressive strivings reanimated by the analytic process and directed toward the analyst. The transference neurosis, arising from repressed conflicts and centering on the analyst, could be observed in a limited or circumscribed form during certain phases of treatment with even such a young child. It was surprising how the child, Anne, was able to confine a repetition of her earlier fears to the analytic situation. According to Harley, "This lasted for a number of weeks, and seemed to fulfill the criteria for a circumscribed transference neurosis." Anne was able to organize not only preoedipal but also phallic conflicts around her anal trauma which then took on the meaning of an oedipal sexual attack.

All these experiences in the transference would support the thesis that the original infantile neurosis and its clinical amplification were not as clear-cut as was originally thought, but contained both preoedipal and oedipal processes.

THE INFANTILE NEUROSIS CONCEPTUALIZED AT THE END OF THE CENTURY

This has truly been the Freudian Age persisting right through the twentieth century. The concept that held true at the beginning of this era underwent modification as psychoanalysis itself gradually evolved and changed. The analytic techniques that were originally devised for the treatment of neurosis are increasingly applied to faults, failures, and frustrations of development before the advent of the infantile neurosis. This shifting viewpoint has been summed up by Anna Freud (1970):

As analysts we propose a multiple view of the infantile neurosis. On the one hand, we regard it as belonging to the realm of psychopathology and realize that in its extensive form it can be severe and crippling. On the other hand, we also know that it has a regular place in the childhood of many individuals whose future adaptation to life is successful, and that the conflicts underlying it are normal ones. Seen from the developmental point of view, the infantile neurosis can represent a positive sign of personality growth; a progression from primitive to more sophisticated reaction patterns and as such, the consequence and, perhaps, the price which has to be paid for higher human development. [p. 202]

Today the mother–infant relationship has extended into the area of infant psychopathology in which the mothering capacity of the caretaker is balanced against the infant's reaction to its environment together with its constitutional capacity. The steadiness and strength of this object relation help to facilitate internalizations and identifications and prepare the ground for neurotic development. The oral and anal component instincts are equally important for the formation of infantile neurosis by preparing the way for regression and compromise formation. The preneurotic symptom formations connected with eating, touching, sleeping, and excreting also play a part, together with conflicts that are still being waged between id drives and the external environment. In the phallic phase, the infantile neurosis peaks and assumes its final shape with advances in structuralization, internalization, and compromise symptom formation.

The complex picture presented by the infantile neurosis today represents an elaborate attempt to deal with conflicting drive derivatives, pleasurable and painful affects, ambivalent attitudes toward objects, together with the whole range of the oedipal and castration complexes set against the background of personal characteristics that have been emerging since infancy and shaped by the fixation point left behind during development. All these interactions are revealed in every analysis of an infantile neurosis.

The cumulative viewpoint covering the history of the Wolf Man strengthens the logic of the neurotic formation: the primal scene observation, the bisexuality, the contributions from morality, the inadequacy of food intake, the urethral eroticisms, the experience of seduction, the early castration threat, the receptive-passive and sadomasochistic tendencies of the anal phase, the earlier fears giving way to guilt, the transformation of sadism into masochism, and the passive homosexual trend that succumbed to the ego's fear of castration in the phallic stage. The anxiety hysteria, the phobia, and the conversion symptoms gradually acquired an obsessional overlay causing the whole upheaval to subside spontaneously with some residue left behind—inhibitions toward women with a new dependency on them, repetitive tendencies, an inclination toward men, an intolerance for narcissistic frustration, and finally conduced to the reactivation of a variegated neurotic disorder in adult life. All this was summed up in masterly fashion by Anna Freud almost sixty years after her father, Sigmund, laid the foundation for our understanding of the infantile neurosis and the neurotic disorders stemming from it. It is a clearer, but not necessarily a larger picture than the one conceived originally by Freud.

There is no doubt that the concept of an infantile neurosis, in the strict sense of the term, has proven to be the cornerstone in the psychoanalysis of neurotic disorders whether in children or adults.

"UNFINISHED HUMAN BEINGS" AND DEVELOPMENTAL MOVEMENT

As Anna Freud (1966) pointed out, "Children of all ages are 'unfinished human beings' striving toward maturity" and this movement can continue to advance, be held up, or reversed. In the reversal, the significant factor is whether the libido alone or the ego as a whole undergoes a regression. If the latter is the case, the child remains infantile and more or less incapable of developing an infantile neurosis (p. 305).

Neurosis is the great paradigm of psychoanalysis, and it comes as a shock when psychiatrists seek to reduce its importance in their nosology. But compared to the other psychopathology that afflicts adults and children neurosis belongs to the minority. As Anna Freud has stated (1956):

> Clinics were open to deal with childhood neurosis, even though it was often time limited and "cured" by further development. What came as a surprise were the types of cases with which the clinics were confronted. The majority of children who were referred did not fit the picture of the infantile neurosis. Many children were seen with difficulties or conflicts that were far removed from the oedipal scene, who had in fact never reached the oedipal level, and consequently could not be described as having regressed from it. It was far from easy to bring order into the chaos of clinical pictures . . . as cases of this kind could crowd out those with phobias and incipient obsessional neuroses. [p. 303]

But one needs to be diagnostically assured that we are not dealing with entities beyond (and before) the infantile neurosis but with unusually intense neuroses. Little Hans might well have grown out of his phobia untreated, but perhaps be at risk for an adult neurosis. The Wolf Man, had he presented himself to an analytic outpatient clinic today, might still have the diagnostician concerned with some more serious type of psychopathology such as a borderline disorder. In fact, Blum (1974) speaks of his borderline childhood that led on to a borderline adolescence and then to an adult borderline personality, and in all three instances, he employed the term "borderline" to describe a condition close to psychosis with severe ego impairment but without the irreversible disorganization and structural fragmentation of psychosis. According to Blum, the patient's infantile disturbances also showed characteristics of severe pathology, undergoing a personality transformation at the age of 2 ½, becoming sadistic, suspicious, stressful, rageful, and violent. However, he clearly developed a latency obsessional neurosis (sometimes seen as a precursor to adult schizophrenia), and the two analysts who saw the Wolf Man after 1956, both diagnosed the disorder as obsessional-compulsive personality. Gardener (1956) reported that after having been in contact with the patient for a period of 43 years she concluded that she had seen no evidence of any psychosis. If the Wolf Man suffered from a borderline psychopathology during early childhood as suggested by Blum, then, according to Anna Freud's dicta he would not have graduated to the level of an infantile neurosis and the rich clinical delineations, formulating the condition, would be lost to us. In addition, there would be less discrepancy between the type of patients seen at the beginning of the century and the nonneurotic cases that swamp our clinics toward the end of it.

WHERE DOES ONE GO FROM HERE?

If there are difficulties in teasing out the various elements that qualify the neurotic process, there has also been a surprising lack of clarity in the recognition of the neurotic disorder, and lists and clusterings of symptoms have not eased the situation to any great extent. The cause for this has been ascribed to the antidiagnostic attitude of traditional child guidance clinics, the resistance to using diagnoses derived from adult classifications, and the repugnance to categorizing a child permanently during the years of development and change (Anthony 1975). There has also been an implicit concept of children as more reactive than introversive and a proclivity toward propositions favoring such nondescript behavioral categories as conduct, habit, and situational disorders.

In the few surveys that have been carried out, neurotic reactions of children have shown a frequency of 5-20 percent of all cases with the different figures reflecting the orientation of particular clinics.

In the report of the Group for the Advancements of Psychiatry (1966) on the classification of psychopathological disorders in childhood, an attempt was made to define neurotic reactions in terms acceptable to anyone working broadly within the psychoanalytic frame of reference. Thus, neurosis in childhood was defined as a consequence of unconscious conflicts over the handling of sexual and aggressive impulses that, although repressed, remained active and unresolved. These conflicts derived from the relation of the child to significant family members and belonged almost exclusively to the preschool years. During early childhood, such consequences could be expressed in various symptomatic reactions, but as the children became older, they became more internalized, encapsulated, and chronic. Many of the milder reactions could resolve spontaneously as the child reworked them at a later stage of development and a higher level of maturation. The symptomatology was composed of both positive and negative phenomena: the positive ones included such reactions as anxieties, phobias, conversions, dissociations, and depressions, while the negative phenomena comprised the absence of demonstrable organic pathology, persistent and consistent intellectual deterioration, any primary disturbance of mood, or failure of reality testing. The neurotic group had to be differentiated from so-called reactive disorders, developmental deviations, normative crises, and psychosomatic disorders. The neurotic process could begin with free-floating anxiety and develop into a full neurosis depending on the intensity and internalization of the conflict. In certain instances, the precipitating situation of stress can be so overwhelming and unexpected that it produces a traumatic neurosis that may be either a severe reactive disorder or a sudden crystallization of a latent or subclinical neurotic state. In certain instances, for reasons that are still not completely clear, the symptom formation may not occur, and instead, the personality structure of the child will be diffusely affected by neurotic conflicts and evince traits that are egosyntonic. Later, these traits may coalesce to form a personality disorder.

In milder cases, the differentiation of abnormal and normal reactions presents some degree of difficulty, since various investigations have shown that almost every child manifests various symptom constellations at different stages of development, including neurotic traits. For example, sleep disturbances may occur in the second and third years, phobias in the fourth and fifth years, obsessional activities from the sixth to the eighth year, and a large assortment of anxieties involving apprehensions to do with disease, disfigurement, disability, and death from the ninth year onward.

There have been recent attempts to base an understanding of neurotic reactions on the person's mode of adaptation to such primary disturbing affects as anxiety and depression. Freud came to regard anxiety as playing a primary role in the development of all other types of disordered behavior, the elements of which could be regarded basically as statistics for reducing or avoiding anxiety. In his second theory, it was anxiety that led to repression and not the reverse. He also began to see the close connection between particular defense mechanisms and a particular type of neuroses.

There are certain sequences that follow the emergence of anxiety. For instance, it may remain undefended without an object and experienced both psychologically and physically as an anxiety reaction; or it may be displaced onto some symbolic object or situation, as in the phobic reaction; or converted into various somatic symptoms as in conversion reaction; or it may overwhelm the individual and cause aimless activity or freezing as in dissociative reaction; or transposed by means of various repetitious rituals and reactions as in the obsessive-compulsive reaction; or it may allay itself by self-deprecation and result in a depressive reaction. These techniques are all available to children from an early stage onward, and clinically one may see the reaction in relatively pure form or accompanied by one or more of the other neurotic reactions. Anxiety, however, remains the chief characteristic of the neuroses.

There has been a tendency recently to treat another basic psychobiological affective reaction, depression, in a similar style. Both anxiety and depression are seen as appropriate reactions under normal conditions of danger and desertion, but both can become abnormal when they occur in inappropriate circumstances, when they persist for an undue length of time, or when the child is unable to make a developmentally appropriate adaptation to them. It has been said that many of the symptoms of neurosis represent a misuse of emergency mechanisms. As with anxiety, the individual develops various mechanisms for dealing with depression, such as the development of core feelings of unworthiness, regression, obsessive-compulsive reaction, reversal of affect, identification with idealized figures, acting out in the form of delinquency, and development of psychosomatic ailments. All these defenses are means of mitigating the overwhelming experience of abandonment and loss. In recent times, it has been thought that anxiety and depression are often conjoined in neurotic formation with anxiety being the predominant affect, but actual or fantasied losses are common during the development, and the individual may react both anxiously and depressively. Neurotic reactions these days may be seen, therefore, as a compendium of preoedipal and oedipal elements of anxiety and depression, and of libido and aggression.

In view of this development, it may seem retrogressive to refer again to circumscribed and diffuse types of neurosis in childhood. The circumscribed is restricted to the phase of conflict; the premorbid history seems relatively peaceful, the parents are more helpful than harmful, constitutional factors are slight, and the prognosis is fairly good both with and without treatment. With the diffuse neurosis, the case is polyphasic, the family more severely disturbed, the early history almost continuous with the psychopathology, and the prognosis, with or without treatment, not too favorable. Anthony (1986) attempted to set up an "experimental" situation. He noted that historically an untreated child with a diffuse neurotic illness grew up to become the Wolf Man, and that his adult treatment was interminable and, in the long run, not too successful. He posed the question, "What if the Wolf Man had also been treated like Little Hans as a child? Would the outcome in adult life have been more successful?" To find even a tentative answer seems to depend on finding two cases, circumscribed and diffuse, and engaging them in psychoanalytic treatment by the same child analyst, using the same technique, governed by the same underlying theoretical assumption and over the same period of time.

Two such cases met these criteria and were treated until the neurotic impediments had been removed and normal development resumed. Anthony provided process notes taken randomly from different stages of the treatment. During the initial phase, the neurotic process at work in the treatment situation had differed markedly in the two cases, and the two children were diagnosable as circumscribed and diffuse by independent review. The neurotic reactions for both boys began gradually to look more alike, although each retained a characteristic style of presenting material. In the third phase of treatment, both underwent a regressive transference, but the neurotic symptoms that made their appearance were circumscribed in one case and somewhat diffuse in the other. In the final phase, they began to seem like two fairly healthy boys, but the therapist had the sense of a less favorable prognosis for the diffusely neurotic patient. He also felt that development had taken an active role as the invisible "co-therapist" in the circumscribed case but that the recuperation in the diffuse case stemmed more from the work of analysis. As seen in the two boys' adolescence, in a follow-up, there were personality differences between them that had not been ironed out by the analytic treatment.

CONCLUSION

Metabletics, or the science of change, has enabled us to look at the psychoanalytically crucial notion of infantile neurosis in a wide variety of ways. With every shift of the kaleidoscope, different perspectives have made their appearance, sometimes opposing and sometimes supporting established viewpoints. The shifts of opinions across the century seemed massive, but on closer inspection, the changes were much less striking than appeared at first. Following the first delineation by Freud, each decade seemed to bring important additions of theory coupled with significant changes in clinical practice and in the nature of the patient's disorder, but the classical case of the Wolf Man was like good vintage wine that retained its richness from the beginning of the century to its end. The case had as much to say to us in the first twenty years as it has in the last twenty years. This speaks very much to Freud's genius and his extraordinary capacity to sense the theoretically and therapeutically worthwhile and epoch-making cases within the average patient load of the practicing therapist. Despite their minority status, the neuroses of childhood will stay with us into the next century and continue to provide the paradigms for understanding and treatment that are so invaluable for the growth of our discipline.

Another new perspective that has entered the picture in the last two decades has been the influence of cognitive and perceptive style on the nature of the neurosis, and this is more obvious with the obsessional disorders in which cognition plays such a large part. It has been suggested that ego styles develop early in childhood and remain fairly permanent during the course of life, perhaps enabling the analytic investigator to predict and confirm the later choice of neurosis (A. Freud 1966). In the case of the obsessional neurosis, there are still unanswered questions of how early it can be detected, what part the mother-infant relationship plays in the genesis, how related it is to the tempo of development, and whether the infantile obsessional neurosis is always followed by an adult one. The traumatic management of the anal phase was at one time considered a popular causal factor, but the obsessional line of development may not be significantly decided by mismanagement in the nursery.

In the other great neurosis of childhood, hysteria, one is also concerned today as to whether it "runs in families, whether it is sex-linked, whether a special kind of environment conduces to it, whether constitutional factors influence its development, and whether psychosocial conflict, as psychoanalysis believes, is crucial to its development" (Anthony 1982). The condition has been an elusive and enigmatic one since ancient times, but it is only since Freud that it became a clinical entity of childhood, one of the offshoots of the infantile neuroses, in which certain features disposed toward it: a triadic conflict, an ambivalent dependency on the mother, an inner struggle between passive asexual relations and phallic-sexual ones, a body valued by the parents but open to injury by them, and a father image appearing as very strong and very weak. These appear in projective testing. Whatever the outcome in adolescence or adult life, these individuals remain, as Freud (1895) once described them, "the flowers of mankind, sterile, no doubt, but beautiful as double flowers"; so promising, so gifted as children but to no purpose.

REFERENCES

Abraham, K. (1924). A short study of the development of the libido, viewed in the light of mental disorders. In *Collected Papers on Psychoanalysis*, pp. 418–502. London: Hogarth Press, 1949.

Anthony, E. J. (1975). Neurotic disorders of childhood. In *Comprehensive Textbook of Psychiatry*, vol. 2, ed. A. M. Freedman, H. I. Kaplan, and B. J. Fadack, pp. 2143–2160. Baltimore: Williams & Wilkinson.

——— (1986). Contrasting neurotic styles in the analysis of two preschool children. *The Journal of the American Academy of Child Psychiatry* 25:46–57.

——— (1982). Hysteria in childhood. In *Hysteria*, ed. R. Alex, pp. 145–163. New York: John Wiley.

Blum, H. P. (1974). The borderline childhood of the Wolf Man. *Journal of the American Psychoanalytic Association* 22:721–742.

Bornstein, B. (1946). Hysterical twilight states. *Psychoanalytic Study of the Child* 2:151–166. New York: International Universities Press.

DSM-III, Diagnostic and Statistical Manual of Mental Disorders (1980). Washington, DC: American Psychiatric Association.

Freud, A. (1954). Problems of infantile neurosis: contribution to the discussion. In *The Writings of Anna Freud*, vol. 4, 1945–1956, pp. 324–355. New York: International Universities Press, 1968.

——— (1966). Obsessional neurosis: a summary of psychoanalytic views. In *The Writings of Anna Freud*, vol. 5, 1956–1965, pp. 242–264. New York: International Universities Press, 1969.

——— (1970). The infantile neurosis: genetic and dynamic considerations. In *The Writings of Anna Freud*, vol. 7, 1966–1970, pp. 189–203. New York: International Universities Press, 1971.

Freud, S., with Breuer, J. (1895). Studies in hysteria. *Standard Edition* 2:3–309.

Freud, S. (1909). Analysis of the phobia in a five-year-old boy. *Standard Edition* 10:5–152.

——— (1913). Totem and taboo. *Standard Edition* 13:1–192.

——— (1918). From the history of an infantile neurosis. *Standard Edition* 17:7–122.

Gardner, M. (1971). *The Wolf Man by the Wolf Man*. New York: Basic Books.
Hall, J. W. (1946). The analysis of a case of night terrors. *The Psychoanalytic Study of the Child* 2:189–228. New York: International Universities Press.
Hartmann, H. (1954). A problem of infantile neurosis. In *Essays on Ego Psychology*, pp. 204–214. New York: International Universities Press, 1964.
Harley, M. (1967). Transference developments in a four-year-old child. In *The Child Analyst at Work*, ed. E. Geleerd, pp. 115–141. New York: International Universities Press.
Klein, M. (1928). The Oedipus complex in the light of early anxieties. In *Contributions to Psychoanalysis 1921–1945*, pp. 339–390. London: Hogarth Press, 1948.
Sylvester, E. (1945). Analysis of psychogenic anorexia in a four-year-old. *Psychoanalytic Study of the Child* 1:167–188. New York: International Universities Press.

2

Symptomatic Disturbances and Clinical Manifestations of Neurosis in Children and Adolescents

Helen R. Beiser, M.D.

I was surprised to realize how difficult it is to describe clinical manifestations of neurosis in children. Should one include every deviation of behavior and affect that may occur, or stick with the definition in use for adult neurosis? (*DSM-III*, pp. 9–19, 364–365).[1] As far as I could determine, the adult definition has several aspects. First, neurosis results from structural conflicts, with symptoms resulting from compromise formation; second, these symptoms have symbolic meaning; and third, they are ego dystonic. Where does this put the behavioral and physical symptoms of infancy which have no basis in organic disease? At what age does the personality have enough of a structure to have a structural conflict? When does one have evidence of symbol formation or other unconscious meaning? What if the child enjoys the deviant behavior, or denies that he/she has a problem? In order to fulfill at least some of the criteria for a neurosis, the child analyst probably has to include the parents as part of the child's personality structure, at least for the very young child. Certainly no neurotic child will be brought for therapy unless the symptom is ego dystonic to the parent. Sometimes it may be

---

1. In 1987, *DSM-III-R* again eliminated the diagnosis of neurosis except as explanatory for dysthymia. This makes the process discussion important as opposed to a descriptive diagnosis.

dystonic to one parent and not to the other, which further confuses the situation.

Diagnosis of neurosis in children may then be quite complicated. Usually a neurosis is a regression from a previously attained level of development. This should differentiate deviant behavior of a constitutional nature from that due to a conflict. For example, if the symptom is enuresis, and the child is of an age at which such control could be expected but has never been dry, pathology in the urinary tract should be investigated before concluding that the symptom is neurotic. The enuresis that is first observed when arrangements have been made for the child to go away to camp is more obviously a psychological evidence of anxiety and is susceptible to analytic therapy. Of course, chronic enuresis on an organic basis may have neurotic consequences due to negative attitudes that exist in the child's environment.

Another problem in diagnosis relates to deciding when a symptom which is expectable as part of a developmental stress has shifted to a well crystallized neurosis. A reluctance to separate from parents at the end of the day, due to the immature child's inability to conceptualize reunion the next morning, may slowly shift to a phobia of the dark or a chronic battle with parents over going to bed. In such situations, parental attitudes and behavior are influential in determining the outcome. The parent, for reasons of ignorance or personal pathology, may be unable to help the child negotiate one or more developmental stresses. It may be hard to say why some children with such parents develop discrete neurotic symptoms, some will develop character traits, and others more total character disorders. It is probable that the latter occurs when the parental attitude is chronic, and the resulting behavior not too unacceptable to the parent. Such deviant behavior may only come to light when the child goes to school and does not fit into that environment. This might make the child and parent see the behavior in a more ego dystonic way, or set up a conflict externally with the school.

TYPES OF NEUROTIC BEHAVIOR

Classification is difficult, and the term "neurosis" was eliminated from *DSM-II*, but reintroduced in *DSM-III*. Because of the protean nature of neurotic symptoms in childhood, it might be helpful to review the major forms of behavior, affective deviation, interpersonal relations, and physical symptoms that *may* be neurotic. *Anything* may be neurotic, but if the definition is adhered to, not *everything*.

Perhaps anxiety is the symptom most clearly associated with neurosis in childhood. If limited to a particular developmental stress situation, it is not neurotic, but if it spreads to a generalized state, even to panic, it certainly is irrational and probably has unconscious meaning. If focused on one or more specific objects or situations, the anxiety then is a specific phobia, whose unconscious meaning may be determined in the course of psychotherapy. If anxiety is repressed, it may be converted into physical symptoms. Conversion reaction such as paralysis of voluntary muscle groups, or sensory symptoms such as anaesthesias or blindness are rare in children. The stomachaches of the phobic child may be a form of conversion reaction. Probably related to anxiety is a character type rather than a symptom, the avoidant personality who stays away from situations that might produce anxiety. Shyness is an avoidant trait, as are some learning problems. Learning may symbolize adult unhappiness, or even death. A different way of dealing with anxiety is through obsessive-compulsive defenses. These may be rituals, obsessional fears, or a personality that is overly conscientious. Actually, it may be difficult to differentiate obsessive fears from anxiety neurosis.

There is a new interest in depression in children, even in the early appearance of bipolar disease, although this cannot be considered a neurosis. Most depressions are a reaction to some real or perceived loss, such as death or disappearance of a family member. Grief can be expected, and is not neurotic unless it is prolonged and there are elements of conflict due to hostility toward the lost person with ensuing guilt. Depressive mood swings are considered by many to be a normal part of adolescence.

A wide variety of problems in interpersonal relationships reflect problems in object relations. They may or may not have neurotic elements to them. Most extreme are autistic children (Mahler et al. 1968 pp. 6–7). At one time this syndrome was considered to be a reaction to faulty parenting, but it is now classified as a developmental disability. Although this is a rare condition, it has been extensively studied, and its response to various kinds of treatment highly controversial. Much more common is the dependent child. The expectation to be taken care of like a younger child may be the result of a physical illness with prolongation of a necessary dependence, or a result of a parental message indicating that the parent, for a number of possible reasons, does not want the child to grow up. In contrast, the oppositional child always seems to oppose the parent, sometimes attempting tasks beyond the level of his or her ability. This is much more likely to be dystonic to the parents. In the male child, the mother might complain while the father feels that his son is "all boy." A step further is the sadomasochistic child. Oppositionalism may become bullying, or provoking someone to punish him/her. In milder form, this may have neurotic features, and be treatable psychoanalytically. Clear, long-term antisocial behavior cannot be treated as a neurosis. It is possible in some cases that if the behavior is controlled, depression or somatic symptoms may appear, which can then be treated as a neurosis (Aichorn 1935). Although signs of deviate gender identity may appear very early, homosexual behavior does not usually appear until adolescence. Stoller indicates that there are more than constitutional factors involved, and if not too crystallized, and if ego dystonic, many sexual disorders of children may be amenable to analytic therapy.

Finally, there is the wide variety of physical symptoms that may have a neurotic component. These include enuresis, encopresis, sleepwalking, nightmares, eating disturbances, hyperactivity, learning disorders, and tics and other movement disorders. Other diseases or symptoms that may have a neurotic component are asthma, neurodermatitis, arthritis, and ulcerative colitis, as well as occasional constipation, diarrhea, and headache and stomachache. Many of these require combined medical and psychiatric diagnosis and treatment.

REACTION TO DEVELOPMENTAL STRESS: THE MODEL FOR NEUROSIS

The human baby is a remarkably immature organism, totally dependent on caretakers. Full maturity takes many years, and has been divided into developmental phases by Freud in his classical essay on the theory of sexuality. Others have elaborated on these or proposed other systems, but the important thing is to recognize the transitions from one phase to another, which are usually accompanied by symptoms of stress. These symptoms are often considered typical for a given phase, and normally do not last long or develop into neurotic symptoms, although there may be a close external similarity.

Infancy

In early infancy stress could be considered that of adjusting to life outside of the womb. Infants express stress through physical symptoms such as excessive crying, difficulty in being soothed, difficulty sleeping, disturbance in gastrointestinal functions, or failure to relate to caretakers. This is hard to diagnose as neurotic, or to predict as a later neurotic disorder. Neurotic symptoms in the mother are easier to diagnose, and may be reflected in her handling of the infant. When there is no organic disease, many of the foregoing physical disturbances may be reactive to high anxiety levels in the mother, to neglect, or to stereotyped handling. I observed, as an intern on a pediatric service, a baby with eczema discharged in the morning with a clear skin and returned the same afternoon covered with a rash.

In the latter half of the child's first year, two new stresses usually arise. Stranger anxiety is the result of neurological maturation, allowing the baby to differentiate mother from strangers, and strangers are greeted by anxious crying or avoidance. In an extremely sensitive baby with a protective mother, this may lay the groundwork for a dependent neurosis or an avoidant personality. A somewhat later development is separation anxiety. Most babies react with crying and clinging when the mother leaves the room. They do not have a concept of time to help them wait, which is part of the process of developing object constancy. If this is encouraged by mothers who are anxious about leaving their babies, separation may be expected to continue into subsequent phases. A neurotic mother may have an obsessional fear of her baby dying while she is away.

The Toddler

In the anal or separation-individuation phase, the child is now mobile and can separate on his/her own initiative. The continuing inability to conceive of the difference between temporary and permanent separations is probably the basis of running away followed by clinging to or following the mother. There may be particular difficulty in going to bed and going to sleep. Although this might be seen as a fear of the dark, it is more likely a fear of separating from mother at the end of the day for fear she will not be there in the morning. Crying on waking up in the middle of the night may have the same meaning. I remember a case where I had consulted with parents who were undergoing a custody battle over their older child. As if sensing the anxiety over separation, the 14-month-old son woke up at night repeatedly and clung to them. The child who walks early who may dash away from mother in a new-found independence may suddenly dissolve in tears when he or she realizes the separation and fright.

The task of controlling sphincters in order to become clean and dry is a new stress in this period. At one time, oppositional behavior was thought to be a product of early, strict toilet training. However, oppositionalism seems to be a characteristic of this stage even with the mildest of training or encouragement toward cleanliness, and Spitz found that the ability to say no was an important milestone in the achievement of autonomy and power. It may develop into a characterologic or neurotic problem if a parent gets into a head-to-head power struggle. If handled punitively, the child is more likely to become hostile, and other defense mechanisms may be involved.

Even if not handled punitively, this phase ushers in a new behavior, which, if seen later, is considered neurotic. The repetition involved in the mastery of new tasks can take on a ritualistic quality. It may be difficult to differentiate pleasurable repetition in order to attain mastery from rituals that defend against hostility or anxiety. The famous example of Freud's grandson repeatedly throwing a spool away and then recovering it was his way of dealing with separation anxiety. There are a number of common pounding toys that allow expression of anger by hitting, as well as repetitive mastery of the mechanism of the toy. Also to be differentiated is the repetition of perseveration due to organic deficit. Clinically, the rituals developed around bedtime are the most frequent, and may last a lifetime without being considered anything more than a personal idiosyncrasy. If intense and prolonged, however, the struggle over bedtime can be considered neurotic. There is certainly a conflict between the physiological need for sleep, and the desire to keep actively involved with the mother. Oppositionalism is also usually involved. Although speculative, it can be assumed that the fear of the dark has an unconscious meaning of fear of loss of mother. Here we clearly approach the adult meaning of neurosis. The relationship with mother in this period, so admirably described by Mahler (1968), is a stress that may also contribute to later neurosis. The conflict between the desire for autonomy and the desire for closeness to mother results in ambivalence, which, depending on the intensity of the conflict and the reactions of the mother, may lay the groundwork for future difficulties in object relations. In general, the stresses in this period provide the basis for the broad outline of personality types. Whether they are oppositional, overly compliant, or anxious depends on the strength of various aspects of the conflicts.

Oedipal Phase

As the child becomes more comfortable in motoric autonomy and develops language and symbolic abilities, the remaining anxieties from earlier phases are more elaborated, and new stresses appear. Waking at night is now more often accompanied by dreams that the child can relate, indicating either a fear of the child's own aggression or a fear of loss of protection. This becomes clinically significant if the child awakens the parents, and they seek professional help, at least partially for their own comfort. I recall the mother of a 5-year-old girl consulting me because her daughter repeatedly woke her up crying about a dream of a lion chasing her. Instead of comforting her or explaining the lack of reality of dreams, she anxiously asked the child, "What color were his eyes?" This is a vivid example of how phase-specific stresses may be supported, and develop into a neurosis.

At this phase or earlier, according to Galenson and Roiphe (1971), children become aware of the differences between the sexes. They also explore their own bodies, including the genitals, which usually results in masturbation. The resulting castration anxiety may lead to inhibition or retaliatory aggression. Sometimes masturbation in boys leads to an actual castration threat from parents. This threat has a different effect than the fantasy of castration, which is more likely to have a neurotic outcome. Girls are likely to believe that they have been castrated, also providing the unconscious elements for a neurosis.

Classically, the main stress of this period is the oedipal conflict, with the wish to possess the parent of the opposite sex and displace the parent of the same sex. The resulting conflict in loyalties may precipitate the child into a regression. The defensive mechanisms used, such as anxious clinging, compulsive rituals, or unmanageable behavior to provoke punishment, vary with the child's previous experiences. Some children may avoid the conflict by precociously concentrating on intellectual activities, although at the same time they may continue to suck their thumb or wet the bed. It may be particularly difficult for children who have lost a parent through death or divorce to negotiate the triadic object relations required to resolve this conflict properly.

Another frequent stress during this phase is the acquisition of a sibling. To the toddler, a baby is simply an annoyance, frequently directly attacked or disapproved of. The negative reaction of parents to such hostility provides the conflict that the child must deal with in his usual way. During the oedipal phase, the child can be better prepared for the arrival of this sibling, and the conflict can be dealt with in more subtle ways. Girls often fantasize that they are the mother, complicating their oedipal conflict. Boys are more likely to stress their superior strength and maturity. Either may regress to clinging or wishing to be bottle fed. Related to the problems of sibling rivalry is the introduction to children outside the family, such as in nursery school. The stress of cooperation may be expressed in inhibition or anxiety or in wanting their own way, a residual of oppositionalism. The simultaneous arrival of a sibling and the start of a group experience may be a particularly difficult stress. In such an outside group, the child also meets new authority or caretaking figures, which may arouse stranger or separation fears. If prolonged, such fears may be considered neurotic. Parents may either be helpful to the child in coping with these new stresses or support the anxiety or clinging.

The expected outcome of the resolution of the Oedipus conflict is to establish gender identity through identification with the parent of the same sex. The awareness of one's gender probably occurs much earlier, and there can be considerable experimentation. It is quite common for children of this age to express a desire to be not only the appropriate parent of the same sex, but also the other parent or a child of the opposite sex. If, for a variety of reasons, internal and external (Stoller 1968), the inappropriate gender is preferred, and development proceeds accordingly, the basis is laid for future problems in identity, as well as for the choice of an opposite love object. If the identity problem is not solidified, and there is still a struggle going on, it may be considered neurotic. Otherwise, it should be considered a fixation.

Another expected outcome of the resolution of the Oedipus conflict is the formation of an internal superego. Although the early outlines of the superego are laid down in the toddler stage with the need for parental training, the oedipal superego arises out of the giving up of the wish for an exclusive relationship with the parent of the opposite sex and an identification with the parent of the same sex, including their values. This addition to the structure of the personality is a classical component of neurotic conflict. During the resolution phase, the conflict is often portrayed symbolically in anxiety dreams, which represent both the wish and the punishment, as in the dream of the lion chasing the little girl. (I knew her father, who had bushy, blonde, curly hair.)

Latency

The relatively long span of years between the end of the oedipal phase and the beginning of adolescence is supposed to be without major stress. Clinically, however, the most referrals for therapy occur during these years. To explain this, one can say that there were problems in negotiating the previous phases and their stresses, or, toward the end of latency, there are stresses in the preparation for puberty and adolescence. This is certainly true, and it is in this phase that it is observed that symptoms that may be considered phase appropriate earlier are now pathological. Early in latency (approximately ages 6 and 7), symptoms of lack of sphincter control, anxiety in new situations, avoidance or inhibition, immature speech or stuttering, or poor relations with peers are common, indicating failure to negotiate one or more previous phases successfully. Parents had either supported them or adjusted to them, but teachers and peers, as new observers, are usually not so tolerant, and provide a new source of conflict. At the other end of the phase (approximately age 10 to 12), concern may occur in parents, school, or the child him- or herself that they are emotionally or physically behind classmates. For a variety of reasons, there may be a neurotic conflict between progressing toward adolescence and adulthood and wishing to remain children. Not as likely to have a neurotic structure are those children who act like adolescents before it is age appropriate. Some of this behavior is considered delinquent, and although of concern to the school, may not be to parents. Those most likely to be brought to therapy are girls who want to dress and act like teenagers and are interested in early sexual relations, often expressing symbolically that they have won in the oedipal struggle. Boys, on the other hand, are usually brought to treatment because they are immature, often expressing the fear of growing up, with a concomitant castration anxiety if they successfully compete with father.

Because the main task of latency is to learn in school and to be able to make relationships with peers and adults outside the family, the resulting stress may precipitate many neurotic symptoms. The conscientious child may be an excessive learner, sometimes at the expense of peer relationships. If, for any reason, there is a learning problem, failure to keep up with peers may precipitate a depression, with feelings of inadequacy, which may be realistic but cause conflicts with parental expectations. Rather than depression, such feelings may produce an angry reaction, with projection of blame and hostile behavior. If the child suffers from guilt over the failures, a pattern of sadomasochistic behavior may result. Difficulties with peer relationships may produce similar defensive measures. Etiology of problems with peer relationships may lie in the failure to resolve the oedipal rivalry or sibling rivalry. Difficulties with new adults such as teachers are usually a direct transference from problems with parents.

Somatic symptoms usually occur in ordinarily well-behaved children. Instead of stubborn behavior, they manage to avoid unpleasant or anxiety-arousing tasks by being sick, usually with stomachaches or headaches. This is most clearly seen in the classic school phobia, now called school avoidance, in which a child refuses to leave home and mother in the morning, and usually also complains of being sick. The basis for such symptoms may be further complicated by the observation that there is preceding illness in either mother or child. Classical conversion reactions are rare, and I have seen only one in long years of practice. An 11-year-old girl presented with a paralysis of the right hand. She could not eat or write with that hand, but she could play a musical instrument. Her parents had wished for a boy, and had given her a name that could be for a boy. Her father had feared that she had an early multiple sclerosis and did not support higher education for females, while her mother had a strong wish for her daughter's school success. The girl's symptoms were a symbolic message of her feeling of being castrated, as well as of her conflict between success and dependency. In fourteen hours of supportive psychotherapy she recovered, but without insight. However, I did not hear of any further problems.

Adolescence

Puberty is a particular stress for many children, especially if the effects of previous stresses are still apparent. The "good" latency child may be upset by puberty, and be reluctant to go into adolescence. I saw one 12-year-old girl who said so very openly, on the basis that she hated to give up her position of indulged baby of the family. Others tend to be overly conscientious or inhibited, with limited social contacts. The conflict is with the wish to be a part of the "popular" peer group. At the other extreme is the child who has never gone into latency, usually because of inconsistent or deficient structure in the family. Puberty is an added stimulus, as well as the occasion for greater social freedom which is allowed at this time. The resulting uncontrolled behavior probably should not be considered neurotic, as it has no unconscious symbolism. Although a certain percentage of incarcerated delinquents are depressed (Chiles et al. 1980), the question of delinquent behavior as a defense against neurotic depression is a controversial one, which can only be decided by finding evidences of guilt and symbolic process.

Conflicts over developing sexuality may precipitate earlier problems of gender identity, inhibitions relating to the opposite sex, or premature or excessive sexual behavior. A serious symptom usually first seen in adolescent girls is anorexia nervosa. The conflicts relate to a number of phases—orality and dependency, control, and the assumption of a mature body habitus. Related is the disorder known as bulimia, alternately overeating and purging. The conflicts are similar, but the unrealistic attitudes about body image are much less. Uncontrolled eating leading to obesity can be seen in both sexes; this also conceals the sexual maturity of the body.

The adolescent task of matching ability to future vocational plans is particularly stressful to many. The dawning awareness of limited ability in relation to earlier fantasied goals may precipitate depression and a loss of desired peer relationships. The depression may be self treated by joining a lower peer group and indulging in delinquent behavior, especially experimenting with mind-altering drugs. If addiction results, along with a commitment to the drug subculture, it is questionable if this constitutes a neurosis. At least it is highly questionable if the ordinary treatment for neurotic disorders is suitable. The depressions accompanied by guilt and feelings of failure which are not realistic are much more likely to take a neurotic form and be amenable to psychoanalytic treatment. Some minor delinquencies, more related to oppositional disorders, and which have specific meanings related to independent strivings from ambivalently perceived parental figures, may also be able to use psychoanalytic treatment.

Adulthood

Although it might be expected that whatever neurotic symptoms that arose in childhood would be repeated under the pressures of adulthood, such is not necessarily the case. Various defenses may be utilized in the course of development, and usually become more complex and elaborate. There is a clearer relationship between childhood personality types and adult personality types. If conscientiousness had been a coping mechanism in childhood, it can be expected to continue into adulthood. On the other hand, the severely anxious or phobic child may not become a chronically anxious adult. He or she may learn to avoid the anxiety-provoking stimulus and simply have a narrow life. The child with separation fears may become a dependent personality, often marrying a parent figure and eventually becoming dependent on children. I have encountered a number of mothers who cannot allow their children to individuate, and who also call their own mothers daily, but they are not symptomatically neurotic. Other anxious children add compulsive defenses in the course of growing up, and appear as rather fragile or unstable compulsive characters. Others may develop counterphobic defenses and look quite different to the casual observer. There also seems to be a relationship between childhood anxieties and somatizing disorders of adulthood, and between early compulsive personalities and later depression. The old-fashioned involutional depressions usually occurred in rather rigid compulsive characters.

As in childhood, symptomatic neurosis is usually a prolongation of naturally occurring stresses. Aside from the stresses of losses and disabilities of various sorts, adulthood has its own developmental phases, with expectable stress. These may be divided into those relating to psychosexual maturity and those relating to vocational identity. Frequently, the stresses come in the two areas at the same time, and that may explain why the life period that Blos (1962) calls postadolescence is so frequently fraught with neurotic or even psychotic breakdown. I have had many referrals during the last year of college, or at the end of some final period of schooling, with depression or physiological symptomatology, as the young person contemplates finding both a job and a mate. The major presenting problems of young people (up to their late thirties) who seek psychoanalysis are failure to find a lasting relationship with a person of the opposite sex and/or failure to find satisfying work. Midlife crises, when sexual life may be diminishing, also overlap the two areas, and there is a realization that there will probably not be any appreciable progress in job success. Aging may bring a loss of work identity as well as losses of family and friends, health, and skills. Adults who are parents have additional stresses, as well as an opportunity to rework certain conflicts as they help their children with the developmental tasks. A particular stress may arise in those parents who have lost one of their own parents in childhood (Altschul and Beiser 1984). They may find it difficult to help their children go beyond the age they were at the time of the parental loss. One can say that certain problems of parenting may be considered neuroses.

Any of the aforementioned stresses may precipitate a neurosis, which may or may not be similar to the neurosis that individual suffered from in childhood. As the lay public has become more sophisticated about neurosis, however, the classical symptoms are not seen as often as in the past. Instead, seemingly rational behaviors can be seen to have the structure of neurosis. All sorts of interpersonal conflicts, such as marital problems, peer problems, problems with bosses or subordinates, as well as difficulties with job performance may be shown to have unconscious symbolic meaning, and not be amenable to logical resolution. During the course of a psychoanalysis, the various layers of defense can be demonstrated, and eventually, through the analysis of the transference neurosis, the origins of the conflicts can be seen in the infantile neurosis. I have frequently found in adult patients with interpersonal problems a history of an early transient school phobia or enuresis, which had not even been mentioned in the early contacts or history. An early trauma, such as the death of a parent or sibling, may also have been considered unimportant, and the unconscious fantasies associated with the trauma may be a very important part of the adult neurosis and only be recovered in analysis. It is unclear why some neurotic conflicts seem to be resolved with a minimum of help, or even corrective life experiences, while others are highly resistant to long and intense psychoanalysis.

TRANSFERENCE MANIFESTATIONS

Transference manifestations in the neuroses of children and adolescents are different from those in the analyses of adults. For children the analyst is first of all a stranger, and will be seen as an ally or enemy, depending partly on the attitude of the parent and partly on the developmental level of the child and his or her relationship with the parent. On the whole, analytic treatment of children depends on the active motivation of the parents. Often, in my experience, one or both parents have been in analytic treatment themselves, and see the analyst as an ally of themselves as well as of the child. This may complicate the situation if the child has a hostile relationship to one or both parents. I have found it advisable to form an alliance with both parents in order to safeguard the analysis of the child. This does not include treatment of the parents, and may only mean keeping lines of communication open and a sufficiently positive relationship to keep up the analysis past the point of symptomatic improvement.

The anxious or prelatency child tends to see the therapist as a stranger, and may show stranger anxiety through openly fearful behavior or separation anxiety by clinging to the parent who brings him. Children, especially those with physical symptoms, may have had traumatic experiences with doctors and show anxiety transferred from those painful medical procedures. Eventually, more specific transference manifestations will be seen. For example, I saw a 7-year-old boy with a school phobia who, after a short period at the beginning of analysis, fought coming into the office at all. In the process of seeing him for several hours along with his parents, I discovered that almost a year ago he had been sent to his grandmother's house in order to ease his mother's recovery from a very serious operation. A family move and new school had precipitated his neurosis, and he saw coming to analysis as being sent away again. This was my first experience with a grandmother transference, and it took me awhile to understand what was happening. Later, his mischievous behavior in the hour, and guilt reaction, helped us understand that he felt his behavior had caused his mother to have cancer, and that he had been sent away as punishment.

The transference in adolescence may be particularly difficult and cause disruption of the treatment. For example, I have found that the transference to a woman therapist of many 13-year-old girls is to sit in stony, hostile silence. In spite of understanding this as a combination of trying to loosen the dependent relationship to mother and a cognitive stage where abstract conversation is difficult and play is considered immature, I have not been able to tolerate this immediate reaction. It certainly has not helped that I was probably a very similar kind of 13-year-old. I have encountered frequent cancellations or outright failures by midadolescents to appear for appointments. Although understandable from the standpoint of strivings for autonomy, the countertransference problems provoked, relating to confidentiality in regard to parents, and the issue of payment for missed hours may make therapy impossible. On the other hand, if the adolescent finds the therapeutic relationship not only comfortable but pleasant, the parent may stop treatment or payment out of jealousy. This can also occur with younger children, which is why it is so important to form a therapeutic alliance with parents, espially the one who is expected to pay the bill. The latter can be seen in cases of divorce, when the noncustodial parent is supposed to be responsible for medical expenses.

SUMMARY

The clinical manifestations of neurosis in children are truly protean, covering almost all possible symptoms. The most common are those that in some way manifest anxiety, and probably next are various somatic symptoms. In recent years, depression in children is being increasingly recognized and investigated. Classical obsessive-compulsive symptoms and conversion hysterias are rare, but closely resemble the adult disorders. Learning and conduct disorders may be neurotic, but need careful differential diagnosis.

In order to diagnose any of these clinical manifestations as neurotic, the metapsychological definition needs to be considered. There must be evidence of a conflict, preferably intraspychic, but in the case of children, especially the youngest ones, one arm of the conflict may be a parent or other external authority. Second, the symptom must represent some form of compromise solution to that conflict, usually by symbol formation. This is certainly not obvious in many situations, especially if the symptom is somatic. Third, the symptoms must be ego dystonic. Again, this is not necessarily true in children, but the parent may be the one to whom the symptom is unacceptable. Especially in children, it is necessary to consider constitutional defects or deviations as well as psychoses, which may appear in severe withdrawals or obsessive-compulsive symptoms.

The more usual differential to be made is between neurosis and a transient reaction to a developmental stress. Each developmental phase has its own expectable stresses, including adulthood. In early childhood, there are certain expectable reactions to these stresses, such as nightmares during the oedipal period, and very individual ways in which parents or families deal with these reactions. The reactions then may be quite temporary, persist as neurotic symptoms, or become a part of a character trait or pattern. Character patterns may be expected to persist into adulthood, but there is less likelihood of the neurosis of childhood being the same as an adult neurosis. During the course of psychoanalysis, however, it can be expected that the infantile neurosis will emerge.

Psychoanalysis is the treatment of choice for neuroses in both children and adults. Psychoanalytic understanding, but also an understanding of development and its normal stresses, is essential in the treatment of many of the clinical disorders of childhood, and I have also found it very valuable in the understanding of transference manifestations in adults.

REFERENCES

Aichorn, A. (1935). *Wayward Youth.* Rev. ed. New York: Viking Press.
Altschul, S., and Beiser, H. (1984). The effect of early parent loss on future parenthood. In *Parenthood: A Psychodynamic Perspective,* ed. R. S. Cohen, B. J. Cohler, and S. H. Weissman, pp. 119–147. New York: Guilford Press.
Blos, P. (1962). *On Adolescence.* New York: Free Press of Glencoe, pp. 148–159.
Bornstein, B. (1949). The analysis of a phobic child. In *Psychoanalytic Study of the Child* 24:181–226. New York: International Universities Press.
Chiles, J. R., Miller, H. L., and Cox, G. B. (1980). Depression in an adolescent delinquent population. *AMA Archives of General Psychiatry* 37:1179–1184.
DSM-III (Diagnostic and Statistical Manual) (1980). Washington, DC: American Psychiatric Association, pp. 9–10, 38–43.
Freud, A. (1965). *Normality and Pathology in Childhood.* New York: International Universities Press, pp. 38–43, 151–154, 192–193.
Freud, S. (1953). Three essays on the theory of sexuality. In *Complete Psychological Works,* vol. 7, pp. 135–144. London: Hogarth.
——— (1955). Analysis of a phobia in a five-year-old boy. In *Complete Psychological Works,* vol. 10, pp. 116–117, 149. London: Hogarth.
——— (1955). Beyond the pleasure principle. In *Complete Psychological Works,* vol. 18, pp. 14–15. London: Hogarth.
Galenson, E., and Roiphe, H. (1971). The impact of early sexual discovery on mood, defensive organization, and symbolization. In *Psychoanalytic Study of the Child* 36:195–216. New York: International Universities Press.
Mahler, M., Pine, F., and Bergman, A. (1968). *The Psychological Birth of the Human Infant.* New York: Basic Books, pp. 52–75.
Spitz, R. (1957). *No and Yes: On the Genesis of Human Communication.* New York: International Universities Press.
Stoller, R. (1968). *Sex and Gender.* London: Hogarth.

3

Transference Neurosis in Childhood and Adolescence

Henry Eisner, M.D.

Transference refers to the revival of feelings from objects, usually parents or parent surrogates, of the past onto the analyst in the present. These feelings have been repressed and are unconscious. All people transfer unconscious libidinal aspects of their relationships from significant figures of the past onto current ones. In neuroses there is only a quantitative difference from the normal. The neurotic derives inadequate gratification from the people in his life due to repression of impulses and complexes, so that unreasonable infantile demands left over from the past are unconsciously and unrealistically pressed on current figures.

The transference occurs because all individuals long for elements of infantile gratification. Derivatives of this longing for infantile gratification (id impulses) provide the motivating force for analytic work and open the individual with a neurosis to suggestion. Both rational capabilities (a relatively intact ego), and irrational factors, the longing for gratification (id), are necessary for analytic work.

Transference phenomena in children and adolescents differ from those in adults for a number of reasons. The adult is removed generally from his infantile objects, his psychic apparatus is matured, his character structure crystallized. In the child and adolescent, parental figures are still present in his life generally, and his character structure is still modifiable by them. It is generally thought that the child has his parental objects still involved through reality in his neurosis (A. Freud 1927, 1946, Ritvo 1978). The child still lives with his parents and is still dependent upon them, so that they are available for drive gratification.

Insofar as that is true, the child has less need to turn to the analyst for this gratification or for that matter for symptom formation. This will be discussed further below.

The issue of deciding what is and what is not transference is extremely important. Moore and Fine (1968) state:

> The transference neurosis is an indispensable therapeutic tool, since the feelings experienced by the patient in the transference have a unique vividness in the present, which makes their interpretation and the sense of conviction about them especially effective. If transference is used by the patient as a resistance that proves difficult to overcome, the possibility of successful psychoanalytic treatment will be correspondingly diminished. [p. 93]

If a piece of behavior from the past is repeated in the transference in the present, the understanding of the past behavior is enriched to a degree of scientific accuracy that can not be obtained in any other way. The essential elements of the infantile neurosis that is itself the symptomatic manifestation of conflicts arising from the oedipal stage of development can be constructed through the medium of the transference neurosis.

Mrs. R. entered analysis in her mid-fifties due to great anxiety. She was reluctant to admit the unhappiness of her marriage, and only after two years of analysis could she acknowledge her hatred of her husband and her uncaring mother. She did things for everyone else, and she complained, "How about me!" In reconstructing her infantile neurosis over long periods of the analysis, she could recall her wish to be rescued, first by Santa Claus at age 4 when she had wandered away from home to the local school flag pole which she thought was the north pole. At age 9 she sang opera in the front window of her home hoping she would be rescued. The opera she sang from was *La Boheme* where she imagined herself Mimi, pale and dying. It was easier for her to think of herself as dying Mimi than to acknowledge her hatred toward her family, especially her mother. She played out this dying, martyred role in her relationship with her mother, her marriage, and in her work after her divorce. It then appeared in the transference in her being the "good" patient who cooperates with the analyst regardless of her personal feelings. Then through dreams and associations the analyst became the knight who would rescue her from her unhappiness. This passive masochistic fantasy of being Mimi was the core of her oedipal fantasy, and the basic complex around which her neurosis was constructed. Unconsciously she avoided doing things in her own behalf in order to promote the opportunity of being rescued because she was so good!

This is an example of how the infantile neurosis with its accompanying oedipal fantasy can be played out over a lifetime and then appear in the transference. But all of the interaction of the child (or for that matter the adult) to the analyst is not transference. When a child communicates with his therapist with words or play, the communications may be in response to the immediate reality in which the child finds himself within the office setting (object relationship), a displacement from the child's present life outside the therapist's office, or an expression of a conflict from the child's earlier life experiences.

A depressed and somewhat masochistic and lonely 12-year-old was upset by the emotional distance of her brilliant, intellectual father. In a therapy session she became provocative with her male analyst, and laughingly pushed the bridge table in the office into him. When this got no punitive response from him, she became bolder and upset the table and its contents into his lap and simultaneously moved closer to him. She was feeling less shy and was smiling though watchful while she did this. The described behavior occurred in the context of her telling how her father, in his awkward attempt to become more interested in her, took her shopping for a camera and hardly talked to her. The analyst interpreted her disappointment with her father, and her attempts to get some kind of reaction from him, the analyst, as compensation for her father's coolness toward her. She replied only: "You're too old anyway!"

This baffling response showed that the analyst was at least partially off target, and it illustrates how difficult it may be to put an exact label on the patient-analyst reactions of children. Was this a transference reaction at all? Or was the 12-year-old simply flirting with the analyst, whom she liked? In other words was this a true object relationship much as a young adult woman patient might have for a young analyst she liked, or was this a compensating displacement from her frustrating relationship with her distant father? Or was she acting out an oedipal fantasy from the past? Or was it a combination of any or all of these? The only way one can be sure would be to have more of the underlying fantasy than the patient expressed.

Because the relationship between patient and analyst may be difficult to define in childhood, it is necessary that we enumerate the possible ways in which patients may interact with the analyst before we discuss the controversial issue of transference neurosis in childhood. We may classify the relationship with the analyst along the following lines, acknowledging that there is a level of arbitrariness about this. Pearson (1968) and Sandler and colleagues (1975) have slightly different classifications.

1. Relation of child to any adult in a true object relationship
2. Treatment alliance or rapport

3. Characteristic ways of this child's relating to any adult with elements of externalization of the self
4. Imitation or identification with the analyst
5. Displacement from current relationships in the child's life
6. Transference from past relationships
7. Transference neurosis

The first category of true object relationship in part refers to the respectful attitude children have for adults, appropriate to the age of the child. The younger the child, the more uncertain or anxious we would expect him to be with any stranger. The child would see the adult as objectively as could be expected of a healthy child of that age. In this category we also find a related phenomenon and quote from Ritvo (1978):

> The child analyst is . . . an external center of psychic activity or object with whom the child interacts at times in his life when new psychic structures are being formed. In the analyst the child interacts with an object who does not respond in the ways characteristic for the particular parents. Presumably the analyst, via his responses to the wishes and fantasies and his verbalization and interpretation of them, offers the ego of the child alternative ways of finding detoured discharge, gratification, or control, which influence the formation of psychic structure or organization. Thereby the child analyst may be instrumental in facilitating the child's fulfilling a developmental need. [p. 302]

Ritvo adds that if we keep this view in mind, it will help us explain why child analysis can help the child resume developmental progress without preventing the need for more analysis later on. Teachers or other respected and loved adults may have a similar effect on the child.

The second category, related to the first, refers to the "treatment alliance," which is a term taken over from adult analysis. It refers to an "alliance between the analyst and the healthy part of the patient's ego" (Bibring 1937). This alliance depends on the child's reality testing, object constancy, impulse control, frustration tolerance, and so forth, much as it would for an adult (Curtis 1979). It allows the child to look at what he is feeling objectively, and to cooperate in the analytic venture. The transference itself, as Freud (1914) pointed out, "is an intermediate region between illness and real life through which the transition from one to the other is achieved." It is this alliance with the analyst that permits the patient to look at aspects of his own personality that include transference phenomena. To that extent the child identifies with the therapist's psychoanalytic stance, takes distance from his conflicts, and tries to understand himself.

In the neuroses the patient cooperates with the analyst because he or she unconsciously fears loss of love and punishment (Bibring 1937). With the neuroses the therapist should be careful not to gratify transference wishes, which will only hamper the analysis. Thus, in the example given on p. 43 the analyst did not gratify the youngster's wish to be attacked for her provocative behavior of pushing the table onto the therapist, but instead waited for his patient to verbalize her fantasy. He already had a therapeutic alliance with her on which he could rely. In this instance the patient, with her masochistic character structure, unconsciously both wished for and feared attack with its sexual as well as punitive meaning. Of course, in the normal child at age 12 we would expect heterosexual impulses to be strongly colored by sadomasochism. Note how this child in her eagerness to gain the analyst's reaction provoked him by pushing the table into him, though playfully. This child dared not do anything provocative at home or either parent would be angry with her. In fact, her parents complained that she was depressed and listless, an unconscious defensive pose that she had assumed in order to avoid her parents' anger. In the relatively permissive atmosphere of therapy, she could spread her wings and express feelings she previously tried to divest herself of. Such freedom to express oneself is not necessarily transference, but simply a realistic assessment of what of the child's behavior will be tolerated in a given situation with an adult. This is what Ritvo was referring to in the quote above.

The child's characteristic ways of relating to all adults will appear especially in the early stages of the analysis once the child feels safe with the analyst. These may include excessive deference, guardedness, sadomasochistic elements, and so on.

A 9-year-old with a mixed picture of neurosis and arrest in his development was very courteous to the analyst for the first three sessions. After he felt safe with the analyst, his "enfant terrible" behavior, so prominent at home and in school, came into the therapy as he derisively threw an eraser at the analyst. He had thrown a bottle at his father, chalk at a teacher in school, and a stone at a peer, all before the analysis began. This was characteristic impulsive behavior toward all people with whom he felt both frustrated and fearful. After two years of analysis such behavior centered more on the analyst, and became a transference phenomenon the meaning of which could be understood as identification with the aggressor. The point here is that throwing objects at people was at first a nonspecific response to frustration, and only later evolved as a specific transference that could be analyzed.

Furman (1980) has written about the normal use of externalization of the superego during early latency. She points out how some children become especially sensitive at this phase of development and complain about adult figures who "yell" at them or are "mean" to them. The child is not yet used to the new intrapsychic superego structure that is forming and externalizes its admonitions. This is not transference when these complaints happen within the analytic situation and must not be handled as such. These are truly externalizations of the self that are phase specific and come under the heading of characteristic ways of relating.

Children and adolescents will imitate or identify with the mannerisms of the people they admire. During the course of a prolonged treatment with a helping adult, the child not only identifies with the psychoanalytic stance of the therapist, which is a desirable form of identification, but with random characteristics, behaviors, and even attitudes. Some of these may constitute forms of resistance in themselves, and must be understood.

Angry and unhappy 9-year-old Eddie, who had been in many fights with peers and done poorly in school, began insisting on sitting in the analyst's chair in his office rather than using the playroom as he previously had done. He had told the analyst how much he wanted to be an analyst himself when he was older. Eddie would put his feet on the ottoman as he had seen the analyst do on occasion. Then he would question the analyst as the analyst questioned him. Attempts to understand this at first met with angry outbursts. Only after some time was it learned that the boy not only admired the analyst but felt that he was being "grilled" by him. The boy said that the analyst's questions were like those of his obtrusive father. The boy was turning the tables on both through this defensive behavior.

In this example we see not only admiration for the analyst but displacement into the analysis of current conflicts with father, of past conflicts (true transference), and identification with the aggressor, the feared analyst. As can be seen from the examples already given, it is not unusual for more than one form of interaction with the analyst to be present in a given behavior, that is, a child can identify with an analyst, demonstrating displacements from outside the analysis, and show a transference phenomenon from the past all in a single piece of behavior. In so far as Eddie could enjoy defeating his father through the analyst, we have an example of transference resistance. Transference resistance is a term that applies to situations in which the patient tries to satisfy urges within the transference rather than do analytic work and understand his present behavior in relation to both his life outside the analysis in the present and in the past. This is exactly what Eddie was doing.

Displacements from current relations in the child's life refer to the common phenomenon seen for example in the famous James Joyce short story "Counterparts" (Joyce 1946). A clerk is furious with his authoritarian boss's rebuke following the boss's giving him more work than he wishes and the clerk not completing it. The clerk leaves work, has too much to drink, and comes home and beats his young son for not working hard enough for him. The anger toward the boss is taken out on the innocent boy who helplessly prays for his father to stop flailing him.

Four-year-old Billy's mother locked him in the closet when he was "bad." Very shortly after therapy began, and Billy felt comfortable with the therapist, Billy began insisting that the doctor go in the closet and the door be locked on him. When the therapist refused, Billy cried in utter helpless frustration until he could be convinced to carry out this "game" with a doctor doll in the doll house. The game went on for weeks before Billy could talk about his rage toward his mother who simply couldn't be convinced to stop this form of punishment.

This example is of a displacement of repressed anger from mother to the therapist during the course of psychotherapy of a boy who lived part-time with his mother, part-time with his grandparents. Billy was too frightened and angry to talk about his mother at first and could only act it out in the play until he both could give up the gratification from direct action and feel safe enough to verbalize his anger, which, through repeated play, he had partially mastered by identification with the aggressor.

Displacements are extremely common during the course of child analysis. Children take out their unhappiness with a poor school grade, a slight from a peer, or a disappointment with a parent or teacher on the analyst whom they know will not retaliate. It is extremely important that the child be able to verbalize the original situation and come to grips with the feelings that accompanied it. Of course, adults are forever telling children "not to feel that way," "not to cry," "put on a happy face," in order to teach children to get along in society. Thus, children frequently become intolerant of certain affects which they cheat themselves from experiencing in order not to lose the approval of adults or peers. These affects must then be reexperienced if the analysis is to go forward.

Transference from past relationships or experiences refers to the way in which fantasies, wishes, conflicts, modes of relating, and defenses from the past are revived during the course of analytic work and as a result of that analytic work. The unconscious fantasy surfaces due to the fact that defenses against its manifesting itself have been weakened by the analytic work. The drives behind these fantasies then reappear in regard to the relationship with the therapist.

Seven-year-old Albert had undergone a urethral dilatation at age 3. His hospitalization had been very traumatic. The night before the procedure, he screamed and tried to climb out of his crib. The nurses tied a net over the crib to restrain him. One year into his analysis he began tying the play dolls in a "fish net," and he tried to tie the analyst with a ball of kite string that he brought and unraveled all over the playroom. Then he poked the analyst with a stick. Over a period of weeks this behavior became clearer and clearer with its reference to the hospitalization. Gradually the memory of the hospitalization was revived as Albert worked out the feelings of intimidation and helplessness he had felt, as well as the loneliness and sadness experienced on being left in the hospital.

In this example the analyst was the inquisitor who had shoved a rod into his urethra, and in the play Albert turned the tables on him. The episode was clearly recalled with all the fantasies that surrounded it. During this time the tying and poking play was entirely confined to the analyst and the playroom. Some children who have undergone such trauma will feel no compunction to keep the revived play in the therapy, but will act it out at home, in school, and in their play with friends. In the adult such behavior would be considered a form of acting out, but in children (Fraiberg 1966) we can not hold the child to confining his reliving to the analytic situation. The child feels free to rework the trauma wherever he pleases. Parents need to be warned in advance that children who were previously very good suddenly may show outbursts of naughtiness in their efforts to master the trauma which they have known. The child may feel free to reproach the parent for subjecting him to the operation, for deserting him in the hospital, for example, as actually happened in the example of Albert, as the infantile object who did these things to him is not only still available but still actively involved in the child's development, including his neurosis.

THE TRANSFERENCE NEUROSIS

Historically, the term transference neurosis was used by Freud to differentiate the psychoneuroses from the psychoses and from the "actual neuroses," and references to this term in Freud's writings reflect this.

Today the term is used differently. Moore and Fine (1968) state: ". . .

transference neurosis is the new 'version' of the neurosis which develops in the course of psychoanalytic treatment, with the analyst as the focal figure upon whom the original childhood conflicts between instinctual drives and the defenses against them are now displaced (p. 93)."

Freud described this in adults in a number of places without referring to it specifically as transference neurosis. Here is one example (Freud 1917):

> ... the patient's illness, which we have undertaken to analyse, is not something which has been rounded off and become rigid but that it is still growing and developing like a living organism. The beginning of the treatment does not put an end to this development; when, however, the treatment has obtained mastery over the patient, what happens is that the whole of his illness's new production is concentrated upon a single point— his relation to the doctor. Thus the transference may be compared to the cambium layer in a tree between the wood and the bark, from which the new formation of tissue and the increase in the girth of the trunk derive. When the transference has risen to this significance, work upon the patient's memories retreats far into the background. Thereafter it is not incorrect to say that we are no longer concerned with the patient's earlier illness but with a newly created and transformed neurosis which has taken the former's place. . . . All the patient's symptoms have abandoned their original meaning and have taken on a new sense which lies in a relation to the transference; or only such symptoms have persisted as are capable of undergoing such a transformation. But the mastering of this new, artificial neurosis coincides with getting rid of the illness which was originally brought to the treatment—with the accomplishment of our therapeutic task. A person who has become normal and free from the operation of repressed instinctual impulses in his relation to the doctor will remain so in his own life after the doctor has once more withdrawn from it. [p. 444]

Does such a transference neurosis occur in childhood and adolescence? The matter is still one of controversy, but in general, the thinking about it has gone through two major phases, which correspond to one major development in child analysis, the introduction of the findings of ego psychology.

Anna Freud (1945) wrote: "[Is] . . . the relationship of the child to the analyst . . . really wholly governed by a transference situation? Even if one part of the child's neurosis is transformed into a transference neurosis, as happens in adult analysis, another part of the child's neurotic behavior remains grouped around the parents, who are the original objects of his pathogenic past" (p. 130). This was a change from her 1927 opinion where she felt no transference formed at all in children

(p. 46). Anna Freud implied that the transference neurosis played a minor part in the analysis of children. Her later discussions say the same (Sandler et al. 1975), and many others have shared this view (for example, Pearson 1968).

Fraiberg (1966) believed that with the findings of ego psychology a major change occurred in analytic technique. Misbehavior in the analytic sessions was no longer viewed as a way of avoiding conflict. In the early days of child analysis up to the 1950s misbehavior was prohibited during the analytic hour with the idea that such prohibition would "convert it into a neurosis," a notion taken over from the therapy of delinquents (Aichhorn 1925, A. Freud 1965), and then the conflicts of the neurosis could be analyzed. In a way, it was mistakenly thought that the misbehavior was a form of transference, which it was not! After the application of the findings of ego psychology, it was seen that misbehavior in the neuroses was a reaction to events or thoughts that stirred anxiety in the child. Technique then changed to one of clarifying for the child how the misbehavior occurred in response to specific situations, or thoughts or feelings within the child, and gaining the child's cooperation in analyzing the unconscious meaning of these external situations or internal events. From there the transference developed along different lines, and instances of true transference neurosis seemed to occur (Brody 1961, Fraiberg 1962, 1966, Kut 1953, Tyson 1978), though the original view was not lost, only modified. At this writing attention seems to be toward those situations in which there were exceptions to Anna Freud's original 1927 view.

Our own experience in the Child and Adolescent Division of the Institute of the Philadelphia Association for Psychoanalysis is that a true transference neurosis may form fairly frequently in children and adolescents, and it fits the criteria in these individuals as much as it does in adults.

The question had remained as to how central a transference neurosis is to the analysis of most children and adolescents, and if it occurs, what are the circumstances that evoke it. Why does it occur in one child and not in another? Pearson and colleagues (1968) answered this question quite succinctly:

> The possibility for development of such a transference neurosis seemed to be more likely the more the child's circumstances permitted a repression of the infantile neurosis; the more the child's gratification of the repressed fantasy through the infantile objects was either not indulged or found to be too threatening; the more independent the child was of the parent figure for gratification of his real needs; the further the progression of the

child's development toward adulthood; the stronger the development of the child's ego (both for containment of the infantile fantasies and for expression of, establishing some distance from, becoming aware of, and working through their derivatives toward the therapist); and finally the more available a treatment setting of analytic neutrality. [p. 344]

The mother of 5-year-old David had a severe back problem that limited her activity, kept her in bed for most of David's second and third year, made her inaccessible to David when he needed her then, and still to some extent when he needed her in the present, and made her feel helpless in disciplining him. In addition to the physical limitation, she got some unconscious enjoyment out of David's acting up and would laugh at his getting his brother to throw a Teddy bear in the toilet, thus blocking it. In his analysis David's reaction to the analyst's vacations was severe and represented the reliving in the transference of the inaccessible mother both of the past and to some extent in the present. The mother's going away on vacation for a weekend with father brought the same overreaction with accompanying misbehavior as happened with the analyst. In the office David threw things when frustrated. Frustrations and tensions at home brought equivalent behavior.

In this example there is poor repression of David's conflicts regarding both being left and frustrations in everyday life. Mother is still to some extent unavailable to him when she must occasionally nap because of her back, and mother is perpetuating his difficulties regarding ordinary frustrations because she gets some mileage out of his defiant misbehavior because of her own still unconscious conflicts. There is both transference and displacement of these problems into the analysis, but no transference neurosis per se because David's fantasies are still discharged with mother. Gradually David was able to verbalize his unhappiness about abandonment and his mother's unavailability, first in the analysis, then later at home. Gradually he was able to verbalize his frustrations, for example, on the first day of second grade when his younger sister got to stay home with their mother and he had to attend school. But work with the mother had to be undertaken to minimize her perpetuating David's problems by laughing at his misbehavior even as she complained about it. In addition, there was no way to separate past conflicts over abandonment from present hurt as the same inaccessibility of mother was still true in the present. What could be done about it was to help David deal with his feelings in a more age-appropriate fashion. The point is that no well-encapsulated fantasy formed to the point where it could be isolated and analyzed. A fantasy regarding an ugly woman who gets buried did in fact appear, but the misbehavior at home always remained on a parallel with that in the office, unlike the situation with a transference neurosis in which the behavior at home becomes normal and the misbehavior or fantasies of misbehavior appear only in the analytic situation.

It is not unusual for parents to stop treatment once a true transference neurosis forms, because as far as the parents are concerned, the child appears well. This may be one of the reasons that we do not see the transference neurosis more often in children. The situation is something like that in psychotherapy where all the parents care about is symptom improvement, and the therapist uses the positive relationship with the child and the transference to obtain a true "transference improvement."

A 7-year-old child's borderline psychotic mother died when the child was 4. Breast feeding had stopped at 3 ½ when the mother's breast cancer had been discovered. The mother hardly disciplined Sarah, and when the father remarried when she was 5, Sarah was still not toilet trained. The stepmother instituted toilet training and consistent discipline, and Sarah became toilet trained but was a severe behavior problem with many tantrums, and seemed to learn nothing in first grade. Her private school refused to take her back for second grade because she couldn't read. Over the course of one and a half years of analysis, a well-encapsulated phobia regarding the stepmother formed, and the child's behavior greatly changed. Then gradually the fear turned to a hate of the stepmother, which Sarah realized was totally unfounded. As we began to talk about this, an uneasy feeling toward the analyst formed and the dread of the stepmother diminished and alternated with dread of the analyst. By this time Sarah's behavior had become exemplary (too much so), and her school work was entirely up to age level. Her father would not listen to either the analyst's, the stepmother's, or Sarah's pleas to continue the analysis. To his mind she was cured!

In this example, the consistent handling by the stepmother, in addition to the unavailability of the original object who nurtured the arrest in development by allowing Sarah overgratification of her impulses, contributed to the repression of the infantile conflict. In this example we might even say that the stepmother's consistent behavior was the first step in "converting" misbehavior into a neurosis (A. Freud 1965). The drives could no longer be discharged directly through soiling, sucking, and the like, and were partially repressed. Further repression occurred in the early stages of the analysis through a technique of education mixed with clarification. A phobia then formed around the person of the stepmother, and gradually, portions of this were displaced onto the analyst. But even here we have to question how much this was transference and how much reality because to some extent the child probably experienced interventions made by the analyst as prohibitions during periods of the analysis which Maenchen (1984) would refer to as "adaptations" of the technique.

Elisabeth Geleerd (Buxbaum 1958) is one of those who does not believe that a true transference neurosis develops until after adolescence. She feels that this is so because psychic structuralization is not complete until adulthood. However, most analysts would disagree with her. The following case history is presented to show the operation of displacement, transference, and transference neurosis in an adolescent boy.

Don was 14 when he entered analysis for school underachievement and poor peer relations. He was forever being teased and attacked by boys whom he provoked with his bossiness. He would cry if corrected by his parents, and they would feel sorry for him and often apologize. In the first three months of his analysis Don began fearing that he would be attacked on the way to my office, especially near my office which is situated adjacent to a public park. This was the first sign of the developing transference, that is, the unconscious wish to be attacked by the analyst.

Despite consciously strong motivation for analysis and a wish to master his problems, Don showed little commitment to school work, making friends, or analysis. And when he was invited to take a long weekend trip, which interfered with analytic hours, he accepted. When his lack of commitment was pointed out to him by the analyst, he cried. This was a displacement of current ways of behaving with parents into the analysis, as well as transference from the past. When this was pointed out to him, he became angered.

In the next hour Don brought in some shop work to show me. It was really very good, but he said that the shop teacher had done it for him. He was embarrassed to show it to me. I pointed out to him that if the shop teacher had done it for him, it was easily understandable why he was reluctant to show it to me as his own. The patient said that he was trying to please me, and that's why he wanted to show it to me, because he had done some of it. I told Don that if he were really trying to please me, he might be using the analysis better than he had been. Don had gotten the shop teacher to help him with his work by feeling helpless and being reduced to tears, and the shop teacher felt sorry for him. I pointed out to Don how he wanted people to do things for him rather than to do things for himself, and how he used crying in order to get this. (This was later connected to the crying in other areas of his life, like camp.) Don cried again and left the office crying.

The next day he came in angrily and said he was going to get back at me for what I had said the previous day. He then changed his story about the shop teacher, saying that he, not the shop teacher, had really done most of the work. I asked him why he had presented it the opposite way before. Don said that this was due to his modesty, that he didn't want to have to take the credit for it because it would be showing off. He argued with me about his trying and said that he had been trying. He now decided not to go on the trip with his family but to continue and not miss any of the analytic hours. He was still angry with me about what I had said to him at the two previous hours. He felt that the way that I confronted him with some of his behavior about his crying and about his lack of commitment was an insult. I pointed out to Don that this behavior was unconscious, and what he had been doing to other people. Now it had come into the analysis and had come out in the relationship with me where we could clearly see it and understand it. It had to do with an unconscious method he used to get people to do what he wanted while doing as little as possible himself, then getting some mileage out of his putting something over on someone else. Don listened and added material of his own, confirming what I was saying, and the many silences that had preceded this hour stopped. He discussed his own provocativeness, how he got people to attack him, and seemed to want me to attack him through his showing me a piece of work he said someone else had done.

About two years after analysis began Don revealed his "true" fear. He was worried that he was homosexual. He had his first orgasm while wrestling with his younger brother Stan when Don was 13. Don said that the first time he ejaculated while wrestling with Stan was accidental. But the next two times it was intentional. Don said he had avoided going out with a girl he had met. He explained that he worried that the analyst might not be interested in him if he was not homosexual. Then he worried that if he was a homosexual an analyst couldn't help you because he remembered that in the movie, *The Boys in the Band*, one of the homosexuals said an analyst can't help homosexuals.

Don was very competitive in his fantasies of smashing opposition. He had been very afraid of these fantasies, and thus, though he competed, he was nevertheless passive in many other aspects of his life. He seemed afraid to assert himself and do well in school because of this. His father had succeeded in medicine, but then failed in his marriage and investments. Don reasoned that this happened to his father because he was overaggressive. His father used to pummel him when he was younger, and Don retained a fear of his father, mixed with contempt. He fantasied his father coming to him begging him for money. Don had enjoyed the fantasy of taking a light job and living off his father, but as the analysis progressed, he realized that his father was foolish with his money, and there wouldn't be any for him.

Some time about a month later the patient talked about his fear that the analyst would die. This came at a time when his father was leaving home prior to divorce. The father had been a "nuisance" in the home. I interpreted Don's fear that I would die as punishment for his wishing that his father would leave. In this instance I believe that we had a true transference reaction in his ambivalent attitude toward his father because of memories from age 5 of fears that his father would die. In addition, because his behavior at home had become normal for a 16-year-old, his school work up to age level, and his peer relations to all outward appearances normal, I believe that we had a true transference neurosis. The past conflicts were now centering solely around the analyst. But even here it is the original object's leaving that provokes the death fear.

Material surfaced regarding Don's wishing to attack and be attacked. He had skipped glee club rehearsal and imagined that I would be angry with him. He was mad that he couldn't play basketball because analysis interfered with it. All of this came up after his seeing *The Godfather*, and the wish to retaliate. Attack was the subject of analysis for a few weeks. He told of his fears of the dark in the context of his anger and frustration with both his parents. His mother didn't protect him, and his father ignored him. On the one hand he wanted to be a professional football player, and on the other hand he was afraid to go to a dentist because he would get hurt.

From here Don said that he was afraid to talk about some things with me that he wanted to, namely some sexual practices, normal and abnormal. But then he didn't talk about it and only used it to tease me, and wished to get me into a tug-of-war with him. This was a repetition of his relationship with his father from the past, when he gave vague answers to simple questions and annoyed his father. Don said that he liked to hold onto things, referring to these secrets. He liked to hold onto tension and then let it go in front of friends by acting in some obnoxious way, making an asshole out of himself. Then he laughed at his own thoughts about shitting on everyone. He said that it was so much fun acting like a good boy, then turning around and shitting on everyone. His falsely accusing me of things he had done in the past was his way of shitting on me after feeling some tension. Then Don seemed angry with me for pointing out ways he handled some of his feelings previously. He recognized how he attempted to get sympathy to cover up some of his aggressiveness: "I suffer so from losses, how can you not be sympathetic with me!"

Don wished that he had a big IQ, which would enable him to have less frustration in attaining academic goals. This led to his saying that he thought that his penis was too small. He measured it with a ruler and it was only five and a half inches long. He worried that he would submit homosexually and get screwed in the ass. He feared he was masturbating too much. He looked in the mirror, he projected his shadow on the wall to make sure he was still big enough after he masturbated. He wanted so much to be big!

Two months later Don said that it was unethical that he paid nothing to come (his parents paid!) because his fantasy was that the analyst would use him for his own homosexual purposes. He wondered how much the analyst cared for him. And then a couple of weeks later he talked about his frustrations and his attempts to get the analyst to be a close friend to him. The analyst pointed out to him that he passed up opportunities with boys who could be his friends. If I were a close friend to him I couldn't help him understand himself.

Three months later Don joked defensively about sitting in silence for twenty minutes daydreaming without talking. He had fantasies about wishing to be attacked from the rear by the analyst. He angrily and defiantly told the analyst that the analyst should tell him why he was having trouble dating. It was pointed out to Don that this was one of his wishes of being attacked from the rear, that is, to be shoved from the rear, in effect, to have a penis shoved up his ass in order to get him moving. Don responded that he had had a fantasy of seducing a man to shove a penis into his anus and snapping his ass closed and catching the penis. I interpreted to Don his idea that he felt that his penis was too small, that he should get the analyst's bigger penis which would then enable him to date.

Don first showed displacements in his relationship with parents, school teachers, and peers in the analysis. Then with the guilt regarding the deathwish toward his father (which also existed in the present) we find oedipal fantasies from the past as well. As the analysis progressed, the father became less available, and Don became more emotionally independent of his parents; he formed a true transference neurosis, with the provocative behavior and homosexual wishes to seduce the power from the analyst being part of a transference neurosis.

In the adult, emotional dependence on the parent or on a spouse may persist and interfere with the formation of a transference neurosis. This situation happens when an adult continues to live with a parent and discharges derivatives of infantile impulses with the parent instead of within the analytic situation.

The lack of formation of a transference neurosis is not always due to the analysand. If the analyst offers too much help, gratifies the patient's needs too much, the impulses are not repressed, and no structured conflict develops that can be analyzed. As Freud pointed out (1919), there are adults who are so infantile in their behavior that technique must be modified in order to best help them adapt to reality. For the transference neurosis to form there must be no opportunity offered by the analyst for gratification by him of his patient's infantile longings: ". . . the patient must be left with unfulfilled wishes in abundance" (p. 164). But he added later: "We cannot avoid taking some patients for treatment who are so helpless and incapable of ordinary life that for them one has to combine analytic with educative influence" (p. 165). This to some extent corresponds with the situation with children due to the child's immature ego.

CONCLUSION

In summary, current consensus is that the transference neurosis can and does form in children, has greater potential in adolescence, and ideally always occurs in adults. It is a vital part of the therapeutic aspects of analysis, the mechanism through which one can be most sure of the validity of his hypotheses. In children we count more on displacements from current situations and transference of past than on the transference neurosis to establish this validity. Nevertheless, the goal in all analytic work should be to approach the ideal of the transference neurosis through careful attention to the individual's ego strengths, his external situation, and the holding so far as possible to ideal analytic technique.

REFERENCES

Brody, S. (1961). Some aspects of transference resistance in prepuberty. *Psychoanalytic Study of the Child* 16:251-263. New York: International Universities Press.
Buxbaum, E. (1958). Panel report: The Psychology of Adolescence. *Journal of the American Psychoanalytic Association* 6:111-120.
Curtis, H. (1979). The concept of therapeutic alliance: implications for the "widening scope." *Journal of the American Psychoanalytic Association* 27 (supp.): 159.
Fraiberg, S. H. (1951). Clinical notes on the nature of transference in child analysis. *Psychoanalytic Study of the Child* 6:286-306. New York: International Universities Press.
―――. (1962). Technical aspects of the analysis of a child with a severe behavior disorder. *Journal of the American Psychoanalytic Association* 10:338-367.
―――. (1961). Further considerations of the role of transference in latency. *Psychoanalytic Study of the Child* 21:213-236. New York: International Universities Press.
Freud, A. (1945). Indications for child analysis. *Psychoanalytic Study of the Child* 1:127-149. New York: International Universities Press.
―――. (1927). Four lectures on psychoanalysis. In *The Writings of Anna Freud*, vol. 1, p. 46. New York: International Universities Press.
―――. (1965). *The Writings of Anna Freud*, vol. 6. New York: International Universities Press, p. 225.
Freud, S. (1917). Transference, in introductory lectures on psychoanalysis. *Standard Edition* 16:444.
―――. (1919). Lines of advance in psychoanalytic therapy. *Standard Edition* 17:164, 165.
Furman, E. (1980). Transference and externalization in latency. *Psychoanalytic Study of the Child* 35:267-284. New Haven, CT: Yale University Press.
Joyce, J. (1946) *Dubliners*. In *The Portable James Joyce*, ed. H. Levin. New York: Viking Press.
Kut, S. (1953). The changing pattern of transference in the analysis of an eleven-year-old girl. *Psychoanalytic Study of the Child* 8:355-378. New York: International Universities Press.
Moore, B. E., Fine, B. D. (1968). *A Glossary of Psychoanalytic Terms and Concepts*. New York: American Psychoanalytic Association, p. 93.
Pearson, G. H. J., ed. (1968) Transference and countertransference. In *A Handbook of Child Psychoanalysis*, pp. 335-355. New York: Basic Books.
Ritvo, S. (1978). The psychoanalytic process in childhood. *Psychoanalytic Study of the Child* 33:295-305. New Haven, CT: Yale University Press.
Sandler, J., Kennedy, H., Tyson, R. L. (1975). Discussions on transference: the treatment situation and technique in child psychoanalysis. *Psychoanalytic Study of the Child* 30:409-441. New Haven, CT: Yale University Press.
Tyson, P. (1978). Transference and developmental issues in the analysis of a prelatency child. *Psychoanalytic Study of the Child* 33:213-236. New Haven, CT: Yale University Press.

4

Traumatic Neurosis in Children

Jules Glenn, M.D.

INTRODUCTION

In a post-traumatic stress disorder, according to the *Diagnostic and Statistical Manual of Mental Disorders*, Third Edition *(DSM-III)* (1980), characteristic symptoms develop "following a traumatic event that is generally outside the range of usual human experience" (p. 236). The diagnostic criteria include (1) The existence of a recognizable stressor; (2) reexperiencing the trauma in recurrent recollections or dreams of the event or feeling as if the occurrence were happening again; (3) numbing of responses to or reduced involvement with the external world; (4) at least two of the following symptoms: startle response, sleep disturbance, survivor guilt, impaired memory or concentration, avoidance of activities that arouse recollection of the trauma, and intensification of symptoms when exposed to events similar to the trauma.

I find these descriptive diagnostic criteria, excellent though they are, lacking. They omit a definition of trauma. And since the psychodynamics are not stated, they fail to recognize that the reactions to the traumatic event can, and often do, become enmeshed in unconscious conflict and the development of psychoneurosis.

The term *trauma* has been used to signify a range of conditions. These include masterable or unmasterable difficulties; externally instigated troubles that result in symptoms or other disturbances; and extreme stimulation which overwhelms the ego. Because there are a variety of definitions, mental health professionals are often at a loss to determine the specific type of trauma referred to in discussions of the matter.

Following Freud (1916-1917, 1920) and Furst (1967), I propose that we restrict the term to overwhelming stimulation beyond the individual's capacity to deal with by his usual psychic mechanisms. I will adhere to this definition, but I will discuss other usage as well.

HISTORICAL CONSIDERATIONS

Freud early on considered trauma important in the etiology of mental disorders, but he used the term loosely. In *Studies on Hysteria* (Breuer and Freud 1893-1895) he and Breuer described disturbing pathogenic precipitating and predisposing events, labeled traumata, that resulted in hysteria and other neuroses. He continued this usage in his Clark University Lectures (Freud 1910). However, when he examined the types of onset of neurosis in 1912, Freud discussed difficulties that cause neuroses, such as frustrations, but did not call them traumata. The observations of soldiers who experienced traumatic neuroses during World War I influenced Freud's thinking (Simmel 1918, Freud 1919). From 1916 on he refined his conceptualization of trauma in children and adults. He wrote that the term "traumatic" applies "to an experience that within a short period of time presents the mind with an increase of stimulus too powerful to be dealt with or worked off in the usual way, and this must result in permanent disturbances of the manner in which energy operates" (1916-1917, p. 275). Traumata of this kind can occur in children when the biological stimulus barrier (or the parental protective shield [Spitz 1965]) fails to prevent overloading of the organism. Overwhelming stimulation may result in anxiety or the individual may develop signal anxiety, which serves as a warning and enables him to avoid the drastic effects of intense stimulation. The latter occurs normally.

As Freud applied the concept of trauma to the ordinary psychoneuroses, he also saw that special mechanisms were employed to deal with traumata. He noted that "the dreams of patients suffering from traumatic neuroses lead them back . . . to the situation in which the trauma occurred. . . . They are attempting to master the stimulus retrospectively" (Freud 1920, p. 32).

Freud erred in stating that patients with traumatic neuroses were not "much occupied in their waking lives with memories of the incident" (p. 13). Actually they do repeat the incident, but often without full awareness of the repetition, which may be disguised. Interestingly enough, shortly after discussing the traumatic neuroses, Freud described the defense mechanisms that typically occur following trauma, but which can be used to deal with other disturbing experiences as well: going from being in a passive situation with attendant discomfort to repeating the situation as an active participant. A child separated from his mother plays a game in which he throws a ball away. He becomes the active "leaver" (of the ball, symbolizing mother), thus mastering the loss and unknowingly expressing his anger. Similarly, after an operation a child will repeat the procedure in play, but pretend to perform the surgery on someone. Again he tries to master the frightening situation actively while avenging himself on a substitute.

Others have built on Freud's description of trauma and mastery. The diagnostic criteria of *DSM-III* are based on his observations. Anna Freud (1936) in *The Ego and the Mechanisms of Defense* described the defense mechanism of the *reversal* from being a passive victim to becoming an active repeater of the event. She also described children's and adults' identification with the aggressor; the reversal here is amalgamated with identification when the child plays the doctor and operates on his friend for instance.

In addition, a variety of traumatic events have been described. Freud was aware of the fact that children may be molested sexually and aggressively, and this has been confirmed repeatedly (Goodwin 1985). At one point Freud thought seduction was the sole pathogenic factor, but he modified this view as he recognized that fantasies as well as actual events may cause mental disorder. Children have also been traumatized by physical abuse (Green 1985), by the Holocaust (Krystal 1968), by observing violent behavior to others (Pynoos and Eth 1985), by the primal scene (Freud 1918), by separation from parents (Robertson and Robertson 1971), by the death of parents (Furman 1974), by illness and surgery (Robertson 1958), by kidnapping (Terr 1983), by natural catastrophes (Newman 1976), as well as other experiences.

TRAUMA AND ITS CONSEQUENCES

I have already stated how I use the term *trauma* in this chapter. I recommend a restricted meaning in order to attain clarity of communication and conceptualization: psychic trauma results from overwhelming stimulation beyond the organism's capacity to master through usual means. This is an economic definition based on the assumption that there is a psychic energy that can flood the organism. External or internal physiological stimulation is somehow converted into this psychic energy. At the time of the trauma the individual is overwhelmed, shocked, and experiences a state of confusion, disorganization, or absence. At that point his usual defenses do not suffice. With time, he attempts to master the situation by repetition as described above, and also through erotization of the memories of the traumatic event. The repetition may succeed in its task of mastery, or it may be traumatic in itself. The individual may repeat the traumatic experience but remain the victim and be terrified once again. The excessive anxiety may be traumatic in its production of further intense and unmasterable stimulation.

Furthermore, unconscious conflict may be intensified by the trauma. The external (or internal) trauma-producing stimulus may be libidinal in nature and may increase the intensity of drive derivatives. The trauma may be viewed by the individual as punishment for some conscious or unconscious crime. He thus becomes inhibited or develops pathogenic defenses against forbidden drives. Also, the ego, made fragile by the trauma, may be less able to perform autonomous ego functions or to defend successfully against drive derivatives and the anxiety evoked. The trauma can give rise to intense rage and aggressive feelings that are forbidden and difficult to deal with.

Although the concept of trauma I am utilizing is an economic, that is, energic, one, other metapsychological points of view are clearly involved. Structural conflict (between ego and id) may be intense and interfere with adaptation.

CLINICAL EXAMPLE: STIMULATION FROM WITHOUT

A clinical example will help us examine a number of the questions that arise when we attempt to conceptualize the role of trauma and to determine whether an event of yesteryear was truly traumatic or simply pathogenic.

Gene was 3 years old when an acquaintance, rushing about in play, ran into a glass storm door and cut his brachial artery. Gene was horrified as he watched the child exsanguinate while he stood by helpless. Even the adults failed to save the boy. The traumatic stimulation originated from the boy's environment. His affect, chiefly panic, probably castration anxiety, may account for most of the stimulus, and most likely aggressive drives were aroused as well. In any case, when I saw Gene at age 13, he was still attempting to master the trauma. Reconstruction of the experience, much of which was denied or repressed, was necessary. A dream early in his analysis helped clarify the trauma and its consequences: The patient was riding in a car that almost ran off a bridge that was incomplete.

Gene's associations were to accidents in which he was endangered and to the event when he was 3. By stopping in time to prevent an accident in the dream, he controlled fate and prevented injury, death, and panic. He told me that his father, a physician, would have been able to save the boy's life by joining the two ends of the severed artery. Gene determined to be a doctor himself, a surgeon who would cut people, but would do so to save lives, not to kill. He would thus master the dangers of life and his own aggressive urges.

Gene was understandably sensitive to illness and accidents and would report them both because they were upsetting to him and because he could use them to once more attempt mastery. When a boy in school cut his hand with an electric saw, Gene responded by telling me the numerous ways one could save the boy's extremity. He reasserted that his father could save people and that he, Gene, as a surgeon could do so as well.

The report of a single session will help clarify some of the issues.

Three days prior to our last session before a summer break, Gene discussed when he would start again in August. He then told me that he was going by propeller plane to a camp in Ithaca and that this worried him. He would travel to the camp at Cornell University with two girls from his high school. One of them had arranged the flight while he had arranged for the limousine to the airport. The girl had told Gene they would take a propeller plane, and he had said he did not like that. He soon forgot about the plane trip only to recall it a few days ago. He knows, he said, that it is safe to fly planes, but worries, or rather had worried, anyway. A propeller plane is less safe than a jet plane. He had stopped being afraid to fly a few years ago when he flew with his two older sisters and not with his parents. Flying over land appears more dangerous than flying over water because water provides for a softer landing in case of a crash. Then after continuing to deny that he worries, the following facts emerged: He doesn't want the girls to know that he is afraid. Everybody had thought that the flight by propeller plane was cheaper, and, with the money saved, Gene hired a stretch limousine with a bar and TV set in it. If he changes flights, he might have to give up the limousine.

The thought of crashing reminded Gene of the accident he witnessed at 3. He described it in more detail than before. He and two other 3-year-old boys were playing at a friend's house. His and another boy's teenage girl baby-sitters were caring for them. Eric and Jean—a different spelling from Gene's, he pointed out—two boys of about 11, were running about the house. Eric chased Jean toward the front door, which was open, though the storm door was closed. Jean ran to the right into a closet, but Eric raced ahead and stretched his arm out as he approached the glass and metal storm door. His arm went through the door and he cut himself from wrist to axilla. Glass fell on both sides of the door. Eric fell to the floor. Gene watched the blood pour out in spurts all over the floor—for what seemed like a few minutes. He didn't know what was happening. There was no shock, he said spontaneously, indicating, I think, his repression of the actual shock experience. One of the baby-sitters said, "Get them out of here," and the three boys were taken to another house across the street. The baby-sitter called an ambulance and the police. The police took Eric to the hospital, but he died. The boys were interested in and looked at the police cars and the excitement. They were especially interested in the CB announcements.

Although Gene, according to his recollection, was not upset or shocked at the time of the accident or when his mother told him later in the day that Eric had died, that night he had a nightmare in which the scene of the accident appeared, the bleeding and all. Gene awoke and went to his parents' bed. From 3 to 13 years of age he had such nightmares about six times a year. In addition, since then Gene has been afraid of cutting himself and bleeding. Once he cut his hand with a Swiss knife and bled a lot. He became frightened. At another time he became very upset when, while backpacking, a tree branch cut his axilla slightly.

Gene dwelt on the fact that he did not understand death at 3. I said that explains why, when the boy cut his hand on the saw at school, he talked about saving the boy's *hand*, not of saving his *life;* it was like a 3-year-old's thinking. Gene replied that he *did* think of saving the boy's life through saving his hand and preventing loss of blood. (Indeed, he had at the time talked of joining the blood vessels so as to stop the bleeding.) Then he added that even now he could not understand death.

This clinical example alerts us to some of the issues one encounters when evaluating psychic trauma. We often cannot rely on the patient's memory, but have to reconstruct the economic (energic) situation at the time of the trauma. Reconstruction may be easy when the patient recalls being overwhelmed or immobilized or disorganized. However, Gene did not remember being overwhelmed, or even panicky, as he watched Eric fall and bleed. We cannot be sure whether denial, repression, or some other mechanism at the time of the accident worked so effectively that Gene was not aware of his responses even then. Nor can we be certain whether Gene was aware of his reaction at the time of the accident and then repressed much of it. We note that he recalled the traumatic effect of the event, as indicated by the start of nightmares that night. In discussing this Gene was inclined to think he had forgotten the shock and fear at the time of the accident. Quite possibly his repeatedly saying he didn't understand death reflected his confusion about what was happening at the time of the accident and when his mother told him the boy died. Yorke and Wiseberg (1976) have pointed out that the "traumatic event itself is rarely forgotten, unlike the dazed period that follows it," suggesting "that the failure to remember the dazed condition is a consequence of the near paralysis of the ego at that time" (p. 131).

The change in the state of consciousness at the time of the trauma interferes with its being remembered.

We also may wonder whether being overwhelmed by an influx of psychic energy is the same as being bombarded by inner physiological or external physical stimulation, as the concept of the stimulus barrier implies. Perhaps stimulation from within or without should be viewed as evoking the excess of the hypothetical psychic energy that provokes the state of trauma.

I must add at this point that I have simplified matters. True, Gene suffered from severe trauma at 3. But a number of other life experiences contributed markedly to his feeling of vulnerability as well. When he was 8, a series of illnesses and deaths upset him to no small degree. During that year his maternal grandfather was operated upon for carcinoma of the stomach in June and died in the hospital of a myocardial infarct in August. In August, while Gene was still at camp, his paternal grandmother died of a breast malignancy. More illness appeared in the family. When Gene was 11 his father had a pulmonary lobectomy for a tumor that turned out to be benign, and when Gene was 12 his mother had a hysterectomy for fibroids. Previously, when Gene was 5, his mother had suffered what the family called a mild coronary for which she was hospitalized.

Some clinicians would say that the series of nontraumatic events (in the strict sense of the term) was more important than the trauma at 3. Some would perhaps emphasize the importance of the fact that Gene's parents argued a great deal, spoke openly of divorce, and deprecated the role of the trauma at 3. They would also underline Gene's father's humorous derision of my patient. Gene was in fact preoccupied with all these events; they appeared in his associations repeatedly. Certainly we should not discount in any way the significance of these events, which accentuated his castration anxiety and his fears that he would lose those close to him, that his aggressive wishes might realize themselves. However, watching the dying boy when he was 3 and his intense emotions at that time also contributed to the pathogenesis of his neurotic disturbance. We see here that shock trauma and other types of stress reinforce one another. In interpretive psychotherapy the role of *all* these factors must be taken into account.

In some cases the early trauma accentuates the disturbing effects of later pathogenic events. In others, events preceding the trauma make the patient more sensitive to the traumatic event. In Gene's case we discovered later in the analysis that his mother's coronary when he was 5 was of overwhelming significance. His father was panicky about the possible loss of his wife, and Gene lost his mother while she was in the hospital. He could not be taken care of sufficiently by the caretaker who replaced his mother. As he perceived his father's terror, his own fear snowballed. His emphasis on the death of his friend at 3 served to defend against his dread about losing his mother.

In addition, intense inner conflict appeared. Tabooed sexual and aggressive urges, accentuated by the numerous traumata in his life, felt even more forbidden because seeing a boy exsanguinate proved to him that one can actually die, that punishment through bodily injury was not a mere fantasy. So too did the deaths in his family confirm for him the fragility of the human body. Gene developed the symptom of obesity to defend himself against the dreaded bodily injury. A heavy person seems more substantial. Furthermore, he said, if one has layers of protective fat, a knife would not penetrate and cut the arteries within as well. The obesity also seemed to serve as a protective shield between oneself and those outside. Emotion could be muted by the barrier, Gene imagined. In addition, the overeating he indulged in dampened the intensity of sexual and aggressive drives, allowed oral satisfaction, and hid feelings of frustration and rage.

The traumata Gene encountered not only led to repeated attempts at mastery, they also accentuated unconscious conflict and produced neurotic symptoms.

CLINICAL EXAMPLE: PARENTAL LOSS

One of the traumata Gene experienced was the loss of his mother. Another illustration will allow us to study further the influence of such loss in more detail.

The parents of Billy, a 3-year-old boy, left him in the care of a strange baby-sitter for ten days while they went to Europe. On their return they found him dejected and distant. He seemed not to recognize them. When he entered treatment at the age of 4 he was still reacting to the traumatic experience. He played hiding games in an attempt to reassure himself that he could find the person he could not see. He loved a book called *Are You My Mother?* about a bird who searches for his lost parent and finally finds her. The hiding games took a variety of forms. He had his analyst hide so that he, Billy, could search for and find him. Then, reversing the game, he hid from the therapist, who had to seek him out. In that game he became the deserter who made the victim feel the terrible loss. Billy also modified the game so that toys, dolls, and even pieces of paper were hidden and sought. These inanimate objects represented the disappearing humans.

The traumatic effects of separation from a mother include the inability to find drive satisfaction when the mother is away. Ordinarily a mother, through her talk and touching, through her feeding and fondling, gratifies drives and provides a means of discharge. She also protects the child from environmental overstimulation with its potentially traumatic effects. Without her palpable presence the child may be traumatized by excessive external stimulation as well as excessive internal drive stimulation.

Billy also developed character disturbances based in part on inner conflict. He pictured his mother as a source of pain, and her image included the distress connected with separation. He sought pain as a means of imagining that his mother was present. For instance, he tried to get his sister to pinch his penis and thus produce pain. A masochistic clinical picture appeared as he eroticized the painful loss. When he entered the oedipal stage, his forbidden sexual wishes were disguised as masochistic provocation became dominant.

CLINICAL EXAMPLE: STIMULATION FROM WITHIN

Generally traumata are thought of as developing after stimulation originating from outside the organism. Indeed, Freud viewed it in that way. The external event may result in intense physiological stimulation from within and an accompanying intense release of psychic energy that floods the organism. There are, in addition, instances in which the original stimulus occurs *within* the organism to produce a traumatic state.

Betty suffered from coeliac syndrome from the age of 1 year 2 months to 2 years 2 months. She had numerous large, smelly, painful bowel movements each day. Overstimulation of her intestines occurred repeatedly. She recovered from the coeliac disorder, but later, when she was 3, she started to retain feces for as long as ten days. She again produced large painful bowel movements. She was repeating in disguised form her early painful traumatic experiences, which she tried to master by retention. During analysis she invented games in which she was the mother who actively tried to toilet train the therapist. She also identified with the therapist/child who refused to be trained.

The reenactment involved unconscious psychic conflict as well as repetition to attempt to master trauma. Betty developed the obstipation at 3 when her mother became pregnant. The bowel movement within Betty represented a baby, and she was the mother she feared losing. Identifying with her mother, she could in fantasy prevent the loss. By being her mother she kept her mother with her.

The bowel movement in her also represented her sibling she wished had not been born. And through its stimulation of the intestine, it produced a pleasurable effect, a precursor of oedipal sexual pleasure. The intestinal stimulation was eroticized and sought. Pain also served as punishment for forbidden wishes to get rid of her sibling and attain the love of her parents.

OTHER VIEWS OF TRAUMA

As I have stated, the term trauma has been defined and employed in many ways, but I advocate a narrow usage. Readers should be aware of other definitions so that they can attempt to ascertain which meaning an author intends. More often than not authors (or colloquial users of the term) do not bother to tell the reader or listener what they mean by trauma. Indeed, they may not be aware that it is an issue.

Greenacre (1967), taking a broad view, includes as traumatic conditions "any conditions which seem definitely unfavorable, noxious, or drastically injurious to the development of the young individual" (p. 128). Kris (1956) labeled as "shock trauma" the sudden overwhelming trauma that I have simply called trauma. He contrasted this with "strain trauma," or "long lasting situations, which may cause traumatic effects by the accumulation of frustrating tensions" (p. 324). Although semantically weak, this definition has clinical validity. We more often find that our patients have been subject to many more tension-producing events than single blasts, and that the long-standing strain can be pathogenic. Khan's (1963) concept of the "cumulative trauma" is relevant. He suggests that the mother not only may fail to protect the infant from overwhelming overstimulation, but also may fail to act as a protective shield in more subtle ways. To illustrate, he quotes Anna Freud (1958), who observed regarding a particular patient "that . . . subtle harm is being inflicted on this child, and that the consequence of it will become manifest at some future date." In one form the mother allows tension to build up through repeated premature separations or failure to allow adequate drive discharge. The child becomes uncomfortable and anxious or dejected over a long period. Memories of shock trauma may be merely defensive screens for the terrible chronic strain and may, as Kris (1956) observed, telescope a number of disturbing events.

At the time of the strain, even an astute observer may fail to note the child's distress. Only later may the pathogenic effect become apparent, as indicated in the following example of chronic strain.

TRAUMATIC NEUROSIS IN CHILDREN

An adult patient of mine suffered from an undetected learning disability as a child. Although she had difficulties in school, somehow the diagnosis was not made. She was considered rebellious. Her antagonism arose in part from her continuous and repeated failure to achieve. She felt inferior, and indeed fantasies that women were inherently deficient and envious of men were intensified by her childhood failures.

Chronic or cumulative strain should be differentiated from repeated episodes of acute and shocking trauma as well as from prolonged trauma in which the individual is overwhelmed for long periods of time. In the Holocaust, for instance, victims were often traumatized (in the sense of intensely overstimulated) for long periods, and were also subjected to brief barrages of acute trauma.

There can be no doubt that chronic or cumulative strain exists. However, I object to calling it "trauma" since it is a different kettle of fish. We have too much trouble understanding one another when we use the same word for different states. The situation has changed little since Anna Freud made the following remarks in the concluding chapter of the book *Psychic Trauma* that Sidney Furst edited in 1967: "I welcome this opportunity to inquire more closely into the current usage of the term 'trauma' and perhaps, to rescue it from the widening and overuse that are the present-day fate of many other technical terms in psychoanalysis and, in the course of time, lead inevitably to a blurring of meaning and finally to the abandonment and loss of valuable concepts" (p. 236).

DIFFERENTIATING THE EFFECTS OF TRAUMA AND OTHER PATHOGENIC EFFECTS

Similar external events may have different effects on people. What external observers may consider traumatic (in the narrow sense) may be pathogenic but not traumatic. I will restrict myself to four situations.

1. The loss of a parent may be traumatic in that the child, overstimulated from within by inability to discharge drives or from without by the absence of the protective barrier, becomes overwhelmed. On the other hand, the family may rise to the emergency and act with haste to protect the child by providing surrogates who comfort and protect. Trauma may then be avoided, but the pathogenic influence of losing the parents may be strong. The child may develop wishes to be with his mother, whose death is denied, and may long for a reunion in death. Denial may come to play a too prominent role in the child's hierarchy of defenses. The

child may feel the loss as a punishment and become inhibited. These pathogenic effects may be potent, but should be differentiated from trauma (Furman 1974, 1986).

2. Even a child who is molested may be free of traumatic effects in the narrow sense of the term. Many children who are seduced by adults are shocked by the experience. Some are not.

An 8-year-old was stimulated genitally by a grandfather she loved. She enjoyed the sexual excitement and was not overwhelmed by it. Nevertheless, she felt the activity was wrong. She did not tell her parents because she did not wish to discontinue the sex play, and because she felt guilty and feared their reprimands. This experience was clearly pathogenic. Severe inhibitions to sexual enjoyment persisted into adulthood.

3. Similarly, observing parents have intercourse may or may not be traumatic. The child may be overwhelmed, his curiosity may be aroused, or his psychic life set on a sadomasochistic course as he imagines his parents hurting each other.

4. Understimulation from the external world may be traumatic when it is accompanied by failure to afford drive discharge, as we have seen in the case of Billy. In addition, understimulation may have other nontraumatic effects. The child's intellectual and affective life may become impoverished. He may come to lack curiosity and gratification in contact with people. Stimulation appears necessary for growth of dentrites.

There are many possible pathogenic effects of nontraumatic experiences. The individual may later repeat the pathogenic experiences in disguise in order to achieve mastery or in order to attain gratification, and may become anxious when the reenactment occurs.

RESOLUTION OF TRAUMA

Following traumatic experience the individual automatically institutes self-healing behavior. He repeats the experience, often in disguised form, usually without full awareness of what he is up to. He may repeat it in the role of the passive victim in the hope that the outcome will be favorable. He often repeats it as the active aggressor, turning the tables and doing to someone else what was done to him so that he is no longer the victim. Doing this he will express the anger he may not have been capable of expressing during the trauma. Parents often encourage the overwhelmed child to deal with the event through calm support, reassurance, and protection. The child will then be able to carry out the therapeutic reenactment with a feeling of relative confidence and minimal fear, and it is hoped, to achieve mastery.

Professional intervention (Sours 1973) is based on the same principles. The therapist encourages the child to repeat the trauma in an atmosphere of supportive neutrality, that is, without unduly inhibiting or criticizing the child's aggression or sexual enactments. The therapist may have to institute some restraint if the patient becomes so hostile as to injure himself or others. Otherwise the child's anxiety may increase as he realizes he cannot control himself and the grownups about him will not aid him. In addition, the therapist can help by explaining to the patient what experiences he is trying to master, and his means of doing so. Of course, once the memories of the traumatic event become enmeshed in neurotic conflict, the situation is more complicated and requires more extensive interpretative work if the patient is suitable for a type of treatment based on insight.

Traumatic events need not have a long-term pathogenic effect. When mastered they may lead to confidence in one's ability to deal with the world, rather than the expectation of catastrophe so often seen after unresolved calamities.

ADAPTIVE ASPECTS

There is no escaping trauma, either defined as overwhelming stimulation or in the sense of other disturbing events in an individual's life. Although either type of difficulty may have pathological effects, they may also produce adaptive solutions.

We saw in Gene's case that psychic trauma in the sense of overwhelming stimulation had adaptive as well as neurosogenic consequences. Gene determined to become a doctor in order to be able to master the traumata he experienced at 3 and later. Such an outcome is not unusual.

Dr. P. had experienced severe shock trauma when he was operated on at the age of 6. He fell unconscious after a surgeon pierced his retropharyngeal abscess without first anesthetizing him. Later he attempted mastery through identification with the aggressor. He played a game in which he stabbed pictures in magazines which he then examined to determine how many throats he had pierced. When he grew up, impotence interfered with his marriage. He could not introduce his penis into his wife because, unconsciously angry at what had been done to him and identifying with the surgeon, he felt he was an attacker who would hurt his wife. His love for her and his conscience forbade him from penetrating her and in fantasy hurting her.

He became a physician as a result of the same mechanism, identification with the aggressor, but was inhibited in his work. The physician after all damages the patient, he imagined. And he wanted to attack and achieve vengeance, even if he had to use a scapegoat. Through psychoanalysis Dr. P. overcame his impotence and was able to function successfully as a doctor and researcher.

Trauma can lead to adaptation in other ways as well. Freud (1926) asserted that inevitable psychic trauma in early infancy resulted in anxiety that the child seeks to control and prevent because of the intense pain involved. Subsequently, he becomes able to deal with danger situations through the development of signal anxiety. When a minute degree of anxiety appears, the individual automatically takes steps to avert the danger, an adaptive outcome. The adaptive mechanisms or defenses that ensue can be totally adaptive or can lead to symptoms.

In the cases of Gene and Dr. P., psychic trauma accentuated inner conflict and gave rise to symptoms. Other types of disturbing events can facilitate conflict and may further the development of symptoms or adaptive outcomes. Life situations may have disturbing affects. For instance, being a twin or an adopted child necessarily leaves a mark on the individual. Twins may suffer because they differentiate self and object representations poorly and because they are burdened by an excess of sibling rivalry and, paradoxically, sibling love. They may suffer unduly in reaction to the unhappiness of others. They may desperately try to establish a firm sense of identity, even if it means avoiding areas of accomplishment that they consider twins' provinces. On the other hand, twins may use their sense of flexible boundaries for creative achievement. Peter and Anthony Shaffer, who are fraternal twins, are successful authors who often create characters that possess the traits of twins (Glenn 1974).

Quantitative factors are important. A constitutionally more vulnerable person will have more difficulty dealing with disturbing events adaptively and will more likely fail to manage inner psychic conflict successfully. However, if the pathogenic event is severe enough, even a well-constituted person will develop a psychoneurosis or psychosis rather than an adaptive outcome.

Inner psychic conflict, like trauma, is inevitable. Hartmann (1965) has described the transformation of conflict-laden defenses into autonomous ego functions. The defense of isolation, which protects people from anxiety due to struggles between the ego and the id, can be used adaptively to facilitate concentration. Similarly, reaction formation may result in a useful orderliness and healthful cleanliness. Defensive neatness or disdain for dirt, a response to drive-dominated wishes to be messy and dirty, become helpful traits.

CONCLUSION

Understanding the traumatic neuroses of children requires a definition of psychic trauma. I suggest that trauma be conceptualized as overwhelming stimulation beyond the individual's capacity to deal with it by his usual psychic mechanisms, an economic (energic) definition. The overwhelming stimulation may be from within or without the organism. Lack of parental care of protection may result in such stimulation. Other metapsychological points of view complement the economic in our understanding the effects of traumata. The trauma will have meaning for the child, signifying punishment for instance. It often increases the degree of psychic conflict and thus produces psychoneurotic symptoms.

Resolution of the disorders associated with psychic trauma may occur through the institution of defenses such as repetition and reversal to accomplish mastery. Psychotherapy and psychoanalysis may facilitate resolution or bring about adaptations that ordinarily would not occur. Psychic trauma can be temporarily or permanently devastating, or can have adaptive consequences.

REFERENCES

Breuer, J., and Freud, S. (1893–1895). Studies on hysteria. *Standard Edition* 2.
Diagnostic and Statistic Manual of Mental Disorders, 3rd ed. (1980). Washington, DC: American Psychiatric Association.
Erikson, K. T. (1976). Loss of communicality at Buffalo Creek. *American Journal of Psychiatry* 33:302–305.
Frederick, C. J. (1985). Children traumatized by catastrophic situations. In *Post-Traumatic Stress Disorder in Children*, ed. S. Eth and R. S. Pynoos, pp. 71–99. Washington, DC: American Psychiatric Association.
Freud, A. (1936). *The Ego and the Mechanisms of Defense*. New York: International Universities Press.
_____ (1958). Child observations and prediction of development. *Psychoanalytic Study of the Child* 13:92–124. New York: International Universities Press.
_____ (1951). Comments on trauma. In *Psychic Trauma*, ed. S. S. Furst, p. 236. New York: Basic Books.
Freud, S. (1910). Five lectures on psycho-analysis. *Standard Edition* 11:1–55.
_____ (1912). Types of onset of neuroses. *Standard Edition* 12:227–238.
_____ (1916–1917). Introductory lectures on psychoanalysis. *Standard Edition* 15/16.
_____ (1918). From the history of an infantile neurosis. *Standard Edition* 17:1–22.

―――― (1919). Introduction to psycho-analysis and the war neuroses. *Standard Edition* 17:205–215.
―――― (1920). Beyond the pleasure principle. *Standard Edition* 18:1–64.
―――― (1926). Inhibitions, symptoms and anxiety. *Standard Edition* 20:75–175.
―――― (1933). New introductory lectures on psychoanalysis. *Standard Edition* 22:1–182.
Furman, E. (1974). *A Child's Parent Dies.* New Haven, CT: Yale University Press.
―――― (1986) On trauma: when is the death of a parent traumatic? *Psychoanalytic Study of the Child* 41:191–280. New Haven, CT: Yale University Press.
Furst, S. S. ed. (1967). *Psychic Trauma.* New York: Basic Books.
Glenn, J. (1974). Twins in disguise. A psychoanalytic essay on *Sleuth* and *The Royal Hunt of the Sun. Psychoanalytic. Quarterly* 43:288–302.
Goodwin, J. (1985). Post-traumatic symptoms in incest victims. In *Post-Traumatic Stress Disorders in Children*, ed. S. Eth and R. S. Pynoos, pp. 155–156. Washington, DC: American Psychiatric Association.
Greenacre, P. (1967). The influence of infantile trauma on genetic patterns. In *Psychic Trauma*, ed. S. Furst, pp. 108–153. New York: Basic Books.
Green, A. H. (1985). Children traumatized by physical abuse. In *Post-Traumatic Stress Disorders in Children*, ed. S. Eth and R. S. Pynoos, pp. 133–154. Washington, DC: American Psychiatric Association.
Hartmann, H. (1965). *Essays on Ego Psychology.* New York: International Universities Press.
Khan, M. (1963). The concept of cumulative trauma. *Psychoanalytic Study of the Child* 18:286–306. New York: International Universities Press.
Kris, E. (1956). The recovery of childhood memories in psychoanalysis. *Psychoanalytic Study of the Child* 11:54–88. New York: International Universities Press.
Krystal, H. (1968). *Massive Psychic Trauma.* New York: International Universities Press.
Newman, C. J. (1976). Children of disaster: clinical observations at Buffalo Creek. *American Journal of Psychiatry* 133:306–312.
Pynoos, R. S., and Eth, S., eds. (1985). Children traumatized by witnessing acts of personal violence, homicide, rape and suicidal behavior. In *Post-Traumatic Stress Disorder in Children*, pp. 17–43. Washington, DC: American Psychiatric Association.
Robertson, J. (1958). *Young Children in Hospital.* New York: Basic Books.
Robertson, J., and Robertson, J. (1971). Young children in brief separation: a fresh look. *Psychoanalytic Study of the Child* 26:264–315. New Haven, CT: Yale University Press.
Simmel, E. (1918). *Kriegsneurosen and "Psychisches Trauma."* Munich. (Referred to by Freud 1919.)
Sours, J. A. (1978). The application of child analytic principles to forms of child psychotherapy. In *Child Analysis and Therapy*, ed. J. Glenn, pp. 615–646. New York: Jason Aronson.
Spitz, R. A. (1965). *The First Year of Life.* New York: International Universities Press.
Terr, L. (1979). Children of Chowchilla: A study of psychic trauma. *Psychoanalytic Study of the Child* 34:547–623. New Haven, CT: Yale University Press.
―――― (1983). Chowchilla revisited: The effects of psychic trauma four years after a school bus kidnapping. *American Journal of Psychiatry* 140:1543–1550.
Yorke, C., and Wiseberg, S. (1976). A developmental view of anxiety. *Psychoanalytic Study of the Child* 31:107–135. New Haven, CT: Yale University Press.

5

The Infantile Neurosis and Neuroses in Childhood

J. Alexis Burland, M.D.

Neuroses have a distinctive appearance, whether they occur in childhood, adolescence, or adulthood. They also follow a similar course when treated by one of the psychoanalytic therapies. A few brief clinical vignettes will demonstrate this point.

CASE A

A 7-year-old boy was brought for psychotherapy because of a phobic fear that there was a dangerous goat on the second floor of his home that would attack him if he went upstairs at night to go to bed. This fear was so intense that over the several months of its duration bedtime had evolved into a tearful, screaming family conflict, with the boy refusing to go upstairs, his parents—especially the father—getting more and more angry and frustrated over his son's seeming irrationality, and everyone losing enough sleep that their daily functioning was affected. In treatment, he took to the doll house, and over a period of a year played out in increasing detail a scenario about an imaginary family at bedtime. By the end of the year, he was also talking increasingly about himself and his actual family's bedtime procedures and rituals in such a way that it was clear that the imaginary family was a fantasy he had been having about his real family.

Three major themes emerged. First, the son was preoccupied with electric gadgets, old batteries, broken radios, and the like, and he would play with them in his bedroom, pretending they were powerful weapons or startling new inventions, and that he was brilliant and powerful for devising them. But this play was accompanied by great fears of an evil monster that lived in the attic above his room who disapproved of what he was doing and threatened to come down through the trapdoor in the ceiling of the boy's closet and punish him. In the transference relationship this young boy for a while duplicated his gadgetry and inventions activities in the office, requesting frequent reassurances from me that this was not a waste of our time, that is, he feared my disapproval as he feared that of the monster in the attic.

Second, the son and his two-years-younger sister frequently played house together, a game that over time got increasingly exciting, culminating in an activity called "playing mommy and daddy" in which they would wrap themselves in a blanket and tickle each other until they were in tears from their giggling and laughing. This game was kept secret from the parents and very cautiously revealed to me.

Third—the last theme to surface—the son could lie in bed and look out through his open bedroom door into the hall where he could see reflected in a large hall mirror the open door to his parents' bedroom. At first he insisted the room was dark and he could see nothing; but in time, and with some difficulty, he admitted he could see them hugging and, he believed, tickling each other. As this last piece of the puzzle surfaced, the patient suddenly recalled that there had been a very special mirror in the hall that somehow fell and broke just prior to the onset of his phobia; the mirror had been in the shape of a goat's head. By this time his phobia, which had been diminishing, totally disappeared.

CASE B

An 8-year-old boy was seen in psychotherapy for another bedtime phobia, this time a fear that a robber was on the roof outside of his window and would break in and kill him. In this family, too, bedtime had gradually become a chaotic situation with the boy tearfully refusing to go upstairs and his parents—again, especially the father—growing increasingly impatient and frustrated.

In treatment, the boy was soon spinning endless tales about his favorite hobby, "bugging devices." This was in the 1960s when governmental bugging of suspected subversives was common knowledge and hobby shops sold a wide array of miniature microphones, pocket receivers, and so on, about which my patient was well informed; this was also where his allowance went. In fact, his tales were fantasy elaborations of actual activities that he and some of his friends engaged in. For instance, they once concealed a microphone in the room where their school held faculty meetings and managed on several occasions to overhear teachers discussing various problems of some of the students. Soon he was fantasizing bugging my office, or better yet, in time, bugging my home so that he could find out about my personal life—especially whether I were married and had children, a frequently used, roundabout way of asking about my sex life.

At this point his phobia had changed to a fear that he was being spied upon by a robber on the roof, rather than being threatened with bodily harm, and as this material was being played out and discussed, he came to a confession. Shortly before the onset of the phobia he had managed to force his 13-year-old brother and his friends to include him in a sleepout in their backyard in a boy scout tent they had just purchased. That night the adolescents engaged in group masturbation and introduced my patient to that practice. He found it pleasurable enough that it had since become a regular bedtime activity. This, he confessed, was what he feared the robber would see him doing through the window. With some difficulty over the ensuing weeks, he revealed that his conscious masturbatory fantasies were of breaking into the girls' locker room at school and catching them unclothed. This fantasy soon changed into one that had been hidden behind the other, in which he would break into his parents' bedroom and catch them unclothed and having intercourse. By this time the phobia had disappeared.

Within a few more weeks he told me that the reason it had ended was because he had stopped masturbating, at least until he was as old as his brother, which seemed to him to be an age at which one could masturbate without getting so upset and anxious.

CASE C

A man in his mid-forties was in analysis with an initial complaint of urinary frequency for which no organic cause could be found. It soon surfaced that he experienced this symptom only at night; furthermore, as he realized that his fear was of wetting the bed, he suddenly recalled that he had been enuretic at ages 6 and 7. It had been the center of an intense power struggle with his idealized but tyrannical father. Prior to that time he had been the apple of his father's eye, and both had shared the dream of a future life in which the son would emulate his father.

However, as my patient grew older and more autonomous, the relationship with the father soured; any sign of independence on his part was viewed as defiance and often brutally squashed. Enuresis developed and became the perfect weapon, as we uncovered later in the analysis. He claimed—and consciously believed—that as he was asleep he had no control over it, so his father, who was enraged by it, would not be able to hold him responsible. But his father did anyway, and one day threatened to "beat the hell out of" him if he did it once more; he did, and he was beaten. He never wet the bed again, but only because he would waken every hour or so and go to the bathroom. That manifest symptom gradually faded by the time of the onset of adolescence, though in the analysis we uncovered a variety of ways in which the persistent unconscious conflicts found other more subtle avenues of expression.

What had precipitated the return of the anxiety in adulthood was a parallel situation at work: my patient, one of the youngest men in his field to achieve an important and prestigious administrative position, had recently endeavored to introduce some innovative if not radical practices, and those who once idealized him and supported his rapid rise up the ladder suddenly grew fearful and critical of his challenge to tradition. In the analysis, the arena in which these same dynamics from childhood were played out in the transference was dream analysis. Of course dreams occur at night, and my patient would worry whether or not he would please me by "being a good boy" in his sleep and do what I wanted of him, namely have dreams. When he would report them in the analytic sessions, a conflict arose over whether his "dream analyzing instrument" was as powerful as mine, and if it were (or if it were superior) would I get angry? Just as we had uncovered that his enuresis had conveyed the message that his penis was somehow ineffective, "good only for pissing " (a self-protective, pseudo-self-castration designed to disarm his father), so too, in the transference he proclaimed his inability to understand his dreams on his own, as evidence that his dream analyzing instrument was less effective than mine. As with the two boys described in the two previous cases, as the memories from the past were recovered and the unconscious dynamics of the transference brought into consciousness, the presenting symptoms abated.

These three brief clinical vignettes of neurotic conflict at work pose the question: How do we understand such clinical psychological phenomena? On a descriptive level it would seem that each patient is at war with himself, afraid of his own drives (primarily sexual but also self-assertive), and resolves the situation by use of a complicated stratagem involving self-inhibition, disguised symbolic gratification, and self-punishment in the form of mental anguish. All of this occurs out of consciousness; bringing it into consciousness is related to the disappearance of the symptoms. The adult patient in the third vignette was reexperiencing a neurosis he had first experienced when he was a child close in age to the younger patients described previously. This demonstrates a relationship between the neurosis the man suffered in childhood and the one he suffered as an adult, and this regularly observed phenomenon needs also to be explained.

Certain other features of the clinical picture are more or less common among the three. First, the material they present is made up of double entendres, of symbolic, that is, disguised, expressions of forbidden wishes, fears, and fantasies. It is possible that as you read the material you sensed this at once, and even found it amusing. There is often a certain playful and humorous dimension to the hide and seek games of neurotic symptoms, for example, the broken hall mirror having a goat's head design, the bugging of the school office, and the competition as to whose dream analyzing instrument was bigger. There is also a creative plasticity at work; whatever life situation is currently extant, each patient found a way to use it according to his inner needs. The transference distortions are examples of this; while consciously viewing our relationship in fairly realistic terms as a cooperative and friendly venture, our interaction was unconsciously viewed as a kind of sexual and self-assertive activity engaged in against the wishes of paternal authority. A parent-child dimension was imposed on our relationship and I was viewed as someone other than who I was, in particular, someone who at least on the surface stood against their seeking sexual gratifications.

This mobility of the neurotic conflict is evident in all dimensions of a patient's life.

Some other examples include a college student whose initial complaint involved being somehow unable to bring to completion any kind of school project. His expectation was always that it would turn out so well he would be applauded by the teacher and also by his peers, who would envy his accomplishment. We discovered in analysis that unconsciously each project was viewed as an instance of masturbation, an act accompanied by dreams of glory in which he outperformed his father and older brother. He had as a young adolescent experienced great masturbation guilt, which he handled by allowing himself to masturbate but stopping just before he achieved orgasm—just as he now stopped short of completing his school assignments.

Another example: A high school student was introduced to the use of marijuana by friends. Soon he was struggling over using it or not, fearing on the one hand that if he did it would make him sterile and ruin his brain, as rumor had it, and on the other hand feeling compelled to seek the pleasures of being high, something viewed as cool and tough by his peers. He left his stash out on his desk "by accident" for his mother to find; she cooperated with his unconscious wish and became, with his father, a strong voice for abstaining from drug use. Yet he needed then to rebel against them, in keeping with his ideal image of himself as independent and in the fast track.

Compare this vignette with that of an adult who recalled of his adolescence in the 1950s, prior to the spread of the drug culture among adolescents in the 1960s, that he feared that masturbation would make him sterile and ruin his brain—as he had heard in the locker room. He left semen stains on his sheets and pajamas with the conscious fantasy that his mother would see them, get angry, and then help him stop the practice. We discovered in analysis that behind this conscious fantasy was an unconscious fantasy that she would be seduced by the evidence of his sexuality. In other words, the same behavior on a conscious level was designed to bring his masturbatory activities to an end, while unconsciously it was a means of gratification of his incestuous wishes. Not surprisingly, his masturbatory fantasies also revealed his ambition to outperform his father in every way: educationally, professionally, and especially sexually, and that these fantasies were in conflict with his simultaneous deep and abiding love and respect for his father, thus generating much of his guilt.

In these two cases we see how current trends in adolescent behavior—here the introduction of the drug culture—will build upon preexisting unconscious neurotic patterns.

And a final example: A 6-year-old girl in play therapy was playing "repair shop." The shop was for the repair of washing machines and automobiles; she took on the job of repairing the washing machines because she understood how all the "tubes and pipes inside" worked, but I was assigned the repair of automobiles because "only a man, like my father, knows how a stick shift works." It may sound like an exaggeration, but for the neurotically conflicted any and all daily tasks, activities, reactions, and fantasies are liable to be made into double entendres for forbidden sexual activity.

THE EVOLUTION OF PSYCHOANALYSIS

The history of psychoanalysis is the history of attempts to understand and explain such features of neurotic activity with the aim of thereby being able to create an effective form of treatment. It has only been in recent years that psychoanalysis has turned its attention to other than neurotic mental conditions, the so-called widening scope of analysis. It has been pointed out that as our ability to assess the totality of mental functioning has improved, some of the cases that served as Freud's clinical data in the formulation of his theories about neurotic mechanisms were probably suffering at the same time from other, more debilitating conditions, for example, borderline states or narcissistic character disorders. But such patients also experienced islands of neurotic conflict and these were Freud's focus. That the psychoanalytic research into the mind began with the examination of neurotic mechanisms probably reflects several factors: in Freud's Vienna, hysteria was common; these patients were referred to Freud by his mentors as he was setting up his practice; neurotic mechanisms are strikingly visible and almost seductive in their colorful and often amusing nature; in self-analysis, the means by which much of Freud's thinking was confirmed for himself, neurotic mechanisms are more readily perceived by the observing ego.

Early Observations

Among the first observations made was that hysterics relive unconsciously in their symptoms past anxiety-generating sexual experiences and that behind the adult neurosis is an "infantile neurosis" (Breuer and Freud 1893). What was relived was first thought to be memories of actual sexual seductions experienced in early childhood, whether intentional (the guilty party was conscious of his or her sexual intent), or unintentional (a mother innocently bathing her child might touch his or her genitals, which would be experienced as sexually stimulating by the child even though that was not the mother's conscious intention). Memories of such events were believed to persist actively in the mind, seeking actualization through their being relived, yet due to the anxiety they generated, needing to be kept out of consciousness. The model of the mind formulated as an expression of this view was topographical: like a map it defined two mental realms, one conscious and one unconscious, with a narrow spit of land between the two—the preconscious, a realm in which memories are only partially unconscious and therefore more readily brought into consciousness.

Although it was and is a fact that such sexual seductions occur, it soon seemed to Freud that in some, if not most, of his patients these memories of seductions were in fact memories of *fantasies* of seductions, fantasies created in response to internal sexual drives, drives that he was discovering through his work with patients and in his own self-analysis (Freud 1892–1899). In fact, even if an actual seduction occurred its impact was related more to what it stirred up within the child through sympathetic vibrations with his own sexual wishes. The neurotic then changed from a passive victim to an active participant in the traumatic events that led to his or her symptoms, and thus, within his or her own mind, in conflict between wishes and fears of those wishes. As Karl Meninger put it in the title of his book that brought psychoanalytic insights to the public: *Man Against Himself.*

The mental model in keeping with this new understanding had to be more complex, a structure that identified the various parts of the mind engaged in this internal civil war: a part that generated the drives, the id; a part that turned parental-derived disapproval toward the drives, the superego; and a central part of the mind that moderated between the opposing internal forces and the demands of external reality and worked out compromises that satisfied all parties to the dispute to some degree, the ego (Freud 1923).

At this point in history the basic dynamic of the neurotic structure— in both the adult neurosis and in the infantile neurosis—was understood essentially as it is today: namely, an instinctual wish, primarily sexual but with self-assertive and aggressive elements as well, that generates anxiety. This anxiety signals the psychic apparatus to institute means of self-protection. This involves a complex amalgam of forces that inhibit the direct gratification of the forbidden wish by disguising gratifications sufficiently to allow for some secret gratification, and by some form of suffering to placate the internalized critical parental images. This process is made more complex by the fact that such compromises are rarely fully effective; some of the wish escapes from control, more anxiety is generated, and secondary levels of compromise formations are then needed, which are in turn less than fully effective as well. Neuroses, then, usually grow and spread and transform themselves over time.

As Freud was discovering from his adult patients what they could recall of their childhood sexual lives, a student of his work wrote him about his 5-year-old son, who was showing evidence of exactly the kinds of phenomena Freud was writing about. Their correspondence continued, with the father writing detailed accounts of his son's fantasies and fears and Freud answering with suggestions as to how the father might respond. This is the famous case of Little Hans (Freud 1909), which was the first recorded instance of the direct observation of a child as a means of learning more about early psychological development. Indeed, it is remarkable how accurate Freud's reconstructed understanding of childhood turned out to be. Little Hans clearly confirmed what he had pieced together from his own self-analysis and the analyses of his patients, particularly about the oedipal phase of development, from the ages of roughly 2½ or 3 to 6 or 7. This infantile neurosis is sometimes so intense that it is evident to the adults around the child that he or she is having neurotic symptoms—like Little Hans's phobia or those of the patients I described earlier. But often, as Freud put it, "the symptoms are dismissed as naughtiness" by the adults, who underestimate the depth and richness of meaning that a child's fantasy life can express. This expression of the child's struggle with oedipal-phase drives, fantasies, and anxieties is understood to be ubiquitous; *all* normally developing children at that age, if examined carefully, reveal neurotic mechanisms in operation. These reflect efforts on the part of the child's psyche to deal with the internal pressures generated by age specific instinctual drives that arise in response to psychophysiological maturational changes. These phenomena, in other words, are cross-cultural because they are biological in origin.

THEMES OF THE INFANTILE NEUROSIS

Sexual Anatomy

Analytic scrutiny of the infantile neurosis reveals that its phenomenology can be explicated in terms of five common themes. The first is the preoccupation with sexual anatomy, one's own and that of the other sex.

Children have been observed to demonstrate a specific interest in their genitals as early as at about 20 months of age, though most researchers date it to 24 months. Even at younger ages erections in boys and vaginal secretions in girls can be observed during feeding and bathing, and younger infants do indeed grab their genitals. But at about 2 there is a striking change in the manner in which children relate to their genitals; they selectively and purposefully reach for them, and they persist in manipulating them with clear concentration and a faraway look that suggests that they are having fantasies related to their masturbatory activity (Roiphe and Galenson 1972). This is believed to reflect the maturation of the sensory pathways that carry sensual and erotic genital zone sensations. Beginning at this age children go out of their way to see the genitals of others as well. For instance, they will watch while siblings or other children are being diapered or bathed, or they will follow their parents into the bathroom to watch them urinate or defecate. They stare at the genital areas of dolls, and animals, which are a ready source of information as animals are not clothed.

At the same time these conscious preoccupations are in evidence, there are also symbolic expressions of genital preoccupations that speak for an unconscious element. Boys are obsessed with phallic symbols: guns, racing cars, swords, space rockets, and so forth linking a kind of macho and cocky self-image to fantasy play with these toys, which are recognized as "boys' toys" by everyone, including other children. Girls prefer play objects that symbolize their genitals, such as purses or knit hats. Girls also play with dolls and doll houses. "Girls' toys" are as commonly identified as such as are boys' toys, and are linked with a sense of femininity. In other words, play activity with symbolically gender-specific toys is used to help build a sense of one's gender identity. Crossplay evokes teasing at this point: boys who play with girls' toys are sissies and girls who play with boys' toys are tomboys. It can almost be said that the whole world is assessed or reassessed in terms of sexual anatomy, and male and female chauvinistic lines are clearly drawn.

Currently, there is a debate around the relative impact of biological versus social factors in the creation of this childhood chauvinism. Although social and experiential factors cannot be altogether discounted, the psychoanalytic evidence is very strong that inherent psychobiological factors are predominant. For instance, it has been observed frequently that in many suburban communities, children are driven mainly in mother's car, with mother at the wheel, but children from such families still identify cars and driving games as boys' toys.

Similarly, in many modern families children are exposed to fathers feeding, diapering, and playing with babies, yet such activities in play are viewed as being only for girls.

Of central importance in the young child's discovery of sexual anatomy is what is referred to as "castration anxiety" (Jones 1933). The initial view was that at first both boys and girls responded to sensations from their phalluses, the penis in boys and the anatomically homologous clitoris in girls. In other words, the initial belief was that there was no anatomical difference between the sexes, that is, everyone has a phallus. This period of naïvete gives way to reality, perhaps because of experience. That is, seeing a member of the opposite sex unclothed, a common enough occurrence, but also perhaps because of inherent knowledge, the child learns that some children have a penis, and some—girls—don't.

Observational data give ample evidence that this discovery upsets both boys and girls; girls get depressed and angry at their mother, whom they blame for their deprivation; boys get anxious with the concomitant fearful fantasy that the penis can be lost, that is, they can be castrated. It is not surprising that with the instinctual and sensory investment in this most exciting part of their anatomy children would be worried specifically about its safety. This initial formulation has been changed recently only to the extent that observational data suggest girls have more awareness of their internal organs than had originally been thought. There is, therefore, a primary feminine identity based on an anatomical awareness in girls. This co-exists with whatever sense of envy they may feel for boys with their penises. As will be elaborated upon later, castration anxiety has a key role to play in the child's struggles over masturbation.

What Happens When Genitals Meet?

A second and related theme concerns curiosity about what happens when the male and female genitals meet, when penis enters vagina. By far the most common fantasies are violent in manifest content even though accompanied by a pleasurable and erotic affect. A 6-year-old girl decided to play "honeymoon": A man and a woman get married and fly to Chicago, but the flight is very bumpy, and the plane—as depicted with dramatic gestures—goes swiftly up and down and up and down, until it crashes in the mountains. The wife escapes, and the husband chases after her, up and down the mountainsides, trying to stab her with a long knife. The child's affect was expressed through somewhat anxious giggling and titillation, in seemingly marked contrast to the violent manifest content of the fantasy. As indicated, phallic toys are most frequently weapons, so it is not surprising that fantasies of intercourse often involve shooting and stabbing. Girls can utilize destructive seeming symbols for their genitals as well: one 7-year-old girl, in play that was clearly about her sexual identity, used as a symbol of her genitals a deep pool under a romantic waterfall but filled with man-eating alligators.

As was true in the first theme, these preoccupations are also expressed simultaneously at a conscious and an unconscious, or symbolic, level. Boys and girls do speak openly with one another and with certain adults in their lives of these matters while gaining mastery over them through symbolic play whose unconscious meaning appears to be unknown to them even when to the analytically sophisticated adult the double entendres seem transparent. For example, a 6-year-old girl was playing bedtime at her doll house: first, the children went up to bed; then the parents went up the stairs, but at the moment they got into bed the whole house rocked and collapsed because there was an earthquake.

The Primal Scene

That fantasy leads directly into the third theme, which relates the first two to the parents, namely, "primal scene curiosity." The term curiosity may be misleading as, regardless of whatever interest there is in collecting information, the oedipal-phase child is driven mainly by sexual urges to participate in erotic activities, including voyeuristic ones, even if they are limited to fantasied occurrences. Primal scene experiences, in other words, are erotic more than educational; in fact, as they may be all fantasy, no unknown information can be conveyed. If actual exposure to parental intercourse occurs, the experience falls upon very fertile soil and stirs up many deep sympathetic psychological reverberations. One of Freud's best-known clinical articles concerned a patient he called the Wolf Man because of the man's frightening dream in which there were wolves in a tree outside his bedroom window (Freud 1918). This nightmare was traced through associations to the psychologically traumatic witnessing of his parents having intercourse when, as a young child, his crib was kept in their bedroom. For such an experience to be psychologically traumatic it must stir up intrapsychic conflicts of sufficient intensity to also stress the ego in its inner directed aspect; the child is not a purely passive victim of primal scene experiences.

The Oedipus Complex

The fourth and best-known theme of the infantile neurosis is the one that gives it its other name, the Oedipus complex. Boys lust for their mothers, girls for their fathers, and boys vie with their fathers while girls vie with their mothers. The parallel to the Oedipus myth, as well as to Shakespeare's *Hamlet*, was noted by Freud, who selected the Greek name for the infantile sexual memories he was uncovering in his mind and those of his patients (Freud 1892–1899). Again, many expressions of this are conscious and familiar; both boys and girls ordinarily enjoy romantic attachments to their opposite-sex parent, usually with the pleasurable encouragement of the parent involved: the father who brings home a baby doll to Daddy's darling daughter, the mother who dances with her son to music on the radio, for instance. Slang makes many uses of this scenario, and we all recall the song: "I want a girl just like the girl that married dear old Dad." Similarly, the competition between father and son and between mother and daughter is equally prevalent and manifest.

An 8-year-old boy was seen for enuresis. He recalled—and his mother later verified—that on the morning of the day it first occurred he had awakened with one of his eyelashes on his cheek. His mother, who is the one who had awakened him, reminded him that when that occurs, one can make a wish that will come true. He wished to take his mother away from home and from daddy, off to a foreign castle, where they could live happily ever after. Both parents thought that fantasy was adorable; the enuresis, however, turned out to express the anxiety that such a directly wish-fulfilling fantasy stirred up inside of the boy.

It is surprising that skepticism exists about the existence of the Oedipus complex as evidence of it is so commonplace. Probably the skepticism is in response to the simultaneously unconscious and defended-against expressions of the same triangle.

A 5-year-old girl could speak openly of her romantic longings for her father. In one session she suddenly jumped unexpectedly into my lap and declared, "I asked father to marry me, but he said he couldn't as he was married to mother, but since you're not married to mother, you can marry me!" In other sessions at that time she used chess pieces to play out a fantasy about an angry queen, a handsome king, and a pretty princess entangled in a conflict-filled romantic triangle. I felt sure that she was referring without conscious awareness to herself and her parents. The evidence was that the affects accompanying the symbolic expression of the triangle were more primitive and naked, whereas the affects accompanying the conscious expression of the triangle were more defended against.

Behind this positive oedipal scenario there often lurks fantasies of a negative oedipal constellation; that is, the child seeks sexual love from the same-sex parent, and competes with the other-sex parent for her/him. This is felt to reflect the as yet unstructured sexual drive derivatives of the child, his or her polymorphous sexuality. The constellation seems to be more significant when the child is reluctant to move on from a dyadic or dependent position, and mixes passive yearnings of a maternal sort with the oedipal drive derivatives. The child, then, assumes a regressive passive position vis à vis both parents, a position that contaminates the more aggressive one of the usual oedipal scenario.

A late adolescent in analysis, complaining of fears that he was homosexual, recalled vividly an early memory of lying curled up next to his father and feeling his father's strength passing into his body, making him feel not only strong, but safe and secure; his memories of his mother were characterized by her cold distance and critical attitudes toward him. As an adult, he was frightened of women, but sought dependent attachments to strong men whose masculine essence he fantasied taking into his body through sexual contacts.

Masturbation

Finally, the fifth theme of the infantile neurosis is masturbation. At first, the interest in masturbation is open and innocent; we are all familiar with the excited child who unselfconsciously manipulates his or her genitals, even in polite company, often to the distress of parents. One progressive set of parents, trying to prevent the kind of masturbatory guilt that had troubled their adolescences, told their just 4-year-old daughter it was all right to masturbate, but that it was a private activity to engage in in her own room. One evening, after a family dinner to which both sets of grandparents had been invited, she cheerily announced to everyone at the table, "Well, I'm going up to my room now to masturbate." But this innocence is short-lived; by the age of 5 or 6 efforts can be seen on the part of the child to suppress masturbation, signaling the child's efforts at entering the latency stage of normal development. In fact, it has been suggested that latency can be understood as a defense against the infantile urge to masturbate (Bornstein 1951). Both of these phenomena—the urge to masturbate, and the later urge to stop—are related to the psychodynamic core of masturbation, which is not the mechanical act itself but the accompanying fantasy.

The masturbatory fantasies include references to the themes described earlier: the love triangle, the genitals, and the parents' genitals and their union in the act of intercourse. Obviously the universal themes that are the basic building blocks of the masturbatory fantasy are influenced by the specifics of the child's situation, both by his or her external reality as well as by those aspects of their internal reality that are unique to them. Examples of this were given in the cases of the 7- and 8-year-old boys that began this chapter. The first boy's masturbatory fantasy included the theme of the all-powerful penis, a challenge and a threat to his father who planned retaliation, a wish for sexual intimacy with his mother, and primal scene curiosity. The second boy's masturbatory fantasy included the theme of primal scene curiosity as its major element, with the challenging of authority (father), curiosity about female sexual anatomy, and dreams of personal potency as subthemes.

The conflict over masturbation arises out of the increasing anxiety the child experiences over his or her sexual interests and thoughts. This is, it would seem from clinical data, not an inherent or biologically determined aspect of normal sexual development. Latency—the period of at least lessened sexual preoccupation that follows the years in which the oedipal complex predominates—has largely social and experiential roots. It is most in evidence where the child is brought up in a relatively stable, nurturant and empathic family setting with predominately loving and gratifying relationships with the parents. The child then experiences an internal conflict, what is sometimes called oedipal ambivalence. On the one hand, his or her sexual and assertive drives stimulate fantasies and wishes of an erotic, competitive, and provocative sort of interaction with the parents; on the other hand, there is a positive investment in good and trouble-free relationships with adults who are loved, trusted, looked up to, and depended upon. Despite the excitement and titillation they arouse, the drive gratifications inevitably seem to be rejected, at least in part in favor of good relationships. The fantasied oedipal parents are relinquished so that the relationship with the real parents can remain relatively trouble free.

The effort at controlling the sexual impulses by means of inhibiting masturbation with its titillating but frightening accompanying fantasies is not reliant solely on the positive rewards of happier interaction with the parents. It is also driven by anxiety, in particular the castration anxiety mentioned previously. Not surprisingly, this fear is evident both on a conscious and an unconscious level of awareness. The large number of jokes about penises falling off or being cut off are examples of both conscious awareness of castration and the use of humor to counter the anxiety generated by the idea. It is of interest that the concept of sex change surgery, even though supported and practiced by adult physicians, is based on the child's fantasy that the presence or absence of a penis determines gender. A man with a penis cut off becomes a "she" and a woman with a flap of flesh sewn on the anatomical site of a male's penis becomes a "he." The unconscious masturbatory fantasy that his lust for his mother was angering his father, who might retaliate by cutting off the offending organ, the penis, was expressed consciously by one 8-year-old boy in the symbolism of the fear that playing too frequently or too roughly with his new water pistol, a toy that elicited negatives from the adults both at home and at school, would lead to its getting broken. A 6-year-old girl confessed that her bad habit of putting her hands in her knitted wool cap and stretching it would both ruin the cap and infuriate her mother. One 7-year-old girl in analysis complained bitterly that in school she got As in every subject but handwriting. In play she would also drop toys or accidentally break or damage a project she was working on, explaining that she was "no good with her hands" and that this always angered her mother. She later charted her progress in treatment by following the improvement in her handwriting grades from D to C to B and, finally, to A. At the end of treatment she offered the view that she had been seen because of her problems with handwriting. And this, despite the fact that the subject of her masturbatory guilt and her efforts at curbing the practice were explicitly acknowledged and discussed.

The child's efforts at suppressing oedipal drive derivatives include the creation of a special function of the ego, the superego. Images of the judgmental parents—both the angry parent critical of bad behavior and the loving parent happy over good behavior—coalesce through a series of steps and become a part of children's sense of themselves. They adopt these values of the parents, and from a situation where the child turns to the parents for guidance and control the child now assumes that responsibility. Separation anxiety and fear of the loss of parental approval and love are replaced by guilt (Sandler 1960). Some children, out of an exaggerated fear of their own drives and a lack of confidence in their ability to contain them, cling excessively to the superego and become hypermoralistic goody-goodies; this form of childhood depressive neurosis, unfortunately, often wins children gold stars for excellence in school rather than the referral for psychotherapeutic help that they really require.

The ubiquity of such amusingly transparent symbolism, as well as of certain obsessive or phobic symptomatic expressions of conflict, raises the question of how one draws the line between normalcy and pathology in need of therapeutic intervention. The usual response to this question is that one takes into consideration factors other than simply the presence or absence of infantile neurotic expressions. The difference between a developmentally "normal" infantile neurosis and a neurosis in childhood that requires treatment is a matter of degree rather than kind. Duration and intensity have to be considered, and the extent to which there is significant and chronic interference with normal everyday functioning at home, at school, with friends, and with relatives. Ordinarily, the infantile neurosis resolves itself as the child opts to internalize the superego and enter the latency phase (Freud 1924). This is the source, probably, of the familiar reassurance that he or she "will grow out of it." Experience with adult patients, however, makes clear that many times this simply means that the conflicts are temporarily buried; the manifest symptoms lessen or disappear, but the potential for full neurotic illness continues into adulthood as a psychological vulnerability waiting for the right mix of circumstances to force it to return to the surface. It is not possible to predict one's future life, of course, so that it is not possible to guarantee that one has ever grown out of it. But this possibility must be considered when weighing the pros and cons of treatment (Tolpin 1970).

REFERENCES

Bornstein, B. (1951). On latency. *Psychoanalytic Study of the Child* 6:279–285. New York: International Universities Press.
Breuer, J., and Freud, S. (1893–1895). Studies in hysteria. *Standard Edition* 2:1–306.
Freud, S. (1892–1899). Extracts from the Fliess papers. *Standard Edition* 1:175–282.
―――― (1909). Analysis of a phobia in a five-year-old boy. *Standard Edition* 10:3–152.
―――― (1918). From the history of an infantile neurosis. *Standard Edition* 17:3–122.
―――― (1923). The ego and the id. *Standard Edition* 19:3–68.
―――― (1924). The dissolution of the Oedipus complex. *Standard Edition* 19:173–182.
Jones, E. (1933). The phallic phase. *International Journal of Psycho-Analysis* 14:1–33.
Roiphe, H., and Galenson, E. (1972). Early genital activity and the castration complex. *Psychoanalytic Quarterly* 41:334–347.
Sandler, J. (1960). On the concept of superego. *Psychoanalytic Study of the Child* 15:128–162. New York: International Universities Press.
Tolpin, M. (1970). The infantile neurosis: A metapsychological concept and a paradigmatic case history. *Psychoanalytic Study of the Child* 25:273–308. New York: International Universities Press.

6

Update on the Concept of the Neurotic Child

Charles A. Sarnoff, M.D.

"Neurotic" is a term that refers to a type of personality organization that is manifested in a mature level of psychosexual and cognitive development that permits repression and the resolution of internally prohibited wish-fantasies through compromise formation using symbols. Usually such resolutions are manifested clinically in the neuroses. These consist of symptomatic disorders of emotional origin such as conversion symptoms, dissociation states, phobias, obsessions, and compulsions. Anxiety is always a concomitant of neurosis. There is also a neurotic state in which anxiety is primary; unconscious fantasy activity lies behind this anxiety. Such anxiety neuroses are often transitional states on the way to a pathological resolution through neurotic symptom formation. In addition, there are neurotic behavior disorders. In these, the disordered behavior is repetitive. The repetitions are determined by fantasies that represent repressed wishes.

There has been a tendency in the delineation of official nosologies in psychiatry to group childhood neuroses and adult neuroses together as a single entity. No separate category of neuroses of childhood is recognized in this approach. This occurs in *DSM-I, -II,* and *-III.* As a result, the concept of the neurotic child has been enveloped in the nosological maelstrom of adult mental diseases and reduced to the status of the homunculus from which the adult neurosis will develop essentially without change.

An exception to this tendency can be found in works written by child psychiatrists for child psychiatrists. These include Sarnoff (1976, p. 385) and the GAP (Group for the Advancement of Psychiatry) report of June 1966. In these efforts, the neuroses of childhood are recognized for the distinct entities that they are.

Placing the neurotic child in a category of his own permits the refinement and development of the concept of the neurotic child from both a theoretical and a nosological point of view. In Shakespeare's felicitous phrasing, when one ". . . gives to airy nothing a local habitation and a name" (*A Midsummer Night's Dream*, Act 5, scene 1), one grants reality, a sticking post, and a starting point for developing a concept that would otherwise be ignored.

CHILDHOOD NEUROSES AS DISTINCT ENTITIES

The GAP report (pp. 229–237) emphasizes the differences between child and adult neuroses. Childhood neuroses are more apt to be transient than are those of adults. Spontaneous resolution as the result of reworking conflicts with a more mature ego permits the child to master previously unresolvable tasks (p. 229). In children, symptoms are at first appearance seen as something foreign and painful and out of one's control less consistently than they are in adults.

Precipitation of a childhood neurosis is apt to be the product of maturational growth associated with the development of conscience, strong repression of affects, and the internalization of conflict. Adult neuroses are more apt to be associated with situational events that mobilize unconscious fantasy in such a way that existing ego organization must be reorganized to deal with them. The neuroses of childhood may be the direct result of parental conflicts. In this regard, one might consider such instances as the mother who will not permit the child to make a decision on his own, will not let the child out of her sight for fear he will disappear, insists on studying the stool of the child each day, takes the child into bed when her husband is gone, gives conflicting messages, and seduces or beats the child. The overly clean parent is bound to set up conflict in the child whose aggressive and mess wishes take the form of a need for disorder. The parent who is conflicted about his own sexual identity often pays so much attention to the child's behavior and tastes that an exaggerated emphasis is placed on such matters in the life of the child, creating areas of conflict and decision where society and the inclinations of the child would have produced no problem. When such parental inclinations occur, it is required that the parent be dealt with if treatment is to be effective. Anxiety neurosis that may persist in a diffuse state in adults usually develops into "one of the more crystallized 'symptom' neuroses" (p. 232). Though hysterical conversion reactions usually occur in hysterical characters in adolescents and adults, in children such symptoms are particularly apt to occur in association with other personality disorders (p. 234). Dissociative states also appear transiently in response to great stress. In children, the intensity of the stress can take precedence causally over the characterological structure of the child.

As the consequence of maturation in children, the ego's changing resources create most of the characteristics in the production of neuroses that differentiate childhood neurosis from the neuroses of adults. Transiency, maturationally based improvements, and inescapable parental pressures create conditions that, though similar in dynamics, are different clinically and require their own set of psychotherapeutic strategies.

Transiency is a characteristic of many childhood hysterical neuroses. This need not always be the case. Clower (1974) reported cases of vaginal anaesthesia that began at age 7 and continued on into adult life. Childhood neuroses are considered to be predominantly transient phenomena by most writers.

The phobias of latency-age children (in this regard see Sarnoff 1987, chap. 6.) are true phobias dynamically speaking. They have peculiarities of their own that set them apart from phobias met with in adults. These differences are useful to know in working with phobic children. Phobias in children are easier to work with. Repression is not as strong. The true object of fear is more easily detected. The parents are still present in the life of the child; therefore, the child's gains from the phobia are primary gains. The earliest relationships are still extant and are preserved by the phobia. In the adult, the phobia is sustained by a link to secondary social gains.

This difference in the role of the phobic symptom in the life of the child, along with the changes in ego structure, cognition, and socialization that occur in early adolescence, usually results in the disappearance of the phobia with the passing of latency. Phobias in early adolescence are replaced by shyness, introversion, asceticism, or withdrawal. Phobias of the adult type usually first make their appearance during the late teens through the early twenties (Laughlin 1967, p. 566). Latency-age phobias can therefore be expected to clear up with age. Laughlin has quoted Meninger to the effect that ". . . about twenty percent of college students have or have had phobias in early years which sooner or later disappeared spontaneously" (p. 566).

What is the dynamic of this process? In early adolescence the symbols of the latency years (ludic symbols) lose their potency. Syncretically, the nature of symbols available to the child changes early in the transition from midlatency to early adolescence. (See Sarnoff 1987, vol. 2, chap. 1.) Psychoanalytic symbols (those with repression of the link between that which represents and that which is represented) dominate fantasy play and dreams in midlatency. Manipulable small-size physical replicas of objects and ideas (Piaget 1945) such as toys, dolls, and two-dimensional images (ludic symbols) can be used as the symbolic manifestations in latency play to represent latent fantasy content. In the same context, daydreams use verbal images; in sleeping dreams, visual components dominate. In day and night dreams, such symbolic representations continue to be used all one's life. Ludic symbols may first be seen at 26 months. They are at their strongest during early to midlatency. The use of ludic symbols in play wanes during mid- to late latency. Except by a very small group (child psychiatrists, puppeteers, and film animators) they drop from use during late latency. This is the process of *ludic demise*. More than any other developmental event, ludic demise marks the end of childhood. As a result, fantasy becomes less effective as a latency defense, and play therapy begins to lose its "play," which is the source of its name and one of its primary means of communication with the secret and unconscious world of the child. Though play ends, fantasy continues, but with other sources for its symbols. By early adolescence, reality objects tend to be recruited to serve as symbols.

When ludic symbols lose their potency (ludic demise) the fantasies that drive the neurotic behavior of the child are forced to find other pathways for expression. Through this step the door is opened to living a fantasy-dominated life or establishing a bridge to the object world and perfecting future planning.

In the transitional phase between midlatency and early adolescence, attempts to resolve problems through autoplastic fantasy activity continue even after ludic demise has begun. During this phase of transition, fantasies are less masked and representations become more explicit. Masochism is represented by fighting or physically hurting oneself. Bisexual fantasies are manifested by effeminacy, or wearing items of mother's clothes, or are defended against in some by lifting weights to assure a manly physique. Scoptophilic fantasies are lived out through illustrated sexual magazines and peeping tomism. Fixation at this level results in such characteristics as residual effeminacy, transvestism, and scoptophilia.

In effect, it may be said that the inner problems of the child remain viable, while their manifestations undergo a metamorphosis. The old wine has been poured into new bottles. If one views the phobias of latency from the perspective that time and medication will heal most of them, one will probably be right. Psychotherapy is still indicated, however, for what is gained in curing the phobia but not the child?

The ego structure that in latency provides discharge through fantasy produces mastery fantasies when its symbols have a low valence for attracting affect (Sarnoff 1976, pp. 25, 162, 341). *Affective valence* is a term adapted from chemistry. It refers to the power of a manifest symbol to represent an unconscious referent shorn of the charge of affect (for example, guilt, depression, shame, humiliation, anxiety) that has forced the referent into the system unconscious. A healthy symbolizing function is able to produce symbols that are free of affect. The fantasy contexts that contain these symbols become the basis for sublimation of drives or of the freeing of neutral energies. The valence for attracting affect of a given manifest symbol among all the symbols available for use is determined primarily by two factors: idiosyncratic experiential factors and near universal human responses to certain symbolic stimuli.

MANIFEST SYMBOLS BASED ON IDIOSYNCRATIC EXPERIENTIAL FACTORS

A child who has had his house robbed may adapt the experience to produce a fear of robbers as a representation of his fear of his own aggression, which he has projected onto his father, who, by displacement, becomes (in masked form) one of the intruders. The fear of aggression projected onto the father is nearly universal. The selection of the robber in this context has been overdetermined by the recent experience. Even more idiosyncratic would be the selection of a benign plant or seaweed to represent the aggressive wishes of a little girl to a mother who goes away too often (Sarnoff 1970). One boy displaced his hostility to his father onto a tale of the killing of a king in a distant time and place. He told the tale with gusto until the moment of the killing. At that point, valence for affect became more intense. He went blank mentally for a moment and directed his attention to the fact that he was thirsty.

MANIFEST SYMBOLS BASED ON NEAR-UNIVERSAL HUMAN RESPONSES

Certain symbols have universal meanings. Others are universally capable of producing an affect if experienced in dreams or in play. Such symbolic representations as shadow, storm, flood, fire, and blood have this capacity. The appearance of such symbols usually indicates a loss of the defensive strength of the symbolizing function. This condition indicates a slipping of the child's emotional adaptation into the borderlands of maladjustment.

Starobinski (1973) noted that Kant was aware of this capacity for distortion of the organization of human reason. In describing the well-defended person, he finds in man a ". . . dimension by which he can outstrip the cosmic forces or historical aggressions that crush him. Storm and tempest, like bullet and blade, herald the destruction of our physical existence . . ." (p. 202). When experienced as sublimations, such as paintings or movies, these symbols "convey a kind of sublimity" (p. 202). Mastery of forces that threaten existence occurs. When experienced on the level of a ludic or an oneiric (dream) symbol, the immanence of the experience of these symbols carries great affective valence. The experience is terror; the effect is not mastery, but regression. From this reaction comes the stuff that many phobias, states of terror, and bad dreams are made of.

The fantasizing function of latency (Sarnoff 1976, chap. 2) produces persecutory fantasies from either type of symbol when displacement is insufficient. As a result, the valence for attracting affect of the persistent implied unconscious referent remains. Thus, the feared aspect of the father becomes represented by an equally feared symbol in the form of a shadowy robber or demon. These persecutory fears of fantastic elements constitute the phobic neuroses of childhood.

The phobic elements of adolescence and adulthood that begin to be seen in the late teens, in contrast to the fantastic persecutors (horses, goblins, monsters, robbers, witches, and so on) of the childhood phobic neuroses of latency, usually consist of fears of places and people in the real world. The bridge that links the two phenomena is the ego structure of latency, which continues to function in adolescence. It plays a role that is a far cry from its function in latency, for the symbol representations through which it works have shifted from fantasy representations to reality elements. This is one of the cognitive maturational changes that accompany the transition from latency to adolescence. The role of the structure of latency becomes that of future planning (a reality-oriented ego function) since reparative fantasies now are synthesized from elements in the real world. In situations that mobilize stressful drive derivatives, the ego mechanisms of latency are evoked to attempt mastery. Due to the shift in symbolic forms that occurs during late latency–early adolescence, the fear fantasies that are produced have realistic persecutory objects and situations.

Thus, phobic reactions involving the fantasy function of the latency-age child are mobilized in the direction of object relations. Drive organization shifts from fantasy objects to objects in the environment for its drive discharge. Adult phobias may then be developed in relation to social situations, while the fantastic persecutors of latency lose their preeminent position.

Frequently, children must develop rituals in order to organize their sleeping or habit training. Psychotic children often defend against their disordered mental function through the use of obsessive-compulsive symptoms. For this reason, obsessive-compulsive symptoms are difficult to diagnose as neurotic. A review of obsessive-compulsive symptomatology has been presented in the excellent paper by Silverman (1972). Obsessive-compulsive symptoms are often seen in late latency during the period of ethical individuation. This refers to the period of superego reorganization when peers (and sometimes parents) are encouraging the child to behave with more latitude than the parents permitted when he was younger. The symptoms resolve the conflict symbolically as well as deflecting attention from it. The terms of the conflict are remarkably close to consciousness and the symptom complexes relatively short-lived. I recall a child of 9 whose extreme counting ritual disappeared over a summer. Phobic and psychosomatic disorders also occur during this phase of ethical individuation. The complex is worth exploring when dealing with the neurotic child with a new symptom at about the age of 9.

The study of the concept of the neurotic child is especially productive when one comes to the area of personality disorder. The GAP report (1966) contains a category of personality disorder that is called the Tension Discharge Disorder (p. 245). "Children in this category exhibit chronic behavioral patterns of emotional expression of aggressive and sexual impulses which conflict with society's norms" (p. 245). This grouping is subdivided into the "impulse ridden personality" and the "neurotic personality disorder" (p. 249).

The impulse ridden personality discharges impulses both sexual and aggressive, immediately and impulsively. There is little anxiety, internalized conflict, or guilt. The content and form of the discharge relates more to the shape and provocativeness of the environment than to the inner fantasy life of the patient (p. 247).

The neurotic-personality disorder children act out their tensions in a superficially similar way. However, their behavior is primarily a response to inner tensions. Their actions are an expression of repressed neurotic conflicts. The neurotic nature of their behavior is revealed by its repetitive character (p. 249).

The difference between these personality types in childhood can be explained on the basis of the presence or absence of an effective symbolizing function during the latency years that will permit and support repression, internalization, and symbolic resolution of conflict. The impulse-ridden child cannot defend against overstimulation through the use of fantasies produced by the ego structures of latency. Since these children cannot master stimulation, they cannot delay responses to stress. This results in poorly structured activity aimed at others. These children tend to act out in an impulsive manner; their hostility is diffusely destructive. They break things belonging to other children, often getting into a fight with the first person they see. Since there is no formed fantasy guiding their misbehavior, one never knows from which direction the misbehavior will come, or what form it will take.

The child with a neurotic personality disorder expresses his conflicts through involvement in actions derived from fantasy content. He tends to produce safety-valve fantasies as a consequence of the activities of the symbolizing and fantasizing functions of the ego in latency. Overstimulation cannot be mastered or processed by the production of these fantasies that usually serve to provide discharge mentally. Mastery is usually the case. Child and play therapy can take advantage of these fantasies, when they are acted out in the playroom, as an entree into the unconscious fantasy life of the child. When the drives become too much to master, the child acts out the fantasy. Since the manifest fantasies so produced are all patterned on the core latent fantasies of the child, they have similarities of action, structure, and content; when acted out, therefore, formed fantasy guides their activities. There is a repetitive and predictive quality to the misbehavior.

CONCLUSION

The clinical findings that support the concept of the neurotic child are alive and dwell in patterned behavioral aberrations and symbolic resolutions of conflict in latency-age children. The heuristic concept of the neurotic child enhances the possibility that child therapists will be able to detect these findings. Alertness to their presence and prescience of their unique characteristics help the therapist both to identify them and to formulate appropriate psychotherapeutic strategies.

REFERENCES

Clower, V. (1974). Panel on the psychology of women: latency and early adolescence. Fall meeting, American Psychoanalytic Association. New York, December 13, 1974.

DSM-I, Diagnostic and Statistical Manual of Mental Disorders (1951). Washington, DC: American Psychiatric Association.

DSM-II, Diagnostic and Statistical Manual of Mental Disorders (1968). Washington, DC: American Psychiatric Association.

DSM-III, Diagnostic and Statistical Manual of Mental Disorders (1980). Washington, DC: American Psychiatric Association.

Laughlin, H. P. (1967). *The Neuroses.* Washington, DC: Butterworths.

Piaget, J. (1945). *Play, Dreams, and Imitation in Childhood.* New York: Dutton, 1951.

Psychopathological disorders of childhood: theoretical considerations and a proposed classification (1966). *Group for the Advancement of Psychiatry* 6:229-237.

Sarnoff, C. A. (1970). Symbols and symptoms: phytophobia in a 2-year-old girl. *Psychoanalytic Quarterly* 39:550-562.

——— (1976). *Latency.* New York: Jason Aronson.

——— (1987). *Psychotherapeutic Strategies.* Vol. 1: *The Latency Years.* Northvale, NJ: Jason Aronson.

——— *Symbols in Psychotherapy, Sexuality and Sublimation.* In preparation.

Silverman, J. (1972). Obsessional disorders in childhood and adolescence. *American Journal of Psychotherapy* 26:362-377.

Starobinski, J. (1973). *1789: The Emblems of Reason.* Charlottesville: University of Virginia Press, 1982.

7

Neurotic Children in the Light of Research

Aaron H. Esman, M.D.

Over a decade ago Shapiro (1975) reviewed the concept of childhood neurosis as it had evolved over the preceding seventy-five years, that is, since Freud conceived it in his own self-analysis and later in the case of Little Hans (Freud 1909). In this chapter I shall, therefore, emphasize researches of the past two decades in an effort to place them in the context of more traditional views and to indicate some of the ways in which recent investigations have required modification of, or have lent support to, those views.

In the traditional (pre-*DSM-III*) literature, the diagnosis of neurosis in childhood was based on (1) the presence of specific symptoms or symptom clusters,[1] that is, anxiety states, phobias, somatoform (hysterical) symptoms, obsessions and/or compulsions, and (2) the absence of evidence of significant deficits in basic adaptive (ego) functions. The neurotic child, then, was seen as a relatively sturdy child with good general personality development who suffered from a specific disturbance of function that was distressing either to himself or to those close to him and that was outside the realm of phase appropriate expectation (for example, the 3-year-old with separation difficulty would not necessarily be seen as neurotic, while an 8-year-old with similar symptoms might).

From the standpoint of etiology, two broad conceptual currents were prominent. The first, broadly conceived as *psychodynamic* or *psychoanalytic*, postulated the existence of underlying unconscious conflicts, of

---

1. I shall not discuss here the "neurotic" depressions, since their nosological status vis à vis the affective disorders is not clearly established. For a thorough review of these questions, see Cantwell (1985).

which the symptom represented a compromise solution, allowing both for disguised expression of an unconscious wish and for the influence of defensive forces designed to oppose its gratification or keep it out of awareness. For example, the fear of being bitten by a dog might represent the compromise between the wish to attack or hurt the father and the prohibition against that wish, expressed by its reversal, projection, and displacement, that is, "It's not that I want to bite daddy, but that a dog symbolizing daddy wants to bite me."

The second etiological theory was the behaviorist one, which posited the symptom as a learned behavior, based on a conditioning model in which reinforcement of a maladaptive pattern encouraged its persistence. The symptom is not seen as deriving from conflict, and has no unconscious meaning. To understand it one must find the circumstances in which it first appeared and the reinforcers that perpetuated it.

Needless to say, different treatment strategies devolved from these radically different etiological theories. The former called for a psychotherapy geared to the exploration of meaning and the uncovering of unconscious conflict, that is, psychoanalysis or psychoanalytic psychotherapy (Shapiro and Esman 1985), while the latter demanded the use of desensitization, operant conditioning, or other learning theory-based behavior modification techniques (Rachman and Costello 1961, Ross 1981). Despite the fact that in practice elements of both approaches tended to be used by the advocates of each, strenuous and at times acrimonious debate reigned as to their respective explanatory and clinical merits.

RECENT DEVELOPMENTS

Perhaps the most striking and certainly the most controversial event in this area in recent years has been the elimination of the term "neurosis" from the standard nomenclature (*DSM-III*) and the development of a new descriptive classification system that, in the view of its authors, is atheoretical (Rutter and Shaffer 1980, Spitzer and Cantwell 1980). Designed to promote communication among theorists of various persuasions, it was also intended to provide operationally defined criteria that would encourage reliable and valid research efforts. *DSM-III-R* specifies a number of childhood onset disorders: separation anxiety, avoidance anxiety, and overanxious disorder. In addition, such adult disorders as simple phobia disorder, obsessive-compulsive disorder, and somatoform disorder can also be diagnosed in children. Characteristically, academic investigators have by and large welcomed this semantic change, while many clinicians have objected to it or ignored it. Achenbach (1980) has described two empirically-based "broad band" clusters of symptoms that he has termed "internalizing" and "externalizing"; the neurotic disorders generally correspond to his "internalizing" cluster. Although there are discrepancies between Achenbach's groupings and the *DSM-III-R* classification, much of the research in this area in the past decade has been guided by the new nomenclature and its descriptively-based categories.

PSYCHODYNAMIC AND DEVELOPMENTAL RESEARCH

Early psychoanalytic studies of childhood neurosis concentrated on the role of oedipal conflict in its genesis (A. Freud 1965, Freud 1905). Recent research has, however, focused its attention on the contribution of earlier developmental periods. In particular, the pioneering research of Margaret S. Mahler and her associates (Mahler 1972, Mahler et al. 1975) has cast light on the impact of the processes of separation and individuation in the first three years of life. Although Mahler was reluctant to associate specific psychopathologies with disturbances in the various subphases of the processes she described, it has seemed evident to many of her colleagues that, at the very least, the failure to traverse adequately this process and achieve a sense of individuality and of object constancy (McDevitt and Mahler 1980) would be likely to predispose the child to persistent separation anxiety and apprehensiveness, as well as to difficulty in resolving ambivalent feelings toward the mother that might predispose to neurotic conflict.

The critical role of separation anxiety has been central to the work of John Bowlby (1969, 1973, 1980). In his view attachment of infant to mother is a primary drive intrinsic in all mammalian species. Disruption of this attachment by premature separation, loss or threat of loss, or the mother's affective detachment leads, he believes, to pathological anxiety responses in the child that may be dealt with by means of various defensive measures appropriate to the child's developmental level. Neurosis is, therefore, redefined as "anxious attachment," and Bowlby reinterprets both Freud's case of Little Hans and Jones's case of Peter (1924) in these terms. Bowlby's view derived in large measure from ethological research, represented more recently by work such as that of Suomi and colleagues (1981), which showed that Rhesus monkeys separated from their mothers in the early weeks of life continued to show fearful behavior in later periods. Harlow's studies (Harlow and Mears 1979) of monkeys deprived of normal attachment experience also played a major role in shaping Bowlby's views. On the other hand, Hersov (1960) observed some time ago that children with school phobia had experienced significantly less separation than had controls.

In more traditional terms, Roiphe (1965) and Galenson and Roiphe (1974) have, using a research model similar to that employed by Mahler, observed very young children in nursery and day-care settings and found evidence of what they term an "early genital phase." In their view, the awareness of anatomical sex differences normally occurs during the second and third years of life (earlier than previously believed), and evokes powerful responses in children of both sexes: penis envy and feelings of defectiveness in little girls, castration anxiety in little boys. In most cases these reactions are transitory, and the new information is integrated into the child's nascent body image. For some more vulnerable children, however, these negative responses are persistent, though repressed, and form the nucleus for later castration reactions that will generate neurotic symptom formations.

Stern (1985) has recently proposed a pattern of mother–child relationship that may underlie certain neuroticlike or preneurotic symptoms seen in very young children. He describes a 9-month-old boy with a fearful reaction to nursing bottles, which seemed to condense and symbolize a complex of conflictual interactions around feeding situations. Stern's suggestion is consistent with his view that complex cognitive functions and a defined self-organization occur in infancy well before the time usually assumed in traditional psychoanalytic developmental theory.

BEHAVIORAL STUDIES

Although most behavioral research in this area has been in the field of therapeutic applications, an important critical reevaluation of earlier studies has led to significant reconsideration of etiological hypotheses about children's fears. Reanalysis of the famous Watson and Rayner (1920) work with Little Albert has led to serious challenges to the classical behaviorist notion that such fears can be explained on the basis of simple conditioning. Harris (1979) and Samuelson (1980) found serious methodological defects in the original work, and, in fact, efforts to replicate Watson and Rayner's findings have been consistently unsuccessful.

Nonetheless, behavioral approaches have been found useful in dealing with children's fears and particularly with school phobias. Modeling procedures (films of peer models approaching the feared situation) have been helpful in dealing with such simple fears as those of the dentist, dogs, and so forth (Bandura et al. 1968, Melamed et al. 1975). Various behavioral approaches have been successfully employed with school phobias (O'Leary and Carr 1982) but largely on a single-case basis and without well-controlled studies. There is a critical need for such systematic controlled research with extended follow-up to substantiate the claims of efficacy that have been offered by behavioral investigators.

EPIDEMIOLOGICAL AND DESCRIPTIVE STUDIES

The prevalence of psychoneuroses or what are regarded as preneurotic disorders has been the subject of many studies, often as an aspect of more generalized surveys of both normal and clinical populations. Characteristic of such reports is that of Wolkind and Everitt (1974), who found in a study of British preschoolers a prevalence of 6 percent of what they term an "early neurotic cluster" of symptoms, including fears, separation anxiety, dependence, and worrying. In the studies of Rutter and colleagues on the Isle of Wight (Rutter et al. 1975) neurotic disorders were found in only 2.5 percent of the population of school age children; however, a similar survey of children in an inner city London borough revealed a prevalence twice as high. It seems probable that, at least in urban centers, the prevalence of anxiety disorders in children ranges from 6 to 7 percent of the population.

Richman and her associates (McGuire and Richman 1986) have developed and applied a preschool screening instrument from which they have derived a number of behavioral clusters, including an isolated-immature cluster that they say is similar to Wolkind and Everitt's early neurotic type. Of the population they studied, 12 percent showed this pattern (compared with 59 percent "normals"). No follow-up data are reported from this study, but in an earlier communication (Richman et al. 1982), it is stated that 3-year-olds with behavioral control and language problems, identified with another survey instrument, tended to have persistent difficulties a year later.

Cox (1978) concludes on the basis of such epidemiological surveys that evidence for continuity between childhood neurosis and adult neurosis is lacking. She quotes Rutter to the effect that "most neurotic children become normal adults and most neurotic adults develop their neuroses in adult life" (p. 41). She challenges the idea of an autonomous neurotic process, and suggests that "genetic, temperamental, and environmental explanations are more frequently applicable" (p. 56). In their recent comprehensive review of the epidemiological literature, Orvaschel and Weissman (1986) conclude that the picture is "confusing." Though anxiety symptoms in children are quite prevalent, their significance is unclear, and the relationship between such symptoms and other indicators of child psychopathology is "contradictory." "Even less," they say, "is known about the long-term significance of anxiety symptoms in children" (pp. 70–71). It seems clear that further epidemiological research is needed to bring clarity to this murky field.

The role of stress factors is unclear. Although most studies discount the importance of acute environmental traumata, Gittelman-Klein and Klein (1980) found that in "80 percent of cases of separation anxiety, onset had occurred after an illness or death in the family, a move of the child's home, or a change of school, all instances in which major change in the children's pattern of attachment had occurred. Therefore, the notion of stress may have to be redefined for an understanding of the psychological factors that can lead to anxiety disorders in children" (Gittelman 1985, p. 78).

As is the case in adult psychiatry, the relationship between anxiety disorders and affective illness in children has been a subject of considerable recent interest, particularly in the wake of some of the psychobiological research described below. Typical is a study by Bernstein and Garfinkel (1986) in which a group of chronic early adolescent school refusers were surveyed for symptoms of anxiety and depression. Of the twenty-six patients studied, 60 percent met *DSM-III* criteria for affective disorder, 60 percent for anxiety disorder, and 50 percent for both. The authors concluded "that severe anxiety disorders in children and adolescents may be clinically indistinguishable from depression" (p. 235). If borne out by further studies, these results may have significant treatment implications.

From the psychoanalytic standpoint, the paradigmatic adult neurosis is conversion disorder (hysteria). *DSM-III-R* attempts to distinguish this pattern carefully from other somatizing disorders (Briquet Syndrome) and from "hysterical personality." The occurrence of hysterical conversion symptoms in children, though not rare, is relatively infrequent (virtually unknown before age 5), and systematic studies are few. Volkmar and colleagues (1984) have reported a study of thirty such cases seen over the period 1970–1981. Of these, six were males and twenty-four females; ages ranged from 6 to 15 years. Outstanding findings included the frequent (50 percent) presence of a model of illness in the family, a high incidence of psychosocial and familial stress, and the extraordinarily high occurrence (90 percent) of a history of sexual stressors. "La belle indifference" was seen in half the sample, but its significance in children was considered unclear. Neurological symptoms were present in 77 percent of cases, although on follow-up only two cases had subsequently received neurological diagnoses, in contrast to earlier reports (Rivinus et al. 1975) of the great frequency of such occurrences.

BIOLOGICAL RESEARCH

In keeping with current trends in general psychiatry, biological research in child psychiatry has made major advances in recent years. Included among significant studies and reevaluations has been the range of neurotic disorders, in particular, anxiety states and obsessive-compulsive disorders. Elkins and colleagues (1980) proposed a neurobiological view of the latter that is, they believe, strongly suggested, if not supported by, a number of lines of investigation, including psycholinguistic tests, association with Tourette's syndrome, and pharmacological studies. From the same laboratory, Flament and colleagues (1985) reported statistically significant improvement in obsessive-compulsive symptoms in nineteen such children treated with clomipramine, though the precise mechanism of its action was unclear. These results, they believe, support the presence of a significant neurobiological factor in this disorder (see Esman 1989).

The relationship between anxiety states and neurobiological abnormalities has long been a question in child psychiatry, beginning at least with Bender's (1956) view that unexplainable anxiety in a child always indicates severe disorganizing pathology. Schaffer and colleagues (1985) have reported that, in a group of children known to have soft neurological signs at age 7, significantly more showed psychiatric disorder at age 17 than did a group of controls. Further, all the girls and 80 percent of the boys with diagnosable anxiety disorders had shown soft signs at age 7. The authors concluded, therefore, that soft signs at age 7 "were strongly predictive of persistent psychiatric disorder characterized by anxiety and withdrawal" (p. 342).

Perhaps the most substantial body of recent psychobiological and psychopharmacological research in child psychiatry has been that in the area of anxiety disorders. Pioneered by the studies of Donald Klein in adult anxiety states, a number of investigators (Berney et al. 1981, Gittelman-Klein and Klein 1973) have been pursuing the effect of antidepressant drugs, particularly tricyclics, in the treatment of school phobia and other anxiety symptoms in children. Gittelman-Klein and Klein reported favorable results (81 percent improvement versus 47 percent on placebo) in a group of school-phobic children treated with high doses of imipramine and parent counseling. The findings led them to challenge theories of separation anxiety that implicated external (that is, parental) influences in the genesis of this disorder. Since Berney and colleagues did not obtain similar results using clomipramine, and since Werry (1982) is skeptical about the value of tricyclics in such cases, further controlled trials in this area seem warranted before general use can be recommended.

Concurrently, the use of benzodiazepines in childhood anxiety disorders has been studied by other investigators (Simeon and Ferguson 1987), moved in part by the greater degree of safety of these compounds. School refusal and other anxiety symptoms appear to respond equally well to chlordiazepoxide and alprazolam as to imipramine, at least in open clinical trials (D'Amato 1962, Garfinkel and Bernstein 1984). No evidence of habituation or dependence was observed. Controlled trials have, however, not been reported as of this writing.

These pharmacological studies offer significant support to the view that there exists a substantial neurobiological component to childhood anxiety disorders, both of the separation anxiety and generalized anxiety types. It is not clear from this work whether the neurobiological disturbance is primary or whether it is secondary or corollary to primary psychosocial etiologies. Further investigations seem clearly to be indicated, although as Simeon and Ferguson (1985) point out, such study is made difficult by the fluctuant character of anxiety in childhood, parental need to minimize or ignore it, clinicians' biases as to its etiology and essential nature, and the lack of clear diagnostic criteria in childhood.

TEMPERAMENT STUDIES

One of the major research efforts of the past two decades has been the exploration of the role of innate temperamental factors in personality development. In a series of communications, Chess (1979), Thomas and Chess (1980), and Chess and Thomas (1984) have described the findings of the New York Longitudinal Study, which has followed a cohort of middle class children from infancy into early adult life. They have described two temperamental constellations—"the difficult child" and "the slow-to-warm-up child"—that are associated with a higher than normal occurrence of pathologies defined generically as behavior disorders. Such pathological outcomes result, they suggest, from poorness of fit between infantile temperamental characteristics and environmental (particularly parental) response.

With respect to anxiety and anxiety disorders, these observers challenge the long-standing psychodynamic view that anxiety is the initiating affective experience for the organization of neurotic or other pathological structures. They believe that their data support the thesis that anxiety is a secondary response.

> A parsimonious view based on the goodness of fit model, in terms of objective and overtly evident characteristics of the child, patterns of parental functioning, and other specific environmental influences, has been sufficient to account for the genesis of the problem behavior. Where anxiety has evolved in the course of the development of the behavior disorder, it has been a secondary phenomenon, *a consequence rather than a cause of symptom formation and expression.* [Chess and Thomas 1984, pp. 282–283, my italics]

Thus in their model the role of intrapsychic conflict is minimized in favor of actual interpersonal conflicts, and defense mechanisms are seen as "behavioral strategies with which individuals attempt to cope with stress and conflict," with no "a priori theoretical formulations of the ontogenesis of stress and conflict."

CONCLUSION

What does this body of recent research, limited though it is, have to tell us about neurotic disorders in childhood? Essentially, it points to a widening of our conception both of etiology and treatment of such problems. Just how the complex set of variables—biological, interpersonal, intrapsychic, and sociocultural—interact in engendering pathological anxiety states is far from clear at this time, but it is evident that a unifocal adherence to a narrowly psychodynamic or behavioral model is rarely tenable. At the very least, biological vulnerability to stress must be considered, perhaps as manifested by early temperamental characteristics, perhaps founded on aberrant neurochemical organization.

At the same time, such investigations as those of Stern (1985) on mother-infant attunement interdigitate with Mahler's separation-individuation research to highlight the contribution of interpersonal—and especially mother-child—communication to the genesis of early anxiety states and, presumably, their continuation in chronic neurotic symptom formations. Every clinician is familiar, however, with the range of children's responses to what appear to the observer to be unfavorable or traumatic life experiences. Freud (1917) early spoke of a "complemental series" of constitutional and environmental factors in neurosogenesis; recent research is only beginning to lend specificity to the component of constitution. Anthony's (1974) studies of "invulnerable" children—those with extraordinary resiliency in the face of severe familial pathology—are relevant here.

The result of this work is a broadening and deepening of therapeutic possibilities. The earlier reliance on a single therapy—psychoanalytic psychotherapy—has given way to a new eclecticism, one that incorporates a multiplicity of treatment modes into the clinician's therapeutic repertoire. For the simple phobias, behavioral methods appear to be effective, while the general anxiety disorders, complex avoidance syndromes, and obsessive-compulsive states seem likely to respond best to multimodal therapies involving a judicious mix of individual, family, and pharmacological elements

This is not to say that psychoanalytic therapy has lost its place in the care of neurotic children. For the appropriate case, where social and familial circumstances permit, the analytic exploration of meaning and the support of an intense sustained relationship with a consistent therapeutic person are invaluable. But in most cases of childhood neurosis less intensive and expensive methods must be resorted to, and the conscientious therapist must know that simple symptom relief can be of great benefit to the child's development and to the enhancement of his self-regard.

Rutter has suggested, as noted previously, that most childhood neuroses are self-limited. Gittelman (1985), however, stated that "the overview of the outcome studies does not provide a clear picture of the psychiatric sequelae of childhood and adolescent anxiety disorders" (p. 73). Kandel and Davies (1986) report that "feelings of dysphoria in adolescence predict most strongly a similar experience in adulthood" (p. 255). We still do not know the full story on this matter. As clinicians we are still concerned to differentiate transitory symptoms, which may be left untreated or dealt with through parental guidance, from fixed, chronic symptoms that may be associated with or lead to serious functional impairment and that, in the current state of knowledge, warrant direct intervention. Careful longitudinal studies are still needed to provide us with clearer guidelines for making this critical distinction. In the end, however, it will still rest with the individual clinician to use his judgment (abetted, no doubt, by objective rating scales and assessment instruments) as to the degree and fixity of interference with normal developmental expectations and to decide which child does and which does not need what kind of treatment.

REFERENCES

Achenbach, T. (1980). DSM-III in the light of empirical research on the classification of child psychopathology. *Journal of the American Academy of Child Psychiatry* 19:395-412.
Anthony, E. (1974). The syndrome of the psychologically invulnerable child. In *The Child and His family*, vol. 3, ed. E. Anthony and T. Koupernik, pp. 529-544. New York: John Wiley.
Bandura, A., and Merlove, F. (1968). Factors determining vicarious extinction of avoidance behavior through symbolic modeling. *Journal of Research and Sociological Psychology* 8:99-108.
Bender, L. (1956). *Psychopathology of Children with Organic Brain Disorder*. Springfield, IL: Charles C Thomas.
Berney, T., Kolvin, L., Bhate, S., et al. (1981). School phobia: a therapeutic trial with clomipramine and short-term outcome. *British Journal of Psychiatry* 138:110-118.
Bernstein, G., and Garfinkel, B. (1986). School phobia: the overlap of affective and anxiety disorders. *Journal of the American Academy of Child Psychiatry* 25:235-241.
Bowlby, J. (1969). *Attachment and Loss*. Vol. 1: *Attachment*. New York: Basic Books.
―――― (1973). *Attachment and Loss*. Vol. 2: *Separation*. New York: Basic Books.
―――― (1980). *Attachment and Loss*. Vol. 3: *Loss*. New York: Basic Books.
Cantwell, D. (1985). Depressive disorders in children: validation of clinical syndromes. *Psychiatric Clinics of North America* 8:779-792.
Chess, S. (1979). Developmental theory revisited: findings of longitudinal study. *Canadian Journal of Psychiatry* 24:101-112.
Chess, S., and Thomas, A. (1984). *Origins and Evolution of Behavior Disorders*. New York: Brunner/Mazel.
Cox, A. (1978). The association between emotional disorders in childhood and neurosis in adult life. In *Research in Neurosis*, ed. H. van Praag, pp. 40-58. New York: Spectrum.
D'Amato, G. (1962). Chlordiazepoxide in the management of school phobias. *Diseases of the Nervous System* 23:292-295.
Elkin, R., Rapoport, J., and Lipsky, A. (1980). Obsessive-compulsive disorder of children and adolescents: a neurobiological viewpoint. *Journal of the American Academy of Child Psychiatry* 19:511-521.
Esman, A. (1989). Psychoanalysis and general psychiatry: obsessive-compulsive disorder as paradigm. *Journal of the American Psychiatric Association* 37:319-336.
Flament, M., Rapoport, J., Berg. C., et al. (1985). Clomipramine treatment of childhood obsessive compulsive disorder. *Archives of General Psychiatry* 42:977-983.
Freud, A. (1965). *Normality and Pathology of Childhood*. New York: International Universities Press.

Freud S. (1909). Analysis of a phobia in a five-year-old boy. *Standard Edition* 10:22-152.
_____ (1917). Introductory lectures in psychoanalysis (lecture 22). *Standard Edition* 16:339-357.
Galenson, E., and Roiphe, H. (1974). The emergence of genital awareness during the second year of life. In *Sex Differences in Behavior*, ed. R. Friedman, pp. 78-93. New York: John Wiley.
Garfinkel, B., and Bernstein, G. (1984). *The pharmacological treatment of separation anxiety*. Presented at annual meeting, American Academy of Child Psychiatry.
Gittelman, R. (1985). Anxiety disorders in children. In *Advances in Clinical Child Psychology*, vol. 8, ed. B. Lahey and A. Kazdin, pp. 53-78. New York: Plenum.
Gittelman-Klein, R., and Klein, D. (1973). School phobia: diagnostic considerations in the light of imipramine effects. *Journal of Nervous and Mental Disorders* 156:199-215.
_____ (1980). Separation anxiety in school refusal and its treatment with drugs. In *Out of School*, ed. L. Hersov and J. Berg, pp. 321-341 London: John Wiley.
Harlow, H., and Mears, C. (1979). *The Human Model: Primate Perspectives*. Silver Spring, MD: V. H. Winston & Sons.
Harris, B. (1979). Whatever happened to Little Albert? *American Psychology* 34:151-160.
Hersov, L. (1960). Persistent non-attendance at school. *Journal of Child Psychiatry and Psychology* 1:130-136.
Jones, M. (1924). The elimination of children's fears. *Journal of Experimental Psychology* 7:382-390.
Kandel, D., and Davies, M. (1986). Adult sequelae of adolescent depressive symptoms. *Archives of General Psychiatry* 43:255-264.
Mahler, M. (1972). On the first three subphases of the separation-individuation process. *International Journal of Psycho-Analysis* 53:333-338.
Mahler, M., Pine, F., and Bergman, A. (1975). *The Psychological Birth of the Human Infant*. New York: Basic Books.
McDevitt, J., and Mahler, M. (1980). Object-constancy, individuality and identity formation. In *The Course of Life*, vol. 1, ed. S. Greenspan and G. Pollock, pp. 407-424. Bethesda MD: National Institutes of Mental Health.
McGuire, J., and Richman, N. (1986). Screening for behavior disorders and neuroses. *Journal of Child Psychiatry* 27:7-32.
Melamed, B., and Siegel, E. (1975). Reduction of anxiety in children facing hospitalization and surgery by use of filmed modeling. *Journal of Consulting and Clinical Psychology* 43:511-521.
O'Leary, K., and Carr, E. (1982). Childhood disorders. In *Contemporary Behavior Therapy*, ed. G. Wilson and C. Franks, pp. 445-504. New York: Guilford.
Orvaschel, H., and Weissman, M. (1986). Epidemiology of anxiety disorders in children: a review. In *Anxiety Disorders of Childhood*, ed. R. Gittelman, pp. 58-72. New York: Guilford.
Rachman, S., and Costello, C. (1961). The etiology and treatment of children's phobias: a review. *American Journal of Psychiatry* 118:97-105.
Richman, N., Stevenson, J., and Graham, P. (1982). *Preschool to School: A Behavioral Study*. London: Academic Press.
Roiphe, H. (1965). On an early genital phase. *Psychoanalytic Study of the Child* 23:348-365. New York: International Universities Press.
Ross, A. (1981). *Child Behavior Therapy*. New York: John Wiley.
Rutter, M., Cox, A., Tupling, C., et al. (1975). Attainment and adjustment in geographic areas: I. prevalence of psychiatric disorder. *British Journal of Psychiatry* 126:493-509.
Rutter, M., and Shaffer, D. (1980). DSM-III: a step forward or back? *Journal of American*

Academy of Child Psychiatry 19:371-394.
Samuelson, F. (1980). Watson's "Little Albert", Cyril Burt's twins, and the need for a critical science. *American Psychologist* 35:619-625.
Shaffer, D., Schonfeld, L., O'Connor, P., et al. (1985). Neurobiological soft signs. *Archives of General Psychiatry* 42:342-351.
Shapiro, T. (1975). Childhood neurosis: the past 75 years. *Psychiatry and Contemporary Science* 4:453-477.
Shapiro, T, and Esman, A. (1985). Psychotherapy with children: still relevant in the 1980s? *Psychiatry Clinics of North America* 8:909-922.
Simeon, J., and Ferguson, H., (1987). Alprazolam effects in children with anxiety disorders *Canadian Journal of Psychiatry* 32:570-574.
────── (1985). Recent development in the use of antidepressants and anxiolytic medications. *Psychiatric Clinics of North America* 8:893-908.
Spitzer, R., and Cantwell, D. (1980). The DSM-III classification of the psychiatric disorders of infancy, childhood and adolescence. *Journal of the American Academy of Child Psychiatry* 19:356-370.
Stern, D. (1985). *The Interpersonal World of the Infant*. New York: Basic Books.
Suomi, S., Kraember, G., Baysonger, C., et al. (1981). Inherited and experimental factors associated with individual differences in anxious behavior displayed by Rhesus monkeys. In *Anxiety: New Research and Changing Concepts*, ed. D. Klein and T. Relkin. New York: Raven Press.
Thomas, A., and Chess, S. (1980). *Dynamics of Psychological Development*. New York: Brunner/Mazel.
Volkmar, F., Poll, J., and Lewis, M. (1984). Conversion reactions in children and adolescents. *Journal of the American Academy of Child Psychiatry* 23:424-430.
Watson, J., and Rayner, R. (1920). Conditioned emotional reactions. *Journal of Experimental Psychology* 3:1-12.
Werry, J. (1982). An overview of pediatric psychopharmacology. *Journal of the American Academy of Child Psychiatry* 21:3-9.
Wolkind, S., and Everitt, B. (1974). A cluster analysis of the behavioral items in the preschool child. *Psychological Medicine* 4:422-427.

PART II

DEVELOPMENTAL AND ETIOLOGICAL CONSIDERATIONS

8

Neurosogenesis

Henri Parens, M.D.

WHAT IS NEUROSIS?

Our central concern in addressing the question of the genesis of neurosis is what causes neurosis. First, a quick look at what neurosis is is needed to address the question of neurosogenesis. To begin, I point to the fact that neurosis, as the *Glossary of Psychoanalytic Terms and Concepts* (Moore and Fine 1968) tells us, is

> the result of conflict between sexual and aggressive drives (id) and ego forces striving to control and limit the expression of these drives. . . . The ego reacts to the possible emergence into consciousness of these instinctual derivatives with anxiety, a danger signal which alerts and stimulates repression and other defense mechanisms. . . . [And] analysis of symptoms show them to be compromised formations, disguised substitute expressions of the instinctual drives combined with manifestations of the repressing forces or even punishment by the superego. [pp. 79–80]

Let us also draw attention to the well-established distinction between what psychoanalysts identify as a *clinical neurosis*—for example, a symptomatic neurosis that most commonly appears after the oedipal phase (2½ to 6 years of age)—and *the infantile neurosis,* a ubiquitous development in normal enough (indeed, even in quite disturbed) children that occurs during (and, in fact, constitutes) the oedipal phase in which the original version of the conflict spoken of above emerges and becomes structured. We will talk about this infantile neurosis a little later.

The essential point we want to make is that neurosis is the product of a repressed and otherwise defended against intrapsychic conflict. In the unfolding of the infantile neurosis, it emerges and is then repressed; in the symptomatic neurosis, a recent event resonates with and enhances the repressed (defended) conflict, thereby giving it greater force and upsetting the repressive (defensive) capability of the ego, leading to a psychic disequilibrium which is then redressed by a new compromise formation and the production of symptoms. Before proceeding, just a note on the models we are using in this discussion.

Models Implemented

Many efforts have been and are being made to provide us with models of the mind that may, in the eye of their originator, serve us better than those that constitute a large part of psychoanalytic metapsychology. Although we are learning more by means of some of these new models, I find their usefulness lies more in their ability to complement rather than replace those that have helped us so enormously over the past six or so decades in the clinical situation and in uncovering critical factors and features of psychic development. I continue to find that the still evolving classical models—the metapsychological and object relations theory models—serve us exceedingly well. Indeed, those proposed to replace them—be it with systems theory models (Peterfreund 1971, Rosenblatt and Thickstun 1977, Sander 1964, 1983), self psychology (Gunther 1980, Kohut 1977, M. Tolpin 1980), affect theories that pressingly dispose of drives (Basch 1976, 1984, Stechler and Halton 1983), or still others (Gedo 1979, Schafer 1976, 1985)—although they do away with some of the problems extant in the metapsychological models and they add to our ability to see and understand, they do not address as well those critical factors and features of both development and clinical phenomena elucidated by the classical models.

I will especially use the several metapsychological models best known to us: the topographic model that proposes mental activity in terms of its conscious, preconscious, and unconscious—with its cardinal "repressed unconscious"—aspects of mental activity, as well as the structural, the genetic, and the dynamic models to discuss the question of neurosogenesis. However, as do most analysts now, I will go beyond psychosexual theory in my implementation of these models; I will amalgamate clinical and observational research-supported concepts from psychosexual theory with contributions from separation-individuation theory and my reformulation of aggression theory. But back to our question. We know well enough what a neurosis is, now we want to look more closely at what causes it.

WHAT CAUSES NEUROSIS?

Given sufficient psychic functional capability, that is to say, sufficient development and healthy enough psychic organization, neurosis is caused by a stable, perpetuated, unresolved, and, by the self, unresolvable intrapsychic conflict. This conflict consists of a wish (drive derivative) encountering an internal opposing reaction to it, be it from the ego (adaptive assessment) or the superego (assessment by conscience and/or ego ideal). The protective defensive operations, as is well known in clinical psychoanalysis, plays a major part in neurosogenesis.

What sustains the production of neurosis and perpetuates the potential for the emergence of neurotic symptoms is the repressed (and otherwise defended against) component of the unresolved, stable, and perpetuated intrapsychic conflict. Therefore, the potential for neurosis exists where an intrapsychic conflict that has undergone repression exists. Repression particularly but some other defenses as well—denial, avoidance, projection, and so forth—we assume, like Keats's *Ode on a Grecian Urn*, makes for unchangeability and with it perpetuation of the intrapsychic conflict.

But why does it undergo repression? Here is a pertinent observation I had the privilege of witnessing in our psychoanalytic direct observational research (see Parens 1979a, chap. 4).

While in the observational setting, where the mothers and their children usually settle, a group of several 2- and 3-year-olds were returning from the snack area accompanied by one of our trainee staff members. Upon entry into the observational setting, the young staff member, charmed and excited by the discussion that had been ongoing in the snack area, suggested to one of the 3-year-old children: "Jane, tell Dr. Parens who you said you are going to marry!" Jane's initial response was one of excitement, her face lit up, and she was on the point of responding. Suddenly, as if by some sharp new awareness of the implications of what she was about to say, Jane became immobilized. Her expression sobered dramatically. Not yet fully tuned-in to what she was asking of Jane, the staff member again prompted Jane to please tell Dr. Parens whom she said she was going to marry. Jane was mortified. She remained mute and continued to be immobilized. Whereas several minutes before she had been able to tell her cohorts gleefully that she is going to marry her daddy—this was in the context of a discussion of whom the children are going to marry, something that arose spontaneously among them—now in the presence of her mother, she was unable to reiterate what she had said so easily before.

The acute anxiety Jane felt and the conflict created in her by the wish she had verbalized just several minutes before led to an apparent immobilization, whether controllable by Jane or not. My impression was that she was not in control of her actions at this point. I had the further impression that Jane had got into the arena of the triadic conflict sphere without thinking, or knowing its consequences until they suddenly occurred to her; before she knew them, she had, so to speak, gotten into the situation too deeply, indeed "over her head." She was mute for several minutes, and then seemed to be taken off the hook only by my verbal assurance to her that all children sometimes wish things they find very upsetting and difficult to deal with it (an intervention consistent with our research approach).

I inferred here the probability that the wish she had so readily expressed minutes earlier had now been repressed. This was so because its mental sequelae had become unmanageable by this 3-year-old child. As has been repeatedly reconstructed and experienced in the clinical situation, Jane had to repress (defend against) what she had earlier expressed because she became acutely aware of the disaster to which her wishes could take her. Interestingly, Jane later developed a notable degree of inhibition. The need for repression, for defense against this previously stated wish, is unavoidable.

CAN NEUROSIS BE PREVENTED?

If neurosis is the product of defense, one could propose that the potential for no neurosis exists. That is, if we could disallow defense, we could prevent neurosis. That, however, as Jane so clearly illustrated, cannot be done; furthermore, it is not desirable. Jane could not do it because her emotional attachment to her mother was of good quality, and her need for her mother continued to be immense. In other words, it cannot be done due to the emotional attachment to love objects and the powerful drive derivatives that these objects gratify: the need for love, for care, for protection, and so forth.

Not only can it not be done, but it would be highly undesirable to try to do so. It would be undesirable because the gains toward growth that these conflicts bring with them (the rapprochement crisis and the Oedipus complex) are enormous, if not indispensable to healthy development. Indeed, we have long known that neurosis—in the genetic sense, arising out of the infantile neurosis—is part of normal development, and that it is the unavoidable by-product of the interplay of the evolution of the self in the context of human relationships. Before elaborating further the loci in development where neurotic conflicts are usually produced, let me comment on a few other issues.

THE INTERPLAY IN NEUROSOGENESIS OF DEVELOPMENT AND INTRAPSYCHIC CONFLICTS

Two cardinal interacting aspects of neurosogenesis are (1) its generation and shaping by the interplay of constitutional givens and experience in the course of development, and (2) its production by the evolving of normal, built-in intrapsychic conflicts. There is a reciprocity in neurosogenesis between development and normal conflicts.

The Generation and Shaping of Neurosogenesis

Development—differentiation, to be more accurately in accord with Hartmann's (1952) definitions of these two terms—dictates *when* these normal conflicts will emerge. Freud spoke of a timetable that leads to the differentiation and emergence of the Oedipus complex at about 2 ½ years of life and to its reactivation with the emergence of adult sexuality (genitality proper, he proposed) at puberty. Experience is the factor that leads from differentiation to development as Hartmann defined these terms. In addition, every current development is shaped by prior developments and by prior existing conflicts. It is well to recall that Freud held the view that neurosis is the product of the complemental series that is "constitution" and "experience," that is, "nature" and "nurture."

The Production of Neurosogenesis

The qualitative aspects of each conflict as it arises at its appropriate phase and of its resolution will set the stage for the qualitative aspects of the conflict that will arise during the next phase of development. In other words then, in addition to their being age-adequate and appropriate, intrapsychic conflicts are prior-development-dependent, and prior-conflict-dependent.

Neurosogenesis, then, is the by-product of the interplay of normal conflicts and development. We note again that Freud held to the view that neurosis is the product of a related complemental series of constitution and experience. We can now ask what conditions generate and produce and what conditions facilitate the emergence of neurosis.

WHAT CONDITIONS GENERATE AND PRODUCE NEUROSIS?

Inherent tendencies that are part of the organism's given constitutional makeup that call for gratification against which an internal opposing tendency emerges generate the conditions necessary for the development of an intrapsychic conflict and then of neurosis. A drive derivative may be opposed by an ego (adaptive) reaction or by a superego dictate or prohibition. Or, a superego prescription may be protested by an ego (adaptive) reaction. A number of such *inter*agency (between psychic structural agencies) conflicts are possible. As analysts have long known, *intra*agency conflicts are also, most commonly, conflicts due to ambivalence, for example, hating a loved object. The drives especially generate neurotic conflict by their inherent nature, giving rise to wishes and demands that impel gratification. Three-year-old Jane illustrated most exquisitely, in *statu nascendi*, her ego and superego reactions to her just-verbalized wish to marry her daddy.

Here is what we know to date regarding the generation and production of neurotic conflicts in the normal child. The origins of and foundation for neurotic conflicts lie in developments that occur during the first six years of life. Subsequent normal stresses and strains of development will play upon and be determined by the qualitative character of the conflicts that stabilize during those years. For example, one of the major conflicts produced by the emergence of puberty (Laufer and Laufer 1984) is significantly determined by the oedipal conflict that occurs during that two-and-a-half- to six-year period. It is useful to consider what occurs at puberty to be a *new* conflict that arises out of an old one. In terms of levels of psychic organization, it is fruitful to bear in mind the structuring of each progressive stage of development upon the earlier ones. This is so with due regard for both continuity and discontinuity theoretical aspects of development.

The Basic Early Conflicts

Assuming that each phase of development brings with it a specific type and level of psychic organization, here are the cardinal normal conflicts that direct child observation have highlighted for me:

1. Conflicts of autonomy from aggression theory (Parens 1979a,b, 1986, Parens and Pollock 1978)—battles of wills, the anal conflicts of psychosexual theory: children vary in their strivings for autonomy, their dispositions, their aggression endowment, and therewith in the production of conflict. And, of course, parents vary in their handling of these (due to parental character formations and residual neurotic conflicts), which contributes significantly to the shaping and intensity of these conflicts in their children.

2. Rapprochement crisis of separation–individuation theory (Mahler et al. 1975, Mahler and McDevitt 1981): patterns of its emergence and experience facilitate or make it more difficult. For instance, a condensed, one-major-episode type of crisis may be more conflict-producing than a gradual, lesser series of crisis episodes that can be dealt with progressively (Parens 1979a, chap. 9). Again, parental handling is a significant contributing factor. A mother who cannot be close emotionally or cannot let her child separate comfortably contributes toward the intensification of her child's conflicts. One who can do both is likely to facilitate her child's coping with and better resolving this developmental crisis.

3. The Oedipus complex of psychosexual theory, the well-known conflict that produces neurosis: the quality of attachment and the quality of sexual drive upsurge both contribute to the child's contribution to this particular conflict. Again, the way parents deal with the child's expressions of sexuality and the change in the quality of object attachment significantly influence the child's ability to deal with the oedipal conflict and its resolution. But a critical question must be asked here: When does a neurosis become possible?

WHEN DOES A NEUROSIS BECOME POSSIBLE?

First, when the child becomes able to disapprove of or feel alarmed (anxious) in reaction to a wish, or when the ego is capable of experiencing co-existing wishes that are at odds with each other. A more elaborate answer is: where there is sufficient structuring of the ego as an agency, and of the superego as an agency to make possible a sufficiently sustained internal reaction to experienced wishes.

It is likely that one of the earliest intrapsychic conflicts arises from the emergence and experience of co-existing wishes that are at odds with each other. This does not require the functioning of a well-structured superego, and beginning ego functioning can suffice as conditions that can create such an intrapsychic conflict. Looking at ambivalence may help us answer the question: When does an intrapsychic conflict and then, neurosis, become possible?

The experience of ambivalence becomes possible (1) when the ego becomes capable of experiencing anxiety, and (2) when co-existing reactivities, feelings, or attitudes that are experienced as being at odds with each other can be experienced simultaneously or in rapid succession. Elsewhere (Parens 1979a,b) I have tentatively hypothesized two basic conflicts of ambivalence during prelatency life. This hypothesis in turn has generated a number of hypotheses relevant to the question of neurosogenesis.

Two Conflicts due to Ambivalence

In 1979(b) I said that

> from a developmental point of view, two factors recommend the proposition that ambivalence evolves through two basic conflicts in early childhood. The two conflicts of ambivalence show (1) significant differences which are determined by their different levels of structural . . . and object related developments; (2) there is an important difference in the path taken by girls and boys in the formation of their ambivalent cathexes. [pp. 387–388]

The first conflict of ambivalence, I propose, "occurs in the context of *dyadic* object relatedness. It seems to originate at the end of the first year during the differentiation-practicing subphases of separation individuation theory, and it gains a large tributary during the rapprochement subphase when it becomes focused, organized, and the preexisting ambivalence may be intensified or ameliorated" (p. 388). *The second conflict of ambivalence,* I suggest, "occurs in the context of first genital [phallic]-phase *triadic* object relatedness. It both arises within the classical Oedipus complex and gives rise to its core conflict. It is largely determined by the then-current status of ambivalence in dyadic object relations and may in turn retrogressively reactivate and/or intensify dyadic object-related ambivalence" (pp. 413–414).

Although I initially conceptualized the first conflict of ambivalence to encompass developments and conflicts that occur during the first 18 to 24 months of age, namely ambivalence arising out of dyadic object relatedness, I have more recently (Parens 1984) found it necessary to detail two preoedipal conflicts that occur under normal developmental conditions.

The first of these is the earliest conflict of autonomy, which emerges from as early as about 10 to 12 months of life and arises especially out of battles of wills between infant and mother. This type of conflict is not only interpersonal, when it produces ambivalent feelings toward the mother, it sets the stage for an intrapsychic conflict (see Parens 1979a,b). This conflict, I have proposed, sets the stage for, and contributes the structure of the battle of wills and ambivalence to, the anal conflict of psychosexual theory that emerges later. It can also be said to occur at the time separation–individuation theory conceptualizes as the practicing subphase.

The second of these preoedipal conflicts is that which arises out of the rapprochement crisis as defined by Mahler and her co-workers. There is a fundamental difference between these two preoedipal conflicts that occur in rather rapid developmental sequence, eventually tend to occur simultaneously (McDevitt 1983), and influence each other intimately. The autonomy conflict initially manifest in battles of wills brings with it a conflict due to ambivalence. The co-existence or rapid alternations of love and hate feelings toward self and love object may bring about splitting not only as a transient defense, but also as the basis for more serious disturbance (as spelled out by Klein [1939], Kernberg, [1975, 1980] and Mahler [1968, 1971] especially). The rapprochement crisis, on the other hand, brings with it a conflict that arises principally out of the infant's experience of anxiety in the face of attempting to separate and individuate from the object. Here the effort is in the direction of the development of the self and of the object as separate entities bound by a highly valenced emotional relationship.

Represented diagramatically for the purpose of elucidation, I would suggest that if the task of rapprochement is to resolve the symbiosis, we can represent it thus:

Diagram 8-1: The Task Of The Rapprochement Subphase

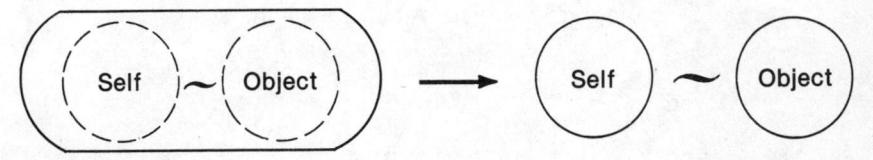

Archaic symbiotic
self-object representation
"I–not-I" (Parens and Saul
1971, Mahler et al. 1975)

End point: sufficient stability in
experiencing self and object as
separate individuals, but tied
by a powerful positive-enough
emotional bond.

And the rapprochement crisis can be represented as follows:

Diagram 8-2: The Rapprochement Crisis

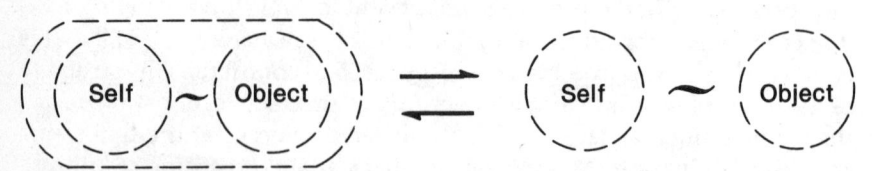

Then the rapprochement subphase conflict can be represented as the following polarization:

Diagram 8-3: Rapprochement Subphase Polarization

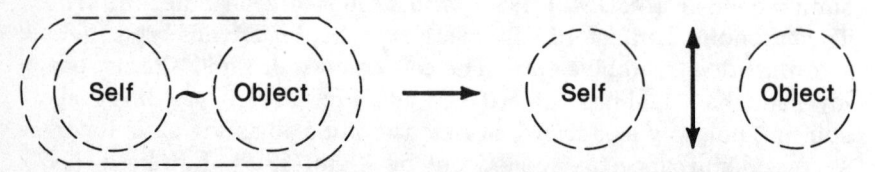

the separation–individuation
line of effort and experiencing

In its simple form, this conflict, which, like all intrapsychic conflicts, has polarizing forces at play, is not however, a conflict due to ambivalence—which, as I have defined it, is a conflict of co-existing love and hate toward the same object. Thus, whereas the rapprochement crisis in its basic form is a crisis of self-object, the poles of which are the self and the object, a conflict due to ambivalence has another polarizing parameter, which is love and hate. The combination of these two conflicts might then be represented this way:

Diagram 8-4: The Ambivalence Axis

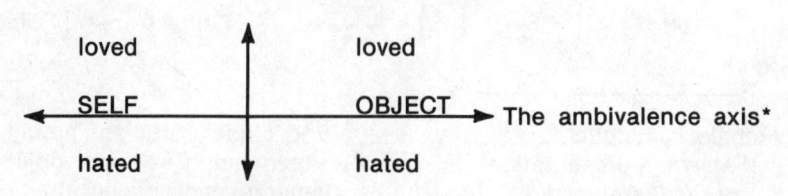

the separation–individuation line

*Kernberg's theory of splitting can be implemented at this point.

The Second Conflict of Ambivalence

The conflict inherent in the Oedipus complex is the paradigm of a triadic intrapsychic conflict that arises out of the first emerging of object-directed genital sexuality. This ambivalence conflict is unique, distinguishable from the preoedipal conflict of ambivalence by virtue of the emergence of object-directed genital sexuality and the structuring of a novel triadic object-related constellation.

Roiphe and Galenson have reported extensively (Roiphe 1968, Roiphe and Galenson 1981) on a prior phase of sexuality, a "prephallic genital phase," which is narcissistic and dyadic in character. Also, although there are pregenital triadic conflicts (see Abelin 1971, Parens and Saul 1971), these triadic pregenital conflicts are less preoccupying and determining of psychic activity and arise out of pregenital need constellations.

A third and critical aspect of the difference between the oedipal and prior conflicts due to ambivalence is the higher level organization and structural development that characterize the later conflict, for example, the differentiation of genital as compared to pregenital sexuality, the ego's ability to fantasize at a new level (Peller 1954), and more (see Rangell 1973).

The oedipal conflict has been amply described in psychoanalysis, but a word on it is warranted here. Freud initially placed the castration complexes at the center of this conflict (1925). Arising out of direct child observations where it is amply evident, I propose (Parens 1989) enlarging on one point Freud stated in 1913 and 1926, which is that the Oedipus complex brings with it and is a conflict due to ambivalence. And although observation amply documents the major part the castration complex plays in the boy's life, we have not found it equally prominent in little girls. Some girls do show a sharp reaction of disappointment and despair at not having a penis, others do not.

My point is that the ambivalence of the Oedipus conflict allows for explanations that address more fully than castration theory alone questions of differences in boys and girls, as well as the question of superego formation in the girl (Parens 1989). Although the castration complex in the boy, as well as in the girl, plays a significant part in the Oedipus complex, in its character and its resolution, viewing the Oedipus complex from its central conflict of ambivalence allows for an explanation that brings us closer to what we invariably encounter in the clinical situation and the analysis of which, I believe, makes for better oedipal conflict resolution than does the (at times) over-emphasized analysis of the castration complex.

Especially highlighted by this proposition is the fact that basing the girl's Oedipus complex—R. Parens (1985, 1986), by the way, insists that the girl's experience is sufficiently different from the boy's complex to warrant our identifying it as the "Electra complex"—and its central conflict due to ambivalence sheds a different light on the development of the girl's superego than that proposed by Freud, an issue addressed by a number of analysts.

Proposing two basic conflicts of ambivalence during the first six years of life reveals that the girl has these two basic conflicts of ambivalence *primarily with her mother*, whereas the boy has his first conflict(s) of ambivalence (autonomy conflict and rapprochement crisis) primarily with his mother and the second (Oedipal conflict) with his father. This proposition allows for the sharp heightening of ambivalence that a girl feels toward her mother, which is central to development of her conscience and explains its stable structuring as well as its often encountered severity. Furthermore, this may well explain the high levels of guilt, inhibitions in success, and depression often encountered clinically in women.

What is required for the production of neurosis is not only the experience of intrapsychic conflict but its sufficiently stable repression. Analysts agree that stably intrapsychically repressed conflict and the production of neurosis become possible during the oedipal phase when the functional capabilities and level of organization that occur at this time obtain. Certainly from the end of the third year of life on a neurosis is possible—both the infantile neurosis and soon, therewith, a symptomatic neurosis.

But there is a gray area before that time when internalized conflicts may occur, especially those determined by ambivalence. Nagera (1966) speaks of preoedipal neurotic conflicts which he contrasts to developmental conflicts. Developmental conflicts, according to Nagera, are normative strains between id, ego, and superego-precursors specific for certain phases of development. He notes that when these developmental conflicts are insufficiently resolved during their normative phase, the residual conflict becomes a neurotic conflict. He further observes that "a neurotic conflict is frequently the continuation of a developmental conflict that has not resolved itself properly at the appropriate time" (p. 49). Nagera gives the example of a $2\frac{1}{2}$ year old who since 9 months of age showed an inhibition of chewing food, and that of another child who at 2 years of age developed symptoms that "amounted to a hand washing compulsion" (p. 52). Much neurotic psychopathology occurs prior to the emergence of the neurotic oedipal conflict, which by virtue of their internalized dynamics produce such neurotic symptoms as sleep disturbances, separation panic reactions, feeding problems, obsessive-compulsive symptoms, stuttering, inhibitions, and more.

It is an error to assume that preoedipal intrapsychic conflicts do not produce ambivalence or compromise formations. It is not clear whether or not they become repressed or just denied, avoided or otherwise defended against. Equally erroneous is the assumption that such preoedipal conflict compromises and patterns of adaptation are not stable. Clinicians know well that efforts at their reduction can encounter much resistance and their persistence is readily inferable in the shape they give to oedipal phase conflict and compromises that follow them. I would say that if there is repression of such intrapsychic conflict and it is stable, it is neurotic. It is, however, unavoidable, because of the momentum of time, that such early neurotic clinical pictures are soon organized and shaped by the Oedipus complex, which emerges quite early in life. The line, then, between oedipal and preoedipal at times becomes blurred as one attempts to sort out what came with the Oedipus complex and what came before it.

What Conditions Facilitate the Production of Neurosis?

Foremost is the quality of experience. Psychoanalysts since Freud (1923, 1939) place large emphasis on the fact that parents, as the representatives of civilization in the rearing of their children, contribute centrally to the experience-determined shaping of the child's ego, superego, and self. This is because experience is principally shaped by the child's parents. As I said earlier, Freud proposed that neurosis is determined by the complemental series of constitutional givens (and timetables) and experience.

This too is where many psychoanalysts, including Kohut, M. Tolpin, and I, coming from different viewpoints, converge: parenting is one of the most critical factors contributing to the development of neurosis and more serious disturbance.

As was noted earlier, the way parents respond to their children's strivings for autonomy is a major contributor to the conflict produced within the child that arises from these strivings. For example, a mother who cannot comfortably enough allow her child to explore the environment will bring into the child's experience more frustration than would a mother who has baby-proofed the house satisfactorily and made more opportunities for safe explorations by her infant. A parent who is in need of overly controlling the whereabouts and the activities of her child is likely, at least in some children, to intensify the possibility of battles of wills, thereby intensifying the possibility for the production of heightened ambivalence and of intrapsychic conflict.

Similarly, a parent who has difficulty with closeness, or with allowing her child sufficient age-appropriate separateness, will create greater difficulty for the child as the child attempts to resolve the rapprochement crisis he or she will experience. Holding onto the baby or pushing the infant away before the infant is ready to separate comfortably will bring difficulty to the child's experience of this conflict and may thereby produce greater polarization of the rapprochement crisis and intensify intrapsychic conflict in the child.

And as we have said already, where parents have great difficulty tolerating the child's sexual behaviors, oedipal feelings, and wishes, or find it difficult to help their child cope with these transgressive wishes, this will also contribute to an intensification of the child's oedipal conflict and may thereby set the stage for or facilitate the intensification of this dramatic intrapsychic conflict that may express itself sooner or later in a symptomatic neurosis. This, of course, is where prevention can be called into play—in parenting (see chapter 9).

CONCLUSION

Neurosis formation occurs where an intrapsychic conflict that is intolerable to the self and the ego is repressed and by remaining repressed, stabilizes in the psyche and cannot be resolved. The repressed conflict holds the capability of producing neurotic symptoms and will do so typically (characterologically), or in response to conditions that produce a disequilibrium in its status quo (events that intensify drive derivatives or superego reactivity or undermine defensive operations). Our discussion of neurosogenesis is stated in concepts of classical models, particularly the topographic, the structural, and the genetic, as well as that of object relations theory. Elements of separation-individuation theory are implemented as well.

There is a significant reciprocal interplay between development and the intrapsychic conflicts that occur in the course of normal development. Some conditions generate neurosis and others facilitate them. Those that generate neurosis are the basic tasks of early development that bring with them intrapsychic conflicts. These are (1) the conflicts of autonomy that result from battles of wills between child and parent and that also bring with them ambivalence from the end of the first year of life—and eventually give shape to the anal conflict of psychosexual theory; (2) the rapprochement subphase conflict produced by its polarizing wishes to separate-individuate versus remaining symbiotically tied to mother; and (3) the well-known oedipal conflict.

Whether these potentially normative intrapsychic conflicts produce neurosis or not is determined by the degree to which they are intensified and repressed. They are also determined by when the psyche is developmentally capable of such repression. We are certain that it is so capable by 3 years of age—during the oedipal phase that begins at about 2½ years.

But there is a gray area prior to this developmental period when intrapsychic conflict seems possible and is likely. Looking at the production of ambivalence, an intraagency conflict, we find it capable of creating intrapsychic conflict that leads to a variety of defensive operations that probably already includes repression during the second year and possibly from the very end of the first year of life. Strivings for autonomy bring with them ambivalence under normal conditions (for example, of limit setting) by the end of the first year of life. At times it is not possible to determine whether such conflicts are simply "developmental conflicts" as proposed by Nagera (1966) or "neurotic" ones. Whether or not they themselves constitute neurosis at its very beginnings or lay the groundwork for it during the oedipal phase cannot easily be determined.

Also, I am suggesting that looking at intrapsychic conflicts from their common nucleus of ambivalence allows for explications of development in boys and girls that enhance our understanding of their intrapsychic conflicts, superego formation, and neuroses. Furthermore, our clinical understanding and treatment of these conflicts are enhanced by the thesis that first and second conflicts of ambivalence are experienced differently in girls and boys.

Finally, looking at neurosis as the product of the complemental series of constitution and experience (nature and nurture) allows the fact that the contribution made by constitution (endowment) is a given that cannot be predetermined or prevented and that the contribution of experience (especially nurture) is the critical modifiable determinant of neurosis. The way parents rear their children, the way they react to and help their children with their unavoidable intrapsychic conflicts, makes a significant contribution to the facilitation of neurosis or to its mitigation.

REFERENCES

Abelin, E. (1971). The role of the father in the separation-individuation process. In *Separation-Individuation: Essays in Honor of Margaret S. Mahler*, ed. J. B. McDevitt and C. F. Settlage, pp. 229-252. New York: International Universities Press.

Basch, M. (1976). The concept of affects. *Journal of American Psychoanalysis Association.* 24:759-778.

———— (1984). Response to Dr. Freedman. In *Psychoanalysis: The Vital Issues*, vol. 1, ed. J. Gedo and G. Pollock, pp. 39-52. New York: International Universities Press.

Freud, S. (1913). Totem and taboo. *Standard Edition* 13:1-161.

———— (1923). The ego and the id. *Standard Edition* 19:3-66.

———— (1925). Some psychical consequences of the anatomical distinction between sexes. *Standard Edition* 19:3-66.

———— (1926). Inhibitions, symptoms and anxiety. *Standard Edition* 19/20:77-94.

———— (1940). An outline of psycho-analysis. *Standard Edition* 23:141-207.

Gedo, J. (1979). *Beyond Interpretation.* New York: International Universities Press.

Gedo, J., and Goldberg, A. (1973). *Models of the Mind.* Chicago: University of Chicago Press.

Gunther, M. S. (1980). Aggression, self psychology, and the concept of health. In *Advances in Self Psychology*, ed. A. Goldberg, pp. 167-192. New York: International Universities Press.

Hartmann, H. (1952). The mutual influences in the development of the ego and the id. In *Essays on Ego Psychology*, pp. 155-181. New York: International Universities Press, 1964.

Kernberg, O. (1975). *Borderline Conditions and Pathological Narcissism.* New York: Jason Aronson.

———— (1980). *Internal World and External Reality.* New York: Jason Aronson.

Klein, M. (1939). *The Psychoanalysis of Children.* New York: Grove Press, 1960.

Kohut, H. (1977). *The Restoration of the Self.* New York: International Universities Press.

Laufer, M, and Laufer, M. E. (1984). *Adolescence and Developmental Breakdown.* New Haven, CT: Yale University Press.

Mahler, M. S. (1971). A study of the separation-individuation process and its possible application to borderline phenomena in the psychoanalytic situation. *Psychoanalytic Study of the Child* 26:403-424. New Haven, CT: Yale University Press.

Mahler, M. S., with M. Furer (1968). *On Human Symbiosis and the Vicissitudes of Individuation.* New York: International Universities Press.

Mahler, M. S., Pine, F, and Bergman, A. (1975). *The Psychological Birth of the Human Infant.* New York: Basic Books.

Mahler, M. S., and McDevitt, J. B. (1980). The separation-individuation process and identity formation. In *The Course of Life*, ed. S. I. Greenspan and G. H. Pollock, pp. 395-406. Bethesda, MD: National Institutes of Mental Health.

McDevitt, J. B. (1983). The emergence of hostile aggression and its defensive and adaptive modifications during the separation-individuation process. *Journal of American Psychoanalytic Association* 31:273-300.

Moore, B. E., and Fine, B. D. (1968). *A Glossary of Psychoanalytic Terms and Concepts.* New York: American Psychoanalytic Association.

Nagera, H. (1966). *Early Childhood Disturbances, The Infantile Neurosis, and the Adult Disturbances.* New York: International Universities Press.

Parens, H. (1979a). *The Development of Aggression in Early Childhood.* New York: Jason Aronson.

_____ (1979b). Developmental considerations of ambivalence. *Psychoanalytic Study of the Child* 34:385–420. New Haven, CT: Yale University Press.

_____ (1984). What is the first conflict of ambivalence? Paper presented to the Regional Council of Child Psychiatry, Philadelphia, January 7, 1984.

_____ (1989). On the girl's psychosexual development: reconsiderations suggested from direct observation. *Journal of American Psychoanalysis Association* (in press).

Parens, H., and Pollock, L. (1978). Film #5b: *Toward an Epigenesis of Aggression in Early Childhood:* No. 2: *Aggression, Ambivalence, and Beginning Separation–Individuation.* Audiovisual Media Section, Eastern Pennsylvania Psychiatric Institute, Philadelphia.

Parens, H., and Saul, L. J. (1971). *Dependence in Man.* New York: International Universities Press.

Parens, R. (1985). The Electra complex in Greek tragedy compared to psychoanalytic findings on the girl. Presented at Meetings of the American Psychoanalytic Association to the Colloquium: Understanding adolescent development through fiction, E. L. Goldberg and S. Wagonfeld, co-chairmen. New York, December 22, 1985 (unpublished manuscript).

_____ (1986). The complexes on family dramas of Electra and Oedipus (unpublished manuscript).

Peller, L. (1954). Libidinal phases, ego development, and play. *Psychoanalytic Study of the Child* 9:178–198. New York: International Universities Press.

Peterfreund, E. (1971). *Information, Systems and Psychoanalysis. Psychological Issues,* Monograph 25/26. New York: International Universities Press.

Rangell, L. (1972). Aggression, Oedipus and historical perspective. *International Journal of Psycho-Analysis* 53:3–11.

Roiphe, H. (1968). On an early genital phase. *Psychoanalytic Study of the Child* 23:348–365. New York: International Universities Press.

Roiphe, H., and Galenson, E. (1981). *Infantile Origins of Sexual Drive* (unpublished manuscript).

Rosenblatt, A., and Thickstun J. (1977). *Modern Psychoanalytic Concepts in a General Psychology. Psychological Issues,* Monograph 42/43. New York: International Universities Press.

Sander, L. W. (1964). Adaptive relationships in early mother–child interaction. *American Academy of Child Psychiatry.* 3:231–264.

_____ (1983). Polarity, paradox, and the organizing process in development. In *Frontiers of Infant Psychiatry,* ed. J. D. Call, E. Galenson, and R. L. Tyson, vol. 2, pp. 333–346. New York: Basic Books.

Schafter, R. (1976). *A New Language for Psychoanalysis.* New Haven, CT: Yale University Press.

Stechler, G., and Halton, A. (1987). The emergence of assertion and aggression during infancy: a psychoanalytic systems approach. *Journal of American Psychiatric Association* 35:821–838.

Tolpin, M. (1980). Discussion of "psychoanalytic developmental theories of the self: an integration" by Morton Shane and Estelle Shane. In *Advances in Self Psychology,* ed. A Goldberg, pp. 47–68. New York: International Universities Press.

9

Neurosis and Prevention

Henri Parens, M.D.

The history of prevention in psychoanalysis is not a long one. It begins with Freud, who on a number of occasions wrote (as he did in 1933) that perhaps the greatest contribution of psychoanalysis would be its "application to . . . the upbringing of the next generation." He believed this contribution to be "so exceedingly important, so rich in hopes for the future" (p. 146).

Although this history is a quiet one, it has already had a pronounced influence. While there have been no national programs to vaccinate all children against learning inhibitions, such problems are no longer viewed as the product of laziness. Nor have there been outspoken campaigns against sexual prohibitions (in fact, the United States Supreme Court has endorsed an intrusive sexual prohibition); yet, the notable social prohibitions against masturbation have dramatically lifted. (Personal prohibitions never will as they arise from the Oedipus complex.) It is a fascinating history, one that warrants more attention. It seems to this writer that despite the fact that neither government nor psychoanalysis has mounted campaigns to enunciate psychoanalytic findings and advance strategies for improving mental health, nevertheless, psychoanalytic findings pervasively influence society and the conduct of our citizens. That we are influenced by unconscious motivations, the play of fantasies in our lives, parapraxes, by the fact that dreams have meanings, by the normality of infantile sexuality, and by many more revelations uncovered by psychoanalysts is now accepted by many people as fact and has enlarged our understanding of ourselves and those about us.

To the degree that psychoanalytic treatment opens to patients a means of understanding their troublesome dynamics and their conflicts and teaches them how to cope better with them, it secondarily prevents mental illness. In this sense, all psychoanalysts, like all physicians, not only treat and sometimes cure, but they also prevent. And in this sense the history of prevention has its start with Freud's early cases.

These domains though, I believe, are not where the preventive strength of psychoanalysis lies. The primary prevention capability of psychoanalysis is in what Freud enunciated in the 1933 quote that opened this chapter. The fact is, Freud was a strong proponent of primary prevention, not only in his belief that psychoanalysis could provide us with a general psychological explanation of mental activity, human dynamics, and development, but particularly because he believed that the knowledge it would bring could be put to use in rearing our children in better health-insuring and growth-promoting ways. But to look at our topic more closely, at both its history and its content, some conceptual clarification is in order.

PREVENTION: PRIMARY AND SECONDARY

Prevention in mental health, specifically in terms of neurosis, is not a single-level phenomenon. For instance, we can prevent some illness from happening at all; we can prevent illness from recurring; we can prevent it from getting worse; we can prevent secondary illness from arising out of a primary illness. Although a more complex system is proposed by Berlin (1979), for our present discussion of the prevention of neurosis, I will simply suggest two levels of prevention, primary and secondary prevention.

Primary prevention is the attempt to prevent the emergence of troubled adaptation and/or symptom formation. It is the addressing of potential symptoms and disorders before they occur. In one of our applications of psychoanalytic concepts, our parent–infant group work (Frank and Rowe 1981, Parens 1985, Parens et al. 1974), we often have the opportunity to prevent certain symptomatic behaviors from appearing by talking about such behaviors with parents, about what gives rise to them and what their consequences might be. For example, in groups of seven to ten mothers with their infants, when we address something that is going on with one particular child and talk openly with that mother about it, we have found, and the mothers have told us, that this discussion is useful for them with their own children. Seeing potentially symptomatic behavior in one child and working jointly with that child's mother to understand what is going on helps the other mothers to deal better with these behaviors when they appear in their own children.

Secondary prevention is the effort to prevent the stabilization and therewith the perpetuation of troubled adaptation and/or presenting symptoms. One of the principles of psychoanalytic treatment is to resolve intrapsychic conflicts that generate and perpetuate neurotic and more serious psychological symptoms. The treatment that succeeds sufficiently in decreasing the influence of intrapsychic conflicts, or of resolving such intrapsychic conflicts, brings with it the decreased possibility of symptom formations. Therefore, psychoanalytic therapy serves not only the function of resolving or lessening symptom formations, but also of preventing their continuing presentation or recurrence. Psychoanalytic treatment then is a vehicle or tool for secondary prevention. This, I believe, is especially true of those engaged in child and adolescent psychoanalytic treatment.

But a critical issue needs our attention before we can talk about prevention, primary or secondary—it is that prevention of illness or disaster is determined by and depends upon what we can influence. This is true for mental illness and for neurosis in particular.

WHAT IN NEUROSIS CAN WE INFLUENCE?

What can we influence? What can we not influence and, therefore, not prevent? What factors contribute to the production of neurosis? Freud held that neurosis is inevitable in all of us. It is so by virtue of the fact that the infantile neurosis occurs in all of us. However, he noted that we are not all equally subject to neurosis, that the outcome of neurosis is the product of a complemental series combining, to varying degrees and in various ways, factors that are inborn (constitutional) and factors that are experiential. A confluence of nature and nurture is at play. A brief look at what is inborn will help define some of the limits imposed on the prevention of neurosis.

We cannot change or prevent that which is inborn.

1. Genetic-constitutional factors that may dispose to neurosis cannot be changed. For instance, shyness that leads to heightened stranger anxiety seems to be a predisposition in certain children. So are low thresholds of irritability commonly found in infants born with central nervous system immaturity; for example, it is quite probable that minimal brain dysfunction contributes to the production of neurosis by the heightened degree of irritability and aggression it brings into play, and the heightened ambivalence that may follow from it.

From the early days of life, Cindy, the smaller of twins, showed a degree of irritability far sharper than her sister's, a much lower tolerance for frustration, and seemed upset by many more stimuli, including loud noises, bright lights, and so on. In the course of her development, Cindy was subject to many more episodes of rage than was her twin. This led to many more unpleasant interactions with her mother, and a much heightened mobilization of hostility and a much greater degree of ambivalence was experienced by both mother and child. In fact, for some time she became the "bad baby" while her twin was "the good baby." Inasmuch as heightened ambivalence and heightened levels of hostility contribute to the development of neurosis, Cindy was more vulnerable to neurosis than was her twin.

2. The qualitative and quantitative inherent thrust of the drives cannot be changed. Our work strongly supports what has long been known among psychoanalysts, namely, that children are endowed differently in terms of their aggression and sexual-drive dispositions (Alpert et al. 1956, Parens 1979). For instance, Mary and Bernie, Jane and Harold were all handsomely endowed in aggression. Some of our other infants were much more passive, from early in life less pressured from within to explore and assert themselves on their environment. Although the tendency is to see such differences in drive endowment more clearly with regard to the aggressive drive, a similar statement can be made about the sexual drive. Variations in the quality of attachment do not only depend on the character of the mother–child relationship. Some infants tend not to want as much holding and closeness as some others; on the other hand, others seem to need more holding and to thrive when this is provided for them. Although the issues are complex and the contributing factors not easily teased out, I believe it an error to assume that there are no variations in the endowment of the libidinal drive.

3. Schedules and timetables of development cannot be changed—except by drastic means. Freud emphasized that the Oedipus complex was scheduled to emerge at about 2 ½ years of age. Our own longitudinal observations over the past two decades strongly support Freud's timing for the emergence of the Oedipus complex (Parens et al. 1976). Nonetheless, although when the Oedipus complex and when puberty tend to emerge has some uniformity among children, there are individual variations. In another area of maturation, for instance, Mary and Bernie had a marked upsurge of aggression at about 7 to 11 months of age, a phenomenon I described in 1979. Jane and Harold, by contrast, both of whom were also handsomely aggressive drive-endowed, experienced an upsurge of aggression that was more gradual. We have found that the gradual emergence of any new psychic differentiation, be it of a drive (manifest in drive derivatives) or of a developmental task (for example the rapprochement crisis described below), tends to present an

easier adaptation challenge for the child than, for instance, a marked or sharp upsurge of aggression as we found in Mary and Bernie does. Such a marked upsurge is difficult not only for the child but often also for the mother, which may then, thereby, create further difficulty.

The same is true for such developmental tasks as we found in Candy, whose rapprochement crisis was sharp and large. It produced an acute conflict for her as well as for her mother (Parens 1979, pp. 223–231,). By contrast, Jane's rapprochement crisis, as well as Cindy's, was gradual, small-dosed, and produced less of a crisis for both infant and mother. We are all familiar with the kind of difficulty early puberty, or late puberty onset, too, may bring to a child. The long and short of this is that we cannot influence schedules and timetables of development, which may bring difficulties with them for the child.

4. We cannot prevent the emergence of the infantile neurosis. Whatever experience produces, except in the most severe disturbance, the infantile neurosis will occur. As we discussed in the chapter on neurosogenesis, the infantile neurosis is a normal development that arises out of the play of the sexual and aggressive drives in evolving object relations. However one explains the motivational systems classical analysis explains in terms of instinctual drives,[1] account must be taken of the maturations and developments of both sexuality and aggression in understanding a child's development. In our two decades of direct observations of young children and their parents, we have amply documented the emergence of those behaviors from which we infer the intrapsychic conflict characteristic of the infantile neurosis (see Parens et al. 1976). In the chapter on neurosogenesis I gave one illustration of such evidence, namely of 3-year-old Jane's acute repression and intrapsychic conflict in *statu nascendi*.

We can no more prevent this differentiation from occurring at about 2½ years of age than we can prevent the emergence of puberty about a decade later.

Parenthetically, let me ask: Even if we could, would we want to prevent the emergence of the infantile neurosis even though we know it brings with it the potential for a future symptomatic neurosis? Consider the experience of the 4- or 5-year-old in the throes of wishing to destroy

---

1. Kohut (1977), Tolpin (1980), and Basch (1984) propose that the infantile neurosis is not a normal development but rather the "breakdown product" of miscarriages of parenting, particularly in the form of failure of empathy. Although I strongly concur with the view that parental empathy is a critical factor for the healthy development of humans, the explanation of the infantile neurosis as a breakdown product is not acceptable. The assumption that the infantile neurosis exists only as the product of faulty upbringing is, I believe, flawed.

one of his or her two primary love objects, as well as the anxiety produced especially in boys by the castration complex. This state of affairs leads to remarkable adaptive, salutary reactions.

The balance between developing a neurosis and developing greater ego-functioning capability, for instance, a better capability to modulate aggression, a more stable identification with the parent of the same sex, a greater capacity for altruism and empathy, greater capabilities to sublimate, and a more mature and benevolent conscience formation, which all follow on the emergence of the infantile neurosis and the child's efforts to cope with it, is one of the remarkable phenomena of psychic life. If we could, would we want to prevent the Oedipus complex, the infantile neurosis? Not I. The contributions to civilization of the fact that humans develop large coping capabilities, especially our sublimations and even—while still seriously wanting—our moral codes, our consciences, owe an enormous debt to the Oedipus complex we all suffer. We cannot prevent neurosis, nor, in fact, do we want to prevent this major fountainhead of symptomatic neurosis, the normal infantile neurosis.

WHAT IN NEUROSIS CAN WE PREVENT?

Analysts say that neurosis is the product of the complemental series givens and experience. The givens (temperament, diatheses, organic dysfunction) and timetables, unpreventable *ab ovo*, can, however, be influenced.

As in embryology, any given genotype allows for a range of phenotypes. The single most significant factor that contributes to any particular development is experience. That is to say, experience determines the development (Hartmann 1952) these givens and their maturations will allow. And it is just in this sphere, in the quality of experience, that the potential for neurosis can be influenced.

Some of the experiential conditions that facilitate the development of neurotic conflicts come from within the child: for example, the child's own perception and interpretation of experience and the child's wishes and fantasies, both conscious and unconscious. Some facilitating conditions come from the environment: for example, the ambience and emotional quality of relationships, of caregiving, and of rearing. And, of course, traumatizing events play their part as well.

One of the major contributions psychoanalysis has made and continues to make is to have begun specifying what in experience facilitates neurosis. Analysts have emphasized—and some at times too much—the large contribution made by those from the environment. It is here that many analysts coming from varied vantage points converge in opinion, from Freud (1923, 1940) through Anna Freud (1965, 1978); M. Klein (1939); Jacobson (1964); Spitz (1965); Winnicott (1965); Mahler and her co-workers (1968, 1975); Kohut (1971, 1977); Fraiberg (1959, 1980); Provence (Provence and Lipton 1962; Provence and Naylor 1983); Sander (1962, 1964, 1983); Parens (1973, 1979; Parens et al. 1974, Parens et al. 1987); Greenspan (1981, 1985); and a number of other authors including Emde, Galenson, Kestenberg, Osofsky, and Stern. All point to the fact that parenting is a critical factor in the facilitation and pathogenesis of neurosis. It is especially here that prevention can be called into play, which led Freud (1933) to say that one of the great contributions psychoanalysis will make will come by means of applying what we learn from it to the rearing of the next generation.

I am firmly convinced that it behooves psychoanalysts to speak out, work, and further elaborate cautiously and thoughtfully what we want parents and all child caregivers to know.

CONTRIBUTIONS OF PSYCHOANALYSIS TOWARD PREVENTION

Led by clinical findings, psychoanalysts have searched for the origins of and contributions to mental illness and neurosis in particular. Vast psychoanalytic clinical experience supports, and theoretical constructions hold to, the assumption that the foundation of personality and of mental health is shaped and structured by the experiences of the first five years of life. Although an overly simplified view of this assumption has recently been challenged by some proponents of discontinuity theory, this assumption, contained in both metapsychological genetic and developmental points of view continues to be held by psychoanalysts and most other child developmentalists and psychotherapists. Much development follows these earliest five years of life, but the foundation and basic structure of personality have been erected and have remarkable stability—as documented by the rigorous and long psychoanalytic therapeutic efforts required to modify troubled beginnings. The assumptions contained in this viewpoint have led a number of clinical researchers to look for the pathogenetic factors operative in neurosis and more severe disturbances in the early years of life.

In their early studies it was not the spoken goal of psychoanalytic researchers to aim at prevention. However, they could not but have shared Freud's conviction that what we learn from the psychoanalytic treatment of individuals and research will find rich application in the rearing of the next generation. It is especially the work of a number of child psychoanalysts—who would most likely be thrust into the exploration of the early years of life not only in the clinical setting but in direct observational research as well—that serves the goal of prevention, even suggesting strategies to do so.

For example, consider the work of only a few of a number of such psychoanalytic researchers. Rene Spitz's work, side by side with that of Anna Freud and her co-workers, and that of John Bowlby represent the pioneers of psychoanalytically oriented direct observational research. Spitz's work on hospitalism (1945) and on anaclitic depression (1946) and his numerous writings on the development of the libidinal object and libidinal attachment (1965) are cardinal studies for prevention.

His work on hospitalism revealed that failure to thrive, and even infantile death, could be the product of overwhelming failures of emotional attachment and emotional nutriment. This finding itself pointed to the remarkable importance to normal development of sufficient emotional caregiving to infants from the first days of life on. This work was strongly supported by the studies of Bowlby (1951, 1960) and Provence and Lipton (1962). The implications for prevention were lucidly evident: in order to develop age-adequately, children need *emotional* nurturance sufficient to the individual child from the first days of life on, a hypothesis that gave rise to a vast literature even in animal studies (Harlow 1960, Harlow and Zimmerman 1959, Liddell 1958, Parens and Saul 1971).

Spitz's study on anaclitic depression taught us that this depression presents during the second half of the first year of life where a sufficiently satisfactory attachment has developed between an infant and its mother and results from the sudden and unreplaced loss to the infant of that libidinal object. Spitz's conceptualizations paved the way for our appreciation that libidinal attachment becomes specific, when it becomes specific, and that it needs to be protected to secure the child's normal development. Where that object is lost to the infant, good substitution can be brought about and anaclitic depression thereby prevented.

By understanding the meaning of the social smiling response, of separation and stranger anxiety, our understanding of the nature of the infant's attachment has made us better able to judge the progression of attachment, to intervene early where miscarriages of that attachment present, and to protect against not only anaclitic depressions but impoverishments of attachment and its many potential consequences as well. Furthermore, the strategies most commonly used in handling difficulties in attachments derive from Spitz's work, as do the insight and prevalent current concern arising from the fact that many mothers have now joined the out-of-the-home work force and leave their infants from the early months of life on. What are the implications of this on the child's attachments and development? These and other questions are given meaning by Spitz's work. Many research efforts have followed from his work (for example, Emde and his numerous collaborators) and that of Bowlby (for example, Ainsworth and her collaborators and students).

The work of Margaret S. Mahler and her co-workers (Mahler and Furer 1968, Mahler et al. 1975) is another case in point. Mahler's work in the 1940s and 1950s on childhood psychosis led her toward an exploration of early pathogenetic and normal developments that resulted in her formulation of separation–individuation theory, which proposes a model of the nature of the child's experience of his or her relationship to the mother. Years of direct observation led Mahler to infer that the infant experiences a basic separation–individuation process from birth to about 3 years of age. In this process the infant experiences him- or herself and the mother as if in a symbiotic oneness; this then evolves through a separation and individuation of self from that object into a relationship where the child experiences both himself and his mother as individuals attached to the other by a powerful emotional tie.

In our work with parents we have found that the experiences the infant undergoes in the course of this unfolding have been highly puzzling to many a mother and her child. For instance, some mothers are troubled by the fact that at the midpoint of the second year of life many infants who have long freely moved away from their mothers, who seemingly have been comfortable separated from her, begin to cling to her again. Many mothers experience this as disconcerting and as a regression. Mahler's explanation that this seeming regression is in fact a further advance in the process of separating and individuating has given an explanatory model that is of enormous value to both clinicians and parents. In the long run then, it is also invaluable for the child.

Our experiences in implementing the work of Mahler in our education for parenting have shown the enormous value of her theory for prevention strategy. That is to say, when a mother understands that what her child is experiencing during rapprochement is not a regression but rather a progression, the quality of how she handles the child's clinging becomes a different experience. Whereas not knowing what this clinging means has led many mothers to experience the infant's clinging with distress and to push the child away, understanding what the clinging is about helps the mother to react to it positively, acceptingly, and constructively, which makes a significant difference both in the child's passage through the rapprochement crisis and in increased positive attachment to the mother.

As we have found on numerous occasions in direct observation and in clinical work, being understood from very early in life facilitates better adaptation, development, and by causing less intense ambivalence, lessens the likelihood of symptomatic neurosis and more severe disturbance. In fact, as the work of many clinicians confirms, feeling understood from early in life is a phenomenon critical to healthy development. Indeed, the Chicago school of self psychology asserts—even at the expense of other necessary capabilities in parenting—that insufficiently empathic parenting is the cardinal underminer of mental health and normal development.

In our own work in education for parenting, the implementation of Spitz and Mahler's theories are major explanatory paradigms for making more understandable to mothers the nature of their child's developing a sense of self and of attachment to them. We have found the structuring of the libidinal object and separation–individuation theories to be very helpful to parents because of their explanatory nature.

Although components of separation–individuation theory have recently been challenged by Daniel Stern (1985), my perception of Stern's challenge is that it is not an opposing but rather a complementary view. Separation–individuation theory made no attempt to explain everything the infant experiences. Stern's contribution is one that, put in the balance with the essence of separation–individuation theory, meaningfully rounds out the picture. Separation–individuation emphasizes the infant's experiencing of self-object attachment, experiencing oneness with the object—"selfobject" (Kohut 1977)—and the differentiation out of that oneness into self and libidinal object. Stern's contribution amplifies the classical concept of primary narcissism, highlighting the infant's experience of some sense of self, however primitive, from its earliest experiences.

We have ourselves been privileged in the course of our observational research to find another area where the implications of psychoanalytic direct observational research findings have enormous implications for prevention. Our own studies of aggression have not only led us to propose a reformulation of the psychoanalytic theory of aggression (Parens 1973, 1979, 1984, 1989a,b), but have also impelled us to recommend strategies for preventing the development of excessive hostility in children (Parens 1979, Parens et al. 1982).

Our findings (Parens 1973, 1979) led us to hypotheses that there are several kinds of aggression, including aggression that is inherently nondestructive as well as aggression that is hostile and destructive. Both types of aggression, or trends in the aggressive drive, have their own histories, developments, and far-reaching implications for healthy adaptation.

Specifically, we have proposed the need for protecting the development of nondestructive aggression as manifested in assertiveness, and for the need to mitigate and, where possible, prevent the development of excessive hostility in children. This latter thesis rides on the hypothesis that it is when we experience excessive unpleasure that hostility is generated within us (Parens 1979). This hypothesis holds that hostility is not an inborn phenomenon, but is the product of experience. And because excessively unpleasurable experiences often can be governed, so can the generation of excessive hostility in humans. Having detailed how hostility is generated and mobilized, having proposed what leads to its generation and how that generation can be mitigated and prevented, we have developed a formal strategy aimed at accomplishing this. Although we have already seen the positive implications of putting these strategies into effect in our work in education for parenting, that is, actually with parents and their children, we have currently developed the methodology (Giacomo et al. 1985, Parens et al. 1986, 1988) for formally studying the effects of our interventions in the hope of documenting the changes that in our prior work we have assessed (by clinical judgment) take place.

The point I want to make is that psychoanalytic research of this kind, which leads to a clearer understanding of factors that contribute to the development of healthy aggression as well as of hostility, has led to the proposition that interventional strategies can be developed to insure healthier development of nondestructive aggression (as implemented in assertiveness and in the achievement of our goals) and lead to the prevention of excessive hostility in children.

The work of the investigators and their co-workers about which I have commented is illustrative of that of a number of psychoanalytic investigators whose contributions can and have been tested in the actual experiences of parents and children with whom we work. In addition, the work of a number of such other analyst–researchers as Anna Freud and many of her collaborators, John Bowlby, D. W. Winnicott, E. Galenson, and H. Roiphe, and others find their way into many clinicians' interventions.

The type of research carried out by these analysts pertains to the development of *the individual child* in the context of the parent–child relationship, particularly the mother–child relationship. In addition, the parent–child relationship itself had been explored by a number of other psychoanalytic researchers.

Sylvia Brody, Eleanor Pavenstedt, Selma Fraiberg, and Sally Provence are all pioneers in exploring within the context of depth-psychology the influences at play in parent–child relationships in families with young children. These psychoanalysts were among the first to conceptualize their findings in contexts that also have significant implications for prevention.

Brody (1956, 1970) was among the first psychoanalysts to study mother–infant interaction in the course of feeding, and to draw inferences from the different types of mothering and interaction between mother and child. In her studies she compared the impact of sufficiently gratifying to frustrating feeding experiences on the infant.

Pavenstedt (1973), in her studies of disadvantaged families, was among the first psychoanalysts to research and report on the ravages to emotional development by some of the consequences of being raised in a disadvantaged family.

Fraiberg's (1980) work, also with disadvantaged families, drew particular attention to how very early in life the experience within the mother–child relationship can have both beneficial as well as detrimental effects on the infant. She was a leading force in the development of infant psychiatry, and went so far as to formulate strategies for therapeutic intervention with infants.

Much influenced by and following on the work of Anna Freud, M. Senn, E. Kris, A. J. Solnit, and S. Ritvo, Provence, whose pioneering study of institutionalized children (Provence and Lipton 1962) has become a classic, more recently developed and reported (Provence and Naylor 1983) on a five-year study of her team's preventive interventions with families of young children. In a broad approach that provided pediatric, nursery, and individual psychological services to a number of families, Provence and Naylor found that these services yielded developments in these families, including mothers and their children, substantially more favorable than they were at the outset of their work or in comparison to norms of the population from which these families come. Furthermore, Provence was the first among us to develop a manual for daycare, *The Care of Infants in Groups*, based on psychoanalytic information (1967).

The focus of these psychoanalytic contributors is the interaction, the reciprocal influences at play in the parent–child relationship. In this sphere the work of Louis Sander has led to a microscopic exploration of the impact of maternal responsiveness on her infant, and that of the infant on the mother. Sander's (1962, 1964, 1980) focus on mother-infant interactive adaptation adds to our ability to propose interventional strategies that can further optimize the parent-child relationship, that cardinal vehicle for human development. We must also add work of Stanley Greenspan (1981, 1985) and that of Robert Emde, who has given us greater details of the child's affective development (Emde 1983). Both have also extended our understanding of development by their extensive research in mother-child interaction (Emde and Esterbrook 1985, Greenspan and Lieberman 1980), as well as by their theories on development (Emde 1988, Emde and Harmon 1984, Greenspan 1981). Also, Daniel Stern has microscopically explored aspects of mother-child play (1974) as well as emotional interaction and "affective attunement" (1985b). This work, as well as his recent conceptualizations of the development of self (Stern 1985a) have substantial implications for prevention.

A salutary phenomenon prevalent during the past two decades clarifies better still the way toward prevention by adding a valuable dimension to the work of psychoanalytic clinical researchers in the treatment of mental health. It is the greater appreciation of the reciprocal implications and value of the work of developmental psychologists, which has developed much more meaningfully during the last 25 years by such researchers as Gouin-Decarie (1965), Ainsworth and colleagues (1978), and others for psychoanalysis, and of psychoanalysis for developmental psychology. Although differences in their respective research methodologies prevail, these differences can bring value to each, where parochialism does not restrict creative problem solving and collaboration. Bridges are being built especially by researchers who bring backgrounds of psychoanalysis and developmental psychology to their studies. In addition to the large potential contributions to psychoanalysis by developmental psychologists, a handful of pediatricians, for example, B. Spock (also a psychoanalyst), J. Richmond, B. Brazelton, A. H. Parmelee, have added a wealth of psychoanalytically-relevant findings and concepts that have already begun to be put into play to an unprecedented level in psychoanalytic theorizing (Emde 1980, Greenspan 1979, 1981, Lichtenberg 1983, Stern 1985) and in clinical work.

Psychoanalysis, from its early decades, has provided a growing pool of information of which many professionals and even nonprofessionals have availed themselves for the purpose of securing healthier development in children (among them Fraiberg [1959] and Buxbaum [1970], and in Spock's several child care books). In this sense, psychoanalysis has already fulfilled to some extent Freud's vision of making meaningful contributions to the rearing of the next generation. The information gathered in the past several decades, complemented by that of developmental psychology, has become an enormous source of information from which strategies for prevention can be proposed.

The work of the foregoing psychoanalytic clinician-researchers has opened major avenues of intervention that are currently in the process of becoming established: (1) *secondary* prevention by means of early intervention therapy, that is, psychotherapy with infants and their parents; and (2) *primary* prevention by means of education for parenting and developmental guidance.

EARLY PSYCHOTHERAPEUTIC INTERVENTION STRATEGIES—INFANT PSYCHIATRY

Dynamic psychotherapies are almost totally indebted to psychoanalysis for their major features. Whether supportive therapy in which the understanding of ego functions, especially adaptive and defensive functions, is essential, or insight-gaining psychotherapies that rely heavily on understanding unconscious phenomena, psychodynamic principles and activity, ego functioning, and more, all, as I see them, are derivatives from psychoanalysis. Their contribution to secondary prevention, although disputed by a number of people, is much believed by those who practice dynamic psychotherapies every day.

However, nowhere can the contribution of a dynamic psychotherapy be more productive of secondary prevention, and even of primary prevention, than in the application of treatment to infants. Formalizing therapies for infants (and their parents) has opened the subspecialty of infant psychiatry.

What we have learned to date of human psychodynamics, human development, intrapsychic conflict, and the development of neurosis, as Freud foresaw, has opened our eyes to the possibility of intervening at or near the threshold of the emergence of neurosis and especially of more severe psychopathology, and gives us the opportunity to prevent its continuing unfolding, stabilization, and enhancing of symptom formations. The work of Anna Freud and her colleagues, Rene Spitz and his colleagues, Winnicott, Erikson, and Mahler and her colleagues has informed us of the beginnings of potential disturbance.

Pathogenesis, we find, emerges even earlier than had been conceptualized. Today's clinicians have learned from their own practices and researches that developmental miscarriages appear even within the first year of life. The range of disorders that can occur during the first three years of life is surprisingly large. It is this fact that has given rise to the subspecialty of infant psychiatry.

I have already enumerated a number of cardinal contributors to what ultimately is prevention by means of very early (infancy) intervention, but I want to note briefly here some of Selma Fraiberg's ideas regarding infant psychotherapies in order to emphasize the contribution this work makes to primary and secondary prevention.

In 1972 Fraiberg developed an interventional program for infants and their families. In 1981, with several colleagues, she reported on the significantly improved status of infants resulting from their therapeutic interventions with these children. Fraiberg (1980) eventually formulated psychodynamically oriented treatment modalities. These include (1) crisis intervention, (2) developmental guidance with supportive psychotherapy, and (3) infant–mother (parent) psychotherapy.

All infant psychotherapies are carried out jointly with infant *and* parent(s). "Infant" here means the child from birth to age 3 years. *Crisis intervention* is self-explanatory. It may suffice by itself, but it may also lead to one of the other two forms of psychotherapy. Developmental guidance with supportive psychotherapy combines classical supportive techniques for both infant and parent(s) with information regarding child development and child rearing issues imparted to parent(s). Infant–mother (parent) psychotherapy is the application of insight-gaining techniques that particularly address the parent–infant relationship, their interaction, and neurotic problems in the parent that directly influence the relationship. Fraiberg rightly emphasized the need to address the troublesome influence of "ghosts in the nursery" (1980).

New especially is Fraiberg's finding the more-than-anticipated value of judiciously bringing into the therapeutic milieu an element of education—imparting information—which in the usual dynamic psychotherapeutic setting we find objectionable and interfering. In our work we also have found it feasible to inform parents, in appropriate settings, of the growing pool of child development and rearing information. Essentially what I have in mind here is that within the context of psychotherapeutically intervening with parents and their young children from birth to age 3 years, a cardinal strategy included in both developmental guidance with supportive therapy and in infant–parent psychotherapy, is a degree of education for parenting that Fraiberg identified as "developmental guidance." The contribution of this strategy to prevention is abundant. Noteworthy is the fact that as early as 1946, Margaret Fries, cognizant of the difficulty and complexity of rearing children, recommended that parents have available to them developmental guidance in the rearing of their children from infancy through adolescence. Our own work tends to support this recommendation, although we do find that parents who get such guidance in their children's early years tend to find ways of applying what they have learned when their children are adolescents.

EDUCATION FOR PARENTING

In the course of our own psychoanalytic direct observational research (Parens 1979), we have learned the feasibility of bringing parents information that we have found to be highly pertinent to their parenting, toward rearing their children in growth-promoting ways (Parens et al. 1974, Parens 1988).

After a year's preparation, in 1970 we started a study that attempted to correlate specific aspects of the mother–child relationship (qualitative interactions) with the development of three specific ego functions in the child (Parens et al. 1970). We were soon impelled by unexpected findings into quite different areas of investigation, one of which was parenting.

This arose out of the fact that we found, beyond what we had expected, a wide range of difficulties already manifest in the infants we were observing during their earliest years and indeed, in some instances, in the early months of their lives. Finding a wide range of potential and already existing emotional and/or developmental problems, we discovered that we could intervene in a manner that seemed clinically helpful to the mothers and infants. Thus, we recognized as we proceeded that we had developed an interventional method, a method of educating parents that has as its principal aim the prevention of experience-derived emotional disorders in children, and the facilitation for the parent of the difficult job of parenting (Frank and Rowe 1981, 1986, Parens 1988, Parens et al. 1974).

We found that there is a great deal we mental health professionals know about child development and rearing that parents do not know. We also found that parents can learn much more of what we know than we had thought possible and that, in turn, we can teach them much more than we had realized. Issues that are at the center of the child psychiatrist's and child psychoanalyst's work are a daily concern to parents. We found that parents often grossly misunderstand what a child's emotional needs are, what thumbsucking is all about, what transitional objects do for children, what causes stranger and separation anxiety, what the separation–individuation process achieves. Many know nothing about the Oedipus complex, what it does *to* and *for* children, or how important it is to the development of adaptive functions, morality, social conduct, and the ability to form good love relationships.

Very briefly, the method we developed for teaching parenting (Parens 1988, Parens et al. 1974) consists of regular weekly one-and-a-half-hour meetings, in a reasonably comfortable setting, of five to ten mothers, their infants and preschool children, and one or two professionals knowledgeable about child development theory. We focus our attention on the child's behavior, with a view to talking about any issue pertinent to that behavior that the mother or child finds puzzling or troublesome. The approach is educational, not psychotherapeutic. Efforts are currently being made (Parens et al. 1986) to document changes in parenting function—toward growth-promoting parenting—arising out of parents' participation in such educational groups. As Provence and Naylor (1983) have reported, early interventional efforts, educational as well as psychotherapeutic, bring results we find clinically convincing, although rigorous research documentation of these findings to date has not yet been achieved.

At present, narrowing such education for parenting efforts to helping parents prevent the development of excessive hostility in their children is in progress. Formal methodologies to document changes are now being developed, look promising, and will be implemented by us when complete (Parens et al. 1986). This effort follows on prior work by Parens and colleagues (1982, Giacomo et al. 1985).

Education for Parenting for School-age Children

The mothers with whom we had the privilege of working opened our eyes to a further, unanticipated possibility. "If only I had known this with my first child," some would say as our efforts began to be useful to them. And we became intrigued with the possibility that perhaps we could help people know more before they become parents. Now, fifteen years later, we know it can be done.

In 1976 a team of three child psychiatrists (two were also child psychoanalysts), three social workers, and three schoolteachers began to work together to develop a curriculum on education for parenting from which we wanted to develop a graduated curriculum for teaching parenting to school-age children grades K through twelve. From those beginnings, at present, our original research group has gone in two directions.

Some of our teachers, spearheaded by Sara Scattergood, have developed an introductory curriculum for teaching parenting to school-age children which they have implemented in a number of private schools and in several of the Philadelphia as well as New York and Chicago Public Schools (Heath et al. 1986).[2]

Our mental health group has been somewhat slower in its progress. We have started to write an extensive source (text) book for teachers who, it is our hope, will eventually participate in a curriculum in parenting. In addition to the source book for teachers, we are also preparing class lesson plans because we have found that mental health professionals are more aware than other professionals of the emotional and mental health concerns parents have.

We have established the criteria our type of curriculum must meet in order to be capable of achieving the primary mental health prevention effort we intend for it.

1. It must have a large emotional element of parenting that addresses child development (for example, attachment theory, separation–individuation, infantile sexuality, and so forth); child rearing issues and methods such as "Am I holding my baby too much?," how to deal with setting limits, temper tantrums, infantile sexuality; as well as parenthood itself (one parent families, when the mother goes to the hospital, object loss, separation and divorce, work outside the home, vacations without the children, for example).

2. It must be for students in grades K through twelve. That elementary school-age children would be receptive to such materials was anticipated by us and was endorsed by Anna Freud (1978). This has been confirmed by our experiences in our pilot school (Germantown Friends School in Philadelphia) as well as by the work of Sara Scattergood and her collaborators. The curriculum we proposed should consist of a pyramid of thirteen grade level courses.

3. The curriculum we have in mind is a laboratory type curriculum. By this we mean that the children should be expected to make live observations as they do in biology, chemistry, and physics courses.

In a personal communication on this issue on October 18, 1978, Anna Freud encouraged our efforts: "I agree with you absolutely that psychoanalytic knowledge can be invaluable if brought to the public in this and other ways, and that at present not enough is done about this."

Let me add that we are not the only ones calling for education for parenting. Over the past twenty years there has been a vigorous call for

---

2. This curriculum is a highly creditable effort, and more than any other has opened the doors to education for parenting in primary and secondary education.

education for parenting from national level administrators in education. Stanley Kruger (1978), at that time from what was then HEW, called for an interdisciplinary effort in the development of education-for-parenting programs. He is well aware of what we have discovered, which is that mental health professionals—and I would say particularly psychoanalysts—know perhaps better than anyone else those ingredients of parenting that will promote better emotional health in children and adults. Our limited experience necessitates the caution that curricula developed by teachers without close collaboration with mental health professionals may lead to emphases that will not promote better mental health.

We believe that through formal efforts to help parents, as well as future parents, psychoanalysis can contribute enormously, as Freud anticipated, toward the rearing of our children in ways that will better secure their mental health by means of better growth-promoting parenting.

PSYCHOANALYSIS AS TREATMENT: SECONDARY PREVENTION

Research in clinical psychoanalysis with children and adolescents is sparse. Only the case study method applies, and such case studies are small in number.

Nonetheless, psychoanalysts who treat children and adolescents attest and assert that the secondary prevention in psychoanalytic treatment with children and adolescents is significant. It is a fundamental principle of psychoanalytic treatment of children (Anna Freud 1965) that the psychoanalysis of children should be undertaken where development is arrested because of neurotic process. Indeed, it was Anna Freud's view that psychoanalytic treatment should be undertaken when such arrest in development presents and that it should come to a conclusion when development has been put back on track. This basic view is enlarged upon by a number of psychoanalysts who venture into the psychoanalysis of children disturbed with more than neurosis, for example, borderline children. They maintain that certain pathological processes that lead to arrests in development and serious deviations in development can be undone only by a psychoanalytic process.

It is also commonly believed among psychoanalysts of children and adolescents that the psychoanalytic treatment of prelatency and latency age children can prevent serious if not disastrous consequences in certain neurotic and borderline children upon their entry into adolescence. In addition, a number of psychoanalysts have spoken of the difficulties inherent in carrying out the psychoanalysis of adolescents (Adatto 1958, Blos 1962, Anna Freud 1958, Kestenberg 1975). Although this view is generally accepted, such treatment (or therapy similar to psychoanalysis) is often warranted in the face of moderate to even severe neurotic conditions. Moses Laufer and Egle Laufer (1984) have recently spoken in favor of such analytic or analysis-near treatment even with well-selected quite disturbed (borderline) adolescents in the hope of preventing the stabilization of significant disturbance and the further breakdown to which it will most likely lead in adulthood.

This discussion of the efficacy of psychoanalytic treatment in reducing and possibly resolving severe disturbance is aimed to underscore the capability of psychoanalytic treatment to prevent, secondarily, the continuing influence of unresolved neurosis and the continuing ravages of more severe disturbance.

CONCLUSION

The contributions of psychoanalysis to prevention are already substantial. Freud's vision of what it can do for the betterment of society has, however, mostly been tested in the sphere of our clinical practices. That psychoanalytic principles can be employed in the rearing of the next generation has been applied only informally, on the initiative of individual writer–psychoanalysts (for example, Fraiberg, Spock, Buxbaum, L. Kaplan, Parens with Scattergood, Singletary, and Duff), and as parents have become better informed about the needs of children and about the consequences of conflict and of impoverished and overly hostile relatedness. However, utilization of psychoanalytic principles in this way has not yet received the formal applications the findings deserve.

Some of us are only on the threshold of attempting such preventive application more formally. Our limited experience over the past two decades suggests that such formal application is feasible and significantly promising. But much work remains to be done to develop the application methods, namely, by means of education for parenting curricula to which psychoanalysts would contribute—research of such applications, convincing of others that such applications are useful—these are all before us. It is this writer's experience and resulting conviction that much more needs to be done; that indeed, as Anna Freud said, "Not enough is being done about this" (1978).

REFERENCES

Adatto, C. P. (1958). Ego reintegration observed in analysis of late adolescents. *International Journal Psychoanalysis* 39:172–177.
Ainsworth, M. D. S., Blehar, M., Waters, E., et al. (1978). *Patterns of Attachment.* Hillsdale, NJ: Lawrence Erlbaum.
Alpert, A., Neubauer, P., and Weil, A. (1956). Unusual variations in drive endowment. *Psychiatric Study of Children* 11:125–163. New York: International Universities Press.
Basch, M. (1984). Response to Dr. Freedman. In *Psychoanalysis: The Vital Issues,* vol. 1, ed. J. Gedo and G. Pollock, pp. 39–52. New York: International Universities Press.
Basic Handbook of Child Psychiatry (1979). Vol. 4, section 1: prevention, ed. I. Berlin and L. Stone, pp. 3–312. New York: Basic Books.
Blos, P. (1962). *On Adolescence.* New York: The Free Press.
Bowlby, J. (1951). *Maternal Care and Mental Health.* Geneva: World Health Organization.
―――― (1960). Separation anxiety. *International Journal Psychoanalysis* 41:89–113.
Brody, S. (1956). *Patterns of Mothering.* New York: International Universities Press.
―――― (1970). *Anxiety and Ego Formation in Infancy.* New York: International Universities Press.
Buxbaum, E. (1970). *Troubled Children in a Troubled World.* New York: International Universities Press.
Emde, R. N. (1980). Toward a psychoanalytic theory of affects: II. Emerging models of emotional development in infancy. In *The Course of Life,* vol. 1, ed. S. I. Greenspan and G. H. Pollock, pp. 85–112. Bethesda, MD: National Institutes of Mental Health.
―――― (1983). The prerepresentational self and its affective core. In *Psychiatric Study of Children.* ed. 38:165–192. New Haven, CT: Yale University Press.
―――― (1988). Development terminable and interminable. *International Journal Psychoanalysis* 69:23–42.
Emde, R. N., and Easterbrook, M. A. (1985). Assessing emotional availability in early development. In *Early Identification of Child at Risk,* ed. W. K. Frakenberg, R. N. Emde, and J. Sullivan, pp. 79–101. New York: Plenum Press.
Emde, R. N., and Harmon, R. (1984). Entering a new era in the search for developmental continuities. In *Continuities and Discontinuities in Development,* ed. E. N. Emde and R. J. Harmon. New York: Plenum Press.
Fraiberg, S. (1959). *The Magic Years: Understanding and Handling the Problems of Early Childhood.* New York: Scribner's.
―――― (1977). *Every Child's Birthright: In Defense of Mothering.* New York: Basic Books.
―――― (1980). *Clinical Studies in Infant Mental Health.* New York: Basic Books.
Fraiberg, S., Lieberman, A. F., Pekarsky, J. H., et al. (1981). Treatment and outcome in an infant psychiatry program; part 2. *Journal of Preventive Psychiatry* 1:143–167.
Frank, E., and Rowe, D. (1981). Primary prevention: parent education, mother–infant groups in a general hospital setting. *Journal of Preventive Psychiatry* 1:169–178.
―――― (1986). Clinical interventions in parent–infant groups around issues related to separation–individuation. In *Infant Mental Health Journal,* vol. 7, pp. 214–224. Fall 1986.
Freud, A. (1965). *Normality and Pathology in Childhood: Assessment of Development.* New York: International Universities Press.
―――― (1978). Personal communication (letter), October, 18, 1978.
Freud, S. (1923). The ego and the id. *Standard Edition* 19:3–66.
―――― (1933). New introductory lectures on psycho-analysis. *Standard Edition* 22:3–182.
―――― (1940). An outline of psycho-analysis. *Standard Edition* 23:141–207.

Fries, M. (1946). The child's ego development and the training of adults in his environment. *Psychiatric Study of Children* 2:85–112. New York: International Universities Press.

Giacomo, L., Parens, H., and Rowe, D. (1985). The continued development and refinement of the excessive unpleasure hostility record (EUHR). Final report to the Fund for Psychoanalytic Research of the American Psychoanalytic Association.

Gouin-Decarie, T. (1965). *Intelligence and Affectivity in Early Childhood*. New York: International Universities Press.

Greenspan, S. (1979). *Intelligence and Adaptation: An Integration of Psychoanalytic and Piagetian Developmental Psychology. Psychological Issues*, Monograph 47/48. New York: International Universities Press.

─── (1981). *Psychopathology and Adaptation in Infancy and Early Childhood*. New York: International Universities Press.

Greenspan, S., and Greenspan, N. T. (1985). *First Feelings*. New York: Viking Press.

Greenspan, S., and Lieberman, A. F. (1980). Infants, mothers and their interaction: a quantitative clinical approach to developmental assessment. In *The Course of Life*, vol. 1, *Infancy and Early Childhood*, ed. S. I. Greenspan and G. H. Pollock, pp. 271–312. Bethesda, MD: National Institutes of Mental Health.

Harlow, H. (1960). Primary affectional patterns in primates. *American Journal of Orthopsychiatry* 30:676–684.

Harlow, H., and Zimmerman, R. R. (1959). Affectional responses in the infant monkey. *Science* 130:421–432.

Hartmann, H. (1952). The mutual influences in the development of the ego and the id. In *Essays on Ego Psychology*, pp. 155–181. New York: International Universities Press, 1964.

Heath, H., Scattergood, S., and Meyer, S. (1986). An introductory curriculum: *Learning about Parenting through Learning to Care* (unpublished manuscript).

Jacobson, E. (1964). *The Self and the Object World*. New York: International Universities Press.

Kestenberg, J. S. (1975). *Children and Parents—Psychoanalytic Studies in Development*. New York: Jason Aronson.

Kohut, H. (1971). *The Analysis of the Self*. New York: International Universities Press.

─── (1977). *The Restoration of the Self*. New York: International Universities Press.

Kruger, S. (1978). Education for Parenthood. Presented at the National Conference of Educators. Philadelphia, PA, November 1978.

Laufer, M. and Laufer M. E. (1984). *Adolescent Breakdown*. New Haven, CT: Yale University Press.

Lichtenberg, J. (1983). *Psychoanalysis and Infant Research*. Hillsdale, NJ: Analytic Press.

Liddell, H. S. (1958). A biological basis for psychopathology. In *Problems of Addiction and Habituation*, ed. P. H. Hoch, and J. Zubin, pp. 94–109, New York: Grune and Stratton.

Mahler, M. S., with Furer, M. (1968). *On Human Symbiosis and the Vicissitudes of Individuation*. New York: International Universities Press.

Mahler, M. S., Pine, F., and Bergman, A. (1975). *Symbiosis and Individuation: The Psychological Birth of the Child*. New York: Basic Books.

Parens, H. (1973). Aggression: A Reconsideration. *Journal American Psychiatric Association* 21:34–60.

─── (1979). *The Development of Aggression in Early Childhood*. New York: Jason Aronson.

─── (1984). Toward a reformulation of the theory of aggression and its implications for primary prevention. In *Psychoanalysis: The Vital Issues*, vol. 1, ed. J. E. Gedo and G. H. Pollock, pp. 87–114. New York: International Universities Press.

─── (1988). A psychoanalytic contribution toward rearing emotionally healthy children. In *New Concepts in Psychoanalytic Psychotheraphy*, ed. J. M. Ross and W. A. Meyers, pp. 120–138. Washington, DC: American Psychiatric Press.

_____ (1989a). Toward an epigenesis of aggression in early childhood. In *The Course of Life*, 2nd ed., ed. S. I. Greenspan and G. H. Pollock, pp. 689–721. New York: International Universities Press.

_____ (1989b). Toward a reformulation of the psychoanalytic theory of aggression. In *The Course of Life*, 2nd ed., ed. S. I. Greenspan and G. H. Pollock, pp. 643–687. New York: International Universities Press.

Parens, H., Giacomo L., and McLeer, S. V. (1982). Toward preventing the development of excessive hostility (Program, p. 20). Presented at the Research in Progress section at the meetings of The American Psychoanalytic Association. New York, December 18, 1982.

Parens, H., Pollock, L., and Prall, R. C. (1974). Film #3, *Prevention—Early Intervention Mother-Infant Groups*. Audio Visual Media section, Eastern Pennsylvania Psychiatric Institute, Philadelphia, PA.

Parens, H., Pollock, L., Stern, J., et al. (1976). On the girl's entry into the Oedipus complex. *Journal of American Psychiatry Association*. 24:79–107

Parens, H., Prall, R. C., and Scattergood, E. (1970). *The Early Child Development Program: Correlations of the "Libidinal Availability" of the Mother with the Development of Psychic Structure in the Child*. (Unpublished manuscript).

Parens, H., and Saul, L. J. (1971). *Dependence in Man*. New York: International Universities Press.

Parens, H., Scattergood, E., Singletary, W., et al. (1987). *Agression in Our Children: Coping With It Constructively*. Northvale, NJ: Jason Aronson.

Parens, H., Singletary, W., Barcan, D., et al. (1986). *The Evaluation of Parenting Activity Scale (EPA Scale): Growth-Promoting versus Growth-Disturbing* (unpublished manuscript).

Parens, H., Singletary, W., Skivone, L., et al. (1988). *Parents Coping with Their Children's Aggression Scale (PCA Scale): Growth-Promoting versus Growth-Disturbing* (unpublished manuscript).

Pavenstedt, E. (1973). *Intervention at Early Age in High Risk Families*. Final report. Bethesda, MD: National Institute of Mental Health.

Provence, S. (1967). *Guide for the Care of Infants in Groups*. New York: Child Welfare League of America, Inc.

Provence, S., and Lipton R. (1962). *Infants in Institutions*. New York: International Universities Press.

Provence, S., and Naylor, A. (1983), *Working with Disadvantaged Parents and Their Children*. New Haven, CT: Yale University Press.

Sander, L. (1962). Issues in early mother–infant interaction. *Journal of the American Academy of Child Psychiatry* 1:141–166.

_____ (1964). Adaptive relationships in early mother–child interaction. *Journal of the American Academy of Child Psychiatry* 3:231–264.

_____ (1980). Investigation of the infant and its caregiving environment as a biological system. In *The Course of Life: Psychoanalytic Contributions toward Understanding Personality Development*, vol. 1: *Infancy and Early Childhood*, ed. S. I. Greenspan and G. H. Pollock, pp. 177–201 Washington, DC: National Institutes of Mental Health.

Spitz, R. (1945). Hospitalism: an inquiry into the genesis of psychiatric conditions in early childhood. *Psychiatric Study of Children*. 1:53–74. New York: International Universities Press.

_____ (1946). Anaclitic depression: an inquiry into the genesis of psychiatric conditions in early childhood. *Psychiatric Study of Children*. 2:313–342. New York: International Universities Press.

_____ (1965). *The First Year of Life*. With W. G. Cobliner. New York: International Universities Press.

Stern, D. N. (1984). The goal and structure of mother-infant play. *Journal of the American Academy of Child Psychiatry* 13:402-421.
—— (1985a). *The Interpersonal World of the Infant.* New York: Basic Books.
—— (1985b). Affect attunement. In *Frontiers of Infant Psychiatry*, vol. 2 ed. J. Call, E. Galenson, and R. Tyson, pp. 3-14. New York: Basic Books.
Tolpin, M. (1980). Discussion of psychoanalytic developmental theories of the self: an integration by Morton Shane and Estelle Shane. In *Advances in Self Psychology*, ed. A. Goldberg, pp. 47-68. New York: International Universities Press.
Winnicott, D. W. (1965). *The Maturational Processes and the Facilitating Environment.* New York: International Universities Press.

10

Neurosis and Object Relations in Children and Adolescents

Leroy J. Byerly, M.D.

Anna Freud (1970), commenting on the state of the infantile neurosis, found it difficult to compare the original formulations with the current formulations. As she pointed out, the propositions on which the past and present formulations were based were "on different grounds and encompassed different concepts." Neurosis in children and adolescents was not a major part of early psychoanalysis. The infantile neurosis, the cornerstone of neurosis in both adults and children, was at that time of primary interest to early psychoanalysis only insofar as it extended their understanding of the adult neurosis. Little Hans and the Wolf Man are both regarded as outstanding examples from Freud's case studies of the infantile neurosis as it was then formulated (A. Freud 1970, Mahler 1975).

DEVELOPMENTAL CONSIDERATIONS

To appreciate the significant differences in our concepts of the infantile neurosis, we need only follow the evolution of the metapsychological points of view. In psychoanalysis, based on our metapsychology, it is our clinical assumption that in order to understand a psychic event completely, it is necessary to analyze it from six different points of view: the topographic, the dynamic, the genetic, the structural, the economic, and the adaptive (Greenson 1967, p. 21). Needless to say, the use of these points of view in actual practice results in a more fragmented and less optimal application than is implied. Nevertheless, from a theoretical stance, our metapsychological views are the minimal, basic assumptions that represent and are contained within psychoanalysis (Rappaport and Gill 1959).

The original formulations of the cases of Little Hans and the Wolf Man were based on only four metapsychological points of view: the topographical, the dynamic, and by implication, the genetic and the economic points of view. The advent of the structural point of view as a direct result of Freud's work (Freud 1923) produced a major reformulation of psychoanalytic concepts and the formulations of ego psychology that followed. A. Freud (1936) with her work, *The Ego and Mechanisms of Defense,* firmly established ego psychology, particularly in child analysis, as an integral part of psychoanalysis. Her subsequent work and that of her colleagues at the Hampstead Clinic, including the conceptualization of developmental lines (A. Freud 1963), has been invaluable in the progression from ego psychology to developmental formulations. It is not possible to enumerate at this time the indispensable and multiple contributions of both child and adult analysts that, in an explosive manner, have contributed to a continuing refinement of development. We are still attempting to integrate many of these discoveries into our psychoanalytic understanding. More in keeping with our subject of object relations, it is important to note that these discoveries and refinements lead inevitably to experiential consideration, that is, the ego's interaction with its constituted environment, both internal and external, and its resultant intrapsychic organization. This aspect of ego psychology and development was formulated by Hartmann (1939) as the adaptive point of view and it completed our metapsychology as we now utilize it.

The significance of our progression in ego psychology, development, and object relations, specifically for the infantile neurosis, is that we now have clearer operational definitions of psychoanalytic terms, a more integrated concept and more encompassing conceptualization of our clinical material. A notable illustration of this is found in Blum's (1974) reconstruction of the preoedipal period of the Wolf Man. Previously, our conceptualizations of the infantile neurosis were divided into oedipal and preoedipal stages. In actuality, further divisions were evident: Freud's autoerotic, phallic, and oedipal stages, a preobject and postobjectal stage as seen in Abraham's (1924) preambivalent, ambivalent, and postambivalent objects; and also, the concepts of narcissistic and neurotic transferences, which implied different levels of structural organization. All of these stages depend on libidinal development as the main criteria for psychic organization. Our present knowledge of developmental stages, reconstruction from adult analysis and direct observation of infants and children no longer makes it feasible to view the infantile neurosis in terms of preoedipal and oedipal issues (A. Freud 1970, Lester 1983). From this vantage point, that is, the extensive mapping of early infantile experiences (A. Freud 1970, p. 193), we can no longer primarily view the infantile neurosis from the Oedipus complex backwards but need to include a forward, unfolding view of the Oedipus complex as it is organized.

Ego psychology, as an aspect of development, forms the present basis for object relation theory. For this reason, it would be profitable to review some fundamental issues around development. The organization of the ego, in psychoanalytic theory, proposes a series of transformations that can be defined in terms of developmental stages. Most research workers in development assume that there are stages of organization or organizational levels of development. In part, these assumptions are based on the evidence of stages or levels of development determined by biological growth. The human organism is described as moving from a state of relative undifferentiatedness towards states of increased differentiation and hierarchial integration by Weiner and Kaplan (1964, pp. 4-8) in their organismic-holistic theory. The movement from an undifferentiated to states of higher organization is development as we have come to understand it. In the context of psychic structuring, particularly the formation of the ego, Hartman (1950) and many other theorists have expressed similar views. Developmental progress is defined operationally and in general terms as differentiation and integration, and in addition, as structure formation and functions. Fundamentally necessary to any formulation of object relation theory are two premises based on these developmental premises:

1. Continuity in development is determined by differentiation and integration; discontinuity is present in evolving or emerging structure formation and functions (Weiner and Kaplan 1964, pp. 7-8). Dynamically, this concept implies not only progression but, critical for normal development and for pathology, regression as well. Development becomes an interplay between progress and regression as well as between differentiation and integration and structure and function.
2. Development takes place in an interactional field. That is, the human organism grows within a particular milieu or *Umwelt*. This environment is described by Weiner and Kaplan (1964) as being "not only

reacted to and acted upon but is 'known' in the form of perceptualized and conceptualized objects" (p. 9) by the human organism. This clearly defines object relations in terms of self-object interaction.

Emde (1983), commenting on this interactional world of the infant, states that this is a new way of thinking. Previously, we tended to conceptualize the infant as having to adapt to a fixed reality. Further, we thought of the infant's adaptations in terms of drive reductionism and reflectology. Now, we speak more consistently in terms of mutuality and the mother-infant unit, in terms of an evolving inner and outer reality based on mother-infant interaction conditioned by the infant's endowment.

The manner in which we conceptualize development will directly influence our use of object relation theory to define both normal and pathological states. For example, Emde (1983, p. 173) proposes that affects emerge from an "affective core" and that affects provide for the continuity in development. That is, the continuing differentiation and integration of affects provides for a sense of continuity in human development. If his formulations on development are not viewed in a larger metapsychological way, we may be imposing an unrealistic limitation on development and may move away from drive theory. Instinctual drive differentiation and integration is also an essential part of continuity in development. We also need to keep in mind that emerging psychic structure and consequential functioning is accompanied intrinsically not only by dynamic features but energy redistribution and energy-related regulatory mechanisms. Our understanding then of object relations will be determined by the organizational groupings we give to developing structures, by the stages we choose to assign to emerging functions, and the emphasis we place on particular levels of integration.

CONSIDERATION OF OBJECT RELATIONS

It is out of the earliest tenets of psychoanalysis that object relations theory emerges. Freud's view of object relations was organized around drive theory. The object was defined as an intrapsychic mental representation, cathected with sexual and aggressive energy. The evolution of self-object differentiation is an intricate part of many of Freud's most significant discoveries. Object relation theory can be said to embrace the central concepts of psychoanalysis such as infantile sexuality, narcissism, identification, introjection, internalization, mourning and loss, and structure formation. It is because it embraces so many fundamental psychoanalytic concepts that it holds such importance for analysts. It is the assumption and fear of some analysts that the far-reaching implications of object relations will control the whole of psychoanalysis. There is a continuing debate, therefore, over the relevance of object relations, its contents and implications, and its significance for psychoanalysis. On an intermediate level, this debate centers around the significance of objects. More specifically, the issues in contention relate to the function of objects and their importance and implication for structure formation, ego psychology, and development. These issues move quickly into debates over internal and external reality, object need-satisfaction, object choice, and drive theory replacement. Buckley (1986), in his introduction to *Essential Papers on Object Relations*, contrasts Arlow's and Fairbairn's view as representative of the two polarities in object relation theory. Arlow's view is cast in terms of classical psychoanalysis where the object is seen as an intrapsychic representation that cannot be separated from the vicissitudes of the drives. Fairbairn's view at the opposite extreme holds that in reality the object becomes the controlling factor in determining psychic structure. The object and gratification are the primary aim of the libidinal drives. In essence, his postulation subjugates the pleasure principle to the reality principle. There is frequently an expressed concern among some analysts that object relation theory does lead imperceptibly to an overcommitment to the reality principle. In such instances, accusations of concepts becoming psychosocial are frequently raised, implying that the importance of intrapsychic concepts is lost.

When we consider the most elementary basis of the object relation debate, we discover that behind these current issues is a fundamental problem that has plagued psychoanalysis since its inception. That is the nature versus nurture argument first raised by Freud. The question posed is then not simply to what extent our experiences determine our psychic development, but also to what extent our constitutional endowment determines our experiences. It was at this junction that many of the most far-reaching contributions to object relations theory were made during the past generation. Much of the progress in object relations was due to the major interest in childhood psychosis at that time. It was in this area that the fundamental issues of nature versus nurture became critical in understanding the complexities of autism and symbiotic psychosis.

Briefly, these critical issues were also polarized by the work of Bender and Katan. Bender's biological orientation was in direct oposition to

Katan's earlier formulations. Beres' emphasis on "varying ego functions," in part, resolved this conflict. But it remained for Weil (1970) with her critical work on the basic core to bridge the gap between Bender and Beres. Weil (1970, p. 442) described the basic core as the interaction between the infant's "equipment and early experiential factors" that leads in a few weeks to the emergence of fundamental trends with which the infant enters the symbiotic phase. That is, the basic core will emerge as a result of the infant's "congenital equipment" (genetic heritage plus irreversible paranatal influences) and after a few weeks of infant–mother interaction. With the mother's attunement, the multiple variants seen in infants will become increasingly evident. The manifestations of individual variations in the basic core will partially determine not only the range of potential trends for normal personality development but also for pathology formation. General patterning and maturation of physiological functionings as well as tensions and anxiety potentials determine these variants. Different constellations of neurophysiological states impinge and interact with the infant's environment further unfolding the basic core. Weil's concepts, defined in terms of neurophysiological and experiential interactions, had a direct effect on our understanding of childhood psychosis. However, her work was equally significant in allowing the integration of Mahler's monumental work on early mother–child interaction (symbiosis and separation–individuation) with the concepts of biological vulnerability.

Between Arlow's view and Fairbairn's, there is a broad continuum of views regarding object relations that influences our present concept of childhood neurosis. Foremost among them, in a summary manner, are the following: E. Jacobson (1964), who carefully delineated the self and object representations of early introjects and clarified the development of these structures; Hartmann (1939), who described the autonomous structures of the ego and their relationship to the conflict-laden sphere of the ego, contributing to our understanding of structure formation; and Spitz (1965), whose work on the first year of life has become an indispensable part of object relations theory. Of particular importance is his work on the "organizers" of the ego, and his early work on the infant–mother matrix. Sandler and Rosenblatt's (1962) formulation on the representational world is utilized by many analysts in determining their concepts of object relations. Their work proposes the establishment of a "representational world" as the result of an ego function, and clarified the relation of the ego to self and object representations. Erikson's multiple contributions include the concept of ego identity which he described as occurring at critical stages of development. And finally, M. Klein's (1946) concept of splitting and its related stage of the paranoid-schizoid position have assumed a central role in both Kernberg's and Mahler's theories.

Kernberg's contributions to object relation theory have been determined by his interest in the borderline patient. His work with borderline patients led him to the conclusion that the differences between the neurotic and borderline patient is that in the borderline patient, the highest levels of superego and autonomous ego functions are missing. But he also concluded in these cases that "the persistence of nonmetabolized early introjections is the outcome of a pathological fixation of severely disturbed early object relation" (Kernberg 1976, p. 34). This fixation is intimately associated with the pathological mechanism of "splitting." He views splitting as a defensive mechanism that exists at earlier stages of structure development which is replaced by repression at later stages of structure development. Anxiety represents the basic motive for the defensive operations of the ego at all levels and is, therefore, the prime motivator for both splitting and repression. It is in connection with the organizing aspect of internalization that splitting occurs.

Kernberg (1976, p. 28) described three levels of internalization: introjection, identification and ego identity. He further describes these processes of internalization as containing (1) object image or object representation, (2) self-image or self-representation, and (3) drive derivatives or disposition to specific affective states. Introjection represents the most basic of primitive levels of internalization organization. Introjects with positive valences and those with negative valences are at first kept separated because of causal relations and the ego's inability to integrate them, but are later kept apart for defensive reasons. That is, the ego actively uses their separation for defensive purposes (Kernberg 1976, p. 35). It is the affective coloring that represents the active valence of an introject, and similar valence introjects fuse. Those introjects that are formed in response to a libidinal gratifying experience are organized as "the good internal object" while those experiences that take place under the negative valence of the aggressive drive derivatives are internalized as the "bad internal object" (Kernberg 1976, p. 37).

Loewald brings an interesting but different perspectus to our understanding of neurosis in terms of object relations. Ego development is viewed as a process of increasingly higher integration and differentiation of the psychic apparatus and does not stop at any given point except in neurosis and psychosis. Development is viewed as interactional (object relations) but intrapsychic processes dominate its progression. He stresses the importance of the concept of a continuing developmental process throughout the life cycle. In intrapsychic terms, the continuing differentiation of the unconscious provides continuing conscious mentation that leads to continued ego growth. In structural theory terms, his concepts are consistent with Schur's (M. Schur 1966) formulations of the organization and structuring of the id. In this manner, the id can then be viewed as ego in *statu nascende*. In Loewald's (1978) words, this continuing differentiation is responsible for giving one's life fluidity. Maturation and ego growth are achieved by repeated integration of experiences at *all* levels of mentation, an adaptive process we would recognize as related to sublimation (pp. 21-25).

Of all the intrapsychic mechanisms that are involved in object relation theory, none are more encompassing than internalization. It provides for an understanding of how interaction with an object can become an internal reality. In general terms, it is defined as "certain processes of transformation by which relationships and interactions between the individual psychic apparatus and its environment are changed into inner relationships and interactions within the psychic apparatus" (Loewald 1960, p. 262). Introjection and introjects, identification and identity are the major components of internalization. It is the structure-building capacity of internalization that we might briefly review in relationship to self-object differentiation.

In the early stages of development when introjection, primary identification, primary narcissism, and primary aggression (primary masochism, Loewald 1960, p. 265) are operative, they are immediately and directly taken into and utilized in forming the emerging ego and the antecedents of the superego. Characteristically, and as a requirement, this stage of development lacks boundaries to the extent that inside and outside reality are not discernible and self-objects have not differentiated. Primary identifications are not the result of relinquishing objects. Through a series of gradual transformations in self-object differentiation and similar drive differentiation, carefully described by Mahler, in the separation-individuation process secondary identification becomes an increasingly stable mechanism in the second to third year of life (rapprochement subphase). Secondary identification requires not only a relatively advanced self-object differentiation but also the capacity to libidinally and aggressively cathect an object. As is repeatedly evident throughout development, giving up the external objects and their internalization, as is the case in secondary identification, involves the process of separation (Loewald 1980, p. 258). The process of separation is similar in many ways to the mourning process and as such is frequently characterized by regressive tendencies, chaotic movement, and a disruption in intrapsychic equilibrium because of the ambivalent nature of human relationships. It is the giving up of the oedipal objects that leads to new structure formation: the superego, as the "heir to the oedipus complex."

Primary narcissism and primary aggression, once established, are followed by a process of externalization. When externalization has occurred, then reinternalization, a process increasingly important for structure formation, may occur. Reinternalization may result in the internalization of libidinal and aggressive drives that have been altered by their contact with the object. This is the mechanism that led to Freud's statement: "The shadow of the object fell upon the ego" (Loewald 1980, p. 265). Externalization will be critical in adolescent development. Both the superego and the ego-ideal have their primitive formation in primary narcissism although their development pathways are different. The superego becomes the agency of prohibition and the ego-ideal the agency of aspiration. The ego-ideal incorporates the desire to attain an omnipotent state of perfection characterized by parental omnipotence and undifferentiated primary narcissism, while the superego contains the internalized demands and expectations of the omnipotently perceived infantile objects. The formal stabilization of the ego-ideal will be the end point of adolescent development.

Loewald's concept formation differs from Mahler and Kernberg's in many regards, both in conceptual terms and in concept formation. However, his approach to psychoanalytic formulations, including the infantile neurosis, is not merely confined to a genetic point of view but is also in keeping with a developmental point of view. That is, his method of understanding the infantile neurosis is not merely retrospective, looking from the Oedipus complex backwards. (For a distinction between the genetic and developmental point of view, see Settlage et al. 1974).

A discussion on the development of narcissism in terms of object relations and its implication for pathological formation would not be complete without including a brief review of Kohut's controversial work regarding narcissistic disorders and the development of the self. Kohut, following Hartmann, defines narcissism as the cathexis of the self. Since he attempts to establish a metapsychology from his concepts, they are involved and not easily integrated into traditional analytic thinking. Kohut (1971) proposes: "[that] the equilibrium of primary narcissism is disturbed by the unavoidable shortcomings of maternal care, but the child replaces the previous perfection (a) by establishing a grandiose and exhibitional image of the self: the grandiose self (b) by giving over the previous perfection to an admired, omnipotent (transitional) self-object: the idealized parent imago" (p. 25).

The narcissistic disorders described by Kohut have their major areas of pathology in preoedipal conflicts of self-object differentiation. Objects are cathected with narcissistic and not object libido. Kohut terms internalization: transmuting internalization. The decathexis of object images and transmuting internalization results in structure formation. The "internal structure now performs the function which the object used to perform for the child" (p. 50). In his clinical approach to the problem of narcissism, Kohut speaks of the "therapeutic activation of the grandiose self and the therapeutic activation of the omnipotent object." The activation of the grandiose self in treatment leads to mirror transference, as the patient merges with the analyst as an extension of the self. The activation of the omnipotent object in treatment leads to the idealizing transference in terms of the patient's relationship with the analyst.

Kohut's theoretical position regarding the transitional self-object approached Winnicott's concept of the transitional object. Kohut (Grolnick 1986, p. 109) granted that archaic objects can be considered transitional, but he considered Winnicott's use of the concept of the transitional object a descriptive entity, in contrast to his own explanation of the phenomena as a metapsychological term (Kohut 1971, p. 33). It was Tolpin, one of Kohut's colleagues, who placed Winnicott's transitional object in the "mainstream of development" (Grolnick 1986, p. 109). Tolpin (1971) did not view the transitional object as fading away, but rather, by transmuting internalization, it became internalized as a self-comforting psychic structure.

Many analysts disagree with Kohut's definition of narcissism: "within my general outlook, [narcissism] is defined not by the target of the instinctual investments (that is, whether it is the subject himself or other people) but by the nature or quality of the instinctual charge" (Kohut 1971, p. 26). Kernberg (1976, p. 115) states that "the nature or quality" of an instinctual charge cannot exist without being related to the respective development of affects and internalized object relations. His position is that if we accept Hartmann's definition of narcissism, it cannot be treated as a drive, independent of internalized object relations or affect disposition. Loewald (1980, p. 350) had similar reservations regarding Kohut's conceptual attempts to relate the self to the id, ego, and superego. He felt there was a lack of clarity in dealing with the self as if it were an agency or constituent of the mind. Also, Kohut's preoccupation with archaic ego structures leads to the possible neglect of ego defenses. Kohut's contributions to object relation theory lies in his forcefully drawing our attention to narcissism as a central point in development and certain pathology, and in stressing self-identity in the formation of the Self.

CHILDHOOD NEUROSIS AND THE SEPARATION- INDIVIDUATION PROCESS

If we begin our exploration of childhood neurosis in a developmental rather than genetic sense, we can find no better guide in mapping the early stages of infancy and childhood than Mahler and her formulations of symbiosis, the separation–individuation process. Lester (1983) and others have regarded this process as "stages in object relations." Although separation–individuation depends upon object relations theory, it encompasses more basically the interrelation of self-object representation, drive development with their inherent conflicts, and with defenses, moods, narcissism, and identity formation (Harley and Weil 1971). In this regard, it is appropriate that I quote in full M. Harley and A. Weil's introductory remarks to Mahler's *Selected Papers* (1979):

> Mahler's intent was not to add new theory, as for example might be erroneously inferred from the phrase "object relation theory." To the contrary, and as she herself reminds us, commencing with the discovery of the infantile neurosis, psychoanalytic theory has encompassed both drives and object relations. Her ultimate aim was to integrate them into our existing body of development knowledge with their numerous variables. Her theoretical frame of reference was fundamentally and consistently psychoanalytical and, although her emphasis was on the ego and self-identity, she was ever aware of the reciprocal relationship between ego and drive development. [pp. xiv–xv]

Over the period of the first three years of life, Mahler delineated three phases of development—autism, symbiosis, and separation–individuation. The separation–individuation phase is further divided into four subphases: differentiation, practicing, rapprochement, and "on the way to object constancy." This last subphase represents the consolidation of the individuation process and is an open-ended subphase (Mahler 1967). Mahler's original concepts of the autistic phase have been challenged in terms of recent findings in infant research. Originally, in describing this phase, her concept embraced those of Freud's in terms of the presence of a "stimulus barrier" and Spitz's formulation of a "coenesthetic organization" of the infant. The stimulus barrier was understood as a barrier that protected the perceptual system of the infant in the first weeks of life from environmental stimuli, resulting in an autistic shell formed around the infant. Coenesthetic organization was Spitz's (1950) conceptualization of the manner in which the newborn infant senses rather than perceptually perceives and was also a mechanism that released inner tensions. Recent developmental research, with advanced techniques to measure infant responses, has shown that the infant at birth and during the first months of infancy responds to a wide range of external stimuli (Stern 1985; Lester 1983). The infant also demonstrates a higher degree of organization during this period than was previously understood. These new findings in infant research permit us a new view of the infant (Stern 1985, p. 4). In the midst of this revolution in infant research, Harley and Weil (1982, p. xiii) remind us of Mahler's basic position regarding the autistic stage of development. Mahler (1974, p. 94) stated that "the main task [of this period] is that with predominantly physiological mechanisms the homeostatic equilibrium of the organism be maintained under the changed post-partum condition." Harley and Weil (1982, p. xiii) suggest the term *quasi-autistic phase* for this period. This would be in agreement with many of Mahler's colleagues' concept of the autistic phase, which they regard as a relative term.

The symbiotic stage has been in many ways overshadowed by the separation–individuation process. Yet, it may well be a profoundly important period for our understanding of later psychopathology, particularly neurosis. It is at the height of symbiosis that the basic core (Weil 1970) is discernible. Recently, Weil (1985, p. 342) stated that "in some patients the significant failure of the symbiotic phase is paramount and the ensuing rapprochement difficulties and the later psychopathology are superimposed and intertwined." In this regard, she is speaking of "early neuronal enmeshing and encoding of the function of internalization and of the emerging self with aggressive drive components" (p. 342). Weil feels that this preponderance of aggressive drives, enhanced by a high potential or by early distress caused by a failure in the symbiotic phase may lead to an early deviational base with which neurotic development may amalgamate at a later stage of development (p. 343).

The symbiotic phase is a metaphorical term and this phase does not represent a true biological symbiosis. The infant's need for the mother is more absolute, while the mother's need for the child is more relative. Importantly, in terms of primary narcissism, this is the stage where the infant "begins to perceive need-satisfaction coming from a need-satisfying part object—albeit within the orbit of his omnipotent symbiotic dual unity with a mothering agency" (Mahler 1967, p. 80). This results in a growing awareness of a sense of separateness. Equally important for this phase is the rudimentary development of sense of identity (Kramer 1986, p. 163). Primary identity formation is the result of mutual cuing or mutual reflections, and especially mirroring. In many ways, it is the elementary sense of well being that is established for the infant in an optimal symbiotic experience. This sense of well being can be expressed in terms of a reserve of primary narcissism that lasts him throughout his life, or the establishment of "confident expectation" (Benedek) or basic trust (Erikson). For the infant, a less than optimal symbiotic phase can have far-reaching implications for pathological formation. Weil proposes that the failure of symbiosis is frequently evidenced by a "prevalence of organismic distress." The symptom picture that, in part, may be the result of a less than optimal symbiotic phase, according to Weil, includes the following conditions: attachment to pain, the masochistic character, the negative therapeutic reaction, and a basic depressive response and anhedonia.

The symbiotic stage ushers in the separation–individuation process. The first subphase is one of differentiation. The differentiation subphase is characterized by gradually maturing sensorium and appearance of the autonomous functions as the child increases its outward directed perceptual activity. Mahler terms this "hatching." The specific smile response and the appearance of stranger anxiety are evidence of increased formation of mental representations. Significantly, this is also the period to which Mahler ascribes defense formation in *statu nascende* (Mahler and McDevitt 1963).

Toward the end of this period and overlapping the early practicing phase, the transitional object and phenomena (Winnicott 1953) frequently appear. Although deceptively simple, the transitional object and phenomena are much too complex for us to explore in any depth. We should at least consider the basic origins from which they arise. Transitional objects are seen as early as age 4 months; most commonly, they are seen in the differentiation and early practicing subphases at a later time. Developmentally, they arise at a time when the infant is moving from a hallucinogenic, delusional state into a relatively more perceptually real world. In terms of boundaries, the infant is moving from an undifferentiated state to one in which boundaries are not clearly defined or formulated. Winnicott describes this as an intermediate area of experiencing to which both inner and external reality contribute. Two quotes from Winnicott are appropriate for continuing our consideration of object relations and neurosis. Winnicott (1953) described the transitional object and phenomena in terms of an intermediate area between inner and outer reality: "an area that is not challenged because no claim is made on its behalf except that it shall exist as a resting place for the individual engaged in the perpetual human task of keeping inner and outer reality separated yet related" (p. 256).

Winnicott supports the concept of extending the transitional object into other aspects of the developing child such as cognition. He writes: "I think there is a use for the root of symbolism in time, a term that describes the infant's journey from the purely subjective to objective: and it seems to me that the transitional object [piece of blanket, etc.] is what we see of this journey towards experiencing" (p. 256).

The most established position for the transitional object and phenomena in psychoanalytic thinking is its progression in development, as a "developmental line" (Grolnick 1986). A. Freud (1965) describes this progression as moving from the body to the toy, and from play to work. A more extensive and encompassing concept of the transitional object and phenomena is proposed by Rose (1978, 1980), who maintains that a transitional process exists and places emphasis on the interaction of the transitional object and phenomena through the life cycle (Grolnick 1986). From this vantage point, the transitional object and phenomena are involved with adaptation, creativity, and to a selected degree, with integration. Winnicott's speculation on the "perpetual human task of keeping inner and outer reality separate but related" speaks to such issues as boundary setting, aspects of continuing differentiation, and a particular form of internalization–externalization interchange. The concept of the potential space in the transitional object and phenomena as a resting place for the individual may speak more directly than we can formulate to such issues as integration, sublimation, and change of function. For example, it is not unusual in analysis to find that after a good piece of analytic work, the patient, in terms of his productions, goes into a resting period which we often view as an aspect of integration. In an intrapsychic manner, the patient may well be struggling with "differences and similarities" (characteristic features of the transitional phenomena as noted by Winnicott), that present no difficulties for the patient in his unconscious, but are not easily assimilated in his preconscious and conscious systems. This interplay between the unconscious and the preconscious will be presented later as another way to view transference. Finally, we should mention that the transitional object and phenomena are also used as a major formulation by many analysts in understanding the transference neurosis.

The practicing subphase (7–8 to 16 months of age) is generally considered in two parts: an early practicing period that can overlap the differentiation phase is characterized by physical separation from the mother by crawling, climbing, and righting himself while holding on; and the practicing period properly characterized by upright locomotion. In the early practicing subphase, Mahler (1972) cites three interrelated developmental contributions that characterize this period: "rapid body differentiation, the establishment of a specific bind with the mother, and the growth and functioning of the autonomous ego apparatus in close proximity to the mother" (p. 124). Patterns of exploring the environment at a physical distance from the mother becomes the key point of the practicing phase. The connection with the mother is maintained through distancing modalities, such as seeing and hearing her. The toddler's constant return to the mother is termed "emotional refueling" (Furer 1976). These new patterns of relating to the mother, according to Mahler (1972), "permits the infant to spill over his interest in the mother onto inanimate objects" (p. 124). One of these objects associated with mother becomes the transitional object.

In the practicing subphase proper, the toddler's increased autonomous functions, especially upright locomotion, result in the child engaging the world with a sense of elation. Mahler (1972) views the child's elation as the result of "the escape from absorption into the orbit of the mother" (p. 127). The continued experienced separation from the mother also leads to increased cognitive and intellectual development. In Piaget's sense, "object permanence" (the fourth sensorimotor stage) is achieved in terms of cognitive and perceptual development. According to Mahler, this is the period in development (the second year of life) in which true representational intelligence develops. Internalization (as defined by Hartmann) through ego identification begins and gradually, at a far distance, will lead to object constancy (Mahler 1967, p. 89). In identity concepts, this advancement leads to the first organized level of self-identity.

The development of moods also becomes an important aspect of the practicing phase. Periods of elation can be followed by low-keyed behavior when the toddler becomes aware of the absence of the mother. In low-keyed behavior, the toddler appears to withdraw from the world and turns his attention inward. This process of inward reflective behavior is termed "imaging" which Mahler (1972, p. 127) attributes to Rubinfine (1961). This special state appears to be "the child's effort to hold onto a state of mind" that Jaffe and Sandler (1965) have described as the "ideal state of self."

Mahler (1972) notes that "peek-a-boo games" at this time turn from passive to active—"the losing and then regaining the love object" (p. 127). The toddler plays with separation. Mahler attributes such behavior as turning the toddler's fear of engulfment from passive to active. A brief vignette from the early life of Chris may illustrate some of the material we have been discussing.

Chris's father was in analysis when over the course of three to four months, he reported the following course of events. Chris was his third child. At age 6 to 7 months, Chris developed a transitional object, a blanket with a satin border, in a usual manner. Chris would frequently collect "fuzzballs" from his blanket. After the initial excitement of his son's birth, the father showed limited interest in his development, being preoccupied with his own work. As a result of many factors in his personal life and in his analysis, he began "looking in" on Chris in the mornings, waking him up and spending time with him. He became aware of Chris' "fuzzballs," and began playing with them. This progressed to their mutually hiding the fuzzballs and finding them. Chris would awaken, wait in anticipation for his father to enter and "search him" for the fuzzballs. Gradually, over the months, Chris began "hiding" himself from his father behind his blanket in a later form of the peekaboo game. This morning play provided Chris and his father with much pleasure, excitement, and satisfaction.

In addition to the important formulations Mahler has given us in understanding the mastery aspect of the peekaboo game at this stage of development, I would like to consider some other factors. I have been particularly impressed with the manner in which infants and fathers become increasingly involved with each other in an engaging relationship at this time in development. There is a contagious atmosphere to the child's increasing mobility, autonomy, and creativity that in a sense seems to draw the father into position with the child. Abelin (1971, pp. 238–239) describes this early form of triangulation as the father being seen by the child as "the other," different, not the same as mother. He also points out the father's role in self-identity and self-constancy (Kramer 1986, p. 164). Chris's use of the transitional object, the potential space (Winnicott), to engage his father in their mutual play leads to further questions regarding the organizing capacity of the transitional object. Grolnick (1986, p. 111) informs us that Spitz, before he died, was working on a project dealing with "the transformational, organizing aspect of the transitional object."

During this phase a more usual form of early identificational patterns used in engaging the father stems from the child's earlier imitative and present actualizing behavior (Kernberg 1976, p. 31). Role definition becomes an increasingly important aspect of the child's development at this time. That is, the child "perceives and 'understands' the functions or role of the mother, etc." (Kernberg 1976, p. 30). Based on interpersonal interaction, these socially recognized functions become increasingly internalized. The child learns roles at first in a passive manner but increasingly in a more active manner that leads to his reenacting these roles. As the child approaches object constancy, these identification patterns stabilize. Kramer (1986) has reviewed this progress of identification through the separation–individuation phase in connection with a clinical case presentation.

In addition to the major implications these early identificational patterns have for ego identity, they can also serve in a reciprocal manner as an avenue for engaging the father in a functional way, providing a means for mutual interaction in the child's life.

Robert was the oldest child of an obsessive-compulsive father who was depressed. The father had many problems in getting up in the morning and facing the world. One of the compulsively related functions he shared with his son was teaching him to brush his teeth. At the age of 14 months, Robert's boisterous, exuberant attempts to engage his father in the morning and get him out of bed were met with indifference on the part of the father. Robert then "took to" appearing each morning in a subdued manner at his father's side of the bed holding two toothbrushes, his and his father's. His father would then dutifully get out of bed and they would brush their teeth together.

In the analysis of the prelatency child, in particular, play and the child's production (drawings and so forth) become the rough equivalents of free association in adult analysis. A frequent aspect of play is the playing out of roles, both on the child's part and in roles assigned by the child to the analyst. It is often possible through such play not only to draw out the child's fantasies and conflicts but also to reveal these early identificational patterns.

It is the rapprochement subphase that commands the most attention in terms of pathological development and future consequences for the formation of the infantile neurosis. Within the rapprochement phase, the rapprochement crisis, its failure or resolution, will influence subsequent development. The rapprochement phase borders the phallic oedipal phase in terms of psychosexual development. That is, the impact of the libidinal and aggressive drives are brought to the fore of development with the advent of toilet training. The force of the drives will continue to direct development until the resolution of the Oedipus complex binds them into a new structure.

Central to an understanding of the rapprochement crisis is the child's ambivalence and ambitendencies, the behavioral manifestations of his ambivalence. It is the child's increasing awareness of his separateness and his denial of separateness that leads to his ambivalence. The accompanying fears of the child are expressed in terms of his fear merging with the mother and a desire to merge with the mother; they are the component polarities in his ambivalent strivings. Mahler (1975, p. 191) describes the child at the height of his awareness of separateness in the rapprochement crisis as "employ[ing] all kinds of partly internalized, partly still outward acted-out coping mechanism in order to deny separateness." Despite such efforts, there is no effective way the child can reestablish the dual mother–child unit that was so important in shaping his world. Mahler (1975) describes the child's dilemma as: "he can no longer enforce her participation in his persisting delusion of parental omnipotence" (p. 191). It is at the crossroads of the rapprochement crisis that heightened separation anxiety dominates the mother–child conflict with coercive, dramatic fights with the mother. Excessive and persistent coercion, darting behavior, shadowing, and temper tantrums are usually regarded as signs of failure to negotiate the rapprochement subphase.

It is of interest to correlate the rapprochement crisis with specific genetic links to acting-out. Blos (1979, pp. 256–257) in a historical review draws our attention to Greenacre's (1950, p. 227) three predisposing factors to acting out:

1. a special emphasis on visual sensations producing a bent for dramatization.
2. a largely unconscious belief in the magic of actions.
3. a distortion in the relation of action of speech and verbalized thought. "This occurs in the second year of life and has to be understood in terms of a defective fusion in word usage of the thing denoted and the emotion associated with it."

Acting out as a resistance to remembering, a form of denial, is an established psychoanalytic concept. The rapprochement crisis may fundamentally contribute to the highly organized and structured mechanism of acting out. The action language of earlier stages of development continues to operate side by side with language development as a form of solving problems and communicating (Blos 1979, p. 257) both in the rapprochement phase and later forms of acting-out. In the phallic oedipal phase, an autoerotic component (phallic masturbation derivatives) will be added to this structured mechanism of acting-out. A distorted sense of reality is also a constituent part of acting-out. Lester (1983, p. 150) has postulated that the cognitive development of the child's sense of reality is a critical factor in resolving the rapprochement crisis. In this period of development, the child "does not simply discover the world around him but may now invent it" (p. 150). It is this form of reality distortion that is so prevalent in acting-out. According to Jacobson (1957, p. 91) acting-out is also associated with a bent for denial. Commenting on denial in the adolescent, Blos (1979, p. 259) relates that his need to deny his helplessness through action is also associated with his need to affirm his independence from the archaic omnipotent mother. The archaic omnipotent mother in this regard may not only be the phallic mother but also the mother of separation.

There is also a whirlpool effect of the three great anxieties of childhood that converge during the rapprochement period. Mahler (1975, p. 192) describes them as follows: the fear of losing the object and fear of losing the love of the object. Fear of losing the object is compensated for by internalizations but "complicated by the introjection of parental demands" and results in the formation of precursors of the superego. The fear of losing the love of the object indicates a "precarious unstable self-esteem," resulting from narcissistic vulnerability. Second, there is anxiety of body functions, particularly over urinary and bowel sensations during the toilet training period. And third, an earlier than usual anticipated discovery by some children of the anatomical sex differences with resultant castration anxiety and penis envy.

Both J. McDevitt and C. Settlage (1971) have examined the pathogenesis of the infantile neurosis in terms of the developmental aspects of anxiety. Clinical material is used to illustrate the preoedipal determinants of an infantile neurosis using the separation–individuation process. Their case studies present us with familiar, recognizable patterns of the antecedents of the infantile neurosis, patterns highlighted by Weil's previously described findings. McDevitt (1971, p. 221) quotes A. Freud (1965) as asserting that, "Children are more likely to fall victim to later neurotic disturbances if they are unable to tolerate even moderate amounts of anxiety" (p. 136). He traced his patient's anxiety reaction from early distress (colic) in her symbiotic phase, which led to an excess of aggression. Her aggression was poorly neutralized and insufficiently counteracted by libido (p. 211). This was followed by an external trauma (a maid being substituted for the mother) during her rapprochement subphase. Failure to resolve the ensuing rapprochement crisis was evident in separation problems manifested by sleep disturbances, shadowing, and excessive clinging to the mother. With her progression to the oedipal period, oedipal-generated death wishes were directed toward her mother; these wishes heightened her aggression which was coupled with penis envy and reached conflict proportions, contributing to symptom formation (p. 211). Settlage (1971) presents the case of a 2-year-old girl who did not show evidence of being in the oedipal stage of development. In outlining her analysis, Settlage presents rather convincing evidence of a reasonably well-organized symptom picture that did not appear transient and that contained neurotic elements as they are generally understood. He proposes a direct relationship between separation anxiety and castration anxieties in which he views separation anxiety as the result of the "earliest fears and anxieties" having to do with separation from the love object. These earliest fears and anxieties merge into castration fears or anxieties. And significantly, Settlage states that both these "categories of anxiety [separation and castration] antedate the development of the Oedipus complex which then provides a further basis for separation and castration fears" (p. 153). Based on his clinical observations, he raises the question of the existence of a preoedipal neurosis that resulted in conflict generated symptom formation.

Anxiety is one of the frequently encountered symptoms in childhood and adult neurosis. In describing the options available to a child who cannot tolerate even moderate amounts of anxiety, Anna Freud (1965, p. 165) lists the following potential neurotic solutions:

1. *The child may deny and repress all external and internal dangers that could possibly cause anxiety.* To which we might add that in the absence of adequately developed defenses of repression and its associated mechanisms, the child may use splitting and its associated mechanisms to deny the dangers causing anxiety.
2. *The child may project internal dangers onto the external world, which makes the world a dangerous and frightening place.* To which we might add that the most fundamental internal dangers which the child encounters are those related to separation issues, anxieties, and fears around the internal aspects of separating from the love object; and the interrelated viscissitudes of narcissism and the instinctual drives, particularly the aggressive drive.
3. *The child may retreat in a phobic manner from the anxiety-threatening situation.* To which we might add that the phobic situation can be viewed as presenting with an admixture of all three great anxieties of childhood—separation anxiety, which at this level of development implies a relatively high level of self-object differentiations; anxiety of bodily function; and castration anxiety resulting from earlier than anticipated discovery by the child of anatomical differences. In terms of conflict, it presupposes the presence of superego precursors from the "introjection of parental demands" (Mahler 1975, p. 192).

The degree of neurotic conflict (intrapsychic conflict) that can exist prior to the oedipal resolution and formal completion of psychic structure remains problematic for some analysts. Mahler has expressed the opinion that we have not fully appreciated the extent to which precursors of the superego can engage already existing psychic structures in conflict at this earlier stage of development.

Further pathological development of a neurotic nature, attributable to the rapprochement subphase, relates to depression. The concept that a basic mood is established during the separation-individuation process is described by Mahler (1966, p. 65). In her terms, depression is viewed as a basic affect reaction, as is anxiety. In depression, there appears to be a developmental procession of "habitual negative affective reactions," as established in the early mother-infant interaction and also in the later mother-child interaction that leads to "the depletion of confident expectation and diminution of self-esteem, with concomitant deficit in neutralized aggression [and] create[s] the libido-economic basis for the depressive mood" (Mahler 1966, pp. 74–75). Again, it is stressed that the proclivity to depression and the dynamic features of depression can occur "before superego precursors are consolidated into a superego structure" (Mahler 1966, p. 75).

In regard to pathological formations during the rapprochement subphase, we should also note that failure to resolve the rapprochement crisis has critical implications for the consolidation of defense formation and patterns of adaptation with resulting characterological pathology. Foremost among these are the narcissistic and borderline personalities. The neurotic symptoms of the narcissistic personality result from the excessive use of the defensive mechanism of splitting of the world into good and bad and excessive ambivalence. The borderline symptomatology that becomes evident in latency and adolescence arises from similar "islands of developmental failures" (Mahler 1975, p. 192) but with profound inability to successfully negotiate the rapprochement crisis.

From our review of the earlier stages of object relation as an intricate part of the separation-individuation process, that is, with the ending of the separation-individuation process as noted in its last phase (on the road to object constancy), we should be able to outline the preconditions necessary for the formation of the infantile neurosis which becomes evident with the resolution of the Oedipus complex. According to Mahler (1977, p. 196), they are the following:

1. Self-constancy, both individual entity and identity
2. Object-constancy which will facilitate triangular whole-object relations cathected with neutralized libido and aggression
3. An emerging and flexible narcissistic genital orientation in terms of psychosexual development
4. The assumption of repression as the major defensive mechanism with concomitant replacement of splitting as a defensive mechanism

We are now in a position to conclude that the complex developmental process of the rapprochement subphase undoubtedly will affect the manner in which the child will subsequently negotiate the oedipal crisis (Mahler 1975). That is, the "visible infantile neurosis may well be shaped by the rapprochement crisis *that precedes it*" (p. 193). The interrelated aspects of the rapprochement phase and the conflicts in the infantile neurosis can be traced in the analysis of Bobby.

Unresolved rapprochement issues in Bobby's development were intricately involved in his oedipal conflict. At the end of his third year, he was much involved in the anatomical differences of the sexes and with wandering around the house at night when everyone was asleep, which had primal scene implications. He would often take down from the cupboard a box of Cheerios cereal late at night, staring at the station signal of an off-the-air TV channel, while eating Cheerios. For this behavior, he was severely reprimanded by his mother, and this was part of an ensuing conflict that developed between them. The first dream he reported in analysis at age 5 was as follows: A "whole bunch of Cheerios" are rolling down a hill. Bobby is curled up as a Cheerio and rolling down the hill with them. A bad witch is following the Cheerios and eating them one at a time. She gets closer and closer to him and to eating him when he awakens in terror.

His mother's prohibition against his eating and wandering behavior (prohibition against his sexual drives) during the rapprochement subphase became an internalized aspect of the parental introject that had implications for his superego formation. Other desires for merger and fears of merger unresolved in the rapprochement crisis were expressed in terms of separation anxieties and fears. These separation fears were intermixed with his castration anxieties and conditioned his oedipal wishes.

These issues of separation are seen in his denial of his castration anxiety in the following incident, related by Bobby after visiting the Statue of Liberty and "crawling inside a woman." He is sitting at the back of his mother's mouth; he is very tiny; he plays with his mother's uvula. If he is not careful, he will slip down into her belly and stay there forever and never get born.

Bobby's mother suffered a profound depression during his first year of life that conditioned his symbiotic relationship. With the limited availability of the mother, his development was precocious in that he tended to initiate stimuli that would normally result from mother-child interaction. His propensity toward depressive moods and withdrawal behavior was evident early in development and became symptomatic. His depressive affect was one of the reasons he was referred by his school for treatment. The birth of his brother, his mother's return to work when he was 2 to 2 1/2 years old, and the more recent birth of his sister were traumatic events for him. His mother was employed as a secretary. During the analysis, in describing his mother's job, he called her a "separator." With his mother's return to work, he was frequently exposed to his father's problems with reasonable judgment. One example may serve to illustrate his father's general behavior and Bobby's exposure to early castration anxieties.

His father built beehives, and took up beekeeping as a hobby. He built the hives immediately adjacent to the walls of the house. The bees extended the hives into the walls of the house and all the children were exposed to repeated and unpredictable bee stings in the house. Toilet training was achieved with difficulty. Bobby's rapprochement subphase was characterized by sleeplessness, excessive wandering both at night and during the day, mixed with excessive clinging to his mother.

A transient phobia occurred in Bobby's analysis which was ushered in by analytic material indicating reemergence of toilet training fears and anxieties. For weeks, he had demanded that his mother not drive past a store called Heine's when coming to analysis. In one session, while eating a ripe plum, the seed fell out. His reaction was one of shock and horror. He withdrew, hid behind furniture, and would not communicate. He then refused to take off his rain boots. He slept in them and insisted he be allowed to bathe with them on. The resulting battle between him and his mother was reminiscent of similar behavior that occurred when he was 2 years old. In the analysis, acting-out behavior dominated his shift to motoric rather than verbal communication. He would unpredictably dart from the office and out into the street, anticipating my following him. The phobic systems resolved through a complicated series of interpretations that led Bobby to describe to me his fears and anxieties over a girl cousin who had her leg amputated because of cancer when he was 2 1/2 years old. Equally significant was his rage and anger over his mother not giving him "seeds" inside of himself with which to have babies. His understanding of his disillusion with the "mother of separation" was a critical point in his analysis and led to his increased understanding and coping with his castration anxieties.

We should consistently hold in mind that the Oedipus complex, "the key to the infantile neurosis," is not only a drive theory that contains the "apex of the libido theory" but, of equal importance, it is also an object relation theory (Mahler 1975, p. 190). The Oedipus complex establishes the boundaries of self-object, the optimal distance (Bouvet 1958) between the self and object world. For these reasons, the Oedipus complex can be considered as an organizer in Spitz's sense (Mahler 1975, Rangell 1972). It will not be until adolescence that we will see such a major organization of the drives and self-object relations.

The shift between a receding dyadic foundation (self-object relations) and the increasingly ascending triangular relations becomes the hallmark of the oedipal conflict, so much so that in our clinical work when we are aware of triangular material from the patient's production, we can assume that oedipal material is not far distant. With the resolution of the oedipal complex, its intensity is dissipated as superego formation binds the drives and self-esteem becomes more internally regulated. The incestuous struggle of the oedipal conflict is frequently transformed into more distant rescue fantasies.

Jonathan, an extremely sensitive child who was basically shy, had a difficult struggle with his oedipal wishes. Strongly attached to his mother, he sought all kinds of ways to maintain his closeness with her. Drive regression to anal and urethral fixation points was evident. In analysis, the sadomasochistic aspect of their relationship became clearer. In an obsessive-compulsive manner, he identified with his father and his sense of duty and responsibility. As his conflicts were slowly resolved, he established a close friendship with a neighborhood girl several months his senior. This relationship contained many of the neurotic elements we had been working with. The girl dominated him in a sadomasochistic manner. Jonathan seemed willing to pay any price to be close to her. During the summer before he ended treatment, he repeatedly played a game in which he was a fireman saving her from the treehouse which they pretended was on fire. Jonathan, in a frustrated, exasperated manner, finally came to grips with the problem. He decided he no longer needed to play with her. No matter how he saved her it was never right. He was either too early or too late, or he did not bring her out of the fire right. He just could not please her. In his words, he stated, "I'm just going to leave her burn."

Jonathan's ability to monitor his own behavior more clearly was dependent on the therapeutic process activating his development and facilitating the resolution of the Oedipus complex. In this regard, the increasing superego functioning was accompanied by a more stable differentiated self-object formation. That is, his ability to deal more competently with his castration fears was based, in part, on the resolution of his sadomasochistic relation to his mother; his ability to more definitively endure separateness with a resultant increase in individuation.

Intimately involved with the resolution of the Oedipus complex and the late oedipal phase is the progressive development of the ego. An important manifestation of this is the increased capacity of the ego to engage in synthetic activity (integrative function). This ego function is enhanced by the development of an observing ego, an organized aspect of the ego that increasingly monitors ego activity. According to Loewald (1957, p. 228), it is the child's arduous search and scrutiny during the oedipal period that results in an organized ego activity that, in part, forms the basis for the working alliance in the analytic situation. In the analytic situation, this is a special variety of object relationship based on previously obtained sublimated, aim-inhibited relationships as Greenson (1967, p. 207) notes. He divides the ego functions in this regard into a reasonable, observing ego and an experiencing ego (pp. 192-193). It is the capacity of the ego to retain contact with reality and still permit regression that makes the observing ego function so indispensible for the analytic situation.

It is not only the working alliance (the therapeutic alliance) that finds its origin in the infantile neurosis but also the transference neurosis. The infantile neurosis is the major pathology of the transference neurosis. (Tolpin 1970, p. 277). Although we generally separate the therapeutic alliance from the transference neurosis, Schowalter notes that the irrational side of the therapeutic alliance is difficult to separate from the transference (Kay 1978, p. 319). Furer (1976, pp. 184-188), utilizing separation-individuation theory, maintains that the early mother-child interaction becomes the foundation of the "non-transference neurosis" involving the analyst. Based on the concepts of empathy, he cites the developmental interaction of emotional refueling and the bridges established between mother and child in the practicing subphase as the model for the analysand-analyst interaction. Loewald (1978, p. 42) would also define a primordial or primary transference in terms of empathy based on a similar unitary libidinal field that involves an earlier mother-infant interaction. Transference proper, that is, transference on the basis of object libido, is established within the context of a transaction based on earlier mother-infant interactions. This transactional field is frequently described in terms of Winnicott's concept of potential space, where boundaries are once more not clearly defined, and serves as an explanation for some of the illusionary qualities of the transference neurosis.

There are two other levels of understanding the transference neurosis, the first, the Sandlers' (1978) concept of "role responsiveness." They remind us that transference is not limited to the distortions of the analyst but also relates to the patient's attempt to create a situation that would be a disguised repetition of an earlier experience or relationship. Perhaps the genetic forerunners of this form of transference may be found in the actualization or role modeling seen in the early identificational patterns of the practicing subphase. Second, Loewald (1978), closely following Freud's concept of the transference, draws our attention to transference as an "interplay of excitation between the unconscious and the preconscious." Both these views permit us to broaden our concepts on transference.

The whole question of transference in child analysis is extensive and controversial. At one time, it threatened the very existence of child analysis as a treatment modality. Gradually, these issues are being resolved. Again, object relations and ego psychology have contributed to this in a major way. A full discussion of these issues is beyond the scope of our topic. In brief, however, A. Freud's (1965) conceptualization of the analyst as a "new object, as an object of libidinal and aggressive transference, and as an object for externalization" has led to increasing refinement and definition of the analyst's role in the transference. For example, as a "new object the analyst may become the focus of evolving libidinal and aggressive phase-specific development that are not repetitions of early phenomena but essentially new levels of organization" (Sharfman 1978, p. 280). With increased clarification, it is generally agreed that capacity to form a transference neurosis increases with increasing levels of development conditioned by pathogenesis. The conditions generally assumed necessary for the capacity to form a transference relation are self-object differentiation, which implies a relative high level of object constancy, and the presence of secondary process thinking and reality testing. Settlage would add that a child needs to achieve some degree of ego autonomy to be able to withstand the lack of gratification of transference wishes. He also feels that superego structuralization is important not only in terms of binding the drives but also because of the internalization of parental values and standards, which permits increased distance from the parents but provides for displacement in the transference of these conflicted values (Sharfman 1978, pp. 283–84). Many of these conditions are fulfilled in the latency child and the intrapsychic structure of the latency child should permit the development of a transference neurosis.

When we speak of the infantile neurosis and its transformation into neurosis, we imply a normal developmental infantile neurosis and a more pathological neurosis. In childhood neurosis, pathological formation may progress uninterrupted from the infantile neurosis in *statu nascendi* so to speak, or it may burst forth in subsequential developmental phases, particularly in adolescence. We anticipate that during the latency period, the normal infantile neurosis will be resolved.

The developmental task of latency is the "step from the triangular oedipal situation into a community of peers" (A. Freud 1965, p. 154). The latency child faced with regression to the oedipal conflict and attempting to distance himself from that conflict, retreats to pregenital levels as a defense against these genital impulses. Every latency child must ward off incestuous fantasies and masturbatory temptations by partial regression. Masturbation becomes the repository of conflicts between pregenital and genital drives and ego derivatives. Reaction formation, the major defense of latency, develops as the "first character change in early latency" (Bornstein 1951, p. 280). It is reaction formation that gives the latency age child his characteristic obsessive-compulsive features. The two most common reaction formations, disgust and shame, are used in latency as defenses against oral and anal impulses and exhibitionism. They will be used to further devaluate the parents and permit the child to move to others as libidinal objects with whom to identify. Kramer (1986, p. 165) has noted the latency child's tendency to replace the father with superheroes whose abilities far exceed those of the now imperfect father. Of all the defenses of latency specifically related with sublimation and the neutralization of instinctual energy, identification retains most clearly the object's libidinal core (Peller 1956). It is through the increased identification, other than with the parents, around which the normal infantile neurosis is resolved. Following this pattern in late latency, the defenses of isolation, displacement, and reaction formation create an aura of obsessive-compulsive behavior. Equally significant, in a defensive manner, is the latency child's propensity for action. The latency child is action oriented. As Kaplan (1965) noted, "in latency the transition is from the unrepressed, freer affect to motor expression to the repressed, purposeful activities, such as the sedentary action of writing and reading, which utilize the new capacity of fine motor organization." Mahler (1949) has noted the ease with which the motor system in the latency child can be involved in neurotic formation, (i.e., "tics"). Acting-out assumes neurotic implications also in this age group. A. Freud (1968, pp. 105-106) designated latency as the developmental stage that separates the age-appropriateness of prelatency children's normal need for acting out, from the significant and therapeutic importance we attach to it during latency. Bornstein (1951), in her brilliant outline of latency, emphasizes that the latency child presents us with defense rather than impulses (Becker 1974, p. 4).

Mahler (Mahler et al. 1975) defines the developmental characteristics of separation–individuation as an intrapsychic process consisting of two intertwined developmental lines. It is the intrapsychic progression of the developmental lines of separation and individuation through the succeeding developmental stages beyond the first three years of life that results in the reverberations of separation–individuation throughout the life cycle (Kramer and Byerly 1978, pp. 211–212). That is, the separation–individuation process (the first three years of life) and the manner in which the mother–infant duality was resolved will continually influence subsequential developmental stages and will in a sense serve as a prototype for future self-object differentiation. The beginning of latency and adolescence can be considered as early stages that are predominantly organized around the intrapsychic consequences and resulting manifestations of the developmental line of separation. Intrapsychic discord, affectual upheavals, and drive regression with weakened ego states characterize these early stages. Separation anxiety is frequently present in a controlling way during these early stages, particularly with increased evidence of pathology. Weiner and Kaplan (1964) and Loewald (1978) divide developmental states into a similar grouping. They describe stages of development as beginning with regressive features, loosening of established gains and previous ties, and some degree of general chaos or disorientation. This, in turn, leads to a reorganization and developmental progression to a high state of differentiation, independence, and autonomy. These attributes are generally regarded as manifestations of the intrapsychic consequences of the developmental line of individuation that controls the later stages of latency and adolescence.

Latency, particularly in its pathological forms, is ushered in with a resurgency of separation anxiety. "Early animal phobias are replaced by a new wave of separation anxiety and open castration fear is substituted by fear of death" (Bornstein 1951, p. 231). With unresolved rapprochement crisis and oedipal issues, separation anxiety can become neurotically manifested around such symptoms as school phobias. As we have seen in the dyadic (mother–child) relationship, the child's disillusion with that relationship, its affective commitment, and its shared omnipotence have important implications of separation. The latency child's separation from the triadic situation produces similar consequences.

It is the heightened state of ambivalence that separates the early and late stages of latency. The child's ambivalence represents the intrapsychic state of disillusionment of the child with the parental aspect of the triadic relationship, the oedipal situation with resultant obsessive defenses. Bornstein (1951) states that this ambivalence is "experienced in the child's behavior by an alternation between obedience and rebellion (p. 280)." The resolution of the child's ambivalence and stabilizing of the psychic structures results in the child's capitulation towards individuation. Bornstein (1951) describes this accomplishment as the result of "the child's increased self-sufficiency and a shift from the belief in the omnipotence of his parents to a greater reliance on his peer group and on other adults" (p. 231).

In late latency, accompanying individuation, the defensive-adaptive patterns are composed of sublimation, neutralization, and related specific defenses. A relative state of equanimity then exists. The reason for this state, as noted previously, is the decreased dependency on oedipal objects through identification, which remains the libidinal core of sublimation and stabilization of the superego and its functions.

A. Freud (1958) states that disharmony in the psychic structure becomes the basic fact of adolescence (Esman 1975, p. 159). In her words, "the relation established between the forces of the ego and the id is destroyed, the painfully achieved psychic balance is upset, with the result that the inner conflicts between the two institutions blaze afresh" (p. 158). In fact, A. Freud questions the adolescent's capacity to form consistent and stable object relations and reminds us "that adolescent manifestations come close to symptom formation of the neurotic, psychotic or dissocial order which merge almost imperceptibly into borderline states" (p. 133). Peter Blos (1962) in *On Adolescence* has outlined the critical stages of adolescence development. These phases are described in terms of phase-specific conflict, a maturational task and a resolution leading to higher levels of differentiation (Blos 1967, p. 156).

In an overall manner, the developmental task of the adolescent is to disentangle (decathect) himself from his primary love objects. Once this has been achieved to a relative degree, he can proceed to investing in other objects. The progression is from increased narcissism to narcissistic object choices and autoerotic behavior. In late adolescence, structural stability is achieved through drive and ego reorganization and heterosexual object choice seeking begins. The final goal of the adolescent process is accomplished not through new structure formation but in a regrouping of the ego-ideal, which plays a major role in the formation of the self.

Esman (1975, p. 155), commenting on Blos's "second individuation," notes that central to his thoughts on the adolescent process is the "phenomenon of disengagement from the parents," and that Blos bases his "formulations on Mahler's fundamental studies on the separation–individuation" phase. Blos maintains strongly that in adolescence, "the danger to ego integrity does not derive alone from the strength of the pubertal drives, but comes in equal measure from the strength of the regressive pull. I came to the conclusion that the task of psychic restructuring by regression represents the most formidable psychic work of adolescence (p. 164)."

The major defense of adolescence is then defined as regression, that is, of both drive and ego forces for the singular purpose of engaging the infantile objects and disengaging (separating) from them. There is no other developmental stage where both ego and drive regression occur together, which makes adolescence not only a turbulent period but also a unique period in development. Regression allows the adolescent to reengage the infantile love objects intrapsychically. "The disengagement from the infantile object is always paralleled by ego maturity" (Blos 1967, p. 159). The establishing of nonincestuous love objects and a hierarchial rearrangement of ego interest and attitudes results in stabilization of the drives.

Returning to the earlier stages of adolescence, we can perhaps illustrate the adolescent process and the interrelated aspects of object relations and neurosis.

Steven, a 10-year-old boy, an artistically creative and athletic child, according to his mother "seemed to be just floundering." His passivity, lethargy, and physiological changes resulted in a constant struggle with his weight. Steven seemed to be "sliding" into adolescence. His close attachment to his best friend, a slender hyperactive child, led to defiance and rebellion toward his parents whenever they were together. He and his male friend explored the woods endlessly, discovering "all kinds of neat things." Specifically, such things included abandoned building sites, lost objects, and "places where you could easily get lost." In therapy, Steven related these activities to implied sexual exploration. Masturbation fantasies appeared centered around similar issues of a sadomasochistic nature. He related, with evidence of genital excitation, stories of exploring caves and mountains and becoming "snowblind" or losing a leg because of a "bad fall." At the height of these revelations, he developed a mouth tic—gapping, twisting movements with his mouth. Long and involved battles with his mother over the treatment of his sister, his room's appearance, and particularly over eating issues ensued. His mother reportedly tried everything. She increased his lessons in art and music and his social activities, former activities that engaged his interest but now did nothing for him.

Preadolescence as a transition into adolescence is a complicated period of development, filled with excitement and new worlds to explore. In some ways, it is reminiscent of the earlier practicing subphase of separation–individuation. As Steven's case material demonstrates, the intersection of physiological change and the beginning disengagement from the parents (regression) was manifestly visible. His defiance and provocativeness with an increase in sadomasochistic behavior toward his mother indicated the regressive quality of his pregenital drive (oral, anal, and phallic) pressure. Repeated battles over pregenital issues such as anality camouflaged and replaced oedipal encounters. The overt presence of a resurgency in castration anxiety pointed directly to oedipal issues that were being reengaged. Conflicts around passivity and activity reappeared. The resolution of passivity and activity in the phallic period contributed significantly to gender identity in the oedipal period. Now passive and active issues led to bisexual solutions and a narcissistic object choice in terms of his best friend. Masturbation increasingly became an apparent act. It served not only as the repository of past infantile and oedipal fantasies but as an integrative force. According to Bernstein (1974, p. 53), it enters into the formation of self-concepts, including body ego; it operates in fusing pregenital and genital and aggressive drives; and, it is involved in object choice and relations. Former means of optimal distancing that worked well in latency no longer worked. It was no longer possible to reduce infantile dependency by the use of identification and increased superego stability.

The case of Judy at age 14 years will illustrate the increasingly complicated issues of the adolescent process and object relation theory during midadolescence.

Judy was brought for treatment because of her learning problem—poor academic performance and behavioral problems. Psychological testing done for diagnostic purposes revealed the presence of "an old-fashioned neurosis" by which the examiner concluded that "she is one of the few individuals one sees whose 'learning problems' are due to emotional factors." Judy exploded into adolescence. It was as if her whole personality was transposed. From an empathetic child who delighted her parents, she began failing in school and became overtly interested in socializing. She entered into a phase of acting-out behavior that included returning home from parties intoxicated, being found upstairs in her bedroom with a boy who was a friend. She was engaged in a "death struggle" with her mother, as her mother described it. Judy was determined that she was not going to be "gay" like her older brother and sister, by which, she meant that she was not going to go through high school in a conservative manner and just study without having any fun. She repeatedly misjudged reality. For example, she had intended to invite a few friends to her home for a party when her parents were away. She "accidentally" told two boys on the football team and thirty or forty people came to her party. The police were called and the downstairs of her home was trashed.

Blos (1963, p. 273) states that the disengagement from the internalized infantile objects leaves the adolescent with a "profound sense of loss and isolation" resulting in severe ego impoverishment. Judy felt, in her words, "utterly abandoned" by her parents. Both her siblings were away at college. She felt alone and deserted because her parents spent increasing time with each other. Her father's usual but seductive behavior of walking into her room unannounced and talking to her made her frantic, despite the fact that she had always enjoyed being his favorite. Her mother did nothing. She found her mother "obnoxious." Her mother was "two-faced" and apparently did have a tendency to bend the truth in her own favor. Judy's reality was impaired by the externalization of her inner realities (a mirror image of her internal conflicts, threats, and comforts) (Blos 1963, p. 273). She easily made transient identifications and played roles (Blos 1979, p. 257). This led to a propensity to act-out, a special form of remembering. The disassembling of her superego, consistent with our understanding of adolescence, revealed increasingly primitive forms of early identification. Oedipal-incorporated standards and values of the parents were rejected. She showed intolerance for delaying gratification. At times, her ceaseless actions seemed aimless and lacked any goal directiveness. Her substitution of her group for her family caused great concern for her parents as did her apparent "object hunger" (Blos 1975, p. 179). The central task of reorganizing the superego and the mutuality of change in the other psychic structure was a formidable task for Judy.

It is the later part of adolescence that is involved with the complex problems of establishing a self-identity. This implies a continuity with the past extending into a tangible future and also implies a sense of continuity with the community's past extended into work accomplishment and role satisfaction (Erikson 1954, p. 53). It is primarily the problems around establishing the ego-ideal that determine the adolescent's transition into adulthood. In part, its resolution is due to the fact that "both the positive and negative oedipus complex come into play again at the termination of adolescence" (Blos 1975, p. 322). The ego-ideal, according to Blos, as it emerges from the end of adolescence, is the "heir to the negative oedipus complex." Its developmental progress is from primary narcissism to merger with maternal omnipotence to oedipal love for the father. It is the regulatory aspect of this component of the superego that is important in establishing a more realistic self-object concept, devoid of excessive self-object idealizations. As such, the ego-ideal becomes the agency of aspiration (Blos 1975, p. 322).

If the case of Judy illustrates an adolescent who made an overcommitment to reality and action to solve her problems, the case of Andrew demonstrates an overcommitment to excitation and affectual experiences to resolve his problems.

At 18½ years of age, Andrew's adolescent problems are representative of late adolescent development. The beginning of his adolescence was characterized by multiple features of the "uncanny" as a result of the regressive pull. Déjà vu experiences were common; there was a great interest in gothic horror stories, and other morbid anxiety states that signaled the return of repressed anxiety from earlier stages of development. In midadolescence, he was repeatedly involved in transient love affairs, wrote long and involved poems extolling the virtues of nature, and searched after absolutes, truth and beauty. An incident he reported is as follows: He was driving his mother and grandmother home. They were both seated in the back of the car. He became mesmerized by his mother's eyes which were framed in the rearview mirror. He entered into a reverie, drove aimlessly, became lost, until his mother intervened. He was aware of thoughts around his mother in a bathing suit that kept trying to emerge.

For some time, Andrew had actively renounced fantasy and was involved in being "more real." He had entered into a serious love affair and was intimately involved with a girl. The above incident was centered around his attempts to compare his girlfriend with his mother libidinally. As Ritvo (1972, p. 247) stated, "In later adolescence when the realistic relationship with the new object is taken up, the individual has to cope with the revival of the libidinal cathexes of the old object as they appear now in the context of the realistic relationship." Andrew's association led to a revival of oedipal and preoedipal material as ties to the infantile objects were continually relinquished. He recalled, with marked affectual responses, his mother and father in their upstairs sitting room having cocktails. His mother is modeling clothing (a bathing suit [?]) for his father. He is sent to his room, and punished, he believes, for masturbating. The bathing suit reminds him of pregenital attachments, and of warm, intimate moments with his mother around being dressed, particularly in the warm relaxed setting of summer.

Andrew became more dedicated to early established ideals around his father. His father, an aviator in World War II, was a formidable hero for him as a young child. Passing through a phase of fantasizing that he and his father were adolescents and friends together, he increasingly identified with his father's "sense of duty and responsibility" and with his father's accomplishments in this world. For Andrew this represented a different solution to his oedipal problems of continued animosity between him and his father. As in the latency child's advancement into his community of peers, the adolescent steps into his community of working peers, into a work-oriented world, bolstered by his aspirations and dreams.

In conclusion, we would again underscore the interaction of the developmental lines of separation and individuation. Blos noted that the ego and the id develop optimally when they progress in concert and are not too distant from each other. The same principle applies to the reciprocal relationship of separation and individuation. Their developmental advancement is most effective when they progress in a more or less mutual manner and are not too distant from each other.

The reverberations of separation–individuation do not end with adolescence but continue throughout the life cycle. The mature adult's commitment to "love and work" (Freud) guarantees the further involvement of object relation, drive progression, and narcissism. Separation–individuation, predicated on the experiences of the first human relationship, will be interrelated with Erickson's concept of generativity, with changes in values and with self-concept in response to physiological and developmental changes of later life. Datan and Thomas (1984, p.

224) summarize these life-cycle transformations in terms of "attachment to others, activity, and the sense of self." The developmental task of distancing ourselves from the basic dyadic relationship of life (mother–infant) at best remains incomplete, and profoundly influences our adult life as it did our childhood and adolescence.

REFERENCES

Abelin, S. (1971). The role of the father in the separation–individuation process. In *Separation–Individuation*, ed. J. McDevitt and C. Settlage, pp. 229–252. New York: International Universities Press.

Abraham, K. (1924). A short study of the development of the libido. In *Selected Papers on Psycho-Analysis*, pp. 418–501. London: Hogarth Press.

Arlow, J. A. (1980). Object concept and object choice. *Psychoanalytic Quarterly* 59:109–133.

Bender, L. (1947). Childhood schizophrenia. *American Journal of Orthopsychiatry* 7:40–56.

Benedek, T. (1938). Adaptation to reality in early infancy. *Psychoanalytic Quarterly* 7:200–214.

Beres, D. (1956). Ego deviation and the concept of schizophrenia. *Psychoanalytic Study of the Child* 11:164–233. New York: International Universities Press.

Blos, P. (1962). *On Adolescence: A Psychoanalytic Interpretation*. New York: International Universities Press.

—— (1963). The concept of acting out in relation to the adolescent process. *Journal of the American Academy of Child Psychiatry* 2:118–136. Reprinted in *The Psychology of Adolescence*, ed. A. Essman, pp. 267–283. New York: International Universities Press.

—— (1967). The second individuation process of adolescence. *Psychoanalytic Study of the Child* 22:112–186. New York: International Universities Press. Reprinted in *The Psychology of Adolescence*, ed. A. Essman, pp. 156–176. New York: International Universities Press, 1975.

—— (1979). *The Adolescent Passage, Developmental Issues*. New York: International Universities Press.

Blum, H. (1974). The borderline childhood of the Wolf-Man. *Journal of the American Psychoanalytic Association* 22:271–742.

Bornstein, B. (1951). On latency. *Psychoanalytic Study of the Child* 3/4:181–226. New York: International Universities Press.

Bouvet, M. (1958). Technical variation and the concept of distance. *International Journal of Psychoanalysis* 39:211–221.

Buckley, P. (1986). Introduction. In *Essential Papers on Object Relations*, ed. P. Buckley, pp. xi–xxv. New York: International Universities Press.

Datan, N., and Thomas, J. (1984). Late adulthood: love, work and the normal traditions. In *Normality and The Life Cycle: A Critical Integration*, ed. D. Offer and M. Sabshin, pp. 204–229. New York: Basic Books.

Emde, R. (1983). The pre-representational self and its affective core. *Psychoanalytic Study of the Child* 38:105–192. New Haven, CT: Yale University Press.

Erikson, E. (1954). The dream specimen of psychoanalysis. *Journal of the American Psychoanalytic Association* 2:5–56.

—— (1956). The problem of ego identity. *Journal of the American Psychoanalytic Association* 4:56–121

_____ (1959). Identity and the life cycle. *Psychological Issues*, Monograph 1. New York: International Universities Press.
Essman, H. (1975). Introduction. In *The Psychology of Adolescence*, ed. A. Essman, pp. ix-x. New York: International Universities Press.
Fairbairn, W. A. (1952). *Psychoanalytic Studies of the Personality*. London: Tavistock Publications.
Freud, A. (1936). *The Ego and the Mechanisms of Defense*. New York: International Universities Press, 1946.
_____ (1958). Adolescence. *Psychoanalytic Study of the Child* 13:255-278. New York: International Universities Press.
_____ (1963). The concepts of developmental lines. *Psychoanalytic Study of the Child* 18:245-256. New York: International Universities Press.
_____ (1965). *Normality and Pathology in Childhood:* New York: International Universities Press.
_____ (1968). Acting-out. In *The Writings of Anna Freud*, 17:94-109. New York: International Universities Press.
_____ (1970). The infantile neurosis, genetic and dynamic considerations. In *The Writings of Anna Freud* (1966-1970), pp. 189-199. New York: International Universities Press, 1971.
Freud, S. (1923). The ego and the id. *Standard Edition* 19:22-66.
Furer, M. (1976). Panel: current concepts of the psychoanalytic process, reporter, S. Morgenstern. *Journal of the American Psychoanalytic Association* 24:184-188.
Greenacre, P. (1950). General problems of acting out. In *Trauma, Growth and Personality*, pp. 224-236. New York: International Universities Press, 1969.
Greenson, R. (1967). *The Technique and Practice of Psychoanalysis*. New York: International Universities Press.
Grolnick, S. (1986). The relationship of Winnicott's developmental concepts of the transitional object to self and object constancy. In *Self and Object Constancy*, ed. R. Lax and A. Burland, pp. 107-134. New York: Guilford Press.
Harley, M., and Weil, A. (1979). Introduction. In *Selected Papers of Margaret J. Mahler*, pp. ix-xx. New York: Jason Aronson.
Hartmann, H. (1939). *Ego Psychology and The Problem of Adaptation*. New York: International Universities Press.
_____ (1950). Comments on the psychoanalytic theory of the ego. In *Essays on Ego Psychology*, pp. 113-141. London: Hogarth, 1964.
Jacobson, E. (1957). Denial and repression. *Journal of the American Psychoanalytic Association* 5:61-92.
_____ (1964). *The Self and the Object World*. New York: International Universities Press.
Kay, P. (1978). Gifts, gratification and frustrations in child analysis. In *Child Analysis and Therapy*, ed. J. Glenn, p. 319. New York: Jason Aronson.
Kaplan, E. B. (1965). Reflections regarding psychomotor activities during the latency period. *Psychoanalytic Study of the Child* 20:222-238. New York: International Universities Press.
Katan, M. (1950). Structural aspects of a case of schizophrenia. *Psychoanalytic Study of the Child* 5:175-211.
Klein, M. (1946). Notes on some schizoid mechanisms. In *Developments in Psychoanalysis*. ed. M. Klein, P. Herman, S. Isaacs, and J. Reviere, pp. 292-320. London: Hogarth, 1952.
Kohut, H. (1971). *The Analysis of the Self: A Systematic Approach to Psychoanalytic Treatment*

of Narcissistic Personality Disorders. New York: International Universities Press.
Kramer, S., and Byerly, L. (1978). Technique of psychoanalysis of the latency child. In *Child Analysis and Therapy,* ed. J. Glenn, pp. 205-233. New York: Jason Aronson.
Kramer, S. (1986). Identification and its vicissitudes as observed in children: a developmental approach. *International Journal of Psychoanalysis* 67:161-171.
Lester, S. (1983). Separation and cognition. *Journal of the American Psychoanalytic Association,* 31:127-155. New York: International Universities Press.
Loewald, H. (1957). On the therapeutic action of psychoanalysis. In *Papers on Psychoanalysis,* pp. 221-256. New Haven: Yale University Press, 1980.
—— (1960). Internalization, separation, mourning and the superego. In *Papers on Psychoanalysis,* pp. 257-276. New Haven: Yale University Press. 1980.
—— (1971). Book review: Heinz Kohut: *The Analysis of the Self.* In *Papers on Psychoanalysis,* ed. H. Loewald, pp. 342-351. New Haven, CT: Yale University Press, 1980.
—— (1978). *Psychoanalysis and the History of the Individual.* The Freud Lectures at Yale University. New Haven, CT: Yale University Press.
—— (1980). *Papers on Psychoanalysis.* New Haven, CT: Yale University Press.
Mahler, M. (1945). Child analysis. In *Modern Trends in Child Psychiatry,* ed. N. Lewis and B. Pacella, pp. 265-289. New York: International Universities Press.
—— (1949). A psychoanalytic evaluation of tics: a sign and a symptom in psychopathology of childhood symptomatics, tics and the tics syndrome. *Psychoanalytic Study of the Child* 3/4:279-310. New York: International Universities Press.
—— (1963). Certain aspects of separation-individuation phase. In *The Selected Papers of Margaret S. Mahler* 2:22-24. New York: Jason Aronson, 1979.
—— (1966). Notes on the development of basic moods: the depressive affect. In *The Selected Papers of Margaret S. Mahler* 2:59-76. New York: Jason Aronson, 1979.
—— (1967). On human symbiosis and the vicissitudes of individuation. In *The Selected Papers of Margaret S. Mahler* 2:77-98. New York: Jason Aronson, 1979.
—— (1971). A study of the separation-individuation process and its possible application to borderline phenomena in the psychoanalytic situation. In *The Selected Papers of Margaret S. Mahler* 2:169-187. New York: Jason Aronson, 1979.
—— (1972). On the first three subphases of the separation-individuation process. In *The Selected Papers of Margaret S. Mahler* 2:119-130. New York: Jason Aronson, 1979.
—— (1974). Symbiosis and individuation: the psychological birth of the human infant. In *The Selected Papers of Margaret S. Mahler* 2:149-168. New York: Jason Aronson, 1979.
—— (1975). On the current status of the infantile neurosis. In *The Selected Papers of Margaret S. Mahler* 2:189-193. New York: Jason Aronson, 1979.
—— (1977). Developmental aspects in the assessment of narcissistic and so-called borderline personalities. In *The Selected Papers of Margaret S. Mahler* 2:196-206. New York: Jason Aronson, 1979.
Mahler, M., and McDevitt, J. (1968). Observations on adaptation and defense in *statu nascendi:* developmental precursors in the first two years of life. *Psychoanalytic Quarterly* 37:1-21.
McDevitt, J. (1971). Pre-oedipal determinants in an infantile neurosis. In *Separation-Individuation,* ed. J. McDevitt and C. Settlage, pp. 201-228. New York: International Universities Press.
Ogden, T. (1986). *The Matrix of the Mind, Objection and the Psychoanalytic Dialogue.* Northvale NJ: Jason Aronson, p. 203.
Peller, L. (1956). The school's role in promoting sublimation. *Psychoanalytic Study of the Child* 11:437-449. New York: International Universities Press.

Rangell, L. (1972). Aggression, Oedipus and historical perspectus. *International Journal of Psychoanalysis* 53:3-11.
Rappaport, D., and Gill, M. (1959). The points of view and assumption of metapsychology. *International Journal of the Psychoanalytic Association* 40:153-162.
Ritvo, S. (1972). Late adolescence: development and clinical considerations. *Psychoanalytic Study of the Child* 26:241-263. New Haven, CT: Yale University Press.
Rose, G. (1978). The creativity of everyday life. In *Between Reality and Fantasy: Transitions, Objects and Phenomena,* ed. S. Grolnick and L. Barkin, pp. 345-362. New York: Jason Aronson.
─── (1980). *The Power of Form: A Psychoanalytic Approach to Aesthetic Form.* New York: International Universities Press.
Rubinfine, D. (1961). Perception, reality testing and symbolism. *Psychoanalytic Study of the Child* 16:131-142. New York: International Universities Press.
Sandler, J., and Rosenblatt, B. (1962). The concept of the representational world. *Psychoanalytic Study of the Child* 17:128-145. New York: International Universities Press.
Sandler, J., and Sandler, M. (1978). On the development of object relationships and affects. *International Journal of Psycho-Analysis* 59:285-296.
Scharfman, M. (1978). Transference and the transference neurosis in child analysis. In *Child Analysis and Therapy,* ed. J. Glenn, pp. 256-309. New York: International Universities Press.
Schur, M. (1966). *The Id and the Regulatory Principles of Mental Functioning.* New York: International Universities Press.
Settlage, C. (1971). Aspects of early psychic development and the genesis of infantile neurosis. In *Separation-Individuation,* ed. J. McDevitt and C. Settlage, pp. 131-156. New York: International Universities Press.
Spitz, R. (1950). Anxiety in infancy: a study of its manifestation in the first year of life. *International Journal of Psychoanalysis.* 31:138-148.
Stern, D. (1985). *The Interpersonal World of the Infant: A View from Psychoanalysis and Developmental Psychology.* New York: Basic Books.
Tolpin, M. (1970). The infantile neurosis: a metapsychological concept and a paradigmatic case history. *Psychoanalytic Study of the Child* 25:273-308. New York: International Universities Press.
Tolpin, M. (1971). On the beginning of a cohesive self: an application of the concept of transmuting internalization to the study of the transitional object and signal anxiety. *Psychoanalytic Study of the Child* 26:316-352. New Haven, CT: Yale University Press.
Weil, A. (1970). The basic core. *Psychoanalytic Study of the Child* 25:422-460. New York: International Universities Press.
─── (1985). Thoughts on early pathology. *Journal of the American Psychoanalytic Association* 33:335-352.
Weiner, K., and Kaplan B. (1964). *Symbol Formation: An Organismic Developmental Approach to Language and the Expression of Thought.* New York: Wiley.
Winnicott, D. (1953). Transitional object and transitional phenomena: a study of the first not-me possessions. In *Essential Papers,* ed. P. Buckley, pp. 254-271. New York: New York University Press, 1986.

11

Parent–Child Dimension of Development and Neurosogenesis

G. Pirooz Sholevar, M.D.

Ego development and psychic structure formation are deeply rooted in the early relationship with parents. Favorable early childhood experiences lead to tolerance of frustration, promotion of ego structuralization, self-object differentiation, and provide the necessary grounds for subsequent oedipal and triadic object relations. Inadequate early experiences and disturbed object relations can interfere with ego development and lead to pathological psychic formations.

The parental personality can act as a prominent factor in the enhancement of ego development, and parental psychopathology can play a decisive role in the genesis and continuation of childhood neurosis and more severe emotional disorders. The presence of the right "fit" between the parent and child can reinforce the equipmental disposition of the child, enhancing ego development and adaptation. A poorly matched parent/child combination can interfere with multiple aspects of ego development and the identification process.

The infant's earliest gratification–frustration experiences with the mother play an important part in stimulating perception and promoting the process of differentiation of the infant's self from the object world (Jacobson 1954). Kris (1953) emphasized that equipmental factors in the child are important in determining what constitutes frustration for a particular child with a particular mother. In the early experience, the child's equipment plays as significant a role as the maternal care in initiating mother–child interaction.

The earliest frustration-gratification experiences of the infant leave their characteristics on the process by which psychic representations of the object are formed. The firm establishment of early object representations plays an essential part in the process of identification. The earlier experiences consequently leave their imprint on later identifications, including superego formation (Freud 1923a, Annie Reich 1954).

A longitudinal study of child development by Ernst Kris and Milton Senn (reported by Coleman et al. 1953) examined the parent/child dimension of development. The investigators observed that a mother's conflictual traits can be intensified as a result of exposure to her child's behavior. Depending on many factors, including the strength of the parent–child relationship, the exposure may lead to a breakthrough and the mother may give temporary free reign to the child's and her own old, regressive pleasures.

Kris's study group (Coleman et al. 1953) underlined the importance of the child's equipment in influencing the parental attitude and determining the character of the child's interaction with the environment. Kris emphasized two extreme possibilities: environmental influences may reinforce the infant's equipment or predisposition or it may act in the opposite direction. The child would have different personality characteristics and adaptation depending on whether his predispositions were reinforced or toned down by the environment.

Friedlander (1949) examined the home background of neurotic children from apparently stable family situations. The outcome depended on the complicated interplay between the child's conflicts about his primitive instinctual urges and the reaction of the environment to the child's needs. In 18 percent of cases the environmental configuration was such that the development of a neurotic constellation might have been predicted. In 82 percent of cases neurotic development could not have been predicted. Here, the child reacted to adverse environmental conditioning, which appeared well within normal limits. Friedlander suggested that there are children whose innate tendencies make them more sensitive to conflictual situations and reduce their capacity to work through their problems without special parental help.

Mahler (1967) has emphasized the importance of innate factors in the child such as the intensity of the child's drives, the harshness of her ambivalence, and other constitutional factors in the genesis of parent-child psychopathology.

In this chapter, the role of the parents in the identification process and the formation of ego ideal will be examined, followed by a description of pathological identifications and ego ideal structure. We will then examine the role of the parental pathology in neurosogenesis and the more severe psychopathology in the children.

IDENTIFICATION

Identifications are defined as components of psychic structure that have their origins in wishful fantasies to be like another person. As a result of these stable behavioral and psychological phenomena, the individual consciously and/or unconsciously thinks of himself as being, acting, or playing the role of, some other person. Even if the individual was conscious of this wish initially, these structures become more or less removed from their sources and gradually evolve into typical modes of psychological functioning (Abend and Porder 1986, Arlow 1986). The object of identification need not be alive or real or accurately apprehended. The "other" is a mental representation in distinction from the self/representation (Abend and Porder 1986).

Identification fantasies, like other fantasies, are the result of compromise formations (Brenner 1982) that invariably combine (1) drive derivatives involving various specific motives for seeking gratification, (2) defensive aspects, whose motive is the diminution of pain, and (3) superego contributions, which add expiatory or punishment motives to the final compromise formations. All instances of identification, however, have in common the idea of being or becoming like someone else as a way of achieving various motives specific to each person.

Identification phenomena can be recognized by searching for some link of likeness, a psychic connection in the patient's associations of similarity to another figure in his or her life. The most significant and useful aspect of the clinical work, then, is to determine the unconscious motives for identification fantasies: various instinctual gratifications, defenses against affects, and superego contributions (Abend and Porder 1986).

Identification is a form of internalization and refers to a process through which the ego introjects an object, with the result that the object itself causes alterations in the ego. The consequences of identification in the ego appear mainly through achievement of autonomy, formation of an identity, and establishment of a relationship with the object in a more realistic pattern; a satisfactory identification reinforces the integration of the ego.

Internalization includes identification and refers to the formation of psychic structures that reflect both actual and fantasied interactions with significant objects under the impact of drive derivatives represented by specific affective states. The basic unit of internalization is a dyadic one; it consists of a self and object representation in the context of a specific affect representing libidinal and/or aggressive drives. Introjection, identification, and identity formation are conceived as a series of progressive levels of internalization (Kernberg 1986).

Introjection is the most primitive form of internalization and occurs during the symbiotic stage of development when self and object representations are not yet differentiated from each other. Identification takes place when self and object representations have been differentiated from each other, that is, in the stage of separation–individuation.

Identity formation refers to the more general intrapsychic process of integration of libidinally and aggressively invested self-representations into a cohesive self, a process parallel to the simultaneous integration of libidinally and aggressively invested object representations into broader representations of significant objects. Ego identity is the result of this process. It includes both longitudinal and a cross-sectional integration of the self.

Incorporation usually refers to a psychological mechanism based upon a physiological prototype which may lead to identification. Freud (1917) and Abraham (1924) emphasized the role of incorporation, particularly oral incorporation both as a prototype and mechanism of identification. However, incorporation is no longer viewed as the primary mechanism for identification and additional or alternate modes are involved. Deferred imitation occupies a position of great importance among the genetic precursors of identification (Blum 1986).

Identification Process

Identification is both a process and a product of that process. The vicissitudes in identification dwell in the process; however, it is through the product that we can observe them first (Blum 1986).

In contemporary structural terms, identification is a process of internalization and structural transformation leading to a change in the self-representation based upon identification with features of an object. However, the process by which the fantasies of being like an object alter the structure has not been clearly identified. Nevertheless, one must distinguish between the dynamics and function of identification from the process or processes by which identification is effected. In identification, the external object goes through the passages to become the internal object and is assimilated by the ego.

Arlow (1986) emphasizes that identifications are not foisted upon the individual. They come into being in response to certain intrapsychic requirements in the context of conflict and serve multiple defensive and adaptational purposes.

Normal identifications are partial or selective. They have progressive or growth-promoting functions. They are modifications of the self-concept under the influence of the object. At the same time, a decrease in the differentiation between the self and object is implied in the incorporation of the different aspect of the object. Identifications may lose much or all of their overt conflictual quality and become stable and relatively harmonious aspects of character formation. Other identifications may remain extremely conflictual.

Kernberg (1986) describes the sequences in the formation of identification. The first step is the realistic perception of an external object and the relationship of one's self to that object under the impact of a determined affect. The second step consolidates an internal representation of the object linked by a specific affect to the corresponding self-representation. The third step is modification of the self-representation under the influence of the current object representation. The fourth step is modification of the general concept of the self to accommodate this particular self-representation. Identification alters the ego and object relationship from which the identification is derived.

The process of identification itself undergoes developmental transformation, and identifications formed in infancy through adolescence are not likely to be based upon the same process. Later identifications are selective and less magical and are probably invested with neutral rather than drive energies. They are less imitative and involve signficant structural transformations. The changes in the identification process parallel changes in the cognitive process and affect regulation and neutralization which in turn may facilitate sublimation (Hartmann 1955). Later superego identifications utilize abstraction and generalization, leading to systems of moral values and precepts abstracted originally from the parents and their authority.

History of the Concept of Identification

In the history of psychoanalysis, emphasis has gradually shifted from identification as simple need gratification and defense to its central position in development and personality organization. Other contemporary foci include the relationship between identification and structuralization and the role of identification in pathogenesis, mastery, sublimation, and adaptation (Blum 1986).

Freud (1913) first examined the concept of identification in the context of the boy's wish to become like his father by orally devouring him. Freud emphasized the basis for identification as the emotional tie to another person. Identification and the formation of psychic structure achieved prominence with the development of ego psychology. Anna Freud (1936) described "identification with the aggressor" as a defense. Mahler (1955) described how the stable image of self depends upon successful identification on one hand and distinction between object and self-representation on the other.

Parens (1971) has summarized the triad of hypotheses in psychoanalysis that clarifies the central position of identification:

1. Ego and superego formations arise largely from identification (Freud 1923).
2. The source of identifications are early love objects (Jacobson 1964).
3. A libidinal object can be given up only by identification with it, by taking the object into the ego (Freud 1917).

Identification has been divided historically into *primary* and *secondary* identifications. This division differentiated between a prestructural relationship and structural transformation. Primary identification was said to both precede object relationships and to be the first form of object relationship, as well as regressively replacing the lost primary object (Freud 1921). It usually refers to the period of nondifferentiation and particularly to the stage of symbiosis and merger from which self-object differentiations emerge (Sandler 1960, Grinberg 1976). However, it is confusing to invoke the concept of identification when there is not yet an emotional tie to a differentiated object with whom to identify (Blum 1968). At present, identification with the primary object is considered a concept of greater utility than primary identification. Early internalizations are antecedent to identification and may influence the stability, coherence, and affective tone of subsequent identifications. They are probably equivalent to the first introjects and gradually and developmentally progress beyond part objects, need-satisfying objects, transitional objects, and emerging self-objects. They are narcissistic identifications with narcissistic objects.

The early identifications undergo a process of selection and integration, a crucial step for the achievement of self and object constancy and the formation of personal and gender identity. Representational constancy in turn then permits identification and structuralization on higher levels of development (Mahler and McDevitt 1982).

Developmental Perspective on Identification

Imitation, occurring as early as the second month of life, may play a role as a genetic precursor, prototype, and mechanism of identification (Gaddini 1969), particularly the higher level imitative identifications found in infancy. Imitation is usually characterized as conscious, superficial, devoid of mental content, and dependent upon the presence of an external model, but deferred imitation is denoted in the absence of such a model and represents a step toward mental representation and structure formation (Blum 1986). Imitation is an increasingly refined re-creation of perceived behavior and may gradually refer to affective as well as sensory motor response and communication. The mother and infant engage in reciprocal, empathic, and mirroring imitative identification (Spitz 1965). The infant gradually uses the mother's selective clues to alter his behavior and potential internalization (Mahler 1968). Mahler (1965) has emphasized the importance of selective mutual cueing on the part of the mother to enhance adaptation and identification of the infant.

At the time of the appearance of tension between the child and the parent, the child can receive some relief from the feeling of helplessness through selective identification with the parents (Mahler and Furer 1968). Successful identification aids individuation, development of sound secondary narcissism, and psychic structure. The more advanced and stable identifications allow the child to separate physically from mother because he has internalized her mothering functions, which previously belonged to the interactional sphere between the child and external environment (Loewald 1962).

Kanzer (1985) describes the evolutionary changes in motives for identification with changing consequences of identification and gradual delineation of self from object representation. Stoller (1968) emphasizes that since the basic identification of children of both sexes is with the mother, the boy must be helped to disidentify from some of the maternal aspects in order to form a masculine identification.

Preoedipal identifications are global, introjective identifications. They are different from oedipal identification where different aspects of the love objects serve as sources of identification in a more controlled, selective, complex manner than earlier ones. Preoedipal identifications are already significant in the second year of life and are important in ego, language, and affect development and for such precursors of superego as the gestural and verbal "no" and incipient internalization of parental permission.

The separation-individuation process bridges the gap between early internalizations that preexist an object and oedipal identifications that eventuate in the structuralization of the superego. Identification with object representations are particularly relevant to the stabilization of self-representations and thence to identity formations.

At the decline of the oedipal period, the child's identification with the *feared* father serves as a component of the superego. The identification with the *loved* father constitutes a component of the ego-ideal. The resolution of the Oedipus complex is achieved largely by means of identification and includes the critical aspects as well as the approving and loving attitudes. In the latency period, nonparental sources of identification include identification with peers, other adults, and "superhero" figures with omnipotent heroism and strength (Kramer 1986).

Earlier partial identifications are continually revised, reorganized, and integrated into an emerging unique ego core or character. They promote strength provided by building structures, restructuralization, and internalization of external controls into autonomous self-control. The neutralization of drives provides the ego with transformed energy; depersonification and abstraction give ascendancy to reasonable, reflective, thoughtful action in place of impulsive and defensive, driven activity. The progressive structuralization occurs with developmental advances.

Children who had fortunate experiences during the preoedipal period construct a high level of ego strength, frustration tolerance, self-control, and secondary process functioning. These qualities enable them to turn to people as whole objects, and develop a focused, excited, optimistic yearning to be like them, to take on their attitudes, standards, and values, pursue them as love objects, and compete with them as rivals in the triadic, oedipal way. Inadequate experiences lead to pathological identifications that interfere with ego development. In optimal circumstances the identifications that are the building blocks for the child's character are modified and become increasingly independent of its source in others.

An external dimension of identification may be recognized in the state of traumatic terrors. Experience with traumatically abused children and terrorized adults have repeatedly confirmed the rather universal response of "identification with the aggressor" (A. Freud 1936) which seems to be an almost obligatory response of the overwhelmed ego. Becoming the aggressor in fantasy imparts a sense of psychological control and mastery of anxiety.

Mahler (1961) and Kramer (1986) draw attention to a significant contemporary issue: the prevalence of multiple caregivers for children due to the ever-increasing number of working mothers. When the multiple caregiving process is functioning smoothly in a relatively conflict-free environment, children develop normally. The child's immature ego absorbs and synthesizes the complex object images without adverse effect and on occasion even with benefit. Thus, the gestalt of the nurse, who may be delegated the function of providing immediate need satisfaction is synthesized with the gestalt of the mother, who may be available only as an additional external ego. Although the mother may be less involved in the actual care of the infant, her image seems to attract much more cathexis than the caregivers and often becomes the "cardinal object" representation (Mahler 1961). However, for this phenomenon to occur, the caregiver should not compete directly with the primary love object.

Kramer (1986) has described the failure of this process in a case report of a borderline adopted boy with school, behavioral, and learning problems.

The boy exhibited problems in identification because his two primary caregivers competed endlessly for possession of him, each demanding loyalty to herself and to herself alone. The boy's identity was confused and his identifications duplicated. The two primary caregivers included the white mother and the black housekeeper who were very much at odds with each other, and related to the boy in such a way as to militate against "synthesis of the gestalts of the two women" and to prevent the image of the mother from becoming the cardinal object representation. The image of the black caregiver was synthesized with the image of birth mother in the mind of the child. The double conflictual identifications with the two caregivers were not integrated or synthesized and gave rise to the fantasy of having a twin: a black boy, related to the caregiver, who was the recipient of the patient's projected badness. The inability to achieve solid identifications with either of the caregivers resulted in poor impulse control. Psychoanalytic treatment enhanced the integration of multiple, conflicting identifications in the patient.

Pathological and Defensive Identifications

The multiple pitfalls of the identification process include the failure of preoedipal narcissistic identifications to establish a solid enough base to permit the child to weather the pressures of oedipal conflict. Furthermore, the oedipal experiences may be so stressful and difficult that they would be beyond the coping capacity of nearly any child. Here, the child regresses to preoedipal, narcissistic modes that impede structuralization and developmental advances. Parental failure to provide optimal modeling for growth facilitating identification is another developmental deficiency (Silverman 1986).

Excessive stress can result in a regressive pull toward the illusion of narcissistic union with an all-powerful parental force for absolute protection. The ego can resist the regressive pull if it has progressed from the initial infantile omnipotence of primary narcissistic identification to mature, differentiated, realistic self-other perception with ego structuralization and internalization of personal and societal value (Silverman 1986).

In psychotic identification, a defensive regression to the symbiotic stage of development occurs. Here, the mental representation of an object relationship is defensively re-fused; re-fusion of the "all-good" self and object representations under the dominance of real or fantasied gratification is a defense against the dread of annihilation. A parallel re-fusion of the "all-bad" self and object representations that reflects internalized object relations dominated by aggression also occurs (Kernberg 1986).

Identifications may also lead to increased instinctualization: the masochist's identification with the sadistic partner; "identification with the aggressor" in some abused children who later become abusive parents; identification with the partner's passion in sexual relationships.

In perversions, preoedipal object relations and conflicts carry over into the oedipal phase, influencing the resolution of crucial conflicts. The vicissitudes of identification in perversions is based on preoedipal, separation, and castration conflicts, which lead to avoidance of oedipal competition, an inverted feminine attitude toward the father, and maintainence of a highly ambivalent attitude toward the mother and women. Arlow (1986) has emphasized the crucial role of the identifications during the oedipal phase in the formation of perversions in spite of the importance of the preoedipal factors.

Identification in Twins

Twins encounter difficulties with the identification process and the establishment of a stable ego identity. Certain psychological processes peculiar to twins frequently conflict with the usual developmental processes. Establishment of clear body boundaries and differentiation between self and nonself is retarded due to early intertwin identification as a result of visual incorporation. The continuing intertwin identification prolongs the mutual interdependence and interferes with object relations to others. The four environmental factors of cultural attitudes, parental attitudes, physical similarity, and economic pressures may further intensify the intertwin identification (Leonard 1961). Factors that diminish the intensity of intertwin identification include the dissimilarity of nonidentical twins and the presence of sibling rivalry (Leonard 1961).

Certain characteristics of intertwin identification can interfere with personality development and increase pathogenicity. They include reciprocity of the identification, identification with an individual on the same level of development, and interference with the relationship with the parent.

Beginning awareness of separation ushers in the process of incorporation of the pleasure-giving object into the ego. Identification with the mother is the result of this early incorporation. The lack of a sharp delineation between the sense of self and the twin described as "syncytium" (Leonard 1961), the intertwin relationship in early childhood, and the double identifications with the twins and mother prevent the complete separation of self and the two object representations. The primary intertwin identification is self-perpetuating and can hinder the development of object relationship.

The identification with the twin often retards the ego development, language acquisition, and formation of other object relationships. The twins may see themselves as two sides of the same personality each of whom is dependent on the other twin in order to become a well-balanced whole. The intertwin identification and the resulting lack of individuation can only become pathological due to intense unadaptive environmental factors resulting in serious ego retardation. The limitation in parental ability to imitate mutually (Spitz 1957) with each twin and the constant presence of the other twin as an object for imitation and identification can result in further ego impediment. Burlingham (1952) emphasizes the importance of being "able to identify with each of twins" in order to love them. If the twins are alike, the mother finds it impossible to identify with each twin and as a result her emotions cannot have free play.

The difficulties of women in unlike-sex twins have been described by a number of studies. Beckwitt (1954) and Abrahams (1963) both describe analytic treatment of the female half of different-sex twins. Both authors emphasize the role of identification with the male twin in the etiology of the neurosis and the tenacity with which patients clung to the fantasy of possessing a penis. Obviously, for a girl to have a male twin adds continued insult to the presumed injury. To maintain equality with the male twin, the intertwin identification must be preserved; therefore, the illusory penis persists and results in the denial of femininity.

The persistence of identity à deux due to primary intertwin identification beyond adolescence enhances the likelihood of a severe pathology in the twins.

Influences of Early Mother–Child Interaction

Ritvo and Solnit (1959) have reported on the vicissitudes of identification in two girls with differing dispositions and their interactions with mothers of markedly different personalities.

In the first case, Evelyn's initial tranquility fitted well with her mother's need for a superficially peaceful compromise with her own conflicts. The mother imposed increasing restrictions early on the child and offered several substitute gratifications. Evelyn's interest in dolls was followed by fantasy play with imaginary companions and advanced fantasy role play. Her imitation served as the earliest active identification and provided a bridge to later partial ego identifications. She exhibited an abundance of neutralized energies in her imaginative paintings and her facility for fantasy served as a tool for the mastery of the separation from her mother. Her characteristic receptivity was well suited to her mother's patterns of mothering; the environment worked in harmony with the equipment. The interaction of the child's equipment and the mother's care was a harmonious one in which frustration and gratification were well balanced and helpful in her development.

In the second case, the relationship of the mother to Margaret was marked by fear and ambivalent feelings about the child. Margaret's irritability made her a difficult child to comfort. This characteristic of the child collided forcefully with the deepest conflicts of the mother. Thus, the close empathic tie with the mother necessary for later successful internalization was hampered. The mother approached Margaret as if control of the child was necessary. She found it difficult to hold and cuddle Margaret, because of the fear that she would damage the child. This approach interfered with those experiences in the child that would lead to fantasy formation. The mother's consistent interference with all of Margaret's activities prevented internalization and did not allow the child to fully take over the maternal functions by identification. As a result, Margaret became bossy, demanding, possessive and overcontrolled, which revealed her defensive identification with the maternal rigidity and constriction.

The capacity for imitation was normal in both children. The contrasting qualities of the mother/child interaction resulted in imitation playing a different role in the development of the two children. In Evelyn, imitation provided a bridge to later partial ego identifications based on the introjection of the object representation. In Margaret, the predominance of unpleasurable experience with the mother interfered with the process of identification and favored the persistence of imitation rather than internalization.

EGO IDEAL: DEFINITION, HISTORY, STRUCTURE, AND PATHOLOGY

Introduction

Ego ideal is a differentiated part of the ego, cathected with narcissistic and homosexual libidos; it has a guiding role similar to that of superego, but it differs from the superego in being more personal and in lacking uncompromising tyranny and primitive cruelty (Blos 1962, 1979, Lampl-de Groot 1962, Reich 1954). Ego ideal attains its definitive organization only belatedly at the decline of the homosexual stage of early adolescence, although precursors of the ego ideal are evident throughout childhood. The irreversible surrender of the negative (homosexual) oedipal position promotes and stabilizes the formation of sexual identity. The content of the ego ideal continues to integrate during adolescence; its structure, however, remains constant and permanent. Ego ideal is goal-directing and choice-determining. The neglect of ego ideal expectations, in contrast to the guilt of superego, results in an assault to the individual's narcissistic balance and subjects the ego to shame and social anxiety (Blos 1979).

Idealizations have their roots in infantile narcissism. The target of idealization may be the object, or regressive, narcissistic self-idealization. Idealization is a primitive mechanism for the regulation of self-esteem and can result in rapid narcissistic fluctuations. Mature ego ideal promotes delay, anticipation, and lifelong striving for perfection. Ego ideal is always striving but will never be fulfilled. In fact, it is the striving for perfection that furnishes a sense of well-being.

The ego ideal, in its typical and predominant form, has its roots in the identification with the parent of the same sex. It receives a decisive formative push during the passing of the Oedipus phase when the child ceases his attempts to be equal to the parent and attempts to become like him. Primitive identification that disregards the distinction between the subject and object is replaced by selective identification with traits, values, and attitudes. These identifications gradually gain ascendency over the precursors of bodily and global idealization of the parent.

The adult ego ideal emerges from the resolution of the negative

Oedipus complex, which gains conflictual prominence at adolescence. Compelled by sexual maturation at puberty, the resolution of the negative oedipal component becomes a matter of developmental urgency. The bisexuality of childhood is brought to an end and a radical step is secured by structure formation. The adolescent negative oedipal cannot be resolved at adolescence by displacement into a nonincestuous object without homosexual dominance becoming a permanent aspect of object relationship. The resolution of the negative Oedipus complex is accomplished through the elaboration of a new structure known as "the adult ego ideal," in contrast with the earlier "infantile ego ideal." From an adaptive or psychological point of view the adult ego ideal can be viewed as the socialization of narcissism (Blos 1979). In the process, all previous ego ideal components ranging from primary narcissism, symbiotic omnipotence, and narcissistic identification to the homosexual object love become integrated in the permanent ego ideal during late adolescence. This process transforms the preoedipal and negative oedipal attachments, and infantile sexual fixations into ego ideal structure (Blos 1962, 1979).

In early adolescence a decathexis of the familiar love objects occurs with the consequent search for new objects. The young adolescent turns to "the friend." The friend acquires a heretofore unknown importance and significance for both boy and girl. The object choice of early adolescence follows the narcissistic model. The idealized friend possesses some admired qualities that the adolescent himself would like to have and in the friendship he possesses it by proxy (Blos 1979).

The ego ideal that the friend represents may yield under the sexual urge and lead to a stage of homosexuality with voyeurism, exhibitionism, and mutual masturbation. The masturbation fantasies generally counteract castration anxiety. If the sadomasochistic heterosexual object themes of such fantasies become disturbing, the adolescent may turn to a homosexual object choice. In these fantasies, the friend, as a comrade in arms, often participates in heterosexual orgies and battles. The strong erotic feelings toward the friend explain the sudden disruption of these attachments. The idealized friend shrinks to ordinary proportions whenever the ego ideal has established itself independently from the object in the outer world.

The libidinal model of "I love what I would like to be" has been described as the homosexual phase of early adolescence. The formation of the final ego ideal organization transforms homosexual object libido into ego libido and establishes heterosexual masculine and feminine polarity (Blos 1962).

Ego ideal has its root in primary narcissism and is closely connected with the narcissistic losses of infancy. It perpetuates an eternal approximation to the narcissistic perfection of infancy and the image of idealized parents. The ego ideal gradually takes over some superego functions in adolescence when the relationship with the ego and superego are being modified.

Ego ideal has the potential to remain an immature, self-idealizing, wish-fulfilling agency, resisting any transformation into a mature, abstract, goal-intentional and action-motivating force, as long as the young man's negative Oedipus complex has not been sufficiently resolved or analyzed in treatment. When the analysis of the negative oedipal conflict has been accomplished, the formation of an adequate, workable ego ideal takes its normal course. "Ego ideal is the heir to the negative oedipus complex" (Freud 1914). Ego ideal can become sexualized in the same manner as superego. It can easily become enmeshed with new drive modalities as well as with new ego competencies.

Genealogy and Theoretical Formulation

Theoretical questions in regard to ego ideal address its relationship and autonomy from superego and ego and the energy source for the ego ideal functioning (Blos 1979).

Freud initially described the ego ideal as a substitute for the lost narcissism of childhood in which the child was his own ideal. In contrast, in 1933, Freud described the ego ideal as the precipitate of the old picture of the parents; the child attributing perfection to the parents. The ego ideal found its secure place in 1923, as the narcissistic component of the superego, within the tripartite structure of the mind. Reassessment of the ego ideal as a psychic agency took place with the enhanced interest in ego psychology. It was universally agreed that ego ideal was rooted in the narcissistic sector of the personality related to the stage of primary narcissism.

Bing and colleagues (1959) see ego ideal anatomically as a part of the ego. Lampl-de Groot (1962), on the basis of genetic and adaptive considerations, concludes that ego ideal is an established substructure or province within the ego and can be looked at as "an ego function." But even in its most highly developed form it "remains essentially an agency of wish fulfillment." Jacobson (1964) states that it is "more correct to consider ego ideal an ego formation rather than a part of the superego system." With progressive ego development, the ego ideal "gradually bridges the two systems and may ultimately be claimed by both." These formulations are in opposition to the views advanced by Hartmann and

Lowenstein (1962), who consider the ego ideal an aspect of the superego system.

Steingart (1969) considers ego ideal in the conceptual framework of psychic apparatus development, self and object representations. Preoedipal ego ideal reflects drive-gratifying wishes of aggrandizement, in contrast to the phallic oedipal period, when idealization encompasses increasingly new issues. Esman (1971) follows the same paths in viewing the ego ideal's changing function in relation to developmental tasks, for example, the support it lends to the sublimatory efforts characteristic of the latency period.

With developmental progression, ego ideal ceases progressively to be the agency of wish fulfillment through either fantasy or identification. It acquires structuralization during adolescence, which then becomes qualitatively different from its antecedent developmental stages. The ego ideal achieves the hierarchical reorganization and final integration of earlier and later values and concepts arising from both systems, ego and superego, into a new coherent structure and functional unit, namely the mature ego ideal (Jacobson, 1964).

Murray (1964) attributes to the early narcissistic state of ego ideal the attitude of *entitlement* (pregenital) and postulates a sublimation of narcissism and of the affects attached to libidinal objects that are part of the ego ideal organization. The narcissistic libido centered in the ego ideal returns to the ego to recathect unconscious latent homosexual elements when the idea is lost or dimmed. Adolescent conflict centers around having to forego pregenital entitlements in favor of the more ideal-oriented relationships with mature libidinal fulfillments. Ego ideal has close ties to the systems ego and superego. The distinctness of the mature ego ideal is defined and preserved by its intersystemic ties.

Piers and Singer (1953) relate the experiencing of shame to tension between the ego and ego ideal and guilt to the tension between ego and superego. They view ego ideal and superego as two entirely separate and independent psychological entities. The superego sets boundaries for the ego ideal goals. Ego ideal has four major attributes: it contains a core of narcissistic omnipotence, and it represents the sum of the positive identifications with the parental images. It contains layers of later identifications that are more readily changeable than the earlier ones, and finally, it contains the goal of the drive to mastery.

The formation of infantile ego ideal coincides with the attainment of object constancy (Aarons 1970) and postambivalent object relations (Blos 1970). Potentially, the ego ideal transcends castration anxiety with feelings of invulnerability and immortality and thus propels man toward incredible feats of creativity, heroism, sacrifice, and selflessness (Piers and Singer 1953). The ego ideal spans an orbit that extends from primary narcissism to the highest level of man's achievement. In its mature form, the ego ideal weakens the punitive power of the superego by taking over some of its functions.

The concept of "ideal self" in distinction from the ego ideal, has been elaborated by Sandler and colleagues (1963). The ideal self contains temporary elements as well as a more stable unconscious core, based upon the ideals created in childhood. It includes the following components:

1. The ideal self-representation or ideal self-image.
2. The ideal parental introjects which serve as models for the self.
3. Certain ego functions which were at one time considered to be functions of the superego (self-observation and defensive function).
4. The individual's reality-based knowledge of his own potentialities and limitations.

The ideal self is far more fluid and flexible than the ideals held up to the child by his introjects, although it will contain a solid core of identifications with the admired parents of his earlier years. In states of regression, the content of the ideal self will approximate more closely the aspects of the idealized pregenital object.

The construction of an ideal self and the efforts to attain it constitute an attempt to restore the primary narcissistic states of the earliest weeks of life. The failure to ready the expectations of the ideal self results in pangs of disappointment because self-esteem is a function of the discrepancy between the self-representation and the ideal self (Jacobson 1954, A. Reich 1960).

The Development of Male and Female Ego Ideal

The development of ego ideal is not identical for boys and girls although for both sexes it influences motivation and has a regulatory function for the sense of well-being. The ego ideal draws the body image into its realm (Blos 1979).

Ego Ideal and the Girl

Jacobson (1964) states that the little girl develops a nucleus of true ego ideal even earlier than the little boy and in connection with the early onset of her castration conflict. She attempts to recover the phallus by turning to her father, a premature relinquishment of genital activities, and with the shift of narcissistic libido from the genitals to the whole body.

Blos (1962, 1979) emphasizes the importance of the stage of being a tomboy when the body-phallus equation is prominent. For the older girl, exhibitionism becomes a controlling and excitatory agent of sexual arousal. She perceives all males as lusting for her. The mature female ego ideal absorbs and replaces forever the "illusory penis" fantasy.

The girl's tendency to regress to the primitive state of her early ego ideal formation complicates or delays the establishment of the mature ego ideal. The attachment of the ego ideal to an outside person is a lasting tendency conserved by the girl. The female ego ideal tends to remain prone to reenmeshment, in the vicissitudes of object relations. The attainment and stabilization of femininity requires the resolution of the regressive incorporation of the paternal phallus as the narcissistic regulator of the sense of completeness and an enduring identification with the mother. The desexualized and deconcretized ego ideal favors transformation of infantile penis envy into striving for perfection as a woman, removed from envy, competition, and rapaciousness (Blos 1979). This transformation includes a general transition from the personalized, dependent, and concrete to the autonomous, impersonal, and abstract ego ideal.

Benedek (1956) has commented on a conflict typical of the modern girl who attempts to integrate opposing goals in her personality: masculine (active) ego ideal rigidly opposed to regression as an essential step in the development of motherliness.

Ego Ideal in the Boy

The first progressive developmental step is away from primary narcissism and delusion of omnipotence shared with the mother to the narcissistic identifications with her idealized image. This narcissistic identification becomes progressively tempered by the reality principle, and the state of infantile omnipotence becomes relegated to the world of fantasy (Blos 1962, 1979).

Preoedipal fixation on the phallic mother weakens the rivalrous, phallic assertions of the boy and the lack of resolution of his Oedipus complex. The apprehension about the mother's powerful position leads the boy to idealize the father's protective and reassuring peership. The newly-found transient feeling of narcissistic grandeur from this comaraderie eventually threatens the arousal of homosexual feelings due to the relatively incomplete solution of the oedipal complex. Resolution of the negative Oedipus complex and the structuralization of the mature ego ideal reduce excessive self and object idealizations and result in more realistic self and object appraisals. From here on the ego ideal derives its momentum from the unending flow of neutralized homosexual libido. "Striving for perfection" becomes the source of narcissistic sustenance (Blos 1979).

The feminine component of the little boy's instinctual life become restrained, restricted, or rejected far more forcefully by narcissistic injunctions. The boy's relationship with the father is never better, that is, less conflicted or more positive than it is at the dawn of puberty (Blos 1962).

Ego Ideal Pathology

Ego ideal pathology refers to the developmental stage of ego ideal and the correspondence between the content of the ego ideal and the level of ego development. Although such pathology can be defined with sufficient specificity, it is frequently and erroneously classified under ego and superego deviations. Ego ideal pathology in adolescent males can exhibit with a symptom complex of high ambitions yet inability to pursue goals, aimlessness, dejection, extreme mood swings, sporadic short-lived bursts of enterprising action, and dreams of glory. The interpretations of oedipal rivalry and castration anxiety do not resolve the symptomatology of the pervasive inhibitions. The analytic themes seem related to the wish to be the recipient of the father's affection, which presents an obstacle to the formation of realistic goals (Blos 1979).

There is an intrinsic connection between ego ideal pathology and insufficiently attenuated homosexual trends (Hunt 1967, A. Reich 1954). This relationship involves the persistence of a magical, omnipotent form with aspirations of creating an ideal state through forming primary identifications with the object (Hunt 1967). Whenever homosexuality, latent or manifest, has become the major regulator of the narcissistic equilibrium, the ego ideal remains arrested on an infantile level. Ritvo (1971) speaks of the reinstinctualization of the ego ideal with predominantly homosexual libido as part of the normative aspects of the adolescent process. The strivings and fantasies for perfection may acquire a prolonged homosexual course, indicating a lack of resolution of the libidinal attachment to the parent of the same sex. The adolescent propensity to idealize persons, ideas, and goals may become greatly prolonged and exaggerated beyond the developmental phase (Blos

1979). Another ego ideal pathology is negative ego ideal, "the introjected negative standard of the parents and of the culture" (Kaplan and Whitman 1965).

Blos (1979) has described the analysis of an adolescent girl with a pathological ego ideal who attempted to gain perfection by incorporating the idealized object, gaining a penis, and intellectual superiority. Aggressive self-idealization blocked the way to the emergence of a deinstinctualized ego ideal.

Blos (1979) has also described the analysis of a boy with an extremely unstable self-representation, difficulties with sexual identity, and academic failure. The analytic themes centered around persistent instinctualization of the ego ideal, preoedipal object ties to the mother, and lack of resolution of the negative oedipal complex.

The normal state of a partially integrated and still externally regulated ego ideal of childhood undergoes a radical and lasting change during adolescence (Reich 1954). The regressive revival of the primitive ego ideal as a phase-specific, but transient, self-esteem regulator can occur later in life as a result of assault on a person's narcissism.

INTERLOCKING PARENT–CHILD NEUROSES AND SIMULTANEOUS ANALYSIS OF PARENTS AND CHILDREN

The concept of interlocking neuroses in parents and children has received attention since the 1950s. The construct is applicable to the clinical situation when a child's neurosis does not yield to the therapeutic intervention with the child alone because the unconscious forces in the parent work in the direction of maintaining the child's psychopathology (A. Freud 1960, Kolansky and Moore 1966). The extreme, pathogenic influence of the parent is generally rooted in the severity of the parental neurosis and the intensity of the parent–child bond. In such situations, neurotic conflicts in the parent diminish the child's therapeutic progress or render the treatment ineffective. Simultaneous analysis of child and parent can elucidate their overlapping fantasies and regressive tendencies and help them progress beyond their positions of fixation.

The mother can be threatened by the analyst as an intruder into her intimate bond with her child (Burlingham 1951). Winnicott (1960) has described the narrow demarcation line that exists between a mother's normal and pathological concerns for her child's body. He described a boy who presented in the office saying: "Please, doctor, my mom complains of pains in my tummy."

Bobby, age 4½ years, and his mother entered simultaneous analysis with two analysts following an unsuccessful and interrupted analytic treatment of Bobby for eating problems, soiling, wetting, and running in front of buses (Burlingham et al. 1955). The treatment data of mother and child revealed many overlapping fantasies and conflicts in the oral, anal, and phallic areas.

Bobby's longstanding eating problems and extreme passivity had begun following his abrupt weaning at age 12 weeks. He felt neglected and deprived. The mother also felt empty, deprived, and unwanted, and had projected the unwanted attitude onto Bobby who has identified with the maternal projections. She felt guilty that her own mother had developed breast cancer after nursing her and therefore abruptly terminated Bobby's nursing because of her own fear of breast cancer.

In the anal area, the mother exhibited lifelong constipation, rooted in her attempts to keep her withdrawn mother with her during the defecation acts. The mother's presence reassured her that her dying mother was not dead yet. This maternal fantasy has resulted later in the creation of a toilet training scene with Bobby where the act of defecation has become a *folie à deux* resembling a love scene. The fantasies of anal union and death wishes gave rise to sadomasochistic and defensive clinging interactions between Bobby and his mother. Their mutual anal birth fantasies included holding back feces to feel full and have excrements as "big as a baby." Defecation resulted in feelings of emptiness, depression, and suicidal thoughts. Bobby identified himself with an anal baby and became fearful that the mother would "drown" his feces in the lavatory.

The overlapping fantasies extended to the phallic-oedipal area, too. The mother's feelings of defectiveness dated back to her feeling castrated in comparison to her brother and her wish to have her brother's and father's penis (penis = baby) to gain parity with them. She treated Bobby as her penis on the one hand and also as a defective and castrated child due to the projection of her own castrated self-image. Bobby has learned that his mother overvalued his phallic organ and that he could dominate her by just exhibiting his penis.

Bobby's tearing himself away from his mother to run in front of buses was related to the mother's adolescent rape fantasies, when her fear and wish of rape was displaced onto fear of being hit by cars. Bobby's fantasies seemed to be a counterphobic extension of the maternal fantasy.

The simultaneous analysis released Bobby to a large measure from the maternal pathogenic influence. The mother's symptoms remained less responsive to the analytic treatment.

Dick and his father entered simultaneous analysis because 13-year-old Dick was passive, noncompetitive, and underachieving in school (Kolansky and Moore 1966). He had been beaten frequently by his father since he was 6 or 7. Dick's passivity transferred readily to the analytic situation where he acted passive and pessimistic. He described his mind as a "steel door" because it would not let anything in or out.

The father was highly conflicted about his competitive and death wishes toward his own father. He projected his competitive and challenging impulses onto his son and then punished the son for his own projected wishes. To the father, Dick represented his own "small penis," his feelings of impotence, and castration anxiety. His use of his hands to "mete out" punishment to his son was a reenactment of his own adolescent masturbatory practice. He equated his son with his own penis, and attempted to keep Dick under control, as he had done with his own penis and masturbation during his adolescence. Dick attempted to defeat the father by making him feel helpless and outraged.

When the father was able to work through sufficiently his passivity and fear of loss of control over his son (Dick = penis), the son could utilize his own psychoanalytic treatment. When the father's anxiety about Dick acting as his uncontrollable penis could be analyzed, the father and son were no longer locked in a neurotic conflict. Dick was then able to utilize the analytic process to relax his pessimistic attitude, improve his study habits and work at his hobbies. The treatment was successful for both the son and father.

THE IMPACT OF SEVERE PARENTAL PSYCHOPATHOLOGY ON CHILD DEVELOPMENT

In this group of childhood disorders, the parental psychopathology exceeds neurosis or neurotic character disturbance and can result in extensive psychopathology in the children with some degree of ego impairment. At times, the parental psychopathology may be moderate but can impact the child at crucial formative periods, thereby resulting in relatively severe psychopathology. A poor match between the parental personality and defensive organization with the child's equipmental sensitivities can also result in severe developmental disorders.

The severe psychopathological states in the children can range from preoedipal developmental arrest (see Kolansky 1966, and Eisner in this volume) to severe ego disturbances including prepsychotic or frank psychotic states. In many of this group of disorders, one or more ego functions may be severely compromised. In preoedipal developmental arrest, the compromise of the ego may be more modest, while in more severe disorders one or more ego functions, such as object relationship, impulse control, regulation of affect and self-esteem, disturbances of the reality testing, the sense of reality, and relationship to reality and cognitive functioning, may be impaired. The self-observing function of the ego is generally undeveloped due to inadequate early parenting.

Freud's (1911) examination of the autobiographical account of Schreber can serve as an instructive example of the impact of the parental psychopathology on a child in light of new findings by Niederland (1974). Schreber suffered from paranoia and emasculation fantasy, and was confined to a mental institution. He thought there was a conspiracy to take his soul, transform him into a female, and sexually abuse him. He believed that he had a mission to redeem the world, but he had to be transformed into a woman before he could achieve this goal.

In his autobiography, Schreber describes his "pathological experiences." Niederland (1959a,b) has examined the early childhood experiences of Schreber based on the examination of his *Memoir* to determine the factors operating in the genesis of symptom formation. Schreber's childhood appears to have been characterized by passive submission to the father's forceful, overpowering, often sadistic (though not entirely unaffectionate) behavior. He suffered early traumatizations through exposure to bizarre "gadget experiences" (bodily overstimulation alternating with mechanical restraint), impairment of the body image by direct and indirect castration threats resulting from the maternal antimasturbation campaign, and Schreber's childhood years in the father's orthopedic institution.

Niederland (1974) has further described Schreber's clear identification with the members of his family: with the tyrannical father who may have been psychotic, and with the neglectful mother into whom he is transformed by an insensitive, abusive, and castrating father. A leading physician of his day, Schreber's father maintained parenting precepts that were nothing short of demanding absolute obedience from the children and denial of their needs. He designed orthopedic apparatus resembling torture devices to restrain, inhibit, and punish children for their sexual and aggressive impulses and for the slightest transgressions (Blum 1986).

Buxbaum (1964) has described the role of the parents in the etiology of learning disabilities as derivative of a partially symbiotic mother–child relationship that prevents the child from becoming completely independent of the mother. The dependence on the mother interferes with the autonomous capacity to test and modify the reality, to adapt and learn. The child's learning capacity, one of the most important ego functions, becomes crippled and disturbed. Learning difficulties rooted in the relationship to the father are usually limited to certain subjects, such as an inability to do arithmetic, and have the characteristics of success neurosis due to the child's fear of competing with a powerful adversary.

In treatment of severe childhood psychopathology, ego supportive (ego building) psychotherapy is the necessary intervention. In less disturbed children, ego supportive psychotherapy can be undertaken by a child analyst or a child therapist in an outpatient setting where the therapist can act as the child's alter ego, attempting to compensate for the missing or underdeveloped ego functions. Through psychotherapeutic relationship and interventions, the therapist helps develop the context and matrix for the compensation for the missing ego functions and paves the way for subsequent development of these specific ego capacities. In more severe states, the ego supportive psychotherapy has to be undertaken in a residential treatment center (Noshpitz 1962) where multiple caretakers can act collectively as alter egos for the patient under the supervision of the primary therapist, who functions as the team leader. The group will collectively enhance and complement the therapeutic goals of the individual sessions. Psychopharmacological agents can be used to stabilize affect, enhance attention span, restore cognitive functions, and improve impulse control.

In the last three decades, relational disturbances as an additional aspect of reciprocal psychopathology between the parents and children have been recognized. The explorations of family relational disturbances and family pathology through psychoanalytic and object relations family therapy have brought to light the role of contemporary family dysfunctions on child development. In contrast to the classical model of neurosogenesis, where the more decisive influence of the parents on child development has occurred at earlier developmental stages, here the parental pathology impacts the developmental process in the offspring in the present sphere through distortions of the contemporary family relationship. At times, the parental pathology may be limited but can result in dysfunctional parent/child interactions and relationships. The use of conjoint psychotherapy for the whole family or concurrent treatment of family members can result in the delineation of the pathological aspect of family relationships. The resolution of such pathological ties can result in the enhancement of adaptation for all family members as well as the resumption of healthier developmental processes in the children. The choice of conjoint or concurrent treatment for family members is dependent on the level of self-observation, maturation, and other issues, such as the need for confidentiality of different family members (Ackerman 1958, Scharff and Scharff 1987, Sholevar 1980, 1982).

CONCLUSION

Satisfactory early parent–child relationships brought about by a good fit between the infant's endowment and parental sensitivity and loving care can enhance optimal ego development. Multiple developmental achievements include the establishment of stable identification and mature ego ideal organization. Parental neurotic pathology can produce complementary neurosis in the children and such interlocking neurosis may only respond to simultaneous analytic treatment of the parent and child. Extensive parental pathology can produce severe psychopathological disorders in the offspring requiring the use of multiple treatment modalities.

REFERENCES

Aarons, Z. A. (1970). Normality and abnormality in adolescence: with a digression on Prince Hal—"The Sowing of Wild Oats." *Psychoanalytic Study of the Child* 25:309–339. New York: International Universities Press.

Abelin, E. (1971). The role of the father in the separation–individuation process. In *Separation–Individuation*, ed. J. McDevitt and C. F. Settlage, pp. 229–253. New York: International Universities Press.

―――― (1975). Some further observations and comments on the earliest role of the father. *International Journal of Psycho-Analysis* 56:293–302.

Abend, S. M., and Porder, M. S. (1986). Identification in neuroses. *International Journal of Psycho-Analysis* 67:201–208.

Abraham, K. (1924a). A short study of the development of the libido, viewed in the light of mental disorders. In *Selected Papers on Psycho-Analysis*, pp. 412–501. London: Hogarth Press, 1949.

―――― (1924b). Character formation on the genital level of libido-development. In *Selected Papers on Psycho-Analysis*, pp. 407–417. New York: Basic Books, 1953.

Abrahams, H. C. (1953). Twin relationship and womb phantasy in a case of anxiety hysteria. *International Journal of Psycho-Analysis* 34:219–227.

Ackerman, N. (1958). *The Psychodynamics of Family Life*. New York: Basic Books.

Aichhorn, A. (1925). *Wayward Youth*. New York: Viking Press. 1935.

Arlow, J. A. (1971). Character perversion. In *Currents in Psychoanalysis*, ed. I. M. Marcus, pp. 317–336. New York: International Universities Press.

―――― (1986). Discussion of papers by Drs. McDougall and Glasser. Panel on identification in the perversions. *International Journal of Psycho-Analysis* 67:245–250.

Beckwitt, B. (1954). Some observations on penis envy in the girl twin. Read at the Los Angeles Society for Psychoanalysis.

Benedek, T. (1956). Psychobiological aspects of mothering. *American Journal of Orthopsychiatry* 26:272–278.

Bibring, G. L. (1964). Some considerations regarding the ego ideal in the psychoanalytic process. *Journal of the American Psychoanalytic Association* 12:517–521.

Bing, J. F., McLaughlin, F., and Marburg, R. (1959). The metapsychology of narcissism. *Psychoanalytic Study of the Child* 14:9–28. New York: International Universities Press.

Blos, P. (1962). *On Adolescence: A Psychoanalytic Interpretation*. New York: Free Press.

―――― (1970). *The Young Adolescent: Clinical Studies*. New York: Free Press.

―――― (1979). *The Adolescent Passage*. New York: International Universities Press.

Blum, H. (1986). On identification and its vicissitudes. *International Journal of Psycho-Analysis* 67:267–276.

Bonnard, A. (1949). School phobia—is it a syndrome? Paper read at the International

Congress of Psychiatry, Paris. Published in *Enfance* 4:183-185, 1951.
Bornstein, B. (1953). Fragments of an analysis of an obsessional child. *Psychoanalytic Study of the Child* 8:313-332. New York: International Universities Press.
Brenner, C. (1982). *The Mind in Conflict*. New York: International Universities Press.
Bressler, B. (1969). The ego ideal. *Israel Annals of Psychology and Related Disciplines* 7:158-174.
Burlingham, D. (1932). Child analysis and the mother. *Psychiatric Quarterly* 4:69-92.
—— (1945). The fantasy of having a twin. *Psychoanalytic Study of the Child* 1:205-210. New York: International Universities Press.
—— (1951). Present trends in handling the mother-child relationship during the therapeutic process. *Psychoanalytic Study of the Child* 6:31-37. New York: International Universities Press.
—— (1952). *Twin, A Study of Three Pairs of Identical Twins*. New York: International Universities Press.
Burlingham, D., Goldberger, A., and Lussier, A. (1955). Simultaneous analysis of mother and child. *Psychoanalytic Study of the Child* 10:165-186. New York: International Universities Press.
Buxbaum, E. (1951). A contribution to the psychoanalytic knowledge of the latency period. *American Journal of Orthopsychiatry* 21:182-198.
—— (1964). The parents' role in the etiology of learning disabilities. *Psychoanalytic Study of the Child* 19:421-447. New York: International Universities Press.
Coleman, R. W., Kris, E., and Provence, S. (1953). The study of variations of early parental attitudes. *Psychoanalytic Study of the Child* 8:20-47. New York: International Universities Press.
Erikson, E. H. (1946). Ego development and historical change. *Psychoanalytic Study of the Child* 2:359-396. New York: International Universities Press.
Esman, A. H. (1971). Consolidation of the ego ideal in contemporary adolescence. In *The Psychology of Adolescence*, pp. 211-218. New York: International Universities Press, 1975.
Freud, A. (1936). *The Ego and the Mechanisms of Defense*. New York: International Universities Press.
—— (1960). Introduction to K. Levy: simultaneous analysis of a mother and her adolescent daughter. *Psychoanalytic Study of the Child* 15:378-380. New York: International Universities Press.
Freud, S. (1910). Leonardo da Vinci and a memory of his childhood. *Standard Edition* 11:59-81.
—— (1911). Psychoanalytic notes on an autobiographical account of a case of paranoia. *Standard Edition* 12:3-84.
—— (1913). Totem and taboo. *Standard Edition* 13:1-164.
—— (1914). On narcissism: an introduction. *Standard Edition* 14:67-104.
—— (1916-1917). Introductory lectures. *Standard Edition* 16:243-481.
—— (1917). Mourning and melancholia. *Standard Edition* 14:237-260.
—— (1921). Group psychology and the analysis of the ego. *Standard Edition* 18:69-143.
—— (1923a). The ego and the id. *Standard Edition* 19:3-16.
—— (1923). The infantile genital organization of the libido. *Standard Edition* 19:141-148.
—— (1933). New introductory lectures on psychoanalysis. *Standard Edition* 22:3-184.
Friedlander, K. (1942). Children's books and their function in latency and puberty. *American Imago* 3:129-150.
—— (1949). Neurosis and home background: a preliminary report. *Psychoanalytic Study of the Child* 3/4:423-438. New York: International Universities Press.
Fries, M. E. (1958). Review of the literature on the latency period. *Journal of the Hillside Hospital* 7:37-48.

Gaddini, E. (1969). On imitation. *International Journal of Psycho-Analysis* 50:475-484.
Grinberg, L. (1978). The 'Razor's Edge' in depression and mourning. *International Journal of Psycho-Analysis* 59:245-254.
Hartmann, H. (1952). The mutual influences in the development of ego and id. *Psychoanalytic Study of the Child* 7:9-30. New York: International Universities Press.
―――― (1955). Notes on the theory of sublimation. *Psychoanalytic Study of the Child* 10:9-29. New York: International Universities Press.
Hartmann, H., and Loewenstein, R. M. (1962). Notes on the superego. *Psychoanalytic Study of the Child* 17:42-81. New York: International Universities Press.
Hellman, I., Friedman, O., and Shepheard, E. (1960). Simultaneous analysis of mother and child. *Psychoanalytic Study of the Child* 15:359-377. New York: International Universities Press.
Hunt, R. L. (1967). The ego ideal and male homosexuality. *Bulletin of the Philadelphia Association of Psychoanalysis* 17:217-244.
Jacobson, E. (1954). The self and the object world: vicissitudes of their infantile cathexes and their influence on ideational and affective development. *Psychoanalytic Study of the Child* 9:75-127. New York: International Universities Press.
―――― (1964). *The Self and the Object World*. New York: International Universities Press.
Johnson, A. M., and Szurek, S. (1952). The genesis of antisocial acting out in children and adults. *Psychoanalytic Quarterly* 21:323-343.
Jones, E. (1918). Anal-erotic character traits. In *Papers on Psycho-Analysis*, 5th ed., pp. 413-437. Baltimore: Williams & Wilkins. 1948.
Kanzer, M. (1985). Identification and its vicissitudes. *International Journal of Psycho-Analysis* 66:19-30.
Kaplan, S. M, and Whitman, R. M. (1965). The negative ego-ideal. *International Journal of Psycho-Analysis* 46:183-187.
Kernberg, O. (1982). Self, ego, affects, and drive. *Journal of the American Psychoanalytic Association* 30:893-917.
―――― (1986). Identification in psychoses. *International Journal of Psycho-Analysis* 67:147-159.
Kolansky, H., and Moore, W. T. (1966). Some comments on the simultaneous analysis of a father and his adolescent son. *Psychoanalytic Study of the Child* 21:237-268. New York: International Universities Press.
Kramer, S. (1986). Identification and its vicissitudes as observed in children: a developmental approach. *International Journal of Psycho-Analysis* 67:161-172.
Lampl-de Groot, J. (1962). Ego ideal and superego. *Psychoanalytic Study of the Child* 17:94-106. New York: International Universities Press.
Leonard, M. (1961). Problems in identification and ego development in twins. *Psychoanalytic Study of the Child* 16:300-320. New York: International Universities Press.
Levy, K. (1960). Simultaneous analysis of a mother and her adolescent daughter. *Psychoanalytic Study of the Child* 15:378-391.
Loewald, H. (1962). Internalization in the development of object relations during the separation-individuation phase. *Journal of the American Psychoanalytic Association* 27:327-345.
Mahler, M. (1952). On child psychosis and schizophrenia: Autistic and symbiotic psychoses. *Psychoanalytic Study of the Child* 7:281-305. New York: International Universities Press.
―――― (1961). On sadness and grief in childhood. *Psychoanalytic Study of the Child* 16:332-351. New York: International Universities Press.
―――― (1967). On human symbiosis and the vicissitudes of individuation. In *Selected Papers*, vol. 2, pp. 76-97. New York: Jason Aronson, 1979.

Mahler, M., and Furer, M. (1968). *On Human Symbiosis and the Vicissitudes of Individuation.* New York: International Universities Press.

Mahler, M., Pine, F., and Bergman, A. (1975). *The Psychological Birth of the Human Infant.* New York: Basic Books.

Mahler, M., and McDevitt, J. B. (1982). Emergence of the sense of self: body self. *Journal of the American Psychoanalytic Association* 30:827–848.

McDevitt, J. B. (1979). The role of internalization in the development of object relations during the separation–individuation phase. *Journal of the American Psychoanalytic Association* 27:327–345.

Meissner, W. (1970). Notes on identification. I: origins in Freud. *Psychoanalytic Quarterly* 39:563–589.

―――― (1971). Notes on identification. II: clarification of related concepts. *Psychoanalytic Quarterly* 40:224–260.

―――― (1972). Notes on identification. III: the concept of identification. *Psychoanalytic Study of the Child* 17:128–145. New Haven, CT: Yale University Press.

―――― (1981). *Internalization in Psychoanalysis.* New York: International Universities Press.

Murray, J. M. (1964). Narcissism and the ego ideal. *Journal of American Psychoanalytic Association* 12:477–511.

Niederland, W. (1959a). Shreber: Father and son. *Psychoanalytic Quarterly* 28:151–169.

―――― (1959b). The "miracled-up" world of Schreber's childhood. *Psychoanalytic Study of the Child* 14:383–413. New York: International Universities Press.

―――― (1974). *The Schreber Case.* New York: Quadrangle.

Noshpitz, J. (1962). Notes on the theory of residential treatment. *Journal of the American Academy of Child Psychiatry* 1:281–292.

Novey, S. (1955). The role of the superego and ego-ideal in character formation. *International Journal of Psycho-Analysis* 36:88–94.

Nunberg, H. (1932). *Principles of Psychoanalysis.* New York: International Universities Press.

Parens, H. (1971). A contribution of separation–individuation to the development of psychic structure. In *Separation–Individuation,* ed. J. McDevitt & C. F. Settlage, pp. 100–112. New York: International Universities Press.

Peller, L. (1959). Daydreams and children's favorite books. *Psychoanalytic Study of the Child* 14:414–433. New York: International Universities Press.

Piers, G., and Singer, M. B. (1953). *Shame and Guilt.* New York: Norton, 1971.

Reich, A. (1953). Narcissistic object choice in women. In *Psychoanalytic Contributions,* pp. 179–208. New York: International Universities Press, 1973.

―――― (1954). Early identifications as archaic elements in the superego. In *Psychoanalytic Contributions,* pp. 209–235. New York: International Universities Press, 1973.

―――― (1958). A character formation representing the integration of unusual conflict solutions into the ego structure. In *Psychoanalytic Contributions,* pp. 250–270. New York: International Universities Press, 1973.

―――― (1960). Pathologic forms of self-esteem regulation. In *Psychoanalytic Contributions,* pp. 288–311. New York: International Universities Press, 1973.

Ritvo, S., and Solnit, A. (1969). Influences of early mother-child interaction on identification processes. *Psychoanalytic Study of the Child* 24:64–91. New York: International Universities Press.

―――― (1971). Late adolescence: Developmental and clinical considerations. *Psychoanalytic Study of the Child* 26:241–263. New York: Quadrangle.

Ruben, M. (1945). A contribution to the education of a parent. *Psychoanalytic Study of the Child* 1:247–261. New York: International Universities Press.

Sandler, J. (1960). On the concept of superego. *Psychoanalytic Study of the Child* 15:128–162.

New York: International Universities Press.
Sandler, J., and Rosenblatt, B. (1962). The concept of the representational world. *Psychoanalytic Study of the Child* 17:128-145. New York: International Universities Press.
Sandler, J., Holder, A., and Meers, D. (1963). The ego ideal and the ideal self. *Psychoanalytic Study of the Child* 18:139-158. New York: International Universities Press.
Schafer, R. (1967). Ideals, the ego ideal, and the ideal self. In *Motives and Thought (Psychological Issues,* Monograph 18/19), ed. R. R. Holt, pp. 131-174. New York: International Universities Press.
_____ (1968). *Aspects of Internalization.* New York: International Universities Press.
Scharf, D. E., and Scharf, J. S. (1987). *Object Relations Family Therapy.* Northvale, NJ: Jason Aronson.
Sholevar, G. P. (1980). Family therapy with psychosomatic disorders. In *Emotional Disorders in Children and Adolescents: Medical and Psychological Approaches to Treatment,* pp. 343-351. New York: S. P. Medical and Scientific Books.
_____ (1982). Current controversies in family therapy, an essay review of Lynn Hoffman's *Foundations of Family Therapy. Contemporary Psychiatry* 1:42-46.
_____ (1985). Marital therapy. In *Comprehensive Textbook of Psychiatry,* 4th ed., ed. H. I. Kaplan and B. J. Sadock, pp. 1443-1450. Baltimore: Williams & Wilkins.
Silverman, M. (1986). Identification in character formation. *International Journal of Psycho-Analysis* 67:201-208.
Solnit, A. J. (1959). The vicissitudes of ego development in adolescence, panel report. *Journal of the American Psychoanalytic Association* 7:523-536.
Solnit, A. S. (1982). Self and object constancy. *Psychoanalytic Study of the Child* 37:201-218. New Haven, CT: Yale University Press.
Sperling, M. (1950). Children's interpretation of their mother's unconscious. *International Journal of Psycho-Analysis* 31:36-40.
_____ (1951). The neurotic child and his mother. *American Journal of Orthopsychiatry* 21:351-364.
_____ (1954). Reactive schizophrenia. *American Journal of Orthopsychiatry* 24:506-512.
Spitz, R. (1957). *No and yes. On the Genesis of Human Communication.* New York: International Universities Press.
_____ (1965). *The First Year of Life.* New York: International Universities Press.
Steingart, I. (1969). On self, character, and the development of a psychic apparatus. *Psychoanalytic Study of the Child* 24:271-303. New York: International Universities Press.
Stoller, R. (1968). *Sex and Gender.* New York: Science House.
Winnicott, D. W. (1960). The theory of the parent-infant relationship. In *The Maturational Processes and the Facilitating Environment,* pp. 37-55. New York: International Universities Press.

12

Neurosis and Femininity

Ruth S. Fischer, M.D.

Claire is an attractive, coy 4½-year-old who was referred for difficulty falling asleep, requiring that a parent sit with her for hours each night. Her history was unremarkable until age 2 when her mother delivered a baby boy with a birth defect. The parents were concerned and preoccupied, but also were aware of Claire and attempted to minimize her anxiety. She enjoyed helping with her brother's care. At times he was a "pain," as he interfered with her relationship with her mother. At 3, she was noted to occasionally withdraw into herself and masturbate. She noted her brother's penis and wondered if it would grow bigger like Daddy's. She demanded her father's exclusive attention and then began to come to the parents' bed at night wanting to sleep with them or to have Daddy sit with her. She had started school where she had many friends, but displayed an apparent disinterest in learning.

In therapy, she was outgoing, warm, seductive, adorable. She was engaging and quickly engaged in treatment. There was minimal difficulty in separating from her mother. Her two favorite games were hide and seek and school. We took turns hiding and finding the pen. In the school game, she was the cruel teacher who gave the analyst difficult work to do. Questions were asked, the answers to which could never be known. She was expressing her difficulty and frustration with school, as well as her need to maintain strict control over pressing wishes, thoughts, and feelings. She had an intense need not to know.

The first game took precedence in the beginning of her therapy. We played it endlessly as we talked about things that are hidden: things she felt she should not know, should not see, things she does know, and how confused she was about all of this. As she pursued this idea, she became silly, giddy, sexually excited, doing gymnastics over the furniture. She sat so that her panties were on display. More and more the dark closet became the hiding place for the pen and then she wanted the analyst to hide there. She kept her there for long periods of time wondering where the analyst was. Suddenly, she would open the door and note her presence with surprise. She also kept the analyst in the closet when she had had enough of what was being said.

At this juncture the schoolteacher game took precedence. Gradually, the teacher became less strict and more sexy. She turned into a rock star with makeup, jewelry, tight, revealing clothes. This material made her uncomfortable. She was too excited and had too much trouble containing it. Then the strict teacher would return and she would turn back to the now more routinized hide and seek.

How do we understand this material? Traditionally, we would say that as Claire entered the phallic-oedipal stage of development, she was faced with the anatomical difference between the sexes. She believed herself to be castrated and she developed penis envy. This was aggravated by the untimely birth of a brother, possibly made worse by his defect. She wanted what she saw that he had. She then turned to her father to get what she wanted (penis, baby) from him. Denial of her castrated state resulted in a learning difficulty. Her preoccupation with the hidden pen had to do with her seeking of her own penis which she believes is hidden somewhere within. The therapeutic goal in this framework is to help Claire come to grips with her penislessness. But suppose that penislessness is not the sum total of her conflicts. Recent advances in our theoretical understanding of female psychology lead us in just this direction.

In order to appreciate our expanded horizon, we must turn back and see from where we are coming. What are the basic theoretical assumptions about female psychology that we are now reviewing and revising?

We start with infantile sexuality, that is, psychosexual development: the child experiencing bodily sensations and organizing him- or herself psychologically in a sequence of stages in response to his awareness of these sensations. Here we have the oral, anal, and phallic stages of development. The importance of these pressing body sensations as initiators of each phase is both an essential component of the theory and a complicating factor in our understanding of female development

TRADITIONAL PSYCHOSEXUAL DEVELOPMENT

Oral sensations focus the child's attention on the mouth. She eats, sucks her thumb, and generally takes in the world through her mouth. She learns about inside and outside, self and other, through manipulations and sensations involving the mouth.

As the nervous system matures, she becomes aware of sensations farther down in her body. Sensation is experienced in the anal zone. Bowel habits change, she picks at her diaper, becomes interested in defecation, in things that go in and come out, and in issues of control. Bodily sensations draw the child's attention to an area, focus interest on activities related to this area of the body, and then go on to related psychological issues. Oral sensations lead to learning about inside and outside, taking in and spitting out, accepting and rejecting, anal sensations lead to holding on and releasing control over oneself and others.

In the phallic phase, sensations are experienced in the phallus: the penis for the boy and its equivalent, the clitoris, for the girl. What is essential to note here is the belief at that time that the only genital organ of which the girl is aware is the clitoris; that there are no vaginal sensations and, therefore, the girl is unaware of her vagina. The only organ that she knows is the one that she can see, touch, or feel, and this is the clitoris. Phallic is not genital. It is penis and clitoris. This is a point to which we will return.

An equality of development is postulated. Girls and boys are the same. The little girl is a "little man" through this stage of development. With increased genital sensation, attention is drawn to the phallic area and anatomical sexual difference is noted. This marks the beginning of the divergence in development of boys and girls.

For the boy, genital sensations become associated with love feelings toward his mother. He loves his mother and is driven to replace his rival, his father, to acquire her. He fears his father's retaliation if he acts on these wishes. Retaliation, he feels, is directed toward his penis, which is the source of the sensations that are driving him toward closeness with mother and wanting to replace father. He must choose between his penis and his love for his mother. The Oedipus complex, his desire for mother, results in castration anxiety, his fear of his father's retaliation, that is, father's revenge against the offending penis. The Oedipus complex is brought to an end as he relinquishes his mother and identifies with his father in order to protect his seemingly threatened penis. This results in the establishment of a firm superego—the internalized, prohibiting, demanding father.

It was assumed that for the girl the same series of events play themselves out only with the roles reversed—the love object being the father; the feared, hated, yet loved rival being the mother. But this was never satisfactory. Too many differences were noted. Castration anxiety was the first problem. To begin with, for the girl, it initiated the Oedipus complex rather than terminated it. The girl becomes aware of anatomical sexual difference, that she is without the prized penis, and has only a poor substitute, the clitoris. She suffers a profound narcissistic blow. She realizes the inadequacy of her clitoris in comparison to the boy's obviously more powerful, gratifying penis. She feels inadequate, deprived, humiliated, envious. This cognitive awareness and the resulting affective humiliation initiate the turn to father with the resulting oedipal complex (rather than the pressing body sensations as with the boy). She turns to her father in the hope of acquiring a penis, to undo her humiliation, her penislessness, her castration. It is the awareness of anatomical sexual difference that initiates her turn to her father. There is, therefore, no castration threat to bring this love affair to an end. There is no castration threat to resolve the Oedipus complex, internalize the father, and establish the superego. There is no motivation to move on in development, to relinquish her tie with father and seek an equal among her male peers, and there is no subsequent moral development.

Up to this point, male and female, boy and girl, have been the same. Now the girl becomes envious, narcissistic, passive, and masochistic. She turns in anger against her loved mother, who deprived her of this organ and has none of her own. She turns to her father in the hope of acquiring a penis to undo her humiliating inadequacy. As there is no castration threat to bring this love affair with father to an end, no identification with father, no internalization of commands and prohibitions, it continues for an indefinite period of time and the girl's superego is weak and inadequate to the cultural contributions of her male counterpart. The effects of the awareness of anatomical sexual difference for the girl are profound and devastating. In this context, it is no wonder that penis envy and castration anxiety would be seen as so central to female psychology and that female morality would be so totally misunderstood.

Male development is taken as the norm from which female development deviates. This is most clearly seen in the understanding of the girl's wish for a baby, which is again explained as an outgrowth of the turn to father in the hopes of acquiring a penis. Later, she substitutes for this wish the desire for a baby from him. Thus develops the first real baby wish. Even this most fundamental aspect of femininity is seen as compensation for her inability to be male. The very essence of femininity, the woman's inner space and ability to procreate, is relegated to a secondary, compensatory status.

Castration anxiety, the awareness of anatomical difference, has dire results for the girl. She turns against her body, feels humiliated, deprived, envious. She gives up her "masculine" sexuality and aggression and is unable to replace it with anything other than neurosis, homosexuality, masochism, passivity, and penis envy. It thrusts her into her oedipal complex. She rejects her depriving, devalued mother, turns to her father for love, for his penis, for his baby. Then, there is nothing to bring this love affair to an end. The boy's love affair with his mother is terminated by his fear of loss of his penis, but for the girl, it is castration anxiety that initiated the Oedipus complex. Therefore, it is resolved late or incompletely and the superego suffers. Even as he wrote this, Freud wondered how much could be attributed to female sexual development and how much was a function of social breeding.

Many key concepts presented here need our attention: primary femininity, the preoedipal attachment to the mother, female masturbation, castration anxiety, penis envy, the wish for a baby, superego development. Much of what Freud observed remains clinically valid and noteworthy as important components of female psychology. However, our understanding of their significance, of their place in female development has been greatly altered.

PRIMARY FEMININITY

Freud believed that the little girl is a little man until she becomes aware of anatomical sexual difference and finds herself without a sexual organ. Until this point in development, boys and girls develop along the same route. In essence, he was saying that the girl has no primary sense of herself as female. This is congruent with the belief that she is unaware of any genitalia other than her clitoris; that there is a lack of awareness of the vagina as there are no vaginal sensations until puberty. Suppose, however, that there are vaginal sensations which the girl experiences before puberty, even from the beginning of life. Increasingly we have become aware of the presence of just such sensations. Girls do experience internal sensations, and from very early are establishing mental representations that include their internal selves. The girl is aware of herself as a girl early in her life. This includes awareness of herself as a person with a genital of her own. She has a basic sense of herself as female. This is a very different starting place from which to understand female psychology.

Here we have a revolutionary new concept—primary femininity. It is revolutionary in the sense that it overturns deeply ingrained basic concepts and requires major theoretical adjustment. At the same time, it seems almost commonplace. How could we have thought otherwise?

Penis envy, castration anxiety, anatomical difference, no longer central to the establishment of femininity, become developmental issues that confront the girl after she has established her gender identity. She deals with her lack of a penis in the context of a basic sense of herself as female.

Primary femininity, a basic sense of being female beginning at birth and continuing and developing throughout life, is what is missing in Freud's understanding of female psychology. It has been explored extensively over the past twenty years by researchers of various persuasions who have focused on different aspects of the issue, and it is to this that I would now like to turn.

Differences between boys and girls are observed at all stages of development. Long ago, Erikson noted that given blocks, boys build towers, girls build enclosures. In latency, girls turn more to fantasy, boys to physical outlets. Girls are more social, outgoing, compliant, educable; boys more independent, less able to sit and learn, explore more, fear physical harm. Girls fear loss of love. How much of this is innate? How much learned? How much is a response to parental expectation or to selective reinforcement?

In an attempt to assess just these social influences, researchers have begun to observe newborns and have noted differences. Children respond differently to stimuli such as food and music. When offered sweetened formula, girls will take more than the usual amount, boys will not change their intake. Boys respond to syncopated beats, girls to jazz—interesting observations. And researchers have turned to observe parents of newborns and note that they hold boys and girls differently in terms of closeness, frequency, and position. They look at, talk to, and touch them differently.

Genetic and hormonal studies are fascinating. What is strongly suggested is that it is the sex in which the infant is reared during the first eighteen months that plays the major role in the establishment of gender identity, not the genetic endowment or the hormonal environment, although they certainly have their influence. The sex in which the child is reared is usually determined by the appearance of the external genitals and the reaction of the parents to them.

Primary femininity, the girl's early and basic sense of herself as female, is determined by many factors: genes and hormones, sex assignment at birth and sex of rearing in the first eighteen months, cognitive factors, and most important, body sensations.

At 18 months, children's behavior indicates that they are experiencing genital sensations. Neurological maturation allows for increased genital sensation, which then draws the child's attention to the area. There is frequent and intense manipulation of the genitals and an upsurge in curiosity about the genitals: one's own and that of others. A new mental image of self and other is formed with the addition of the genital zone. Play and speech indicate that all areas of functioning are influenced and organized by this new genital awareness Reaction to the anatomical difference is noted. Many children develop symptoms: negativism, increased dependency, sleep disturbances, bowel and bladder disturbances, nightmares, fears of being bitten (note here Little Hans). Boys fear their penises will fall off. Girls wonder at the absence of a penis. There are associated fears of object loss and self-annihilation. These new body sensations profoundly influence object relations, ego and superego development, as well as gender development.

The importance of body sensations is not new to psychoanalytic theory. It is the core of our theory. It is psychosexual development—the progression from the oral to anal to genital phases. What is new is the new appreciation of these genital sensations in the female genitals for the female toddler. These sensations affect gender identity. They draw the girl's attention to this area, foster integration of this part of her body into her mental representation, promote dealing with gender difference, push her into another developmental phase, turn her inward, and promulgate certain types of ego activities, superego development, and object relatedness, which are typically feminine.

It is these same sensations that lead to masturbation and for us, a need to reevaluate our understanding of female masturbation. Girls do masturbate contrary to established theory, and concordant with clinical observation. Female masturbation, like male, is important in establishing a sense of self, of one's body, of gender identity, and especially important for the girl, in establishing a mental representation of her genitals.

Why is this so important for the girl? Because by the end of the second year, the boy is more knowledgeable of his genital anatomy than the girl is of hers. This is due to the lack of visibility, the inaccessibility, the unitary function of the female genital, the diffuseness of female genital sensations that lead inward, and frequently, to different parental reactions. There is also a striking cognitive difference, which is that the girl's organ often has no name. The boy has a penis; to the girl, a bottom or, at best, the entire area is her vagina. Naming is such an important tool for mastery and it is absent here. Why? The freedom to masturbate is essential for the integration of the genital into the child's concept of her body. It will be practiced under normal circumstances.

In considering the factors that determine gender identity, primary femininity, a core sense of self as female, we have noted genes, hormones, cognition, language, parental influence, nervous system maturation, body sensations, and masturbation. Of utmost importance, of course, is object relations. The mother–daughter relationship, at this point, almost goes without mentioning. The attachment to the mother is profound, and influences gender identity, identifications, and all ability to relate to others.

What is new is our understanding of the complexity of the relationship with the father, which begins not with castration awareness, the turn to the father for a penis, but from the very beginning of the child's life. From the beginning, the child has a different and special relationship with the father. Later, he becomes important in helping the girl resolve her relationship with her mother, in pulling her out of the symbiosis, in resolving the dyadic tie, in moving on from rapprochement, in becoming a separate and independently functioning adult who is comfortable with both dependency and autonomy.

Further into her development, as her relationship with her father takes on a more genital nature, with awareness of sexual difference and entrance into the Oedipus, her femininity takes on a new complexity and richness. With reinforcement of the girl's feminine behavior, the affection for and attachment to the father is augmented, as is her femininity.

Traditionally, we have understood that the girl is disappointed in her penislessness. She turns to father in hopes of restitution. This wish for a penis from her father becomes a wish for a baby from him. This is the source of the girl's wish for a baby. Now we understand that the relationship with the father begins not with an awareness of sexual difference, with the objective of obtaining a penis, but from the very beginning of the girl's life, the object being relatedness. And the wish for a baby does not begin with the awareness of sexual difference and feeling castrated, the baby being a compensation for penislessness, but rather, it is a basic feminine wish that grows out of awareness of her inside organ, her closeness with her mother, and her relationship with her father, and all that is the essence of her femaleness, which she experiences both inside of her body and outside, in her relationships with the environment and with those around her.

This is the revolutionary idea—that a girl is a girl from birth. It hardly sounds revolutionary. We must wonder why it was never addressed before. A growing fund of knowledge makes the concept of primary femininity irrefutible. We note the importance of the organizing factor of genital sensations prior to castration anxiety and the oedipal complex; the importance of the father prior to as well as during the oedipal period, the importance of cognitive factors, in particular, language and labeling. Penis envy and feelings of inferiority are present, but constitute a less necessary and less central place in the establishment of femininity. They are central factors in enhancing femininity.

PENIS ENVY—NEW UNDERSTANDING

I have focused on a core femininity: the girl's sense of herself as female. It has displaced penis envy as the central factor in femininity; displaced but not discarded, penis envy continues to play an important role. It needs, however, to be reintegrated into our new understanding of a female psychology based on a core sense of femaleness.

What we have been doing is making a beginning in the development of a line of female sexual identity beginning with a core gender identity or primary femininity. With awareness of sexual difference, a richer, more complex femininity is established. This relates to the Oedipus complex, penis envy, castration anxiety, and triangulated object relationships. It was with this more complex femininity that Freud was occupied and which served as the basis of his theory of femininity. It continues to have great clinical relevance, especially when understood as superimposed on a primary sense of femaleness.

Penis envy, castration concerns, rivalry with mother, denigration of women, love for father, masochism, feelings of inferiority, and shame are all elements of every woman's psyche. We need to understand them in context. They are not the bedrock of femininity, the biological basis of woman's sense of inferiority. These are feelings experienced developmentally and resolved. When they persist and become overwhelmingly significant in a woman's life, we must wonder why it is that she feels so inferior, envious, masochistic, rivalrous, or unable to compete. Why must she procreate or refuse to procreate?

What I am saying is that penis envy is a psychodynamic issue, a symptom, not the normal state of femininity, the bedrock that requires acceptance. It is a multidetermined issue which, when persistent, requires analysis of its component parts.

What are some of these component parts? To begin with there is narcissism. Acceptance of sexual difference is a coming to terms with one's loss of omnipotence. One cannot be all things, both boy and girl, man and woman. Penis envy is often a wish for a penis *too*, not a desire to be masculine rather than feminine. Penislessness as an indication of not having or being everything and therefore not being omnipotent, is a narcissistic blow to which a girl is particularly vulnerable if her narcissism is precarious—usually the result of a poor early caretaking relationship or some early body trauma. Prolonged or intense penis envy, then, expresses poor narcissistic balance, an inadequate sense of one's own worth.

Another determinant of excessive penis envy is a desperate attempt at differentiation from mother. Differentiation is difficult for the girl. Fusion is fostered as mother and child feel that they are the same—both female. Identification is with the same person from whom the girl is trying to separate. Genital sensations, experienced as diffuse, not well defined and separate, augment this sense of lack of differentiation. The wish for a penis, at times, is the wish for something that would aid in differentiation.

Penis envy, of course, relates to attempts at oedipal resolution: loving father and competing with mother; loving mother and competing with father, identifying, expressing, denying, defending against all these fears and wishes. Penis envy is also a means of dealing with the fear of penetration.

Penis envy is not the expression of some biological bottom line female inferiority that needs to be accepted, but is, rather, a developmental experience indicating awareness of sexual difference. It may persist, and when it does, it requires an understanding of its underlying components and conflicts. It is the manifest content, the symptom, that needs to be analyzed. It may be the result of any of the factors mentioned above: poor narcissistic balance, difficulty with differentiation from mother, unresolved oedipal conflict, penetration fear, or even more likely, some highly personal conflict involving several of these factors complicated by individual life circumstances.

In order to illustrate this point of the multideterminants of the symptom of penis envy and how it interdigitates with specific individual life circumstances, I would like now to return to Claire. My hope here is to provide some understanding of the new female psychology as it is put into practice and to illustrate the greater depth of understanding that can be attained when penis envy is approached as a symptom that needs to be analyzed into it component parts.

Claire

Claire is a child with a good basic start in life, trusting, outgoing, vivacious, and typically feminine. Gender identity is firmly established. She lives, acts, dresses, and thinks like a 4-year-old girl. At 20 months, her mother became pregnant with her only sib. She felt insecure in her relationship with her mother, sought closeness with mother and was relieved when she got it. Also noted was an increased maternal identification. This was age appropriate but exaggerated. Her mother's pregnancy came at a time of increasing consolidation of her sense of herself as female with the possibility of bearing a child. She was dealing with the upsurge and control of her own pleasant, frightening genital sensations. Mother's pregnancy was taken as all too clear evidence of what it means to be female. This wonderful, powerful, amazing, frightening event that was going on inside her mother's body may one day go on inside her own. That the wish for this was greater than her fear of it was indicated by her increasing maternal identification.

Her brother was born when she was 2½. Her reaction to his birth parallels her reaction to the pregnancy. She was anxious, demanded closeness, and was reassured by it. She took pleasure in helping care for her brother. Mostly, she resented his intrusion into her relationship with her mother. The major stress seemed to be in the breach in the relationship with her mother. This increased her insecurity and threatened her self-esteem.

Several months later, her parents noted increasing masturbatory activity and interest in brother's and father's penis. This is unremarkable. However, her curiosity escalated into an intense preoccupying concern.

Her affectionate demands for father that followed shortly thereafter indicate that oedipal feelings were now also involved. At home, her fears were multiplying, her demands escalating. Although more in control at school, she paid the price of being unable to learn. By the time she was approaching 4, her behavior was most worrisome.

Claire at 3 was a girl with a good basic sense of herself. She trusted and related well. As a girl and as an individual, she has a solid sense of self. There were no concerns about her until anxiety erupted over genital oedipal issues. We can only speculate as to the cause of her distress, whether it was the coincidence of the pregnancy with her early genital stage of development, her brother's gender, his defect, some prior shakiness in the relationship with her parents, or some combination of factors. We could understand this as normal, expectable penis envy and castration anxiety due to her dealing with the anatomical sexual difference with which she must come to terms or, as the analysis progresses, we can look for the determinants that have made the genital difference an issue of insurmountable difficulty for her.

In therapy, the game of hide and seek was pressing. It was used to express her concerns over genital differences. Who has the pen/penis and who does not? Where is it hidden? Will she find it? She wonders what I will do if I cannot find it. She must find it. At times there is a desperation in her need to find it.

Slowly other aspects of the missing/hiding pen/penis begin to emerge. She is preoccupied with death. What happens to the body after death? Where does it go? What does it feel like to be buried? She recalls a child who died. Maybe her brother will die. The hidden pen now takes on a new meaning. It no longer represents simply the hidden penis, but also the dead, buried, suffocated, mutilated body which is in some mysterious, hidden location.

Her interest turned from the pen/penis corpse to the hiding place. Where does the body go? Where is it hidden? The coffin is the box that hides the body and this brings us back to genital difference, to her box, her vagina in which the body penis is placed. This was what was so exciting, so frightening. Her body has a special box in which a baby could grow and could also be suffocated, maimed, or born with a defect. The uterus is both life-giving and life-threatening.

As the autumn passed, Claire, as so many other children her age, was fascinated with and preoccupied by the holidays. For her, the preoccupation had a special meaning. Halloween meant mostly haunted houses and ghosts. Her haunted house was her inner space, which she feared would be destructive in some way. Was she responsible for bringing this defective brother into the world? She had been so identified with mother. She wished for it so much. It was as if she herself had been pregnant and had born her brother. And the ghosts were the destroyed children with no special place of their own in which to live. They were the children killed in the womb and the bad children punished with having no home, having to roam the earth. Thanksgiving gave us another opportunity to rework these concerns. The turkey in the oven was a very clear representation of pregnancy, full blown. The child is healthy and whole and about to be eaten.

We have come a long way, Claire and I, from our original understanding of the hide and seek game. She was concerned with genital difference. She was looking for the penis. To stop here, however, would have been to lose the depth and richness of the material and to do her a grave disservice. It would have been to miss the interrelatedness of these issues with issues of destruction, separation, and loss. It would have been to lose the highly specific meaning of this game and of penis envy to Claire and it would have been to focus on the defense—the penis envy behind which hide her concerns about her hiding place, her box, her coffin, her vagina. It would have been to shift the focus onto the hidden object and to miss the importance of the place in which the object is hidden.

For Claire, what she could not let herself know and therefore could not learn is not that she was castrated or that she had no penis. This, she could talk about. She could not allow herself to think about her own body, her box, her coffin, her vagina, the place that might hold the penis, the baby. It was thoughts about the hiding place that led to sexual excitement, giggling, gymnastics, and displaying her bottom. It was to prohibit such thoughts that the mean teacher was called into play. She tried desperately to keep sexual thoughts and feelings under control. It was long into treatment before it became apparent that it was not penis envy that was her concern, but the sexy rock star with tight clothes, makeup, jewelry, hairdos, and outfits. She needed to keep her female sexual feelings under wraps. That was what had caused the worrisome birth defect. Her vagina was a coffin. Her sexual feelings were very frightening.

Penis envy may be a very persistent and pervasive concern. When it is, we must seek out the underlying anxieties and conflicts that make it necessary to maintain this position. Anxiety about not having a penis was present in this case, but it was anxiety about her own genitals and genital strivings that was of primary concern for Claire. It was only with this more complete understanding that we were able to help her with her specific feminine concerns.

REFERENCES

Abelin, E. (1980). Triangulation, the role of the father, and the origins of core gender identity during the rapprochement subphase. In *Rapprochement*, ed. R. Lax, S. Bach, and A. Burland, pp. 151–169. New York: Jason Aronson.

Bergman, A. (1982). Considerations about the development of the girl during separation–individuation. In *Early Female Development*, ed. D. Mendell, pp. 61–80.
Bernstein, D. (1983). The female superego: a different perspective. *International Journal of Psycho-Analysis* 64: 187–202.
Blum, H. (1976). Masochism, the ego ideal and the psychology of women. *Journal of the American Psychoanalytic Association*. 24(supp):157–192.
Chasseguet-Smirgel, J. (1970). Feminine guilt and the Oedipus complex. In *Female Sexuality*, pp. 94–134. Ann Arbor: University of Michigan Press.
_____ (1976). Freud and female sexuality *International Journal of Psycho-Analysis* 57:275–286.
Clower, V. (1976). Theoretical implications in current views of masturbation in latency girls. *Journal of the American Psychoanalytic Association* 24(supp):109–126.
Edgecumbe, R., and Burgner, M. (1975). The phallic-narcissistic phase: a differentiation between preoedipal and oedipal aspects of phallic development. *Psychoanalytic Study of the Child* 30:161–180. New Haven, CT: Yale University Press.
Fast, I. (1979). Developments in gender identity—gender differentiation in girls. *International Journal of Psycho-Analysis* 60:443–453.
Freud, S. (1905). Three essays on the theory of sexuality. *Standard Edition* 7:125–245.
_____ (1925). Some psychological consequences of the anatomical distinction between the sexes. *Standard Edition* 19:248–260.
_____ (1931). Female sexuality. *Standard Edition* 21:223–246
Galenson, E., and Roiphe, H. (1971). The impact of early sexual discovery on mood, defensive organization and symbolization. *Psychoanalytic Study of the Child* 26:195–216. New Haven, CT: Yale University Press.
_____ (1976). Some suggested revisions concerning early female development. *Journal of the American Psychoanalytic Association* 24(supp):29–58.
Gilligan, C. (1977). *In A Different Voice*. Cambridge, MA: Harvard University Press, 1982.
Greenson, R. (1968). Disidentifying from mother. *International Journal of Psycho-Analysis* 49:370–376.
Grossman, W., and Stewart, W. (1976). Penis envy: from childhood wish to developmental metaphor. *Journal of the American Psychoanalytic Association* 24:193–212.
Jacobson, E. (1937). Ways of female superego formation and the female castration conflict. *Psychoanalytical Quarterly* 45:525–538.
Jones, E. (1933). The phallic phase. *International Journal of Psycho-Analysis* 14:1–13.
_____ (1935). Early female sexuality. *International Journal of Psycho-Analysis* 16:263–273.
Karme, L. (1981). A clinical report of penis envy: its multiple meanings and defensive functions. *Journal of the American Psychoanalytic Association* 29:427–446.
Kestenberg, J. (1968). Vicissitudes of female sexuality. *Journal of the American Psychoanalytic Association* 16:456–520.
_____ (1968). Outside and inside, male and female. *Journal of the American Psychoanalytic Association* 16:456–520.
Kleeman, J. (1976). Freud's view on early female sexuality in the light of direct child observation. *Journal of the American Psychoanalytic Association* 24(supp):3–17.
Kohlberg, L. (1966). A cognitive developmental analysis of children's sex role concepts and attitudes. *The Development of Sex Differences*, ed. E. Maccoby, pp. 82–193. Stanford, CA: Stanford University Press.
Korner, A. (1973). Sex differences in the newborn. *Journal of Child Psychoanalytic Psychiatry* 14:19–29.
Lerner, H. (1976). Parental mislabeling of female genitals as a determinant of penis envy and learning inhibitions in women. *Journal of the American Psychoanalytic Association*

24:269-283.

Mahler, M., Pine, F., and Bergman, A. (1975). *The Psychological Birth of the Human Infant*. New York: Basic Books.

Mayer, E. (1985). Everybody must be just like me: observations on female castration anxiety. *International Journal of Psycho-Analysis* 66:331-348.

Money, J., and Ehrhardt, A. (1972). *Man and Woman, Boy and Girl*. Baltimore: Johns Hopkins University Press.

Parens, H., et al. (1976). On the girl's entry into the Oedipal complex. *Journal of the American Psychoanalytic Association* 24:79-108.

Person, E. L. (1983). The influence of values in psychoanalysis: the case of female psychology. *Psychiatry Update* 2:36-50, ed. L. Grinspoon.

Silverman, M. A. (1981). Cognitive development and female psychology. *Journal of the American Psychoanalytic Association* 29:581-606.

Stoller, R. J. (1976). Primary femininity. *Journal of the American Psychoanalytic Association* 24:59-78.

Tyson, P. (1982). A developmental line of gender identity, gender role and choice of love object. *Journal of the American Psychoanalytic Association* 30:61-86.

13

The Neurotic Adolescent

Robert C. Prall, M.D.

Knowledge of the developmental stages of normal adolescence and the defenses the ego employs in coping with the adolescent upheaval is essential to understanding the psychopathology of this complex period.

Thus, this chapter follows the developmental line of the stages of adolescence as enunciated by Peter Blos (1962, 1967, 1974, 1976, 1979), with an examination of drive development, both sexual and aggressive, the sociocultural aspects, group and peer relations, fantasy life, cognitive development, and the second individuation process in the emancipation from parental object ties.

The development of the ego, superego, and ego ideal is also traced. Normality and pathology in adolescence are explored, and clinical case material encountered in practice is used to illustrate facets of the common psychopathology during the various phases of adolescence. The relationship of defenses to psychopathology is explored, and pathology is also considered from the viewpoints of Mahler's (1968) theory of object relations and from Erikson's (1968) life crises and stages of development. The chapter concludes with a composite table summarizing these points of view.

DEFINITION OF ADOLESCENCE

Adolescence covers a wide expanse of time, characteristics, and behavior, making it difficult to define in totality. The second decade of life is involved in the adolescent process, which is characterized by massive upheaval, both physical and psychological, following the relative calm and stability of the latency period. Latency, with its (1) ego achievements in school learning, (2) peer relationships, (3) sports and social activities, (4) relatively stable defenses, (5) resolution of the oedipal conflicts, (6) superego reinforced by adherence to the rules of the game, and (7) early ego ideal identifications, is comparatively free of the turmoil, similar to that of the prelatency period, that occurs again in adolescence.

The successes and failures of the developmental processes in the earlier stages of life, particularly the preoedipal phase, determine to a large extent the degree of turmoil and the strengths and weaknesses with which the adolescent will face the inevitable upheaval. Oral, anal, and phallic-oedipal fixations, and conflictual elements from the early mother–child dyadic relationship, especially failures in symbiosis and undue stresses in the rapprochement subphase of the separation–individuation process, are reactivated in adolescence and cause greater than usual upheaval, which is characteristic of adolescence.

In general, adolescence is characterized by marked contrasts with the relative stability of latency. There are evidences of increased conflicts in many areas, shown by fluctuations between regression and progression, dependency and self-reliance, male versus female, passivity versus activity, and control and mastery versus submission. Conflicts also occur between enthusiasm and boredom, fascination and disinterest, withdrawal versus social and interpersonal relatedness, love and hate, elation and depression, and narcissistic self-absorption and self-examination with selfish disregard for others versus altruistic interests.

The hormonal upheaval that drives the adolescent process causes marked instability in emotional balance, seen in the rapid oscillations in mood and irritability as well as inconsistency and vacillations in affect and behavior. The adolescent may one minute be calm, considerate, and quite reasonable while at the next moment one notes depression or preschool-like temper tantrums, tears, and screaming demands for his or her own way.

There is great individual variation in onset and timing of the physiological changes that mark the beginning of puberty. In girls, there is an average two-year lead over boys in physical development, and their cognitive advances usually far exceed those of boys during the early phases of adolescence.

On the whole, feeling lonely, isolated, and confused, the adolescent is like a ship adrift on a rough uncharted sea with torn sails, damaged rigging, and a leaky hull (the fragmented body image). There is mutiny against the captain (rebellion against old parental standards), and no helmsman at the wheel (disorganized ego).

With no map or compass, no rudder by which to steer a course (unstructured ego ideal), and no anchor to hold it firm (adolescent disorganized superego), the ship is at the mercy of the waves and winds (the impulses) and is in danger of swamping or crashing on the rocks (personality disorganization or psychosis).

THE TASKS OF ADOLESCENCE

The developmental tasks of adolescence are, in general, (1) emancipation from parental control and maturation of self-dependence—autonomous and independent functioning; (2) establishment of new loyalties, identifications, and intimacies outside the family setting; (3) establishment of a sense of self, identity, and sexual identity; (4) rendering innocuous the bisexual propensities; (5) establishment of mastery and control over drives, both libidinal and aggressive, by means of a restructuring of the psychic apparatus including the ego, superego, and the ego ideal; (6) a final resolution of the Oedipus complex, both positive and negative aspects, facilitated by a temporary regression to earlier levels of conflict. A major goal of adolescence is (7) the achievement of genital primacy.

The final outcome, in normality, is a restructured, more mature personality and stabilized character formation with a stronger ego capable of withstanding frustration and the increased strength of the drives, and an ego ideal that has become consolidated as a psychic structure, along with a strengthened, restructured superego.

LITERATURE ON ADOLESCENCE

The first psychoanalytic exploration of adolescence was Freud's (1905) "Three Essays on the Theory of Sexuality" in *The Transformations of Puberty*. He noted the role of infantile sexuality in puberty and highlighted possibilities for pathology if fixation on the infantile erotogenic zones and component instincts results from an unusual amount of pleasure. He discussed the importance of masturbation and outlined the nature of male and female masturbation. In males, the erotogenic zone does not change in adolescence but remains in the penis, while in the female it must change from the clitoris to the vagina. Freud also outlined the nature of incestuous object choice and taboos in their influence on adolescent object choice. He concluded by indicating that far too little was then known about the entire process of adolescent sexual development, and opened the way for subsequent psychoanalytic workers to fill in the gaps. This has been admirably done by Blos, Erikson, and Anna Freud, among others.

An early psychoanalytic understanding of delinquent adolescents was offered by Aichhorn (1925) in his landmark book, *Wayward Youth*. Erikson (1950, 1956, 1959, 1968) considers adolescence a "normative crisis," a normal phase of increased conflict characterized by fluctuations in ego strength. He states that what may appear to be the onset of a neurosis often is but an aggravated crisis that may contribute to the process of identity formation. He elaborated his concepts of phases in the life cycle of man and related their implications to the adolescent process. These concepts will be related to pathology in adolescence later in this chapter.

The Second Individuation

Another useful viewpoint from which to view adolescent development is the second individuation process of adolescence, as explicated by Peter Blos (1967). He indicates that this is a mandatory part of normal adolescent development in which there is a reworking of the earlier separation–individuation process of the first three years of life which plays a vital role in progressive development.

In the second instance, during adolescence, the individuation takes place by way of separation from the intrapsychic infantile object ties and dependencies in the process of separating from family ties and turning to group and peer object relationships. This is a formidable psychic task and involves obligatory drive and ego regression with the struggle to loosen the ties to the infantile objects.

Insistence upon autonomy and individuation from family involvement is matched in equal measure by the energetic merger into the peer group in which adolescents immerse themselves. The process is accompanied by both depressive affects at the loss of earlier object ties and elation and exhilaration at the development of independent, autonomous functioning. It is also characterized by much ambivalence, rapid mood swings, and conflicts marked by alternations between activity and passivity, fascination and disinterest, and progression and regression.

As Blos puts it, ". . . the task of psychic restructuring by regression represents the most formidable psychic work of adolescence. Just as Hamlet, who longs for the comforts of sleep but fears the dreams that sleep might bring, so the adolescent longs for the comforts of drive gratification but fears the reinvolvement in infantile object relations. Paradoxically, only through regression, drive and ego regression, can the adolescent task be fulfilled" (p. 171). Adolescents cope with the anxiety and tension created by this process either by withdrawal and inactivity or by motor activity, which may take on frantic proportions in their efforts to escape loneliness and boredom.

Blos also indicates that the object hunger and ego impoverishment of adolescence find temporary relief in group activities and relationships that are often transient and rapidly shifting. He adds that the ambivalence of early object relations reappears. ". . . It is the ultimate task of adolescence to strengthen postambivalent relations" (p. 179). If ambivalence inundates the autonomous ego functions, the result is lability and contradictions in affect, drive, thought, and behavior. The ego may find the ambivalence intolerable, leading to the defensive operation of "negativism, oppositionalism, indifference, etc., . . . manifestation[s] of an ambivalent state that has pervaded the total personality" (p. 179).

Depending on the nature of the earlier object relations and separation–individuation process, the adolescent may either succumb to the turmoil and anxiety generated by the regressive process of adolescence and retreat into psychosis or other pathology, or emerge with a restructuring of the personality and a higher level of maturity.

The infantile aspects of the object relations with the parents are replaced, at least to some extent, by contemporary parental relations of a less ambivalent nature. Some of the libido withdrawn from the internal infantile objects returns to invest the self and results in the self-centeredness, self-absorption, and self-aggrandizement and overestimation of the body and mind. Blos concludes that the internal changes of individuation represent a psychic restructuring characterized by ". . . a general instability, a sense of insufficiency, and estrangement. In the effort to protect the integrity of the ego organization, a familiar variety of defensive, restitutive, adaptive and maladaptive maneuvers are set into motion before a new psychic equilibrium is established. We recognize its attainment in a personal and autonomous life style" (p. 182f).

Blos indicates that both ego and drive regression reverberate through adolescence. He also points out that by surrounding himself with pictures of his idolized persons (for example, current rock stars), the adolescent takes part in an experience that makes him an empathic member of his peer group. ". . . The new social matrix at this stage of life promotes the adolescent process through participation in a symbolic, stylized, exclusive, tribal ritual" (p. 184).

Much typical adolescent behavior can be traced to the struggles and conflicts generated by the regression involved in the second individuation process. The frantic efforts to keep reality-bound are seen in the increased level of activity, the need for excitement, and doing things for kicks.

Group belongingness is used as a substitute for the family, to seek empathy and reassurance, and to be able to express loyalty and devotion. Typically, adolescents show the need to belong outside of the family setting by joining groups, for example, "preppies," "eggheads," "druggies," "punks," "jocks," or "dropouts." The need may be met in extreme instances by following more pathological group formations such as the cults of Bagwan Shree Rajneesh, Hari Krishna, the Rev. Moon, satanic worship groups, and the Peoples Temple at Jonestown, which represent to many adolescents a substitute family.

The need to break away from the early objects by pulling away from family standards leads to espousal of such antifamily cults as the punk and hard rock groups with their devil worship and defamation of all that is sacred to parental standards and their urging the adolescent to let it all hang out, use drugs, and seek sex and discharge aggression in an unbridled fashion. (See Demski 1986, 1988.)

Defenses of Adolescence

Anna Freud (1936) points out that in adolescence, as in early childhood, a relatively strong id confronts a relatively weak ego and defensive measures are necessary. Anna Freud (1958) also indicates that the increased drive activity of puberty forces abandonment of the latency character structure to allow adult sexuality to become integrated, thus initiating the adolescent upheaval. She points out that the differentiation of normality and pathology in adolescence is a difficult distinction: ". . . adolescence constitutes by definition an interruption of peaceful growth which resembles in appearance a variety of other emotional upsets and structural upheavals. The adolescent manifestations come close to symptom formation of the neurotic, psychotic or dissocial disorder and merge almost imperceptibly into borderline states . . ." (p. 267). She concludes that if the pathogenic danger situation is in the superego with the anxiety felt as guilt, adolescent upsets take on the appearance of a neurosis. If the danger lies in the increased power of the id, which threatens the integrity of the ego, they resemble psychotic disturbances. The clinical appearance depends on the nature of the id drives and the defenses which the ego uses to ward off the impulses.

Anna Freud (1958) discusses four major defenses against the infantile object ties common during adolescence, in order of increasing pathology: (1) displacement of the libido from the preoedipal infantile objects to parental substitutes (diametrically opposed to the parents) and to peers and the group; (2) the defense of reversal of affect to defend the ego by turning the emotions felt toward the parents into their opposites thus changing ". . . love into hate, dependence into revolt, respect and admiration into contempt and derision" (p. 270); (3) defense by withdrawal of libido to the self, leading to cathexis of the ego and superego with ideas of grandeur and fantasies of unlimited power over people or of becoming a champion. The persecuted ego may assume Christlike fantasies of saving the world. With cathexis of the body, hypochondrical sensations and feelings of bodily changes may result, as in early psychosis; (4) defense by regression with increased anxiety aroused by the object ties and a state of primary identification with the objects may occur, which implies regressive changes in the ego and the libido similar to psychosis. Projection and diminished reality testing with reduced distinction between external and internal worlds leads to a state of confusion, emotional surrender, and fear of loss of identity.

If the defenses against the infantile objects fail, clinical pictures resembling borderline and psychotic illnesses may occur. In these states, defenses against the impulses described by Anna Freud include asceticism, which may be employed by the adolescent to fight all the impulses (preoedipal, oedipal, sexual, and aggressive) when the ego fears being overcome. These young people may turn to the monastic life of such groups as Hari Krishna renouncing all worldly pursuits. The uncompromising adolescents, who are equally abnormal, show far more exaggerated lack of compromise than the average adolescent. This defense represents a strong resistance to treatment.

Concluding her observations of the concept of normality in adolescence, Anna Freud (1958) indicates that there is a disruption in the psychic structure, with the battles between the ego and the id, as attempts are made to restore equilibrium. The defenses described above are normal unless used to excess.

Normal adolescents are inconsistent and unpredictable: they fight and accept their impulses, love and hate their parents, revolt against, are dependent upon, and are ashamed of them while longing for closeness with them. They also thrive on imitation and identification with others while searching for their own identity. They are more idealistic, artistic, generous, self-centered, and egoistic than at any other time of life. They may suffer, but do not usually require treatment unless severe pathology occurs with prolonged regression or extreme anxiety which interferes with ego functioning. Rather, it may be the parents who need help. (See also Anna Freud on puberty [1936, pp. 149-189].)

THE STAGES OF ADOLESCENCE

Since there are marked differences in characteristics of the phases of adolescence, it is useful to define and describe the stages. Blos (1962, 1965, 1979) has divided adolescence into the following stages: preadolescence, early adolescence, adolescence proper, late adolescence, and postadolescence. Each period has its own stage-specific tasks, conflicts, and drive and ego modifications as well as failures and deviations. It is important to note that there are great individual variations in the timing of onset and duration of the stages, and that no exact age limitations can be given. There are no sharp demarcations between stages, rather they merge into one another with intrapsychic and behavioral phenomena defining where an individual is on the developmental ladder.

Preadolescence

Blos (1962) defines puberty as the physical manifestations of sexual maturation, and adolescence as ". . . the psychological process of adaptation to the condition of pubescence" (p. 2). Prepuberty refers to the period prior to development of primary and secondary sexual characteristics. Preadolescence is the psychological stage prior to adolescence, which may remain overly long, independent of physical maturation.

After weathering the storms of the phallic-oedipal period, latency offers the child the opportunity to master reality, expand horizons into education and the community, and to master the drives through sublimation. Blos (1962) indicates that if the oedipal conflicts are not resolved, the child develops a neurosis and does not enter latency. Likewise, unless there is a successful passage through latency, there cannot be a satisfactory adolescent passage, since each stage of personality development is predicated on the adjustment in the preceding phases.

The termination of latency is brought about by biological maturation, regardless of the state of psychological developmental readiness, and puberty creeps up on every individual, ready or not. Rapid physical growth takes place, and the preadolescent feels unfamiliar with the rapidly changing bodily configuration, which causes discomfort and anxiety. The stability and integration of the body image characteristic of latency are lost, and the youngster feels awkward and ungainly in the new body shell. Motor awkwardness related to uneven bone and muscle growth occurs.

Increased endocrine and hormonal activity lead to enigmatic, unsettling feelings and impulses. Much confusion and ambiguity occur with rapidly vacillating moods of elation and desperate depression, and petulant, demanding, turbulent behavior. One often notes alternating periods of furious motor activity or withdrawal and passivity during which the preadolescent withdraws to a room to listen to loud rock and roll music, out of contact with everyone, lost in lonely fantasies.

The successful balance between impulses, ego, and superego of latency with the insistence on rules of the game is lost. In its place there is rebelliousness and opposition to authority and rules and a general defiance toward adults, especially the parents. In preadolescence, the conflicts of the phallic period are reactivated and the Oedipus complex must finally be resolved. The love for the parent of the opposite sex increases and bisexual tendencies are reactivated. However, the masculinity and feminity that became submerged in latency can no longer be dealt with and efforts at defense are made. A major task of adolescent oedipal resolution is to transmute the negative Oedipus complex (the sexual love for the parent of the same sex).

In the process of separating from family ties, the preadolescent is absent from home a great deal and may spend large amounts of time with a peer and the peer's parents, to whom a close attachment may form. These adults often rave to the parents about what a wonderful child they think their youngster is. This frequently comes as a shock to the parents, who may be having great difficulty getting a civil one-word reply from their offspring.

Physical complaints and symptoms may occur, as somatization is a common defensive operation invoked in desperate attempts to deal with the new and unsettling bodily feelings and impulses which are poorly integrated.

Male Development

With the physical changes of puberty, nocturnal emissions usually begin a year or two later. The median age for the onset of nocturnal emissions in boys is between 12.5 and 14 years (Sahler and McAnarney 1981). Masturbatory activity assumes a major role, accompanied by a rich and varied fantasy life that may involve any facet of psychosexual development: oral, anal-sadistic, phallic-penetrating, or polymorphous perverse. In boys there is an increase in restless motor phenomena and interest in gadgets and mechanical devices, weapons, rockets, airplanes, and cars, along with exhibitionistic, counterphobic reckless speed on bicycles, skateboards, and motorbikes.

Blos (1965) describes an increase in phallic aggression and sadism and a turning away from the opposite sex with the increased drive pressure and an upset of the balance between the ego and the id achieved in latency. Object libido gratifications are blocked and regression to the preoedipal "witch-mother" is resisted. The father is aggrandized and becomes an ally in the battle to ward off the archaic preoedipal mother who is seen as evil and castrating. Sadistic fantasies, echoes of the earlier sadomasochistic struggles with the mother, become prominent. Aggression is manifested in fantasy, play, and acting out or in predelinquent or delinquent behavior.

Blos (1962) indicates that, in boys, castration fear from the archaic mother may become so absorbing that resolution of the Oedipus complex becomes impossible and preadolescent fixation may result in a homosexual orientation. The passive drive pathology permeates the ego functions and a state of failure or dissatisfaction results. Blos states that ". . . regression is phase specific for the boy in preadolescence" (p. 110). There is ample clinical evidence seen in their messiness, unwashed appearance, untidy long hair, and their preoccupation with scoptophilia and anal humor and noises.

When pathology develops in boys, delinquency represents an aggressive struggle with school and public authority figures displaced from the parents.

Sexual Conflicts. The bisexual drives lead to sexual curiosity and experimentation with members of the same sex, and some efforts at peeping at the opposite sex. In recent years the availability of sexually explicit magazines, cable TV, and R-rated movies has increased early adolescents' ease of access to voyeuristic opportunities and may have removed some of the prohibitions and taboos of a few decades ago. (This is borne out by clinical encounters as in the case of Wilson, described on p. 256.)

In this stage of adolescence, bisexual conflicts are often pronounced, as illustrated by the following case, which shows clear evidence of the inherent male-female conflicts characteristic of preadolescence.

Ben, at age 13, began to develop pubic hair and genital changes. He showed considerable conflict about his bisexual identity. He had engaged in some typical preadolescent mutual masturbation and exhibitionistic play at camp. At the height of the conflict he shaved off his pubic hair and would stand naked in front of the mirror hiding his penis between his legs folding his arms across his chest to puff out his pectoral area simulating breast formation, fantasizing about what it would be like to be feminine. The other side of the conflict was shown in his masturbating while standing naked in front of the window facing the neighbor's house, fantasizing about heterosexual relations and hoping that the girls next door would see that he, in truth, really had a penis. He dressed in girls' clothes for one Halloween party and in a pirate outfit for another, revealing his identity confusion.

One of the major conflicts of the preadolescent phase is the fear of being overpowered and controlled versus the passive wishes. This is reflected in the fear of passivity, fear of surrender to the preoedipal witch-mother, aggressive impulses toward her, and castration fears at her hands. The penis becomes an aggressive weapon. Fear of castration leads to counterphobic daring and accidents in an attempt to ward off the castration fears.

Edgar, when seen at age 13, had developed marked school difficulties and was repeating seventh grade. He was a handsome, very intelligent youngster, the second child from a well-to-do family, with an older sister who had just started college. She was a brilliant student, much admired by the parents and frequently held up to Edgar as an example. His relationship with his father was tenuous, and the father was quite critical of his son. His father revealed that he, too, had had trouble at this point in school and that Edgar reminded him of his own shortcomings. This irritated him and caused him alternately to criticize the boy and to give up in despair and ignore him. Edgar was quite close to his mother, who was overly concerned, tried to overprotect him, and attempted to make up for father's negative attitude to her son by her solicitousness.

Edgar resisted his mother's overconcern and defended his bodily integrity from her intrusiveness by his reckless accident proneness. He was an avid skateboard addict, much to his mother's concern. He would ride the board in the streets at night without lights and under all kinds of risky conditions. Daily he tried more and more difficult stunts. He would come to therapy proudly displaying his latest brush burns and bruises from falls. These wounds had the quality of his "red badge of courage," revealing his fear of passive surrender to the mother's overprotective ministrations.

His mother's distress also focused on his repeatedly wearing out one pair of sneakers after another as he used his feet for skateboard brakes. The damage to his feet and foot coverings represented a downward displacement, and it became evident that his reckless behavior was a counterphobic defense against his severe castration fears. Edgar seemed to be saying by his behavior, "See, I am [it is] invincible and indestructible," revealing the unconscious equation between body and phallus.

Normally, during this phase for boys there is little hostility to the father, who is sought as an ally against the mother, with the central conflict ambivalence to the preoedipal castrating mother. Unfortunately for Edgar, the father was not available as an ally and contributed to his self-doubts and low self-esteem by his criticism and constant carping.

In healthy development, the ego normally emerges from the regression of the preadolescent phase strengthened from the struggle with the archaic mother.

Female Development

Girls approach menarche with the beginning of secondary sexual characteristics. The acquisition of pubic hair, breast development, and the onset of menarche constitute a major developmental challenge. Many whispered comparisons of who has started her periods and who hasn't take place when the girls share their sexual secrets with a close friend. Wide variation occurs, with some girls showing fully developed secondary sexual characteristics by 12 or 13 years of age while others are just beginning to develop. According to Tanner (1978), the average age for menarche is between 12.8 and 13.2 years. Lipsitz (1980) indicates that since 1840 the average onset of puberty in girls has advanced four months each decade, so that while the average age used to be 17, it is now 12.9 years.

Goldings (1979) points out that for girls there are two hazards: (1) a regressive attachment to the preoedipal mother with whom she has become allied in her final oedipal identifications, and (2) renewed difficulties in dealing with bisexual strivings. The girl resists the regressive pull to the preoedipal mother, turning the object libido to the close friend. She tends to seek a single friend and forms a close quasi-homosexual, intimate relationship. These relationships may become too intense and the homosexual strivings may be warded off by rapid termination of relationships. This accounts for the frequent shifts of loyalties in this age range. The best friend may be very close one day and an enemy the next, only to become the best friend again soon afterward.

Some of the libido is turned to the self and results in preoccupation with bodily sensations, discomforts, and physical symptoms. Preoccupation with bodily configuration may lead to dietary abuses and anorexia as a defensive operation in an attempt to delay the budding physical maturation and feminine development.

Mizzy, one of 11-year-old identical twin girls with two older sisters, was seen in the hospital in a state of severe regression, near death from anorexia nervosa. She was in bed with intravenous fluids and was being tube fed, having lost nearly half of her body weight.

In the analytic therapy begun immediately, it became evident that when the twins were born, the father had very much wanted a boy. By the time the twins had reached latency age, Mizzy had assumed a boy's name and became the father's constant companion and helper on the farm. She helped him with the animals, building repairs, and chores while Lizzy sat around reading comic books. Mizzy had developed a masculine identification in an attempt to please her father, while Lizzy was "mother's girl" and had a feminine identification. Mizzy had also assumed the role of superego for the twinship while Lizzy represented their id expression.

As puberty approached, Mizzy started furiously exercising and running and stopped eating in hopes of "not developing a front" (breasts). She had fantasies of oral impregnation which were related to her failure to eat. Her identical twin sister developed puberty changes and menstruation a full year ahead of Mizzy, evidence of the powerful impact of psychological regressive trends on physical maturation.

In some cases, the reactivation in adolescence of preoedipal oral fixations may lead to overeating or drug and alcohol abuse. In preadolescent girls a vacillation occurs often between anorexia, overeating, and bulimia.

Tomboyishness may be used as a defense against the feminine urges that are threatening to the ego as well as a defense against the regressive pull to the preoedipal mother (Blos 1962). Frequently, when the parents (especially the father) are disappointed in having a girl, this may be suspected from the young lady's name, for example, Georgette or Roberta. In such family constellations, preadolescent girls may identify with the father's interests in sports and attempt to compete with boys as physical equals. Recent court decisions regarding the admission of girls to Little League and school sports attest to the tenacity with which these girls, and their fathers, cling to the need to deny their femininity. Very recently in the author's home town, a legal battle forced the school board to permit a junior high school girl to play on the boys' football team. Dalsimer (1979) gives an insightful analysis of Carson McCullers' description of the transition from preadolescent tomboy to early adolescent girl in *The Member of the Wedding*.

In girls, delinquency typically takes the form of sexual acting out as the girl displaces her oedipal wishes from the father to other male figures, often older, in an effort to seek physical comfort, cuddling, and affection. Their sexual acting out represents an early preoedipal rather than a genital level, and they universally report that they do not achieve orgasm.

Fantasy Life

Throughout all the stages of adolescence, the fantasy life is of paramount importance. In preadolescence with the endocrine upheaval, physical changes, and bisexual urges, fantasies take on a predominant role. As the youngster struggles against the sexual urges in school or while attempting to do homework, fantasies intrude with powerful force. The variety of the fantasy life is extremely broad and includes all types of wish-fulfilling, exciting, megalomanic, aggressive, sadomasochistic, and polymorphous perverse sexual aspects. Current comic books, movies, and television programs involving super heroes and villainous characters dovetail with the young adolescents' fantasy life and absorb much of their time. The popularity among adolescents of the genre of movies such as *Friday the Thirteenth*, *Halloween*, and *The Texas Chainsaw Murders* is due to their magnetic attraction to the ubiquitous fantasy life at this stage of development.

With preadolescent boys, the popular game of Dungeons and Dragons is related to the proclivity for the fantasy life to include dungeon fantasies and a fascination for medieval torture methods. Girls' fantasies center on love, courtship, marriage, penetration, pregnancy, and the pain and fear of childbirth.

Fantasies change with the stages of adolescence depending on the success with which the young people accomplish the tasks of progression through the stages. When there is failure to progress to maturity, one encounters fantasies with patterns similar to Thurber's *The Secret Life of Walter Mitty* or to the anarchy in Golding's *Lord of the Flies*.

A case illustration will serve to highlight the nature of a young adolescent's fantasy life.

Mizzy, described previously, indulged in extensive masturbation fantasies with sadomasochistic elements and an unusual aspect related to her twinship, namely, "triplet fantasies." When the twins were little, they had slept together and sucked each other's thumbs and masturbated each other. However, by puberty, masturbation was solitary. Mizzy had difficulty distinguishing between her repetitive waking fantasies and her dreams, which revolved around kidnap-rape-beating fantasies. She would be kidnapped by a black-bearded bad man who would take her to a cabin in the woods and beat her entire body with a baseball bat and then have intercourse with her from behind, "the way the sheep do on the farm."

Many of her fantasies focused on the farm's sheep. She often helped her father castrate the lambs and dock their tails. Her conflict showed as she professed that she hated these procedures and felt repulsed, but was, at the same time, fascinated by them and continued to participate, ostensibly to please her father, but secretly because they dovetailed with her inner sadistic fantasy life. She revealed vivid fantasies and dreams about going to the butcher shop where she saw her "favorite sheep hanging up, skinned alive, looking reproachfully at me, as though they were saying, 'how could you do this to us when we thought you were our friend?' The next thing I knew, they had done the same thing to me" (i.e., skinned her alive).

An unusual aspect of the fantasies emerged as she told of feeling that there was another one of them besides the twins, a triplet named "Kitchie," who was perfect and never argued or fought. She did everything right and was the best helper and rider on the farm. In one fantasy, she and her twin were upstairs in the house when the bad man came looking for them. She hid under the bed and he grabbed Kitchie and dragged her downstairs. When she crept down, Kitchie was dead. The bad man had tied her up and tried to give her a baby but she had refused and he killed her.

In discussing these fantasies with Anna Freud and Dorothy Burlingham (1968), both of them agreed that this was a most unusual fantasy that neither had encountered previously in their analytic work with twins. These fantasies served a function similar to the normal twin fantasies described by Burlingham (1945). Kitchie represented an alter ego who could have all of the attributes that Mizzy wished she had: to be perfect, never angry or jealous of her twin. She could also express her unconscious death wishes to her twin by having the triplet killed.

Social Development

In normal adolescence, identity formation begins with group identity as belonging to a clique or group serves as a defense against identity confusion. The feeling of "if I belong to something, I know who I am," leads teenagers to associate with any ego-syntonic group with whom they can feel at ease whether it be the jocks, eggheads, artists, musicians, honor students, and cheerleaders, or the misfits, druggies and pot heads. The sense of belonging to a group aids identity formation and facilitates the separation from the nuclear family. As part of this break, adolescents develop their own idiosyncratic language, little understood by their parents. This language is based on "the ever-changing vocabulary of adolescent slang (which) illustrates well the linguistic originality of each generation" (Blos 1976, p. 25).

Healthy ego growth leads to increased social competence, physical prowess, and team-oriented, aim-inhibited competition. The preadolescent also strives for an emancipation of the body from parental, particularly maternal, control. In spite of their efforts to pull away from the family setting, these adolescents also frequently return to the fold and seek parental advice and comfort, thus revealing the ambivalence and inconsistency so characteristic of this phase.

Sociocultural changes reflected by television, movies, rock concerts, and magazines, to which teenagers are exposed, offer massive sexual overstimulation to the preadolescent. (See Demski 1986, 1988.) The increase in the divorce rate, single-parent families, and changing lifestyles have contributed to a marked alteration of sexual behavior in this age group. One finds boys and girls attempting to practice adult forms of sexual behavior at increasingly earlier ages. It is not uncommon for junior high school children aged 11 to 13 to be "going steady" and engaging in regular sexual relations. In part, this may be attributed to lack of parental supervision, when children this age have unsupervised boy-girl overnight parties with alcohol and drugs while parents are out of town.

Lipsitz (1980), in her discussion of early adolescent pregnancies, points out that the only age group for whom the birthrate is not declining is girls of 15 and under. With adolescents biologically capable of reproduction at a shockingly early age and the sociocultural changes that have encouraged earlier sexual activity, there has been a drastic increase in early teenage pregnancies. Unfortunately, although preadolescents are maturing biologically much earlier, they are not psychologically equipped for the complex tasks and demands of parenthood. They are ill prepared to assume responsibility for their sexual behavior. The implications for immature junior high school mothers with their potential for child abuse, neglect, and severe psychopathology in their offspring are self-evident.

Two case illustrations will serve to highlight the problems of the recent social changes, earlier sexual development, and the permissiveness of some parents.

Wilson, a 12-year-old boy of a divorced family, previously a good student, began failing in school. He showed behavior problems and an inability to pay attention in school and was constantly daydreaming. After a bitter divorce struggle, the boy had visitations with his father every other weekend. He reported that while his swinger father was out dating during the visits, he would repeatedly watch his father's pornographic videotapes including *The Devil in Miss Jones*, *Deep Throat*, and *Behind the Green Door* while masturbating. The massive degree of sexual overstimulation was invading his ego functioning to the extent that he was failing in school and was constantly preoccupied with explicit sexual fantasies. He had great difficulty warding off spontaneous erections, and provoked the adults around him to constant harassment and punishment as a result of the guilt feelings brought on by his intense sexual preoccupation. The behavioral difficulties included sexual exploits with a succession of girls and a rebellious disregard of rules and regulations in school and at home. It became apparent that the boy's acting out was unconsciously being fostered by the father's permissiveness, in the sense of Johnson and Szurek (1949, 1952).

Marisella, a Mexican-American, Catholic 13-year-old girl, was admitted to a residential treatment center with the chief complaints of drug and alcohol abuse, defiance of rules, sexual acting out, frequent truancy, and running away. She had four police records for running away. She also had depressive and suicidal thoughts and had made several suicide attempts. Her history revealed that the mother was a depressed, acting-out, rebellious girl of 16 when Marisella was born out of wedlock from an unwanted pregnancy. The father was jailed for drug involvement and was unavailable. The early mother–child attachment was most inadequate and the mother ran away when the baby was 2 months old, leaving her in the custody of the maternal grandmother who raised the child. She was formally adopted by the grandparents at 8 months of age. She did reasonably well in her early years. The grandparents (*de facto* parents) divorced when she was age 3 years, and the grandmother, whom she called "mother," remarried when the child was age 8. The stepgrandfather, an ex-military man, was physically abusive to Marisella as a result of her misbehavior which began soon after the marriage. She began acting out in school and there were intense conflicts with the stepgrandfather.

After Marisella's early sexual development at age 10, she was sexually abused by adolescent boys and a woman babysitter. She was sent to California to live with her biological mother (whom she regarded more as a sister), and a succession of mother's boy friends. She began heavy drug and alcohol use and her school work deteriorated. The mother set no limits, and the child had a wild time with the mother and her friends. She became involved in shoplifting and was arrested and placed on probation. Since her mother's home was adjudged "unfit," she was held in juvenile detention and then placed in a group home from which she ran away. After placement in a temporary foster home, she was returned to the maternal grandmother's custody. There she continued to be rebellious, lied, ran away, stole and wrecked a car, acted out sexually without birth control, and twice became pregnant and had two abortions.

Upon admission she revealed that she hated being Mexican and insisted upon being called "Mary." She told of her mother (grandmother) taking her to a Mexican "witchdoctor-lady" who performed voodoo rituals over her to make her stop acting out. She had become engaged to a 14-year-old boy whom the family liked. They wanted her married to avoid the stigma of more pregnancies and abortions. She stated that she got pregnant to have a baby to cling to. She was hoping vicariously to meet her unmet preoedipal needs for nurturance, which she had missed with her own mother, through a symbiotic relationship with a baby.

This youngster was suffering from severe identity conflicts—wanting to deny her Mexican background and wishing to change her name, wanting to be wild like her delinquent biological mother, but also wanting to be married and become more stable like the grandmother.

This case confirms studies that report earlier age for conception among Hispanic teenage girls in America, who, on the average, mature much earlier than their Anglo peers. (Smith and Wait 1986). They report that in Texas alone, 449 Hispanic teens age 14 and under gave birth in 1984. This study highlights the need for family planning education.

Cognitive Development

In this phase of adolescence, in addition to the changes in physical, social, and intrapsychic development described above, there are also rapid spurts of cognitive development. According to Piaget's formulation of cognitive development, by early adolescence (i.e., 12 plus years), the "concrete operations period" is replaced by the "formal operational period" (Piaget 1957; Inhelder and Piaget 1958). This is characterized by the ability for abstract thinking with comprehension of purely abstract or symbolic content and development of advanced logical operations (complex analogy, inductive reasoning, and higher mathematics). Operations of this level of thinking are necessary for experimentation in physics and chemistry. However, adolescents do not always employ formal operational logic in interpersonal relationships due to the strains—sturm und drang—of emotional maturation.

Early Adolescence

According to Blos's formulation (1965), in the next phase, early adolescence, there is a very rapid rate of growth and marked change in body structure for both boys and girls. For both sexes there are wide variations in the timing and completion of the various spurts of growth during this time. Some boys and girls develop pubertal manifestations as early as 10 or 11 years while others are delayed until age 15 or 16 (Malmquist 1979).

For both boys and girls, facial changes and adolescent acne, more prevalent in boys than girls, often pose major problems in self-esteem and self-image. By age 15 the earlier motor awkwardness has largely corrected itself, and participation in organized team sports is a central focus for both boys and girls. In boys the voice changes and deepens and facial hair increases during this phase.

In boys, the beginning of puberty is characterized by increased size of the testes and penis followed by pubic, axillary, and facial hair, and rapid bone and muscle growth. Ejaculations occur and nocturnal emissions begin about two years later. These changes may lead to anxiety. Other sources of anxiety include the extremes of puberty development, both early and late, since adolescents have a propensity for peer comparison and are prone to develop feelings of inferiority and self-doubt if their growth patterns vary widely from the norm. A common problem for a number of boys (up to 33 percent) is the presence of some breast development during this phase of adolescence, sometimes unilateral, which leads to great concern, as in the following case.

At age 14, Judd began to forget his gym clothes and sneakers and eventually refused to attend gym, causing the school to refer him for psychiatric evaluation. From the history and the evaluation interviews it became clear that the major problem resided in Judd's marked delay in biological maturation. He had no signs of secondary sexual characteristics, had a rather chubby baby-faced appearance, and small, uneven breasts. His refusal of gym class was based on his fear of undressing and being teased by the other boys in the locker room. He envied the more mature boys' genital changes and was afraid that he was deformed and that he would never enter puberty. He repeatedly tried to avoid facing the whole situation by refusing gym class. His avoidance of gym class was in part motivated by a homosexual panic and fear of a feminine identification.

Aggression

During this stage there is a further increase in drive development, which gives rise to an increase in aggressiveness in a variety of forms including provocative behavior, milder forms of mischief such as papering the principal's yard, or putting graffiti on school buildings. More serious expressions include preoccupation with matches and fire-setting, cruelty and sadism, stealing and lying, running away, fighting and vandalism, and aggressive forms of sexual acting out. Physical expressions of aggression toward siblings and parents are noted in sudden outbursts of temper and shouting. The increased aggression calls into play a variety of defenses including projection by which the adolescent externalizes the aggression and feels under attack from without. As self-control threatens to break down, anxiety results from the increase in aggressive impulses, and the ego comes under internal pressure.

Depression and Suicidal Trends

The mood swings and unpredictable emotional outbursts of the average adolescent include periods of depression alternating with elation. The incidence of depressive equivalents is quite high. They include withdrawal, school failure, acting out, truancy, and running away. The expression of suicidal thoughts in a histrionic fashion during a temper tantrum when the youngster shouts, "I wish I was dead!" are different in quality from the more profound preoccupation with suicidal ruminations of the seriously depressed child.

In more severe pathological states, withdrawal, escape into fantasy, or serious depressive and suicidal ideation may occur. When the aggression is turned inward upon the self and against the internal "bad objects," the risk of suicide is much greater and requires different therapeutic handling than hysterical, attention-getting suicidal threats. If an adolescent girl locks herself in the bathroom during a fight with her mother and screams, "I'm taking all of your birth control pills! I want to die!" she is calling for help, and the risk of suicide is much less than if she were to go off quietly and take a large number of pills, telling no one.[1]

Regression

During this stage of adolescence, the conflict between progression and regression continues and signs of regression are ubiquitous. Parents complain about the disaster area conditions in their youngsters' rooms. The regression to the anal phase is attested to by their failure to bathe and tendency to wear messy, dirty, smelly clothes and filthy, worn-out odoriferous sneakers. Often after interviews with a "holy unwashed" teenager, it is necessary for the therapist to open windows and attempt to ventilate the office before the next patient.

Group Identifications

What the parents fail to notice is that the costume of the adolescent is in conformity with the group norm and represents an effort to comply with the group's expectations in the hope of acceptance. Erikson (1950) points out that, in their struggle to avoid the danger of role diffusion in the quest for identity, adolescents temporarily overidentify ". . . to the point of apparent complete loss of identity, with heroes of cliques and crowds" (p. 228).

This mass overidentification is seen in the audiences at rock concerts, where the adolescents wear identical T-shirts with the logo of the band, paint their faces to look like KISS, rip the sleeves out of their clothes,

---

1. The problem of adolescent suicide has increased out of proportion to population growth. From 1960 to 1983 the annual suicide rate for teenagers increased from 425 to 1,677. There are estimates that approximately 10 percent of adolescents may become seriously depressed, and with over 18,500,000 teenagers in America, this represents a sizable number.

and dye and cut their hair in punk style to match the punk rock performers. Other evidences of overidentification are seen in fierce loyalties to local athletic heroes and teams. Adolescents show exaltation and elation following a victory for the home team by shouting, "We won!" as they speed all over town in cars. Crushes on contemporary athletic and entertainment stars are a normal part of this stage.

Adolescents in this age range are more mobile and begin to drive, thus enabling them to be away from home more of the time and to date more readily. Many young people wait to begin dating until someone in the group can drive to avoid dependence on parents for driving them places.

As they break away from their families, still more than in preadolescence, and turn toward the group culture, young people in this age group would rather not go out to eat with their families. They prefer to be with their peers and follow their own idiosyncratic diets of junk food and soft drinks. Greasy french fries, hamburgers, and pizza comprise a major part of their diet at a time of the most rapid physical growth when nutritional demands are the greatest and nutritional deficiencies may occur in spite of voracious appetites. The deterioration in table manners is a means of expressing further rebellion against parental wishes. A degree of alienation from parents is part of the process of breaking away from the earlier internal attachments, an obligatory task of adolescent development.

Sexual Conflicts

In addition to the increase in aggressive drive components, there is a simultaneous upsurge in libidinal drive. The sexual urges are anxiety-producing since they occur out of the individual's control and represent a threat of being controlled by some unseen inner force over which the youth has no control. The fear and dislike of being controlled by inner forces is as threatening as being controlled by the adults of the external world. Strenuous defensive efforts are brought into play in attempts to control the sexual impulses.

Male Masturbatory Conflicts and Exhibitionism. Infantile masturbation is revived in adolescence with the upsurge of endocrine activity in puberty. As Blos (1962) indicates, masturbation serves as a regulator of tension and bearer of fantasies linked to the incestuous wishes toward the primary love objects. Masturbation may either advance forward movement of the instinctual drive or may hold back development by perpetuating infantile sexual positions. Blos states that: "Total absence of masturbation during adolescence indicates an incapacity to deal with the pubertal sexual drives" (p. 161). The accompanying fantasies may exert a harmful influence due either to severe superego anxiety and guilt, or to amalgamation of masturbation with infantile sexual aims that will result in arrested development. "An astounding tolerance of the most bizarre and perverse fantasies exists and is attached to genital masturbation in adolescence" (p. 162). They may either promote a disengagement from infantile gratification or a closer tie between pregenital and genital drives depending on the strength of the fixations and the ego's susceptibility to regression.

Masturbation normally counteracts regression but according to Blos (1962), dependence on masturbation can prevent object libido from flowing outward. "A concentration of narcissistic libido on one's own genital is accompanied by voyeuristic and exhibitionistic tendencies" (p. 162). When masturbation and fantasies are blocked, symptom formation may occur with obsessions, compulsions, phobias, psychosomatic disorders, depression, and inferiority and guilt feelings. Blos also states that there may be the appearance of ". . . neurasthenic symptoms, such as headaches, gastrointestinal disturbances, and fatigue. The adolescent's need for physical activity and social interaction; his inability to be alone without becoming restless and anxious; and his habit of combining his solitary study with listening to music . . . represent typical maneuvers in the battle against masturbation" (p. 163).

Blos highlights the many forms of masturbatory equivalents: "Scratching, nose picking, cuticle tearing, nail biting, hair twisting, pencil chewing, endless play with rubber bands or other objects, . . . [which may lead to] self-accusations, guilt and inferiority feelings. . . ." (p. 163). He adds that gambling, reckless driving, and some forms of procrastination that invite catastrophe may also be viewed as masturbatory equivalents. In connection with the accident proneness of adolescents, he adds that: "The need for punishment and wish for castration are usually both at the source of such self-induced accidents" (p. 165). (See Edgar, p. 251.)

In boys, a major conflictual area is concern over masculinity and sexual adequacy with the conflicts centering around masturbation. The adolescent is driven by the endocrine upsurge to seek physical gratification and release of tension by masturbation. In spite of sex education efforts to teach that masturbation is not harmful per se, anxiety about causing harm to the genitals or fear of damaging the reproductive capacity occurs. Because of castration fears, the boy may be driven to frequent masturbation to prove his manhood, which, in turn, increases the fear of self-injury and leads to efforts to resist the masturbatory impulses. However, the urge is so persistent that the adolescent finds it difficult to resist the temptation and finally succumbs. These intrapsychic conflicts often lead to obsessive compulsive neurotic formations.

Scott, age 15, suffered from massive castration anxiety, which had led to marked inhibition of intellectual functioning and subsequent school failure. He was most concerned about his masculinity and was afraid that he had damaged himself by his frequent masturbation. In order to reassure himself that his genitals were not injured, he resorted to repeated masturbation several times each day. This led to more guilt, shame, and anxiety about self-harm and a perpetual conflict over masturbation. The more he masturbated, the more he feared he had hurt himself, and the more he had to attempt to prove that he had not been harmed (i.e., castrated). At times his violent masturbatory activity actually caused abrasions on his penis, which only served to convince him that he was damaged; this did not stop the compulsive masturbation.

In normal adolescence, exhibitionistic sexual play with group or mutual masturbation frequently occurs, along with comparisons of genital equipment and prowess, for example, competing to see who has the largest penis or who can masturbate the fastest or the longest without ejaculation. The exhibitionistic play often includes regressive anal and urethral level activities such as lighting flatus gas and urination contests. It is unusual for the exhibitionistic quality of their masturbatory conflicts to involve the opposite sex, as seen in the following cases.

Clark, a 14-year-old boy with a sister age 11, was raised by a borderline, narcissistic, non-caring mother who set no limits. She was libidinally unavailabile to her children throughout their lives [in the sense of Mahler et al. (1975)]. She had often left them together, untended and unkempt in their urban apartment. The parents were divorced and the mother frequently traveled abroad and would deliver the children to their father without warning. Clark became closely attached to his father, who was more libidinally available than the mother. Soon after the father married an attractive young woman 20 years his junior and only a few years older than Clark, the mother sent the children to live with him permanently. Clark was annoyed at his father for remarrying and showed much jealousy toward the new stepmother. Both of the children intruded on the couple's privacy in their bedroom. Clark would walk in at night without knocking which greatly distressed the young bride. However, the father said nothing to him and refused to put a lock on their door. Unconsciously, he seemed to relish Clark's acting out.

Chaos resulted when the children constantly tested the limits and refused to accept any direction from the stepmother. The father condoned Clark's acting out behavior by saying, "Oh, he's only being a boy," and by failing to support his young wife's desperate attempts to set realistic limits. For example, despite the stepmother's protests, when Clark invited his girl friend to spend the night, the father allowed the two to sleep in Clark's bedroom along with the sister and the boy she had invited.

Clark was alternately rebellious and insolent with his stepmother and, at other times, very seductive. Over her protests, he insisted on putting up in his room posters of nude women over which he and his father joked together about the big breasts. He often made sexually tinged innuendos to the stepmother as well as to his sister. One day after dinner, while his father was away on business, Clark refused to help clean up and said to his stepmother in front of his sister, "I'm going upstairs to play with myself. Do you want to come and watch?" There was ample evidence of an incestuous tie to his sister, who was afraid to sleep alone and insisted on sleeping in her brother's room. The incestuous feelings were warded off by sadistic provocation and teasing of his sister and stepmother.

In this case one sees a close attachment to the father and overtly incestuous oedipal wishes toward the young stepmother and sister along with a distinctly exhibitionistic quality to the sexual drive. This reflects what Blos calls "the oedipal defense" characterized by a flight into pseudoheterosexuality in attempts to keep the negative oedipal wishes for the parent of the same sex in repression.

In another case of a 14-year-old boy, Sam, from a chaotic family, there was ample evidence of physical abuse by the parents and sexual abuse by a four-years-older sister. There was much disorganization in the home and the mother had several divorces and transient sexual relationships. The boy had witnessed primal scene episodes, drunkenness, and drug addiction among the adults in the home. No one set limits for him. His external life was in chaos, with much acting out in school and the community in efforts to seek punishment. On several occasions, when home alone with his sister, age 18, he came into her room naked with an erection and proceeded to insert the handle of a crochet hook into his urethra. He reported that he had also placed BB pellets in his urethra during masturbation, a painful but erotically intense experience. He had also been involved with various homosexual activities in which he was mainly the passive recipient.

This boy suffered from intense bisexual identity conflicts. His behavior revealed his gender conflicts and attempts at denial of his masculinity by proving to himself and his sister that he not only had a phallus, but also a genital with a "hole." The degree of masochism in this boy's exhibitionistic sexual behavior reflects the impact of the sexual and physical abuse on his psychic economy.

Both of these boys, Clark and Sam, showed rather intense incestuous wishes toward their sisters as displaced oedipal figures and there was evidence of excessive early sexual overstimulation. Their overt exhibitionistic behavior was quite different from the typical early adolescent behavior which usually involves only male peers.

Resolution of the Negative Oedipus Complex. Blos (1965) indicates that in terms of drive manifestations, with boys the aggression shifts in early adolescence from the mother to the father and there develops the passive position of the negative oedipal complex which is stoutly defended against. With attempts to keep the negative oedipal love for the parent of the same sex in repression, dread of homosexuality may occur with a flight into pseudoheterosexuality and the oedipal defense. There is a loosening of early object ties, and with the drive development directed toward coming to terms with the central conflict of the father as the oedipal love object, there occurs displacement onto peer male relationships with adolescent homosexual activities. This, in turn, may lead to rapid termination of relationships when the intensification of instinctual drives results in homosexual panic. The negative Oedipus complex is ended by internalization and development of the new institution, the mature ego ideal, which Blos calls the heir of the negative Oedipus complex, binding the narcissistic, homosexual object libido. Blos (1965) considers the resolution of the negative Oedipus complex and the establishment of the ego ideal as a psychic institution one of the major developmental tasks of early adolescence. Violations of the ego ideal's goals lead to shame, while affronts to the superego, which sets up the boundaries, lead to guilt and superego anxiety.

Female Masturbation Conflicts and Exhibitionism. In girls, the changes consist of further breast development, pelvic and hip changes, and pubic and axillary hair along with the onset of menses if menarchy has not occurred earlier. Anxiety may accompany the beginning of menstruation especially with girls who have not been adequately prepared or who have undergone traumatic experiences including medical trauma and sexual abuse. Some types of pathological family relationships (incestuous relationships with fathers, brothers, or others) often result in guilt and anxiety over the emerging sexuality.

Gwen, at age 14, was greatly distressed about her menses. Her anxiety was manifested by marked bodily preoccupation and intense curiosity about her bleeding. She repeatedly attempted to examine her vagina with a mirror, cried, and became extremely anxious with each period. The anxiety began at her menarche when she was age 13. The situation became so stressful that she was finally referred for therapy. As therapy unfolded, it became evident that she had repressed the memories and painful affects associated with an injury sustained when she was age 3. She had fallen while attempting to copy her older brothers walking on a picket fence and had received severe lacerations of the perineum requiring hospitalization and rather extensive surgical correction.

Following this traumatic experience, she recovered quite well and developed a rather stable latency adjustment. However, she tended to be somewhat tomboyish and enjoyed playing baseball with her older brothers. There were no evident signs of a residual traumatic neurosis until the onset of menstruation when the repressed memories of the early physical trauma to her genitals began to seek expression in consciousness. (See Glenn's discussion on Trauma in Chapter 4.)

In early childhood, female masturbation is morphologically similar to boys' since it takes place through clitoral stimulation. With the absence of a visible sexual organ, it is possible for the female to indulge in masturbation in a more covert fashion by thigh pressure, rocking on the arm of a chair, horseback riding, and so forth. In addition to the necessity of changing her primary love object from the mother to the father, the girl must also renounce clitoral masturbation and transfer the site of stimulation to the vagina or she will remain frigid later in life. The adolescent female gives up masturbation much earlier than the male, usually with menarche, and the libido shifts to the body as a whole. She then turns her libidinal attention to adorning herself, her hair, face, and clothing. Much time is spent on make-up and choosing clothes. She shares her concerns about her appearance with an intimate friend or with her diary, a frequent confidante for the adolescent girl, as exemplified by *The Diary of Anne Frank* (1947). Blos (1962) pointed out that "the diary stands between the daydream and object world, between make-believe and reality, and its content and form change with the times; for material that once was kept as an anxiously guarded secret today is openly expressed" (p. 94).

Exhibitionistic fantasies are common and may take a variety of forms. The defense against the exhibitionistic wishes leads to shyness, self-consciousness, and avoidance of being on public view. In neurosis, this may reach the extent of a street phobia, while in character and personality disorders, it may be acted out.

Female exhibitionism takes on different qualities from that of the male, and involves objects of the opposite sex as displaced oedipal figures. Tight sweaters, low-cut blouses, short shorts, and bikini bathing suits become fashionable. The adolescent girl, frustrated in her attempts to lure the father away from the mother, particularly when there has been sexual overstimulation or sexual abuse, may turn to overt exhibitionistic behavior in her efforts to get the attention of males. She may become a go-go girl, a topless waitress at a bar, or work in a massage parlor, which is a thinly disguised front for a place of prostitution.

Misty, at age 16, looked like a streetwalker, dressed in a tight-fitting blouse unbuttoned quite far down and a short, tight skirt. She had dyed blond hair and wore ample eye make-up and long dangling earrings. She was chewing gum, and her manner alternated between seductiveness and indifferent boredom. She had been referred because she was depressed and had made several suicide attempts. She was raised by an alcoholic, borderline mother and a succession of alcoholic stepfathers, several of whom had sexually abused her from the age of 8 years. She developed sexually quite early and by age 13 appeared more like an 18-year-old. At that time her chronically depressed mother attempted suicide and was hospitalized. Rather than remaining at home alone with her stepfather, who made increasing sexual demands on her, she ran away and worked at various bars as a topless waitress in a distant city. She enjoyed exciting the male customers and frequently went out with them late at night. Because of her pregenital fixations, she never enjoyed intercourse. She tried to excite men by her exhibitionistic behavior but wanted to stop short of intercourse. This had led to several nasty episodes when men had become rough and forced her to have sex.

The revealing of the masochistic job choice and sadomasochistic episodes stirred up marked anxiety and finally led to her recalling the first forceful sexual attack by a drunken stepfather. After this seduction, she had learned to excite her stepfathers by walking around the house scantily clad in order to elicit attention and get affection and physical closeness which she had never received from her mother. Her sexual acting out was on a pregenital level. Because of very low self-esteem and a debased self-image, she never developed relationships with peers outside of the home since she felt she was unworthy of normal heterosexual relationships. Instead she strove to excite older men who represented the father figures in her life who had paid attention to her, mainly in response to her exhibitionism.

This case illustrates how the pregenital conflicts influence adolescent behavior, and especially how lack of maternal libidinal availability may force the child to turn to males through seductive behavior to gain their approval and attention.

Normal Sexuality

In normality, as development progresses, there occurs a new characteristic of drive quality as pregenitality loses its satiatory function, and forepleasure becomes a new drive modality which ". . . eventually elevates genitality to a place of dominance" (Blos 1965, p. 160). In addition, new ego organization and defensive patterns emerge during this phase of adolescence, and superego consolidation takes place by way of new identifications.

Social Development

Interest turns to more activities and relationships outside of the home including extracurricular programs, sports, and group (or gang) activities. The search for new ideals and new identifications is accompanied by sudden crushes on peers, teachers and coaches, and male and female entertainers whose names are on the T-shirts they wear as identification symbols.

Much of what happens in terms of social development in this stage of adolescence depends on the selection of the peer group. If young people choose to associate with the "drug freaks" or "losers," or with a black leather-jacketed motorcycle gang, their development may take a deviant turn. If they choose to relate to the peer culture involved with supervised programs such as Scouts, church or synagogue youth groups, 4-H clubs, after-school activities, or athletic teams where the coach imposes strict rules and demands respect and compliance, a different outcome is likely. If one has his heart set on becoming an Eagle Scout, on making a varsity team, or going to the Air Force Academy, the adolescent turmoil will be far different from that of one who becomes involved with a drug group in an attempt at a chemical escape from adolescent pain, conflict, and boredom by means of drinking, smoking, and drugs.

Some adolescents attempt to hide under the banner of impulse groups to shield the fact that they are *not* acting out. These groups may maintain strong latency qualities with platonic friendships that protect against sexual involvement. On the other hand, Scout and other camp experiences and church youth groups may serve as thinly disguised sexual arenas. In therapy, one frequently hears about seduction of children by adult leaders in group settings.

Although psychodynamic forces determine the object choice to some extent, elements of opportunity and chance enter in. Peers who happen to be readily available, as well as the location and atmosphere in a particular school and neighborhood have a bearing on the peer culture choice. In an inner city ghetto it is difficult, if not self-destructive, to avoid joining a neighborhood gang. Stable, intact families tend to facilitate an easier adolescent passage, while disrupted and disturbed families foster far more adolescent turmoil.

Social development involves much time spent with the peers who are the objects of their libidinal attachment during and after school and on the phone. The need for a sounding board and for an understanding listener is met by adolescents' capacity for empathic understanding. Every social move is talked over and the outcome of each interaction rehashed. When teenagers feel depressed, they turn to peers, not to parents, for help. The peer group functions to offer emotional support during crises and to provide feedback about appropriate behavior in relation to members of the opposite sex and to adults.

Experimentation with dating and sexual behavior involving petting and bodily explorations occurs in this stage. Current mores permit earlier intercourse, and teenagers are far more knowledgeable about sex than in the past through exposure to TV, movies, and open discussions within the school and family. Sexual intercourse tends to occur in bed more often than in the back seat of a car. Petersen and Offer (1979) state that ". . . by age eighteen or nineteen—coitus is more accepted and expected and premarital intercourse becomes normative" (p. 222).

Cognitive development continues to increase as the formal operational stage becomes more firmly entrenched, permitting mastery of more complex logical constructs, scientific problems, and the ability to think, "What if?" about the consequences of one's actions.

Adolescence Proper

During this stage in males, the peak velocity of growth is reached, while in females, growth is nearly completed. The intrapsychic and social processes set in motion in the early stages are extended and consolidated. Cognitive development becomes more firmly anchored in the formal operational mode, and the capacity for more complex reasoning and logic increases. This allows the study of higher mathematics and sciences. Many adolescents develop a philosophical bent and pursue new avenues of thought and new, often radical, political causes. Preadolescent egocentrism and narcissism are replaced by a capacity for empathy.

In adolescence proper, there is ". . . a decisive turn toward heterosexuality and the final and irreversible renunciation of the incestuous objects occurs." (Blos 1962, p. 72). The defenses of intellectualization and asceticism belong to this phase along with the tendency to inner experience and self-discovery. The feeling of being in love and concern with philosophical, political, and social problems occurs here, according to Blos (1962). Sexual experimentation continues but begins to be associated with intimate, longer-lasting relationships. In college settings, many young couples choose to live together and recent studies show that the incidence of premarital coitus is far higher than in past generations.

A decisive break with childhood and a profound reorganization of the emotional life takes place. The sense of identity becomes more firmly established and includes the process of career choice as the individual struggles with the question, "Who am I?" One must decide whether to seek higher education, career training, or employment. Again, social, cultural, and economic factors play a vital role. Among black and Hispanic urban youths the dropout rate for high school students is exceedingly high. In the author's municipality, one out of two Hispanic students drops out of high school. The disproportionately high unemployment in these groups poses severe problems for constructive development in adolescence.

Faced with no prospects for gainful employment or for getting out of the ghetto, these unfortunate young people may turn to drugs and alcohol to escape their misery, and delinquent and criminal behavior often results from expensive drug habits. An increase in depressive reactions may also occur among those who have neither achieved a stable career choice nor defined their goals.

In adolescence proper, further development of the second individuation process occurs with continued expansion of peer relationships and widening of horizons. The adolescent who chooses college away from home has the opportunity to enlarge the circle of friends and to seek new object relationships. However, many college freshman girls have a number of stuffed animals as transitional objects in their dormitory rooms, revealing the need for this type of symbolic representation of the mother during their second separation–individuation process. (See Winnicott 1953, 1958.)

From Erikson's point of view, the answer to "Who am I?" as a sexual person has become more firmly defined. The sense of identity has become more clearly established and role confusion decreases. The question now becomes "Who am I in relation to other people and the future?" The adolescent has become more comfortable with his or her body, and the body image, sexual role, and gender identity have been firmly established. There is increased self-concept, self esteem, and interest in the future with commitments to career choice.

Late Adolescence

Blos (1962) summarizes late adolescence as a phase of consolidation, which involves "(1) a highly idiosyncratic and stable arrangement of ego functions and interests; (2) an extension of the conflict-free sphere of the ego (secondary autonomy); (3) an irreversible sexual position (identity constancy), summarized as genital primacy; (4) a relatively constant cathexis of object- and self-representations; and (5) the stabilization of mental apparatuses which automatically safeguard the integrity of the psychic organism" (p. 129). There is consolidation of the ego and shaping of lasting character formation. There are always remnants of residual phenomena, "partial retardations," from previous stages due to incomplete working through of the earlier phases.

Blos indicates the developmental task of late adolescence to be ". . . the elaboration of a unified ego which fuses in its exercise the 'partial retardations' with stable expressions through work, love, and ideology, eliciting social articulation as well as recognition" (p. 130). With the closing phase of adolescence, the individual shows ". . . gains in purposeful action, social integration, predictability, constancy of emotions, and stability of self-esteem. [There is] greater unification of affective and volitional processes, [and] the amenability to compromise and delay" (p. 128). Blos indicates that the late adolescent defines concerns that really matter in life, which may not tolerate compromise or postponement even if this results in frustration, struggle, and pain. In spite of this, he or she adheres to these choices as avenues to self-realization.

The Role of Trauma and Fixation

As Glenn has pointed out in Chapter 4, there are two types of psychological trauma that are significant in child development—acute and chronic. Acute trauma includes death of a parent, medical or surgical conditions, accidents, and witnessing frightening events. Chronic, day by day, insidious trauma, such as chronic physical or sexual abuse, oversolicitous application of enemas, force feeding, repeated belittling or criticism, and libidinal unavailability of the mother, in the sense of Mahler and colleagues (1975), also have serious and long-lasting effects on the growing child.

Blos (1962) outlines the role of trauma and fixation in the process of establishment of character structure in late adolescence. The negative aspect of trauma is that fixation on the trauma leads to a static position, while the positive aspect of trauma lies in the ever-present urge to rework the trauma in order to achieve mastery over it. He states, "Residual traumata furnish the force (repetition compulsion) which pushes unintegrated experiences into the mental life for eventual mastery or ego integration. The *direction* this process takes—its preferential emphasis on drive discharge, sublimation, defense, ego deformation, and so on—is to a large extent controlled by superego and ego-ideal influences. The *form* the process takes is influenced by the environment, by social institutions, tradition, mores and value systems. . . . within the confines set by constitutional factors, such as physical and mental endowment" (p. 134). Thus, infantile traumas are not removed at the end of adolescence but become integrated in the ego as life tasks. "Every attempt at ego-syntonic mastery of a residual trauma, often experienced as conflict, enhances self-esteem" (p. 134).

By the end of late adolescence ". . . the self-representations assume a stable and dependable fixity. . . . the heir of adolescence is the self" (p. 136). During the final stage of late adolescence the task of "finding new identifications, loyalties, and intimacies outside the accustomed family dependencies . . . is most urgent . . ." (Blos 1965, p. 146). Through the process of regression in the service of development described above, the late adolescent reaches the point of structuralization of ". . . the permanent ego ideal that coalesces during the terminal stage of adolescence. From here on, the ego ideal remains an unalterable psychic structure which extends its influence on thought and behavior over a much larger sector of the personality than was the case before adolescence" (Blos 1974, p. 49).

With the final resolution of both aspects of the Oedipus complex, negative and positive, the result is self-determination, a realistic adult life, and tolerance of self-limitations that was not possible earlier. A precondition is the deidealization of the self and objects which is a major task of late adolescence. Blos (1979) states that ". . . the process of deidealization of object and self represents the most distressful and tormenting single aspect of growing up . . . comparable to the Copernican revolution, which deprived man of his place in the center of the universe—a truly sobering existential awareness" (p. 486).

The newly restructured adult ego ideal, including the body image, becomes an agency of aspiration and failures lead to feelings of shame. The restructured superego is an agency of prohibition and trespasses lead to feelings of guilt.

According to Blos (1974), the ego ideal counteracts regression and shapes adult commitments. Its structuralization in adolescence determines the end of the adolescent process and of psychological childhood. In late adolescence, commitments attain mature form and self-idealization is replaced by a mature sense of self-esteem. The ego ideal represents a "lifelong striving for perfection [which] can never be fulfilled; in fact, it is the sustained striving for perfection that furnishes a sense of well being" (p. 46f).

Blos (1979) concludes that in the consolidation of the stage of late adolescence, ". . . psychic structures acquire a high degree of irreversibility" (p. 496). This results in the finality of character formation with a reconciliation and compromise between such opposite strivings as the active and passive, and masculine and feminine strivings. Preferences for recreation, hobbies, and devotions emerge with equal strength as for the pursuit of work and love, according to Blos (1962).

When the adolescent process is incompletely resolved, efforts at postponement occur as seen in prolonged adolescence. There may be complete failures with regression to psychosis or borderline conditions, or, with "incomplete adolescence," neurotic formations may occur. Erikson (1956) describes late adolescent breakdown as a failure of the maturational task of this stage—the establishment of ego identity—with the persistence of identity confusion.

One of the important tasks of this phase is the formation of a stable and irreversible sexual identity. Failures are seen in the development of homosexual orientations, transvestitism, and perversions. Finally, as Blos (1962) states, "The consolidation of personality in late adolescence brings greater stability and evenness into the feeling and action life of the young adult. There is solidification of character . . . creative imagination fades . . . and adventurous and artistic endeavors decline until they gradually disappear" (p. 146).

Postadolescence

After the storms of adolescence have subsided, we find the ship still afloat, the storm wreckage has undergone some major repairs, and the hull is largely intact (improved body image). The mutiny has subsided and there is once again a captain in charge (strengthened ego). There is now a compass and map to follow and a newly fashioned rudder by which to steer (ego ideal goals). A new anchor is in place (reorganized superego), and the storm winds and waves (id impulses) have decreased in strength but will never disappear altogether.

The task of postadolescence is the stabilization and consolidation of the personality developments of adolescence proper and late adolescence. Blos (1962) points out that this phase represents the transition from adolescence to adulthood and is often referred to as young adulthood. After the resolution of early adolescent bisexual conflicts and the loosening of the early object ties in adolescence proper, along with the selection of life tasks through consolidation of social roles and irreversible identifications in late adolescence, the personality still lacks harmony. The postadolescent must harmonize and integrate the components of the personality along with occupational choice and defining social role, courtship, marriage, and parenthood. The impulses and the ego must reach a harmonious balance, and the mental life must be integrated into a functioning whole which Blos considers the developmental task of postadolescence.

He states that ego-integrative processes undergo their most essential modifications in this phase when permanent settlements of intrasystemic conflicts are brought about and disharmonies in the ego are resolved. Sexual identity exerts a lasting influence on the ego. Experimentation takes place in regard to both sexual love objects and ego interests. The goals and life tasks defined in late adolescence are implemented in permanent relationships, roles, and choices of location. The ego ideal assumes much of the role of the superego with the emphasis on personal dignity and the moral personality. Self-esteem replaces superego dependency and instinctual gratification.

In any of the earlier phases of adolescence, if there is an inadequate resolution of the conflicts or an insurmountable obstacle blocks further progress, development may not proceed and prolonged adolescence may occur. If the organization of the stable self is not attained or if the ego fails to render the conflicts ego-syntonic, there will be deviations of the postadolescent task. Rescue fantasies, where solutions of conflict are avoided or left to the environment, are a remnant of the mother as the reliever of tension and regulator of self-esteem. These fantasies take the form of "If only things were different"—a different job, different location, and so forth—everything would be all right. The abandonment of such adolescent fantasies can be a major task of postadolescence.

While the loosening of the infantile object ties was the task of adolescence proper, in postadolescence the task is to integrate parental ego interests and attitudes, particularly of the parent of the same sex. "In order to reach maturity the young man has to make peace with his father image and the young woman with her mother image. Failure at this junction of development will result in regressive solutions, ego deformations, or a break with reality" (Blos 1962, p. 157).

Incomplete solutions may be reflected in later relationships with a child of the same sex by unconscious substitution. In the rebellions of adolescence proper, the adolescent attempts to detach himself from the parents and their views of morality and reality. After the infantile sexual ties are dissolved, there can be acceptance of parental social and cultural traditions, and the postadolescent becomes more firmly anchored in society. Instinctual conflicts recede and ego integration becomes prominent. "By processes of integration a state of stabilization and irreversibility is finally reached" (p. 158).

PATHOLOGY

Thus far the focus has largely been on the normal adolescent developmental processes and conflicts. As Anna Freud (1958) indicated, it is difficult to differentiate normality and pathology in adolescents as the typical upheavals described above can simulate a wide variety of pathological manifestations.

Erikson's Stages of Development

Erikson's (1950) stages of development and their dangers offer one frame of reference for viewing pathological outcomes of development.

Stage 1, Trust versus Mistrust

(Oral Phase) With insufficient maternal libidinal availability, abandonment, neglect, or abuse during the first year, there will be defects in the sense of basic trust. The absence of basic trust is a paramount feature in childhood psychosis and with abused and neglected children. When there is insufficient basic trust, difficulties will occur during the subsequent phases. In adolescence, reflections of the lack of trust may take the form of withdrawal and isolation. Such adolescents are afraid to face the demands of the outside world and avoid social contact, often remaining isolated in their rooms. As Erikson points out, if the early mother–child relationship is adequate, there remains ". . . the basic faith in existence, which is the lasting treasure saved from the rages of the oral stage" (1950, p. 223). The inability to trust others impairs the ability to trust one's self and the capacity of one's organs to cope with urges. In adolescence, fear of the impulses may lead to an inability to move forward in development and to face the inevitable struggles for independence from the parents. Thus, the absence of rebellion is pathological.

Petersen and Offer's (1979) summary of Erikson's life cycle crises in relationship to the conflicts of adolescence is helpful. They point out that Erikson (1968) relates the first life crisis (oral stage) of trust versus mistrust to a vital role in the adolescent conflict of temporal perspective versus time diffusion. With a sense of basic trust which facilitates the delay of gratification and establishment of a sense of time, the adolescent becomes able to coordinate the past with the future and develops the ability to delay gratifications. By late adolescence, the ability to differentiate between time proper and the measurement of time is developed.

Stage 2, Autonomy versus Shame and Doubt

(Anal Phase) The life crisis of autonomy versus shame and doubt is reflected in adolescent conflicts centering around self-certainty versus self-consciousness. The phenomenon of the imaginary audience is related to the degree of egocentrism, self-consciousness, and the sense of self-certainty. Young adolescents show a tendency to embarrassment and anxiety when they are in public view in sports, in front of the class, or on stage, and feel that others are as concerned about their performance, appearance, and dress as they are. They overgeneralize and feel that all of their concerns are shared by others.

In this phase, the major conflict is holding on versus letting go. Denied autonomy by coercive toilet training, the child may turn the destructive forces against the self with the development of a precocious conscience and obsessive, repetitive attempts to repossess the environment and gain power by stubborn control, which is ". . . the infantile model for a compulsion neurosis" (Erikson 1950, p. 222). There will be the potential for anarchy unless the parents set firm and realistic limits and support the child's ego in control of the impulses.

In the absence of autonomy, shame and early doubt develop. Shame is the feeling of being completely exposed and conscious of being looked at — self-consciousness. Erikson states that shame involves a turning of rage against the self, and that shaming leads to a sense of smallness (lowered self-esteem). If the mother shouts at her child, "Look at you! You are such a mess! How could you do that to me?," her child will feel small and bad and will develop a sense of doubt.

Erikson defines doubt as the consciousness of having a front and back, a "behind," which can be dominated and invaded by others who attack one's autonomy and consider anal products as bad or evil. The aftermath of the basic sense of doubt is compulsive doubting and fears of hidden persecutors.

The obsessive compulsive neurotic remains fixated at the anal level and continues to suffer from obsessive doubts and struggles for autonomy. In more severe pathology, the schizoid or psychotic isolated individual cannot form group identifications and remains fixated at the oral and anal levels and is unable to make the transition from the earlier infantile objects to the group relationships which is obligatory for progressive adolescent development.

Stage 3, Initiative versus Guilt

(Oedipal Phase) According to Erikson, this phase centers on "making" and "being on the make." There is pleasure in attack and conquest—boys in the intrusive mode and girls in catching, snatching, and bitchy possessiveness—or in making oneself attractive and endearing. The danger is the sense of guilt over aggression and coercion involved in the jealousy and rivalry for the attentions of the parent of the opposite sex, and ". . . the inevitable failure leads to resignation, guilt and anxiety" (p. 225). This stage is characterized by fantasies of being a giant and by dreams and nightmares in which the child retreats in terror from the projected images of its own aggression.

The castration complex comes into being with the fear of losing the eroticized genitals as punishment for the fantasies. The superego develops and can be primitive, cruel, and uncompromising to the point of self-obliteration. "One of the deepest conflicts in life is the hate for a parent who has served as the model and the executor of the superego . . ." (p. 225f), but who tried to get away with things the child cannot. Pleasure in this phase accompanies accomplishment with tools, weapons, and toys, and in caring for younger children, according to Erikson.

In pathology, Erikson postulates that conflict over initiative may result in (1) hysterical denial, which leads to repression, organ paralysis, or impotence; (2) overcompensatory showing off as the child "sticks his neck out" (as in the case of Edgar's (p. 251) counterphobic overcompensatory skateboard activity); and (3) psychosomatic disorders, which Erikson believes are due to weakness in underlying trust, which makes autonomy bothersome and leads to regression.

The life crisis of initiative versus guilt is related to the adolescent identity crisis connected with the conflict between role experimentation and role fixation, or negative identity. Experimentation with new roles is a normal part of adolescent development, along with exploring new values and ideals as influenced by the social milieu in the move away from the family values. In pathology, when there is no experimentation with roles, Erikson considers this to represent "identity foreclosure" or "role fixation." Anxiety, withdrawal, and inhibition may interfere with the neurotic adolescent's ability to participate in the normal role experimentation characteristic of this age

Jason came for analysis at age 18 after failing his senior year in high school. He was of superior intelligence, with two professional parents and a younger sister age 16. He had always done well in school until this year when, close to graduation and plans for going away to college, he suddenly stopped working in school and began to fail. He had attempted to make up the required courses in summer school but was completely paralyzed academically. In analysis, he reported that he had always been quite athletic, but now he was unable to do well at anything. When ahead of tennis opponents, he was unable to beat them as he would fail to get his serves and usually well-controlled shots into the court. In wrestling at school, he could make a first period "take-down" and be on the verge of pinning his adversary when he would become weak and allow himself to be rolled over and pinned. It was as if all of his phallic prowess had left him. It was obvious from the analytic material that the sense of impotence was displaced upward, leading to the inability to use his good muscles or brain. He would study hard for a test and then the next morning wake with severe anxiety, nausea, and vomiting so that he could not go to school. If he did go by sheer force of will power, he would forget everything he had learned the night before.

Socially he was unable to date and participate in peer activities due to his excessive anxiety. He lived at home and spent much of his time helping his mother with her professional tasks. He had very little contact with his father and tried to avoid him whenever possible.

As the analysis uncovered the source of his pathological symptom formation, it became evident that there was an unresolved oedipal situation with a driving, competitive father and a doting, oversolicitous mother to whom Jason was extremely attached. The threat of leaving home to attend college represented leaving mother and was one dynamic factor that contributed to the school failure. The main unconscious contributing force was fear of his aggression toward the father, which became displaced onto competition in sports where every opponent represented the father in his unconscious. In addition, to succeed in school and to pass exams was unconsciously equated with killing his father.

By the end of analysis, the oedipal conflicts were resolved and he had become an effective individual. He attended a local university and was elected to the student council as well as president of his fraternity. He was chosen to represent the school at a meeting in the state capital and was an excellent debater and fine student. His athletic abilities were restored and he became captain of the tennis team. He had begun to date and establish normal adolescent relationships. After graduation he went on to law school in another city.

Jason was suffering from a full blown hysterical success neurosis which inhibited his adolescent development. He was fixated at the oedipal stage of development which interfered with his adolescent progress. Feelings of inferiority, impotence, and upward displacement of the castration complex and the feelings of phallic inadequacy had stopped his academic and social progress. Conflicts over initiative and the regressive pull to the preoedipal mother were in the ascendency. His ego had used the mechanisms of inhibition and restriction of the ego, in the sense of Anna Freud (1936), to ward off his unconscious aggression and sexual impulses which had resulted in a virtual paralysis.

Stage 4, Industry versus Inferiority

(Latency) In latency, the child learns to sublimate the oedipal aggression and to win recognition by producing things. Industry develops and competition is an aim. Dangers involve the sense of inadequacy and inferiority, and if the skills and tools are faulty, the youngster abandons hope and despairs of his equipment and his anatomy and feels doomed to mediocrity and mutilation.

In adolescence, when fixated at this stage, there is a sense of inadequacy and inferiority, and the adolescent conflict of apprenticeship versus work paralysis. Selection of occupational roles is a major task for adolescents, and the inability to plan ahead in this area indicates a pathological fixation in this crisis period. Occupational role clarification may also be delayed if there are unresolved conflicts here or in earlier stages of development. Pathological educational inhibition in adolescence may be related to these conflictual areas as well, since education is the major work task of adolescence. Unresolved oedipal conflicts have a particularly powerful impact on educational inhibitions. When feelings of inferiority and fear of failure are intense, they may interfere with the capacity for academic work and young people are unable to complete tasks they have begun. School papers and projects are postponed to the last minute and often are left incomplete or become lost. Boys' efforts to build models end in failure with parts lost and tasks are never completed. They tend to jump from one interest to another without finishing any. They take apart radios or cars and never succeed in putting them back together. Their yards look like auto junkyards with disassembled wrecks in need of repairs. Their cars are never good enough and require constant modification and embellishment since they represent the adolescent's body-phallus and self-image, which is faulty and requires constant external bolstering.

Stage 5, Identity versus Role Diffusion

(Adolescence) In Erikson's schema, with the advent of puberty and adolescence and the addition of physical genital maturity, a new integration of the sense of identity develops that represents the sum of childhood identifications integrated with the libido, aptitudes, and social role opportunities and the promise of a career. The danger in this stage is the conflict between identity and role diffusion. Occupational uncertainty is a disturbing factor to young people of this age and contributes to role diffusion. When this is based on previous doubt about sexual identity, delinquent and psychotic episodes may occur; however, promptly treated, they are not as serious as at other ages.

Erikson states: "It is primarily the inability to settle on an occupational identity which disturbs young people. To keep themselves together they temporarily overidentify, to the point of apparent loss of identity, with heroes of cliques and crowds" (p. 228). Adolescents are concerned with how they appear to others compared to their self-perceptions. "The sense of ego identity, then, is the accrued confidence that the inner sameness and continuity are matched by the sameness and continuity of one's meaning for others, as evidenced in the tangible promise of a 'career'" (Erikson 1950, p. 228).

Thomas was 17 when he began to show rather bizarre behavior in school and at home. He tried to change his appearance by strange haircuts and insisted on wearing the same torn shirt daily. He attracted attention to himself in class by calling out remarks unrelated to the class content. He had been a good student with no behavior abnormalities. He was troubled by severe acne, could not keep his hands away from his face, and obsessively picked at and squeezed his pimples. When he came to school one day with his face painted green, the school suggested psychiatric evaluation. In brief, Thomas showed a looseness of associations, some magical omnipotent thinking, and a few neologisms. He was struggling with a severe masturbatory conflict with rather bizarre sadomasochistic fantasies. The struggle to stop his pimple-picking was obviously a masturbatory equivalent. Painting his face green was related to handsome prince–ugly frog fantasies. He had hoped that a pretty girl would kiss him and that he would turn into a handsome prince free from acne and endowed with riches.

Prior to his acute illness, he had been struggling with career choices, debating whether to go to college, join the army, or seek a job, and had been unable to resolve this dilemma. Socially he had been involved in early adolescent bisexual behavior and was envious of his older brother who had a steady girlfriend. He was somewhat inhibited with members of the opposite sex and had attempted to live out his wish-fulfilling fantasies with the face-painting episode. He was obviously having difficulties with role definition and doubts about his sexual identity. With ego-supportive therapy and the use of antipsychotic medication, this youngster was able to reconstitute his ego integrity and his sense of identity was clarified. With the ego reintegration, he chose to go to college and did well.

Stage 6, Intimacy versus Isolation

(Young Adulthood) The life crisis of intimacy versus isolation has its forerunners in adolescence in terms of gender identity formation—sexual polarization versus bisexual confusion conflicts. Erikson indicates that most young adults develop intimate relationships with a member of the opposite sex, and that the bisexual experimentation of preadolescence facilitates this process by helping to define male and female. He states that a firm sexual role differentiation is vital to the formation of the sense of individual identity.

According to Erikson, with moving into the intimacy of mature object relations, the goal is genitality with orgastic potency free of pregenital influences allowing heterosexual mutuality with sensitivity of both penis and vagina. The danger is avoidance because of fear of ego loss and a resultant sense of isolation and self-absorption. "Satisfactory sex relations thus make sex less obsessive, overcompensation less necessary, sadistic controls superfluous" (p. 230). A paraphrase of Erikson's summary of genitality includes mutuality of orgasm with a loved partner of the other sex with whom one may share mutual trust and regulate the cycles of work, procreation, and recreation. These qualities provide a setting that will also secure a satisfactory development to the offspring.

Unfortunately in America today, the frequency with which young adults fail to provide a secure environment in which their children may develop is increasing rapidly. Failures in reaching this optimum state of genitality among young adults are obvious to all who work with children or adults. The prevalence of infidelity, repeated separations and divorce, devaluation of the family, and abandonment of the children and spouse by both men and women is all too familiar.

According to the 1985 Census, 8.8 million families (26.3 percent of families with children) were one-parent families, more than double the 12.9 percent in 1970. The necessity for working mothers to endow their children with latch-key status and the general lack of solid family structure, with mother and father setting realistic examples of family life as models with which their children can identify, contribute to a generation of troubled children who will undoubtedly have similar difficulties establishing enduring families and homes to serve as models for identification in securing satisfactory development for their offspring. Inevitably, the sins of the fathers will be visited unto subsequent generations.

The typical cases cited above show how unwanted teenage pregnancies, child abuse, sexual abuse, and abandonment affect psychological development. One wonders how the vicious cycle of generational patterns can ever be interrupted. A case report will suffice to illustrate the pathology of failure of genitality and gender identity in this phase.

Fred, an only child, was raised by a powerful phallic mother and a passive, submissive father who seldom raised his voice in protest as the mother preempted the child's autonomy. She force-fed him when he resisted food, and in toilet training, overpowered him with repeated enemas and manual manipulation of his anus. Throughout the preoedipal years and into latency, she continued to bathe him and frequently beat his bare buttocks. He developed a passive, withholding, inadequate personality structure and limped through life hampered in every aspect: social, educational, interpersonal, and sexual, and lived in a world of sadomasochistic sexual fantasies. As an adolescent he was unable to complete genital masturbation to the point of orgasm and regressed to anal masturbation. He began a series of transient homosexual relationships without libidinal attachment to the partners. He invariably took the passive receptive role and allowed anal intercourse but was unable to participate in an active role due to his impotence.

When he was 20 years old he sought help because of depression and hypochondriacal preoccupation with his body. He felt most inadequate and inferior in all of his relationships since he could not achieve orgasm. He had held various menial jobs but had no real "career." Clinically, there were depressive features along with a passive, inadequate personality disorder.

In two attempts at a heterosexual protest against his homosexuality, he had tried to have intercourse with prostitutes but was totally impotent. The most satisfying sexual experiences in which he came close to orgasm were painful episodes of fisting where the partner inserted a fist in his rectum. These encounters stirred up memories of his mother's sadistic attacks on his "rear end" and brought on anxiety and resentment toward the all-powerful preoedipal mother.

It is apparent that this young man, chronologically in late adolescence, had not progressed psychologically beyond the anal stage. He had been unable to work through the oedipal struggles and remained fixated in an anal sadomasochistic, passive position. He suffered from such castration anxiety that he was totally impotent. There was a passive feminine identification and also identification with the passive, ineffectual father. He displaced his fear of the castrating powerful, preoedipal mother onto women in general. The painful overstimulation of his anal region and aggressive attacks on his buttocks by his mother had led to a sadomasochistic anal fixation contributing to the sexual perversion. As a result of these conflicts, this patient was not able to reach the Eriksonian stage of intimacy, but suffered from the opposite pole, isolation.

Stage 7, Generativity versus Stagnation

(Middle Years) The life crisis of generativity versus stagnation has its precursors in late adolescence in terms of conflicts between leadership and following and authority confusion. As the late adolescent moves from the family to society and the workplace, leadership and followership roles inevitably become involved. Competing and conflicting demands may lead to authority confusion.

The danger in pathology is regression to obsessive pseudointimacy with repulsion and a sense of stagnation and interpersonal impoverishment. Clinically this pathological mode is seen in adults of all ages who are unable to maintain a constant relationship with one partner and who engage in numerous affairs often followed by repulsion toward the partners. They disregard their children's needs and abandon them with few qualms. The high incidence of divorce appears to be related to the failures in development of the stages of intimacy and generativity.

Stage 8, Ego Integration versus Despair

(Maturity) The life crisis of integrity versus despair is related to the adolescent struggle of ideological commitment versus confusion of values. Erikson (1950) indicates that only one who has taken care of things and people and adapted to the triumphs and disappointments of being the originator of other people, things, and ideas can have genuine ego integrity. The lack of ego integrity leads to the fear of death and to despair hidden by disgust.

In the postnarcissistic state, a new and different love of one's parents becomes possible. If the stage of ego integration is reached, there is the willingness to defend one's own life-style, and death loses its sting. He adds that ". . . healthy children will not fear life if their parents have integrity enough not to fear death" (p. 233). The presence of ego integrity permits followership and the responsibility of leadership. In pathology, the lack of ego integrity leads to the fear of death, and despair that life is too short to start over. Disgust comes to hide the despair.

Numerous case examples of people who have not reached the stage of ego integrity come to mind. For example, a man who is unable to exert a leadership role in the home and allows his wife to take all of the responsibility for discipline and guidance of the children may also refuse promotions at work from fear of his inability to exert leadership capacity. This type of man usually lives in dread of losing his job and of financial collapse, and despairs of anything being able to improve his lot. Behind this lies a fear of death and a pessimistic bent.

The children in such families often suffer from a sense of insecurity with the failure of their parents to offer a safe haven in which the young people themselves can reach a state of integrity and ego identity. These children are more likely to suffer from anxiety about the potential disasters facing youth today, for example: nuclear disasters, economic collapse, and social disorders.

NEUROTIC CONFLICT AND SYMPTOM FORMATION

The neurotic adolescent shows more anxiety and symptom formation of a persistent nature than the average adolescent. There are more profound interferences with development and longer lasting symptoms. Because of the upward pressure for recognition that adolescence brings, the unconscious impulses, with their attendant cognitive representations, affects, and traumatic memories, constantly strive to reach consciousness. When dreams, slips of the tongue, inhibitions, automatic actions, and behavior give the ego evidence of underlying unconscious manifestations, anxiety arises and the ego brings into play defenses with which it attempts to protect itself from the unwanted encroachments. When the defenses fail to keep the unwanted contents unconscious, substitute symbolic formations take place and neurotic symptoms are the result.

With Gwen (p. 265), we see an example of the unconscious memories of a childhood trauma to her vaginal area seeking expression at puberty, resulting in a neurotic symptom formation. In the case of Jason (p. 278) his ego's inability to cope with the upsurgence of unconscious oedipal impulses in adolescence brought about the symptoms of anxiety, school failure, and collapse of his athletic abilities. Mizzy, the identical twin (pp. 252ff.; 254ff.), was suffering from a severe pan neurosis (Mahler 1964). At puberty, the resurgence of her unconscious sadomasochistic sexual fantasies and unconscious aggression toward her twin sister and mother brought on severe neurotic inhibition and anorexia with which her ego attempted to arrest her physical maturation. In each of these cases, therapy brought to consciousness the nature of the repressed unconscious, restored their functioning to normal, and removed their symptoms, permitting adolescent development to go forward in response to the maturational urge.

DEFENSES AND PATHOLOGY

Differential diagnosis in adolescence is often difficult and may be facilitated by the study of ego defenses. (See Anna Freud 1936). When under pressure from within or without, the ego invokes a wide variety of defenses designed to keep the unwanted impulses from entering consciousness. Chief of these is repression, which, within limits, is a normal defense. If repression fails, the ego is flooded with unacceptable ego-dystonic id contents. Mahler and Elkisch (1953) have described the devastating effects of failure of repression in childhood psychosis. In addition to repression, sublimation is considered a normal defense involving the displacement of instinctual aims. Reaction-formation, within limits, is also a normal defense, as it converts jealousy into pity and envy and greed into altruism and generosity. However, the defense may be used too extensively.

In the process of development, the ego selects various defensive measures but as time goes on, the defensive processes become dissociated from their original situation and become fixed, permanent character traits, what Reich calls the "armour-plating of character."

In neurosis, when repression threatens to break down, anxiety is felt as the ego-alien repressed impulses seek consciousness and the simplest form of neurosis, anxiety hysteria, is the result. Anna Freud (1936) notes that ". . . hysterical patients . . . exclude from consciousness the ideational representatives of their sexual impulses" (p. 37), and it is these impulses seeking expression that give rise to anxiety and symptom formation. In conversion hysteria, if repression does not suffice to keep the id contents out of awareness, the ego invokes the use of somatization, which may result in hysterical paralyses and dysfunctions. Prolonged somatization may also lead to psychosomatic disorders and, in the extreme, to hypochondriasis, which also requires an overcathexis of the body ego with narcissistic libido withdrawn from the object world.

In the phobias, repression falters and the defenses of reversal, regression, projection, and displacement are brought into play. Freud (1909), in his description of Little Hans, showed that the basis of the child's phobia was the boy's love for his mother, which led to the conflict between his aggressive impulses toward his father and his affection for him. Reversal of the aggression to father turned it into anxiety of his being hurt (castrated) by the father, followed by outward projection of the unconscious rage and its displacement onto the horses in the street. Regression to the oral stage occurred, as seen in his fear of being bitten. Neurotic inhibition caused Hans to stop going outside. He successfully employed denial of reality in fantasy in his dreams of having a large penis like his father and babies like his mother.

Anna Freud (1958) pointed out that in neurosis the danger to the ego is the pressure from the superego, which leads to anxiety and guilt and to neuroses, while Blos (1962) said that if the oedipal conflicts are not resolved, neurosis will result.

In the obsessive-compulsive disorders, regression, doing and undoing, reaction-formation, isolation and denial of the affect, denial in word and deed, intellectualization, and rationalization enter the defensive arena. Isolation ". . . removes the instinctual impulses from their context, while retaining them in consciousness" (A. Freud 1936, p. 37f). The obsessive patient isolates the affect from these ideas which he is able to express consciously. Doing and undoing represent attempts to undo what has been done—or thought about. Hand-washing and other cleaning compulsions are defensive operations against the messy anal impulses and represent an attempt to undo the anal wishes. Touching compulsions represent efforts to undo the impulse to touch parts of the body, which was forbidden by the parents and later by the superego, as for example, regarding masturbatory impulses.

With neurotic depressions, the mechanisms of denial and inhibition of the aggression are involved, as the individual attempts to ward off the aggression that is intolerable to the superego. Anxiety and guilt result from the ego's awareness of the emerging impulses, and more strenuous defenses are invoked resulting in the use of turning the aggression against the self, reversal of the instincts, and introjection (of the "bad object"), which become prominent features of defense. Masochism is the end result as the aggression turned inward endows the superego with its cruel characteristics. This is clearly demonstrated in the case of Mizzy, (pp. 252ff.; 254ff.), with her sadomasochistic kidnap-rape-beating fantasies.

In psychotic depressions, more pathological defenses are involved as regression and the denial of reality take place and self-denigrating delusions occur. These patients blame themselves for all sorts of tragedies through a projection of their own self-criticism.

In manic conditions, self-aggrandizement and megalomanic delusions are defensive attempts that the ego employs to ward off the underlying ego-dystonic depressive feelings.

Borderline conditions are related to fixations at, and regressions to, the rapprochement subphase of development. Splitting as a defense becomes prominent, and there is a failure of fusion of the infantile split self- and object-representations that leads to the clinical phenomena so frequently noted in the transference where the therapist at one moment is aggrandized and the next moment totally denigrated. This results from projections in the transference of the unfused good and bad mother/father images onto the therapist. One of the aims of treatment is the healing of the split to allow further progress in development to occur. (See Mahler 1971, 1975; Kernberg 1967, 1975; and Settlage 1980).

Withdrawal of the libido to the self occurs with the narcissistic disorders. The body ego and superego are hypercathected, leading to ideas of grandeur and power and to hypochondriasis. This condition may result from insufficient cathexis of the infant in the early mother–child relationship, which leads to failures in self-esteem. The grandiosity is a defensive attempt to compensate for the feelings of emptiness and inferiority.

In paranoia the early oral mechanisms of introjection and projection are involved. When projection is used as a defense against homosexual impulses, it combines with reversal of love into hate and results in the development of paranoid delusions. "The effect of the mechanism of projection is to break the connection between the ideational representatives of dangerous instinctual impulses and the ego" (A. Freud 1936, p. 132). Erikson (1950) states that late adolescent psychotic breakdowns resulting from prolonged adolescent regression show a persistence of identity confusion. Anna Freud (1958) says that the danger of id impulses threatening an already impoverished ego leads to psychotic disturbances.

In adolescent forms of schizophrenia, more bizarre mechanisms are used, including symbolization, inversions, and reversals, similar to the dream-work process. In catatonic schizophrenia, massive inhibition, restriction and constriction of the ego, and regression render the patient mute, immobile, incontinent, and often huddled on the floor in a fetal position. Erikson states that in schizophrenia there is an absence of the sense of trust. This adds to the therapeutic difficulties.

In behavior and character disorders, the defensive operations center around acting out. These egos have not developed the capacity to tolerate frustration or delay of gratification. When an impulse is felt, it is acted out promptly, as these people cannot tolerate anxiety generated by delaying discharge of sexual or aggressive impulses, and other higher level defensive patterns are not available to deal with the impulses. A prominent defensive operation is identification with the aggressor representing an identification with the dreaded object. Anna Freud (1936) points out that in identification with the aggressor, the child introjects the adults' aggression that was directed at him and reverses passive into active, leading to an active attack on the outside world. The attacked becomes the attacker. The processes of introjection and internalization of other people's criticism that later leads to superego forma tion is truncated by the discharge of aggression and ". . . the mechanism of identification with the aggressor is supplemented by another defensive measure, namely, the projection of guilt" (p. 128). The prohibited impulses are projected outward, thus avoiding self-criticism.

In passive, unassuming types of character formations, the mechanisms of projection and identification permit vicarious pleasure from the gratification of forbidden impulses by others with whom the person can identify. Altruistic surrender takes place and is used to overcome narcissistic mortifications. Asceticism is a defense used to deny the presence of unacceptable impulses.

Anna Freud (1936) points out that inhibition relates to the sexual impulses, which are warded off, while restriction of the ego is related to the aggression.

In adolescent drug and alcohol abuse, there is failure to reach the stages of industry and identity with fixation at the stages of inferiority and role diffusion. These young people use the mechanisms of avoidance and flight along with acting out and regression in their attempts to escape their painful situations, as in the following case illustration.

Betty, at age 13, was a teenage alcoholic. She began drinking her parents' liquor at age 11 when tensions in the home had become intolerable. Both parents, chronic alcoholics, fought constantly, especially over their daughter's behavior and discipline. With chaos in the home, Betty had started staying away from home at friends' houses for long periods. She attempted to deal with her anxiety and distress by escaping reality through chemical means. She stole "white-out" from the stores to sniff and get high. She drank whatever alcohol she could get and also used pot and speed, becoming thoroughly chemically dependent. By age 13, as she could not face a day in school without drinking, she kept a bottle in her school locker. Inevitably, the school authorities became aware of her condition and she was referred for residential treatment.

MAHLER'S OBJECT RELATIONS THEORY AND PATHOLOGY

No discussion of pathology would be complete without reference to Mahler's views on psychopathology. In her developmental schema of the stages of human object relations from normal autism through symbiosis and the separation–individuation process, it is possible to trace the roots of pathological formations based on fixations at, and regressions to, these various stages of infant development.

Normal Autism

During the first two to three months of life, the infant is in a state of primary narcissism with a lack of awareness of the outside world and little or no attachment to the caretaking persons. Fixation at this stage results in what Mahler calls "primary autism." If the infant fails to cathect the mothering person and remains withdrawn in an autistic shell, one finds the severe pathology of infantile autism. If the child begins to form some early object attachment to the mother and progresses somewhat in development, he or she may regress, often with minimal trauma, for example, mother's having another baby. The child may lose speech, toilet training, and other ego functions in a regression to the autistic position in what Mahler refers to as "secondary autism." (See Mahler 1968.)

Symbiosis

From about age 2 months until age 6 months, the child enters the close mother–child need-fulfilling tie of symbiosis that is essential to the psychological growth of the human infant (Mahler et al. 1975). There is a specific attachment to and smile of recognition for the mother. If there is a failure in this process, there will be serious consequences in terms of later pathology. Spitz's (1945, 1947) "hospitalism" and anaclitic depression are related to loss of the mothering function in those infants he described. Depressive reactions later in life also have their roots in the object loss of the early stages of the development of object relations. With a satisfactory symbiosis (Winnicott's [1958] "good enough mothering"), there develops a sense of confident expectation (Benedek 1938), which readies the child for the rigors of the separation–individuation process.

The Separation–Individuation Process

In discussing the subphases of the separation–individuation process, it is essential to keep in mind that the ages given are approximate and that the subphases merge gradually into one another as new trends and capacities emerge.

Between approximately 6 and 9 months, the process of differentiation takes place during which a sense of "me and not me" and the sense of self and identity begins to develop. A dawning recognition of the mother and the self as separate takes place as the child "hatches" from the dual unity of the mother–child symbiotic orbit. Mahler and colleagues (1975) term this "the psychological birth of the human infant." Failures and fixations in this subphase show their reverberations in the adolescent process in failures of ego identity, Eriksonian "negative identity," and identity diffusion. The sense of self is not fully developed and self-esteem regulation may be problematic. Difficulties also occur in formation of the ego ideal.

In the practicing subphase, between ages 10 and 14 months, limitations of motor exploration, either as a result of physical handicaps, for example, casts or physical defects, or through the mother's intervention in the process, will interfere with the smooth progression through this stage (as in Barney's case; see Mahler et al. [1975]). The child's "love affair with the world" (Greenacre 1957) will be abortive and the pleasure in mastery of motor activities will be disturbed. In adolescence, these youngsters may show motor inhibition and conflicts around expression of their motoric urges. Inhibition and restriction of the ego often results.

Following the joyful period of practicing, a more tumultous process occurs during the rapprochement subphase between about age 15 and 24 months. Cognitive abilities increase to the point of greater awareness of separateness, which brings on anxiety and a seeming regression with clinging to the mother, which had been given up in the exuberance of the practicing subphase. At about 18 months, the ambitendency heightens and the child struggles simultaneously for separation from and reunion with the mother, resulting in the "rapprochement crises" that may be severe and quite difficult for some mothers to handle. With the simultaneous pull toward and pushing away from the mother, the child experiences powerful ambivalence and tremendous conflict. Fixation at this phase has its aftermath in borderline and narcissistic disorders and in heightened ambivalence of adolescence. The conflicts between dependency and independence, relatedness versus withdrawal and isolation, and passivity versus activity have many of their roots in this subphase (Mahler 1971, 1975).

The last subphase of the separation–individuation process, on the way to object constancy, from 24 months onward, has many pitfalls, which show their aftereffects in failures in the development of object constancy. The development of separate self- and object-representations takes place and self and gender identity become more firmly entrenched. In this stage there develops the ability to see others as separate individuals and the capacity for intimate relationships without the danger of losing one's identity in merging with others. In adolescence, such difficulties interfere with the development of healthy object relations both in and outside of the family unit and with the smooth transition from the family to relationships in society. When there have been problems in the development of object constancy, the process of disengaging the libido from the internalized objects in adolescence is much more difficult. Such youngsters may show schizoid or withdrawing personality disorders as they find forming object relations an anxiety-producing process; the development of intimacy will suffer and isolation will likely occur. Generativity and maturity are impossible when the capacity for object constancy is impaired.

PROGNOSIS

With an average degree of adolescent upheaval, the prognosis is usually favorable; forward development continues, impelled by the developmental thrust, and eventually, maturity is reached. However, a variety of influences may interrupt the process. As noted above, incomplete development in any of the earlier stages impairs the adolescent's ability to cope with the tremendous conflicts and intrapsychic struggles of this tumultuous phase of life.

The prognosis for recovery in the neuroses is favorable provided adequate treatment is available. Prolonged neurotic inhibitions involving interferences with academic functioning require intervention to avoid disruption of educational progress, school failure, and dropout. In these conditions, with adequate treatment, the prognosis is usually quite favorable, as with Mizzy, Gwen, and Jason. The more complex the defensive structure, the more severe the neurosis, and the less favorable the prognosis. Thus, the obsessive-compulsive disorders are more difficult to treat than the hysterical neuroses and phobias, and the character disorders, perversions, and psychoses are even more challenging to treat.

It is obvious that acting out is a prominent feature of adolescence and, only if it persists, is excessive, or threatening to the self or others, should it become a focus of therapeutic intervention. As Anna Freud (1958) indicated, it may be the parents who need the help rather than the youngster. When the acting out involves self-destructive behavior such as sexual activity without birth control or the danger of harm to the self or others, treatment is indicated. If severe enough to indicate a serious risk, residential or hospital treatment may be appropriate. With involvement of the character structure in the neurotic process, the prognosis is less favorable as treatment becomes more difficult with increased "armor-plating of the character."

The success of treatment with gender identity disorders and perversions depends on the degree of anxiety and ego-syntonicity of the disorder. Without anxiety, an ego-syntonic gender disorder will not lend itself to therapeutic intervention due to lack of motivation. Cases referred by the courts will often fail to respond to treatment.

In the schizoid, narcissistic, and borderline personalities, the prognosis is more guarded, and treatment is much more difficult and prolonged because of the failures in basic trust early in life and the incomplete passage through early stages.

Drug and alcohol addictions are particularly treatment-resistant states unless motivation for change exists from within. Pressures from outside sources (family, school, friends, employer) are stoutly resisted as the pleasure principle is in the ascendency. Because of the tenacity of the physiological addiction and the severity of withdrawal symptoms, tremendous ego strength is required to withstand the frustration and the psychic and physical pain of withdrawal. If the individual has insufficient ego strength to cope with these demands, in-patient treatment will be necessary to effect withdrawal. Unfortunately, relapses often occur unless the patient has adequate follow-up out-patient therapy after the withdrawal.

Adolescents are more likely to recover from acute transient psychotic episodes than those in other stages of life. Prolonged regression in adolescence that does not respond to ego supportive treatment is an unfavorable prognostic sign. The more entrenched psychotic processes including paranoia and the various forms of schizophrenic reactions offer a much more difficult prognosis.

TREATMENT

Goals of Treatment

The goal of psychoanalytic treatment of adolescents is the furtherance of the maturational processes of adolescence by removing the blockages, fixations, and resistances to further growth and progress. Resolution of unresolved earlier conflicts, including the oedipal conflicts, is essential to this process. Often one must work through regressive trends to the early preoedipal phases to permit a passage through latency and adolescence. Symptom removal is, of course, one aim of treatment;

however, transference cures often tend to relieve symptoms without making the basic changes in personality structure necessary for lasting improvement and continued progressive development. Thus, symptomatic improvement alone is insufficient evidence of definitive progress.

This poses a major problem in technique since part of the motivation for seeking and continuing treatment is the presence of symptoms. The therapeutic alliance must be strong enough to maintain treatment after symptomatic improvement has been reached, in order to permit continuation of therapy to the point of resolution of the intrapsychic conflicts and permanent personality change. Therapeutic intervention in adolescent psychopathology requires variations of technique from classical psychoanalytic work with adults. As the adolescent is in a state of severe conflict and disorganization of the entire personality (ego, superego, and ego ideal), it is necessary to constantly keep these points in mind.

EGO SUPPORT

The ego needs the support of the therapist's external ego in its struggle to maintain some semblance of reality testing. Often the adolescent feels that he or she is going crazy and the therapist may have to offer reassurance. We may also be obliged to assist with reality testing by pointing out what is realistic and what is not, being careful to avoid a disapproving tone. For example, if an adolescent girl is acting out sexually without birth control, one may need to help her become aware of the implications of this behavior and assist her with getting some form of contraception, rather than waiting to see what happens.

With the more seriously depressed adolescent, antidepressive medication may provide sufficient ego support to avoid the need for hospitalization. In my clinical experience, I have found it advisable to avoid hospitalization if at all possible, since being hospitalized constitutes an affront to the ego and the narcissism, and tends to foster the regressive, passive-dependent side of the conflicts. By promoting improved mood, sleep patterns, and outlook, the medication may relieve considerable fatigue, anxiety, and distress and serve as a helpful ego-supportive adjunct to therapy. In any use of medication, one must involve the patient's ego by stressing that these are temporary measures to help get beyond the acute symptoms to permit therapy to deal with the underlying issues. One must be wary of adolescents' pull toward drug dependency and wish for easy, simple solutions, and attempt to avoid their becoming drug dependent.

With excessive anxiety and panic states, the temporary use of antianxiety medication may prove helpful in establishing a working alliance with the extremely distressed adolescent. With borderline and acutely decompensating psychotic processes, antipsychotic medication may prove ego supportive and permit therapy to become more effective.

Superego Reinforcement

The shaky superego needs the therapist's help in terms of realistic limits and guidance. Adolescents push the limits with adults, looking for someone to say "no" to help them control their burgeoning impulses. Limits from the therapist in terms of the structure of therapy (appointment schedules and time limitations), our indicating what we may feel is going too far in acting out, and pointing out the consequences of behavior in attempts to curtail the acting out all help reinforce the superego. The old childhood identifications that make up the superego are in the process of being discarded and reorganized. New identifications will take their place, and the kind but strong, firm image of the therapist can serve as a powerful force in the restructuring of the superego. Thus, one should not appear to aid and abet the acting out through such countertransference processes as vicariously enjoying the adolescent's expression of sexual and/or aggressive impulses.

In residential or hospital treatment settings, one may encounter staff difficulties when adolescents attempt to split the staff as they managed to split their parents previously. It is imperative to help the staff avoid being caught in loyalty conflicts and splitting attempts by teenage patients in order to escape continuation of these destructive patterns. Occasionally, a staff member may overidentify with an adolescent and allow favoritism, thus facilitating that youngster's acting out. If the staff is afraid of the patient's aggression and gives in or fails to adhere to the rules, this undoes the therapeutic effect of the milieu.

In in-patient settings, one often encounters extremes of violent and destructive behavior directed toward both the outside and the self. When this occurs, the judicious use of physical holding and restraint is both ego- and superego-supportive. By not allowing the patient to harm him- or herself or others, we show that we care and that we will not tolerate the destructive behavior to which the adolescent responds with a tremendous sense of relief.

Ego Ideal Reorganization

The therapist may assist in the reorganization of the ego ideal by serving as a role model by being punctual, reliable, and trustworthy, and by a constant therapeutic, helpful attitude. How many of us have had our adolescent patients indicate that they are thinking of becoming psychiatrists, psychologists, or social workers by way of identification with their therapist as part of the restructuring of their ego ideals?

The Therapeutic Alliance

In the treatment of adolescents, the therapist fills the role of a new object as well as a transference object. It is often difficult to distinguish between these two roles. The transference aspects represent past struggles in early object relations projected onto the therapist and are, therefore, regressive manifestations. Since adolescents resist the regressive pull, the transference may come to oppose the obligatory push of the maturational forces. The elements of the real object come into play as the adolescent relates to the therapist in the present and may form a positive attachment and/or a negative relationship in which he or she attempts to fight out the rebellious adolescent struggles. To avoid these pitfalls requires considerable skill and modification of therapeutic technique. In view of these two tendencies, building a therapeutic alliance is essential to successful work with adolescents. This invariably requires considerable effort on the part of the therapist. Showing that you understand the conflicts can assist in this process. Helping adolescents realize that they are not the only ones who struggle with similar conflicts can prove helpful.

One must appeal to the positive strengths of the ego in siding with the ego against the self-destructive and antisocial urges. For example, with an adolescent who is failing school in a struggle for autonomy from parental domination, one may say, "I know how much the sensible part of you wants to get ahead in life and wants to conquer the part of you that is fighting your parents and making you do poorly in school. We must work together to help you overcome the forces that are pulling you backwards and keeping you from getting ahead as you would like to do." This is both ego-supportive in our siding with the progressive forces against the regression and also tends to ally us with the positive side of the ego and superego. Another example of a similar ego-supportive technique would be with an adolescent who has acted out in a particularly destructive fashion, for example, speeding and wrecking the family car. One might say, "You and I both know that you wish to God that you wouldn't have to do that sort of thing and we must do our best to work together to help your inner police force keep an eye on the wild part of you that wants to get out of control and cut loose. I'll help you with it if you let me know when it starts to act up."

With the severely depressed suicidal adolescent who states at the end of an appointment that no one cares and that there is no use in going on living, the most therapeutic thing is to show that *you* care. One might say, "Damn it all! I won't let you hurt yourself, not over my dead body! If you feel like seriously hurting yourself, call and let me know and we'll do something about it. We can consider helping you by using the hospital temporarily, if need be, but I would rather trust you to not hurt yourself and to get yourself here so that we can work on what's making you so damn furious that you want to take it out on yourself!" Such a statement is designed to show the patient that you care, while simultaneously indicating that the self-destructiveness is related to turning the aggression against the self. One also hopes to help the patient to externalize the anger in the transference by setting an example— showing that we are not afraid of our own aggression. One must also attempt to make a contract with the patient in the form of a promise not to hurt him or herself without getting in touch with the therapist. We must later on, as time permits, attempt to uncover the sources of the rage. One should also consider antidepressive medication at such points. However, the thoroughly depressed adolescent will often fail to take the medication regularly or may use it to overdose.

With delinquent adolescents, as Aichhorn (1925) pointed out from his early psychoanalytic explorations of delinquent behavior, it is necessary to control the acting out in order to convert the alloplastic disorders into autoplastic conditions so that they may become susceptible to therapeutic intervention. Thus, the use of in-patient treatment may be required to limit the delinquent's acting out.

Transference Problems

Since adolescents are struggling against their bisexual strivings, one of the problems in the transference is the fear of allowing themselves to get too close to a therapist of the same sex, which may lead to homosexual panic and flight from treatment. With male therapists and adolescent girls, the transference dangers lie in the defenses against the oedipal wishes. With female therapists, teenage girls may have to defend against the regressive pull to the preoedipal mother and may attempt to flee treatment.

A further adolescent transference struggle lies in the area of dependency conflicts. The typical fight against the passive-dependent wishes toward the parents readily tends to be displaced into treatment leading to resistance to becoming dependent on the therapist. Transference interpretations must be made in an effort to ward off premature termination of treatment in these situations.

Countertransference Problems

One of the major attitudes to avoid is the tendency to overidentify with the adolescent and to support unconsciously the acting out of sexual or aggressive impulses. Vicarious enjoyment of the rebellion because of one's own unresolved adolescent rebellion is another pitfall to be avoided (Prall and Stennis 1964). Countertransference problems are particularly frequent in work with psychotic youngsters as described by Prall and Dealy (1965).

It is essential to avoid treating adolescents either as adults or as younger children. If one loses sight of the incompleteness of their development and their inability to assume total responsibility for their actions, one may expect too much maturity and overestimate their controls. One should not expect the adolescent to respond to adult techniques of free association and abstain from acting out. On the other hand, adolescents often complain if the therapist treats them like children, which offends their narcissism. One must be flexible in technique and walk a tightrope between treating them either like children or adults.

Another pitfall is siding with the patient against the parents, which invariably leads to difficulties since the ambivalent adolescent may complain bitterly about the parents but still loves them. In handling the negative aspects of feelings toward parents, one should look for opportunities to point out both sides of the ambivalent conflicts rather than emphasizing only one side. For example, one may say, "You have been telling me how much you hate your parents, but we see two sides to it since you find it difficult to let yourself be away from them during vacations. You have very mixed feelings about your parents." This approach is more ego-syntonic and will meet with less resistance, since even the most abused children will come to their parents' defense. If we say they are rotten parents, they will shout, "Don't you talk that way about *my* parents!"

One other countertransference *caveat* is the problem of handling the positive transference. If one gains gratification from patients' admiration instead of having one's libidinal gratifications met outside of the therapeutic situation where they belong, dangers will occur. In handling the positive transference with both children and adolescents, Mahler continually stressed in her psychoanalytic seminars that one should avoid interpreting the positive transference by itself. There will be ample ev-

TABLE 13-1. Erickson's Stages of Life Crises and Mahler's States of Development of Object Relations

Erikson's stages of life crises	Age	Stage-related conflicts	Adolescent conflicts	Pathology	Mahler's object relations phase	Pathology in regression
Oral-sensory	1	Basic trust vs suspicion	Temporal perspective vs time diffusion	Failure to trust others, withdrawal, schizoid and paranoid personalities	Autism, symbiosis, differentiation, early practicing	Autistic and symbiotic psychosis, depression, identity and autonomy conflicts
Muscular-anal	2	Autonomy vs shame and doubt	Self-certainty vs self-consciousness	Failure of autonomy, obsessive/compulsive doubting; neurosis and/or character disorders	Late practicing, rapprochement, on-the-way to object-constancy	Inhibitions, borderline conditions, difficulties with object relations
Locomotor-genital, phallic-oedipal	3–6	Initiative vs guilt	Role experimentation vs role fixation	Negative identity, academic/work inhibition, and success neurosis	Object-constancy	Gender disorders and perversions
Latency	6 to 9–10 years	Industry vs inferiority	Apprenticeship vs work paralysis	Despair of one's anatomy, fear of mutilation, inadequacy, inferiority	Latency	Early phase problems lead to regression

Puberty and adolescence	10–20	Identity vs role diffusion	Identity vs role diffusion	Lack of ego and sexual identity and confidence, career failure, role diffusion	"Negative identity," identity diffusion, regression
Young adulthood	20+	Intimacy vs isolation	Sexual polarization vs bisexual conflicts	Isolation, withdrawal, sexual conflicts, impotence/frigidity	The second individuation process
Adulthood		Generativity vs stagnation	Leadership and followership vs authority confusion	Work and marriage conflicts, divorce and abandonment, rebelliousness	Failures in relationships if object-constancy was not reached—neuroses and character disorders
Maturity		Integration vs disgust and despair	Ideological commitment vs confusion of values	Fear of death, despair, disgust, pessimism	Failures in marriage if object-constancy was not reached—neuroses and character disorders
					Depressions, neuroses, and character disorders may occur if mature object relationships not reached

Adapted from *Childhood and Society* by Erik H. Erikson, by permission of W. W. Norton & Company, Inc. Copyright © 1950, © 1963 by W. W. Norton & Company, Inc. Copyright renewed 1978 by Erik H. Erikson. By permission of Catto & Windus/Hogarth Press.

idence of the positive transference in frequent insistent questions about the therapist—"Are you married? Do you have children? Are they boys or girls? Where do you live?," and so on. If one interprets the positive transference by indicating that the youngster likes the therapist, there may be an immediate rejoinder, "Don't think I like *you*, you old fart!"

One may, however, interpret the positive transference judiciously by pointing out both sides of the conflict. For example, if a youngster is repeatedly late and misses appointments, but also repeatedly phones one at night or is reluctant to leave at the end of appointments, one may interpret the ambivalence as follows: "We see two sides to how you feel *about this place*" (rather than *about me*, since this is more acceptable to the child's ego and will be tolerated more readily). "On the one hand, you are often late and miss appointments, but on the other hand, when your time is up, you have a hard time leaving. You have very mixed feelings *about being here*" (rather than *about me*). This will usually lead to further material regarding the ambivalence toward the therapist rather than to a negative rejoinder.

CONCLUSION

Understanding the developmental stages of normal adolescence, the defenses employed by the ego in coping with the tremendous psychic and physical upheaval, and the pyschopathology of this evolutionary decade can assist the professional person in the difficult task of treating the enigmatic adolescent.

It can be very rewarding to be able to assist disturbed adolescents in overcoming the interferences with development that might have led to a lifetime of escapism, addiction, job dissatisfaction, and problems in object relationships, marriage, and child-rearing, as well as the inability to achieve their potential. Therapy can serve to free disturbed adolescents from inhibitions, restrictions, and other interferences with development and set free the full power of the developmental forces that will propel them to maturity.

Having rounded the Cape of Good Hope, with our help in charting the course and in repairing the ravages of the stormy passage through the shoals of adolescence, the more mature individual will then be able to be the captain of his or her own refitted ship and weather future life crises independently.

A schematic view of some additions to Erikson's chart of the stages of life crises (see Table 13-1) may be helpful in visualizing his and Mahler's concepts in relationship to normal adolescence and psychopathology.

REFERENCES

Aichorn, A. (1925). *Wayward Youth*. New York: Viking Press, 1965.
Benedek, T. (1938). Adaptation to reality in early infancy. *Psychoanalytic Study of the Child* 7:200–214. New York: International Universities Press.
Blos, P. (1962). *On Adolescence*. New York: Free Press.
_____ (1965). The initial stage of male adolescence. *Psychoanalytic Study of the Child* 20:45–164. New York: International Universities Press.
_____ (1967). The second individuation. *Psychoanalytic Study of the Child* 22:162–186. New York: International Universities Press.
_____ (1974). The genealogy of the ego ideal. *Psychoanalytic Study of the Child* 29:43–88. New Haven, CT: Yale University Press.
_____ (1976). The split parental imago in adolescent social relations. *Psychoanalytic Study of the Child* 31:7–33. New Haven, CT: Yale University Press.
_____ (1979). *The Adolescent Passage: Developmental Issues*. New York: International Universities Press.
Burlingham, D. T. (1945). The fantasy of having a twin. *Psychoanalytic Study of the Child* 1:205–210. New York: International Universities Press.
Dalsimer, K. (1979). From preadolescent tomboy to early adolescent girl: an analysis of Carson McCullers's *The Member of the Wedding*. *Psychoanalytic Study of the Child* 34:445–461. New Haven, CT: Yale University Press.
Demski, R. S. (1986). Update on the pornographic rock controversy. Presented to the Texas Society of Child Psychiatry, fall meeting. Lakeway, Texas, August 16, 1986. Unpublished.
_____ (1988). The dangers of noise-induced hearing loss in children and adolescents. *American Academy of Child and Adolescent Psychiatry Newsletter*, p. 6.
Erikson, E. H. (1950). *Childhood and Society*. New York: Norton.
_____ (1956). The problem of ego identity. *Journal of the American Psychoanalytic Association* 4:56–121.
_____ (1959). Identity and the life cycle. *Psychological Issues*, Monograph 1, pp. 1–171. New York: International Universities Press.
_____ (1968). *Identity, Youth and Crisis*. New York: Norton.
Frank, A. (1947). *The Diary of a Young Girl*. New York: Doubleday, 1952.
Freud, A. (1936). *The Ego and the Mechanisms of Defense*. New York: International Universities Press, 1946.
_____ (1958). Adolescence. *Psychoanalytic Study of the Child* 13:255–278. New York: International Universities Press.
Freud, A., and Burlingham, D. (1968). Personal communication in a discussion of the case of Mizzy. New Haven, CT, April 20, 1968.
Freud, S. (1905). Three essays on the theory of sexuality. *Standard Edition* 7:135–243.
_____ (1909). Analysis of a five-year-old boy. *Standard Edition* 10:5–149.
Glenn, J. (1990). Traumatic neurosis in children. In this volume, pp. 59–74.
Goldings, H. J. (1979). Development from 10 to 13 years. In *Basic Handbook of Psychiatry*, ed. J. D. Nosphitz, pp. 199–205. New York: Basic Books.
Greenacre, P. (1957). The childhood of the artist; libidinal phase development and giftedness. *Psychoanalytic Study of the Child* 12:27–72. New York: International Universities Press.
Inhelder, B., and Piaget, J. (1958). *The Growth of Logical Thinking from Childhood to Adolescence*. New York: Basic Books.

Johnson, A. M. (1949). Sanctions for superego lacunae of adolescents. In *Searchlights on Delinquency*, ed. K. R. Eissler, pp. 225–245. New York: International Universities Press.

Johnson, A. M., and Szurek, S. A. (1952). The genesis of antisocial acting out in children and adults. *Psychoanalytic Quarterly* 21:323–343. New York: International Universities Press.

Kernberg, O. F. (1967). Borderline personality organization. *Journal of the American Psychoanalytic Association* 15:641–685.

——— (1975). *Borderline Conditions and Pathological Narcissism*. New York: Jason Aronson.

Lipsitz, J. S. (1980). Adolescent psychosexual development. In *Adolescent Pregnancy: Perspectives for the Health Professional*, ed. P. B. Smith and D. M. Mumford, pp. 1–13. Boston: Hall.

Mahler, M. S. (1964). Personal communication at a case presentation of Mizzy in a child analysis seminar. New York, February 1, 1964.

——— (1968). *On Human Symbiosis and the Vicissitudes of Individuation*. Vol. 1: *Infantile Psychosis*. New York: International Universities Press.

——— (1971). A study of the separation–individuation process: and its possible applications to borderline phenomena in the psychoanalytic situation. *Psychoanalytic Study of the Child* 26:403–422. New York: Quadrangle Press.

Mahler, M. S., and Elkisch, P. (1953). Some observations on disturbances of the ego in a case of infantile psychosis. *Psychoanalytic Study of the Child* 8:252–261. New York: International Universities Press.

Mahler, M. S., Pine, F., and Bergman, A. (1975). *The Psychological Birth of the Human Infant*. New York: Basic Books.

Malmquist, C. P. (1979). Development from 13 to 16 years. In *Basic Handbook of Child Psychiatry*, vol. 1, ed. J. D. Noshpitz, pp. 205–213. New York: Basic Books.

Patersen, A. C., and Offer, D. (1979). Adolescent development: 16 to 19 years. In *Basic Handbook of Child Psychiatry*, vol. 1, ed. J. D. Noshpitz, pp. 213–233. New York: Basic Books.

Piaget, J. (1957). *The Language and Thought of the Child*, trans. M. Gabain. New York: Meridian Books.

Prall, R. C., and Dealy, M. N. (1965). Countertransference in therapy of childhood psychosis. *Journal of Hillside Hospital* 14:69–82.

Prall, R. C., and Stennis, W. (1964). Common pitfalls in psychotherapy with children. *Pennsylvania Psychiatric Quarterly* 4:3–11. Commonwealth of Pennsylvania.

Sahler, O. J. Z., and McAnarney, E. R. (1981). *The Child from 3 to 18*. St. Louis: Mosby.

Settlage, C. F. (1980). The psychoanalytic understanding of narcissistic and borderline personality disorders: advances in developmental theory. In *Rapprochement: The Critical Subphase of Separation–Individuation*, ed. R. F. Lax, S. Bach, and J. A. Burland, pp. 77–100. New York: Jason Aronson.

Smith, P. B., and Wait, R. B. (1986). Adolescent fertility and childbearing trends among hispanics in Texas. *Texas Medicine* 82:29–32.

Spitz, R. A. (1945). Hospitalism: an inquiry into the genesis of psychiatric conditions in early childhood. *Psychoanalytic Study of the Child* 1:53–74. New York: International Universities Press.

——— (1947). Anaclitic depression. *Psychoanalytic Study of the Child* 2:313–342. New York: International Universities Press.

Tanner, J. M. (1978). *Fetus into Man*. Cambridge, MA: Harvard University Press.

Winnicott, D. W. (1953). Transitional objects and transitional phenomena. *International Journal of Psycho-Analysis* 34:89–97.

——— (1958). *Collected Papers*. New York: Basic Books.

14

The Adulthood of the Neurotic Child—Developmental Perspectives

Sol Altschul, M.S., M.D.

The fate of the neurotic child as an adult is part of a broader concern about the vicissitudes and consequences of development. While growth and development may proceed in a relatively uneventful fashion, some degree of struggle, emotional trauma, and conflict is inevitable as the child progresses through the developmental phases. Struggle, which leads to the development of neurosis, is but one manifestation of the back and forth fluctuations of progression, regression, disorganization, and reorganization inherent in childhood growth and development. Other outcomes and variations occur and include a range of possibilities from the development of character traits typical in normal development to distortions, deficits, deviations, and instances of arrested development with different degrees of significance.

CONTINUITY-DISCONTINUITY

Of importance in understanding the outcome of childhood developmental vicissitudes is the question of whether or not there is continuity or discontinuity in development. Continuity of development, which has traditionally been at the base of psychoanalytic theory, implies that what has taken place earlier in the chronology of growth and development predisposes the individual child to a particular sequence and unfolding of personal characteristics. Discontinuity, on the other hand, implies that earlier traumas and developmental struggles may not appreciably affect later development or at least not by direct extension. For example, a child may have difficulty and experience delays or even deviations in its earliest development and yet be able to traverse later developmental steps with comparative ease and without demonstrating significant or harmful effects related to the earlier period or phase.

There has been a shift in recent literature that allows for greater flexibility in developmental theories and leaves room for including diverse views of continuity and discontinuity regarding the affect of earlier experiences. Stern (1985) states, "Development is not a succession of events left behind in history. It is a continuing process, constantly updated" (p. 260). As Rutter (1984) expresses it, "the concept of continuity implies meaningful links over the course of development—not a lack of change" (p. 62). In general, it is evident that what has occurred before is bound to have some influence on the course of development, even though it may be subtle, indirect, and/or minimal, particularly as far as behavioral expression is concerned. It may be that the dynamic process of life with its tendency for growth and development follows a course that includes fluctuations and interactions of regression and advance. Disorganization and reorganization has within it the capacity for reworking and/or correcting prior solutions even though remnants of disequilibrium, conflict, and fixations more or less leave their mark on the personality and character of the developing child. For example, a young oedipal girl may, within the range of expectable behavior, still develop inhibitions in the areas of aggression and competition that interfere with her natural intellectual and physical talents. Later, when adolescence is reached and her struggles with the maternal imago over sexuality and ambition are reawakened, there occurs the opportunity to reexperience and rework the conflicts. The results may end up with the same or even more severe inhibitions, but there are instances where the budding young woman with her more developed capacities can find more desirable solutions and capitalize on her innate abilities without fearing damage to herself or her competitors. Yet, while there will be less interference with her natural talents, probably some remnants of the old inhibitions in competing with women will remain. This is most likely to reveal itself in her personality traits when she is dealing with potential heterosexual rivals.

EFFECT OF CHILDHOOD NEUROSIS IN THE ADULT

Many questions come to mind as we proceed with the study of the neurotic child as an adult. What happens to a child who has suffered a neurosis in the formative years? Is his or her future destined to be burdened by the effects of such a childhood experience or are there pathways and new solutions possible for the still developing child? What do we have in mind when we refer to a childhood neurosis? Do we mean the infantile neurosis with or without symptomatology (Greenacre 1954), or do we have in mind a classical structural conflict with overt symptomatology? What place do preoedipal or pregenital influences have in the development and structure of a childhood neurosis? Do we consider only the conflicts belonging to the oedipal period with the degree of structural formation that period of development entails, or should we also include conflicts or distortions from earlier periods in the concept of childhood neurosis? There will, of course, be a range of possibilities and categories from a relatively pure oedipal conflict to emotional conflicts that represent an admixture of conflicts from earlier periods exerting their effect on the outcome of neurotic symptomatology. Davidoff-Hirsch (1985) indicates that "understanding of separation–individuation must be *added* to understanding of ego functions, psychosexual development and the management of aggression, character structure and defensive modes within the individual personality." Later she adds, "Early separation–individuation events most likely to be enshrined in character often become the fixation points to which regression occurs under stress" (p. 838). Those neurotic or neurotic-like disorders of pregenital origin will usually carry with them more troublesome symptomatology more resistant to change. Pregenital issues generally become imbricated in the development, resolution, and configuration of the oedipal phase and may play a significant part in the subsequent characteristics of both childhood and adult neurosis. In the example of the oedipal-phase girl mentioned earlier, if her preoedipal period had been characterized either by traumatic separations or by grossly erratic and/or inadequate parenting, the child would in all likelihood present a more complicated picture when the oedipal phase was reached. One would probably be able to observe a frightened child who had already experienced severe attacks of anxiety upon separation. Therefore, in addition to inhibition in the competitive arena, the child would very likely also experience increased anxiety and fear of abandonment along with fear of loss of love when aggressive and competitive issues arose. Reactivation of the configuration in adolescence, while on the one hand, with increasing maturation of the child, might offer the opportunity for resolution, the more likely consequence of the reactivation of heterosexual interest would be the production of excessive anxiety along with severe inhibitions.

Other questions arise when one considers whether therapy (or some intervention) has been available to the symptomatic child or whether the child has had to struggle with conflicts predominately by himself, and whether subsequent life events may have ameliorated earlier insults.

Approaches and Methods

There are a number of ways we can approach and observe the outcome of developmental difficulties or childhood neurosis in the adult and attempt to answer some of the questions that have been raised. Particularly instructive are reported psychoanalytic treatment cases of children who are observed and reevaluated later in adult psychoanalytic treatment.

Ritvo (1966), in reporting the classic case of Frankie, demonstrates the areas of continuity in the child's development but with a shift in the symptoms from phobic to obsessional neurosis. "Every conflict and symptom of the childhood phobic neurosis had its continuing representation in the psychic life of the patient. The effect was analogous to a telescoping or layering with the old phobic neurosis much of the time hidden beneath or within the obsessional neurosis. The old conflicts and symptoms had the qualities of enduring psychic structures which were amalgamated in character traits most of the time but at times of stress constituted fixation points to which the patient rapidly regressed." Ritvo adds, "The report correlates the predominate clinical form of the neurosis in each period, that is, the phobic neurosis of childhood with the obsessional neurosis of adulthood, and shows [that] the shift from one to the other was related to a normal developmental change in the child, a change which was facilitated and potentiated by the child analysis" (pp. 131–132).

Longitudinal studies supply another dimension to the subject of the consequences of the childhood conflicts and neurosis in the adult. Studies such as psychoanalytic observations of children over time contribute to the understanding of the lasting effects of earlier psychic development. Solnit (1982) was able to combine direct observations of both childhood and adult psychoanalytic treatment data with continuing follow-up of psychoanalytically informed observations of his patients. His focus was on the "fate of the libidinal attachment to the primary love object," and while he felt that the effects of the past on the present are at best useful approximations, he concluded that "early psychic development unfolds . . . in powerfully influential ways [and] remains constant during a twenty-year period of life experience and personality development from the school-age period into early adulthood" (pp. 34–35). As psychoanalysts we most commonly have access to childhood emotional conflict and the resultant neurotic solutions through the study of adults in psychoanalytic treatment. There, through the therapeutic regression and the recovery of memories in the transference neurosis, one learns about or can get an approximation of the childhood conflicts, compromises, symptoms, and solutions. In instances of distorted development such as those observed in developmental arrest, personality characteristics of the child may be observed almost directly in the adult patient (Fleming and Altschul 1963, Seidenberg 1988, Brockman 1988, and Forman 1988).

I would like to present the findings in a man with a history of a clear-cut clinically demonstrable neurosis in childhood that went untreated at the time of onset of symptoms.

Mr. P. entered psychoanalytic treatment at the age of 34 complaining that he had difficulties maintaining relationships with women and was experiencing increasing dissatisfaction with himself at work. In particular, he has had difficulties in sustaining a relationship that might lead to marriage. He had two or three relationships that he entered enthusiastically, but after six months to a year he became disappointed because he could not continue to feel romantic, found flaws in these women that he could not tolerate, and had to end the relationship. He recognizes that these women were reasonable people, decent, and attractive but he could not continue to relate to them, and he began to wonder why he felt that way and why the outcome was always the same. At work, the disappointment is with himself. His supervisor finds his work and productivity satisfactory but remarks in his evaluations that Mr. P. could be more productive if he were less rigid and perfectionistic.

Mr. P. is moderately depressed and easily moved to tears as he relates his current history. The tears are clearly a mixture of sadness, frustration, and anger. He conveys a sense of having been treated unfairly and of looking for restitution.

Mr. P. was raised in a small, midwest farming community. He was the oldest of three children, with a sister three years younger and a brother five years younger. The parents were both living and both worked at semiskilled occupations at a local industrial complex. The parents' marriage was unhappy and there was constant bickering with threats of divorce during Mr. P.'s formative years. Arguments centered around financial matters and the mother resented having to work, feeling that the father should have been more ambitious and successful. The height of the parents' difficulty came when Mr. P. was about 7 years of age and continued until he was 10 when the parents apparently became reconciled to their situation and much of the bickering decreased significantly. In the time Mr. P. was 7 to 10, however, there were violent verbal outbursts and several short separations. During this period, the mother often turned to Mr. P. for solace and comfort. She confided in him about her difficulties with his father and constantly urged Mr. P. to avoid his father's model by being more diligent and working harder himself. She had great ambitions for her oldest son, while at the same time she was disappointed in him and frequently compared him unfavorably to other young boys in their circle of friends. The mother often expressed her wish that Mr. P. would learn from his parents' experience and be sure to provide a better life for his future wife. Mr. P. remembers these times as both exciting and frustrating. He tried strenuously to live up to his mother's ideals for him and there were moments of intense closeness and gratification, while at the same time he experienced contradictory feelings that his efforts were useless and that he was a disappointment to his mother. His father appeared more shadowy, and was relegated to the background. He became more aloof in his relationship to the children. Essentially, he withdrew and assumed a passive position in the household except for occasions when he would go into towering rages that terrified the children.

Under the pressure of this parental conflict and his own strivings, Mr. P. developed a number of persistent compulsive rituals. He would spend endless time counting and checking various items. He would count to a specified number, but he would then obsess as to whether he had been accurate. If he doubted whether he had done so correctly, he would then have to start all over again. He constantly had to check the gas jets to make sure they were turned off or he repeatedly had to make sure that windows and doors were closed. These acute symptoms started when he was around 7 years of age, persisted for about two and a half years, and then seemed to taper off with periodic return of symptomatology under personal or family stress. The family would at times become annoyed by Mr. P.'s compulsions, but in general his behavior was ignored and no one considered treatment for him. At one point when he went to his physician for a routine examination, the physician noted the boy's tenseness and tried to give fatherly advice about relaxing. Mr. P. appreciated the physician's interest but could not use his advice. The intensity and frequency of the rituals gradually decreased although remnants of them at a lower and more subtle level were to persist into adulthood. This could be seen in many areas when he was a child, but was most dramatically apparent in Mr. P.'s attitudes toward his academic subjects and in his participation in games and general play. He had to be the best or at least near the top or he would feel inadequate and even at times withdraw from the activity or game. The fact that he was able to be an excellent student and outstanding athlete helped him to be very successful and thus protect him from again developing overt symptoms. However, the core infantile configuration ("the inner structure of infantile development" [Greenacre 1954]) remained at the center of his personality. During adolescence, Mr. P.'s character essentially took its current shape as the traits of rigidity and perfectionism became deeply ingrained and set the stage for expressing his conflicts and complaints as an adult in his heterosexual relationships and internalized struggles at work.

As the treatment began, Mr. P. tried his best to be a "good patient" and free associate, but often got bogged down in lengthy detailed descriptions of his work and relationships but without much introspection. Many episodes of disappointments with women or feeling criticized by co-workers were reported.

Initially, Mr. P. could not understand or recognize his own issues and contributions to these episodes but saw them only as reality disappointments.

As these issues were elaborated and worked on, the analyst began to have more importance to Mr. P., who then began to feel more comfortable and secure in the analytic situation. The transference clearly became one of trying to please the analyst and get the analyst's admiration and attention. At the same time, Mr. P. became curious about the analyst's other patients and was convinced that the analyst saw them as more competent, successful, and likable. Interpretations of his wish to please were characteristically experienced by him as criticism and he would get despondent and in effect vow to try harder. Over time, after repeated experiences of this constellation of trying to please, interpretation, and feeling criticized, Mr. P. was gradually able to appreciate the significance of the interaction between himself and the analyst as it related to his past relationships with his parents, particularly his mother, and to be able to tolerate the experience and increasingly be able to utilize the interactions for further investigation of his problems. He began to be more introspective and to be better able to free associate and to participate more fully in the analytic process.

He slowly but progressively began to recover memories of his earlier life experiences. As the therapeutic alliance improved, his intense discomfort in the childhood home became conscious and he remembered how frightened he had been when his parents argued and how he feared they would divorce. He remembered the rage he felt when many planned family outings were spoiled by some minor incident or mistake that led to one or another parental outburst and cancellation of the plans. At these points he could also remember wishing the parents would proceed with a divorce and then would feel remorse and guilt over these thoughts. Early in the treatment, Mr. P. could not recognize the connection between his rages and the compulsive rituals such as counting or checking the doors and gas jets. Clarification and recognition became possible when, as the analysis deepened, the trauma was reenacted in the transference.

Weekend separations became extremely painful and he missed the analyst and became more and more preoccupied with fantasies of the analyst's activities during absences, vacations, weekends, and holidays. Who was the analyst with? What activities was he engaged in? Did he have children? These were some of the questions asked. He would occasionally drive past the analyst's home to try to observe any activities that might be going on. He had fantasies that the analyst and his wife would be entertaining and would not only invite him in, but the analyst would then proceed to introduce the patient proudly to his guests. Almost simultaneously, Mr. P. would also wonder if in reality the analyst was entertaining another patient or worse yet, his children. Following such an absence and fantasy, the patient would usually come to his next appointment depressed and complaining that the treatment wasn't working but instead was making him worse. He would complain that he had difficulty falling asleep, that he would get anxious and had to keep getting out of bed to check that the doors were locked or that the gas jets were turned off.

As such episodes were repeated, the connections between the return of his childhood symptomatology and his anxiety, disappointment, and rage could be interpreted. The patient could then recognize that the depression and return of his symptoms had been precipitated by the fantasies and the recognition of his wishes and subsequent hurt and disappointment. Mr. P. could then corroborate the interpretation and elaborate upon it by relating how angry and lonely he had been that his wishes to be part of the analyst's "happy" family were not gratified. This in turn produced more memories of his unhappiness during the years when he was 7 to 10 and to his childhood fantasies and wish for a happy home. As these events and memories were worked on in the analysis, and Mr. P. could contrast his childhood limitations in coping with his anger and disappointment to his present-day abilities to deal with these affects, the compulsive symptoms reflecting his childhood neurosis abated. Further work on the complex and ambivalent heterosexual relationships could then come into focus.

In a fashion similar to the resolution of the compulsive symptomatology, the attraction to and subsequent rejection of women was reactivated in the transference, both in relationship to competition with the analyst in what Mr. P. saw as rivalry between the analyst and himself for the attention of attractive women and in regard to his contradictory feelings about his mother's leaning on him and then being disappointed in him. On one occasion, for example, when the analyst pointed out that Mr. P. saw a serious flaw in one of his woman friends, the patient at first reacted with feelings that the analyst was jealous and was telling him that he couldn't have a relationship with her. The patient felt as though the analyst wanted the woman for himself. After some reflection, Mr. P. could evaluate more appropriately his own questions about this woman and consider her erratic and irrational behavior toward him as unsuitable. It was also possible to connect it to his mother's contradictory behavior toward him, and led to more suitable feelings and behavior toward other women in his life.

I have chosen in this presentation to limit the clinical details to how Mr. P., in response to his fears, frustrations, overstimulation, disappointment, and anger as a child, developed compulsive neurotic symptoms, which decreased in intensity and became essentially latent while the underlying complex continued and became manifest in adolescence and adulthood in characteristics of rigidity and perfectionism. Only under the influence of psychoanalytic treatment, when old conflicts were reactivated in the transference, did the compulsive symptoms return as a new edition in the transference neurosis. In regard to questions about the fate of the infantile neurosis, both senses that Greenacre (1954) described could be seen in the patient presented here. The outbreak of overt neurotic symptoms was, of course, reported by Mr. P. as he related his childhood history. After 10 years of age, except for momentary lapses, symptoms did not overtly return until psychoanalytic treatment proceeded to the point where symptoms erupted as a new edition in the transference and continued for a period of time while the underlying conflicts were addressed. The second sense of "the inner structure of infantile development, with or without manifest symptoms, which forms, however, the basis of a later neurosis" (p. 18), could also be observed operating in Mr. P. The developmental conflicts and struggles produced both character traits and overt symptoms at different points in Mr. P.'s life and the effects of his character development, with variations and modifications, could be observed and detected into adulthood. The characterological traits representing the core infantile experience were present throughout his life. It was only with the revival of conflicts and working them through during treatment that Mr. P. was able to be more tolerant of his affects and ambivalent feelings and thus come to grips with his anger and oedipal wishes, leading to some readjustment of the forces in his core infantile experience. Nevertheless, the infantile neurosis remains at the core of his personality although the shift in the internal forces makes any future outbreak of symptomatology less likely.

As indicated previously, Davidoff-Hirsch (1985) states that the addition of preoedipal concerns does not diminish "the importance of the Oedipus complex in adult neurotic illness," that the "area of analytic reconstruction has widened to include preoedipal phenomena" (p. 838). However, Seidenberg (1988) demonstrates the effects of preoedipal development and in particular the vicissitudes of separation–individuation on the formation and persistence of symptoms from this period as primary symptoms in the adult emotional problems. His patient's father died when she was 17 months old and this was immediately followed by her mother's withdrawal and depression. The patient's inability to deal with this double loss impaired her capacities to deal with the separation–individuation issues characteristic of that developmental phase. The same immaturity, impaired capacity for personal relationships, and inability to tolerate frustration persisted into adulthood and in the psychoanalytic treatment almost unchanged from the original behavioral expressions. This demonstrates conflict and symptoms continuing from the childhood infantile neurosis, in the sense of an overt outbreak of symptomatology, as opposed to the return of symptoms after a latent or quiescent period, as in the transference neurosis of Mr. P. In similar fashion, Brockman (1988) demonstrates how his patient was arrested in his development in the preadolescent phase as a consequence of his father's death, and continued to act in ways as an adult that were more characteristic of a preadolescent boy. This was manifest in his relationships to both men and women. Forman (1988) details how the fantasies and play of an oedipal girl, who lost her father by death at age 6, persisted into adult life in an almost direct fashion, essentially unchanged from the time she was 6.

RESOLVING CONFLICTS—NEW STRUCTURAL DEVELOPMENT

To this point, the emphasis has been on the continuity of development and the persistence of neurotic symptoms, conflict, and structure from both preoedipal and oedipal phases into adulthood. Earlier, I suggested that the life process has within it psychic mechanisms that allow for reworking and resolving conflicts and structural development from earlier periods. If continuity were so fixed, change would not be possible, either through life events or therapy. Elsewhere, in a discussion of trauma, mourning, and adaptation, I have indicated that

> mourning, as observed in the adult, is the model mechanism for working through the loss of the loved object. It is also the prototype for *working through of all traumatic events*; that is, the piecemeal process of recall and remembering with affective reexperiencing whereby the individual is gradually able to achieve emotional distance from the disturbing event, gradually integrate the event, and reestablish equilibrium in his everyday life. Even normal development, which may in general be proceeding smoothly, has critical periods and phases characterized by episodes of disorganization and reorganization preliminary to growth and development. [Altschul 1988, p. 10]

It should be added that such a mechanism with the potential for solving problems anew in life is always available to the individual child or adult in much more frequent and subtle episodes of disorganization and reorganization.

Correction or reorganization of emotional conflict from previous phases of development is potentially always possible as the child enters the next developmental phase. Previous conflicts may be reworked, and with the growth and addition of new ego capacities, a phobic child may be able to now master a previously frightening situation. As Ritvo has pointed out, it is also possible for the symptoms to shift in the new phase and take on new expressions and manifestations such as an obsessional neurosis (Ritvo 1966). In the adult as well, childhood conflicts may be reworked and resolved through adult life experiences, although the earlier the conflict and the more fixed the character traits are, the more difficult the recovery process becomes. Caution must be taken with this concept because life experiences by themselves do not necessarily provide the opportunity to make for psychic reorganization; more typically what occurs is a reactivation of old conflicts with repetitive neurotic solutions. Often psychoanalytic treatment offers the only or best life experience to foster changes. Parenthood, however, can be one of the life experiences that may provide the stimulus and opportunity for reworking the parents' residual developmental conflicts (T. Benedek 1959, 1970) by reviving in the parent unresolved issues from the developmental phase the child is undergoing. Benedek (in a personal communication) used to remark how the mother of an adolescent girl could become anxious and even develop symptomatology when the daughter began to date, which stirred up the mother's unresolved conflicts around sexuality. H. Hurn (in a personal communication) described the psychoanalytic treatment experience with a man with narcissistic problems who initially could not work within the psychoanalytic treatment situation because he was too ashamed of having symptoms and could not tolerate these intense affects in himself. He could not continue the treatment and left after a brief trial of therapy. At a later date, after the birth of a son, he returned and resumed psychoanalysis. Under these circumstances and conditions, the patient was able to identify and experience his own feeling and conflicts, first, by observing the same issues in the child and then, by reorganizing the same or similar constellations in himself. This then served as a pathway for the ultimate solution of the patient's conflicts by allowing him to face the intense affects that previously had been intolerable and needed to be avoided.

Another man in psychoanalytic treatment, who had been struggling with inhibitions regarding his aggressive and assertive feelings and impulses, was able to make inroads toward the resolution of these conflicts and forge ahead to use these impulses in constructive creative ways after his adolescent son led the way by successfully engaging in competitive activities. This provided the stimulus to allow the parent to reevaluate his own neurotic inhibition. While the disorganization was not evident to the casual outside observer, the reorganization manifested by the patient by a freeing up of creative capacities was quite evident to him and was experienced by the patient as liberating and as being directly related to the unfounded fear that his aggressions would bring harm to himself or his loved ones.

In conclusion, we have discussed the fact that while there are both continuities and discontinuities in development, it is clear that what takes place in development in prior phases unquestionably is a force in shaping later development. While behavioral manifestations may not persist or be in evidence, the underlying conflicts, traits, and configurations do persist and have their effect from one developmental phase to another. As Blum (1971) has indicated, "Premature ejaculation during a phase of psychoanalysis may be traced to the reactivation of enuretic conflicts, but premature ejaculation is not identical with the childhood enuresis" (p. 47). Later he points out: "Infantile reactions, such as temper tantrums, screaming outbursts, sphincter incontinence, are rarely seen in adult transference *neurosis* in their original form, but in attenuated homologues" (p. 47). The methods of studying the fate of childhood neurosis in the adult through longitudinal studies and psychoanalytic treatment have been outlined, and a psychoanalytic treatment case has been presented focusing on the accessibility for study of a childhood neurosis through the reactivation of childhood symptoms in the transference. An attempt has also been made to differentiate between the unresolved childhood neurosis, the infantile neurosis, and the transference neurosis. Finally, there has been a discussion of the dynamic process of growth and development based on models of mourning, adaptation, disorganization, and reorganization that makes changes possible in an otherwise continuous chain of development, either through the reactivation of old conflicts in the treatment process or through fortunate life experiences that allow for reevaluation and change in those individuals who are appropriately and/or ideally constituted to benefit from such fortuitous events. It should, however, be emphasized that while the potential for reorganization is present in life events or new phases of development, the conflicts that are thereby reactivated may not be available to the individual for working over and resolution but may, instead, be the stimulus for the formation of symptomatology and the onset of neurosis.

REFERENCES

Altschul, S. (1988). Trauma, mourning and adaptation: a dynamic point of view. In *Childhood Bereavement and Its Aftermath*, ed. S. Altschul, pp. 3–15. New York: International Universities Press.

Benedek, T. (1959). Parenthood as a developmental phase. *Journal of American Psychoanalytic Association* 7:389–418.

―――― (1970). Parenthood during the life cycle. In *Parenthood: Its Psychology and Psychopathology*, ed. E. J. Anthony and T. Benedek, pp. 185-206. Boston: Little Brown.

Blum, H. P. (1971). On the conception and development of the transference neurosis. *Journal of American Psychoanalytic Association* 19:41–53.

Brockman, D. D. (1988). Preadolescence and early adolescence. In *Childhood Bereavement and Its Aftermath*, ed. S. Altschul, pp. 351–376. New York: International Universities Press.

Davidoff-Hirsch, H. (1985). Oedipal and preoedipal phenomena. *Journal of American Psychoanalytic Association* 33:821–840.

Fleming, J., and Altschul, S. (1963). Activation of mourning and growth by psychoanalysis. *International Journal of Psycho-Analysis* 44:419–431.

Forman, M. (1988). Two defenses against the work of mourning. In *Childhood Bereavement and its Aftermath,* ed. S. Altschul, pp. 377-390. New York: International Universities Press.

Greenacre, P. (1954). Problems of infantile neurosis: a discussion, chairman E. Kris. *Psychoanalytic Study of the Child* 9:16-71. New York: International Universities Press.

Ritvo, S. (1966). Correlation of a childhood and adult neurosis: based on the adult analysis of a reported childhood case. *International Journal of Psycho-Analysis* 47:130-131.

Rutter, M. (1984). Continuities and discontinuities in socioemotional development. In *Continuities and Discontinuities in Development,* ed. R. N. Emde and R. J. Harmon, pp. 41-68. New York: Plenum Press.

Seidenberg, H. (1988). Report of a psychoanalysis and follow-up: severe emotional trauma by parent loss at seventeen months: consequences for development: formation of borderline syndrome. In *Childhood Bereavement and Its Aftermath,* ed. S. Altschul, pp. 309-349. New York: International Universities Press.

Solnit, A. J. (1982). Early psychic development as reflected in the psychoanalytic process. *International Journal of Psycho-Analysis* 63:23-37.

Stern, D. N. (1985). *The Interpersonal World of the Infant.* New York: Basic Books.

PART III

THERAPEUTIC ISSUES

15

The Fantasy World of the Child as Revealed in Art, Play, and Dreams

Jules Glenn, M.D., and Isidor Bernstein, M.D.

Fantasies, which may be conscious or unconscious, are woven into the fabric of the personality. They influence the individual's behavior, dreams, and symptomatology, and affect his perception of reality (Arlow 1969a,b). Like other productions of the mind, they are the outcome of the interaction of drives, ego functions, and, once it is established, the superego. Fantasies, including those accompanying masturbation, are thus compromise formations consisting of hostile as well as sexual wishes that have been altered by defenses mobilized to protect the individual from anxiety and other painful affects that might otherwise appear. The raw, elemental wishes and urges must therefore be disguised sufficiently to meet the demands of reality and the child's superego.

To cite an example, the appearance of an only child's imaginary companion had many determinants. He felt lonely and unloved and therefore fantasized that he could love this "friend" and be loved by him. The boy was upset that his mother was away a great deal, leaving him lonely and sad. He could counteract these feelings by having an affectionate bond with the friend who substituted for his mother. It helped him to avoid anger at his mother when she was away. Also, he could hide more direct sexual feelings for his mother by experiencing the soothing presence of his companion. The anger at and love for his mother and the rage at his father, who he believed kept his mother from him, were forbidden and even dangerous. Such feelings could invite attack in retaliation. He thus defended himself against recognizing his libidinal and hostile wishes by having the disguised satisfaction through the relationship with his imaginary companion. Indeed, in his games with this boy, he could compete and beat a rival.

This example illustrates our intention to examine, in this chapter, the multiple functions of the fantasies of children and adolescents and their manifestations in art, play, and dreams. We will look at the biological basis for the drives that are expressed in modified form in their wishful fantasies. We will also consider the way physiology and anatomy direct the expression of physical and mental activity. The latter includes cognitive thinking and dreaming. In addition, we will take into account the importance of the environment and changing interpersonal relationships.

FANTASIES

Children's fantasies and their manifestations vary with their developmental levels. They can be expressed in words and in the children's play and dramatization, their stories, their drawings, their dreams and daydreams, and their symptoms. They appear spontaneously in psychoanalysis and psychotherapy, thus providing a unique opportunity for their study and interpretation. In this chapter we will offer a clinical perspective supplemented to a degree by descriptions of experimental studies. We will emphasize play, art, and dreams as fantasy products.

Murphy (1947) defines a fantasy as "a wish-fulfilling imaginative process" (p. 986). The American Heritage Dictionary (1982) states that it is "an imagined event or condition fulfilling a wish" (p. 489). Moore and Fine (1968) concur: It is "a product of mental activity which usually exists in the form of images and ideas and fulfills a wish" (p. 46) and may be conscious or unconscious. It is thus primarily unrealistic, but they add that it may also "serve as preparation for realistic action appropriate to the requirements of the environment" (p. 46). We may note that fantasy can be used to master traumata of different types, and in the service of defense (A. Freud 1936). In addition, fantasies may include realistic perceptual elements from the past or present.

Fantasies vary in complexity with the maturity of the child, adolescent, or adult. They are overdetermined compromise formations with contributions from the ego, drives (both libidinal and aggressive), and, when it appears, the superego.

It is difficult to know how early phenomena that can be classified as fantasies occur. Freud (1900) suggested that the infant imagines being fed through a hallucination of the breast, but this cannot be proved, nor the age ascertained. Some have suggested that this occurs as early as 3 months. The occurrence of a hallucinatory experience, identified by Isakower (1936) in latency children and adults, suggests that a wish-fulfilling image of feeding and of feeling a union with the mother occurs early in the child's life. Isakower observed that some people, when going to sleep or lying on the analytic couch, vividly imagine that a mass is entering their mouths and that they are fused with their environment. Their hands and lips feel large and swollen and their mouths dry and sandy. Such hallucinations, which the individual realizes are not real, occur in normal people. Although we can speculate that such imagery occurs in children under a year of age, we cannot be certain. Our hypotheses about children's fantasies are sounder when they can talk about them in a therapeutic situation.

Fantasies have been studied in relation to libidinal stages around which they are often organized, and developmental lines that involve ego, id, and superego working together. Freud (1905) observed that children progress through a series of psychosexual stages. The oral stage is followed by the anal stage and then the phallic stage. The child's major interest (cathexis) during these successive stages switches from one bodily area to another. The early infant is occupied with feeding and hence has oral interests, which involve other bodily sensations as well. The 2-year-old is ready to be toilet trained and is concerned with anal and rectal sensations and pleasures. At around 3 the genitals, especially the penis and clitoris, become more significant and the child masturbates more. Soon, while the genitals are still most significant, the oedipal stage occurs and the infant becomes involved in complicated love and hate relations with his parents. Usually love of the parent of the opposite sex and hatred for the parent of the same sex predominate.[1] The oedipal child fears injury, including castration, for his forbidden wishes.

With the organization of the superego, the part of the personality that establishes ideals to be achieved and punishes the individual if he fails to live up to moral standards, the situation becomes more complicated. Fantasies then include this aspect of the personality. A period of latency

---

1. This description, while essentially correct, is oversimplified for the purpose of exposition. For instance, Roiphe and Galenson (1972) have described an early genital stage at 18 months. And we have glossed over negative oedipal configurations in which the child loves the parent of the same sex.

appears, in which the demands of the superego make the libidinal and aggressive wishes go underground. The latency child, except during relatively brief times in which latency is interrupted, becomes more civilized in his demeanor. Fantasies are there but disguised and hidden. The child uses his energies for educational purposes.

We will resume our description of libidinal stages later when we discuss adolescence. At this point we will turn to manifestations of fantasies in childhood. In doing so we want to emphasize that lines of development, including drives, ego, and superego, will be taken into account.

The Isakower phenomenon is a splendid example of wish-fulfilling imagery with an oral organization. It entails a symbiotic ego state in which the infant imagines himself united with his caretaker. It appears as a regressive experience when a person feels threatened by oedipal desires. So too do other oral fantasies defend against more advanced but frightening wishes. As the child of the oral stage becomes somewhat independent of his mother he often acquires soft, cuddly objects, such as a comfort blanket, called transitional objects (Winnicott 1951) to soothe himself. Such an object represents both mother and child.

A 4-year-old, who entered analysis for separation anxiety, and his mother enjoyed a teasing flirtatious interchange in the waiting room. When the boy joked that he had seen his mother naked, his mother blushed with excitement and delight. Then, wary of his success, he changed his tactics and disguised his intent. He picked up his mother's fur jacket and cuddled it. Instead of being the sexual conqueror of his mother, he became the baby whose sensuous pleasure derived from contact with a transitional object.

Another child, Betty, a 3-year-old girl, fed a baby doll with joy and contentment. She then placed the doll's bottle into her own mouth and feigned drinking as she sucked the nipple. She was both the feeding mother and the infant finding oral gratification. Her fantasy was: "I am fed like a little baby. I prefer that to watching my little brother being fed, which makes me angry." The fantasy reinstated the feeling of being the baby that she once was.

Anal stage issues can also be depicted in fantasies.

At about the same time that Betty sought her mother's love through feeding, she was engaged in a serious conflict with her mother over toilet training. She expressed her fantasied wish to thwart her mother in a game with her analyst. She had the analyst, identified with her mother, command her to have a bowel movement in the toilet. But before she could get to the potty, she (in play, not in actuality) soiled on the floor. The analyst/mother, in her scenario, became distraught and frustrated.

She would then reverse the story roles. She, as the mother, demanded that the analyst, now playing the role of a child, go to the toilet. Sometimes he succeeded, but at other times he had a bowel movement on the floor. Here the patient fantasied herself the powerful mother who could boss the child rather than the powerless child. But at times the mother/enemy was represented as powerless as the patient identified with the child who was the victor.

We have already seen that the oedipal child can imagine himself the successful suitor of his mother, but that this can frighten him so that he gives up his victory and becomes a small child. The little boy who wins his mother may retreat because he fears injury.

Another example will reveal an imagined injury more clearly.

Betty started to masturbate when she was 4 years old. Along with this she expressed oedipal fantasies. She told her analyst she loved the man who had just left the office, her father, and that she had angry feelings toward her mother. She told her analyst that she wanted to bite his, the analyst's, penis and possess it, and indeed lunged toward his penis impulsively only to then control herself. After that, when she saw a paper she had once colored red she became alarmed. She worried that she would be hurt. It wasn't only her genitals—her bottom, she called it—that could be injured. So, too, could her brain, and she could be exiled as punishment.

She played Pinocchio, who was punished for lying by being sent to Pleasure Island where one could enjoy oneself, but where one also is changed into a stupid donkey. She had the analyst become a donkey. He had to kneel and bray, "Hee haw."

Children of the oedipal age express their fantasies vividly. Their superegos have not been fully developed and therefore these oedipal children are less inhibited than latency children. Further, the intensity of their drives pushes them to open expression. Also, the balance of primary and secondary process is such as to encourage creativity. (Primary-process thinking consists of illogical, poorly organized, somewhat flighty ideation, while secondary-process thinking is more logical, reality oriented, and organized.)

With latency, the conscience asserts itself, inhibiting the child's direct expression of his fantasies. Nevertheless there are periodic interruptions of latency during which drive derivatives break through, permitting unsublimated aggressive and libidinal behavior, including masturbation. A transition from sublimated and organized behavior to imaginative, drive-dominated fantasies and behavior is seen in Jim's sessions.

In one session Jim brought a model of an aircraft carrier, the Hornet, he had constructed. Very proudly he described the details of his work. He showed his analyst the planes that landed on the carrier, the ropes that control the planes as they land, the elevators that allow the planes to rise and descend, the area where the planes are stored.

We see here the thinking of the "ideal" latency child. He uses his energies for constructive activity, activity that is socially approved and that involves control. You might guess that behind these sublimations lie aggressive and possibly sexual wishes and fantasies, but these are well disguised and made more acceptable.

As the session proceeded, Jim's controlled behavior started to deteriorate. He became anxious as aggressive thoughts emerged. Eventually Jim's fantasies became somewhat primitive as primary-process thinking became more pronounced. This demonstrates the vulnerability of recently acquired mechanisms of neutralization and sublimation.

Jim told how the original Hornet had been bombed and damaged. He referred to spies and secrets. He had told his mother the secret he would soon reveal to me, but his mother could not tell her friend, David's mother, about this lest she hit him with a brush for doing something bad. Indeed, Jim, identifying with David, started to hit himself on the behind in an excited way. He obviously was enjoying the beating fantasy.

Jim said that he and David had found a Tommy gunner in the nearby woods. They saw a truck with keys in it in this area. When they returned later the truck was gone. They imagined that the truck driver was a thief and that if they caught him they'd receive reward money. Because trespassing in the woods was forbidden, they could not tell David's mother about their escapade. Jim would have to collect the reward money himself and, perhaps, give David half of it.

The reader will see that the fantasy became somewhat wild and unrealistic and logically impaired. Forbidden aggressive drives were appearing along with masochistic derivatives. Ego, id, and superego joined in producing this fantasy. For instance, aggressive and sexual wishes (his beating himself while imagining a woman was doing it) evoked punishment (again his self-flagellation). The ego was not only the instrument through which the wishes and punishment expressed themselves, it also disguised these conflicting forces.

Even more primitive fantasy play occurred in the final third of the session. Jim stuck a pencil into a ball of clay he made and then put it first through a hole in a cup cover that was on top of a cup of warm water. He wanted the clay, now getting soft, to remain on the end of the pencil.

We could understand the fantasy depicted here in a few weeks. Jim's parents were planning to have him circumcised because he had developed a sore on his foreskin as a result of masturbating. Jim had mixed feelings about this. He knew it would please his mother and he also thought it would make his penis look nicer and neater, more masculine. He would appease his superego, which opposed the masturbation. A major masturbation fantasy as it emerged was: "I want to please my sadistic mother by undergoing a castrative operation." On the other hand, Jim was opposed to the painful cutting. The conflict was depicted in the fantasy play with the clay, and the masturbation fantasy.

FANTASIES IN NEUROSIS AND NORMALITY

Fantasies and their manifestations in play, dreams, and art are universal phenomena. They can occur both normally and in neuroses. Fantasies, as we have seen, are compromise formations resulting from the interaction of id, ego, and superego elements. Aggressive and libidinal drives participate, and past and present reality contribute to fantasy formation. They may be unconscious and express themselves as character manifestations, behavior or symptoms. They may serve adaptive functions or be maladaptive. They are often used in creativity and communication.

A single fantasy may appear in different forms. Let us take the family romance fantasy (Freud 1909) as an example. In this more or less universal fantasy, the individual imagines that he was born of royalty and that the father and mother he lives with adopted him. This fantasy, which may be conscious but is often unconscious, has a number of adaptive purposes. It enables the child to tolerate current antagonisms toward the unhappy feelings about his parents. Also, incestuous feelings toward the parents may be dealt with by imagining they are not one's true parents. Paralyzing guilt and anxiety can thus be avoided.

The family romance fantasy may appear in dreams and play in more or less disguised form. It may reveal itself in literature. Sophocles' *Oedipus Rex* is a play about a child who was sent away by his royal parents to be killed but was instead adopted by another family. He was nevertheless fated to murder his biological father and marry his biological mother. Mark Twain's novel *The Prince and the Pauper* tells about a prince who accidentally finds himself cast out of his royal status when he changes places with a poor child who looks exactly like him. In the story, the pauper had played games in which he enacted the role of a king. The very frequency of the family romance fantasy enables the tales to touch the reader, who identifies with the characters (Glenn 1988).

At times the fantasy appears in neurotic symptoms. An adopted child's conscious fear that he will be kidnapped may derive from an unconscious anxiety that his biological parents will try to reunite with him or be a manifestation of a belief that his parents originally kidnapped him. Here we see a neurotic manifestation of a fantasy with symptom formation. Defenses have failed to avoid anxiety.

Optimally, adaptation occurs when defenses serve as adaptive mechanisms and can be used flexibly without painful affects. When an individual uses the same defenses repeatedly no matter what the circumstances, the fixed patterns of behavior and interaction may cause trouble. For instance, when the defensive grandiose aspects of the family romance fantasy are emphasized excessively and repeatedly, the individual may become unable to accept the blows to his narcissism that reality deals. The resultant rage may evoke anxiety, depressive affects, or guilt.

The aim of defense is to modulate and control these emotions. Not only may rigidity deter their effectiveness; if the drives are excessively strong or the superego too primitive, the defenses will fail to accomplish their aims and neurosis may result. Environmental pressures may have similar effects.

The child may use his fantasies adaptively in creative endeavors and communication. It is difficult to determine precisely when and in what form children begin to think in an imaginative and creative form. We may assume that there will be considerable variations depending on genetic and constitutional factors, as well as developmental factors such as maturation and stimulation from the child's surroundings, including that from the nurturing person.

The ordinary or normal child doubtless will be using his ability to imagine in order to satisfy his instinctual needs, either libidinal or aggressive, or to cope with the anxieties and traumata that he experiences in the course of development. How successful he will be will depend upon the nature of the tasks with which he is confronted and the capacities or talents available to him. A verbally gifted child may use his talent to relate stories, while a musically or artistically gifted child may compose music or drawings. The neurotic child may fail if he is too limited intellectually, linguistically, or physically to have the means to express himself. Or he may fail if the emerging fantasy is too exciting or threatening, either to himself or to those receiving his productions. If the child's cognitive, linguistic, or artistic productions (drawings, music) are too heavily charged with erotic or aggressive energy he may feel forced to contain them, which results either in inhibition of his capacity to speak, draw, or play, or that the productions become repetitive, trite, or stereotyped. Not all such productions have a communicative function. They may be for the child's own gratification through discharge or as a form of entertainment.

Psychic trauma produces particular problems. In an attempt at mastery the individual may repeat the traumatic event, usually in a disguised form, with the hope of achieving a satisfactory outcome. Mastery may be accomplished, but in some cases the repetition may evoke intense anxiety, so great that the healing function fails and the patient becomes the victim of a prolonged traumatic neurosis in which anxiety dominates the clinical picture.

FANTASIES AND PSYCHIC TRAUMA

Originally, Freud (1900) believed that dreams were disguised wish fulfillments and that symptoms had a similar structure. Only later (Freud 1933) did he recognize a group of dreams that were "beyond the pleasure principle," and that sought not direct gratification but attempted to master traumata. These were usually repetitive dreams which contained in open or disguised form a disturbing event that the patient tries to deal with (see chapter 4). He then also described the use of play to achieve mastery (Freud 1920).

An 8-year-old boy, anticipating a herniorrhaphy, played games in which doctor and nurse puppets examined a child puppet and performed surgery. In these repetitive games no one was hurt and the outcome was satisfactory. The boy identified with the medical personnel and thus actively attacked the patient, in that way avoiding being the victim who was hurt. At other times the boy was the patient who could control the surgical procedure and thus avoid danger to a degree. In either form the fantasy play was reassuring. The defense of denial helped avoid painful affects.

In this case the repetition succeeded in avoiding traumatic anxiety. In other cases neurosis ensues. The fantasies intended to overcome the effects of the trauma become enmeshed with conflictual aspects of the personality, fixed and frightening.

Sandra, an 8-year-old girl, was brought for treatment because of intense fears of being stung by spiders. The fears had reached the point of interfering with her being outdoors and being able to walk to and from school. She was equally afraid of receiving injections for necessary immunizations. The drawing she made during her sessions made the phallic significance of the stinger and needle quite obvious. She dated the onset of her fears to about 5 years of age. This was after an illness which had necessitated treatment by a series of injections.

The girl enjoyed teasing her father and being teased by him. The teasing enabled Sandra to initiate and control attacks on her. The teasing was a provocative attempt to master the traumatic influence of her receiving injections.

It quickly became incorporated into the Oedipus complex. She was rivalrous with her mother and was often angry at her. Her guilt about her pleasure with her father and irritation toward her mother caused her to behave in masochistic ways.

As positive feelings toward the therapist developed, she became frightened of the taxi driver who brought her to and from his office. Her fantasy was that he would bring her to the wrong place, either on the way to the analyst's office or on the way home, that is, he would kidnap her. The displacement from analyst/father to the taxi driver became clear.

In a subsequent session she intentionally rang the office bell for a long time to get her analyst angry. Her fantasy was that he would punish her either by sending her home, by throwing her off the roof, or by not letting her go home. She offered him her address and telephone number, revealing her wish that he visit her and she visit him. At this point, she returned to the fantasy that her analyst would not let her leave—he could kidnap her and she would be his child. On a deeper level, she was expressing her incestuous wish for her father's love.

CHILDREN'S ART

Having discussed children's fantasies in general terms, we can now turn to more specific manifestations in art, play, and dreams. We have provided examples of these forms of expression as they are common means of communication and discharge in children.

Children find it natural to draw or paint in analysis or therapy. They find art work a pleasant, soothing activity which can allay anxiety. Occasionally the child finds himself drawing something that is upsetting, but he usually avoids this. Art, like play, is a form of drive discharge that utilizes cognitive capacity and defense mechanisms and can be used adaptively to communicate and find pleasure.

The cognitive aspect is significant (Gesell et al. 1940). A 13-month-old can make a mark on a paper. An 18-month-old scribbles. A 2-year-old tends to make circular markings. At 3, children can name the drawings, even though to the adult the names may seem farfetched. The 4-year-old's drawings often appear even to the adult to have a content, but they are rather crude pictures. A house, a nose, the eyes are named by the child. The names the child of 5 gives a drawing are easily recognizable to the adult. Many draw identifiable persons or buildings. The 6-year-old is more accurate, precise, and detailed in his art.

Goodenough (1926) has developed an intelligence test in which drawings of persons are rated. The child progresses from drawing an incomplete face to drawing one with features, to drawing figures with limbs coming from the head, to drawing a head attached to a torso with limbs, to drawing a full figure with neck included. Points are given for details, including fingers, hair, eyes with or without lids and lashes, clothing, and so forth; by adding the points awarded, the test can estimate the child's intelligence quotient.

Emotional factors influence drawings. Girls tend to draw girls and boys to draw boys. If a child spontaneously and consistently depicts children of the opposite sex one may well suspect a gender identity problem. Children who are old enough to include the correct number of fingers but omit some digits may suffer from excessive castration anxiety. The same is true of the children who leave a gap in the genital area. Some young artists draw unstable persons with thin legs, an indication of a feeling of instability, insecurity, and anxiety. Dark pictures, especially black ones when the child has colored crayons available, lead one to suspect depressive affect, while prominent eyes suggest suspiciousness or voyeurism. Relationships with family members may become transparent when the child draws them.

Other symbolism has been used to interpret drawings (Freud 1900). The sun often represents the father, and a house, the artist or his mother. A tree can symbolize male genitals. A frequent drawing of a girl entering puberty consists of a cute, budding girl with prominent eyelashes standing between two curtains as if on a small stage. The exhibitionism may be apparent, but the depiction of the female genitals as two curtains surrounding a body may not.

The therapist of a child who draws has a host of sources of information to rely on before he interprets the picture. Often he will choose not to tell the child his interpretation lest he frighten him and interfere with sublimation. Children may decide to refrain from drawing after a premature interpretation.

One source of information is the immediate setting in which the drawing is made, what the child was doing or saying before and after the drawing. Another is the circumstances of the child's life as the child or his parents describe them to the therapist. The child may expand on his drawing through talking about it. It is unusual for a child to associate directly and intentionally to the picture or its details. Sometimes symbolism can help one to understand the picture, but one must be cautious about this.

Jack required therapy because of three intertwined sets of experiences. He had as a small child been a bowel movement retainer, and as a derivative of this he became a taciturn, withholding boy. Then, when he was in latency, a teacher of a course he was taking seduced him and a number of other boys. A few months before Jack started therapy the seducer had been apprehended and the boys suspected of being molested were interviewed repeatedly by the police. Jack revealed nothing, but there was plenty of evidence from other kids that he had been seduced. In addition, he had a learning disability. A diagnosis of attention deficit disorder had been made on the basis of mild neurological signs, restlessness in school, and difficulty concentrating.

Jack at 11 was reluctant to enter therapy, but his parents insisted. His schoolwork had been terrible and he was disruptive there and at home, often being aggressive to his younger brother. He was reluctant to talk in therapy, but expressed himself by drawing pictures, which he took home and collected. It was necessary with Jack to use information gathered from parents and his own current and past speech in therapy to understand the pictures and make appropriate comments. He did very little associating to the elements of the pictures although he did describe what was going on and identify parts of the pictures when the therapist asked. In one session he first drew a picture of a movie screen with people in the audience watching. It reminded the therapist of the class and the seduction with people watching, but he said nothing about that. Then he drew the beachside pool of Jim, a friend whose magnificent house and grounds he had drawn before. After he finished the drawing he added a box with FIREWORKS written on it (Figure 15-1). He had been to a party at this friend's house, he told the therapist, and they had had fireworks. When the therapist asked who had fired the fireworks he said that Jim and he had.

The therapist knew a lot about Jim's family. Jack's parents objected to Jim and his parents because the parents were unprotective; they even violated laws. They had recently taken Jack into Chinatown and bought firecrackers. When Jack's parents learned of this they criticized Jim's parents. They also knew that they allowed Jack to ride dangerous vehicles on land and a dangerous "jet ski" in the water. Indeed Jack had told his therapist this independently, and had described his excitement.

After Jack drew and described and talked about the picture, the therapist drew some tentative conclusions, most of which he kept to himself. The drawing depicted Jack's desire to do forbidden, exciting, dangerous things, and possibly reflected his parents' and his conscience's opposition. (He also thought it possible that Jack's own aggressive urges were being expressed.) He asked whether Jack wanted to show his parents what happened by taking the picture home, but Jack saw no problem. His parents knew about it. The therapist was surprised and repeated what they had talked about before—that Jack's parents didn't like Jim's parents because they weren't protective enough. They had objected in the past to the boy's parents taking Jack into the city to buy fireworks.

Jack didn't budge. He drew another picture—of a building with a big sign on it: BUY FIREWORKS (Figure 15-2). This was a sign of defiance. No one was going to stop him!

Figure 15-1

Figure 15-2

PLAY

In the section on fantasy we noted that play is often the vehicle for its expression. In this section we will be more explicit about play itself.

Although play is an essential activity in childhood and even in adulthood, its definition is elusive. Dictionaries include so many activities under the name of play that the issue becomes confused. We counted more than thirty-five entries on the verb *to play* and ten definitions of the noun in the American Heritage Dictionary (1982). Many of them are only peripherally related to the clinical usage or to the understanding of children's play. The definitions include: to occupy oneself in amusement, sport or other recreation; to take part in a game; to bet or gamble; to perform on a musical instrument; to act or perform in a dramatic presentation; to pretend to be or to mimic.

Despite a lack of clear definition when we talk of children's play, we have a sense of what is meant. It makes sense when we say a child progresses along a developmental line from play to games to work. And the concept of preplay antedating play appears reasonable.

Childhood play takes a variety of forms including (1) pleasant interactions with other children or adults, (2) enacting of stories the child has heard or made up, (3) repetitions of happy or disturbing events, (4) participation in more or less formal organized games, and (5) imitations of others (including adults).

Using observations primarily but not totally derived from the child analytic situation, Neubauer (1987) has denoted a number of characteristics of play in children.

1. In play the child carries out a physical act.
2. The child knows the enactment in play is not real, while in work the child considers the activity "real."
3. In play the child carries out an exploration, a "trying on," an attempt to try new solutions to problems. This, Neubauer observes, is true of work too.
4. Play expresses a fantasy that may be conscious or unconscious. Drives, both aggressive and libidinal, are discharged, giving pleasure, but sublimation may occur (it often does not), and the fantasy is disguised so that the child does not have to recognize the full significance of his urges.
5. The fantasy can be enacted without concern for the reality consequences, the reactions of the outside world, and with little concern about guilt. We may add that the play and the fantasies behind it,

being compromise formations, contain ego, id, and when it develops, superego elements.
6. Play is a means of communication and is thus useful in analysis and therapy.

Play is a step in the direction of greater maturity in the ways Neubauer describes. It also serves to help the child master difficult situations including shock trauma. By repeating a toilet training situation or a traumatic event directly or in disguised form the child attempts to alleviate the anxiety associated with these occurrences. The defense mechanism used by the child may be identification with the aggressor. Identification with grownups allows for mastery over object loss, facilitates object constancy, and prepares the child for adult roles.

As the child's cognitive capacity matures, the type of play the child can engage in changes. Piaget (1932) has observed that symbolic play starts at 1 1/2 years and that games without fixed rules precede playing with codified rules. An example of symbolic play is the child's using a block or a doll to represent a baby, whom the child rocks. In a classic study Piaget examined the rules of the game by watching children play marbles and interrogating the players. This study of the stages of play also traces aspects of morality and the progression from egocentrism to social awareness. He found four stages.

The first stage is purely motor and individual in character. The child handles marbles according to the dictates of his personal desires and motor habits. More or less ritualized schema appear. There are no truly collective rules, only something that may be called the individual's motor rules. The child may pick up the marbles, look at them, place them in his mouth, drop them, and so forth. The child may conceive of the marbles symbolically, calling them animals or people for instance.

Piaget calls the second stage, which starts between 2 and 5 years of age, egocentrism. The child receives examples of the codified rules, but uses them only to imitate the examples he sees and without understanding the rules. He plays by himself in the presence of others, or with others without trying to win; everyone can "win" during this stage.

The third stage, cooperation, appears between 7 and 8. Children only vaguely understand the rules, according to Piaget. Each child plays according to his own rules, and each child tries to win.

The fourth stage, starting between 10 and 12, entails a codification of the rules which every child knows and plays by in a competitive way. They even know variations in the rules.

There are other progressive sequences. The peekaboo game is a case in point. At first the mother institutes the game. The child is unable to do so because of cognitive and physical limitations. The mother covers her own face or the child's and then uncovers it, to the delight of the infant. The game acts as a reassurance that the mother will not disappear forever. It helps to master separation anxiety.

Later the child can cover his face, keep his mother out of view, remove the cover and delight in her reassuring reappearance. Still later the game becomes one in which the child hides behind chairs or in closets and then appears. When he is older he will enact hiding and seeking without the organized structure of a hide-and-seek game. In the full game, rules include the child who is "it" covering his eyes at home base and counting to one hundred while the other players hide. When the child who is it finds another player, he races back to home and tries to touch it before the other child. Whoever touches home first wins that segment of the game. This version of hide-and-seek is quite complicated and has incorporated into it competitive strivings and mastery of physical capacities as well as mastery over loss of objects. An oedipal element appears in which the winning child wins home, symbolically the mother, from his or her opponents.

Hide-and-seek, although complex compared to peekaboo, is not as complicated as organized games like Chutes and Ladders, Monopoly, checkers, and chess. The more complicated games utilize a variety of cognitive achievements, contain oedipal significances, and often prepare the child for adult work.

Monopoly entails calculating, planning strategies, and competing to acquire wealth in ways based on actual adult real estate practices. Chess involves even more complicated cognition used in an adversative attempt to conquer, capture, and destroy the opponent. In the end the king, symbolizing the father, is killed, as the winner declares, "Checkmate!" ("The king is dead!")

These organized games require so much concentration and are so structured that they have limited value in therapy and analysis. Some children use the games to develop a relationship with the therapist that is close but not too close. Others use the games to hide their feelings. Sometimes, however, the intensity of the desire to win becomes apparent, as does the willingness to cheat to achieve this aim. The competitive feelings may be successfully interpreted but they may nevertheless conflict with the therapeutic alliance.

Other mother–child interactions that can be called play or preplay prepare the child for speech and enhance the warmth of the parent–child relationship. When the child makes certain sounds the mother repeats them. The child then imitates the mother, continuing the cycle. This imitation will eventually become not a game but a serious learning experience in which the child learns and practices sounds especially utilized in his society, individual words, and then phrases.

We have already provided some examples of imaginative play as it appears in treatment in the section on fantasy. We will now offer further examples.

A 5-year-old boy, Charles, was in conflict about his competitive feelings toward his father. During treatment sessions he played a game that involved shooting rubber darts at a target. Each shot was scored on the basis of its closeness to the center. He would insist on playing the game until he scored higher than the therapist and then he would give the therapist another chance to win. The boy also played with toy guns. The play was based on TV westerns. Charles took shelter behind a cabinet and challenged the therapist to beat him to the draw. He instructed the therapist to play dead but then he revived him to play the game again. The game was designed to master the anxiety and guilt over his competitive and murderous wishes toward his ambivalently-loved father.

Frank, a 9-year-old boy, was brought for analytic treatment because of persistent thumbsucking, immature behavior, and poor schoolwork. He was in conflict about his passive dependent relationship with his mother. She was herself involved in trying to free him and herself from a quasi-symbiotic tie between them. Oral needs and wishes figured prominently in his behavior and fantasies. The boy was frightened of his own wishes for engulfment and fusion with his mother. He played out this conflict with sink, bathtub, and toilet as props. For instance, he filled the sink with water and submerged containers, figures, or other objects. He occupied himself with the alternatives of their being lost, destroyed, going down the drain or recovered by emerging unharmed. In another session he filled the sink with water, submerged a man, and then snatched the man out of the water, exclaiming that the man was nearly dead because six minutes had passed and the man would die if he couldn't get air. Frank oscillated between the regressive pull of strong oral-dependent wishes expressed by the desire for fusion with the mother (dramatized by submersion and going down the drain in the sink) and the forward striving for assertive independence. He equated independence, however, with abandonment by others, starvation, and death. He dealt with the resulting fears in play by refueling the engines of the boats in the sink. The boat represented him being fed and cared for by his mother.

DREAMS

The psychoanalytic study of children's dreams has lagged behind that of adult dreams (Gillman 1987). This may be because children generally do not associate directly to the different elements of the dream. The analyst's interpretation will often be based on the general situation in which the dreams occur and on the comments of the child patient. The therapist will make use of information the parents impart to help understand the dream. Indeed the child sometimes tells the parents, rather than the therapist, the dream. The father and mother may then relay the information to the therapist. They may also provide him with information about the child's past or current experiences that cast light on the dream.

A great deal of information about the physiological conditions of dreaming has emerged for children, adolescents, and adults (Hartmann 1967). During sleep, specific cycles occur that are associated with specific electroencephalogram changes. Dreaming usually occurs during periods of REM sleep, so-called because the subject's eyes undergo rapid movement at that time. The electroencephalogram (EEG) displays a typical configuration during REM sleep. The rapid eye movement (REM) state appears after about one and a half hours of sleep. When the individual is not in REM sleep he passes through sleep stages 1 to 4, each with its own EEG configuration. The typical sequence is: awake—stage 1—stage 2—stage 3—stage 4—stage 3—stage 2—stage 1—REM—stage 1—stage 2—stage 3—stage 4, and so forth. The individual may awaken spontaneously after stage 1.

In adults there are typically four or five cycles per night, each lasting about 1½ hours. REM periods are ten to fifteen minutes long. The sequences of the cycle are the same in children, but the percentage of REM sleep and total sleep varies with the age, as indicated in the following table.

TABLE 15-1

Subject's age	REM sleep at % of total time asleep	Total REM sleep per night
Neonate 1–15 days	45–65	9 hours
Infant under 2 years	25–40	4.5 hours
2–5 years	20–30	2.6 hours
5–13 years	15–20	1.7 hours
13–18 years	15–20	1.6 hours
Adult	18–25	1.4 hours

From E. Hartmann, *The Biology of Dreaming*, 1967. Courtesy of Charles C Thomas, Publisher, Springfield, Illinois.

Note that REMs occur in early infancy and in the womb, thus indicating that they antedate dreaming.

Although most dreaming occurs during REM sleep, it is not entirely so. There are periods of less organized dreaming during stages 1–4. *Pavor nocturnus* (a type of nightmare called night terrors) generally occurs during deep non-rapid eye movement (NREM) sleep. Enuresis, previously thought to be accompanied by dreams, actually usually occurs during NREM sleep at a time that REM sleep, which ordinarily would appear, fails to appear.

These physiological changes do not contradict Freud's (1900) assertion that dreams are wish fulfillments, but they do appear to contradict his statement that they are the guardians of sleep. REM periods occur automatically. An increase in the intensity of wishes that threaten to wake the individual is not required to produce a dream.

Freud (1900) stated that dreams were wish fulfillments, but that the wish was almost always disguised by the workings of the dream. He later added that dreams may repeat traumatic experiences in an attempt at mastery (Freud 1920b). In addition, we know that superego derivatives reveal themselves in dreams and that defenses modify and disguise them.

Freud (1900) described a number of children's dreams in his classic book, *The Interpretation of Dreams*. The first, a dream his daughter Anna had when she was 14 months old, was, he said, a direct and undisguised wish fulfillment. She had been kept from eating one entire day because of an attack of vomiting. That night she called out in her sleep: "Anna Fweud, stwawbewwies, wild stwawbewwies, omblet, pudden!" (p. 130). His daughter, the author said, "was in the habit of using her own name to express the idea of taking possession of something" (p. 130). In the dream she named the foods she wanted to eat. The dream also expressed her retaliation against her nurse's belief that strawberries had caused her illness. In another dream, a 22-month-old nephew of Freud, after objecting to giving Freud a gift of cherries, dreamed that he had eaten all the cherries himself.

These dreams directly expressed wishes, as often occurs in small children's dreams, but not all children's dreams are undisguised wish fulfillments. Freud, as an adult, analyzed a dream he had when he was 7 or 8. "I saw my beloved mother, with a peculiarly peaceful sleeping expression on her features, being carried into the room by two (or three) people with birds' beaks and laid upon the bed" (p. 583).

Freud awoke in terror. His associations thirty years later included his recollection that a boy had told him the vulgar word for copulation, one connected with the word for birds. Little Sigmund must have guessed the significance of the word. The anxiety of the dream "can be traced back . . . to an obscure and evidently sexual craving that had found appropriate expression in the visual content of the dream" Freud wrote, (p. 584).

Another set of associations that Freud dismissed as unimportant because they were secondary had to do with a fear that his mother was dying and reassurance that she was not dead. We may surmise that Freud was trying to deny a hostile wish toward his mother.

Child analysis adds to our understanding of dreams. Gillman (1987) has described a rather impressive but unusual analysis of a latency child's dream in which the patient actively helped to interpret it and to recognize her ambivalent feelings toward the analyst.

Jennifer, then 8 years old, dreamed: "I went to see the Mona Lisa, but the museum had tables we were eating at. I looked up and saw the Mona Lisa was missing from its frame. It had torn, cut edges. I was the first to see and told the guard, and the next day told my class in school, and I felt proud I was the first to know" (p. 265).

Jennifer talked about the dream for five successive sessions. The following summary of the work does not include many of the details but will serve our purpose. Jennifer said she and her mother and grandmother had gone to a local gallery to see the famous painting while her sister, who was too young to go, went to her father's office. The analyst asked a few questions. The patient did not want to talk about something's being missing, but she did say she had lost a mitten. She also said she was proud she had corrected her little sister's baby talk.

As Jennifer talked, she drew a two-headed lady and animals at the zoo. The next day her drawings included a 1-month-old girl baby whom the king favored, and Cinderella in rags, downcast but smiling to hide her feelings. When Jennifer examined a picture of Rome in the office, the analyst asked whether it was connected with the Mona Lisa dream. The patient denied this, but the therapist said, "Thoughts stay in the back of your head and come out in dreams" (p. 266), with which the patient agreed.

The following day Jennifer drew pictures of a girl and some two-headed people, which reminded her of a play about a girl named Annette she had written for school. She also dreamed about college girls, some of whom were pretty and whom she ranked according to meanness and popularity. Being pretty, she said, doesn't matter. The analyst dealt with the defense by remarking that some people believe one way but feel the opposite, with which she agreed. Her father had taken her book away, she added, indicating her mixed feelings toward him.

The next two sessions Jennifer played that there were lots of food, drink, and toys in the consultation room, pictured as a museum, where analyst and patient slept, locked in. When the patient called the room an office, the analyst reminded her that her younger sister had gone to their father's office, and she recalled they had drunk Sprite™ there. Mona Lisa's being cut out reminded her that she was cut out. She could see that she had mixed feelings about treatment. She had, she said, been "framed" into coming into analysis and wished she did not have to continue any longer. But she liked it. The two-headed girl represented her two feelings toward the analyst, which in turn derived from her ambivalence to her father. Although she felt she shouldn't have angry rude feelings, she recognized that she did.

The patient thus recognized her hateful and loving feelings toward her analyst, displaced from her father at whom she was angry for favoring her sister. She could see her anger at her sister and some of the defenses she used.

As we stated, children generally do not try to analyze dreams so persistently.

A 9-year-old boy had, the history from the parents indicated, been very jealous of his baby sister when she was born. His anger at his mother and sister persisted, but he had difficulty admitting it. In a number of sessions he filled the bathroom sink with water and submerged mother and child dolls for long periods and then lifted them out. When he reported a dream in which he rescued his young sibling from drowning, the analyst jokingly commented that he did not know he loved her so much. The patient replied, "Oh that was only a dream." He came to understand the difference between the manifest content and what was not so conscious, his wish to get rid of his sister.

A particular type of dream, *pavor nocturnus* or night terrors, is especially difficult to deal with because the dreamer usually does not remember his experiences. It occurs during stages 3 and 4 and not during REM sleep. The child (or adult) undergoes a terrifying screaming attack, may get out of bed, talk to those about him, describe horrible experiences, but is not awake. Eventually the person becomes calm and returns to normal sleep (Dowling 1982, Hartmann 1984). Although some believe they are meaningless psychological events, it is sometimes possible to analyze these dreams by confronting the patient with the forgotten manifest content as related by the parent (J. Perman, personal communication).

Hartmann (1984) differentiates night terrors from true nightmares. The latter, "sometimes called dream anxiety attacks, are long, vivid, frightening dreams which awaken the sleeper and are usually clearly recalled" (p. 5). Nightmares occur during REM sleep.

A 7-year-old boy was referred because of emotional problems affecting his school work; his mother had noticed that he had been "somber and depressed." In the course of taking his history, it was learned that several weeks before, Fred had reported that while he was ill with a strep throat one week ago, he had a "waking nightmare" during which he heard voices coming from the water and somebody screaming. The evening of the day that he told this to his parents, he called his father and informed him that he was having a nightmare. The father described a faraway look in the boy's eyes and added that Fred was aware of his surroundings. Fred's father then interrogated him at some length. The boy said that the voices scream at him in a mean way and don't leave him alone. The voices say they hate him. On further questioning, Fred said that he could not see them—they were in his imagination. They could talk to him and he could talk to them in his mind. In the analytic session the boy remembered the dream vividly, suggesting it was a nightmare rather than *pavor nocturnus*.

The boy had been bursting with rage toward his mother and younger sister ever since that sister had been born when he was 3 years old. He felt abandoned and replaced because the mother would take care of the baby girl before she attended to his needs. He made it so difficult for the mother that she sent him to a day camp and then to nursery school. His anger found expression in his becoming such a behavior problem on the bus that the driver threatened to "drop him off in the middle of the street." It seems clear that the anger was projected onto the threatening figure in the dream whom he had named Killer ("kill her"). Asked to draw a picture in the course of therapy, he produced vicious monsters with many sharp teeth and jagged dentate-shaped appendages and limbs, each with four sharp fingers or toes (Figure 15-3), a killer indeed.

ADOLESCENT FANTASY FORMATION

Fantasy formation and its manifestations become more complicated during adolescence (Blos 1962, A. Freud 1958). Puberty, with its physiological, especially hormonal, changes, leads the child into that developmental stage. The increased cognitive capacity of teenagers enriches their ego structure and affects the way they deal with and control their drives and the external world. Personal, family, and societal demands add to the challenges and conflicts. The imagined or actual perils of impending maturity evoke defenses against its achievement and the development of adaptive mechanisms to attain it.

Fantasies manifest themselves within and outside of the adolescent's treatment. They generally do not appear in the teenager's psychotherapy as play or art. Rather, the patient in treatment verbalizes, even free associates, and behaves more like an adult than a child. Fantasies enter into the formation of symptoms, in acting out, in the adaptive planning of behavior, in dreams, and in the verbal associations during treatment.

The adolescent may, depending on his social environment, engage in displaying his newfound energies and abilities. Internal psychic activity may produce fantasies or dreams of limitless physical and intellectual achievements or sexual exploits. One boy was convinced that he understood politics better than his teachers, parents, and friends. He also pictured himself physically powerful, and eventually he became a

Figure 15-3

weight lifter. Bill, another adolescent, had fantasies of being invisible, creeping into bedroom after bedroom and engaging in sexual intercourse with innumerable women. The omnipotent fantasy, an expression of his biologically-based confidence, also had its defensive aspects. The patient masturbated compulsively with these fantasies, and as an adult, he engaged in a numbers game of promiscuously scoring with successive women. He would count the number of times he had orgasms and the number of women he seduced.

There is a relighting of oedipal strivings and conflicts with the onset of adolescence. Incestuous wishes may occasionally be expressed directly in behavior or through fantasy with thinly disguised incestuous objects. Bill, for instance, masturbated thinking of the mother of his friend. Ordinarily the adolescent will begin some sexual experimentation with social contacts. Rites of passage for males may include group sex or (before Acquired Immune Deficiency Syndrome [AIDS]) introduction to prostitutes by more experienced peers or even fathers. Unfortunately, the adolescent's proclivity to deny vulnerability and realistic consequences may lead to disease or unwanted pregnancy.

Mothers may be attracted to their sons and fathers to their daughters at this time. This may lead to parental seduction of the adolescent with varying degrees of traumatization. One male patient described how, in his adolescence, his mother allowed him to see her nude, touch her breast, and fondle her, but stopped him at the point when he attempted to press his erect penis against her body. She also invited him into the parental bedroom while she and his father were lying embraced at the foot of the bed. He surmised that they had just previously engaged in sexual intercourse. He dealt with his feelings of excitement, frustration, and jealousy by having fantasies of the father sadistically tearing at the mother's face and splitting her apart with his "telephone pole" penis. His identification with this sadistic father led to recurrent episodes of impotence in his later life. His fear of his wish to hurt women caused him to lose his erection or ejaculate prematurely.

The resurgence of oedipal fantasies includes fears of being castrated. The teenager may attempt to counter these fears by an exceptionally daring attitude or bold behavior. He may picture himself invulnerable, like Superman, rather than threatened. Unfortunately, engaging in risky adventures may heighten fear rather than alleviate anxiety.

Sports provide a less hazardous outlet for the intensified energies of teenagers of both sexes and can elevate the individual's self-esteem in a socially acceptable way. However, fantasies of becoming the outstanding baseball player or tennis star can lead to unrealistic overexertion and even physical injury. The competitive aspect can be a stimulus or a threat. A young woman entered into a series of tennis tournaments in hopes of becoming a national star. However, her fear of incurring the displeasure of her defeated rival (unconsciously, her mother) limited her success.

Doubts about one's intelligence or attractiveness, or other imagined personal deficiencies may derive from castration anxiety and may lead to compensatory overachievement. For example, a young man had doubts about his intellectual ability because his grades fluctuated so wildly. As a result, he concluded that he really wasn't very bright. He decided that he would do better by concentrating on financial achievement. Indeed, he was able to learn how to initiate and execute complicated financial transactions in business and became wealthy. He needed to continue to expand his activities and achievements to defend against and compensate for his persistent doubts about how smart he was.

Despite frequent doubts about his intelligence, the teenager actually undergoes a leap in cognitive ability (Inhelder and Piaget 1958). The increased cognitive capacity of the adolescent enables him or her to abstract and hypothesize. He thus develops more abstract ideals and plans his future more imaginatively and often more realistically. However, the teenager's lack of experience limits his ability to plan adaptively, especially if adults do not help guide him. Although he can plan and achieve, he is also likely to attempt to attain unrealistic goals based on fantasies and unrealistic wishes. Nevertheless, his imagination may spur him on to creative efforts that may result in actual achievements.

Indeed, fantasy can prepare the teenager for mature behavior. Masturbatory activity and the accompanying fantasies can enable him to experience sexual activity under controlled conditions. Later he can apply his solitary sexuality to a heterosexual setting.

Many teenagers become fascinated with interpreting dreams, partly because it appeals to their intellect, partly because they become convinced of its therapeutic efficiency. They then report their dreams and associate to them much as an adult usually does.

Richard entered psychotherapy at 9 years of age because of pains all over his body and difficulty in school. His somatic symptoms were in part a result of identification with his mother whom he loved and feared losing, and who had been ill with similar symptoms. The pains also expressed self-attacking punitive aspects of his personality. Richard's pains resulted from an unconscious fantasy: I love my mother but should be punished for it.

We came to see that this patient's conscience was often inconsistent and corrupt, allowing him to violate its demands, but neverthess punishing him. A dream when he was 14 years old helped clarify the role of the superego. His associations to parts of the dream were limited, but our understanding of the background events in his current and past life helped to interpret the dream.

"I am home in my house, in my mother's bedroom, watching TV. My brother and parents are not there. A man got into the house, a genius technician who could bypass the alarm system. I open the door and see a man with an axe downstairs. I quickly lock the door and push the emergency button. I call the police but the phone isn't working. I take apart the alarm and cross wires. The terrorist with the axe runs into the kitchen and slams the alarm box with the axe. Things go into the burglar mode."

Richard associated to parts of the dream to a degree. Watching television reminded him that he sometimes violates the rules and doesn't study when his parents are away. (Actually, this is a very frequent occurrence.) The therapist suggested that he is punished in the dream for these violations. He then remembered that what is his mother's room in the dream is actually the bedroom of both his parents. He added that he did not mind his mother's buying food, but he objected to her buying a toy car for his younger brother the same day.

The dream is about Richard's conscience's demanding punishment for not studying. The attacking burglar represents his conscience. There is good reason to believe that behind the violation of the rule that he study lay other emotional violations. Both the therapist and the patient had long recognized his anger at both his parents. The man with the axe was not only his conscience, but also his angry self. More specifically the dream depicts Richard's anger at his mother, who showed her affection for his brother. The patient wished she would love only him, that he could be alone with her, in her room, without his father or brother as rivals. The reader may suspect that the man with the axe also stood for Richard's father who, he thought, was furious at him for attacking both his father and brother, or for wanting to have his mother. Although his father was consciously irked at Richard's antagonism, there was no evidence that he objected to Richard's loving his mother.

It is interesting that one figure in the dream can symbolize several different real or imaginary persons. The man with the axe stood for the patient, his father, his mother, and his conscience. The natural tendency of dreams to become condensed is supplemented by a specific mechanism. The formation of the conscience (the superego, to be technically more correct) involves identification with the parents as the individual views them.

CONCLUSION

Man's ability to imagine is a wonderful, possibly unique capacity that helps him achieve, adapt, and entertain himself and others. Imagination enriches the individual's mental and emotional life and contributes in important ways to artistic, cultural, and scientific endeavors. The child instinctively begins to fantasize as soon as he is able to remember, and he expands its use as his mind develops.

We have demonstrated the ways in which imagination finds expression through the medium of play, artwork, and dreams. Our examples illustrate the ways this function of the mind operates at succeeding developmental levels. We have shown how the child uses fantasy to help him cope with phase-related anxieties, intrapsychic and interpersonal conflicts, and maturational tasks. Also, we have given examples of how the psychoanalytic therapist uses his understanding of the child's productions to help the child free himself from conflicts that impede his growth and development.

REFERENCES

The American Heritage Dictionary (1982). 2nd College Edition. Boston: Houghton Mifflin.
Arlow, J. A. (1969a). Unconscious fantasy and disturbances of conscious experience. *Psychoanalytic Quarterly* 38:1–27.
―――― (1969b). Fantasy, memory and reality testing. *Psychoanalytic Quarterly* 38:28–51.
Blos, P. (1962). *On Adolescence*. New York: Free Press of Glencoe.
Dowling, S. (1982). Mental organization on the phenomena of sleep. *Psychoanalytic Study of the Child* 37:285–302. New Haven, CT: Yale University Press.
Freud, A. (1936). *The Ego and the Mechanisms of Defense*. New York: International Universities Press.
―――― (1958). Adolescence. *Psychoanalytic Study of the Child* 13:155–178. New York: International Universities Press.
Freud, S. (1900). Interpretation of dreams. *Standard Edition* 4:1–338/5:339–625.
―――― (1905). Three essays on the theory of sexuality. *Standard Edition* 7:123–245.
―――― (1909). Family romances. *Standard Edition* 9:235–241.
―――― (1920). Beyond the pleasure principle. *Standard Edition* 18:1–64.
―――― (1933). New introductory lectures on psychoanalysis. *Standard Edition* 22:1–182.
Gesell, A., et al. (1940). *The First Five Years of Life*. New York and London: Harper and Brothers.
Gillman, R. D. (1987). A child analyzes a dream. *Psychoanalytic Study of the Child* 42:263–273. New Haven, CT: Yale University Press.
Glenn, J., ed. (1978). *Child Analysis and Therapy*. New York: Jason Aronson.
―――― (1988). Twinship fantasies in the work of Mark Twain. In *Fantasy, Myth and Reality*, ed. H. Blum, et al. New York: International Universities Press.
Goodenough, F. L. (1926). *Measurement of Intelligence by Drawing*. Yonkers, NY: World Book Co.
Hartmann, E. (1967). *The Biology of Dreaming*. Springfield, IL: Charles C Thomas.
―――― (1984). *The Nightmare*. New York: Basic Books.
Inhelder, B., and Piaget, J. (1958). *The Growth of Logical Thinking from Childhood to Adolescence*. New York: Basic Books.

Isakower, O. (1936). A contribution to the psychopathology of phenomena associated with falling asleep. *International Journal of Psycho-Analysis* 19:311-334.

Mahler, M. S., Pine, F., and Bergman, A. (1975). *The Psychological Birth of the Human Infant.* New York: Basic Books.

Moore, B. E., and Fine, B. D. (1968). *A Glossary of Psychoanalytic Terms and Concepts*, 2nd ed. New York: The American Psychoanalytic Association.

Murphy, G. (1947). *Personality.* New York and London: Harper and Brothers.

Neubauer, P. (1987). The many meanings of play: introduction. *Psychoanalytic Study of the Child* 42:3-10. New Haven, CT: Yale University Press.

Perman, J. Personal communication.

Piaget, J. (1932). *The Moral Judgment of the Child.* Glencoe, IL: The Free Press.

Roiphe, H., and Galenson, E. (1972). Early genital activity and the castration complex. *Psychoanalytic Quarterly* 41:334-347.

Twain, M. (1882). *The Prince and the Pauper.* Boston: Osgood.

Winnicott, D. (1953). Transitional objects and transitional phenomena. *International Journal of Psycho-Analysis* 34:89-97.

16

A Historical Perspective on the Treatment of Neurotic Children

Bertram A. Ruttenberg, M.D.

This historical account of the development of the concept and treatment of the psychoneuroses of childhood reflects, in a sense, my own contact with the history as I experienced it from those of my teachers who were the makers of that history and from their pupils. There was also the experience of face-to-face meetings with Anna Freud and her colleagues at Hampstead in London, in Philadelphia, in New Haven at Yale, and New York, and with Marianne Kris, AnnaMarie Weil, Erik Homberger Erikson, Sylvia Brody, Margaret Mahler, Peter Neubauer, Berta Bornstein, Phyllis Greenacre, and others.

In my first year of psychiatric residency, an unforgettable month with psychoanalytic historian Gregory Zilboorg added to my vicarious participation in the history of the analytic movement and of the development of the concept of the neurosis. In my analytic training, Robert Waelder, the youngest of Freud's original circle, made the history of the psychoanalytic movement come to life with his anecdotes and vignettes. He described the evolution of the concept of infantile neurosis, among others, and related how the work of Anna Freud with young, disadvantaged children provided verification of the concept. Berta Bornstein, as my child analytic supervisor, demonstrated how to mirror the role of the child, and shared with us the adaptive techniques practiced by the European, particularly Viennese, child analytic groups. Phyllis Blanchard, my first child analytic supervisor, brought me an updated version of the concept of transference and transference neurosis in children, and showed how, indeed, a transference is important and necessary for the resolution in depth of the conflicts in childhood neurosis. She first demonstrated to me how bypassing the conflict and affective expression of the child by getting the information from the parents, or by bringing in reality and corrective teaching too early, can be turned into a resistance that undermines the analysis. Yet I learned that in reality the child is dependent and vulnerable vis-à-vis his parents, so the confidentiality of the child must be respected if trust is to be established and the child protected. Thus, the therapeutic alliance must be with the child, but with the support of his parents.

I was able to see firsthand the impact on neurotic children of applying adult psychoanalytic techniques rigidly without adapting them to the realities of the child's developmental needs to communicate with his parents and to establish peer and school group relationships. For instance, advising parents to tell a child who wants to discuss something and to share his feelings to "save it for your analyst," or insensitively scheduling analytic hours during prime school hours, deprives the child of important social experience, marks him as "different" in the eyes of his peers, to the child's agonizing mortification, and denies the child's reality-based affective approaches. Yes, this was still done in the 1960s, as was misinterpreting the child's desperate struggle to meet phase specific developmental needs as resistances.

Dr. Gerald Pearson opened up for us the world of the developing infant and child with seminars about the work of Spitz, Jacobsen, Zetzel, and Piaget. Pearson's studies of developmentally and neurotically based learning disorders and school phobias are classic, as is his *Adolescence and the Conflict of Generations*. And Mitchell Dratman, in the mid-1950s demonstrated the application of analytic principles to the study and treatment of the developmental disabilities, including autism and symbiosis. With classic clinical examples, he showed that severe, even life-threatening disorders such as anorexia nervosa, asthma, exfoliative dermatitis, ulcers, and ulcerative colitis may indeed be analyzable where the symptomatology symbolically represents a return of the repressed conflict, and which, in his cases, could be traced to infantile neurotic oedipal and preoedipal traumata, and as such were severe conversion neuroses and not psychophysiological at all.

When I originally began writing this chapter, I wavered between concentrating heavily on the psychoanalytic contributions in the historical literature and on other approaches to the neuroses, undoubtedly reflecting my more recent involvement with infantile autism, the childhood psychosis, and the developmental disabilities. Then, a reading of Marjorie Harley's highly personal tribute to Marianne Kris in "Child

Analysis 1947–1984" in the 1986 *Psychoanalytic Study of the Child* made me realize what was bothering me: I was leaving out my own forty-seven years of personal participation and historical sense of the evolution of the concepts and treatment of the childhood neurosis. Harley's retrospective covered the same period of time as my experience. The evolution of theory and practice she had outlined was remarkably similar to my own and provided a kind of validation and support. This account is thus an amalgam of my experiences and published historical reviews.

In order to gain a perspective of the history of the treatment of childhood neurosis, the development of the awareness of the existence and nature of mental illness in children must first be charted. Next, the evolution of the very concept of the neurotic child must be considered, inasmuch as the APA's *DSM-III* has now discarded the classification "Neurotic Disorders" in favor of descriptively coherent categories (such as affective, somatoform, dissociative).

Whereas *DSM-II* categories (psychosis, neurosis, personality disorder, and psycho-physiologic, reactive, and behavior disorders, for example) were grouped according to the severity of ego dysfunctions and were process oriented, *DSM-III* categorization is on a categorical-symptom-oriented behavioral basis.

While the *DSM-III* categorizations may facilitate behavioral research and statistical data reduction and symptom-targeted behavioral and chemotherapeutic approaches, it has severely limited the capacity to classify a mental illness fully according to severity of ego dysfunction, psychic structure, and developmental and environmental adaptive parameters—concepts that clinicians working psychodynamically and in depth, particularly with the neuroses, could account for in using *DSM-II*.

HISTORY OF THE RECOGNITION OF MENTAL ILLNESS IN CHILDREN

With a few isolated exceptions, there is little evidence that mental illness in children was recognized before the late nineteenth century, or that organized psychotherapeutic methodology existed before the early 1900s. This is related to the attitudes toward children that prevailed before the mid 1800s. Despert (1965) writes that children were chattel, possessions over which their parent/owners had absolute life or death control, and could be sold (p. 15).

Severely disturbed children, when described at all, were described without compassion as wicked, possessed, incorrigible—with the onus on them. The descriptions were devoid of any consideration of the environment as an etiological factor. (It would seem that with our current emphasis on intrinsic neurobiological factors we are again moving in that direction.)

Despert notes that in Greco-Persian-Roman and pre- and parabiblical times, children were ritually sacrificed, cast out if inferior, and were sometimes instruments of vengeance (killing of the firstborn). The rights of mothers to care for and protect their offspring were not recognized. However, the Hebrews, perhaps as a function of a monotheistic religious state, developed a more unified family structure in which children were valued to carry on the tradition of learning. In the Middle Ages a child's life was not worth much. Infanticide was common. Clergy influenced attitudes about children's impulses and affective life. The burden of original sin and guilt for jealousy, hatred, and self stimulation lay on the infant and child. "Mental illness (in terms of being possessed), hallucinatory experiences, and *folie en masse* and demonology were noted in children. Abandonment, corporal punishment, and selling children into bondage in marriage or servitude were well recorded, and abandoned children became serfs. Such children became a highly suggestible group of followers, one example of which was the Children's Crusade.

The Renaissance brought a more balanced and mellow family unity, without the patriarchal right of life or death over the child. Recognition that children were different, not just miniature adults, began to appear in more progressive writings. Education of children was emphasized. Alternatives to discipline through love and example rather than by fear and physical punishment, were emphasized. Yet, there was little, if any, mention of mental illness during the Renaissance.

In Colonial America, complete obedience and submissiveness were expected of the child. Hedonism and frivolous amusement compromised his chances of salvation. Strict rules of behavior were laid down, yet behind all this sternness was caring, and private warmth and tenderness.

Even in eighteenth- and nineteenth-century Europe poor children went into servitude in workhouses. Charles Dickens' novels depicting these horrible conditions did much to bring attention to the plight of children and stimulate public reaction to end these abuses.

However, the attitude that infants and children were insensitive chattel who cannot react or remember persisted to the early 1900s. People of conscience would had to have believed that children are incapable of feeling or remembering to have treated them as they have through the ages. That attitude dies hard today—witness the prevalence of sexual and physical abuse. Surgeons in the 1930s and 1940s still performed twenty to thirty tonsillectomies, one after the other, completely insensitive to the wide-eyed terror of the children waiting their turn as the bloodied, anesthetized child just operated on was wheeled past, with the two ball-like tonsils sitting in a tray by his face. Even today some surgeons on rounds stand at the foot of the child's bed and go into gory details of the operation, completely oblivious of any impact on the child.

I have recounted attitudes over the ages toward children as a background for understanding the lack of awareness that they have psychological disturbances. With a few notable exceptions, the recognition and care of emotionally disturbed adults, relegated to madhouse and chain, was not much further along. Pinel in Paris as head physician of the mental institutions the Bicêtre (1792) and the Salpêtrière (1794), and Benjamin Rush in Philadelphia in the mid- and late 1700s, representing a spirit of social enlightenment associated with the French and American Revolutions, unlocked the shackles, transferred the concept of a madhouse as a prison warehouse to a place of humane hospital care with physical and emotional aspects, and opened the way for similar concerns about children. Rousseau by 1762 had prepared the way with his plea for the liberation of the developing infant and child (and their mothers) from the restrictive influences of the day so they could be educated according to their individual capacities, with full parental participation (Despert, p. 92; Adams, p. 207).

Handicapped children, primarily the deaf, mute and blind were the first to receive constructive attention. Itard, while trying to teach a feral child, "the wild boy of Avignon" (Kanner 1967, p. 1313), developed methods of teaching the severely retarded. Social and educational movements in the 1800s and early 1900s called attention to the needs of handicapped, orphaned, and misused children. As mentioned, Charles Dickens' writing called the treatment of children as chattel and the exploitation of orphaned and disadvantaged children to the world's attention.

Alexander and Seleznick (1966) in their classic *History of Psychiatry* note that in the 1800s psychiatrists (there was no child psychiatry) were interested in the classification of the child psychoses: Maudsley (1828) wrote on the "insanities of early life." Esquiral (1838) differentiated the mentally defective from the psychotic child. Griesinger (1845), however, continued the little homunculus notion of children, and classified the mental disorders of children under the same headings as those of adults. He believed there were both psychological and organic predisposing causes. The general attitude was one of irreversibility.

Studies were descriptive accounts, with the notable exception of Emminghaus's *Psychic Disturbances of Childhood* (1877). He presented an epidemiologic study that differentiated psychoses caused by brain disease and those caused by fear and anxiety. He noted that disorders of childhood were often produced by poor home, educational, and social conditions, and he discussed disorders of thinking and imagination. Delinquency was due to illness, not poor morals. Unfortunately, he was ahead of his time and therefore ignored.

Studies of normal development began in the late 1800s. Darwin (1876) wrote a "biographical sketch of an infant" after studying the expression of the emotions in humans and animals (1864), and described the caring responses that the shape of infant and puppy physiognomy elicited from caretakers. This anticipated the more recent observations of developmental researchers that infants can actively elicit caretaking responses. The importance of developmental studies were realized, as was the observation that a child's play revealed his mental process. Stanley Hall initiated developmental psychology measurement techniques in the late 1800s.

The first decade of the twentieth century (1900–1909), under the impetus of societal concern, began looking past the what to the why. The findings of the newly established juvenile courts and social agencies brought requests to psychiatrists for help. Fortunately, from 1895–1910 Adolph Meyer was challenging the Kraepelinean notion of mental disorder as organic disease of the nervous system and, taking note of Freud's dynamic theories, proposed mental illness as disorders of personality and behavior, associated with the impact of family and social settings. He advocated psychiatric consultation to the schools. He also stressed the concepts of endowment potential and preventive intervention. His eclecticism provided the basic conceptual framework for the child guidance movement founded through the efforts of William Healy, the same year (1909) that the National Committee for Mental Hygiene was established to address the problems of delinquency. Dr. Healy, noting that the only two places in the United States testing children psychologically were Goddard's clinic in Vineland, New Jersey, and Witmer's clinic for the mentally retarded at the University of Pennsylvania, obtained private funds to found the Juvenile Psychopathic Institute in Chicago. In 1912, with his influence, the Boston Psychopathic Hospital was established. At the core of the child guidance process was the multidisciplinary team of child psychiatrist, psychologist, and psychiatric social worker which provided individual direct therapy, psychological testing, and working supportively with home and school.

In 1922, the Commonwealth Fund, which had provided grants for establishing demonstration community child guidance clinics, established grants for the training of child psychiatrists. Psychoanalysts and psychiatrists who had learned child psychiatry on their own became the teachers and trainers of professionals as well as researchers and therapists.

An organization of members of these disciplines, (the American Orthopsychiatric Association, which continues to this day) initiated by a meeting of six psychiatrists and psychoanalysts led by Dr. Karl Menninger, a psychoanalyst, was formed in 1924 to further the work of the child guidance movement through scientific meetings, social advocacy, and a journal.

THE ORIGINS OF THE CONCEPT OF PSYCHONEUROSIS OF CHILDREN

Psychiatric historians uniformly date the clinical delineation of the psychoneuroses to Sigmund Freud's (1895) "Studies on Hysteria" and the publication of the case of Anna O. wherein he established the relationship of neurosis to early childhood experience. His "Project for a Scientific Psychology," formulated in the same year, and which sought a unified theory of psychic function and abnormality in terms of neurophysiological correlates, laid the groundwork for his drive theory and his structural concepts of psychic function and neurotic disorder and its origins in infancy and childhood. After all, by 1890 Freud enjoyed a wide reputation as a child neurologist. In 1891 he had published a treatise, "On Aphasia," which adapted Hughling Jackson's holistic approach to brain function and disorder, taking it past the strictly localizing and mapping approach of Broca and Wiernicke. Here was the first use of the concept of overdetermination, which Freud applied to speech function and the concept of dynamic processes rather than static conditions. Before Freud, the term "neurosis" referred descriptively to psychophysiological disturbances that were functional in origin, expressed through the autonomic and neuroendocrine systems and accompanied by severe anxiety and disturbed affect.

Freud used the terms *neurosis* and *psychoneurosis* descriptively to delineate conversion hysteria, anxiety, depression, and phobic and obsessive compulsive conditions that were painful and debilitating yet in which, unlike in psychosis and perversions, reality awareness and drive inhibition or displacement were maintained. Freud's major addition was to demonstrate the etiological process involved. *Unconscious* conflicts between opposing wishes or between drives and inner or outer prohibitions caused anxiety, then repression, and a use of defense mechanisms with a return of the repressed to consciousness in the form of symptoms, dreams, and altered character. From his very first case of Anna O., Freud established the causal relationship between the particular neurotic symptoms and childhood experiences and reactions, which he later called the *infantile neurosis*. It was Freud's work that led to the application of the term neurosis to certain emotional disorders and syndromes in children that were beginning to be noticed as more attention was being paid to children in court-associated juvenile mental hygiene centers and child guidance clinics and their equivalents in Europe, especially by the early psychoanalytically oriented and trained therapeutic nursery teachers, some of whom became child analysts (cf. Anna Freud and her Vienna group).

The first evidence for the existence of the infantile neurosis came from the reconstruction of early childhood events in the analyses of adult neurotics. Freud considered the infantile neurosis to be the manifestation in psychological symptomatology of a universal conflict occurring at the phallic-oedipal stage of development. Whether it was healthy or pathologic as measured in painful intensity and persistence depended on the nature of the earlier preoedipal experiences and fixations and how they influenced or distorted the resolution of the Oedipus complex. Symptoms included nightmares, phobias, rituals, obsessions, inhibitions, and regression to eating and bowel disturbances. The infantile neurosis was sometimes continued as a childhood neurotic disorder, and was similar but not identical with the neurotic disorders that began to be reported in children.

The Basis for Psychoanalytic Treatment

The conceptual basis for the psychoanalytic treatment of children with neurotic disorders was laid down by Sigmund Freud (1905) in his "Three Essays on the Theory of Sexuality," which reconstructed the childhood experiences of his adult analysands. He established the existence of overt sexuality in normal children and outlined his theories of infantile sexuality and the etiology of childhood neurotic disorders, which he felt were rooted in various vicissitudes of an unresolved Oedipus complex and/or actual sexual overstimulation or seduction.

True psychoanalytic treatment of children began indirectly in 1906 with Freud's application of psychoanalytic principles to the case of Little

Hans (published in 1909) through supervision of and consultation with the boy's father. This 5-year-old boy had a severe phobia of horses and a ruminative preoccupation with penises. His phobia had been precipitated by the parental threat of castration when he had been discovered masturbating. The horse was unconsciously equated by Hans with his father, whom he feared would bite off his penis because of Hans's unconscious oedipal hostility to his father and desires for his mother. His phobic neurosis was a compromise formation, the true essence of which was buried by repression and returned as his phobic symptoms. Freud's explanation to the father of the meaning of his symptoms and guidance as to how to respond to the child alleviated the boy's symptoms. This case used a parental intermediary and heralded one of the differences that was felt necessary in adapting psychoanalytic technique to the treatment of children (that is, the involvement of the parents in the process).

The case of the Rat Man, begun in 1907 and published in 1909, and the Wolf Man, begun in 1910 and published in 1918, while reporting the psychoanalyses of two young adults, tended to corroborate Freud's ideas about the childhood neuroses. The Rat Man's obsessional neurosis derived from regression from oedipal conflicts to anality and homosexual defense. The Wolf Man's mixed neurosis resulted from a series of traumatic events in his early years: witnessing parental intercourse at 1½ years, seduction by an older sister at 3¾ years, and a threat of castration by a nursemaid for masturbating at 4 years old. A wolf phobia at 4½ years developed into an obsessive neurotic religiosity.

Sandor Ferenczi, a pupil of Freud in 1913, reported an attempt to apply unmodified psychoanalytic techniques directly to a child without involving the family. It failed; the child became defensively bored and wanted to return to his toys.

It was a decade after Freud's Little Hans before a successful case of psychoanalytic treatment of a child was reported in 1919 by Hermione von Hug-Hellmuth, who demonstrated that a child should, indeed, return to his toys. She realized that a child expresses himself more directly in play than through verbalization alone. In her publication *A Study of the Mental Life of the Child*, she demonstrated that a child's play expresses his fantasies and is the royal road to his unconscious—the child's equivalent to free association. She thus introduced the technique of play therapy, which provided a direct therapeutic approach to the child and thus enabled child psychoanalysis and analytically-oriented child psychotherapy to evolve.

The treatment of the neuroses of children through psychoanalytic means followed two major lines of development, reflected in two schools whose leaders were Melanie Klein and Anna Freud. Melanie Klein (1932) noted in the introduction to her text on the psychoanalysis of children that Hug-Hellmuth did not go on to evolve a system or body of rules for treating the neuroses of children. Melanie Klein, however, did just that. A pupil of Ferenczi's in the early 1920s and later of Karl Abraham, Klein applied Abraham's and Freud's concepts of unconscious life and symbolic meaning to the earliest months of an infant's life. She believed that a child's play was a way of mastering anxiety by reenacting traumatic family situations, so she at first observed her young patients in their family milieu, and later provided a playroom within her office, where she observed and interpreted its symbolic meaning to the child.

Erik Homberger Erikson, who published a comprehensive review on the psychopathology of childhood in 1926, applied Melanie Klein's early concepts of child's play as both expressing and working through unconscious ideas and recreating and mastering anxiety situations, to his analyses of children.

Klein attributed complex ideational concepts to the thinking of infants and developed and interpolated clinical psychopathological sets seen in adults such as paranoid and depressive to the early psychodynamic processes of infants. She felt that the Oedipus complex and superego developed in the first year of life in defensive response to the infant's own hostile and paranoid feeling. She interpreted deeply and immediately to the child his sexual and aggressive impulses, believing that what went on in the playroom implied a transference relationship. Klein, by the mid-1920s, was already taking little interest in the day to day experiences of the child or in the family relationships, feeling that the young child's neurosis was strictly a result of inner struggles about aggressive impulses that had developed in infancy. Early interpretation strengthened the child's ego. Kleinian theories were first presented in London in 1925 and profoundly influenced the British psychoanalytic movement.

At first glance, Klein seemed to follow closely the classic Freudian concepts by retaining the form and the clinical sets and nomenclature. Freud, however, did not believe that the analysis of conditions of preoedipal origin was possible. By attributing the origins of the neuroses to very early traumatic and inner developmental disturbances, Klein, in fact, stimulated the study of early infant development and influenced the shift of the schedule of appearance of the anal and phallic-oedipal stage toward earlier ages. Kleinian theories led to greater attention to the impact of early mothering on the feelings of the developing infant and away from focusing on the Oedipus complex as the source of the neuroses, and had great influence on the later work of Bowlby, Winnicott, and others. The roots of the concepts of the good and bad mother images were contained in her theories.

In the same period of time in Vienna, Anna Freud, in conjunction with work being done by teachers in preschool and early school programs for homeless children and in the child guidance clinic sponsored by the Vienna Psychoanalytic Society, began her psychoanalysis of children with neurotic symptoms. She first reported her work in 1926 in Vienna under the title *Introduction to the Techniques of the Psychoanalysis of Children*. This stimulated the formation of a working group of child analysts from Vienna, Prague, and Budapest who met regularly to present cases and refine techniques.

Her concepts and methods differed from those of Melanie Klein in a number of ways. Klein and her disciples emphasized the id and early superego guilt and inner fantasy about its immediate caretaking world. Anna Freud and later Hartmann and Erikson focused more on the developing ego and formation of object relations with its expanding outer world, beginning with the mothering object. Anna Freud, noting the child's realistic continuing dependence on parents, stressed the importance of collaborative contacts with the parents, while establishing a positive relationship with the child, forming trust and motivation to explore the meaning of his symptoms and behavior patterns. She emphasized that the child's ego functions were still developing, and therefore the analyst not only interpreted unconscious conflict but also represented adaptation and reality. She noted the contribution of maturational processes to the resolution of neuroses at certain developmental nodal points. Clearly psychoanalysis, which had defined the psychoneuroses, and as adapted by Klein and Anna Freud and their schools for use with children, became the treatment of choice for the childhood neurosis. Their centers became the foci for psychoanalytic study of children.

EGO PSYCHOLOGY, STRUCTURAL THEORY, AND THE EVOLVING TECHNIQUE OF THERAPY OF THE NEUROSES OF CHILDHOOD

In 1937, Anna Freud's *Ego and the Mechanisms of Defense* outlined the ego adaptations and defenses, including denial through act or fantasy and identification with the aggressor that, in addition to repression, must be addressed in treatment of the neurosis of childhood. She also described the states of inhibition and ego restriction that evolve as activity-limiting defenses. She addressed the infantile neurosis and neuroses of the latency and pubertal periods, but not the preoedipal factors.

The Viennese group relocated mainly in London and America after 1938. The postwar Hampstead Clinic for Children replaced the wartime Hampstead Nurseries and became the focus and wellspring of the systematic psychoanalytic study of the child and the psychoanalysis of neurotic and other childhood disorders. The basis of its research investigation became the Developmental Diagnostic Profile (1962) and the concept of developmental lines of object relations and various key ego functions, which complemented the stages of psychosexual development.

Psychoneuroses in children were seen as distorting or delaying emotional development in one or more of these key lines of development. Solnit, in his 1975 review of developments in the previous twenty years, described how coteries of psychoanalyzed and psychoanalytically trained workers were developed to address the particular focus of interest in each decade, first addressing infantile sexuality and its transformation. When early education and child upbringing became the focus, parents, nursery school workers, and teachers were psychoanalytically trained. Later, social workers and psychologists and other mental health professionals from the juvenile justice and child guidance clinics were similarly trained. These groups provided psychoanalytic study of normal, neurotic, delinquent and psychotic children, and objective, psychoanalytically oriented, direct observation of these children. Thus, psychoanalytic studies spread their influence to the courts, the child guidance clinics, and to direct observers of infant and child development.

This developmental and ego psychology structural orientation expanded the therapeutic focus to conflictual and developmental issues occurring before and beyond that of the Oedipus complex and the infantile neurosis. H. Nagera (1966), as a member of the Hampstead group, differentiated childhood neurosis with true unconscious conflicts from other childhood disorders representing developmental conflict interferences and transitory reactive conflicts. True childhood neurosis could also develop and be approached therapeutically pregenitally and in latency, prepuberty, and adolescence.

INFANT OBSERVATION AND RESEARCH IN EARLY DEVELOPMENT

I have described how the psychoanalytic understanding of the emotional disturbances in children increased in terms of development. Child development was seen as a sequential and adaptive interplay between constitutional givens, phase specific maturational unfolding, and the environment (nature/nurture). These psychoanalytic studies of the child as reported in the annual *Psychoanalytic Study of the Child* (1949-1989), had contributed much to the theoretical understanding of the psychic development of the infant and child and its deviations, thus opening the way for therapeutic innovations.

Hartmann and Kris's (1945) important article, "The Genetic Approach in Psychoanalysis," set the stage for further direct observation of infants and children—or, more properly, recognized the burgeoning activity and interest in early child development that was taking place in the mid-1940s and which would continue in the late 1940s and early 1950s by both child psychoanalysts and child development researchers. Their paper noted that the genetic approach went beyond anamnestic data and "how the past is contained in the present" to why one solution or adaptation to a conflict was selected over others and the causal relation between these early solutions and later developments.

The two authors, with the addition of Lowenstein (1946), outlined the "Theory of the Formation of Psychic Structure" and provided a conceptual framework and guide for the understanding of direct observations of infant and child development. Their paper emphasized the constitutional givens in the form of early ego capacities, and that the children's capacity to perceive the attitudes of their caretakers develops at an extremely early age. It outlined the differentiation of ego out of an undifferentiated matrix and noted that this differentiation and integration are at least partly regulated by a biologically based maturational sequence, which, however, is influenced by environmental conditions.

The authors differentiated between maturation and development and stressed the role of experience and learning in the adaptive use of the maturing ego apparatus. They described lasting object relations that developed by the end of the first year of life. Learning through mastery of reality and control of instinctual drives were seen as essential in the formation of defenses against external and internal danger. They saw early identifications as the major contributor to the formation of personality and character. They described the formation of the superego and saw it as relatively independent of maturation and more under the influence of social/environmental influences. They traced its progression into and through latency, providing important theoretical aspects of the genesis of neurosis of childhood.

They noted that psychoanalytic hypotheses about early learning experiences take into consideration (1) the stage of maturation of the apparatuses, (2) the reaction of the environment, (3) the tolerance for deprivation, (4) the types of gratification afforded by the process of learning and the satisfactions that can be obtained as consequences of mastery.

This classic paper contained the theoretical basis for much of the direct studies made by child analysts and child and infant developmental specialists. Gesell and his colleagues had already described, in their *First Five Years of Life* and *Infant and Child in the Culture of Today*, the developmental schedules that alerted parents and practitioners to normal expectable behavior and schedule of their developing child. Spock's *Baby and Child Care* was to follow as the all-time popular manual for the parent. One cannot overemphasize the importance of the burgeoning interest and work in early child development in the history of the concept and treatment of the childhood neuroses.

The early issues of the *Psychoanalytic Study of the Child* contained seminal papers on various aspects of infant development and of the impact of mothering patterns, stresses, and deprivation, and the deviant development. These papers, which often developed into classic books on the subjects (for example, Spitz's *First Year of Life*, and *No and Yes*, Sylvia Brody's *Patterns of Mothering*, Jacobson's *The Self and the Object World*, and somewhat later, Sybille Escalona's *The Roots of Individuality*), recognized and confirmed the pregenital origins of most neurotic disturbances of early and later childhood and their role in shaping the individualized nature of an infantile neurosis precipitated by oedipal conflicts, and indeed the very nature of the individualized resolution of the Oedipus complex. Aspects of oedipal conflicts were seen to begin by age 2½ to 3 years, earlier than previously thought.

It is impossible to more than spot-list some of the contributions. In the first five volumes of the *Psychoanalytic Study of the Child* alone there were studies on the importance of the developmental stimulus of the birth process (Greenacre), on the acquisition of hand/eye/mouth coordination and the development of the body ego (Hoffer), and on direct infant observation (Spitz). Spitz also wrote on the genesis of psychiatric conditions in early childhood, the impact of stimulus deprivation (hospitalization) and of early maternal loss (anaclitic depression). Beres wrote on the impact of deprivation on ego development.

Papers appeared both on the classic phobic and obsessive disorders, and on children with physical symptoms that had been considered psychophysiologic and psychosomatic disorders. As I have indicated, in certain cases these symptoms were found to be symbolic expressions of internal conflict and hence amenable to psychoanalysis, that is, sleep disturbance (Fraiberg), masturbation (Lampl-de Groot), psychogenic anorexia in a 4-year-old (Sylvester), the reaction of infants to stress (Leitch and Escalona), preschool dreams (Despert), the analysis of a

5½-year-old phobic child (the classic case of Frankie) (Bornstein), psychogenic constipation in a 2-year-old (E. Sterba), tics (Mahler), feeding problems of psychogenic origin (Lehman). In the 1950s there were papers on separation, object loss, and the grief and depression they caused. Dorothy Baruch's *One Little Boy* (1952) chronicled the analysis of a 7-year-old whose asthma symbolized the cry of the abandoned child. Margaret Ribble's classic article "Rights of Infants" (1949), describing the needs of infants, and the ongoing studies of Margaret Fries (since 1928 in the mental hygiene and wellbaby clinic movements) demonstrated that the three main influences in the child's psychic development were constitution, habit training, and the emotional stability of the parent. Their work had a profound impact on pediatrics, and their role in teaching and influencing through maternal support, on the development of young children. Both Ribble and Fries, though analytically oriented (the latter also trained), were operating outside the psychoanalytic mainstream. Their work was reviewed in the first volume of the *Psychoanalytic Study of the Child* and thus came to the attention of the child analysts and served to effect liaison between the pediatric and child analytic communities.

In New Haven at Yale, Milton Senn bolstered this liaison by supporting the child psychoanalytic group led by Marianne Kris, which was in close contact interchange with Anna Freud and the Hampstead group. Sally Provence was brought into the group by Dr. Senn. Many influential and productive child analysts including Solnit, Sam Ritvo, and M. Harley were trained there.

In the late 1940s and 1950s a number of psychoanalytically-oriented child psychiatry clinics were organized, often under the leadership and supervision of members of the child psychoanalytic training programs of the regional psychoanalytic institutes. In these clinics both psychoanalysis and psychoanalytically-oriented psychotherapy of children was pursued and developed, and, concomitantly, infant and child development observations were made; many child psychiatrists were trained, a number of whom went on to child analytic training. For example, in Philadelphia, Herman Belmont's Clinic at Hahnemann Hospital had the interest and input of the Philadelphia Association's Gerald Pearson, John Eichholtz, and Mitchell Dratman; Berta Bornstein commuted from New York for "master class" supervision. Selma Kramer and Henri Parens, in their clinic at Medical College of Pennsylvania, made developmental studies and carried out and enlarged Margaret Mahler's approach under her supervision and mentorship.

Just a few of those who contributed to the scope and richness of the analytic input were Margaret Mahler, John McDevitt, and Anni

Bergman at the Masters clinic in New York City; Peter Neubauer, Sylvia Brody, and AnneMarie Weill at the Child Development Clinic in New York City; and Beata Rank and Sam Kaplan in Boston at the James Jackson Putnam Center. Evoleen Rexford, Eleanor Pavenstadt, and George Gardner were also in Boston, at the Judge Baker Center. Marianne Kris and Al Solnit at the Yale Child Study Center kept close supportive contact with Anna Freud and the Hampstead Clinic; Mauritz and Annie Katan in Cleveland provided, in the Hampstead tradition, child analytic training for nonphysicians—training there has continued under Bob and Erna Furman. Ann Arbor, Michigan, had Selma Fraiberg, Saul Harrison, and Humberto Nagera; Topeka, Kansas, and the Southard School had, of course, the Menningers and J. Cotter Herschberg; E. J. Anthony taught in St. Louis. In the Washington-Baltimore area were Sid Berman, Joseph Noshpitz, M. Harley, Reginald Lourie, J. Waelder Hall, and more recently, Stanley Greenspan. The Riess Davis Clinic in Los Angeles had Rocco Motto, Rudi Ekstein, Kato Van Leeuwen, and Leo Rangel. At San Francisco's Langley-Porter Clinic were Karl Bowman, S. Szurek, and Irving Berlin. As already noted, the Chicago group contributed over the years to the activities of the I.J.R. Rene Spitz, settling in Denver Colorado, fostered early infant and child development studies through clinical observation.

Erikson (1945) wrote about cultural and anthropological differences and the impact of social forces on the development of personality and identity. His *Childhood and Society* (1950) provided an epigenetic theory of psychosocial development that described the unfolding of increasingly complex and differentiated sequential phases of psychosocial capacities and behavioral descriptions of the corresponding failures. His schema, though psychoanalytically based, was to influence the development of extraanalytic approaches to the treatment of the childhood neuroses.

Later, Mahler (1963, 1975), after years of observation of mother–infant pairs in their first three years of life, set forth a schema of the development of the self vis-à-vis object relationships—in terms of separation–individuation with differentiation, practicing and rapprochement subphases, which has become a widely used frame of reference for the observation of infants and for the conduct of the analysis and psychotherapy of children with neurotic problems.

These reports and studies enabled Cramer (1959), in his review of the common neuroses of childhood in the *American Handbook of Psychiatry* to delineate specific neurotic conditions in the first three years of life that are strongly colored by phase specific adaptive problems reflected in disturbances of feeding, sleep, activity, mood (anxiety, crying), and persistent thumbsucking, as differentiated from the classic infantile neuroses of the oedipal period and those of latency, which can be seen in adaptive failure (social or school), delinquency and other disturbances of conduct, tics and stammering, and inhibitions, as well as the classic obsessive-compulsive, phobic, and conversion phenomena.

In addition to these areas, latency and adolescence were also represented in the studies in the first five volumes of the *Psychoanalytic Study of the Child*. Bornstein's (1951) classic article, "On Latency," in volume six soon followed, as did Gerald Pearson's (1952) "Survey of Learning Difficulties in Children" (in volume seven), which preceded his masterful books, *Psychoanalysis and the Education of the Child* (1954) and *Adolescence and the Conflict of Generations* (1958), which applied psychoanalytic understanding to learning disorders and school phobias as often being of neurotic origin. The neuroses that develop in adolescence were seen as developmental in origin and related to intergenerational conflicts.

Psychologist Lois Murphy and associates (1956) reported methods of studying children in nursery situations that had been carried on since 1940 and formed the basis of expanded play therapy techniques used by psychoanalysts and other psychotherapists.

In 1986 Pearson and his colleagues from the Philadelphia Association for Psychoanalysis published *A Handbook of Child Psychoanalysis*, a state of the art delineation of the classical techniques of the psychoanalysis of children and adolescents as differentially applied to the various age groups.

RECENT TRENDS IN INFANT OBSERVATION AND EARLY DEVELOPMENT

I have already noted the impact in the 1960s of Anna Freud's concept of developmental lines and Mahler's schema of separation–individuation.

Rene Spitz (1959) in his *A Genetic Field Theory of Ego Formation* clearly differentiated inherent biological maturation from psychological development, and went on to describe how the interplay of these two processes produces stages of affective development that act as organizers of the psyche. The first organizer, being biologically and maturationally rooted, is the social smile and motor responsiveness of the early infant; the second is more psychologically rooted in the stages of psychosexual development; and the third organizer is represented in language and communications. He postulated that developmental imbalances and delays in their deployment form a complemental series in the etiology of the neuroses.

Louis Sander also was a pioneer in combining psychoanalytic and biologically-oriented observations of infancy and parent–child interactions. Spitz and Sander pioneered methodology for systematically recording and quantifying the many variables involved in infant observation and parent–infant interactions. Their younger colleagues and pupils—Emde and Harmon in Denver, who produced a comprehensive and composite model for the study of affects; Brazelton and Als in Boston, with a more ethological approach; developmental psychologists Ainsworth and Sroufe (in the U.S.), and Papousek (in Berlin) studying and developing theories of attachment; and many others—produced research paradigms to study the role of parenting on the development of trust, self-confidence and other adaptive mechanisms, as well as the innate capacity of the infant to elicit and activate parenting responses.

Kagan at Harvard and Bruner at Harvard and Oxford, respectively, have studied the development of early cognitive abilities and language and communication. Daniel Stern, combining psychoanalytic and psychobiological concepts, has demonstrated in his recently published *The Interpersonal World of the Infant* how the infant comes into the world prewired for early relationships and affect attunement.

Indeed, these new developmental researchers of the mid 1970s and 1980s have demonstrated that early on the young infant is more resilient and capable of more perception and response, and relatability and elicitation of response from adults, than we had ever imagined. These studies were important in shaping our current concepts of prevention and early intervention in infant and early childhood disturbances. This new information is a result of close cooperation among child analysts, child psychiatrists, and developmental psychologists, and is reflected in the formation and membership of the World Association of Infant Psychiatry and Allied Disciplines and in the Society for Research in Child Development.

Stanley Greenspan, a child and infant psychiatrist and psychoanalyst, has integrated development and structure in his *Intelligence and Adaptation: An Integration of Psychoanalytic and Piagetian Developmental Psychology*. His studies show how the individual organizes his experience at each stage of development, resulting in a system of developmental stages and biological adaptational processes vis-à-vis which pathology can be delineated and intervention made. His schema is particularly well adapted for assessment of the child in his caretaking milieu and for the understanding of the etiological considerations of maladaptations that may eventuate into full-blown neuroses or developmental disabilities and suggests a comprehensive intervention rather than just psychotherapy for the child.

Recent work by Galenson and Roiphe on gender identity and the anal stage in the second year of life, and by Paulina Kernberg on transference manifestation in the analytic treatment of very young children, have had significant technical application. Margaret Harley (1986), reviewing the nature and validity of transference phenomena in child analysis (*Psychoanalytic Study of the Child*, vol. 41) notes that though acceptance of transference as an intrinsic ingredient of the analytic process with children became universal by the 1950s, only later was the importance of allowing a negative transference and its analysis realized. She noted that Robert Tyson had pointed out that influences from the past are important in the selection of which conflicts appear in the transference in treatment—that is, derivatives or the return of the repressed. Preformed transference expectations also occur.

Inasmuch as a child's loyalties are felt to be divided between parents and analyst, building the therapeutic alliance that also involves a close association with the parents is often a necessary adjunct, a technique Anna Freud had stressed years before. Sandler and colleagues (1980) published an important book, *The Technique of Child Psychoanalysis as Practiced at the Hampstead Clinic*.

THE HISTORY OF OTHER PSYCHOTHERAPEUTIC APPROACHES

While psychoanalysis has been considered the ideal treatment of choice for the childhood neuroses, by virtue of time, availability and cost, and now through increasing limitations imposed by third-party payers, it has not been, in practice, the treatment provided for the majority of patients.

You will remember that the child guidance movement first addressed itself to the delinquent child, and the socioeconomic roots of delinquency (Healy). The psychiatrist/social worker team that studied the child in school and at home was in part inspired by the work of Adolph Meyer, the "common sense" eclectic who, as I have described earlier, encouraged a study of the biological and social and biographical factors, and working with the home and school environments. Mrs. Meyer, in carrying out this aspect of her husband's approach, had become the first social worker by 1904 (Wittmer [1946], and Adams [1979]).

August Aichhorn, an Austrian educator working with delinquents, acquired psychoanalytic training in the early 1920s and published *Wayward Youth*, which established that delinquent behavior was often the outward manifestation of an underlying neurosis in children who had never established satisfactory relationships with parents. His work had considerable impact on the guidance clinics that were discussing and treating many varieties of childhood emotional disturbance, including neurotic children. Clear definition of diagnostic categories would have to await the development of more detailed systems of classifications (DSM, Group for the Advancement of Psychiatry [GAP], International Classification of Diseases of the World Health Organization [ICD], and so on). Whereas child guidance clinics originally focused more on doing *for* the child, other clinics, more clearly child psychiatry clinics, evolved, which though still following the psychiatry/social worker dyad model, focused more on the direct therapeutic activity *with* the child. These were often associated with pediatric departments. Leo Kanner's clinic at Johns Hopkins in Baltimore (1930) was one of the first. The core of the therapeutic approaches was play therapy as introduced by child psychoanalysts, particularly Anna Freud. Child psychoanalysts were often the teaching supervisors of the child guidance and child psychiatry teams.

Certain child psychiatrists with other than psychoanalytic orientation and training developed important therapeutic approaches that were variations on the original play therapy/rapport model. Leo Kanner (1935), working closely with Adolph Meyer, extended his psychobiological approach to the early observation of children and worked closely with pediatricians in obtaining a careful developmental history, noting the family and environmental impact. His textbook, *Child Psychiatry*, was the first on the subject in English and approached child neurotics in a holistic way, with direct supportive consideration of symptoms and interventions with the family and with the larger social and educational environment in the child's behalf. The role of unconscious conflicts rooted in the past was minimized.

Frederick Allen, who organized the Philadelphia Child Guidance Clinic in 1925, emphasized the "here and now," noting that in child guidance one dealt with the manifestations of conflict in the current living situations, in contrast to psychoanalysis that dealt with the more deeply rooted sources of the conflict. He felt that the therapist was not a part of the past, but of present reality; that the child's disturbed feelings no longer are part of the past but are now in the immediate treatment situation and can be dealt with by child and therapist in terms of the present. He presented himself to parents and child as a warm, empathetic human being who listened. He promoted identification with his attitudes as an ego ideal, and gave the child an opportunity to work out his transference feelings on the therapist. His theme was that children had potential, and his aim was to help them help themselves and transfer their identification with his attitudes to other social situations and relationships.

Allen also worked with parents and children to work out problems in their interrelationships by acting as a mediator and leading them to insights. His approach contained the forerunner of family therapy, and later, transactional approaches.

Despite his emphasis on the here and now he worked very closely with early child psychoanalysts in Philadelphia such as Phyllis Blanchard and Gerald H. J. Pearson. Pearson's pioneering textbooks *Common Neuroses of Children and Adults* (with O. Spurgeon English in 1937) and *Emotional Disorders of Children* (1949) presented the psychoanalytic orientation. Allen's *Psychotherapy with Children* (1942) emphasized the child's active participation in the therapeutic process (in contrast to the earlier child guidance practice of focusing on modification of the parental and social impact), regarding the child as a human being with the capacity for change rather than an object to be changed.

Although he applied his methods to neurotic children, Allen recognized that it was the personality and behavior problems that were being addressed, and that what characterizes the neurotic child is his inability to be free from a past he will not or cannot part with. His therapeutic effort with neurotic children was to help them free themselves from these attachments.

David Levy (1938) introduced a positive, helpful, supportive educational approach that he called *relationship therapy*. Like Anna Freud and Allen, he formed a therapeutic alliance with the child. However, he did not employ the free play technique, akin to free association in adults, used by the child analyst. He felt that his permissive, accepting attitude would enable the child to be freer with him than with his parents. He also set up his playroom to encourage the reenactment of previous situations that from the history given by the parents, he felt were traumatic and responsible for the child's neurotic posttraumatic behavior, "controlled play," which encouraged abreaction, that is, "release" therapy (Levy 1939).

Virginia Axline (1947, 1969) outlined basic principles for nondirective play therapy. Margaret Gerard (1946), who pioneered the understanding of the origins of the psychosomatic disorders in children, emphasized, with Greta Bibring, that the technique of free play had structure and limits and was not the same as allowing the child to go wild and give vent to all his impulses in a chaotic fashion. Structure and limits were needed to prevent disintegration of ego function.

Lauretta Bender (Lawrey and Bender 1955), at Bellevue Hospital in New York, used puppets selected by the child rather than the therapist to reenact traumatic situations and express his feelings, thus allowing more contacts with the repressed. Her overall concepts included biological predisposition and vulnerability, and greatly influenced the work of B. Fish, L. Eisenberg, A. Freedman, T. Shapiro, G. Faretra, and others.

Group therapy was extended to children (Slavson [Slavson and Schiffer 1975]), and Moreno (Haas and Moreno 1951) used his psychodrama techniques to elicit both abreaction and reenactment of past traumata.

All of these had considerable impact as teachers and trainers of many important child psychiatrists.

Though child analysis remained the treatment of choice for neurosis, it was these "cost effective" compromises, analytically and nonanalytically oriented, that became more readily available. The psychoanalytically oriented therapies recognized the unconscious and repression, leading the child to an awareness of the unreality of his anxieties, fantasies, and defenses against what he subconsciously perceived as dangers (Berman 1979).

OTHER THEORIES OF PERSONALITY DEVELOPMENT AND PSYCHIC FUNCTION UNDERLYING THE THERAPEUTIC APPROACHES

So far we have mainly been considering the psychodynamic theory of conflict and defense and the structural theories that underlay the psychoanalytic approach. Other theoretical models include the social learning-behavioral, family systems, developmental, humanistic, and biological (Harrison 1985).

The Social Learning-Behavioral Theory

This theory, with its roots in the Pavlovian conditioning experiments, is neurobiologically based on the stimulus/response/reflex model. The response may be positively reinforced or extinguished by other positive or negative stimuli. Learning theory states that all behavior—adaptive or maladaptive—is acquired by the same principles. It is either learned or unlearned. What makes behaviors acceptable or maladaptive are their social consequences and reaction. Behavioral disorder can come from either failure to learn or from learning inappropriate or maladaptive responses. Neuroses are considered patterns of behavior that are maladaptive personally and socially. Focus is on the current precipitants of behavior rather than the underlying causal factors. Thus, therapies based on social learning-behavior theory focus on the modification of behavior and symptom removal rather on the gestalt. Other aspects of learning theory—modeling of behaviors, imitative learning by example, and learning of values, mores, and attitudes—have been lost sight of in the current fashion for operant conditioning. Therapeutic technique for symptom removal is described in terms of desensitizations, aversive conditioning, assertiveness training, token economy, and behavior modification either by positively reinforcing desired behavior with rewards or by extinguishing undesirable symptoms through aversive means such as punishment, pain, or deprivation.

The Family Dynamics or Systems Theory

This theory considers the child in his family, and his neurosis as a result of a breakdown or malfunction of the family transactional process. The concepts of the neurosogenic family began with analytically oriented psychiatrists such as Nathan Ackerman and Eric Fromm in the late 1940s and early 1950s. The family was considered to be a relatively self-contained, dynamically evolving and fluctuating system with great impact on the captive child. (Today, families include one-parent and extended family alternative models.) Understanding the etiology of a child's neurosis in terms of family dynamics includes the concepts of scapegoating and double-binding, with the child caught in the middle of parental conflicts, and the parent using the child as an extension of the self or to rework his or her own unresolved conflicts. Such family transactions as manipulating the child by producing guilt, sabotaging, undermining, seductiveness, and rejection to enhance or break down the child's own ego defenses and in turn, the child's manipulative capacities, have led to the development of family therapy techniques to correct these neurosogenic family interactions. Family therapy may be seen as an adjunct to individual therapy or vice versa. Another extreme view (Jay Haley [1971], S. Minuchin [1974]) is that there is no child therapy, only family therapy. Regardless, the concepts noted here that have been derived from family systems theory have been quite useful to the psychoanalyst and psychotherapist alike for understanding the family dynamics operating in the genesis and continuation of neuroses and sometimes refractoriness to individual approaches.

An offshoot of both the family and social learning theories was the contributions of Harry Stack Sullivan (1953), which emphasized the prime importance of *interpersonal relationships*. Fromm, too, felt that the central problem was the breakdown in human relatedness and that childhood neuroses were precipitated by the child's inability to otherwise defend himself against the real impact of the irrational imposition of parental and later teacher authority on the powerless child. He felt that it was this reality, not the theoretical construct of the Oedipus complex that led to development of neuroses in children.

Developmental Theory

As noted earlier, a number of developmental schema have shed light on aspects of child development, which contributed to the understanding of the origins of the neuroses of children and which suggested therapeutic approaches. I have mentioned Freud's stages of psychosexual development, A. Freud's series of developmental lines of object relationship, play, and so forth, and Mahler's separation–individuation formulation. Gesell's descriptions of average expectable age-appropriate behaviors, Piaget's schema for the development of the intellectual-cognitive adaptive stages, and Erikson's epigenetic theory of stages of psychosociocultural development have been major contributions.

The child's neurosis and personality must be viewed in terms of the profile of developmental delay, and future goals in terms of next and future developmental steps. The concept of the phase specificity of certain disturbed behavior helps determine which symptoms' behaviors are developmentally on line and which may be symptoms of developmental deviation or a neurotic regression or fixation. A developmental frame of reference is of prime importance in assessing the necessity for psychotherapy in establishing the short- and long-term goals, and determining and measuring the impact of the therapeutic intervention.

Existential Theories

Paul Adams (1979), in the *Basic Handbook of Child Psychiatry*, wrote that existentialists often state that neurosis is an escape from a fuller, more vital experiencing of life. He quotes Maslow: "We fear our best as well as our worst" (p. 222). Kurt Goldstein talks of "self-actualization" as a phenomenon of growth, and thus neurosis is a failure of growth (p. 222). Maslow put basic needs in a sequential hierarchal series: (1) basic physiological needs (food, warmth), (2) the need for safety and freedom from fear or pain, (3) need for love, which depends on fulfillment of the first and second needs, and (4) the need for esteem and self-esteem, and finally, if the first four are in place, (5) the need for (and drive for) self-actualizing can be attained (p. 222).

This schema—not too far removed from Erikson's—has emphasized a growing and developing individual and hence the need for a child advocacy. Again, however, this focuses on the need to improve the support system—home, school, welfare, and medical care that will provide the milieu for growth. Child care practitioners in child development in preschool, nurseries, and early intervention and preventive facilities have been influenced both by Maslow and Erikson in this regard.

Biological Theories

Most recent in the conceptual approaches to the etiology of the childhood neuroses are the theories of deficient and deviant neurophysiological function, or genetic or congenitally based predispositions or vulnerabilities. The concept of neurophysiological correlates of the psychological manifestations of the neuroses and a possible biological basis, yet to be discovered, goes back to Sigmund Freud.

Lauretta Bender (1947) described childhood psychoses in terms of the psychophysiological dysfunctions such as plasticity, pallor, flushing and other autonomic reactions, dyscoordination, and vestibular self-stimulation, and used chemotherapy in the treatment. In practice, this was extended to address the anxiety, jumpiness, and tenseness of nonpsychotic emotionally disturbed children. Benadryl (diphenhydramine), a precursor of the phenothiazides and an antihistamine was used for sleep disorders and the anxiety symptoms.

Magda Campbell, Barbara Fish, and Theodore Shapiro are among her early students who have used chemotherapy effectively as an adjunct in a more comprehensive approach including psychotherapy and environmental support and orientation.

Chess and colleagues' (1968) classic study established the role of constitutional factors in ordaining temperament, and their influence on early relationships and the development of emotional disorders. As we learn more about brain function and its neurochemistry and the role of different classes of neurotransmitters, it is becoming more and more evident that there are neurobiological factors in certain neurotic conditions formerly thought to be of purely psychosocial origin. Included in this category are certain depressive disorders, phobias, enuresis, certain disorders of attention and hyperkinesis, and anorexia.

The use of imipramine with enuretic children is almost a specific, as are the tricyclics for childhood depressions. Paul Adams (1979) describes the widespread use of Atarax, Vistiril, and Mellaril by pediatricians and family practitioners for anxious, fearful, hysterical, and obsessive-compulsive children, most of whom never get to a child psychiatrist or analyst. In a previous generation, phenobarbital (Luminal) was used. Adams calls these medications "the great subduer of childhood neurosis in America" (p. 231). Often they are used to take the edge off the painful symptom and make the child more accessible to psychotherapy. Many clinical as well as research studies are going on in this area. Morton Reiser, Donald Cohen, and Theodore Shapiro are examples of psychoanalysts who have been active in coordinating psychobiological approaches to the understanding and treatment of childhood disorders, which in their views represent the interaction of biological endowment and experiential and maturational factors (Adams, p. 189).

FUTURE CHALLENGES FROM THE PERSPECTIVE OF HISTORY

I have described the gradual recognition of children as human beings and their emotional disorders, from which the specific categories of childhood neuroses were delineated only about eighty years go. I have described the evolution of the concept of childhood neurosis, first as an extension of a universal infantile neurosis based on conflict and defense and psychosexual development. Then, pregenital roots and types of neuroses, as well as those in latency and adolescence, were recognized, and new concepts of neuroses—in terms of the ego structural theory of psychic structure and development—were noted. Direct observations of infant and child development, studies of psychopharmacological and neurobiological function, and the application of schemas and conceptual frameworks explaining psychic function and disorder have contributed to the understanding of the neurotic processes in terms of learning and family systems theory. The net result is an ever-increasing wealth of information which must be assimilated and applied. The challenge of the future is to integrate this knowledge into a cohesive multidimensional transdisciplinary approach that can assess a child's dysfunction and provide an individualized profile of etiology and process that can be translated into a dynamic evolving treatment plan and procedure in a cost-effective, accountable manner available to children of all socioeconomic and racial backgrounds. Though psychoanalysis remains the ultimate treatment of choice (for the neuroses of childhood) where available, the various therapeutic and conceptual approaches need not be mutually exclusive, and techniques for determining the type, scope, and intensity of therapy in each particular case need to be developed.

Child advocacy is a necessary preliminary step and must be an ongoing watchdog to assure the availability of proper and adequate intervention for all who need it. Historically, it has been so at every stage of development in the care and treatment of children. First came advocacy movements in behalf of the mentally retarded, then the delinquent, then the psychotic and developmentally disabled, and then, for each, the proper therapeutic interventions follow. The growing incidence of one-parent and disrupted families, of child abuse and the behavior disorders and neurotic conditions associated with it, now mandates our concern and advocacy. Let us not throw out the baby with the bathwater. Quality care in depth, treating etiology and process instead of symptom alone, and reactivating development in place of behavior management and suppression should not be discarded in favor of cost-cutting. Clinically useful classification by severity of ego functions should not be sacrificed for classification by symptoms because it is more amenable to statistical evaluations.

Neurosis of children has been known as the middle-class disorder, and psychoanalysis and psychoanalytically-oriented psychotherapy as the treatments of choice are available by and large only to those who can afford it. Those who will not attain resolution of their neurotic conflicts without psychoanalysis or in-depth psychotherapies should have these interventions, regardless of ability to pay. To some extent this is happening at Hampstead Clinic in London, in Cleveland, Ohio, and New Haven, Connecticut. Alex Burland (1986) in Philadelphia has been able to analyze several disadvantaged children through Medical Assistance. The social challenge rivals the technical challenge in importance. From the perspective of history we need not reinvent the wheel. History indeed is repeating itself, but with each revolution, each turn of the wheel, the repetition is on a higher level of knowledge, competence, and scope of endeavor.

REFERENCES

Ackerman, N. (1958). *The Psychodynamics of Family Life:* New York; Basic Books.
Adams, P. (1979). Psychoneurosis. In *Basic Handbook of Child Psychiatry*, vol. 2, ed. J. Noshpitz, part 12, pp. 207–211. New York: Basic Books.
Aichorn, A. (1925, 1935). *Verwahrloste Jugend.* Vienna: Weiner Psychoanalytischer Verlag. *Wayward Youth.* New York: Viking Press.
Alexander, F., and Seleznick, S. (1966). *The History of Psychiatry.* New York: Harper & Row.
Allen, F. (1942). *Psychotherapy with Children.* New York: Norton.
Anthony, E. J. (1967). Psychoneurotic disorders. In *Comprehensive Textbook of Psychiatry*, ed. A. M. Freedman and H. I. Kaplan, pp. 1387–1405. Baltimore: Williams & Wilkins.
Axline, V. M. (1947, 1969). *Play Therapy.* Boston and New York: Houghton Mifflin and Ballantine.
Baruch, D. (1952). *One Little Boy.* New York: Julian Press.

Bender, L. (1947). Childhood schizophrenia: clinical study of one hundred schizophrenic children. *American Journal of Orthopsychiatry* 17:40–56.
——— (1955). Therapeutic play techniques. *American Journal of Orthopsychiatry* 25:574–585.
Bender, L., Waltham, A. S., Lawrey, L. G., et al. (1936). Use of puppet shows as a psychotherapeutic method for behavior problems in children. *American Journal of Orthopsychiatry* 6:341–348.
Berlin, I. N. (1976). *Bibliography of Child Psychiatry and Child Mental Health*. Washington, DC: American Academy of Child Psychiatry.
Berman, S. (1979). The psychodynamic aspects of behavior. In *Basic Handbook of Child Psychiatry*, vol. 2, ed. J. Noshpitz, part A: etiology, pp. 3–28. New York: Basic Books.
Bibring, G. (1957). Personal communication—workshop notes.
——— (1968). *The Teaching of Dynamic Psychoanalytic Psychiatry*. New York: International Universities Press.
Brill, A. A. (1938). *The Basic Writings of Sigmund Freud*. New York: Random House.
Broca, P. (1861). Remarques sur la Fiège de la Faculté du Language Articule. Paris: Bulletin de la Société d'Anthropologie (6).
Brody, S. (1956). *Patterns of Mothering*. New York: International Universities Press.
Burland, A. (1986). The vicissitudes of maternal deprivation. In *Self and Object Constancy*, ed. R. Lax, S. Bach, and J. Burland, pp. 324–347. New York: Guilford Press.
Call, J., Galenson, E., and Tyson, R., eds. (1983, 1984). *Frontiers of Infant Psychiatry*. New York: Basic Books.
Campbell, M., and Shapiro, T. (1975). Therapy of psychiatric disorders of childhood. In *Manual of Psychiatric Therapeutics*, ed. R. I. Schrader, pp. 137–162. Boston: Little, Brown.
Cohen, D. J. (1974). Competence and biology: methodology in studies of infants, twins, psychosomatic disease and psychoses. In *International Yearbook, International Association for Child Psychiatry and Allied Professions*, vol. 3: *The Child in His Family—Children at Psychiatric Risk*, ed. E. J. Anthony, pp. 361–394. New York: John Wiley.
Cramer, J. (1959). Common childhood neurosis. In *American Handbook of Psychiatry*, vol. 1, ed. S. Arieti, pp. 797–815. New York: Basic Books.
Darwin, C. (1872, 1898). *The Expression of Emotions in Man and Animals*. London and New York: Murray and Appleton.
——— (1876). *Biological Sketch of an Infant*. Outlined in E. Tinbergen and N. Tingbergen.
——— (1972). *Early Childhood Autism: An Ethological Approach*. Berlin and Hamburg: Verlag Paul Parey.
Despert, J. L. (1965). *The Emotionally Disturbed Child, Then and Now*. New York: Brunner.
DSM-II (Diagnostic and Statistical Manual of Mental Disorders), 2nd ed. Washington, DC: American Psychiatric Association, 1969.
DSM-III (Diagnostic and Statistical Manual of Mental Disorders), 3rd ed. Washington, DC: American Psychiatric Association, 1980.
Emminghaus, H. (1877). Die Psychischen Störungen des Kinderstalters (Psychic disturbances of children). In *Handbuch der Kinderkrankheiten*. Tübingen: Verlag der H. Laupp'schen Buch handling.
English, O. S., and Pearson, G. H. J. (1937). *Common Neuroses of Children and Adults*. New York: Norton.
Erikson, E. (1950). *Childhood and Society*. New York: Norton.
Escalona, S. (1968). *The Roots of Individuality*. Chicago: Aldine.
Ferenczi, S. (1950). A little chanticleer. In *Contributions to Psychoanalysis*, vol. 1, pp. 240–252. New York: Robert Brunner.
Freud. A. (1946). *Ego and the Mechanisms of Defense*. New York: International Universities Press.
——— (1948). *The Psychoanalytical Treatment of Children*. London: Imago.

17:149–158. New York: International Universities Press.
Freud, S. (1905). Three essays on sexuality. *Standard Edition* 7:123–243.
_____ (1953). *The Standard Edition of the Complete Works of Sigmund Freud.* London: Hogarth.
_____ (1953). *On Asphasia.* New York: International Universities Press.
Fromm, E. (1941). *Escape from Freedom.* New York: Rinehart.
_____ (1947). *Man for Himself.* Greenwich, CT: Fawcett.
_____ (1968). *The Revolution of Hope: Toward A Humanized Technology.* New York: Bantam.
_____ (1970). *The Crisis of Psychoanalysis,* Greenwich, CT: Fawcett.
Gerard, M. (1946). The psychogenic tic in ego development. *Psychoanalytic Study of the Child* 2:133–162. New York: International Universities Press.
Gesell, A., et al. (1940). *The First Five Years of Life.* New York: Harper Brothers.
Gesell, A., and Ilg, F. (1943). *Infant and Child in the Culture of Today.* New York: Harper and Brothers.
Greenspan, S. (1979). Intelligence and adaptation: an integration of psychoanalytic and Piagetian developmental psychology. *Psychological Issues.* Monographs 47/48. New York: International Universities Press.
Haas, R. B., and Moreno, J. L. (1951). Psychodrama as a projective technique. In *An Introduction to Projective Techniques,* ed. H. H. Anderson and G. L. Anderson, pp. 662–675. Englewood Cliffs, NJ: Prentice Hall.
Haley, J. (1971). A review of the family therapy field. In *Changing Families,* ed. J. Haley, pp. 1–12. New York: Grune and Stratton.
_____ (1974). Personal communication at a conference at the Philadelphia Child Guidance Clinic.
Harley, M. (1986). Child analysis 1947–1984, a retrospective. *Psychoanalytic Study of the Child* 41:129–153. New Haven, CT: Yale University Press.
Harrison, S. (1980). Child psychiatry, psychiatric treatment. In *Comprehensive Textbook of Psychiatry,* 3rd ed., ed. A. M. Freedman and H. I. Kaplan, pp. 2647–2667. Baltimore: Williams & Wilkins.
_____ (1985). Individual psychotherapy history. In *Comprehensive Textbook of Psychiatry,* 4th ed., ed. H. I. Kaplan and B. J. Sadock, p. 1766. Baltimore: Williams & Wilkins.
Hartmann, H., and Kris, E. (1945). Genetic approach to psychoanalysis. *Psychoanalytic Study of the Child* 1:11–30. New York: International Universities Press.
Hirschberg, J. C. (1980). History of child psychiatry. In *Comprehensive Textbook of Psychiatry,* 3rd ed., 34:1:2417–2420. Baltimore: Williams & Wilkins.
Hug-Helmuth, H. (1919). *A Study of the Mental Life of the Child.* Washington, DC: Nervous and Mental Disease Publishing.
International Classification of Diseases of the World Health Organization (ICD) (1978). 9th rev.: *Clinical Modification.* Ann Arbor, MI; Geneva, Switzerland.
Jackson, T. H. (1932). *Selected Writings.* London: Hodder and Stoughton.
Jacobson, E. (1964). *The Self and the Object World.* New York: International Universities Press.
Kanner, L. (1967). History of child psychiatry. In *Comprehensive Textbook of Psychiatry,* 38:1:1313–1315. Baltimore: Williams & Wilkins.
_____ (1972). *Child Psychiatry.* Springfield, IL: Charles C Thomas.
Kernberg, P. (1985). Transference manifestations in the psychoanalysis of the preschool child (unpublished report). Seminar on Transference in Early Childhood Analysis, American Psychoanalytic Society mid-winter meetings, New York.
Klein, M. (1932). *The Psychoanalysis of Children.* London: Hogarth.
Levy, D. (1938). Relationship therapy. *American Journal of Orthopsychiatry* 8:64–83.
_____ (1939). Release therapy. *American Journal of Orthopsychiatry* 9:713–736.

Mahler, M. (1963). Thoughts about development and individuation. *Psychoanalytic Study of the Child* 18:307–324. New York: International Universities Press.

Mahler, M., Pine, F., and Bergman, A. (1975). *The Psychological Birth of the Human Infant—Symbiosis and Individualism.* New York: Basic Books.

Minuchin, S. (1974). *Families and Family Therapy.* Cambridge, MA: Harvard University Press.

Murphy, L. B. (1956). *Methods for the Study of Personality in Young Children.* New York: Basic Books.

Nagera, H. (1966). Early childhood disturbances, the infantile neuroses, and the adulthood disturbances. Monograph 2, published by *Psychoanalytic Study of the Child.* New York: International Universities Press.

Pearson, G. H. J. (1949). *Emotional Disorders of Children.* New York: Norton.

—— (1954). *Psychoanalysis and the Education of the Child.* New York: Norton.

—— (1958). *Adolescence and the Conflict of Generations.* New York: Norton.

—— (1968). *A Handbook of Childhood Psychoanalysis.* New York: Basic Books.

Piaget, J. (1954). *The Origins of Intelligence in Children.* New York: International Universities Press.

—— (1962). *Plays, Dreams and Imitation in Childhood.* New York: Norton.

Provence, S. (1987). Some thoughts about approaches to the vulnerable child, then and now. Presented at the Vulnerable Child Workshop, Association for Child Psychoanalysis. Key Biscayne, FL, April 1987.

Psychoanalytic Study of the Child. Vols. 1–25 (1945–1970). New York: International Universities Press. Vols. 26–42 (1971–1986). New Haven, CT: Yale University Press.

Psychopathological disorders in children: theoretical considerations and a proposed classification (1966). New York: Group for the Advancement of Psychiatry (GAP).

Reiser, M. (1985). Converging sectors of psychoanalysis and neurobiology—mutual challenges and opportunity. *Journal of the American Psychoanalytic Association* 33:11–35. New York: International Universities Press.

Roiphe, H., and Galenson, E. (1981). *Infantile Origins of Sexual Identity.* New York: International Universities Press.

Sandler, J., Kennedy, H., and Tyson, R. (1980). *The Techniques of Child Psychoanalysis.* Cambridge, MA: Harvard University Press.

Slavson, S. R., ed. (1947). *The Practice of Group Therapy.* New York: International Universities Press.

Slavson, S. R., and Schiffer, M. (1975). *Group Psychotherapies for Children.* New York: International Universities Press.

Solnit, A. J. (1975). Developments in child psychoanalysis in the last twenty years. Monograph 5, pp. 1–31. Monograph Series, *Studies in Chidl Psychoanalysis Pure and Applied,* published by *Psychoanalytic Study of the Child.* New Haven, CT: Yale University Press.

Spitz, R. (1957). *No and Yes.* New York: International Universities Press.

—— (1959). *A Genetic Field Theory of Ego Formation.* New York: International Universities Press.

—— (1965). *The First Year of Life.* New York: International Universities Press.

Spock, B. (1951). *The Pocket Book of Baby and Child Care* (20th printing). New York: Pocket Books.

Stern, D. N. (1985). *The Interpersonal World of the Child.* New York: Basic Books.

Sullivan, H. S. (1953). *The Interpersonal Theory of Psychiatry.* New York: Norton.

Wernicke, C. (1874). *Der Aphasische Symptomen-komplex.* Breslau: Cohn & Weigart.

Witmer, H. (1946). *Psychiatric Interviews with Children.* New York: The Commonwealth Fund.

Zilboorg, G., and Henry, G. (1941). *A History of Medical Psychology.* New York: Norton.

17

The Neurotic Child and Response to Treatment

Martin A. Silverman, M.D.

The treatment of choice for neurotic children and adolescents is psychoanalysis. Although a number of treatment modalities can alleviate or ameliorate neurotic symptoms, psychoanalysis is the best by far at providing access to the deeper, unconscious mental and emotional struggles that generate the symptomatology observable on the surface. This allows psychological problems to be tackled at their very source, which not only is most likely to lead to lasting symptom relief but also yields invaluable, additional benefits. Assistance can be provided to help the child resolve the core internal conflicts, undo the pathological identifications, and correct the distorted perceptions and attitudes that have been responsible for the child's difficulties. Emotional resources and energies that have been utilized in the service of maintaining neurotic compromise-formations can be freed up for more constructive purposes. Psychoanalytic treatment thus offers more than relief from immediate suffering. It also fosters developmental progress that otherwise would not have taken place. The gains obtainable through the psychoanalytic treatment of children are both extensive and lifelong in their overall impact.

DIFFICULTIES IN THE WAY OF TREATMENT

Multiple external and internal factors, however, interfere with the possiblity of providing psychoanalytic treatment to more than a fraction of the children and adolescents who might benefit from it. The external factors are the easier ones to define. For one thing, properly trained psychoanalysts (let alone child analysts) are relatively few in number, and they tend to be concentrated in or near a few urban centers. They may not be available, therefore, or they may be available only at a considerable distance from the child's home. Parents may be unable or unwilling to undergo the expenditure in time and money that is involved in placing a child into analysis. Parents often are ignorant of or ill-informed about the merits and limitations of the different treatment approaches that are available, and they may be offered poor advice by those to whom they turn for guidance. Cultural factors also may prevent a family from availing itself of child analytic services that are readily available, either privately or in a clinic setting, within the family's means and in an accessible location.

The emotional equilibrium in a family may be such, furthermore, that there is reluctance to take a chance on upsetting the existing balance of forces, or there may even be fear of adversely affecting the precarious psychological state of some other family member should a child who is overtly symptomatic become free of his or her crippling neurotic symptoms and grow emotionally strong and independent. At times, the child's problems interdigitate closely with those of another member of the family. Sometimes, they are associated with neurotic or perverse gratifications and defensive operations of a parent which the latter is not inclined to give up. There are some children and adolescents who can only enter analysis or intensive psychotherapy if one or both parents do so as well.

The internal factors affecting the ability of a youngster to participate in psychoanalytic treatment are more difficult to describe, since they are subtle and complex. They can be divided, in a roughly cross-sectional and longitudinal fashion, into two categories, one diagnostic and the other developmental (although the two cannot be absolutely demarcated from one another, since they overlap and merge). From a diagnostic viewpoint, it is evident that children are best able to make use of analysis when their core conflicts are largely on an oedipal level of object relations, rather than there being a preponderance of very early, preoedipal conflicts. The latter at times can seriously compromise developmental progression. It can burden a child with developmental arrests, emotional neediness, object hunger, distrust of the outside world, fear of change, specific ego disturbances and general ego weakness, and dread of intense emotional excitement. It can be extremely difficult for such a child to participate in an intensive, exploratory, psychoanalytic treatment process.

Regressive flight from triadic, oedipal conflicts back to seemingly simpler, preoedipal ones is a more or less regular aspect of the clinical picture encountered in the intensive treatment of the neurotic child, but this is a very different state of affairs. The preoedipal struggles are largely secondary ones in such children. Their ego organization has developed sufficiently for them to be able to tolerate the kinds of pressures and temporary deprivations that are involved in analysis and they are able to participate in the collaborative, intrapsychic investigative tasks that are at the heart of it.

A certain amount of primary early emotional disturbance is consistent with analytic work, so long as it does not play a predominant role. For analytic work to take place, a child needs to possess sufficient frustration tolerance and tension tolerance and enough trust and faith in the adult world as a reliable source of assistance that he can work together with the analyst for a relatively long period of time during which there is very little drive gratification and, as yet, no symptom relief. The child must be able to wait for the self-understanding, sense of mastery, and resolution of neurotic problems that ultimately are obtained. Not all children are capable of this.

RECEPTIVENESS TO INTENSIVE TREATMENT

There are some children who, even at a very young age, are quite remarkable in their intuitive awareness that forces within them play a part in shaping the problems that trouble them, and they are impressive in their capacity to understand the psychoanalytic point of view. Abbate (1967) and Kelly (1970) have described such children.

A 9-year-old girl brought to me recently wanted very much to go to sleepaway camp for the first time, but was unable even to sleep at a friend's house without experiencing intense anxiety. During her first visit, she said some things that suggested the possibility that she worried about her mother when she was away from her. It seemed that she had to be with her mother in order to make certain that no harm had befallen her. When I put this into words for her, she was puzzled. She had not been aware of such feelings. Then she opened her eyes wide with excitement, and said that I might be right after all. At times when her mother had complained about her sleep being cut short by having to come and fetch her daughter from a friend's house in the middle of the night, the girl not only had felt annoyed at her mother but also had found herself worrying about her mother's health and well-being.

But that was *after* she had been nervous and unable to stay at the friend's home, she added, with a note of confusion in her voice. Was I saying that she actually had been worrying about something happening to her mother *before* she had spoken to her, without knowing what she was feeling inside? The idea intrigued her. Of course, people could think things inside them and not know about it until later on. Sometimes she dreamt things that made her realize that certain matters had been on her mind one way or another without her being aware of it until the dream called her attention to it. She provided an illustrative example (which seemed to me to involve her mother), after which she defensively retreated to doubts about the role of worries about her mother playing a part in her nocturnal anxieties. She made a mild attempt to disown responsibility for her dreams entirely, in fact. I explained that she was the one who created her dreams. She listened closely, and did not appear to be troubled by the idea. Something about it, in fact, seemed to appeal to her. When the time available to us came to an end, shortly thereafter, she readily agreed to return the next day.

My young acquaintance began the next session by stating, "You were wrong, Dr. Silverman. You said I write, produce, direct, and star in my dreams [a metaphorical construction I had chosen in consideration of her profound interest in and enjoyment of dramatics]. But you were wrong. Something *inside* me writes, produces, and directs my dreams . . . [her voice grew sad and plaintive] *and I have to star in them!"*

She also had given some thought, she stated, to what I had said to her about the possibility that feelings about her mother were involved in her difficulty sleeping over at friends' houses. At times she got very angry at her mother, she said, even though her mother was a very good mother and she loved her. This especially occurred when her mother told her what to do or stopped her from doing something she wanted to do. Her mother interfered, for example, when she wanted to eat fattening foods. She would get furious and throw a huge tantrum, far out of proportion to what her mother had said.

At this point, or shortly thereafter, she introduced me to another of her symptoms. This one had troubled her much less than the one that threatened to block her from going to sleepaway camp. It involved an occasional, mild eating inhibition. After we had reflected on it together for a while, I called attention to the sequence of her thoughts and told her that it was possible that when she got so angry at her mother for telling her not to eat the fattening things she wanted to eat, she felt in her anger like biting her mother into little pieces and eating *her* up. With a devilish look, she opened her eyes wide and, with mock fiendishness, replied, "I'll put her in my soup, and eat her up."

After a few more sessions, in which her thoughts went off in multiple directions, including one that reflected oedipal rivalry and anger over primal scene exclusion (with a number of allusions to oedipal transference readiness), she excitedly told her mother that she thought that she and I could figure out what caused her problems. She insistently told her mother that she needed to see me as often as possible, at least three times a week and maybe even more often. Her parents, alas, were not quite ready to agree with her.

Unfortunately, a child like this is the exception rather than the rule. Most children who are brought for emotional assistance do not recognize that they are in need of help and are not able to appreciate the value of what they are being offered. They tend to be wary about strangers inquiring into their personal lives, however kind, interested, and understanding they might be. This applies especially to youngsters who are not undergoing a great deal of conscious suffering as a result of their internal problems.

Many children are brought for help because of difficulties that are more apparent or more troublesome to others than to them. It is their parents and teachers who are concerned about their inhibitions, their compulsions, their social withdrawal, their underachievement, their disturbed behavior. Unlike the girl I have described, they themselves are far less concerned, at least consciously, with those problems. These are the children whose overt symptoms are largely referable to the effect of unconscious defense activity of which they are not consciously aware but which, within them, they very much feel they need. The symptomatology that troubles the people around them is a price that they consciously are willing to pay in order to obtain a measure of relief from the inner terrors, torments, and wrenching emotional conflicts which to them are far worse than the symptoms.

A child who is consciously very anxious or very unhappy may be glad to receive an offer of help in getting rid of the anxiety or unhappiness. Children who are brought for help mainly because others are concerned about them, however, tend to view treatment as a threat, since it pits itself against the very neurotic mechanisms they have been employing to deal with their internal problems. With such children, as Freud (1909), Anna Freud (1927, 1970), Geleerd (1967), Schowalter (1976), and others have noted, parental assistance is of utmost importance in getting the treatment going. It is also necessary to keep it going despite the tensions and discomforts the child experiences in the course of it, until a therapeutic alliance has been established with the analyst that obviates the need for further such ongoing parental, surrogate ego assistance. Even then, however, there may be periodic need for parental support and assistance if the analysis is to be saved from foundering during one of the periodic transference storms and developmental crises that threaten to abort the trip before the destination is reached.

BUILDING A THERAPEUTIC ALLIANCE

Of course, children differ from one another, and some, as Abbate (1967) has pointed out, "can be analyzed without active participation of the parents so long as they are convinced of the need for analysis" (p. 23). We have come a long way from the formulaic belief that child analysis invariably requires concomitant regular frequent sessions with parents for information about the child's present and past life and for clarification of what the child is expressing in his or her sessions. There are many child analysts who have come to believe that dependence upon parental assistance in the best of circumstances need be no more than a temporary feature of child analysis. They believe it can very often be reduced or eliminated as the child eventually becomes able to proceed without the need for such ancillary parental participation. Schowalter (1976) has put it as follows: "In some cases, especially with quite young children, beginning the work requires relatively close contact with the parents, but this contact is usually kept to the minimum necessary to allow the analysis to run smoothly; and as the therapeutic alliance with the child strengthens, meetings with the parents usually become less frequent or not necessary at all" (p. 419).

Building a therapeutic alliance is no easy matter, however. It is difficult enough for an adult to accept a therapeutic approach that offers deferred relief sometime in the future, rather than providing immediate removal of pain and discomfort in the present. Adults have trouble understanding the value of facing the things from which they have been inclined to turn away and to talk about them with someone who can help them make changes in themselves so that they can more effectively deal with what has been troubling them.

Children are even less capable in this regard than grownups are. They do not yet have a mature enough perspective to look at their current problems from the point of view of long-term goals and ultimate aims and ambitions. They function very much in the present, and have great difficulty accepting the long-range value of bearing with and exploring their current pain while they put off obtaining relief from it until later on. They do not possess the capacity (or at least they do not know that they possess it) to tolerate increases in the anxiety, sadness, humiliation, defeat, or sense of loss and loneliness that they have been experiencing, however temporary *we know* they will be, en route to the greater strength, mastery, and effective control over their internal and external environments that we know we are offering them if they only will be a little patient. Children are very much aware of the relative weakness of their ego capacities and are understandably reluctant to abandon or even to loosen the grip they have been able, albeit imperfectly and at considerable cost, to maintain over painful affects, let alone over their urges and impulses. They do not trust themselves to be able to regain control if they relax their guard and permit freer, more direct expression of their feelings and thoughts. And the failure of their current mechanisms to contain reliably and effectively all the negative forces by which they feel assailed does not inspire them with confidence in their ability to elaborate new and better ones should they give up some of the mechanisms they have been employing.

Furthermore, children and adolescents for the most part are action-oriented in their approach to life. They are not inclined to believe that words can be tools of mastery. A psychoanalyst working with children has to devote himself, carefully, patiently, and with a great deal of restraint, tact, and sensitivity to the task of demonstrating the value of verbalization as a means of effecting mastery over oneself and in relation to the world around one. In doing so, the analyst not only has to respect the child's developmental immaturities but needs to work with the child in such a way as to enhance ego development so that the limitations imposed by developmental immaturity can be overcome. Ritvo (1978) has emphasized the significance in child analysis of developmental limitations in the child's capacity for self-awareness, objectivity, toleration of emotional tension, and intellectual comprehension over the course of the analysis. The ego of the neurotic child feels weak, helpless, and in great danger of being overwhelmed by drive pressures. Direct references to drive derivatives and to defensive responses to them cannot be tolerated. "The child responds in analysis," as Ritvo (1978) has put it, "as though most of the time he can tolerate only the indirect recognition of his wishes, his fears, and his ways of defending himself as they are disguised on his fantasy play. . . . The interpretation and analysis of conflict and defense within the fantasy play afford the ego a degree of mastery and relief. However, due to the developmental limitations the full resources of the mature ego cannot be brought to bear on the neurosis" (p. 303). The child analyst has to take care to frame his interventions so that they are addressed mainly toward affects and defenses and refer only indirectly to drive aspects, carefully remaining within the child's capacity to grapple with what is involved. He does not do this merely out of deference to the child's limited capacity to respond to more direct interpretations. The far more important consideration is that of supporting and facilitating the child's innate thrust toward progressive ego development, by working with the child at a level that moves slowly but increasingly closer to the drive contents, with the aid of the increasingly stronger ego capacities that emerge out of their work.

AN EXAMPLE OF THE ESTABLISHMENT OF AN ALLIANCE

Even when children accept the idea of outside intervention, the tendency is to look for assistance in dealing with what is perceived as problems presented by people in the outside world rather than searching within themselves for answers.

Seven-year-old Billy, for example, readily accepted the offer of help when it was made to him. He had been referred because of underachievement at school that was so serious he was faced with expulsion from the excellent private school he was attending. He was the picture of dejection as he sat on the couch and recounted a tale of woe. How could he concentrate on his schoolwork, he asked, when he had so many things on his mind to worry about? His parents kept arguing, and he was worried that they would get a divorce. His mother was ill a lot and he worried about her. His little sister clearly was favored by his parents. She could get away with anything. He tried to keep her out of his room, but she kept coming in and getting into his things. Complaining to his mother didn't do any good, and if he yelled at or hit her he would only get into big trouble. There was *nothing* he could do. He was helpless. His big sister was no help. She not only took his little sister's side most of the time, but she was mean and bossy with him and teased him unmercifully about his bedwetting and tearfulness. He couldn't understand his sister's teasing him about wetting the bed at night. After all, he did everything he could to prevent it. He avoided liquids before bedtime, and allowed his father to wake him up during the night and take him to the bathroom. He couldn't help it that his body behaved that way. And anyone who had to put up with all that he had to contend with would cry a lot. It was not his fault.

Billy was grateful for the offer of help in tackling his problems. He had his own idea of how to go about it, however. If only I would speak to his parents, let them know how he was suffering, and tell them what to do, his problems would be over. Maybe I could talk to his big sister, too, and tell her to leave him alone. If he could get some help in dealing with her, it would relieve his burdens enormously. At this point, I questioned his idea that he was unable to look out for himself. Had he ever stood up to his sister, I asked. Had he ever fought back? He'd never dared. She was much bigger than he was, and she could be very mean when she was crossed. Had she ever really hurt him, I asked. No, she hadn't. He had never thought about that before. It was worth thinking about, I said. Maybe he underestimated the effect he could have if he stood up for himself. Maybe his sister continued to push him around, I added, *because* he never fought back. He had been a pushover.

Billy thought about this, and we discussed it periodically. It took weeks, however, before he summoned up the courage to take matters in his own hands instead of looking for me to intercede on his behalf. One day, he lost his patience and screamed at his sister when she tormented him. Not only did she back off, but to his astonishment, she responded by treating him with a respect she had never shown him before. He was very impressed. At first, he was very reluctant to do the same thing with the boys at school who had been teasing and pushing him around. They were even bigger, tougher, and more forebidding than his sister. He wistfully hoped that I could do something to help him at school. Maybe I could talk to the headmistress or to his teachers about his need for better protection. He certainly couldn't talk to them, or the boys would make it even worse for him *after* school. I questioned the validity of his ideas about what the boys would do to him if he were to stand up to them. I wondered whether his continual show of fear and his deferential meekness might not even be serving as an unwitting invitation to them to attack him. (A cautiously tentative, very mild allusion to his unconcscious, masochistic *desire* to be assaulted drew an anxious denial and a resistive withdrawal, which was not surprising, as he was not yet ready to acknowledge his internal, neurotic wishes.)

We looked together into a brief transference reaction in which he anxiously expected me to become very angry at him and to attack him for having committed an infraction of the analytic "rules" by failing to show up for a session. When I was able to show him that he had not been realistic but had projected onto me something from his own inner feelings and expectations, he became more open to the idea that his fear of the boys at school might also have been exaggerated and worth further consideration. We came to see that his view of himself as powerless against overwhelmingly superior outside forces that were determined to subject him to cruel, vindictive attacks stemmed from more than merely the external realities of sibling rivalry and some bullies among his schoolmates. There was something he was contributing from within himself. His overblown fear of the boys at school diminished enough for him, for the first time, to defend himself instead of submitting meekly or running away. Once again, he discovered that standing up for himself earned him respect rather than getting him destroyed. He began to win some mild acceptance among his male peer group at school, and he even made a friend or two instead of being a solitary outcast.

Billy's confidence grew, and with his improved self-esteem came an appreciation that he possessed resources of which he had not been aware. The discovery that he was not really so weak and helpless with regard to his external problems as he had thought permitted him to begin to approach his internal problems differently as well. The natural thrust of his ego progression had been thwarted by the stultifying effect of a dispiriting series of terrifying experiences and overwhelming defeats which he had gone through (the impact of which we eventually were to analyze together). That thrust had begun to regain momentum now. He was beginning to believe in himself once again, albeit in a relatively small way, which provided him with the courage to respond more acceptingly to my efforts to stir his interest in exploring the forces within him that had been contributing to his feeling frightened, discouraged, and defeated.

The problems in school had lessened, as he had come to feel better about himself and to concentrate better on his schoolwork, but they had not gone away. Feeling stronger and more vigorous now, he responded to my invitation to pursue his inner demons, which earlier he had rejected as a hopeless and terrifying idea.

As we explored the sources within him that contributed to his learning problems, we were greeted with some surprises. We discovered, for example, that Billy's inability to conquer the world of mathematics stemmed from unconscious, symbolic connections of which he had not been evenly dimly aware. Addition stumped him, we found, because it reminded him of his mother's pregnancies and of his younger sister's birth. Subtraction reminded him of the multiple miscarriages his mother had experienced. Eventually, his teacher had said, he would learn multiplication. "And you know," he said with a shudder, "what rabbits do!" Division, we found, also worried him. It reminded him, we came to see, of his fear that his parents' frequent quarreling would one day lead to a divorce.

He would sneak up to his parents' room and listen to their arguments, he said, with a pounding heart and a fascination that puzzled him. It was as though he *had* to listen, even though at the same time he did not want to hear what was going on. The primal scene excitement that was involved, outside of his conscious awareness, came to be a subject of our careful and cautious scrutiny, as we worked together to understand what went on within his mind. We could not go very far with this at first, of course, and Billy turned his attention away from it to water play, in the little kitchen adjoining my consulting room.

As he played with the little paper boats he made, spinning out scenarios of boats sinking in terrible storms or as the result of violent sea battles, it emerged that there still was a good deal of fright in his family whenever he became even mildly ill, that he was placed on antibiotics everytime he developed a cold or sore throat, and that he still checked his urine every day for albumen even though it had been clear for a long time. A few years earlier, he had been hospitalized with a sudden and mysterious case of nephrosis, an experience he claimed had been brief, no more than a minor annoyance (after all, his mother had stayed with him, there had been no pain, and he had completely recovered, he said), something he had forgotten and had no reason to remember or think about.

My musings about a possible connection between his water play and the water retention that had been the principal symptom of the nephrotic syndrome for which he had been hospitalized struck him as absurd, and he irritatedly told me to forget it. There was something much more important on his mind, he said. He had a birthday coming up, and, since I claimed to be a friend and ally and he expected presents from the grownups in his life, he was wondering what he would receive from me. A number of possibilities occurred to him, but the two that appeared to have the most emotional valence were a certain kind of truck with moving parts he had seen advertised, and a chemistry set. The analysis took place some time ago, at a time when cookies and milk, gifts, assistance in carrying out projects, and similar things children expect from adults were considered to be ordinary, acceptable aspects of child analysis. I elected to give Billy a simple chemistry set for his birthday, although in retrospect it would have been technically more advisable to discuss the possible meanings of the gifts he thought of receiving from me (which we did do) without actually giving him one. He was pleased with the gift, even if he was a little nervous as we talked about his mixed feelings about wanting to know what was taking place in his genito-urinary system. He made a seeming shift in focus to an interest in cartooning that had not been apparent until then. The underlying anxieties revealed themselves in the themes of attack, injury, defect, and loss portrayed in his cartoons. Billy suddenly realized that the "M.D." after my name on the sign next to the front door meant that I was a doctor. A transference storm gradually developed that centered about the fantasy that I was a "mad scientist" who was out to "transform" him in possibly dangerous ways. It took a long time, but we eventually analyzed this in great depth in terms of his illness and hospitalization several years earlier and its meanings to him in connection with his concurrent oedipal conflicts.

Not all analyses demonstrate the sequence from an external to an internal orientation as clearly and dramatically as this one does, but it is a more or less regular feature of child analysis. Children in general, aware of their immaturity, feel relatively powerless against the forces at play within them. They are much more likely to focus their attention on the outside forces with which they feel they must contend, and to look to the analyst for help in dealing with them rather than acceding to the analyst's inward-looking approach. It takes a great deal of work addressed to the child's need for assistance in appreciating his or her ego strengths and in developing them so that they can be utilized to grapple with the internal conflicts that ultimately are the central focus of analytic work. "We try not only to remove obstacles to orderly development," as Kestenberg (1969) puts it, "but to ally ourselves with the progressive developmental forces of a given phase [Anna Freud 1965]" (p. 359).

WORKING WITH PRESCHOOLERS

With very young children, the analyst needs to respond to the child's need for help from the adult world in developing the ego resources that are needed for the kind of productive self-investigation that psychoanalysis has to offer. We eventually want to help children to think and talk about their feelings and fantasies and to use their intellectual and emotional tools to resolve their conflicts, grow in self-reliance, and gain mastery over their urges and impulses. First, however, we need to attend to the ego developmental requirements of the child. With regard to preschoolers, Kestenberg (1969) puts it this way:

> We assist the two-to-four-year-old to achieve a meaningful *integration* of units of achievement, memory fragments, body feelings, words, and concepts. We respect the *global growth* of the four-year-old and help him cope with the suddenness and the intensity of his new excitement. We help the five-year-old in his attempts to *differentiate* between children and adults, fantasies and actions, the good and the bad, the socially desirable and the condemned. [p. 359, italics mine]

Emmy was 4 years old when she entered analysis for encopresis and enuresis. Angry, vindictive, thoroughly confused about her feelings, her body, and her relationships, she required a long period of extensive clarification about the difference between thoughts and deeds, between facts and fantasies, between internal body contents and outside objects, between feces and babies, and so on, before we could turn our attention to the emotional conflicts underlying her symptoms. Fraiberg (1965) has described the analysis of a 5-year-old boy that proceeded in two stages. In the first, he disowned his inner conflicts and problems, which he presented by externalizing and transferring them in play to an imaginary figure outside himself. After a year and a half of work that centered mainly about the fostering of the child's ego development, he became able to shift to observing, reflecting upon, and talking about the drive derivatives he was playing out. It was evident that his newly-found capacities were not merely chronological in origin.

It is not chronological age, but developmental age and defensive age that determine what a child is able and inclined to do. Erna Furman (1967), in a case similar to that described by Fraiberg, has described a latency age but developmentally regressed and fixated girl who had to make extensive use of the analysis to effect necessary ego and superego advances before she could use the treatment to explore and resolve the emotional conflicts that were impeding her maturational and developmental progress.

THE EARLY LATENCY CHILD

Unlike the prelatency child, who tends to welcome the analyst as a valuable assistant, the early latency child, whose ego controls are not yet strong and consistent, tends to project its primitive, harsh, unreliable superego criticisms onto the analyst. Even the mildest of the analyst's clarifications, confrontations, and interpretations tend to be heard as painful, threatening criticisms from which the child has to defend himself. Paradoxically, the analyst's uncritical acceptance of the expression of drive derivatives tends to be experienced as dangerously seductive (Williams 1972). Fortunately, the analyst also tends to be viewed, however grudgingly, as a necessary ally who can help the child ward off the surging pressure of drive derivatives and obtain a greater measure of self-control (at least until midlatency, when the child begins to feel more secure in the efficacy of his or her defense mechanisms and tends instead to view outside intervention as a threat to a system that is working, rather than greeting it as the arrival of welcome reinforcements to relieve the beleaguered troops). At times, there is a tendency to instinctualize the assistance offered by the analyst into a form of sadomasochistic gratification.

Johnny, for example, was brought for help at the age of 5½ years because of enuresis and a behavioral disturbance stemming from inadequate impulse control. Aggressiveness toward his younger sister was the most obvious expression of this, but he also used to provoke his mother into chasing after him to contain and control him and used to elicit punishments from his father for flagrant misbehavior. When he became excited, early in the analysis, he often would spring into wild behavior, which could not always be controlled by interpretation alone, although the oedipal and preoedipal components usually were quite clear. At times, I had to restrain him physically, such as when he ran out to turn on the sprinkler and direct the stream at the door to my office in an enactment of a primal scene fantasy (see R. Furman 1967). Most often, he welcomed my efforts to help him control himself, especially since he was terrified of his fantasies of horrendous retaliation, but on occasion he would complain that he was afraid of me because I "squeezed too hard." At one point, he barricaded himself in the family car outside my office and used juice-sippers to set up a series of gunlike weapons in cracks above the windows because he feared I would pursue and attack him. This turned out to have a transference component. A session later he recalled a babysitter who several years earlier had lost her temper when he had squirmed in opposition to her changing his diaper and, in frustration and anger, had leaned over and bitten him.

AN EXAMPLE OF ANALYSIS IN EARLY LATENCY

A more typical experience with a late oedipal–early latency child is that of a 5-year-old girl who was brought for treatment because she needed to be able to talk to someone about the effects upon her of some marital discord taking place between her parents. She found it so useful to discuss her feelings about her parents that she gratefully accepted the offer to help her understand and overcome her separation problems and phobic anxieties as well. At this point, she became increasingly agitated and excited during her sessions. She put on seductive gymnastics exhibitions and voluptuous dances for me, which made her fidgety and anxious afterwards and in subsequent sessions, made her reluctant to leave the waiting room to come with me to the playroom to work with me. She began to stay in the waiting room with her mother, crawling into her mother's lap and hugging and kissing her so hard that she hurt her. She put on exciting plays in the waiting room, involving violent activities going on in the dark in which murders took place and a woman's head was cut off. I was assigned the role of a guard who maintained order and kept things from getting out of control.

At first, when the observation was offered to her that she seemed to be afraid of hurting her mother's feelings and perhaps even of losing her mother if she chose to leave her to go with me, she became able once again to accompany me to the playroom. She was unable to stay there with me, however; she had to bring the play back to the waiting room each time. The themes emerging in her play began to oscillate between badgering her mother for attention via affectionate displays that also contained elements of hurting her and making her uncomfortable, and making dramatic displays of dislike for me, accompanied by raining torn-up bits of paper on me and hurling ill-defined insults at me. Interpretations of her behavior in terms of fear of positive feelings for me and the need to reassure her mother that she loved her appeared to reduce her anxiety somewhat and to permit her to express her fantasies somewhat more easily. What emerged, however, involved allusions to attacking and biting her mother and to fear of loss of control of her excited behavior when she was with me.

With regard to both of these, furthermore, she demonstrated very little ability to take responsibility for what she felt and did. She tended to distrust her own ability to control her urges and impulses, and to phobically project and externalize them to outside stimuli which she could avoid or manipulate. She would cast blame upon her mother or, more often, upon me if she violated standards of performance or behavior. "Look what you did" was a frequent cry after she had dropped or spilled or torn something or had failed to carry out some intended action satisfactorily. After she had expressed a thinly disguised fantasy of biting her mother, she became afraid of the "meat-eating dinosaurs" in the playroom. When she had become overexcited with me and felt in danger of losing control, she tended to become afraid of me and angry at me, or even to become claustrophobically unable to be in the same room with me, or, at one point, even inside the building with me.

As she became more and more excited, her behavior, regressively, became increasingly disorganized, wild, and out of control, with an outpouring of disconnected bits and pieces of raw fantasy. She became bossy, imperious, tyrannical, then hurtful, cruel, sadistic. She became increasingly biting, sarcastic, and insulting, as she barked orders at me in the master-and-slave games that alternated with the exciting fantasies that tumbled out in the plays we quickly wrote, hastily rehearsed, and then put on in the waiting room for her mother as the audience. If I were to comment on any of this as something we might think about and understand together, she would become anxious and push me away by expressing anger and hostility towards me. She even might rush out to her mother in the waiting room to complainingly cry out, "I don't want to come here anymore. He says bad things to me!" When she began to lose control of herself, throw things around, and break things, she welcomed my assistance in reestablishing order.

She played out fantasies involving crooks and policemen, shooting and being shot, robbing and being robbed. She restrained herself from shooting first me and then her mother. She played first at being a sheriff killing me or subjecting me to painful imprisonment and torture and then at being a little girl who is kidnapped by a terrifying pirate, who casts her into a dungeon to be tortured. The heater had to be turned on each time to make it unbearably hot for the prisoner. She retreated from this in subsequent sessions to maneuvers that distanced her from her awareness of being a little girl who felt overwhelmed by excitement she felt helpless either to suppress or to control. She became a dog who needed a doghouse to contain and restrain her, or she became a grownup lady who was far too busy drawing up important shopping lists to talk to me about little girl things. Either way, she became intensely bossy and controlling. She either ordered me to "arf up" (dog language for "shut up," she informed me) and obey the orders she barked out to me, or imperiously demanded that I "shut up" and do all the little things that, as a grand lady, she ordered me to do to facilitate her work.

I indicated that I was willing to assist her in expressing the things inside her that troubled her so that she could understand and control them better, but that I could not permit her actually to do anything that would hurt either of us in any way. I objected, for example, to her using the blocks to *really* hurt us during the punishment and torture sequences or to her throwing them about or using them in a way that might possibly cause her pain and injury. I also called attention to her telling me to arf up when I hadn't said anything at all, and raised the possibility that when she thought she was telling *me* to shut up she might actually have been trying to quiet something inside herself that criticized, berated, and threatened to punish her for transgressions. I shared with her, in the course of yet another session, my impression that it was when she was feeling out of control that she became very bossy with me.

In response to this, she became able to reduce her defensive distancing of herself from me enough to invite me to "play with" her. She elaborated play themes that shed increasing light upon her inner emotional conflicts, the meaning of the ways in which she struggled with them, and the difficulty she was having in making use of my assistance to understand and resolve her problems. She made a great deal of progress from this point on, during which it was very clear that the opportunity analysis offered her was a twofold one. At first, her utilization of me as a partner in an ongoing effort to undergo necessary ego and superego growth was the more prominent aspect of the work she chose to do with me.

My participation had to be limited predominantly to serving as an assistant to her in creative, constructive, and expressive play activities of her choosing that appeared to serve the functions of building tension tolerance, frustration tolerance, impulse control, verbalization, cooperation, self-observation, reasonable and tolerant self-judgment and self-criticism, and so forth. My activity had to be limited largely to assisting her in these efforts and to interpreting affects and (reasonably accessible) defenses rather than drive-related content. As her ego resources grew and her superego structure matured, she became increasingly able to make use of me as an assistant in exploring and working out her inner, unconscious emotional conflicts and difficulties. Space does not permit a detailed explication of the way in which this took place.

MIDLATENCY RESPONSE TO TREATMENT

By midlatency, executive and defensive ego capacities have advanced sufficiently and have acquired enough stability that children tend much less to perceive the analyst either as a harshly critical observer or as a seductive Pied Piper than they might have a little earlier. Although one might expect that the analyst's job would be much easier than it had been before, this is not very often the case. In certain ways the midlatency child is freer to accept assistance in exploring his inner thoughts and feelings, but in other ways he is not. One set of causes for resistance to analytic intervention has evaporated, but another one has appeared to take its place. Children tend now to guard against disruptive invasion of defensive systems that now are working reasonably well. Anyone who treats children who are in this developmental phase must respect this need to protect defensive activity that is succeeding and to be tactful and patient if effective work is to be carried out. As in earlier phases, the thrust of innate developmental advance needs to be given equal consideration alongside classical interpretative intervention to facilitate resolution of the neurotic conflicts that have been interfering with that advance. One is as much a part of child analysis as the other, and it is necessary to move very carefully between the two.

Little Johnny, for example, who had been so wildly out of control during the early part of his treatment, which began when he was just 5 years of age, made use of analytic assistance to move into very different behavior by the time he had reached the age of 7. At that point, he shifted from poorly controlled behavioral expression of his inner conflicts, in response to which I had helped him gain control over himself via a combination of confrontation, clarification, interpretation, and intermittent admonition and restraint when necessary, to firming up of his newly gained capacity for self-control via repetitive construction with blocks and engagement of me in playing out one table game after another with him. There was a recurrent theme in his block play of inviting me, in the form of an animal or a soldier or an automobile, to invade a building he had constructed to try to capture his secret treasure, only to be caught in a trap and either inextricably imprisoned or, less often, destroyed altogether. At times, this alternated with automobile races, paper airplane bombing runs against each other's territory, or competitions in games of skill that he devised in which we rolled balls into compartments of different value that he had constructed out of various materials. He almost always made sure to win in these competitions, and was noticeably distressed and vindictively angry on the few occasions when he lost. The same held for the table games.

He permitted me to interpret these behaviors in terms of the oedipal conflicts and sibling rivalry to which I saw periodic connections. He also allowed me to connect them with the dreams he brought in, at his parents' suggestion, of flying saucers invading his home, of an assortment of space monsters with multiple arms, many eyes, and lots of sharp teeth (which he drew for me even if he would not reflect upon them), and of a boy who could not stop himself from robbing the bank again every time he escaped from jail, even though it only led to his being caught and returned to jail by the sheriff. He would not think about them himself, however, nor would he think about his frequent urges to violate or change the rules of the games we played so that he could win. He preferred to let me do the talking while he concentrated on controlling himself better (in the sessions with me as well as at home and in school) and increasing his ability to accept losing games and to accept losing out at home to his siblings or to his father. At times, he was under greatly increased stress at home, for example, when his mother decided to go back to school and then out to work, when a new housekeeper he had come to accept suddenly left the family, when his beloved former babysitter experienced a series of terrible events affecting one of her children and threatening her life, and when his parents quarrelled intensely and began to speak of obtaining a divorce. At those times, he reverted back to fantasy play that revealed his inner concerns and conflicts in a relatively transparent way. He temporarily lost some of the improved capacity for self-control that he had acquired (especially at home and at school rather than in his sessions with me). At such times, he worked with me at reflecting and understanding what was going on within him, and seemed grateful for the assistance I was offering him. As soon as he felt more in command of himself, however, he would turn away from my efforts to continue our thinking together about what was happening in his life and about his inner emotional response to them and revert back to his preference for the table games and construction with blocks.

Johnny's pattern is quite typical for the midlatency child. In this developmental period, children tend a large part of the time to be closed up, contained, secretive, and more concerned with maintaining the status quo and fortifying it than with wrestling with emotional conflicts and making changes. Periodically, however, when they find themselves under unexpected stress and are in need of help or, paradoxically, are feeling secure and safe enough to relax their guard, they open up and offer access to their sexual and aggressive conflicts. At such times, they can work very well for a while analytically, until they retreat once again behind a veil of impenetrability. While it lasts, they are a delight to work with. In contrast to the early latency child, because of their greater emotional strength, stability, and defensive confidence, they also are much less prone to react with narcissistic hurt and injury to analytic interventions that are imperfectly phrased or are not optimally timed. If one is able to be patient and to be content with intermittent analytic work, it can be very satisfying to work with these children.

THE LATE LATENCY CHILD

By the time children reach late latency they generally have built up an elaborate defensive system to which they adhere rigidly as they ward off external interference with it. Those who are symptomatic and are brought for treatment for the first time have reached this point in their development only partially, since in certain respects there has been developmental failure and the necessity to establish neurotic pseudosolutions of unresolvable emotional conflict. The combination of a rigid defensive system that does not work effectively and the carrying forth of the kind of harsh, primitive, yet weak superego organization more typical of a much younger child can make it very difficult for the child to enter an exploratory treatment situation (see Williams 1972).

Ego and superego weakness and rigidity, together with a tendency to be suspicious of critical, intruding adults and to react against excessive dependence upon parents, perceived as having all the strength and power, by being rebellious and insistently pseudoindependent, can lead such children to respond in such a way to treatment that it becomes an impossible situation. This can be an extremely difficult time to take a child into treatment. A great deal of tact, sensitivity, and patience are necessary on the analyst's part if treatment is to be possible. It may be necessary to start slowly and cautiously rather than moving directly into an intensive, analytic treatment situation. Not infrequently, children who are in this period vehemently refuse to enter treatment or quickly need to withdraw from it, only to enter treatment later on and do well with it.

Midlatency and late latency, of course, are only terms of convenience. They are not clearly distinguishable from one another as developmental periods, tend to evolve fluidly from one to the other, and do not correlate more than very roughly—and quite variably—with chronological age.

A typical late latency child I recall was one who entered intensive psychotherapy at the age of 4½ because of anxious, agitated, driven behavior in his nursery school classroom, where he was so distractible and was so busy flitting from one thing to another, as though he was searching and searching for something, that he could not participate in the program, could not establish meaningful relationships with anyone, and so on. Not only was he going through all the intense feelings that are inevitable in a child whose parents are in the midst of an acrimonious divorce, but, as we discovered, he also was driven at the time I met him by intense anxiety over the repeated disappearance out of his scrotum of highly retractile testicles.

We worked very hard together to analyze and understand his conflicted feelings and the complicated defensive maneuvers he was employing to grapple with them, and we both felt we were doing a pretty good job of it. It was almost startling, therefore, when shortly after his eighth birthday, he stopped working so vigorously and enthusiastically, albeit with intermittent resistive defensiveness, of course, at exploring within himself. He retreated instead into a protracted removal of himself behind comic books, homework that "had to" be done immediately, and insistence that all his problems had been solved and under control. Even his testicles, he averred, had grown large enough that they could no longer fit through his inguinal rings and disappear up into his body. He expressed resentment of what he perceived as my intrusive insistence on opposing his efforts to take care of himself responsibly and grapple with things on his own instead of depending on other people for help. Hadn't I called his attention in the past to his tendency to act as though he were helpless and to look to others to do things he could do himself? Wasn't I now abandoning my own point of view about the value of his taking charge of his own life? It was only when a remark by his mother about his sitting in the tub and taking long, hot baths caught my attention that I began to have an inkling of the extent of his denial and retreat into hiding in identification with his testicles. It eventually became clear that his testicles were disappearing up into his inguinal canals for as much as a day or two at a time. An orchiopexy was carried out soon thereafter. It was yet another while before he returned to an approximation of the cooperative joint effort in which he had participated with me during the first few years of our working together. Billy, the early part of whose treatment has been described above, went into a similar pattern of retreat and withdrawal behind a curtain of books, seemingly urgent homework assignments, and repetitive games he invented when he was about 9 years of age. It was self-limited but prolonged, and it was understandable, similarly, in very large part in developmental terms.

EARLY ADOLESCENTS IN TREATMENT

Again, the demarcation between late latency and early adolescence (which Peter Blos 1962, subdivides into *preadolescence*, in which latency-like features are prominent, and *early adolescence* proper) is not sharply etched, so it is appropriate to make a few comments about the latter. Pubertal and immediately postpubertal youngsters, as Harley (1970) has aptly described, are struggling with heightened sexual arousal, which they are struggling to master and to incorporate into their self-image and coping patterns. They are trying to loosen their preoedipal and oedipal childhood object ties to move toward independence, self-reliance, and self-assertion. They are casting about for new (at first largely narcissistic) relationships. They tend to view the analyst, when they are brought for assistance, in multiple ways: as an extension of the parents, upon whom they depend and who represent old superego standards; as new objects in their lives who can be employed to fill the void left by emotional removal from the objects of their past; and as objects of instinctual drive gratification. All this threatens their quest for independent, instinctual control and is very frightening, especially since they are in a regressive state in which they are invoking old response patterns to deal with states of excitation for which they are not quite ready. The bisexuality characteristic of this period also presents problems in the form of fear of revealing humiliating sexual fantasies and activities and fear of being taken unawares in a premature confrontation with their sexuality.

There are powerful resistances to analysis at this time. One tendency is to fear the analyst as a seducer who will lead the youngster into revealing sexual fantasies and practices that he or she would prefer to keep secret.

Twelve-and-a-half-year-old Sara, for example, was restless, fidgety, and hypersensitively vigilant to any indication that anxiety-producing topics might be raised during the initial sessions, although she had quite agreed that her volatile mood swings, interpersonal problems, and extremely unhappy relationships with her parents necessitated intensive exploration and resolution of what obviously was troubling her very much inside. She was ready to burst into tears and was strongly inclined to flee. Insults to her intelligence and threats to her established means of coping with her responsibilities and with her external problems were repeatedly perceived in even the slightest expression of interest in her problems and in her feelings. She resorted to the structure and safety afforded by various word games, but then felt guilty about wasting the time and her parents' money by engaging in such activities. Rationalizations were employed to restrict the frequency of the sessions temporarily and then to cancel sessions because of apparent conflicts with personal and academic responsibilities. She shifted some appointments only to come for the substitute sessions at the wrong time. There were clear indications of the wish to gratify curiosity about my other patients and of competitive feelings involving them, but all that she could let herself be aware of were her guilt feelings, and even then the guilt was experienced as fear of accusation and recrimination and an urgent need to cast blame outward and hurl counteraccusations at me before anything might be directed against her.

Despite repeated threats to quit, she continued in treatment. One day, she arrived scantily dressed in a costume she had had to wear for a play rehearsal at school just before her session. She was keyed up and excited about the dramatic activity. Certain aspects of it reminded her of experiences at summer camp involving a counselor who wore very revealing clothes, talked a great deal about her activities with boys, and once at lakeside got up from sunbathing in a prone position with her bathing suit top still untied, so that her breasts were exposed briefly before she replaced the top. At this point, in the session with me, she suddenly began to rail against the treatment as getting her nowhere, and against me as unable to understand her. She insisted that she was going to leave and not return. Although she derided my assertion that she was reacting to the discomfort she had felt talking with me about what had happened at camp, lest, like the counselor, I too would let things get out of control, she became calmer and did return for the next session. She carefully chose more or less neutral topics to bring up in the next few sessions, and chose to devote a sizable portion of each session to word and card games.

After a couple of weeks of this, she returned to the theme that had given her so much trouble, announcing at the beginning of a session that she'd seen something on television about a young woman who had been raped and physically abused. She immediately switched from speaking with me to playing word games, brushing aside my comment about the nervousness she once again had felt talking to me about things involving sex. At the beginning of the next session she expressed interest in obtaining some help from me with a math problem, only to drop the idea quickly and irritatedly, express scorn and derision about her treatment with me, and switch to playing games. My linking her apparent need to turn away from her interest in having me help her with problems with the anxiousness she had felt the previous time speaking about something involving a young woman and sex fell on seemingly deaf ears. For a while thereafter, she could *only* play games, and allowed me to say no more than that I appreciated how difficult it was for a girl her age to talk about very personal things, which included thoughts about sexual matters, with a man. At home, she expressed guilt over her inability to do more than play checkers with me, but for a while could not do more than that with me.

It is not always this difficult, of course, but it is never easy for an early adolescent to enter into an intensive, exploratory type of treatment. A relatively frequent approach employed in this phase is to turn attention away from what is going on inside and to level an unwavering attack upon the external, adult world. An effort can be made by such adolescents to enlist the analyst into siding with them in negative, hostile attitudes toward parents (Harley 1970), as with the 12-year-old girl with whom I worked who for a year railed against her mother and read books to me about wicked stepmothers, only to get eventually to her sadness about the growing gulf between them and her yearning for loving closeness with her.

Early adolescents tend very much to externalize their inner control problems and superego onslaughts as they complain about the restrictions and limits placed upon them by their parents and about their parents in general. One needs to be careful not to oppose directly or question too strongly the validity of these complaints, since it can feel to adolescents like siding with their parents. It is equally unwise to join with them against their parents in a mistaken attempt to forge a therapeutic alliance. The former approach is fraught with danger, as I discovered very early in my career when, misreading the significance of a persistently critical, derisive attack leveled at the beginning of treatment by a 13-year-old boy against certain adults around him, I questioned his complaints and connected them with feelings to which he had alluded involving his father. His response was to redirect his scorn and derision wholeheartedly toward me, which made for serious problems in the analysis.

Siding with the youngster against the parents can be equally unwise, however. This is likely to be viewed not only as seductive but also as evidence of misunderstanding what is taking place within the youngster. At the beginning of adolescence, there is an obligatory deidealization of the parents en route to detaching themselves eventually from their instinctual involvement with them and their dependence upon them for external restraint and control over their impulses. The issue is not really the parents, however real the nuggets of truth around which the criticisms and complaints about the parents are formed. The real issue is the youngster's inner problems involving self-control of exciting sexual and aggressive feelings, urges, and fantasies. The task is to help the patient find a way to get to these, while accepting and appreciating the need to externalize the problems and focus attention on the parents and other adults who are so desperately needed as assistants in maintaining self-control. There is a need to deny and turn away from the necessity to have parental guidance and restraint, but if the need for the parents that lurks behind the complaints is not recognized, the youngster will feel very much in danger and the treatment will be jeopardized. As a 14-year-old girl once put it, "My parents are good people; they mean well. They don't want me to get into trouble. And I know I'm not really able yet to run my own life by myself. It's just that my parents don't know how to do it. I'm their oldest, and maybe they're learning too."

There are other aspects of the response to treatment of early adolescents that also are important. These include incorporation of the analyst or therapist into the quest for new objects and use of him or her as a new source of needed, external strength and control to fill the void left by increasing detachment from internal parental images. They also include the tendency to seek an idealized parental object with whom to identify as they disidentify with parents, the recognition of whose defects and limitations contributes to narcissistic injury and the removal from whom leads to narcissistic depletion. Young adolescents tend to respond to the therapist's attempt to establish an exploratory treatment approach that aims at fostering understanding and reflection into a corrective emotional experience in which use is made of him or her as a real object rather than as a transference figure and reflective assistant. The developmental processes taking place need to be comprehended and respected if one is to have a chance to help the patient eventually do more than merely make use of the treatment opportunity to negotiate a developmental crisis. Skill and deftness are required if analytic goals are to be fulfilled as well. This is a complex matter that deserves a fuller, more detailed examination than space permits at this time, however.

CONCLUSION

In this chapter, I have attempted to focus upon the neurotic child's response to treatment both in general and in regard to the specific issues that are of particular importance during successive developmental periods. Treatment of children aims not merely at obtaining symptom relief, but even more important, at resolving internal emotional problems that are impeding developmental progress from being made. The main goal, optimally, of treating neurotic children is to restore their capacity to develop in accordance with their innate potentials. In attempting to arrive at this goal, as I have emphasized, developmental considerations are paramount in shaping the problems encountered, as well as in determining the technical means that are most likely to be useful both in overcoming them and in maximizing the ultimate personal therapeutic gains that are being sought. It probably is true of adults as well, though in much more subtle ways, so that it is less obvious, but for children there is little doubt, in my estimation, that the key to successful treatment is an understanding and an appreciation of developmental principles.

REFERENCES

Abbate, G. M. (1967). Notes on the first year of the analysis of a young child with minimum participation by the mother. In *The Child Analyst at Work*, ed. E. R. Geleerd, pp. 1–13. New York: International Universities Press.

Blos, P. (1962). *On Adolescence*. New York: Free Press of Glencoe.

Fraiberg, S. (1965). A comparison of the analytic method in two stages of a child analysis. *Journal of the American Academy of Child Psychiatry* 4:387–400.

Freud, A. (1927). *The Psycho-Analytical Treatment of Children*. New York: International Universities Press, 1959.

───── (1965). *Normality and Pathology in Childhood*. New York: International Universities Press.

—— (1970). Child analysis as a subspecialty of psychoanalysis. *Writings* 7:204–219.
Freud, S. (1909). Analysis of a phobia in a five-year-old boy. *Standard Edition* 10:3–149.
Furman, E. (1967). The latency child as an active participant in the analytic work. In *The Child Analyst at Work*, ed. E. R. Geleerd, pp. 142–184. New York: International Universities Press.
Furman, R. A. (1967). A technical problem: the child who has difficulty in controlling his behavior in analytic sessions. In *The Child Analyst at Work*, ed. E. R. Geleerd, pp. 59–84. New York: International Universities Press.
Geleerd, E. R. (1967). Introduction. In *The Child Analyst at Work*, ed. E. R. Geleerd, pp. 1–13. New York: International Universities Press.
—— (1967). Intrapsychic conflicts as observed in child analysis. In *The Child Analyst at Work*, ed. E. R. Geleerd, pp. 288–310. New York: International Universities Press.
Harley, M. (1967). Transference developments in a five-year-old child. In *The Child Analyst at Work*, ed. E. R. Geleerd, pp. 115–141. New York: International Universities Press.
—— (1970). On some problems of technique in the analysis of early adolescents. *Psychoanalytic Study of the Child* 25:99–121. New York: International Universities Press.
Kelly, K. (1970). A precocious child in analysis. *Psychoanalytic Study of the Child* 25:122–145. New York: International Universities Press.
Kestenberg, J. (1969). Problems of technique of child analysis in relation to the various developmental stages: prelatency. *Psychoanalytic Study of the Child* 24:358–383. New York: International Universities Press.
Maenchen, A. (1970). On the technique of child analysis in relation to the stages of development. *Psychoanalytic Study of the Child* 25:175–208. New York: International Universities Press.
Ritvo, S. (1978). The psychoanalytic process in childhood. *Psychoanalytic Study of the Child* 33:295–305. New Haven, CT: Yale University Press.
Schowalter, J. E. (1976). Therapeutic alliance and the role of speech in child analysis. In *Psychoanalytic Study of the Child* 31:415–436. New Haven, CT: Yale University Press.
Williams, M. (1972). Problems of technique during latency. *Psychoanalytic Study of the Child* 27:598–617. New Haven, CT: Yale University Press.

18

Current Perspectives on the Treatment of Neuroses in Children and Adolescents

J. Alexis Burland, M.D.

A factor that needs to be taken into account when assessing the need for treatment for neurotic symptoms is the wider psychological context in which they occur. The concept of the "normal neurotic" is that of a child, or for that matter an adult, who has a circumscribed neurotic symptomatic illness but that in all other aspects of his psychological life is functioning without significant problem. Such patients are generally conceded today to be quite rare; some wonder if they exist at all, or ever did. It was believed for many years that they were plentiful, but the growing awareness of and sensitivity to the much harder to detect evidences of pre- or other-than-oedipal conflict have given us the capacity to recognize and identify hitherto invisible aspects of mental life that might have gone unnoticed before.

Nevertheless, relatively uncomplicated neuroses respond well to psychoanalytic psychotherapies, which are particularly effective as they were devised specifically with the dynamics of neuroses in mind. The history of psychoanalysis is in one sense the history of the treatment of neuroses. For instance, the initial discovery was that neuroses in adults (as well as, we now realize, in the postoedipal or latency age child and adolescent) expressed memories of past psychosexual conflicts that were repressed, that is, kept out of conscious awareness by the expenditure of mental energies. This led Freud to make his famous statement: "neurotics suffer from reminiscences" (Breuer and Freud 1893, p. 7). Though these memories are held in repression, they surface indirectly in disguised form, often in such everyday forms as slips of the tongue, humor, dream symbols, transitory mild symptoms, or more complexly, as the reliving, symbolically, of the past in current relationships, or, of course, within the symptoms themselves of a neurotic illness.

As psychosexual conflict—the infantile neurosis—is a ubiquitous phenomenon, common to all children, how does one draw the line between health and illness when dealing with such an unstable repression? The mere presence of unconscious conflict alone cannot be the basis for such a determination; normalcy cannot be defined by the presence or absence of a dynamic. One must widen one's perspective, and consider the success and efficiency with which the psychic apparatus as a whole operates. Starting with the child's efforts at entering latency, there is increasingly elaborated a means of accomplishing this repression of early sexual conflict. The oedipal child, in order to rescue the good, real, loving, and dependent tie to the benign and loving parents, relinquishes that demand for sexual instinctual instant gratification that generates conflicts within those parent–child relationships. This inevitably involves the creation of the internal policing agency, the superego, and with its help, a variety of self-inhibiting processes occur: some conscious suppression, the breaking of bad habits as children often describe it; the elaboration of reaction formations, in particular of reactive character traits—as seen in the age-appropriate hypermoralism of the latency age child; and repression of fantasies and events that express drive gratifications and/or anxiety over them. The oedipal wishes are also subject to sublimation in the form of fantasy play and idealisms relating to aspects of sexual identity, heroes, villains, and love affairs.

Though much is accomplished for the child to truly enter latency, the final step in the total process is when in young adulthood the individual finally relinquishes the acting out of the desire for incestuous relationships and enters into an intimate, loving relationship with a peer. The unconscious, however, is never obliterated, and as has been said, there are always six people inhabiting the honeymoon bed: the bride and her two parents, the groom and his. Nevertheless, these invisible members of the party do not necessarily cause mischief; it depends upon how stable and efficient is the mix of suppressive, repressive, reactive, and sublimatory activities holding them in check, under the direction of the superego, and upon the nature of the stress; that is, a stressful and conflicted marriage is more likely to feel the intrusion of parental mental images from within the psyches of the partner(s). The same can be said for post-oedipal (that is, latency age) children and adolescents; both of these developmental phases can be upset by the breakthrough of oedipal conflict for the same reasons: the instability of the ego defenses and the degree and kind of life stress.

The goal of treatment, then, can be understood as the reestablishment of the normal balance of forces when they have been overthrown; this is a significant shift from Freud's initial therapeutic goal of simply bringing into consciousness the repressed memories that generated the symptom-producing anxieties. The first area of interest in this broadening of the therapeutic focus was the preoedipal period of development, that is, the developmental crucible that determined the nature of the psychic apparatus as it first confronts—successfully or not—the challenges of the phallic-oedipal phase. That this was an issue was recognized early in psychoanalysis, even though the focus at the time on the vicissitudes of oedipal neurotic conflict retained center stage status. Freud wrote that it was simply an inadequacy on his part that made it difficult for him to either stimulate or perceive maternal transference manifestations from the earlier preoedipal years of the mother–infant dyad, although women analysts associated with him, he reported, seemed able to do so (Freud 1931). And Ernest Jones, writing of the phallic phase of psychosexual development, the phase that just precedes and in fact interdigitates with the oedipal, claimed that clinical evidence made clear that confidence over possession of the penis was directly related to a preexisting confidence in the availability of the nipple, that is, that oral phase phenomena influenced phallic phase competence. But he added that research—particularly infant observational research—would be needed to explicate just what the connection between the two was, something that at that time remained obscure (Jones 1933). That he was not alone in this belief is evidenced by the fact that it was in the 1930s that infant observational research began; it has grown in interest since then, and has been perhaps the central focus of psychoanalytic research for the past fifty-odd years. It has brought forth a wealth of data and theories concerning preoedipal psychological development. The recognition and understanding of dyadic transferences are no longer rarities; nor are they limited to analyses conducted by women—dissemination of such information makes it available to any and all therapists who wish to make use of it.

Preoedipal factors can play two roles: as reasons why the child is unable to deal adequately with the phase-specific challenges of the Oedipus, and as generators of separate but co-existing and mutually influencing other-than-neurotic-oedipal psychopathology. Neurotic conflict, for instance, can—and usually does—exist amid or within a certain character structure, which can be in and of itself maladaptive and symptomatic. Or neurotic conflicts over oedipal issues can exist side by side with neurotic conflicts over oral or anal drive derivatives or other earlier developmental challenges. Multiple and inconstant neurotic structures are a frequent element of borderline personality disorders; in the early efforts at explicating this severe character disorder it was even called "pseudo-neurotic schizophrenia" because of this feature of its profile. Both of Freud's best-known case histories, the so-called Rat Man and Wolf Man, involved patients with what we now would recognize as severe character and structural problems in addition to the neurotic complexes upon whose explication through psychoanalysis Freud focused (Freud 1909, 1918).

A 6-year-old girl was referred for symptoms that were clearly neurotic in nature: phobic fears of tight or wrinkled clothing, fairly common and recognizable symbolic expressions of anxiety over the subjects of pregnancy and delivery, sexual penetration and genital anatomy, as well as free-floating anxiety around a preoccupation with the romantic content of certain television soap operas she was watching behind her mother's back. But there were also other complaints that dated back to her infancy. She was a precocious, overenergetic girl who pushed for autonomy at an early age but beyond her ability to cope; for instance, as a toddler she would push away from mother and throw herself into activities only to get upset shortly about something; she then would come running back to mother, in acute distress, only to push away from her the moment she tried to comfort her or inquire as to what was wrong. This became a character trait still in evidence at the time treatment began: getting in over her head but then rejecting the offers of help her distress elicited from others. Instead, she would comfort herself with regressive transitional phenomena, or, as we later learned, masturbation. In treatment she revealed this problem by throwing herself into blatant infantile neurotic material, with transparent sexual double entendres, only then to stop suddenly, run to the couch that was at the other end of the office, lie down, suck her tongue, and stroke her soft cotton undershirt. She called this, after we had begun to try to understand it, "getting a shot of mommie." The first year of psychoanalysis dealt primarily with this severe self-generated separation anxiety. She was a good example of the difficulties a gifted child can get into: the precocious maturation of such autonomous ego functions as memory and perception, as well as either more intense drives or greater than average internal responsiveness to drive derivatives, pushed her into inner driven, autonomous activities and precocious independence from mother; but this degree of cognitive precocity made her more aware than she could tolerate of her sense of separateness so that she would suddenly feel out on a limb and panic. In addition, her mother, perplexed by the child's behavior, was unable to find an effective way to be emotionally available and nurturant to her, so that there was a less than optimal opportunity for the internalization of comforting experiences. In other words, she ended up deprived, in effect, and this handicap prevented her negotiating the challenges of the Oedipus more effectively. Once, through treatment, she could confront and master her unresolved rapprochement struggles (using Mahler's terminology), the focus of the analytic work could shift to the neurotic elements per se.

Her two clusters of conflict, one oedipal and one dyadic, revolved around fantasied scenarios with different casts of characters. In neurosis, the mother and father are viewed as separate objects, as autonomous individuals, toward whom the child directs sexual and competitive wishes as well as real day-to-day loving and dependent feelings. When preoedipal development has been delayed, aborted, or incomplete, the child's relationship to the parents is different, contaminating oedipal issues with preoedipal ones. For instance, the infantile mother is experienced as a necessary part of the self, as a "selfobject," and is omnipotent, the giver and taker of life; the relationship to such a mother is far more intense, carries with it primitive fears and aggressive feelings, and the anxiety generated by conflicts in the relationship is about separation, about the dangers of collapse in the face of the absence of the needed dyadic partner. Competitive feelings toward such a mother on the part of a daughter will therefore be far more complex and explosive. Similarly, sexual wishes toward such a mother on the part of a son will generate more primitive levels of anxiety than simply retaliatory castration. Structuralization of the ego and the neutralization of aggression are both important preoedipal development achievements that make it more possible for the child to deal with the oedipal neurotic scenario. When they are less than adequately achieved, they can generate symptoms on their own as well as make it impossible for the child to resolve the oedipal complex and move into the latency phase of development (Burland 1980).

Preoedipal libidinal fixations can also contaminate the dynamics of the oedipal situation; for instance, a late-adolescent woman was in analysis because of being unable to establish the kind of romantic relationship with a man that she wished. She longed to have a penis inserted in her vagina so that she would feel herself to be a woman; but behind this primarily phallic fantasy was another one, of which she was not initially conscious. It related to her feeling deprived by what she remembered as a depressed and self-absorbed mother when she was a little child. This fantasy was of mother's nipple being inserted into her mouth, and her thereby being created as a person. The parallel, in her mind, between penis-in-vagina and nipple-in-mouth led to a two-tiered symptom complex in which the more superficial phallic-oedipal one could not be adequately resolved until the underlying oral anxieties could be first resolved.

Another developmental line that can influence the outcome of the phallic-oedipal phase is that of normal narcissism (Kohut 1971, Mahler and McDevitt 1980). It is hypothesized that infants experience what has been termed a sense of omnipotence; that is, they have the illusion that the world revolves around them, an illusion of well-being and safety that is necessary for the optimal realization of the infant's developmental potential. As suggested by the findings from reconstructive work in the intensive analysis of the more primitive transferences, to the infant, his or her hunger, for example, creates the nipple, or his or her feeling cold creates the comforting warmth. Part of normal psychological development is dealing, then, with the day by day process of disillusionment as, starting in the middle of the first year and continuing throughout our lives, we are confronted by our separateness, vulnerability, relative helplessness and mortality (Winnicott 1960). A strong sense of our capacities and a view of ourselves as comfortably autonomous and functionally self-reliant help us cope with this loss of infantile omnipotence.

A 7-year-old boy was in treatment for a variety of immature behaviors: bedwetting, thumbsucking, "silliness," and "mindlessness" that led to impulsive behaviors for which other children teased him. A small boy, with thick corrective glasses, he was born at a time of family strife and received less than optimal attention as everyone's main focus was elsewhere; further, he had three older brothers, all of whom teased him, put him down, and humiliated him repeatedly as a way of venting their own frustrations. In play therapy, his interests were on but one of the themes of the infantile neurosis; he was exclusively preoccupied with phallic symbols—guns, rockets, spaceships, superhero dolls, and war games in which a small underdog managed to overwhelm the much more powerful bad guys. He would get so intensely involved in his play activity of super powerful characters locked in ferocious competitive warfare that he would "forget" where he was and not even hear me speak. He was unable to play even simple board games as he had always to win; if it seemed in my turn that I had gained any advantage at all, he had to cheat to make sure he felt in the lead again. He also bragged about the size of his muscles (which were, if anything, remarkably small), his strength (which was not impressive), and even wore to school superhero costumes, the kind worn by children on Halloween, earning himself a poor reputation of which he seemed oblivious. This preoccupation with the phallic narcissistic aspect of the infantile neurosis prevented his moving on to its later and more object related aspects. He had such low self-esteem, felt internally so inadequate, so much the family runt, that he needed a constant flow of restitutive and compensatory fantasies of phallic grandiosity to protect him from his underlying narcissistic depression.

The diagnosis of neurosis, then, must also include references to the broader, overall state of the individual's psychic apparatus, not only as a predisposing cause for the neurosis in the first place but as part of an assessment of the individual's resources, assets, and other liabilities needed to determine the optimal form of therapy and predict its likely course and the degree of its success (Mahler 1975).

Along with this broadening of the psychoanalytic diagnostic perspective, in response to the increasingly more sophisticated understanding of the structure of the psychic apparatus as a whole, the technique of psychoanalytic treatment has changed in focus in three significant ways. First, resistances against remembering are better recognized and understood; the work of treatment, then, instead of simply attempting to overpower them, as with hypnotism or suggestion or by simply telling patients what the therapist believes are the contents of their unconscious conflicts, concentrates more on identifying and interpreting the resistances to memory, so that their diminution through the working-through process will make possible the recollections they are designed to prevent (Freud 1914).

Second, the recognition of the fact that repressed memories are inevitably projected by the patient onto the therapist-patient interaction has led to an increased focus in interpretive work on the transference and countertransference dimension of the therapeutic process. It is possible that this was not one of Freud's initial discoveries, as his personal analysis was a self-analysis, and he had less firsthand personal experience with the power of the transference until he discovered its operation during his efforts at analyzing others. In a sense this holds true today; one's personal analysis remains the most effective means of discovering the power of the transference.

Finally, as developmental theory has expanded to include all aspects of a person's psychological life over time, deep and thoroughgoing psychoanalytic treatment also has as one of its goals the explication of the patient's entire mental life narrative, tracing the vicissitudes of early problems through all of their metamorphoses and permutations.

Where the treatment for neurotic conflicts becomes more difficult is when they are accompanied by pathological states that respond less effectively to psychotherapy—for example, when multiple and inconstant neurotic conflicts are part of a borderline character disorder or where significant character pathology creates defenses and resistances that bend reluctantly to the therapeutic process.

One 11-year-old boy was in treatment for temper tantrums and social problems. Anxious and defensive at first, he hid from the therapist by burying himself in games devoid of revealing fantasy content and refusing to confront any of the problems he knew full well he was there to discuss. Over time, the provocative quality to this resistance became increasingly clear from the feelings roused in the countertransference, and it could be understood as an invitation to the therapist to engage in a sadomasochistic power struggle. As this was interpreted, the boy became more communicative about his inner life and shared a series of conflicted but exciting sexual fantasies involving his parents. At first, the specifics of the fantasies involved primal scene images of genitals meeting; but over time this meeting was portrayed as increasingly violent, so that problems with aggression seemed more prominent than problems with sexuality. Finally the scenario shifted from intercourse to a spanking fantasy in which his father ferociously whipped his mother's buttocks until they were red—graphically depicted in a series of colored drawings the boy made.

Our sessions were now the high point of his day as he came to indulge himself with increasing excitement and more and more openly in his drawings of sadomasochistic scenes. The transference became central as his drawings shifted to his being beaten by the school disciplinarian (in part, a disguise for the therapist); this escalated to his depicting himself in his drawings as being hung on a gibbet while he was being spanked and whipped, on some days to the point of death. This obsessive self-gratification in our sessions acted as a severe resistance against treatment; interpretations were ignored, partly as he was not interested in interrupting his pleasure, partly as a provocation to actualize his sadomasochistic perception of our relationship. He was so overwhelmed by the force of his drives, so unable to contain their push for gratification, so lost in acting them out in the transference, and so comfortable with his sadomasochistic preoccupations, therapy became stalemated. Over a two-year period of time, the intensity of his activities diminished; there was some softening of his sadism (in large measure through identification with the therapist), but the basic core of his problems never surfaced in a therapeutic manner.

Treatment was interrupted after some three and a half years because progress, though evident in improved academic and social functioning, had slowed to a crawl. This boy's poor grasp of reality, his inability to form object relationships, his sexual drive fixations, the intensity of his preoccupations with aggression, his inability to contain or defend against his anxiety—all of these deficits in ego structuralization prevented the kind of relatively smooth resolution of the infantile neurosis conveyed in the content of some of his fantasy play activity. Treatment then is best conceptualized as treatment of the patient, not simply of the neurosis.

In summary, neuroses are specific islands of intrapsychic conflict in which infantile sexual wishes, accompanied by affects appropriate to them, generate sufficient anxiety that the person must direct mental energies against their conscious recognition. In this psychodynamic course of events, the neuroses resemble the normal developmental challenges that characterize the phallic-oedipal stage of psychosexual development except that where treatable illness occurs, it is because the resolution of these conflicts is less than satisfactory and symptoms interfere with life. Such unsuccessfully repressed conflicts continue to cause problems; leakages occur that require the elaboration of more repressive strategies. The symptoms of a neurosis include the subjective experience of the anxiety in response to these leakages and the nature of the defenses utilized—phobic avoidances, for instance, or obsessive intellectualizations. The need for treatment depends upon the overall state of the patient's mental functioning. Where neurotic structures predominate, the goal of treatment is to bring into consciousness the nature of the repressed wishes, the anxieties they generate, and the means devised by the patients to protect themselves from conscious psychological discomfort. This is accomplished especially through the vehicle of interpreting the conflict's reappearance in the transference. Other coexisting areas of conflict require the simultaneous use of other therapeutic techniques appropriate to their unique structure and psychodynamics.

REFERENCES

Breuer, J., and Freud, S. (1893–1895). Studies in hysteria. *Standard Edition* 2:1–306.
Burland, J. A. (1980). Unresolved rapprochement conflict and the infantile neurosis. In *Rapprochement: The Critical Subphase of Separation-Individuation*, ed. R. Lax, S. Bach, and J. A. Burland, pp. 377–416. New York: Jason Aronson.
Freud, S. (1909). Notes upon a case of obsessional neurosis. *Standard Edition* 10:153–318.
——— (1914). Remembering, repeating and working-through (further recommendations on the technique of psycho-analysis II). *Standard Edition* 12:145–156.
——— (1918). From the history of an infantile neurosis. *Standard Edition* 17:3–122.
——— (1931). Female sexuality. *Standard Edition* 21:223–246.
Jones, E. (1933). The phallic phase. *International Journal of Psycho-Analysis* 14:1–33.
Kohut, H. (1971). *The Analysis of the Self*. New York: International Universities Press.
Mahler, M. (1975). On the current status of the infantile neurosis. In *The Selected Papers of Margaret Mahler*, vol. 2, pp. 189–194. New York: Jason Aronson, 1979.
Mahler, M., and McDevitt, J. (1980). The separation-individuation process and identity formation. In *The Course of Life*, ed. S. I. Greenspan and G. Pollock, pp. 395–406. Bethesda, MD: National Institutes of Mental Health.
Winnicott, D. W. (1960). The theory of the parent-infant relationship. In *The Maturational Process and the Facilitating Environment*, pp. 37–55. New York: International Universities Press, 1965.

Index

Aarons, Z. A., 212
Abandonment, 352, 363
Abbate, G. M., 381, 383
Abelin, S., 174
Abend, S. M., 199
Abraham, K., 13, 160, 200, 358
Abrahams, H. C., 207
Abuse
  adolescent treatment and, 398
  developmental stages and, 281–282
  historical perspective on, 352–353, 375
  identification and, 206
  incest, 263–266, 269, 343
  sexual molestation, 61, 70
Academic functioning. See Education
Accident proneness, 262
Achenbach, T., 103
Ackerman, N., 220, 371
Acquired Immune Deficiency Syndrome (AIDS), 343
Acting out, 50, 176–177, 185
Adams, P., 353, 372, 374
Adatto, C. P., 154
Adolescence, 241–302
  adolescence proper stage, 269–270
  aggression and, 250, 259, 265, 286
  body ego and, 188–189
  borderline disorder and, 154
  case examples of, 79–80
  childhood neurosis and, 184
  cognitive development in, 258
  confidentiality, 38
  conflict and, 34, 188–189, 242, 261–267
  countertransference, 38
  defenses and, 187, 246–247
  definition of, 241–243
  delinquency during, 34, 250, 259, 270
  denial and, 176–177
  depression and, 34–35, 259–260, 270, 286, 296
  developmental stages and, 241, 279–280
  developmental stress and, 34–35
  developmental task of, 187
  dream analysis and, 344–345
  early adolescence stage, 258–269
  eating disorders in, 34
  ego and, 189–190
  ego ideal and, 209–210, 212, 215
  ego supportive treatment in, 293–298
  endocrine system and, 242
  epidemiological research into, 106
  externalization and, 167
  fantasy and, 253–255, 341–345
  historical perspective on, 365
  homosexuality and, 28, 210, 252, 259, 265, 287, 296
  hysterical conversion reactions and, 93
  infantile sexuality and, 243
  interpersonal relations and, 34–35
  late adolescence stage, 270–273
  latency phase and, 33
  masturbation, 188–189, 191, 243 249, 286
  mood swings in, 242, 249, 259–260
  neurosis manifested during, 34–35, 284
  normal sexual development and, 267–268
  object relations and, 188–191, 288–291
  Oedipus complex and, 249, 250, 265
  parents of, 400
  passivity, 188
  peer groups and, 34–35, 260–261
  phobia and, 96

Adolescence (*continued*)
  postadolescence stage, 273–275
  preadolescence stage, 248–258
  preoedipal phase, 242
  prognosis in pathologies of, 291–292
  regression and, 187, 260
  research on, 243–247
  secondary prevention and, 154
  second individuation process in, 244–246
  separation–individuation process and, 187–191, 242
  sexuality and, 34, 261–267
  social development in, 255–258, 268–269
  stage development and, 248, 275–284
  symbolism and, 94
  task of, 243
  teenage pregnancy rates, 256
  transference neurosis and, 37–38
  treatment (psychotherapeutic) and, 292–298
  treatment goals in, 292–293
  treatment outcomes and, 397–401
  treatment with ego support in, 293–298
  vocational choice, 34–35
Adult neurosis, 303–315. *See also* Childhood-to-adult neurosis continuum; Childhood neurosis; Infantile neurosis; Neurosis
  childhood diagnosis of, 102
  childhood neurosis and, 92–93, 105–106, 304–311
  conflict resolution and, 312–314
  continuity-discontinuity in, 303–304
  definition of, 25
  infantile neurosis and, 4, 7, 10, 18, 77–78, 159, 184
  manifestation of, 35–36
  phobia and, 96
  transference and, 41
  transference neurosis and, 49
Adult psychotherapy, child analysis contrasted, 350
Affect(s)
  developmental considerations and, 162
  research in, 366
Affect theory model, 118
Age level. *See also* Developmental factors
  body image and, 258–259
  borderline disorder and, 17
  developmental factors and, 138

  diagnosis and, 26
  dreams and, 337
  ethnic differences in maturation rates, 257–258
  fantasy and, 320
  gender disorders and, 28
  genital awareness and, 83, 104
  infantile neurosis and, 8
  latency phase and, 32–33
  menarche onset, 252
  neurosogenesis and, 148–149
  Oedipus complex and, 121, 362
  puberty and, 242
  sadomasochism and, 45
  separation–individuation process and, 289–290
  symbolism and, 94
  symptom manifestation and, 18–19
  therapeutic relationship and, 44
Aggression
  adolescence and, 250, 259, 265, 286
  depression and, 260
  drive theory and, 138
  fantasy and, 324
  identification and, 206
  infancy and, 358
  infantile neurosis and, 18, 139, 177
  neurosis and, 123
  object relations theory and, 167
  oedipal phase and, 31
  symbiotic stage and, 170
  Tension Discharge Disorder and, 97
  types of, 145
Aichhorn, A., 28, 50, 244, 296, 301, 367
AIDS (Acquired Immune Deficiency Syndrome), 343
Ainsworth, M. D. S., 143, 147, 366
Alcohol abuse. *See* Substance abuse
Alexander, F., 353
Allen, F., 368–369
Alpert, A., 138
Alprazolam, 108
Altschul, S., 36, 303–315
Ambivalence, 124–129, 175–176, 186
Anaclitic depression, 142–143, 362. *See also* Depression
Anal stage and anality. *See also* Separation-individuation process; Toddler phase
  autonomy versus shame and doubt stage and, 276

developmental stages and, 229
fantasy and, 322-323
latency period and, 185
neurosis and, 123, 282
neurosis manifestation during, 29-30
research in, 366
Analytic transference neurosis. *See* Transference neurosis
Anatomy. *See* Sexual anatomy
Animal studies
neurosis and, 8, 10
separation anxiety and, 103-104
Anna O. case, 355, 356
Anorexia nervosa
adolescence and, 34, 252-253
child analysis and, 350
transference neurosis and, 13-14
Anthony, E. J., 3-23, 110, 364
Antisocial behavior, 27-28
Anxiety. *See also* Developmental stress; Stress
adolescence and, 245, 247, 258-259, 261, 285
childhood/adult neurosis compared, 92-93
childhood neurosis classification and, 26-27
developmental factors and, 10, 277-278
dreams and, 340-341
fantasy and, 343
female adolescence and, 265
infantile neurosis and, 4, 18-19, 177-179
Little Hans case, 5
neurosis and, 91, 117, 178
psychoanalysis and, 81, 356
rapprochement subphase and, 177
research into, 106, 107-108
splitting and, 165
temperament studies and, 109
Anxiety reaction, 19
Arlow, J. A., 163, 164, 199, 201, 206, 319
Art, fantasy and, 328-332
Asceticism, adolescence proper stage and, 269
Asthma, 350, 363
Atarax, 374
Athletics
adolescence and, 255, 258, 268
fantasy and, 343-344
femininity and, 253
group identification and, 261

Autism
child analysis and, 350
classification of, 27
normal, 289
phase challenged, 169-170
Autonomy versus shame and doubt stage, 276-277
Avoidance, stranger anxiety and, 29
Avoidant personality, 27
Axline, V., 369

Bandura, A., 105
Baruch, D., 363
Basch, M., 118, 139n
Basic trust, 171, 275-276
Beckwitt, B., 207
Bed wetting. *See* Enuresis
Behavioral theory, historical perspective on, 370-371
Behavior disorder, adolescent pathology and, 287
Behaviorist approach, 102, 104-105
Behavior modification techniques, 102
Beiser, H. R., 25-39
Belmont, H., 363
Benadryl (diphenhydramine), 373
Bender, L., 107, 163-164, 369, 373
Benedek, T., 171, 214, 289, 313
Benzodiazepines, 108
Beres, D., 164, 362
Bergman, A., 363-364
Berlin, I., 136, 364
Berman, S., 364
Berney, T., 108
Bernstein, G., 106, 108
Bernstein, I., 188, 319-347
Bibring, G., 44, 45, 369
Bing, J. F., 211
Biology, 107-108, 352, 373-374
Bipolar disorder, 27. *See also* Depression
Bisexuality
adolescence and, 249, 250-251, 252, 264-265, 398
ego ideal and, 210
intimacy and, 281
latency and, 94
Little Hans case, 5
Blanchard, P., 349, 369
Blos, P., 36, 154, 176, 187, 189, 190, 209, 210, 211, 212, 213, 214, 215-216, 241, 244, 245, 248, 250, 253, 255, 258,

Blos, P. (*continued*)
 261–262, 264, 265, 266, 267–268, 269, 270–271, 272, 273, 274, 286, 341, 397
Blum, H., 17, 160, 200, 201, 202, 203, 313
Board games, 335
Body ego, 188–189, 362
Body image. *See also* Sexual anatomy
 adolescence and, 252–253, 255, 258–259
 adolescence proper stage and, 270
 female adolescence and, 265
 late adolescence and, 272
 postadolescence stage and, 273
Borderline disorder
 adolescence and, 154, 247, 286–287
 adolescent pathology prognosis in, 292
 childhood neurosis and, 17
 identification and, 205
 object relations theory and, 165
 treatment perspectives and, 406, 409–410
Bornstein, B., 184, 185, 186, 349, 363, 365
Bouvet, M., 181
Bowlby, J., 103, 142, 143, 145, 359
Bowman, K., 364
Brazelton, B., 147, 366
Breast, 10
Breast development, 259, 265
Brenner, C., 199
Breuer, J., 60, 80, 403
Briquet syndrome, 106
Broca, P. P., 355
Brockman, D. D., 306, 311
Brody, S., 50, 146, 349, 362, 364
Buckley, P., 163
Bulimia, adolescence and, 34, 253
Burland, J. A., 75–90, 375, 403–411
Burlingham, D., 207, 216, 255
Buxbaum, E., 53, 147, 154, 219
Byerly, L. J., 159–195

Campbell, M., 373
Cantwell, D., 101n, 102
Caregivers, 204–205, 220
Carr, E., 105
Castration anxiety
 adolescence and, 250, 251
 art and, 329
 childhood and, 84
 early genital phase and, 104
 ego ideal and, 212

 fantasy and, 343, 344
 female developmental stages and, 229–231
 infantile neurosis and, 179
 latency phase and, 33
 Little Hans case, 357
 male adolescent sexuality and, 262–263
 masturbation and, 210
 neurosogenesis and, 127
 oedipal phase and, 31, 277
 rapprochement subphase and, 177
Character disorder, 287–288, 291
Chess, S., 108, 373
Child abuse. *See* Abuse
Child advocacy movement, 375
Child guidance movement, 354, 367–368
Childhood neurosis. *See also* Adult neurosis; Childhood-to-adult neurosis continuum; Infantile neurosis; Neurosis
 adult neurosis and, 303–315
 classification of, 8, 9, 91–92
 definitions of, 101
 diagnostic problems in, 25–26
 distinct entity of, 92–95
 etiology of, 101–102
 historical perspective on, 359–360
 incidence of, 105
 infantile-to-adult neurosis continuum and, 184
 manifest symbols and (experientially-based), 95
 manifest symbols and (universally-based), 95–98
 research into, 101–113. *See also* Research
 transference neurosis questioned in, 53–56
Childhood-to-adult neurosis continuum
 conflict and, 312–314
 continuity-discontinuity issue in, 303–304
 epidemiological research into, 105–106, 110–111
 lifecycle and, 304
 object relations and, 306–307
 Oedipus complex and, 311
 psychoanalysis and, 312–314
 separation–individuation process and, 305
Chiles, J. R., 34
Chlordiazepoxide, 108

INDEX

Chronic strain, trauma contrasted, 68–69
Classification. *See* Nosology
Clinical manifestation, 25–39. *See also* entries under names of specific disorders
   adolescence and, 34–35, 284–298
   adulthood and, 35–36
   diagnostic problems, 25–26
   historical perspective and, 362
   infancy phase and, 28–29
   infantile neurosis and, 4, 5, 6
   latency phase and, 32–34
   neurotic behavior types, 26–28
   oedipal phase and, 30–32
   phobia case examples, 75–77
   psychoanalysis and, 117
   toddler phase and, 29–30
   transference manifestations, 37–38
   traumatic neurosis examples, 62–68
Clitoris, 229, 266
Clomipramine, 107, 108
Clower, V., 93
Cognition
   adolescence and, 258, 269, 341, 344
   infancy and, 358
   play behavior and, 334
   research in, 366
Cohen, D., 374
Cohort analysis, 109
Coleman, R. W., 198
Communication
   child analysis and, 350
   fantasy and, 326
   research in, 366
Competition. *See* Athletics
Compulsive ritual, 308, 309. *See also* Obsessive-compulsive disorder
Conditioning, 104
Confidentiality, 38, 350
Conflict
   adolescence and, 34, 188–189, 242, 250–252
   adolescent neurosogenesis and, 284
   adult neurosis and, 25
   childhood-to-adult neurosis and, 312–314
   infantile neurosis and, 12, 18
   neurosogenesis and, 7–8, 117, 119, 122–123, 124–129
   neurotic personality disorder and, 98
   separation–individuation process and, 30

   transference neurosis and, 14
   trauma and, 62, 72
Conscious mind
   fantasy and, 320
   transitional object and phenomena, 172
Continuity-discontinuity. *See* Childhood-to-adult neurosis continuum
Conversion disorder. *See also* Hysterical neurosis
   adolescent pathology and, 285
   epidemiological research into, 106–107
   psychoanalytic perspective and, 106
Conversion reaction
   age level and, 8
   anxiety and, 19
   childhood neurosis and, 93
   Dora case, 9
   incidence of, 27
   latency phase and, 33–34
Costello, C., 102
Countertransference, 38, 297–298. *See also* Transference; Transference neurosis
Cox, A., 105
Cramer, J., 364
Creativity, fantasy and, 326
Criminality, 270. *See also* Delinquency
Cult membership, 246
Culture
   adolescence and, 255–256, 260–261
   ego ideal and, 216
   nosology and, 3
   treatment decision and, 380
Cumulative trauma, 68
Curtis, H., 44

Dalsimer, K., 253
D'Amato, G., 108
Darwin, C., 354
Datan, N., 191
Davidoff-Hirsch, H., 305, 311
Davies, M., 110
Dealy, M. N., 297
Death. *See* Parental death
Defense mechanism
   adolescence and, 187, 246–247, 252–253, 259, 344
   adolescent pathology and, 285–288
   adulthood and, 35
   childhood psychopathology and, 8
   dreams and, 338
   fantasy and, 325–326

Defense mechanism (*continued*)
  identification and, 206
  latency period and, 184–185, 394
  neurosis and, 4, 119
  psychoanalysis and, 356
  splitting and, 165
  trauma and, 61
  traumatic neurosis and, 72–73
Delinquency, 375
  adolescence and, 34, 250, 259
  adolescence proper stage and, 270
  female adolescence and, 267
  historical perspective on, 354, 367–368
  latency phase and, 33
  psychoanalysis for, 296
  transference neurosis and, 50
Demski, R. S., 246, 256
Denial, 178
Dependency
  adolescent psychotherapy and, 296–297
  adulthood and, 35
  anorexia nervosa and, 34
  neurosis and, 27
  stranger anxiety and, 29
Depression
  adolescence and, 34–35, 259–260
  adolescence proper stage and, 270
  adolescent pathology and, 286
  adolescent psychotherapy and, 296
  anaclitic depression, 142–143
  anxiety and, 19
  delinquency and, 34
  infantile neurosis and, 19–20
  neurosis and, 27
  psychopharmacological treatment for, 374
  separation–individuation process and, 179
Desensitization, 102
Despert, J. L., 351, 352, 353, 362
Developmental disabilities, child analysis and, 350
Developmental factors. *See also* Age level; Object relations; Separation–individuation process
  adolescence and, 241
  childhood-to-adult neurosis continuum and, 303–304
  direct observational research and, 360–365
  ego ideal and, 212
  Erikson's stage theory and, 275–284, 299–300
  fantasy and, 321
  femininity and, 228–232
  historical perspective on, 354, 372
  identification and, 203–205
  life cycle perspective on, 165–166, 172, 185, 275–284, 304
  Mahler and, 288–291
  maturation contrasted, 361
  nonpreventable quality of, 138–139
  object relations and, 159–162
  parental psychopathology and, 218–220
  parenting and, 197
  play behavior and, 334–335
  recent research trends in, 365–367
  separation–individuation process, 169
  treatment outcomes and, 390
  treatment perspectives and, 409
Developmental psychology, mental health and, 147
Developmental stress. *See also* Anxiety; Stress
  adolescence and, 34–35
  adulthood and, 35–36
  childhood neurosis classification and, 26–27
  infancy phase and, 28–29
  latency phase and, 32–34
  oedipal phase and, 30–32
  toddler phase and, 29–30
Diagnosis
  childhood neurosis, 25–26
  treatment and, 380, 408–409
Diagnostic and Statistical Manual-I, 91, 368
Diagnostic and Statistical Manual-II, 26, 91, 351
Diagnostic and Statistical Manual-III, 351
  adult neurosis and, 25
  epidemiological research and, 106
  neurosis and, 3, 26, 91, 102, 103
  trauma and, 59, 61
Dickens, C., 352, 353
Differentiation
  parenting and, 197–198
  penis envy and, 236
Differentiation subphase, 171
Diphenhydramine (benadryl), 373
Direct observational research
  alternative psychotherapeutic approaches and, 368

INDEX

Direct observational research (*continued*)
  historical perspective and, 360–365
  prevention and, 142
  recent trends in, 365–367
  separation–individuation theory and, 143, 144
Displacement, 47
Dissociative state, 19, 93
Divorce, 256, 283
Dora case, 9
Dowling, S., 340
Dratman, M., 350, 363
Dream(s)
  adolescence and, 344–345
  fantasy and, 336–341
  mastery and, 327–328
  oedipal phase and, 30–31, 32
  symbol and, 96
  trauma and, 338
Dream analysis
  adult therapy and, 77–78
  trauma and, 60
Drives and drive theory
  adolescence and, 244–245, 246, 250, 259
  fantasy and, 319, 320, 324
  infantile neurosis and, 139
  neurosis and, 78, 122
  nonpreventable quality of, 138
  object relations theory and, 163
  psychoneurosis concept and, 355–356
  rapprochement subphase and, 175
  seduction hypothesis and, 81
  trauma and, 62
Drug abuse. *See* Substance abuse
Duff, A., 154

Early adolescence phase, 258–269
Early genital phase, 104
Eating disorders, 34, 252–253
Education
  adolescence proper stage and, 270
  adolescent pathology prognosis and, 291
  latency phase fixation and, 279
  parenting education, 150–153
Ego
  adolescence and, 189–190, 246–247, 255, 270–271, 341
  adolescent pathology and, 285, 286
  borderline disorder and, 165
  childhood neurosis and, 93
  developmental considerations and, 161–162
  ego ideal and, 209
  fantasy and, 319, 320, 324
  identification and, 199, 201, 202
  infantile development of, 361
  infantile neurosis and, 12
  latency and, 95, 394, 396
  mastery and, 96
  neurosis and, 117, 119, 122
  object relations theory and, 164, 165, 167
  Oedipus complex and, 182–183
  parenting and, 197
  postadolescence stage and, 273, 274
  psychoanalysis and, 81, 359
  psychopathologic parents and, 218–219
  separation–individuation process and, 290
  shame and, 212
  substance abuse disorder and, 292
  superego development and, 10
  transference and, 41
  trauma and, 59, 62, 72
  treatment and, 44, 295, 381, 384
  twin studies and, 207
Ego-dystonic disorder, 3, 25
Ego ideal, 209–216
  adolescent sexual development and, 265
  adolescent trauma and, 272
  genealogy/theoretical formulations of, 211–213
  identification and, 204
  overview of, 209–211
  pathology and, 215–216
  postadolescence stage and, 273
  reorganization of, during adolescent psychotherapy, 294–295
  sex differences and, 213–215
Ego integration versus despair, 283–284
Ego psychology
  ego ideal and, 211
  historical perspective on, 359–360
  identification process and, 202
  object relations theory and, 161
  psychoanalysis and, 160
  transference and, 183–184
  transference neurosis and, 49–53
Eichholtz, J., 363
Eisenberg, L., 370
Eisner, H., 41–57, 218

Ejaculation, 258
Ekstein, R., 364
Electra complex, 128
Electroencephalogram (EEG), 337
Elkins, R., 107
Elkisch, P., 285
Emde, R. N., 141, 143, 147, 162, 366
Emminghaus, H., 354
Empathic understanding, 269
Endocrine system, 253–254, 261
   adolescence and, 242
   puberty and, 249
   sex differences and, 232
English, O. S., 369
Entitlement, 212
Enuresis, 86
   adult neurosis and, 77–78
   childhood-to-adult neurosis and, 313–314
   diagnosis and, 26
   oedipal phase and, 31
   sleep and, 338
Epidemiology, 18, 105–107
Erikson, E. H., 148, 164, 171, 190, 191, 232, 241, 244, 260, 270, 273, 275–284, 287, 290, 298, 299–300, 349, 358, 359, 364, 372, 373
Escalona, S., 362
Esman, A. H., 101–113, 186, 212
Esterbrook, M. A., 147
Eth, S., 61
Ethnic differences, in maturation rates, 257–258
Everitt, B., 105
Exfoliative dermatitis, 350
Exhibitionism
   art and, 329
   female adolescence and, 265–267
   latency period and, 185
   male adolescence and, 261–265
Existential theory, 372–373
Externalization, 167

Fairbairn, W. A., 163, 164
Family. *See also* Father and fathering; Mother and mothering; Parents and parenting
   adolescence and, 244, 246
   adolescence proper stage and, 270
   adolescent peer groups and, 255
   childhood psychopathology and, 8

   dependency and, 27
   diagnosis and, 25, 26
   historical perspective on, 352–353
   infantile neurosis and, 18
   neurosogenesis and, 129–130, 198
   oedipal phase and, 31
   therapeutic alliance and, 367
   treatment decision and, 380
Family dynamics theory, 371–372
Family romance, 8, 80–81, 343. *See also* Oedipus complex
Family therapy, 371–372
Fantasy, 319–347
   adolescence and, 249, 253–255, 341–345, 398–399
   age level and, 320
   anal stage and, 322–323
   artistic manifestations of, 328–332
   castration anxiety and, 277
   childhood-to-adult neurosis and, 311
   defined, 320
   developmental level and, 320, 321
   dreams and, 336–341
   family romance and, 325. *See also* Parental seduction fantasy
   identification fantasy, 199
   infancy and, 321
   latency and, 321–322, 323
   male adolescence and, 262
   mastery and, 95
   masturbation and, 87–88, 344
   neurotic/normal compared, 325–327
   oedipal stage and, 323–325
   oral stage and, 322
   personality and, 319–320
   phobia and, 96–97
   play manifestations of, 333–336
   postadolescence stage and, 274
   sadomasochism and, 210
   seduction hypothesis and, 81
   symbol and, 96
   trauma and, 327–328
Faretra, G., 370
Father and fathering. *See also* Family; Mother and mothering; Parents and parenting
   adolescence and, 251, 253, 264
   ego ideal and, 214
   female development and, 229–230, 234–235
   identification and, 202, 204

INDEX

latency period and, 185
separation–individuation process and, 174–175
Fears, 104. *See also* Phobia(s)
Femininity, 227–240. *See also* Masculinity; Sex differences
  adolescence and, 249
  case example of, 227–228, 237–239
  developmental stages and, 228–232
  object relations and, 234–235
  penis envy and, 236–239
  sex differences and, 232–234
  tomboyishness and, 253
Ferenczi, S., 357, 358
Ferguson, H., 108
Fine, B. D., 42, 48–49, 117, 320
Fire-setting, 259
Fischer, R. S., 227–240
Fish, B., 370, 373
Fixation
  adolescence and, 243
  adolescent trauma and, 271–273
  childhood-to-adult neurosis and, 305
  infantile neurosis and, 12
  latency and, 94, 279
Flament, M., 107
Fleming, J., 307
Forman, M., 306, 311
Fraiberg, S., 48, 50, 141, 146, 147, 149, 154, 364, 390
Frank, E., 136, 150
Free association
  dreams and, 336–337, 339
  play compared, 175
Freedman, A., 370
Freud, A., 11, 14–15, 16, 21, 41, 49, 50, 52, 61, 68, 69, 103, 141, 142, 146, 148, 152, 153, 154, 159, 160, 161, 172, 184, 185, 186, 187, 202, 204, 216, 244, 246, 247, 255, 275, 279, 285, 286, 287, 288, 291, 320, 338, 341, 349, 356, 358, 359, 360, 363, 364, 365, 367, 368, 369, 372, 383
Freud, S., xi, 4, 5, 6, 7, 8, 9, 12, 16, 19, 28, 30, 44, 48, 49, 56, 60, 67, 72, 80, 81, 82, 85, 101, 103, 110, 121, 127, 129, 135, 136, 138, 141, 142, 147, 148, 154, 159, 160, 162, 163, 167, 169, 177, 191, 198, 200, 202, 211, 219, 231, 232, 243, 285, 321, 325, 327, 329, 338–339, 349, 354, 355, 356, 357, 358, 372, 383, 403, 406
Friedlander, K., 198
Friendship, 210, 252. *See also* Peer relations and peer groups
Fries, M., 149, 363
Fromm, E., 371
Furer, M., 143, 183, 203
Furman, E., 45–46, 70, 364, 390
Furman, R. A., 364, 391
Furst, S., 60, 69

Gaddini, E., 203
Galenson, E., 31, 83, 104, 127, 141, 145, 321n, 366
GAP report. *See* Group for the Advancement of Psychiatry (GAP)
Gardener, M., 17
Gardner, G., 364
Garfinkel, B., 106, 108
Gedo, J., 118
Geleerd, E. R., 53, 383
Gender identity
  female developmental stages and, 231–232, 233, 235
  oedipal phase and, 32
  postadolescence stage and, 274
  research in, 366
Gender identity disorder
  adolescent pathology prognosis in, 292
  age level and, 28
Generativity, 291
Generativity versus stagnation, 183
Genetics
  ego ideal and, 211
  genotype/phenotype interaction, 140
  historical perspective and, 361
  neurotic factors and, 137–138
  object relations theory and, 164, 167
  rapprochement subphase and, 176
  sex differences and, 232
Genitals. *See* Clitoris; Penis; Sexual anatomy; Vagina
Gerard, M., 369
Gesell, A., 328, 362, 372
Giacomo, L., 145, 151
Gill, M., 160
Gillman, R. D., 336, 339
Gittelman-Klein, R., 106, 108, 110
Glenn, J., 59–73, 271, 319–347,
Golding, W., 254
Goldings, H. J., 252

Goldstein, K., 372
Goodenough, F. L., 328–329
Goodwin, J., 61
Gouin-Decarie, T., 147
Government, 135
Graham, P., 107
Grandiose self, 167–168
Gratification-frustration experience, 197–198
Green, A. H., 61
Greenacre, P., 11, 12, 68, 176, 290, 305, 310, 349, 362
Greenson, R., 159, 182
Greenspan, B., 141
Greenspan, N. T., 141
Greenspan, S., 141, 147, 364, 366
Grief, 27
Grinberg, L., 202
Grolnick, S., 168, 172, 174
Grooming, 260
Group for the Advancement of Psychiatry (GAP), 18, 92, 97, 368
Group identification. *See* Identification; Peer relations and peer groups
Group therapy, 370
Guilt, 27
  developmental issues and, 10, 277–279
  ego ideal/superego tension, 212
  superego and, 209
Gunther, M. S., 118

Haas, R. B., 370
Haley, J., 371
Hall, J. W., 13, 264
Hall, S., 354
Hallucination, 321. *See also* Fantasy
Halton, A., 118
Hampstead Clinic for Children, 360
Handicapped children, 353
Harley, M., 14, 169, 170, 350–351, 363, 364, 367, 397, 399
Harlow, H., 104, 142
Harmon, R., 147, 365
Harrison, S., 364
Hartmann, E., 337, 340
Hartmann, H., 12, 72, 121, 140, 160, 161, 164, 167, 173, 201, 211, 359, 361
Hatching concept, 171
Healy, W., 354, 367
Heath, H., 152
Here and now approach, 368–369

Herschberg, J. C., 364
Hersov, L., 104
Heterosexuality, 269
Hide-and-seek games, 335
Hispanics, maturation rates among, 257–258
Hoffer, E., 362
Holocaust, 61
Homosexuality
  adolescence and, 252, 265
  adolescent pathology and, 287
  age level and, 28
  ego ideal and, 209, 210, 212, 214–215
  late adolescence and, 273
Homosexual panic, 259, 296
Homeostatic equilibrium, 170
Hormones. *See* Endocrine system
Hospitalism, 142
Hospitalization, 362
Hug-Hellmuth, H., 357, 358
Hunt, R. L., 215
Hurn, H., 313
Hysteria, 80
Hysterical neurosis, 291. *See also* Conversion disorder
Hysterical reaction. *See* Conversion reaction
Hysterical reaction, 8

Id
  adolescence and, 246
  fantasy and, 324
  infantile neurosis and, 12
  neurosis and, 117
  object relations theory and, 166
  psychoanalysis and, 81
  transference and, 41
  traumatic neurosis and, 72
Idealization, ego ideal and, 209
Ideal self, ego ideal contrasted, 213
Identification, 199–209
  defined, 199
  developmental perspective on, 203–205
  ego ideal and, 209
  group, in adolescence, 260–261. *See also* Peer relations and peer groups
  history of concept of, 201–202
  mothering and, 208–209
  object relations theory and, 165, 166
  pathological/defensive forms of, 205–206
  process of, 200–201

INDEX

symbiotic phase and, 170–171
twin studies of, 206–208
Identity, 255
Identity versus role diffusion, 279–280
Imagination, 326. *See also* Fantasy
Imipramine, 108, 373
Imitation, 203, 208
Impulse ridden personality, 97–98
Incest. *See also* Abuse
 adolescence proper stage and, 269
 fantasy and, 343
 female adolescence and, 265–266
 male adolescence and, 263–265
Incorporation, 200
Individual differences, 164
Industry versus inferiority stage, 279
Infancy. *See also* Infantile neurosis
 autism phase challenged, 169–170
 cognition and, 358
 neurosis manifestation during, 28–29
 psychotherapeutic intervention during, 148–150
Infanticide, 352
Infantile depressive position, 10
Infantile gratification, 41
Infantile neurosis. *See also* Adult neurosis; Childhood neurosis; Infancy; Neurosis
 adult neurosis and, 159, 184
 case examples of, 75–80
 contemporary concept of, 14–16
 defined, 117
 developmental issues and, 16–17, 160–161
 future concepts of, 17–20
 genetics and, 167
 historical perspective on, 356
 incidence of, 18
 masturbation and, 87–90
 nonpreventable quality of, 139–140
 Oedipus complex and, 86–87
 original formulation of, 4–13, 80–82
 pathogenesis of, 177–179
 primal scene and, 85
 psychoanalysis and, 159–160
 rapprochement subphase and, 175
 reenactment of, in child analytic transference neurosis, 13–14
 separation–individuation process and, 177–178, 183–185
 sexual anatomy and, 82–85
 transference example of, 42–43
 universality of, 404
Infantile sexuality, 243
Inhelder, B., 258, 344
Initiative versus guilt stage, 277–279
Instinctualization, 206
Intellectualization, 269
Interlocking neurosis, 216–218. *See also* Family
Internalization
 identification and, 199–200, 202
 object relations theory and, 165, 166
 self psychology and, 168
International Classification of Diseases (ICD, WHO), 368
Interpersonal relations, 371. *See also* Peer relations and peer groups
 adolescence and, 34–35
 latency phase and, 33
 neurosis and, 27–28
Intimacy versus isolation stage, 281–282
Introjection, 165, 199–200
Isakower, O., 321, 322

Jackson, H., 355
Jacobson, E., 141, 164, 176, 197, 202, 211, 212, 213, 350, 362
Johnson, A. M., 256
Jones, E., 84, 103, 405
Joyce, J., 47
Juvenile delinquency. *See* Delinquency

Kandel, D., 110
Kanner, L., 368
Kant, I., 96
Kanzer, M., 203
Kaplan, B., 161
Kaplan, E. B., 185, 186
Kaplan, L., 154
Kaplan, S., 364
Kaplan, S. M., 216
Katan, A., 364
Katan, M., 163–164, 364
Kay, P., 183
Keats, J., 119
Kelly, K., 381
Kernberg, O., 125, 126, 165, 167, 174, 200, 201, 206, 287
Kernberg, P., 366
Kestenberg, J., 389
Kestenberg, J. S., 141, 154

Khan, M., 68
Kidnap fantasy, 325–326
Klein, D., 108
Klein, M., 10, 11, 13, 125, 141, 164, 358, 359
Klein, R., 106
Kohut, H., 118, 129, 139n, 141, 144, 167–168, 408
Kolansky, H., 216, 217, 218
Kraepelin, E., 354
Kramer, S., 170, 174, 185, 204, 205, 363
Kris, E., 68, 146, 197, 198, 361
Kris, M., 349, 350–351, 363, 364
Kruger, S., 153
Krystal, H., 61
Kut, S., 50

Lampl-de Groot, J., 209, 211, 362
Language
  acquisition of, 30
  adolescence and, 255
  mastery and, 385
  rapprochement subphase and, 176
  research in, 366
Late adolescence stage, 270–273
Latency
  childhood neurosis and, 8, 10
  described, 241–242
  developmental stages and, 279
  developmental task of, 184–185, 248
  ego ideal and, 212
  fantasy and, 96, 321–322, 323
  historical perspective on, 365
  identification and, 204
  infantile neurosis resolved in, 184
  neurosis manifestation during, 32–34
  phobias and, 93
  sex differences during, 232
  symbols and, 94
  transference neurosis and, 37
  treatment outcomes and, 390–397
Laufer, M., 122, 154
Laufer, M. E., 122, 154
Laughlin, H. P., 93
Lawry, L. G., 369
Learning disabilities, 350
  anxiety and, 27
  historical perspective on, 353
  parental role in developing, 219
Learning theory, historical perspective and, 361–362

Leonard, M., 206–207
Lester, S., 161, 169, 170
Levy, D., 369
Libido. *See also entries under* Sexual; Sexuality
  adolescence and, 245, 246–247, 250, 252
  adolescent pathology and, 287
  ego ideal and, 212
  identification and, 202
  object relations theory and, 163
Lichtenberg, J., 147
Liddell, H. S., 142
Lieberman, A. F., 147
Life cycle development
  childhood-to-adult neurosis issue and, 304
  Erikson's stage development theory of, 275–284
  object relations theory and, 165–166
  separation–individuation process and, 185
  transitional object and phenomena and, 172
Lipsitz, J. S., 252, 256
Lipton, R., 141, 142, 146
Little Albert case, 104
Little Hans case, xi, 4, 5–6, 9, 11, 17, 20, 82, 101, 103, 159, 160, 233, 285–286, 356–357
Loewald, H., 165, 166, 167, 182, 183, 186, 203
Lourie, R., 364
Lowenstein, R. M., 212, 361
Ludic symbols, 94

Mahler, M., 27, 30, 103, 110, 123, 125, 141, 143, 144, 148, 159, 164, 165, 166, 167, 169, 170, 171, 172, 173, 174, 175, 176, 177, 178, 179, 180, 181, 185, 198, 202, 203, 204, 205, 241, 263, 271, 284, 285, 287, 288–291, 349, 363, 364, 365, 372, 408, 409
Males. *See* Masculinity; Sex differences
Malmquist, C. P., 258
Manic disorder, 286
Masculinity, 249, 262–263. *See also* Femininity; Sex differences
Maslow, A. H., 372–373
Mastery
  adolescence and, 269

developmental issues and, 361
dreams and, 327–328, 338
ego and, 96
fantasy and, 95, 98
female developmental stages and, 233–234
language and, 385
separation–individuation process and, 30, 174
trauma and, 61, 62, 71
Masturbation
adolescence and, 188–189, 191, 243, 249
adolescent pathology and, 286
castration anxiety and, 210
fantasy and, 319, 343, 344
female developmental stages and, 233, 265–267
infantile neurosis and, 87–90
latency period and, 184
male adolescence and, 261–265
oedipal phase and, 31
sex differences and, 243
social norms and, 135
Maturation, 283
development contrasted, 361
ego growth and, 166
play and, 334
separation–individuation process and, 291
McAnarney, E. R., 249
McCullers, C., 253
McDevitt, J. B., 103, 123, 125, 171, 177, 202, 363, 408
McGuire, J., 105
Mears, C., 104
Mellaril, 374
Menarche. *See* Menstruation
Menninger, K., 81, 355, 364
Menstruation, 252, 265
Mental health, 135. *See also* Prevention
parenting education and, 153
psychoanalysis and, 147–148
Mental hygiene movement, 363
Mental illness, recognition of, in children, 351–355. *See also* Childhood neurosis
Mental retardation, 353, 354, 375. *See also* Learning disabilities
Metabletics, 3, 21
Metapsychology, 118, 159–160
Meyer, A., 354, 367, 368

Minuchin, S., 371
Mirroring, 171, 203
Mirror transference, 168
Misbehavior (in therapeutic session), 50. *See also* Acting out
Mixed neurotic reaction, 8, 9
Modeling procedures, phobias and, 105
Molestation. *See* Abuse; Sexual molestation
Mood swings, 242, 249, 259–260
Moore, B. E., 42, 48–49, 117, 320
Moore, W. T., 216, 217
Moreno, J. L., 370
Mother and mothering. *See also* Family; Father and fathering; Parents and parenting
basic trust development and, 275
drives and, 138
female development and, 234
historical perspective and, 362
identification and, 203, 208–209
infancy and, 358–359
infant developmental stress and, 28–29
infantile neurosis and, 15
mutuality in, 162
neurosis and, 104, 123
neurosogenesis and, 140, 282
play behavior and, 335–336
prevention strategies and, 143–144
psychopathology and, 11
rapprochement subphase and, 175–176
self psychology and, 167–168
separation anxiety and, 103
separation–individuation process and, 29–30, 173, 290
symbiotic phase and, 170–171
working mothers and, 143
Motto, Rocco, 364
Multiple caregivers. *See* Caregivers; Working mothers
Murphy, G., 320
Murphy, L., 365
Murray, J. M., 212

Nagera, H., 128, 360, 364
Naming, mastery and, 233–234
Narcissism
defined, 168
ego ideal and, 210–211, 213
object relations theory and, 167–168
penis envy and, 236
primary narcissism, 167, 171

Narcissistic personality disorder
  adolescent pathology prognosis in, 292
  childhood-to-adult neurosis and, 313
Narcissistic transference, infantile neurosis and, 160
National Committee for Mental Hygiene, 354
Nature/nurture problem
  historical perspective and, 361
  object relations theory and, 163–164
Naylor, A., 141, 146
Neubauer, P., 333, 334, 349, 364
Neurobiology, 107–108, 352. *See also* Biology
Neuropsychology
  historical perspective on, 373–374
  object relations theory and, 164
Neurosis. *See also* Clinical manifestation
  causes of, 117–133. *See also* Neurosogenesis
  definitions of, 18, 91, 117–118
  Diagnostic and Statistical Manual-III and, 3
  femininity and, 227–240. *See also* Femininity
  historical origins of concept, 355–359
  prevention possibility discussed, 120–121
  separation anxiety and, 103
Neurosogenesis, 117–133
  age level and, 148–149
  ambivalence conflicts and, 124–129
  causation, 119–120
  conditions facilitating, 129–130
  conditions required for, 122–123
  ego ideal and, 215–216
  generation and shaping of, 121
  identification and, 205–206
  infantile neurosis and, 139, 177–179
  latency and, 186
  mothering and, 282
  parent-child dimension in, 197–220. *See also* Parents and parenting
  production of, 121–122
  psychoanalysis and, 140–141
  theoretical models and, 118
  twin studies in, 207
Neurotic personality disorder, 3, 97–98
Neurotic process, 3–4
Newman, C. J., 61
New York Longitudinal Study, 109

Niederland, W., 219
Night terrors, 338, 340–341
Nocturnal emission, adolescence and, 258
Normal autism, 289
Normal neurotic concept, 403
Noshpitz, J., 220, 364
Nosology
  culture and, 3
  neurosis and, 26
Nursery school, 31–32. *See also* Caregivers
Nutrition, adolescence and, 261

Object choice, adolescence and, 243
Object relations, 118, 159–195
  adolescence and, 188–191, 245
  adolescent pathology and, 288–291
  childhood-to-adult neurosis and, 306–307
  developmental considerations and, 159–162
  female development and, 234–235
  historical perspective on, 361
  identification and, 206
  infantile neurosis and, 139–140
  intimacy and, 281–282
  nature/nurture problem and, 163–164
  neurosis and, 27–28
  Oedipus complex and, 181
  psychoanalytic origins of theory, 162–163
  separation–individuation process and, 169–191, 290–291. *See also* Separation–individuation process
  spectrum of views in theory of, 164–168
  transference contrasted, 44
Object representations, identification and, 204
Obsessional neurosis, childhood-to-adult neurosis and, 306, 312
Obsessional reaction, age level and, 8
Obsessive-compulsive behavior, latency period and, 184–185
Obsessive-compulsive defenses, anxiety and, 27
Obsessive-compulsive disorder
  adolescent pathology and, 286, 291
  anality and, 276–277
  anxiety and, 19
  biological research into, 107
  historical perspective on, 362
  latency and, 97

Rat Man case, 9
Occupational choice. See Vocational choice and identity
Oedipal stage
  fantasy and, 323–325
  identification and, 206
  neurosis manifestation during, 30–32
Oedipus complex, 120
  adolescence and, 249, 250, 265
  age level and, 121, 138, 362
  childhood-to-adult neurosis and, 305, 311
  developmental stages and, 229, 277–279
  ego ideal and, 209–210, 211, 215
  fantasy and, 325, 343
  female developmental stages and, 229–230
  identification and, 204, 205
  infancy and, 358
  infantile neurosis and, 4–5, 86–87, 160–161, 356
  Klein and, 10
  late adolescence and, 272
  latency period and, 184, 186
  neurosogenesis and, 123, 124–129
  object relations theory and, 166–167
  penis envy and, 236–239
  rapprochement subphase and, 175, 178
  separation–individuation process and, 179–183
  treatment perspectives and, 407–408
Offer, D., 269, 275
O'Leary, K., 105
Omnipotence, 343, 408
One-parent family. See Caregivers; Single-parent family
Operant conditioning, 102
Oppositionalism, 29–30
Orality
  anorexia nervosa and, 34
  developmental stages and, 228–229
  fantasy and, 321, 322
  identification process and, 202
  latency period and, 185
  trust versus mistrust stage and, 275
Original sin, 352
Orvaschel, H., 106
Outcomes. See Treatment response

Panic, 26
Paranoia, adolescent pathology and, 287
Paranoid-schizoid position, object relations theory and, 164–165
Parens, H., 118–133, 135–158, 202, 363
Parental death
  anaclitic depression and, 362
  trauma and, 66–67, 69–70
Parental seduction fantasy, 8, 80–81, 325, 343. See also Incest; Seduction
Parents and parenting, 197–225. See also Family; Father and fathering; Mother and mothering
  adolescent pathology prognosis and, 291
  adolescent psychotherapy and, 297
  centrality of, 197–198
  childhood-to-adult neurosis and, 313
  education in, 150–153
  ego ideal and, 209–216
  Fraiberg's study of, 149
  identification and, 199–209
  interlocking parent-child neurosis, 216–218
  postadolescence stage and, 274
  prevention strategies and, 143–144
  psychoanalysis and, 359
  psychopathological parents and, 218–220
  research in, 145–147
  sex differences and, 232
  therapeutic alliance and, 400
  treatment outcomes and, 382–383
Parmelee, A. H., 147
Passivity, adolescence and, 188, 251
Pathogenesis. See Neurosogenesis
Pathology. See Psychopathology
Patient-therapist relationship. See Therapeutic alliance; Therapeutic relationship
Pavenstadt, E., 146, 364
Pavor nocturnus. See Night terrors
Pearson, G. H. J., 43, 50, 350, 363, 365, 369
Peek-a-boo games, 173, 174, 334–335
Peer relations and peer groups
  adolescence and, 34–35, 245–246, 255–258, 260–261, 268–269
  body image and, 258–259
  child analysis and, 350
  latency phase and, 33
Peller, L., 127, 185
Penis, childhood development and, 10

Penis envy
  components of, 236-239
  early genital phase and, 104
  female developmental stages and, 230
  primary femininity and, 235
  rapprochement subphase and, 177
Penis-nipple parallel, 407
Perman, J., 340
Persecutory fantasy, latency and, 96
Perseveration, 30
Personal grooming. *See* Grooming
Perversions
  adolescent pathology prognosis in, 291, 292
  identification and, 206
  late adolescence and, 273
Peter case, 103
Peterfreund, E., 118
Petersen, A. C., 269, 275
Phallic stage
  adolescence and, 249
  developmental stages and, 229
  infantile neurosis and, 15
Pharmacology, 220
  historical perspective on, 373-374
  neurobiological research and, 107-108
Phenothiazides, 373
Phobia(s)
  adolescence and, 96
  adolescent pathology and, 285, 291
  age level and, 8
  animals and, 10
  anxiety and, 19, 27, 178
  case examples of, 75-77
  childhood neurosis and, 93
  childhood-to-adult neurosis and, 306
  fantasy and, 96-97
  historical perspective on, 362
  infantile neurosis and, 18
  latency and, 95
  Little Hans case, 9, 357
  school phobias, 350
Physical symptoms
  latency phase and, 33
  neurosis and, 28
Piaget, J., 94, 173, 258, 334, 344, 350, 372
Piers, G., 212-213
Pinel, P., 353
Play behavior and play therapy
  adolescence and, 249, 254
  age level and, 83
  child analysis and, 357
  definitions of, 333
  fantasy and, 333-336
  historical perspective on, 354, 368
  ludic symbols and, 94
  origins of, 357
  role playing and, 175
  sex differences and, 232
  sexual content of, 85
  transference and, 358
Pollock, L., 123
Porder, M. S., 199
Positive transference, adolescent psychotherapy and, 297-298
Postadolescence stage, described, 273-275
Post-traumatic stress disorder, 59
Practicing subphase, described, 172-175, 290
Prall, R. C., 241-302
Preadolescence stage, described, 248-258
Pregenital stage
  childhood-to-adult neurosis and, 305
  neurotic origins and, 362
Pregnancy (teenage), 256, 281, 343
Premature ejaculation, 313-314
Preoedipal factors
  adolescence and, 242, 253
  treatment outcomes and, 380-381, 389-390
  treatment perspectives and, 405-407
Preoedipal identification
  described, 203
  pathology and, 205, 206
Prevention, 135-158
  history of, 135
  infant psychiatric intervention and, 148-150
  neurosis, 120-121
  nonpreventable factors in neurosis, 137-140
  parenting education, 150-153
  preventable factors in neurosis, 140-141
  primary/secondary definitions, 136-137
  psychoanalysis as treatment, 153-154
  psychoanalytic contributions to, 141-148
  secondary prevention, 135-136
Primal scene, 61, 70, 85
Primary aggression, 167. *See also* Aggression
Primary autism, 289

Primary femininity. *See* Femininity
Primary identification. *See also* Identification
  defined, 202
  symbiotic phase and, 170–171
Primary narcissism. *See also* Narcissism
  object relations theory and, 167
  symbiotic phase and, 171
Primary prevention. *See also* Prevention
  defined, 136
  infant psychiatry and, 148
Procrasination, adolescence and, 262
Prognosis, adolescent pathologies, 291–292
Projection, anxiety and, 178
Prostitution, adolescence and, 267
Provence, S., 141, 142, 146, 363
Pseudo-neurotic schizophrenia, 406
Psychoanalysis. *See also* Psychotherapy; Treatment perspectives
  adolescent pathology and, 292–293
  alternative psychotherapeutic approaches and, 367–370
  childhood neurosis and, 101–102
  childhood-to-adult neurosis and, 312–314
  children and, 356–359
  clinical neurosis and, 117
  conversion disorder and, 106
  dream analysis, 336–341
  evolution of, 80–82
  history of, xi, 349–378, 403–404
  identification concept and, 201–202
  infantile neurosis and, 159–160
  mental health and, 147–148
  neurosogenesis and, 140–141
  object relations theory and, 162–163
  obstacles to treatment with, 379–381
  parent-child interlocking neurosis, 216–218
  prevention and, 141–148
  research and, 103–104
  secondary prevention and, 135–136, 137, 153–154
  treatment of choice, 367, 379
Psychoneurosis, 355–359. *See also* Neurosis
Psychopathology. *See also* Adult neurosis; Childhood neurosis; Infantile neurosis; Neurosis; Psychosis
  adolescent defenses and, 285–288

childhood and, 5, 6, 8
ego ideal and, 215–216
identification and, 205–206
parental, 197, 218–220
rapprochement subphase and, 175
symbiotic stage and, 170
twin identification studies, 207–208
Psychopharmacology. *See* Pharmacology
Psychosis, 375
  adolescence and, 247, 286, 291, 292
  biological approaches to, 373
  childhood development and, 10–11
  identification and, 206
  object relations theory and, 164
  ritual and, 97
  separation–individuation process and, 143
Psychosomatic disorder
  adolescent pathology and, 285
  history of research in, 369
Psychotherapy. *See also* Psychoanalysis; Treatment perspectives
  adult/childhood therapy compared, 350
  childhood neurosis and, 102
  future trends in, 374–375
  historical perspective on, 349–378
  infant interventions, 148–150
  origins of, xi
Puberty. *See also* Adolescence
  age level of onset, 242
  body image and, 258–259
  defined, 248
Pynoos, R. S., 61

Quasi-autistic phase, 170

Rachman, S., 102
Rangell, L., 127, 181, 364
Rank, B., 364
Rappaport, D., 160
Rapprochement subphase
  adolescent pathology and, 290
  infantile neurosis pathogenesis and, 177–180
  Oedipus complex and, 180
  separation–individuation process and, 175–179
Rat Man case, 9, 357, 406
Rayner, R., 104
Reaction formation
  adolescent pathology and, 285

Reaction formation (*continued*)
  latency period and, 184–185
  traumatic neurosis and, 72–73
Reality testing, 3, 44
Regression
  adolescence and, 187, 244, 245, 247, 252, 260
  childhood-to-adult neurosis and, 305
  fantasy and, 322
  identification and, 206
  infantile neurosis and, 4, 15
  late adolescence and, 272, 273
  latency period and, 184–185
  male adolescent sexuality and, 262
  middle years of life, 283
  oedipal phase and, 31
  treatment outcomes and, 380–381
Reich, A., 198, 209, 213, 215, 216
Reiser, M., 374
Relationship therapy, 369
Religion, 352
REM (rapid eye movement) sleep, 337–338, 340
Repetition, separation–individuation process and, 30
Representational world, object relations theory and, 164
Repression
  adolescent pathology and, 285
  anxiety and, 19, 27, 178
  Little Hans case, 5
  neurosis and, 117–118, 119
  psychoanalysis and, 356, 403–404
  splitting and, 165
  transference and, 41
  transference neurosis and, 14
  treatment perspectives and, 409
Research, 101–113
  adolescence, 243–247
  behaviorist-oriented, 104–105
  biologically-oriented, 107–108
  epidemiological/descriptive studies, 105–107
  parenting and, 145–146
  prevention and, 142
  psychoanalytically-oriented, 103–104
  recent developments and, 102–103
  temperament studies, 108–109
  theoretical perspective and, 101–102
  working mothers and, 143

Resistance
  child analysis and, 350
  treatment perspectives and, 409
Retardation. *See* Mental retardation
Reversal of affect, adolescence and, 247
Rexford, E., 364
Ribble, M., 363
Richman, N., 105
Richmond, J., 147
Ritual, latency and, 97
Ritvo, S., 41, 44, 45, 146, 191, 208, 215, 306, 312, 363, 385
Robertson, J., 61
Roiphe, H., 31, 83, 104, 127, 145, 321n, 366
Role definition, separation–individuation process and, 174–175
Role diffusion, developmental stages and, 279–280
Role responsiveness, transference neurosis and, 183
Rose, G., 172
Rosenblatt, A., 118
Rosenblatt, B., 164
Ross, A., 102
Rousseau, J. J., 353
Rowe, D., 137, 150
Rubinfine, D., 173
Rush, B., 353
Ruttenberg, B. A., 349–378
Rutter, M., 102, 105, 106, 110, 304

Sadomasochism
  adolescence and, 250, 259, 284
  adolescent pathology and, 286
  age level manifestations and, 45
  ego ideal and, 210
  fantasy and, 324
  female adolescence and, 267
  identification and, 206
  latency and, 94
  male adolescent sexuality and, 264
  neurosis and, 27
  trauma and, 67
Sahler, O. J. Z., 249
Salpêtrière, 353
Sander, L. W., 118, 141, 146–147, 365–366
Sandler, J., 43, 164, 173, 183, 202, 213, 367
Sarnoff, C. A., 91–99
Saul, L. J., 142

Scattergood, S., 152, 154
Schafer, R., 118
Schaffer, D., 107
Scharff, D. E., 220
Scharff, J. S., 220
Scharfman, M., 184
Schiffer, M., 370
Schizoid personality disorder, adolescent pathology prognosis in, 292
Schizophrenia, 287, 292
School avoidance, latency phase and, 33
School phobia
  behaviorist approach and, 105
  separation anxiety and, 104
  treatment perspectives on, 350
Schowalter, J. E., 183, 383, 384
Schur, M., 166
Scoptophilic fantasy, 94
Secondary identification, 202. *See also* Identification
Secondary prevention. *See also* Prevention
  defined, 137
  infant psychiatry and, 148
  psychoanalysis as treatment, 153–154
Second individuation process, 244–246. *See also* Separation–individuation process
Seduction, adolescent treatment and, 398
Seduction hypothesis, 8, 80–81, 343. *See also* Incest
Seidenberg, H., 306
Seleznick, S., 353
Self-actualization theory, 372–373
Self-esteem
  ego ideal and, 209
  postadolescence and, 274
Self psychology, 118, 144
Senn, M., 146, 198, 363
Separation, adolescent peer groups and, 255
Separation anxiety
  adulthood and, 35
  centrality of, 103–104
  epidemiological research into, 106
  infant developmental stress and, 29
  infantile neurosis and, 178
  psychopharmacology and, 108
  rapprochement subphase and, 176
  separation–individuation process and, 29, 30, 186

Separation–individuation process, 169–191
  adolescence and, 187–191, 242
  adolescent pathology and, 289–291
  challenges to, 144
  childhood-to-adult neurosis and, 305
  differentiation subphase of, 171
  identification and, 203–204
  infantile neurosis and, 177–179
  latency period and, 184–187
  neurosis and, 123
  neurosis manifestation during, 29–30
  Oedipus complex and, 179–183
  practicing subphase of, 172–175
  psychosis and, 143
  rapprochement subphase in, 175–179
  research and, 103
  second individuation process and, 244
  sub-phases in, 169
  transference neurosis and, 183–185
  transitional object and phenomena, 171–172
Settlage, C., 167, 177, 178, 184
Sex differences
  adolescence proper stage and, 269
  adolescent sexuality and, 261–267
  art and, 329
  conversion disorder and, 106–107
  developmental stages and, 229
  ego ideal and, 213–214
  femininity and, 232–234
  identification and, 203
  latency phase and, 33
  masturbation and, 243
  neurosogenesis and, 127–128
  oedipal phase and, 31
  play behavior and, 83
  preadolescence and, 249–253
  puberty onset and, 242
  twin identification studies, 207
Sex role
  child's play behavior and, 83–84
  developmental stages and, 281
Sexual abuse. *See* Abuse
Sexual anatomy
  adolescence and, 258–259. *See also* Body image; Puberty
  awareness of, 104
  childhood development, 10
  developmental stages and, 233

Sexual anatomy (*continued*)
  female adolescence and, 265, 266
  infantile neurosis and, 82–85
Sexual conflict, adolescence and, 261–267
Sexual identity. *See* Gender identity
Sexual intercourse, 269–270
Sexuality. *See also* Libido
  adolescence and, 34, 250–252, 256, 267–268, 343, 398–399
  adulthood and, 36
  age level and, 45
  children and, 356
  drive theory, 138
  infantile neurosis and, 18, 139
  intimacy and, 281–282
  oedipal phase and, 31
  social norms and, 135
Sexual molestation, 61, 70. *See also* Abuse
Sexual stimulation, infancy and, 12
Shaffer, D., 102
Shakespeare, W., 86
Shame
  ego ideal/ego tension and, 212
  late adolesence and, 272
Shame and doubt, developmental stages and, 276–277
Shapiro, T., 101, 102, 370, 373, 374
Shock trauma, 68
Sholevar, G. P., 197–225
Shyness, 27
Siblings
  latency phase and, 33
  oedipal phase and, 31
Silverman, J., 97
Silverman, M., 205, 206
Silverman, M. A., 379–402
Simeon, J., 108
Singer, M. B., 212, 213
Single-parent family
  adolescence and, 256
  increase in, 375
Singletary, W., 154
Slavson, S. R., 370
Sleep, 337–338
Sleep disorders, 18, 373
Smith, P. B., 258
Social class. *See* Socioeconomic class
Social development, adolescence and, 255–258, 268–269
Social learning theory, historical perspective on, 370–371

Social work, 367, 368
Sociocultural factors. *See* Culture
Socioeconomic class
  child analysis and, 375
  delinquency and, 367
  parenting and, 146
Solnit, A. J., 146, 208, 306, 360, 363, 364
Sophocles, 325
Sours, J. A., 71
Spitz, R., 60, 141, 142–143, 144, 148, 164, 169, 174, 181, 203, 207, 289, 350, 362, 364, 365
Spitzer, R., 102
Splitting
  adolescent pathology and, 286
  object relations theory and, 164–165
Spock, B., 147, 154, 362
Sports. *See* Athletics
Starobinski, J., 96
Stechler, G., 118
Sterba, E., 363
Stern, D., 104, 110, 141, 144, 147, 170, 304, 366
Stimulus deprivation, 362
Stoller, R., 28, 32, 203
Strain. *See* Chronic strain
Stranger anxiety, 29
Stress. *See also* Anxiety; Developmental stress
  epidemiological research into, 106
  identification and, 206
  infantile neurosis and, 18
Sublimation
  latency and, 185, 279
  symbol and, 96
Substance abuse, 253, 268, 270, 288
Substance abuse disorder, adolescent pathology prognosis in, 292
Suicide, 259–260, 296
Sullivan, H. S., 371
Suomi, S., 103
Superego
  adolescence and, 246
  adolescent sexuality and, 262, 265
  adolescent trauma and, 272
  appearance of, 10
  borderline disorder and, 165
  developmental stages and, 229
  dreams and, 338
  ego ideal and, 209, 211
  fantasy and, 319, 320, 321–322, 324

female developmental stages and, 231
formation of, 361
guilt and, 212
identification and, 202, 204
infancy and, 358
latency and, 396
neurosis and, 117, 119, 122
object relations theory and, 167
Oedipus complex and, 32, 181–182, 277
postadolescence stage and, 273, 274
psychoanalysis and, 81
reinforcement, during adolescent psychotherapy, 294
separation–individuation process and, 179
transference and, 46
Superhero figure, identification and, 204
Supreme Court (U.S.), 135
Sylvester, E., 13, 362
Symbiosis
adolescent pathology and, 289
child analysis and, 350
Symbiotic stage, 169, 170–171
Symbol and symbolism
age level and, 94
art and, 329
experientially-based, 95
play and, 334
universally-based, 95–98
Symptomatic disturbance. *See* Clinical manifestation
Systems theory, 118, 371–372
Szurek, S. A., 256, 364

Tanner, J. M., 252
Teenage pregnancy, 343
developmental stages and, 281
increases in, 256
Temperament studies, 108–109
Tension Discharge Disorder, 97–98
Terr, L., 61
Therapeutic alliance
adolescent psychotherapy and, 295–296
child analysis and, 350
establishment example, 385–389
infantile neurosis and, 183
parents and, 400
relationship therapy and, 369
research in, 367
transference contrasted, 44–45
treatment outcome and, 383–385

Therapeutic relationship. *See also* Therapeutic alliance; Transference; Transference neurosis
transference identification and, 43–48
traumatic neurosis and, 71
Therapist-patient relationship. *See* Therapeutic relationship
Thickstun, J., 118
Thomas, A., 108
Thomas, J., 191
Thurber, J., 254
Time sense, adolescence and, 276
Toddler phase, 29–30. *See also* Anal stage and anality; Separation–individuation process
Toilet training
fantasy and, 322–323
rapprochement subphase and, 175
separation–individuation process and, 29–30
shame and doubt and, 276
Tolpin, M., 90, 118, 129, 139n, 168, 183
Tomboyishness, 253
Tourette's syndrome, 107
Transference, 41–57
adolescent psychotherapy and, 295, 296–297
child analysis and, 183–184, 349–350
defined, 41
identification of, 42–43
infantile neurosis and, 160
play and, 358
research in, 366–367
self psychology and, 168
therapeutic relationship and, 43–48
Transference neurosis
adolescence and, 37–38
adulthood and, 49
child analysis and, 349–350
childhood and, 37
childhood-to-adult neurosis and, 314
defined, 48–49
ego psychology and, 49–53
existence questioned, in childhood, 53–56
infantile neurosis and, 13–14, 183
research in, 367
transitional object and phenomena, 172
Transiency
childhood neurosis and, 93
early genital phase and, 104

Transitional object
  fantasy and, 322
  object relations theory and, 171–172
Transmuting internalization, 168
Transvestitism, late adolescence and, 273
Trauma and traumatic neurosis, 59–73
  adaptive solutions to, 71–73
  chronic strain contrasted, 68–69
  classification of, 59–60
  clinical examples of, 62–68
  defined, 59–60, 61
  differentiation of other pathogenic effects from traumata in, 69–70
  disturbed psychic processes caused by, 61–62
  dream analysis and, 338
  epidemiological research into, 106
  events causing, 61
  fantasy and, 327–328
  fixation in adolescence and, 271–273
  historical perspective on, 60–61
  infantile neurosis and, 8
  primal scene and, 85
  resolution for, 70–71
Treatment alliance. *See* Therapeutic alliance
Treatment perspectives, 403–411. *See also* Psychoanalysis; Psychotherapy
  borderline personality and, 409–410
  diagnosis and, 408–409
  goals and, 405
  infantile neurosis and, 404
  normal neurotic concept and, 403
  oedipal factors and, 407–408
  pre-oedipal factors and, 405–407
  technique changes and, 409–410
Treatment response, 379–402
  adolescence and, 397–401
  child's receptiveness and, 381–383
  latency child, 390–397
  obstacles to treatment, 379–381
  preschoolers and, 389–390
  therapeutic alliance and, 383–385
  therapeutic alliance example and, 385–389
Tricyclics, 108, 374
Trust versus mistrust stage, 275–276
Twain, M., 325
Twin studies
  adolescent fantasy and, 255
  identification and, 206–208

Tyson, P., 50
Tyson, R., 367

Ulcerative colitis, 350
Ulcers, 350
Unconscious
  anxiety and, 26, 27
  fantasy and, 320
  infantile neurosis and, 18
  Little Hans case, 5
  neurotic process and, 3–4
  oedipal phase and, 31
  psychoanalysis and, xi, 356, 358
  transference and, 41
  trauma and, 65
United States Supreme Court, 135
Universal symbols, 95–98. *See also* Symbol and symbolism

Vagina, 229, 231
Van Leeuwen, K., 364
Vienna Psychoanalytic Society, 359
Vistiril, 374
Vocational choice and identity
  adolescence and, 34–35, 280
  adulthood and, 36
  postadolescence stage and, 274
Volkner, F., 106
Voyeurism, male adolescent sexuality and, 262

Waelder, R., 349
Wait, R. B., 258
Watson, J., 104
Weil, A., 164, 169, 170, 177, 349, 364
Weiner, K., 161, 186
Weissman, M., 106
Wellbaby clinic movement, 363
Werry, J., 108
Whitman, R. M., 216
Wild boy of Avignon, 353
Williams, M., 390, 396
Winnicott, D. W., 141, 145, 148, 168, 171, 172, 174, 183, 216, 270, 289, 322, 359, 408
Wiseberg, S., 64
Wish fulfillment
  dreams and, 338
  ego ideal and, 211, 212
  fantasy and, 320, 322, 324

Wolf Man case, 4, 5, 6, 7, 9, 10, 11, 12, 15, 17, 20, 85, 159, 160, 357, 406
Wolkind, S., 105
Working mothers
  identification and, 204–205
  research on, 143

World Health Organization (WHO), 368
World War I, 60
Yorke, C., 64
Zilboorg, G., 349
Zimmerman, R. R., 142